# AVENUES TO ANTIQUITY

Readings from
**SCIENTIFIC
AMERICAN**

# AVENUES
# TO ANTIQUITY

*With Introductions by*
Brian M. Fagan
*University of California, Santa Barbara*

W. H. Freeman and Company
*San Francisco*

Some of the SCIENTIFIC AMERICAN articles in
AVENUES TO ANTIQUITY are available as separate
Offprints. For a complete list of more than 950 articles
now available as Offprints, write to W. H. Freeman
and Company, 660 Market Street, San Francisco,
California 94104.

**Library of Congress Cataloging in Publication Data**

Main entry under title:

Avenues to antiquity.

   Bibliography: p.
   Includes index.
   1. Archaeology—Addresses, essays, lectures.
I. Fagan, Brian M.   II. Scientific American.
CC65.A87     930'.1     75-42293
ISBN 0-7167-0542-7
ISBN 0-7167-0541-9 pbk.

Printed in the United States of America

9 8 7 6 5 4 3 2 1

# PREFACE

The articles in this volume represent a broad cross section of archaeological research, covering a timespan extending from the earliest humans up to the threshold of modern times. The first section covers early prehistory, the vast period of time when hunting and gathering were the only viable means of human subsistence. Two shorter collections of articles cover the origins of food production and the beginnings of cities and civilization. Both topics are major issues of concern to archaeologists studying world prehistory. The concluding articles bring us into more recent times, and deal with a wide range of archaeological situations and prehistoric and historic peoples. The close interfaces between history, archaeology, and anthropology are clearly demonstrated by these articles.

The objective of this anthology is to highlight some of the major controversies, discoveries, and research projects in New World and Old World archaeology. A major fascination of archaeology is the light it throws on humankind's evolving behavior during the past three million years. The articles in this volume are among the better attempts to show how skillful fieldwork and laboratory work by archaeologists can contribute to our understanding of human behavior.

*April 1975*                                                    Brian M. Fagan

# CONTENTS

# V   ARCHAEOLOGY AND ARCHAEOLOGICAL ISSUES

*Note on cross-references:* References to articles included in this book are noted by the title of the article and the page on which it begins; references to articles that are available as Offprints, but are not included here, are noted by the article's title and Offprint number; references to articles published by SCIENTIFIC AMERICAN, but which are not available as Offprints, are noted by the title of the article and the month and year of its publication.

# AVENUES TO ANTIQUITY

# I

# EARLY PREHISTORY

# EARLY PREHISTORY  I

## INTRODUCTION

In the beginning God created the heaven and the earth." The Biblical legend of the Creation is but one of many such tales, which are handed down from generation to generation, often as part of religious dogma. Humankind has always sought explanations for its history, intellectual justification for its existence and for the situations in which it finds itself. The quest for human origins has been a pervasive interest of intellectuals for thousands of years, but only during the past two centuries has this quest become systematic. The science of prehistoric archaeology, which is one means of pursuing the search for human origins, has resulted largely from intellectual endeavors of the past 150 years.

Archaeologists have worked with prodigious energy to uncover the impressive array of prehistoric cultures that are now common knowledge. The Sumerians of Mesopotamia, the peoples of the mysterious Indus civilization, the Minoans of prehistoric Crete—all were unknown a century and a half ago. No one had any idea how long humankind had dwelt on earth. Inquiries into human origins were shackled by theological beliefs that God had created the world in six days, that the story of Adam and Eve was literally true. In the seventeenth century, Archbishop James Ussher of Northern Ireland had calculated that the Creation took place in 4004 B.C., a calculation based on the genealogies in the Old Testament. Most people were quite content to believe that humankind was but six thousand years old. Clerics and scientists alike firmly believed in the Ussherian chronology, secure in their unwavering belief that the Bible was the true account of human origins.

The archaeologists of the early 1800's were, however, increasingly confused by an enormous proliferation of new sites and human artifacts. Burial mounds and stone implements, hillforts and bronze swords, were jumbled together in a confusing mass of discoveries. The trouble was that no one knew how old anything was, or how to relate one site to another. Danish scholars took a first step toward reducing the confusion by proposing a "Three Age" classification of prehistoric times, dividing prehistory into a Stone Age, a Bronze Age, and an Iron Age, a technological classification based on the materials from which tools were made. This basic classification, much refined and amended, still remains in use today in the Old World. Although the Three Age system presupposed that stone was used before metal, an assumption later proved by excavation, the Danes had no idea how long humankind had inhabited Europe, nor how far back human origins might lie.

At the same time as the Danes were classifying the past, European geologists were looking closely at the Earth's strata. The British geologist William Smith examined thousands of geological exposures and concluded that the earth and present landscape had been formed by continuous natural processes, such as erosion, weathering, and flooding, rather than by the catastrophic floods and upheavals postulated by earlier scientists to explain the extinction of animal species. Under the old doctrine, humankind had originated after the last major "catastrophe," as a result of divine intervention. If this were true, the bones and tools of humans could not be found alongside the remains of extinct animals, simply because they belonged in different worlds. Unfortunately for traditionalists, people were beginning to find human artifacts in the same geological layers as extinct animals, in situations where the traces of human behavior were obviously much older than 4004 B.C. Was, then, the world older than the Biblical Creation story would have one believe? Thus developed one of the great intellectual controversies of the nineteenth century, that surrounding the Antiquity of Man.

British archaeologist Glyn Daniel, a leading historian of archaeology, describes the events which led up to a wide acceptance of a great antiquity for humankind, in the first article in this volume. Once the dramatic discoveries of John Frere, Boucher de Perthes, and the geologists were accepted by leading scientists, it was possible to envisage a huge, and unlimited, span of time to encompass the gradually unfolding story of human prehistory. Much of the story of archaeology in the past century and a half is the story of world prehistory. Archaeologists have begun to write an outline account of the major landmarks in our gradual evolution from apelike hunter-gatherers to urban dwellers surrounded by the awesome technology of twentieth-century society.

Archaeology is far more than a means of writing the history of humankind before literate civilization. Its raw material, archives if you will, is the artifacts, ruined structures, storage pits, and multitude of finds from excavations and survey work. Much of archaeology is descriptive, the cataloging of minute stylistic differences in pottery decoration or stone-tool design. Meticulous records of excavations and articles are essential to archaeology's primary objectives, those of reconstructing and explaining the past. But it is not enough to describe the long sequence of technological changes that occurred throughout prehistory; one must also explain why such changes took place, and what their consequences were, in terms of human behavior. A major focus in modern archaeology is on the changing trends of human behavior and settlement patterns, fields of enquiry that demand meticulous research and a huge base of information from excavations.

The world of archaeology encompassed in this volume ranges from the very earliest human origins up to Medieval times. Method and theory in archaeology have mushroomed in complexity since the controversies of the nineteenth century. Accurate time scales now straddle over 2.5 million years of human experience, a far cry from the 6,000 years of Archbishop Ussher. Archaeologists and historians collaborate over medieval Winchester; frozen subsoil conditions preserve the minutest details of Scythian burials for us. Each and every archaeological site poses different problems and challenges. A cross section of modern archaeology is presented here.

The very beginnings of human origins are shrouded in mystery, although the dedicated researches of the Leakey family and others in East Africa, so familiar to readers of the *National Geographic*, have extended to the most distant millenia of the Pleistocene epoch, if not earlier. The earliest human camp sites yet discovered have been located on the shores of desolate Lake Turkana in northern Kenya and in the steep walls of Olduvai Gorge, a jagged gash in the Serengeti Plains of northern Tanzania. Human artifacts have been dated back at least 2.61 million years in the Lake Turkana area using radioactive dating techniques. Fragments of ape-men known as Australopithecines (*Australopithecus*—"Southern Ape," after the first finds in South Africa) together with the bones of extinct animals have been found over a wide area to the east of the lake. At Olduvai Gorge, actual camp sites—scatters of broken animal bones, simple stone choppers, and, in rare instances, the bones of the ape-men themselves—have been excavated intact. The camp sites had been on the shores of a vast shallow lake which later dried up. Its deposits, and the camp sites around its shores, were accidentally exposed in the walls of Olduvai Gorge by an earthquake that cut through the site of the old lake. The oldest living floors at Olduvai are at least 1.75 million years old.

A great deal of controversy surrounds the early evolution of humankind. Most scientists agree that the ancestors of modern humans became distinct from their nearest living relatives, the apes, at least five million years ago and probably much earlier. Unfortunately, no one has yet found enough fossils from the Miocene and Pliocene epochs to establish the exact relationships between apes and humans during this critical period in their evolution. The earliest ape-men so far discovered date to the very early Pleistocene, some five million years ago, by which time apes and humans were clearly separated. More fossil discoveries will be needed to clarify these relationships. Promising results have been obtained by studying the behavior of nonhuman primates, such as the baboon and chimpanzee, and using the results of these researches to speculate about very early human behavior. University of California anthropologist Sherwood Washburn, whose article, "Tools and Human Evolution," appears here, was a pioneer in this research, which has involved in-depth studies of chimpanzees and other primates in Africa and elsewhere. Washburn believes that the development of toolmaking as opposed to tool-using was an event of major importance for human origins. As Jane van Lawick-Goodall observed in Tanzania, chimpanzees will commonly use and modify a twig to dig out grubs from termite heaps. But there is a world of difference between using a twig and making hundreds of identical, manufactured tools to fulfill a specific function like butchering game. A new acceleration of human evolution resulted directly from the invention of toolmaking. The chopper tool, with its simple jagged cutting edge, remained in day-to-day use as a major element in the human toolkit for about two million years. These distinctive artifacts have been found on early camp sites in East and Central Africa, in the Near East, and possibly in Europe too.

We know little of the way of life or behavior of the earliest humans. Their settlements are mainly confined to subtropical parts of the Old World, as if humans were not yet able to adapt to more extreme climates. Most scientists feel that Africa may have been the cradle of humanity, but it is quite possible that future discoveries will bring to light settlements of the earliest humans in Southeast Asia or other regions.

The story of human evolution unfolded against a background of major world climatic changes during the Pleistocene epoch. The Pleistocene began about five million years ago and is principally famous for its tremendous climatic fluctuations, or "ice ages," when much of the temperate portions of the northern hemisphere were subjected to periods of arctic cold separated by intervals of much warmer climate. During the first 4.5 million years of the Pleistocene, the world population of humans was extremely small, being confined for the most part to tropical regions. But by 500,000 years ago, new and more advanced humans had appeared in several parts of the Old World, hunters and gatherers who could adapt to a far wider range of environmental conditions.

*Homo erectus*, as discussed in the article by William W. Howells, possessed a larger brain and stood fully upright, his limbs and hip bones being virtually identical to those of modern people. However, his skull was flatter, with a retreating forehead and prognathous face. Many people believe that *Homo erectus* had vastly improved communication skills, including fully articulate speech. Certainly traces of fire have been found in the caves and open campsites inhabited by these hunters. Their toolkit was much more sophisticated and often included fine "handaxes," multipurpose tools probably used for butchering animals and digging up roots as well as for woodworking.

The first discoveries of *Homo erectus* were made in China and Indonesia, especially in the great cave of Choukoutien near Peking. But recent excavations have been concentrated in Europe and Africa, where camp sites of these early hunters have been uncovered *in situ*. Henry de Lumley's excavations at Terra Amata near Nice in the South of France, as described in his article, "A Paleolithic Camp at Nice," are remarkable for the complete information they yielded on the inhabitants of a temporary camp site by the seashore. The hearths and shelters of the hunters could be reconstructed from archaeological evidence. We even know the time of year when the settlement was occupied. Terra Amata is typical of many Middle Pleistocene hunting camps, occupied for a few weeks, located in an area whose food supplies were abundant at certain times of the year, a locality visited at regular intervals by generations of hunters. Most Middle Pleistocene sites are the remains of transitory camps occupied by hunters and gatherers dependent for their livelihood on migrating game and seasonal vegetable foods. Although the world's population was still tiny, by the end of the Middle Pleistocene, about seventy thousand years ago, humankind was living successfully in Africa, in temperate Europe, and in northern China, the last two being regions where winters of arctic intensity were commonplace. Increasingly successful adaptations to a variety of Pleistocene climates were now a reality.

Our much polluted world boasts a remarkable diversity of human populations, with differing cultures, adaptations, and physical characteristics. Although the concept of "races" has been in vogue for at least a century, in reality all humans belong within the same family. The present distribution of the world population results in part from massive resettlements in the past five hundred years and also from population movements that took place many thousands of years ago, some of them as long ago as the Upper Pleistocene.

Considerable academic debate surrounds the date for the appearance of modern man; there are several world prehistories available which summarize the latest evidence. By 35,000 years ago, however, the hunting populations of Western Europe were biologically indistinguishable from modern man, and the roots of modern world-population distributions date to the then ensuing period of prehistory. Hunters and gatherers had settled in Australia by 30,000 years ago and in the New World by 25,000 years ago, at the latest. Dense populations of hunters flourished in the deep river valleys and natural rockshelters of southwestern France from 30,000 years ago.

Most of the Upper Pleistocene unfolded during the last great "ice age," the so-called Weichsel glaciation, which mantled Scandinavia and much of Canada in deep ice sheets and brought arctic conditions to temperate Europe. The hunters of southwestern France flourished under these conditions, living in huge overhanging rockshelters and evolving a whole series of distinctive and highly specialized hunting cultures. The Solutrean culture, described in the article by Philip Smith, was one of the most shortlived but remarkable of these cultures. The Solutreans are famous for their fine flint lanceheads, made by skillful application of a "pressure flaking" technique. Reindeer and other arctic species provided much of the hunters' diet. Smith's article gives an impression of the remarkably diverse material culture available to Europeans some fifteen thousand years ago, complete with specialized hunting and craft tools and a distinctive art tradition. The technological sophistication of the Solutrean is a far cry from the simpler cultures of *Homo erectus* or the chopping tools of the earliest humans.

The hunters of southwestern France were the first people to develop their own artistic tradition, engraved and painted on the walls of caves or rockshelters, and carved on small pieces of bone or reindeer antler. Upper Paleolithic art was first identified in the mid-nineteenth century, but the authenticity of the cave paintings and engravings remained in doubt until French scientists had convinced themselves of the antiquity of the art by finding long-sealed painted caves and comparing the style of the wall art with engraved artifacts found in occupation levels in painted rockshelters. Now hundreds of painted and engraved sites are known from southwestern France and northern Spain. Several styles of cave and rockshelter art were identified by a celebrated French prehistorian, the Abbé Breuil, who devoted his entire lifetime to a study of Paleolithic art. The most famous paintings are those from the caves of Altamira and Lascaux, where bison, wild horses, primeval oxen, and stags dance along the walls of long-abandoned caverns with a sense of life and movement that delights the eye. Much speculation has surrounded Upper Paleolithic art, its significance, and its stylistic development. No one disagrees that there was a gradual move towards greater realism, but the details of stylistic change, worked out by close scrutiny of superimpositions of different paintings and by Professor Leroi-Gourhan's statistical analysis of the clusters of drawings and engravings, remain highly controversial. Leroi-Gourhan, in his article, "The Evolution of Paleolithic Art," identifies several chronological benchmarks for the art, with the first cave-art styles evolving during Solutrean and Magdalenian times, after 17,000 B.C. The art vanished after 9000 B.C., as ice sheets retreated and the hunting cultures of western Europe became impoverished and more specialized. The purposes of this earliest human artistic tradition will always remain uncertain, but most people feel that it had some magico-religious significance, connected with the seasons of game and the chase. To judge from Australian aboriginal art, some of the ritual and symbolism connected with the paintings and engravings must have been both elaborate and highly abstract, so much so that we are unlikely ever to recover the details.

The last 25,000 years have witnessed the peopling of the world by hunters and gatherers, and, after about 8000 B.C., by agriculturists as well. Many of the details of this rapid expansion of world population remain obscure, for archaeological research in the more remote parts of Africa, Asia, and the U.S.S.R. has hardly begun. Hunters and gatherers were settled in much of Siberia by 20,000 B.C., and Stone Age bands were living in Australia by at least 30,000 B.C. The New World was settled across the Bering Straits sometime before 20,000 or 25,000 B.C., and we summarize some of the latest findings below.

University of Chicago archaeologist Richard Klein is one of the few Western archaeologists who have studied the prehistory of Russia and Siberia in any detail. The frigid plains of western Russia were first settled by big-game hunters about 45,000 years ago or somewhat earlier, during the Weichsel glaciation. The steppe country of the Ukraine supported a rich and varied fauna, including reindeer, wild horse, and bison. Although the hunters lived off a variety of game, they relied on the bones of the mammoth for construction materials for their large shelters. The limb bones, tusks, and other carefully selected bones from long-dead mammoths were used for this purpose, and the hunters clothed themselves in the skins of wolves, arctic foxes, and other animals. In "Ice-Age Hunters of the Ukraine," Klein describes the salient details of a distinctive hunting adaptation that survived for thousands of years in the inhospitable river valleys of the Ukraine, one of many specialized adaptations that emerged in the world during the Weichsel glaciation.

In some parts of the world, Stone Age hunters and gatherers have survived virtually unscathed into the twentieth century. The Bushmen of the Kalahari desert in Southern Africa and the Australian aborigines are two excellent examples of hunting and gathering societies whose economy and material culture have given us valuable insights into prehistoric lifeways. Many archaeologists have turned their attention to "living archaeology," examining the remains of recently abandoned camps and hill sites and comparing them to prehistoric settlements in the same area. The objective is to develop viable analogies from close observation of modern hunters and gatherers to aid in the interpretation of prehistoric sites and settlement patterns.

The prehistory of the Australian aborigine began at least 300,000 years ago and ended with the arrival of the first British settlers near Sydney in 1788. Many aboriginal bands survived into our century and their camp sites, rock art, and complex social organization have been used as a basis for interpreting a surprisingly complex archaeological record. John Mulvaney's article, "The Prehistory of the Australian Aborigine," describes some of the recent excavations, as well as the artifacts made by prehistoric Australian hunters. He emphasizes the cultural continuity between the prehistoric and modern inhabitants in an area of the world that was among the last to be colonized by Stone Age hunters. The type of archaeology described by Mulvaney has been neglected in many parts of the world, which is a pity, for the cultural institutions of the Stone Age still form an important element in the world's diverse cultural experience. "Archaeological anthropology" is capable of yielding vital information on human culture history, and Australian archaeologists have pioneered in this important field.

Over 90 per cent of the human experience has been based on a hunting and gathering way of life. Human society was based for the most part on small bands and extended family organizations. The massive social and economic changes of the past ten thousand years have involved humankind in a totally new experience, much of which is completely alien to the lifeways of most prehistoric times.

# The Idea of Man's Antiquity

# 1

Glyn E. Daniel
*November 1959*

*When Father MacEnery found flint implements in the same stratum with the fossils of extinct animals, he pushed human history far beyond 4004 B.C., the date most people took as man's beginning*

Digging near the Bavarian city of Bayreuth in 1771, Johann Friedrich Esper found human bones at the same level as the remains of extinct animals. He was more startled than elated by his find, because it confronted him with a disturbing anachronism in the then-accepted timetable of the world's history. In the preceding century Archbishop Ussher had worked out this chronology from the complicated genealogies of *Genesis;* he concluded that the world and man had been created in 4004 B.C. Six millennia took in everything, and man was only a trifle younger than time itself. In this view of human history there was no inkling that sources other than written ones existed. The antiquaries of the time were concerned with describing monuments and cataloguing portable relics; they had no idea that history lay in the soil, much less any notion of how to wrest it from its grave. Samuel Johnson spoke for the prearchaeological scholar when he declared: "All that is really known of the ancient state of Britain is contained in a few pages. . . . We can know no more than what old writers have told us."

Except for a few pagan myths, the old writers did not suggest that there were men before Man. Geology in Esper's and Johnson's time was little more than an elaboration of the Biblical story of Creation and the Flood. In accordance with that tradition it was easy, and not without logic, to explain fossils and river gravels in terms of the Flood, or sometimes of several floods. This was catastrophist or diluvialist geology. There was, to be sure, some talk of animals antedating 4004 B.C., but their fossils were believed to be the remains of creatures discarded by the Creator before his culminating creation: the world of Genesis. But with the creation of Adam, according to the doctrine, further creation ceased. Opposed to this account were the antediluvians—the near-heretics who held that man may have lived before Adam. This was the danger apprehended by Esper, and it caused him to ask: "Did [the bones] belong to a Druid or to an Antediluvian or to a mortal man of more recent time? I dare not presume without sufficient reason these members to be of the same age as the other animal petrifactions. They must have got there by chance."

The "sufficient reason" Esper asked

**FLINT TOOL FROM HOXNE IN SUFFOLK is typical of the discoveries that caused speculation about man's antiquity. This hand-axe, dated according to the stratum in which it was found and** the workmanship it displays, belongs to the Lower Paleolithic of about half a million years ago. The illustration appeared in 1800 in *Archeologia,* a publication of the Society of Antiquaries of London.

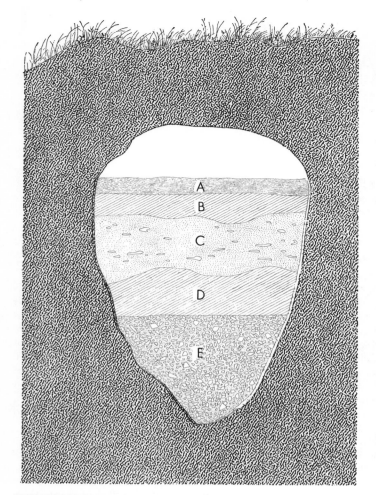

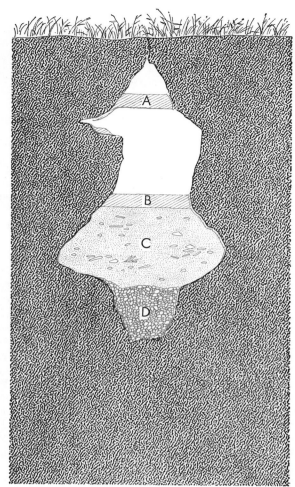

**DEVON CAVES IN ENGLAND** figured prominently in establishing the antiquity of man. Kent's Cavern (*left*) was the earlier find. Under surface layer (A) lay a stalagmite stratum (B) which sealed the cave earth (C) containing human artifacts amid the remains of extinct animals. Layers D and E are stalagmite and breccia. The floor of the 600-foot long Brixham Cave (*right*) had once been at A, but when excavated in 1858 the stalagmite at B was the cave floor. In the six feet of cave earth (C) were remains similar to those found in Kent's Cavern. Level D is gravel bed. Both the caves measure more than 20 feet from roof to gravel-bed bottom.

for was soon to be forthcoming. James Hutton, in his *Theory of the Earth*, published in 1785, offered the first persuasive alternative to cataclysmic geology. He suggested that the stratification of rocks was due not to floods and other supernatural calamities but to processes still going on in seas and rivers and lakes. He wrote: "No processes are to be employed that are not natural to the globe, no action to be admitted except those of which we know the principle." Hutton's reasoning was carried forward by William Smith—"Strata" Smith as he was called—who assigned relative ages to rocks according to their fossil contents, and who argued for an orderly, noncatastrophic deposition of strata over a long period of time—much longer than 6,000 years.

But the climate of opinion was still catastrophist. In 1797, just 26 years after Esper's discovery, John Frere, a gentleman of Suffolk, sent to the Secretary of the Society of Antiquaries of London some hand-axes and other implements of flint found at Hoxne, near Diss. In his accompanying letter he wrote: "If [these] weapons of war, fabricated and used by a people who had not the use of metals . . . are not particularly objects of curiosity in themselves, they must, I think, be considered in that light from the situation in which they are found, [which] may tempt us to refer them to a very remote period indeed; even beyond that of the present world."

They were indeed to be referred "to a very remote period": modern archaeologists would place them in the Lower Paleolithic of perhaps half a million years ago. But at the time no one took Frere's speculations seriously.

William Buckland, Reader in Geology at Oxford and later Dean of Westminster, perhaps typified catastrophist thinking. In 1823 he published his great book *Reliquiae Diluvianae, or Observations on the Organic Remains contained in Caves, Fissures and Diluvial Gravel, and on Other Geological Phenomena attesting the Action of an Universal Deluge*. Buckland himself had found evidence of the antiquity of man, but he refused to believe it. He had excavated Goat's Hole Cave near Paviland in South Wales and amid Upper Paleolithic implements had found the skeleton of a young man. (He believed it to be that of a young woman, and it is still referred to as the Red Lady of Paviland.) But he insisted that the skeleton was "clearly not coeval with the antediluvian bones of the extinct species" of animals. He made similar discoveries in the caves of the Mendip Hills of southwestern England but again refused to believe they were antediluvian. He argued instead that the caves had "been used either as a place of sepulture in early times or resorted to for refuge by the wretches that perished in it, when the country was suffering under one of our numerous military operations. . . . The state of the bones affords indication of very high antiquity but there is no reason for not considering them post-Diluvian."

When a Roman Catholic priest, Father MacEnery, discovered some flint implements at Kent's Cavern near Torquay in Devon, he wrote of them to Buckland. Buckland reacted characteristically. The flints had been found amid the stratified remains of rhinoceros and other animals under the unbroken, stalagmite-sealed floor of the cave. Buckland avoided the implications of this sealed evidence and offered another ingenious and tortured explanation that preserved catastrophist doctrine. He told MacEnery that ancient Britons must have camped in the cave; they had probably scooped out ovens in the stalagmite and in that way the flint implements had got below. Thus, according to Buckland, the association of the flints with the skeletal remains of extinct animals was only apparent. It was all very reasonable, except that, as MacEnery noted, there were no such ovens in the cave. But Buckland was insistent, and out of deference to his views MacEnery did not publish his evidence.

At about this time, however, the National Museum in Copenhagen had been opened to the public with its antiquities arranged in three ages: Stone, Bronze and Iron. This classification was the work of Christian Jurgenson Thomsen, director of the Museum, and he set forth its underlying idea in a treatise that served as a guidebook to the display. His three-age system has been described very properly as "the cornerstone of modern archaeology"; it helped to secure recognition for the view that the human species had come through a long prehistory. (The word "prehistory" did not appear in print until 1851, when Daniel Wilson used it in *The Archaeology and Prehistoric Annals of Scotland*.)

The 1830's were eventful for the emerging new science of archaeology. In 1833 Sir Charles Lyell published his *Principles of Geology*, a powerful contribution to the cause of the fluvialists, as the supporters of Hutton and Smith were called. This book was in its way as important as Darwin's *Origin of Species*. Lyell took the many fragmentary observations and insights of the fluvialists and organized them into a coherent system. He stated the principle of uniformitarianism: the central geological idea that strata could only be interpreted correctly by assuming that the agencies that formed them had operated at a uniform rate and in a uniform way, just as they work in the present. Lyell's great book was a staggering blow to catastrophist geology. But though the discoveries of Esper and Frere were thus rationalized, and the work of Hutton and Smith endorsed, this was not yet sufficient to swing general opinion behind belief in the true antiquity of man. More evidence was needed to shatter the old view and establish the new one; it soon came from Devon and northern France.

Boucher de Perthes was a customs official at Abbeville in the north of France. He had become interested in archaeology when he encountered neolithic artifacts and bones—"Celtic" remains as they were called—brought up by the dredging of the Somme Canal. His interest grew as more remains of "diluvial" man and animals were found in the quarries of nearby Manchecourt and Moulin-Quignon. By 1838, some five or six years after Lyell's *Principles* had appeared, de Perthes set forth his views in a five-volume work entitled *De la création: essai sur l'origine et la progression des êtres*. At about the same time he was exhibiting *haches diluviennes*, roughly chipped hand-axes, before the Société Imperiale d'Emulation de la Somme in Abbeville and at the Institut de Paris.

He was received with the same coldness suffered by his fellows in England, and like them he was regarded as a crank. "At the very mention of the words 'axe' and 'diluvium,' " he once remarked, "I observe a smile on the face of those to whom I speak. It is the workmen who help me, not the geologists." But de Perthes worked on and accumulated more evidence. The association he observed of human artifacts and extinct animals in the Somme gravels was compelling and no longer to be explained by the diluvial theory. In 1847 he published the first part of a three-volume work entitled *Antiquités celtiques et antédiluviennes*. The very title of the work indicates the effect his researches had on his thinking: the *haches diluviennes* were now *haches antédiluviennes*.

In England, meanwhile, the new archaeology had found other champions. William Pengelly, a schoolmaster, reworked MacEnery's cavern in Kent and,

SKULL OF NEANDERTHAL WOMAN was found in Forbes Quarry at Gibraltar in 1848. First believed to be a new species, Neanderthal was later seen to be a human variant. Missing portions of skull are outlined in this drawing from Hugo Obermaier's *Fossil Man in Spain*.

viewing the evidence there in terms of Lyell's uniformitarianism, saw it as proof of man's antiquity. But he realized that objections could be raised because the cavern had been disturbed by other workers. He found an entirely new site in an undisturbed cave across the bay in Devon above Brixham Harbour—Windmill Hill Cave. To supervise his excavations here he enlisted a committee of distinguished geologists in London. Pengelly, carrying out the actual digging, worked from July, 1858, to the next summer. It was a successful year. On the floor of the cave "lay a sheet of stalagmite from three to eight inches thick having within it and on it relics of lion, hyena, bear, mammoth, rhinoceros and reindeer." Below the floor Pengelly found flint tools.

The Brixham discoveries were compelling. Sir Charles Lyell said of them: "The facts recently brought to light during the systematic investigation of the Brixham Cave must, I think, have prepared you to admit that scepticism in regard to the cave evidence in favour of the antiquity of man had previously been pushed to an extreme."

The revolution was nearing a crisis: within the immediately foreseeable future man's history was to reach back beyond Archbishop Ussher's 6,000 years. The catastrophist theory was once and for all to be discarded and with it the Biblical notion that the world and man represented unalterable acts of special creation.

In 1858, while Pengelly was digging in the Brixham cave, the Scottish geologist Hugh Falconer visited Boucher de Perthes at Abbeville. De Perthes' evidence of man's antiquity immediately convinced Falconer. When he returned to London, he persuaded the geologist Joseph Prestwich and the antiquary John Evans to go and see the finds of Abbeville for themselves. As Evans was leaving for France, he wrote of the widely separated events that were revising men's beliefs: "Think of their finding flint axes and arrowheads at Abbeville in conjunction with the bones of elephants and rhinoceroses 40 feet below the surface in a bed of drift. In this bone cave in Devon now being excavated . . . they say they have found flint arrowheads among the bones and the same is reported of a cave in Sicily. I can hardly believe it. It will make my ancient Britons quite modern if man is carried back in England to the days when elephants, rhinoceroses, hippopotomuses and tigers were also inhabitants of the country."

Evans then records what happened

when they got to France. De Perthes showed them his collection of flint axes and implements "found among the beds of gravel, . . . the remains of a race of men who existed at the time when the deluge or whatever was the origin of these gravel beds took place. One of the most remarkable features of the case is that nearly all . . . of the animals whose bones are found in the same beds as the axes are extinct. There is the mammoth, the rhinoceros, the urus, . . . etc." Then they arrive at the actual gravel pits: "Sure enough, the edge of an axe was visible in an entirely undisturbed bed of gravel and eleven feet from the surface. We had a photographer with us to take a view of it so as to corroborate our testimony."

The evidence at Abbeville convinced Evans and Prestwich as it had convinced Falconer, and this, with Pengelly's work at Windmill Hill Cave, brought the whole matter to a head. When they got back to London, Prestwich read a paper to the Royal Society in which he said: "It was not until I had myself witnessed the conditions under which these flint implements had been found at Brixham that I became fully impressed with the validity of the doubts thrown upon the previously prevailing opinions with respect to such remains in caves." That famous meeting of the Royal Society was on May 26, 1859, and of it John Evans wrote: "There were a good many geological nobs there: Sir Charles Lyell, Murchison, Huxley, Morris, Dr. Perry, Faraday, Wheatstone, Babbage, etc. . . . . Our assertions as to the finding of the weapons seemed to be believed."

A week later Evans read a paper on the same subject to the Society of Antiquaries of London. In his account of this meeting he remarked: "I think I was generally believed in."

In August Sir Charles Lyell himself went to see the evidence of the Abbeville pits. He too was convinced, and a month later, in his presidential address to Section C of the British Association for the Advancement of Science, with Prince Albert presiding, he said: "I am fully prepared to corroborate the conclusions recently laid before the Royal Society by Mr. Prestwich." The battle was over; the great antiquity of man was an established fact. Victorian thought had to adjust itself not only to organic evolution but also to the antiquity of man; 4004 B.C. was forgotten.

It is perhaps strange that Charles Darwin himself was not at first impressed by the findings of de Perthes. Later in life he confessed: "I am ashamed to

think that I concluded the whole was rubbish. Yet [de Perthes] has done for man something like what Agassiz did for glaciers." Perhaps Darwin held back because he did not want to involve his theory of evolution, at least at the outset, in anything so controversial as the ancestry of man. In the first edition of the *Origin of Species* he refused to discuss the relationship of evolution to man, and made only one cryptic statement on the general thesis of his book: "Light will be thrown on the origin of man and his history." In later editions this sentence was modified to: "Much light will be thrown. . . ."

But Darwin threw no light, not at any rate until 1871, when he published his views on the relation between man and general evolutionary theory in his *Descent of Man*. But this was eight years after T. H. Huxley's *Evidence as to Man's Place in Nature* had been published, and a dozen years after the climactic events of 1859. Thus whatever contribution Darwin made to the discovery of the antiquity of man, it was indirect and unwitting. It consisted entirely in the new way of thinking that he exemplified: uniformitarianism and evolution. The doctrine of evolution had man evolving from a prehuman ancestor; obviously there must somewhere be evidence of his passage from savagery through barbarism to civilization. The roughly chipped tools from Devon and the Somme now were more than credible, they were essential. People now had to accept the discoveries of de Perthes and Pengelly, where only a generation or two before, when the immutability of the species and catastrophist diluvialism were the dominant ideas, such discoveries had been scorned or ignored. Thus though Darwinism did not create prehistoric archaeology, it did give a great impetus to its acceptance and study; it helped set the stage for the acceptance of the idea of man's antiquity.

But even after the idea seemed well established, many students of the mid-century discoveries had misgivings about them. There was one particularly troublesome point: Men had left their axes but no trace of their physical selves, no bones. "Find us human remains in the diluvium," some of de Perthes' countrymen said to him, "and we will believe you." For de Perthes it was a sad challenge; this was 1863 and he was an old man of 75. Unable to dig for himself, he offered a 200-franc reward to the first quarryman to find human remains. With four months' wages as the prize, the quarrymen could not leave it to honest luck. Soon after the offer was made, they "found" human remains; first a human tooth; five days later a human jaw.

Boucher de Perthes was vindicated, and his French colleagues were at last satisfied. But the drama had not played out. Some British archaeologists had long suspected that de Perthes' gravel pits were being salted, and they proved that the jaw and several hand-axes had been inserted into the gravel faces by some of his workmen. It was a cruel blow.

Fortunately the case did not hang by so meager a thread. There was genuine skeletal evidence of man's antiquity. Two years before the 1859 pronouncements about the antiquity of man, the long bones and skullcap of a manlike being had been discovered in a limestone cave in the ravine of Neanderthal near the Rhenish city of Düsseldorf.

Hermann Schaaffhausen, who first described these remains, noted the large size, low forehead and enormous browridges of the skullcap. He believed that the Neanderthal skeleton belonged to "a barbarous and savage race," and he regarded it "as the most ancient memorial of the early inhabitants of Europe."

There was still more evidence. A female cranium had been found nine years before that, in 1848, during blasting operations in the Forbes Quarry at Gibraltar. The significance of the relic was not realized at the time, but at this juncture, in 1859, George Busk read a paper on it before a meeting of the British Association. The ebullient Falconer, who had persuaded Evans and Prestwich to visit de Perthes six years before, again apprehended the importance of a crucial find. He perceived that here was a new species of man; he proposed to name it *Homo calpicus*, after Calpe, the ancient name for Gibraltar. He wrote his suggestion to Busk, referring somewhat redundantly to his "Grand, Priscan, Pithecoid, Agrioblematous, Platycnemic, wild *Homo calpicus* of Gibraltar." It was only later realized that this "grand, primitive, manlike, wild-eyed, flat-headed, wild Calpic man of Gibraltar" was not one of a new species but a member of that curious human variant, Neanderthal man.

And so by 1859 all the evidence for proper recognition of the antiquity of man was available: artifacts from the Somme and south Devon and fossils from Neanderthal and Gibraltar. The century since then has been given to building on that premise, to filling in its outlines with new evidence of man's physical and cultural evolution.

# Tools and Human Evolution

by Sherwood L. Washburn
*September 1960*

*It is now clear that tools antedate man, and that their
use by prehuman primates gave rise to* Homo sapiens

A series of recent discoveries has linked prehuman primates of half a million years ago with stone tools. For some years investigators had been uncovering tools of the simplest kind from ancient deposits in Africa. At first they assumed that these tools constituted evidence of the existence of large-brained, fully bipedal men. Now the tools have been found in association with much more primitive creatures, the not-fully bipedal, small-brained near-men, or man-apes. Prior to these finds the prevailing view held that man evolved nearly to his present structural state and then discovered tools and the new ways of life that they made possible. Now it appears that man-apes—creatures able to run but not yet walk on two legs, and with brains no larger than those of apes now living—had already learned to make and to use tools. It follows that the structure of modern man must be the result of the change in the terms of natural selection that came with the tool-using way of life.

The earliest stone tools are chips or simple pebbles, usually from river

gravels. Many of them have not been shaped at all, and they can be identified as tools only because they appear in concentrations, along with a few worked pieces, in caves or other locations where no such stones naturally occur. The huge advantage that a stone tool gives to its user must be tried to be appreciated. Held in the hand, it can be used for pounding, digging or scraping. Flesh and bone can be cut with a flaked chip, and what would be a mild blow with the fist becomes lethal with a rock in the hand. Stone tools can be employed, moreover, to make tools of other materials. Naturally occurring sticks are nearly all rotten, too large, or of inconvenient shape; some tool for fabrication is essential for the efficient use of wood. The utility of a mere pebble seems so limited to the user of modern tools that it is not easy to comprehend the vast difference that separates the tool-user from the ape which relies on hands and teeth alone. Ground-living monkeys dig out roots for food, and if they could use a stone or a stick, they might easily double their food supply. It was the success of the simplest tools that started the whole trend of human evolution and led to the civilizations of today.

From the short-term point of view, human structure makes human behavior possible. From the evolutionary point of view, behavior and structure form an interacting complex, with each change in one affecting the other. Man began when populations of apes, about a mil-

lion years ago, started the bipedal, tool-using way of life that gave rise to the man-apes of the genus *Australopithecus*. Most of the obvious differences that distinguish man from ape came after the use of tools.

The primary evidence for the new view of human evolution is teeth, bones and tools. But our ancestors were not fossils; they were striving creatures, full of rage, dominance and the will to live. What evolved was the pattern of life of intelligent, exploratory, playful, vigorous primates; the evolving reality was a succession of social systems based upon the motor abilities, emotions and intelligence of their members. Selection produced new systems of child care, maturation and sex, just as it did alterations in the skull and the teeth. Tools, hunting, fire, complex social life, speech, the human way and the brain evolved together to produce ancient man of the genus *Homo* about half a million years ago. Then the brain evolved under the pressures of more complex social life until the species *Homo sapiens* appeared perhaps as recently as 50,000 years ago.

With the advent of *Homo sapiens* the tempo of technical-social evolution quickened. Some of the early types of tool had lasted for hundreds of thousands of years and were essentially the same throughout vast areas of the African and Eurasian land masses. Now the tool forms multiplied and became regionally diversified. Man invented the

**OLDUVAI GORGE** in Tanganyika is the site where the skull of the largest known man-ape was discovered in 1959 by L. S. B. Leakey and his wife Mary. Stratigraphic evidence indicates that skull dates back to Lower Pleistocene, more than 500,000 years ago.

bow, boats, clothing; conquered the Arctic; invaded the New World; domesticated plants and animals; discovered metals, writing and civilization. Today, in the midst of the latest tool-making revolution, man has achieved the capacity to adapt his environment to his need and impulse, and his numbers have begun to crowd the planet.

The later events in the evolution of the human species are treated in other articles from the September, 1960 issue of SCIENTIFIC AMERICAN. This article is concerned with the beginnings of the process by which, as Theodosius Dobzhansky says in the concluding article of the issue, biological evolution has transcended itself. From the rapidly accumulating evidence it is now possible to speculate with some confidence on the manner in which the way of life made possible by tools changed the pressures of natural selection and so changed the structure of man.

Tools have been found, along with the bones of their makers, at Sterkfontein, Swartkrans and Kromdraai in South Africa and at Olduvai in Tanganyika. Many of the tools from Sterkfontein are merely unworked river pebbles, but someone had to carry them from the gravels some miles away and bring them to the deposit in which they are found. Nothing like them occurs naturally in the local limestone caves. Of course the association of the stone tools with man-ape bones in one or two localities does not prove that these animals made the tools. It has been argued that a more advanced form of man, already present, was the toolmaker. This argument has a familiar ring to students of human evolution. Peking man was thought too primitive to be a toolmaker; when the first manlike pelvis was found with man-ape bones, some argued that it must have fallen into the deposit because it was too human to be associated with the skull. In every case, however, the repeated discovery of the same unanticipated association has ultimately settled the controversy.

This is why the discovery by L. S. B. and Mary Leakey in the summer of 1959 is so important. In Olduvai Gorge in Tanganyika they came upon traces of an old living site, and found stone tools in clear association with the largest man-ape skull known. With the stone tools were a hammer stone and waste flakes from the manufacture of the tools. The deposit also contained the bones of rats, mice, frogs and some bones of juvenile pig and antelope, showing that even the largest and latest of the

SKULL IS EXAMINED *in situ* by Mary Leakey, who first noticed fragments of it protruding from the cliff face at left. Pebble tools were found at the same level as the skull.

SKULL IS EXCAVATED from surrounding rock with dental picks. Although skull was badly fragmented, almost all of it was recovered. Fragment visible here is part of upper jaw.

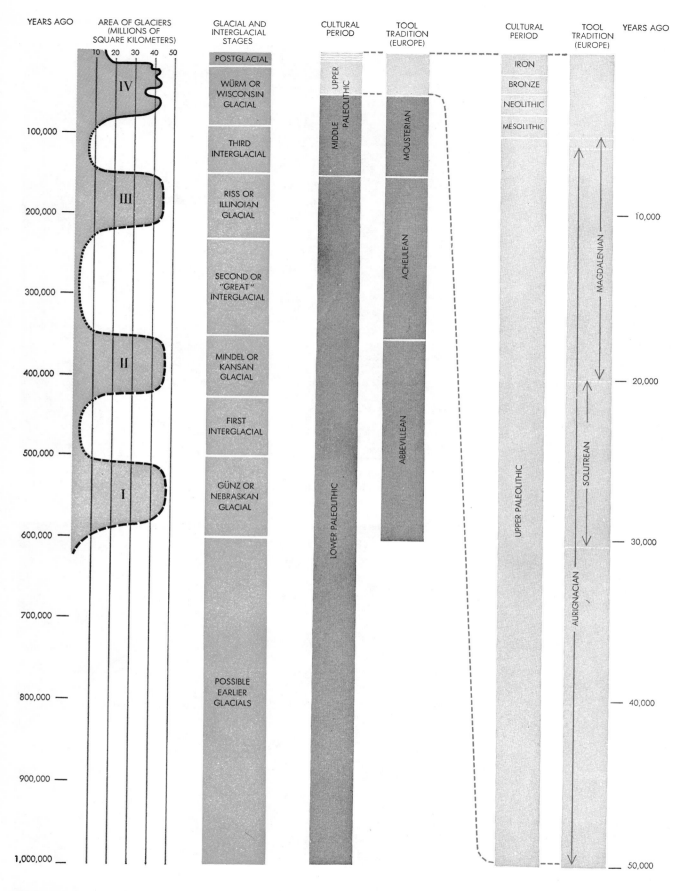

| YEARS AGO | AREA OF GLACIERS (MILLIONS OF SQUARE KILOMETERS) | GLACIAL AND INTERGLACIAL STAGES | CULTURAL PERIOD | TOOL TRADITION (EUROPE) | CULTURAL PERIOD | TOOL TRADITION (EUROPE) | YEARS AGO |

**TIME-SCALE** correlates cultural periods and tool traditions with the four great glaciations of the Pleistocene epoch. Glacial advances and retreats shown by solid black curve are accurately known; those shown by broken curve are less certain; those shown by dotted curve are uncertain. Light gray bars at far right show an expanded view of last 50,000 years on two darker bars at center. Scale was prepared with the assistance of William R. Farrand of the Lamont Geological Observatory of Columbia University.

man-apes could kill only the smallest animals and must have been largely vegetarian. The Leakeys' discovery confirms the association of the man-ape with pebble tools, and adds the evidence of manufacture to that of mere association. Moreover, the stratigraphic evidence at Olduvai now for the first time securely dates the man-apes, placing them in the lower Pleistocene, earlier than 500,000 years ago and earlier than the first skeletal and cultural evidence for the existence of the genus Homo [*see illustration on next two pages*]. Before the discovery at Olduvai these points had been in doubt.

The man-apes themselves are known from several skulls and a large number of teeth and jaws, but only fragments of the rest of the skeleton have been preserved. There were two kinds of man-ape, a small early one that may have weighed 50 or 60 pounds and a later and larger one that weighed at least twice as much. The differences in size and form between the two types are quite comparable to the differences between the contemporary pygmy chimpanzee and the common chimpanzee.

Pelvic remains from both forms of man-ape show that these animals were bipedal. From a comparison of the pelvis of ape, man-ape and man it can be seen that the upper part of the pelvis is much wider and shorter in man than in the ape, and that the pelvis of the man-ape corresponds closely, though not precisely, to that of modern man [*see top illustration on page 23*]. The long upper pelvis of the ape is characteristic of most mammals, and it is the highly specialized, short, wide bone in man that makes possible the human kind of bipedal locomotion. Although the man-ape pelvis is apelike in its lower part, it approaches that of man in just those features that distinguish man from all other animals. More work must be done before this combination of features is fully understood. My belief is that bipedal running, made possible by the changes in the upper pelvis, came before efficient bipedal walking, made possible by the changes in the lower pelvis. In the man-ape, therefore, the adaptation to bipedal locomotion is not yet complete. Here, then, is a phase of human evolution characterized by forms that are mostly bipedal, small-brained, plains-living, tool-making hunters of small animals.

The capacity for bipedal walking is primarily an adaptation for covering long distances. Even the arboreal chimpanzee can run faster than a man, and any monkey can easily outdistance him.

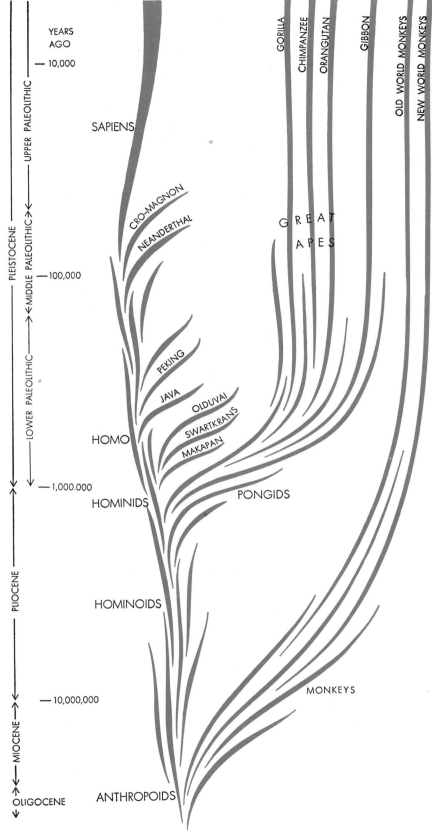

**LINES OF DESCENT** that lead to man and his closer living relatives are charted. The hominoid superfamily diverged from the anthropoid line in the Miocene period some 20 million years ago. From the hominoid line came the tool-using hominids at the beginning of the Pleistocene. The genus *Homo* appeared in the hominid line during the first interglacial (*see chart on opposite page*); the species *Homo sapiens*, around 50,000 years ago.

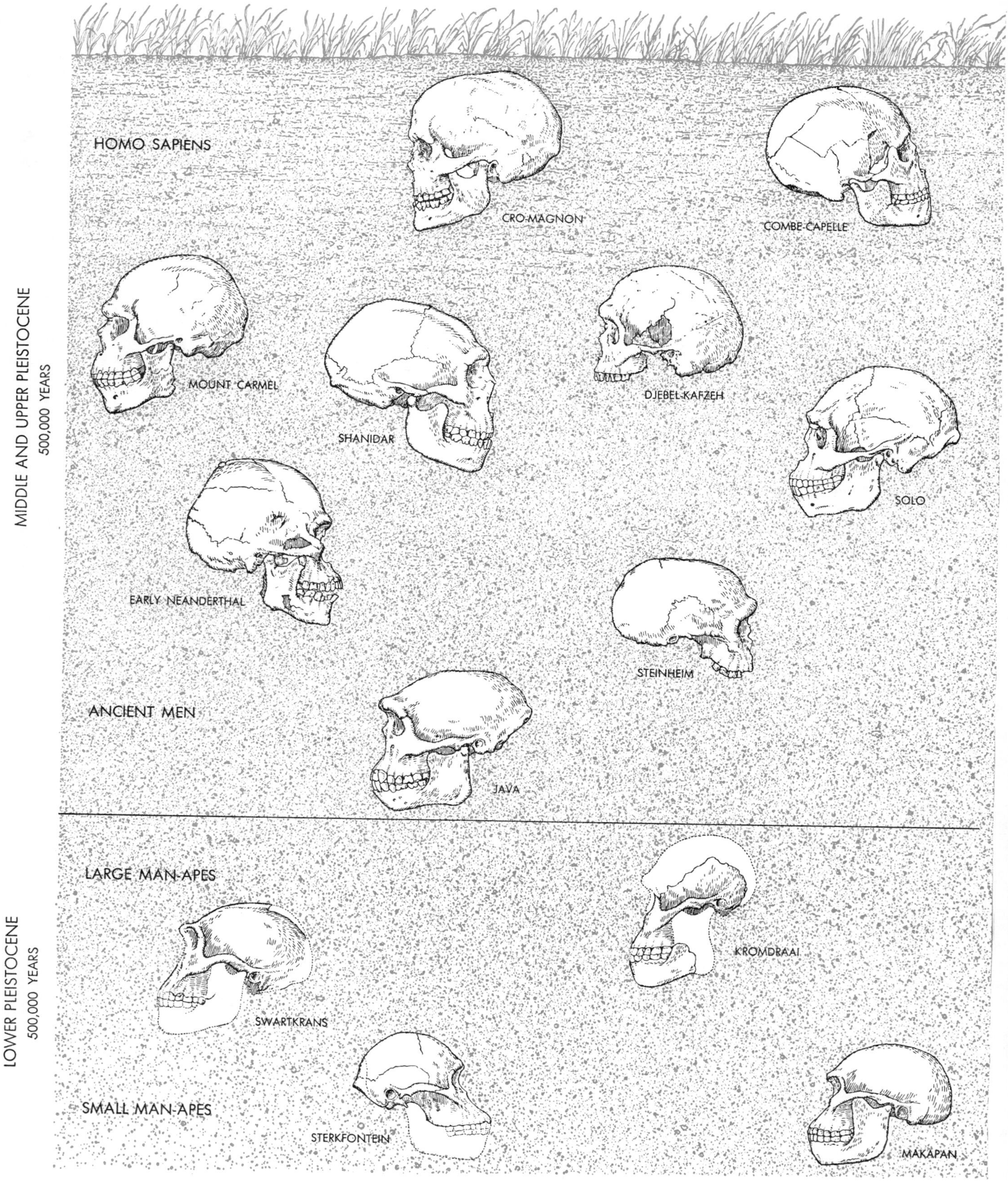

HOMO SAPIENS

CRO-MAGNON

COMBE-CAPELLE

MOUNT CARMEL

SHANIDAR

DJEBEL-KAFZEH

SOLO

EARLY NEANDERTHAL

STEINHEIM

ANCIENT MEN

JAVA

LARGE MAN-APES

KROMDRAAI

SWARTKRANS

SMALL MAN-APES

STERKFONTEIN

MAKAPAN

MIDDLE AND UPPER PLEISTOCENE
500,000 YEARS

LOWER PLEISTOCENE
500,000 YEARS

FOSSIL SKULLS of Pleistocene epoch reflect transition from man-apes (*below black line*) to *Homo sapiens* (*top*). Relative age of intermediate specimens is indicated schematically by their posi- tion on page. Java man (*middle left*) and Solo man (*upper center*) are members of the genus *Pithecanthropus*, and are related to Peking man (*middle right*). The Shanidar skull (*upper left*) be-

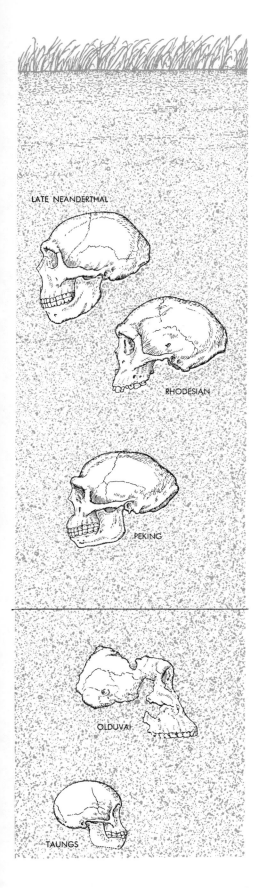

LATE NEANDERTHAL

RHODESIAN

PEKING

OLDUVAI

TAUNGS

longs to the Neanderthal family, while Mount Carmel skull shows characteristics of Neanderthal and modern man.

A man, on the other hand, can walk for many miles, and this is essential for efficient hunting. According to skeletal evidence, fully developed walkers first appeared in the ancient men who inhabited the Old World from 500,000 years ago to the middle of the last glaciation. These men were competent hunters, as is shown by the bones of the large animals they killed. But they also used fire and made complicated tools according to clearly defined traditions. Along with the change in the structure of the pelvis, the brain had doubled in size since the time of the man-apes.

The fossil record thus substantiates the suggestion, first made by Charles Darwin, that tool use is both the cause and the effect of bipedal locomotion. Some very limited bipedalism left the hands sufficiently free from locomotor functions so that stones or sticks could be carried, played with and used. The advantage that these objects gave to their users led both to more bipedalism and to more efficient tool use. English lacks any neat expression for this sort of situation, forcing us to speak of cause and effect as if they were separated, whereas in natural selection cause and effect are interrelated. Selection is based on successful behavior, and in the man-apes the beginnings of the human way of life depended on both inherited locomotor capacity and on the learned skills of tool-using. The success of the new way of life based on the use of tools changed the selection pressures on many parts of the body, notably the teeth, hands and brain, as well as on the pelvis. But it must be remembered that selection was for the whole way of life.

In all the apes and monkeys the males have large canine teeth. The long upper canine cuts against the first lower premolar, and the lower canine passes in front of the upper canine. This is an efficient fighting mechanism, backed by very large jaw muscles. I have seen male baboons drive off cheetahs and dogs, and according to reliable reports male baboons have even put leopards to flight. The females have small canines, and they hurry away with the young under the very conditions in which the males turn to fight. All the evidence from living monkeys and apes suggests that the male's large canines are of the greatest importance to the survival of the group, and that they are particularly important in ground-living forms that may not be able to climb to safety in the trees. The small, early man-apes lived in open plains country, and yet none of them had large canine teeth. It would appear that the protection of the group must have shifted from teeth to tools early in the evolution of the man-apes, and long before the appearance of the forms that have been found in association with stone tools. The tools of Sterkfontein and Olduvai represent not the beginnings of tool use, but a choice of material and knowledge in manufacture which, as is shown by the small canines of the man-apes that deposited them there, derived from a long history of tool use.

Reduction in the canine teeth is not a simple matter, but involves changes in the muscles, face, jaws and other parts of the skull. Selection builds powerful neck muscles in animals that fight with their canines, and adapts the skull to the action of these muscles. Fighting is not a matter of teeth alone, but also of seizing, shaking and hurling an enemy's body with the jaws, head and neck. Reduction in the canines is therefore accompanied by a shortening in the jaws, reduction in the ridges of bone over the eyes and a decrease in the shelf of bone in the neck area [*see illustration on page 24*]. The reason that the skulls of the females and young of the apes look more like man-apes than those of adult males is that, along with small canines, they have smaller muscles and all the numerous structural features that go along with them. The skull of the man-ape is that of an ape that has lost the structure for effective fighting with its teeth. Moreover, the man-ape has transferred to its hands the functions of seizing and pulling, and this has been attended by reduction of its incisors. Small canines and incisors are biological symbols of a changed way of life; their primitive functions are replaced by hand and tool.

The history of the grinding teeth—the molars—is different from that of the seizing and fighting teeth. Large size in any anatomical structure must be maintained by positive selection; the selection pressure changed first on the canine teeth and, much later, on the molars. In the man-apes the molars were very large, larger than in either ape or man. They were heavily worn, possibly because food dug from the ground with the aid of tools was very abrasive. With the men of the Middle Pleistocene, molars of human size appear along with complicated tools, hunting and fire.

The disappearance of brow ridges and the refinement of the human face may involve still another factor. One of the essential conditions for the organi-

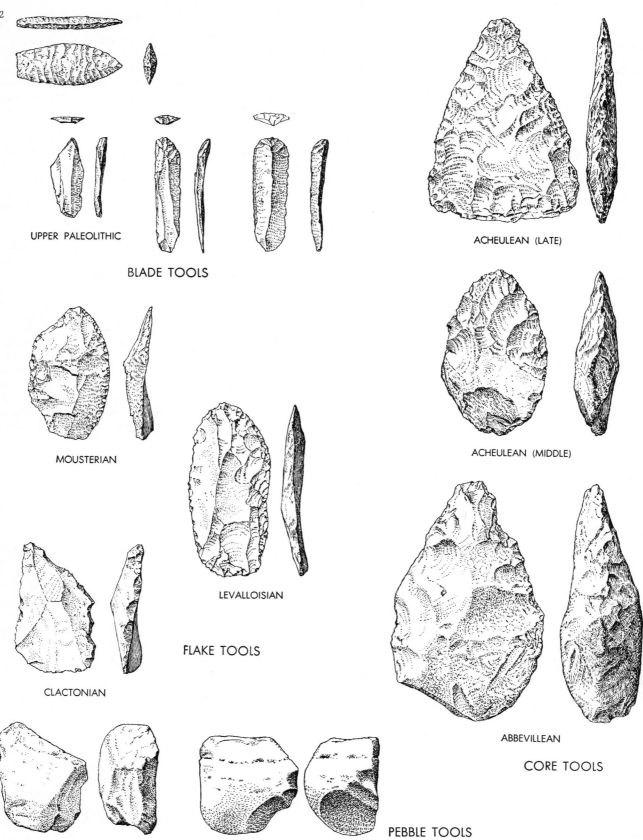

UPPER PALEOLITHIC

BLADE TOOLS

ACHEULEAN (LATE)

MOUSTERIAN

ACHEULEAN (MIDDLE)

LEVALLOISIAN

FLAKE TOOLS

CLACTONIAN

ABBEVILLEAN

CORE TOOLS

PEBBLE TOOLS

**TOOL TRADITIONS** of Europe are the main basis for classifying Paleolithic cultures. The earliest tools are shown at bottom of page; later ones, at top. The tools are shown from both the side and the edge, except for blade tools, which are shown in three views. Tools consisting of a piece of stone from which a few flakes have been chipped are called core tools (*right*). Other types of tool were made from flakes (*center and left*); blade tools were made from flakes with almost parallel sides. Tool traditions are named for site where tools of a given type were discovered; Acheulean tools, for example, are named for St. Acheul in France.

zation of men in co-operative societies was the suppression of rage and of the uncontrolled drive to first place in the hierarchy of dominance. Curt P. Richter of Johns Hopkins University has shown that domestic animals, chosen over the generations for willingness to adjust and for lack of rage, have relatively small adrenal glands. But the breeders who selected for this hormonal, physiological, temperamental type also picked, without realizing it, animals with small brow ridges and small faces. The skull structure of the wild rat bears the same relation to that of the tame rat as does the skull of Neanderthal man to that of *Homo sapiens*. The same is true for the cat, dog, pig, horse and cow; in each case the wild form has the larger face and muscular ridges. In the later stages of human evolution, it appears, the self-domestication of man has been exerting the same effects upon temperament, glands and skull that are seen in the domestic animals.

Of course from man-ape to man the brain-containing part of the skull has also increased greatly in size. This change is directly due to the increase in the size of the brain: as the brain grows, so grow the bones that cover it. Since there is this close correlation between brain size and bony brain-case, the brain size of the fossils can be estimated. On the scale of brain size the man-apes are scarcely distinguishable from the living apes, although their brains may have been larger with respect to body size. The brain seems to have evolved rapidly, doubling in size between man-ape and man. It then appears to have increased much more slowly; there is no substantial change in gross size during the last 100,000 years. One must remember, however, that size alone is a very crude indicator, and that brains of equal size may vary greatly in function. My belief is that although the brain of *Homo sapiens* is no larger than that of Neanderthal man, the indirect evidence strongly suggests that the first *Homo sapiens* was a much more intelligent creature.

The great increase in brain size is important because many functions of the brain seem to depend on the number of cells, and the number increases with volume. But certain parts of the brain have increased in size much more than others. As functional maps of the cortex of the brain show, the human sensory-motor cortex is not just an enlargement of that of an ape [*see illustrations on last three pages of this article*]. The areas

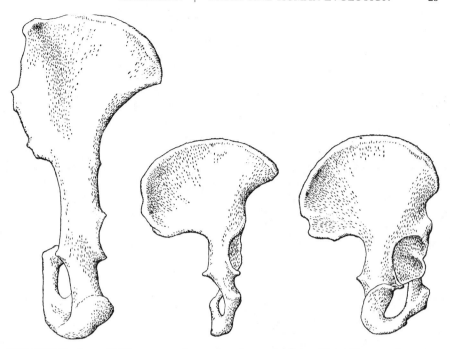

**HIP BONES** of ape (*left*), man-ape (*center*) and man (*right*) reflect differences between quadruped and biped. Upper part of human pelvis is wider and shorter than that of apes. Lower part of man-ape pelvis resembles that of ape; upper part resembles that of man.

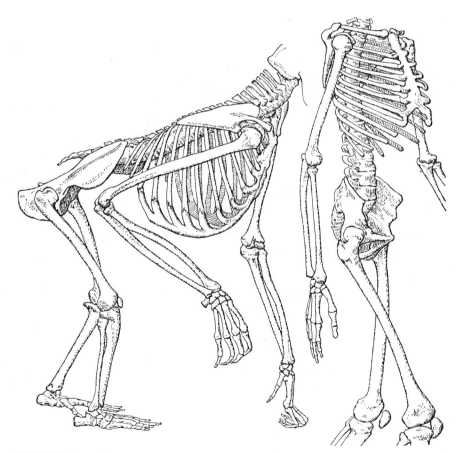

**POSTURE** of gorilla (*left*) and man (*right*) is related to size, shape and orientation of pelvis. Long, straight pelvis of ape provides support for quadrupedal locomotion; short, broad pelvis of man curves backward, carrying spine and torso in bipedal position.

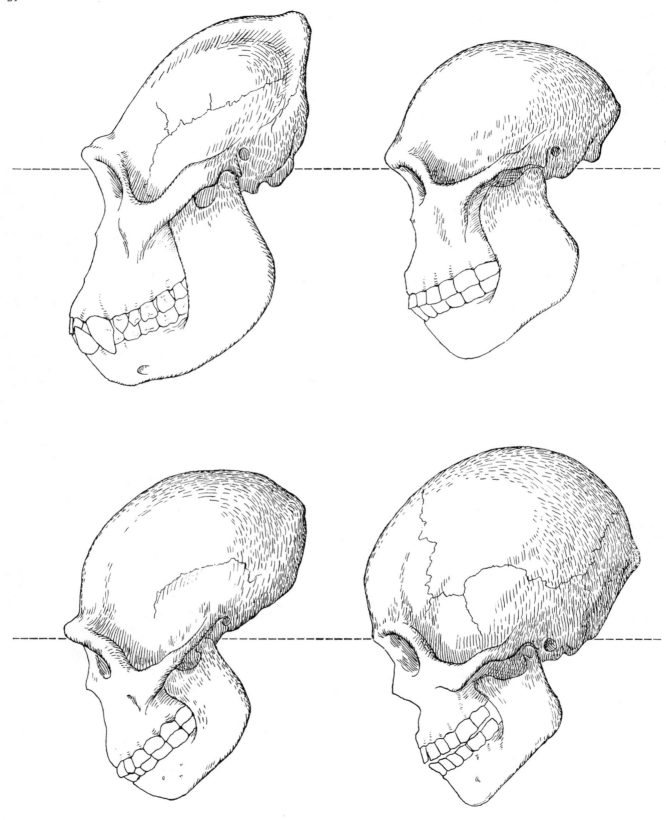

**EVOLUTION OF SKULL** from ape (*upper left*) to man-ape (*upper right*) to ancient man (*lower left*) to modern man (*lower right*) involves an increase in size of brain case (*part of skull above broken lines*) and a corresponding decrease in size of face (*part of skull below broken lines*). Apes also possess canine teeth that are much larger than those found in either man-apes or man.

for the hand, especially the thumb, in man are tremendously enlarged, and this is an integral part of the structural base that makes the skillful use of the hand possible. The selection pressures that favored a large thumb also favored a large cortical area to receive sensations from the thumb and to control its motor activity. Evolution favored the development of a sensitive, powerful, skillful thumb, and in all these ways —as well as in structure—a human thumb differs from that of an ape.

The same is true for other cortical areas. Much of the cortex in a monkey is still engaged in the motor and sensory functions. In man it is the areas adjacent to the primary centers that are most expanded. These areas are concerned with skills, memory, foresight and language; that is, with the mental faculties that make human social life possible. This is easiest to illustrate in the field of language. Many apes and monkeys can make a wide variety of sounds. These sounds do not, however, develop into language [see "The Origin of Speech," by Charles F. Hockett Offprint 603.] Some workers have devoted great efforts, with minimum results, to trying to teach chimpanzees to talk. The reason is that there is little in the brain to teach. A human child learns to speak with the greatest ease, but the storage of thousands of words takes a great deal of cortex. Even the simplest language must have given great advantage to those first men who had it. One is tempted to think that language may have appeared together with the fine tools, fire and complex hunting of the large-brained men of the Middle Pleistocene, but there is no direct proof of this.

The main point is that the kind of animal that can learn to adjust to complex, human, technical society is a very different creature from a tree-living ape, and the differences between the two are rooted in the evolutionary process. The reason that the human brain makes the human way of life possible is that it is the result of that way of life. Great masses of the tissue in the human brain are devoted to memory, planning, language and skills, because these are the abilities favored by the human way of life.

The emergence of man's large brain occasioned a profound change in the plan of human reproduction. The human mother-child relationship is unique among the primates as is the use of tools. In all the apes and monkeys the baby clings to the mother; to be able to do so,

**MOTOR CORTEX OF MONKEY** controls the movements of the body parts outlined by the superimposed drawing of the animal (*color*). Gray lines trace the surface features of the left half of the brain (*bottom*) and part of the right half (*top*). Colored drawing is distorted in proportion to amount of cortex associated with functions of various parts of the body. Smaller animal in right half of brain indicates location of secondary motor cortex.

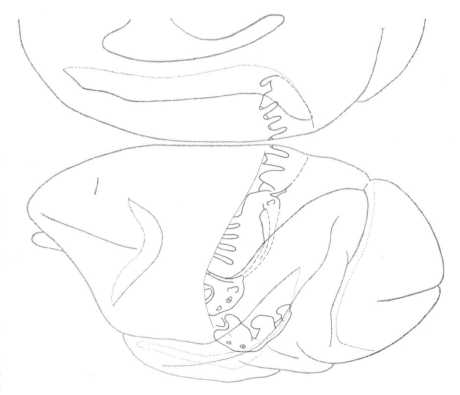

**SENSORY CORTEX OF MONKEY** is mapped in same way as motor cortex (*above*). As in motor cortex, a large area is associated with hands and feet. Smaller animal at bottom of left half of brain indicates location of secondary sensory cortex. Drawings are based on work of Clinton N. Woolsey and his colleagues at the University of Wisconsin Medical School.

the baby must be born with its central nervous system in an advanced state of development. But the brain of the fetus must be small enough so that birth may take place. In man adaptation to bipedal locomotion decreased the size of the bony birth-canal at the same time that the exigencies of tool use selected for larger brains. This obstetrical dilemma was solved by delivery of the fetus at a much earlier stage of development. But this was possible only because the mother, already bipedal and with hands free of locomotor necessities, could hold the helpless, immature infant. The small-brained man-ape probably developed in the uterus as much as the ape does; the human type of mother-child relation must have evolved by the time of the large-brained, fully bipedal humans of the Middle Pleistocene. Bipedalism, tool use and selection for large brains thus slowed human development and invoked far greater maternal responsibility. The slow-moving mother, carrying the baby, could not hunt, and the combination of the woman's obligation to care for slow-developing babies and the man's occupation of hunting imposed a fundamental pattern on the social organization of the human species.

As Marshall D. Sahlins suggests ["The Origin of Society," SCIENTIFIC AMERICAN Offprint 602], human society was heavily conditioned at the outset by still other significant aspects of man's sexual adaptation. In monkeys and apes year-round sexual activity supplies the social bond that unites the primate horde. But sex in these species is still subject to physiological—especially glandular—controls. In man these controls are gone, and are replaced by a bewildering variety of social customs. In no other primate does

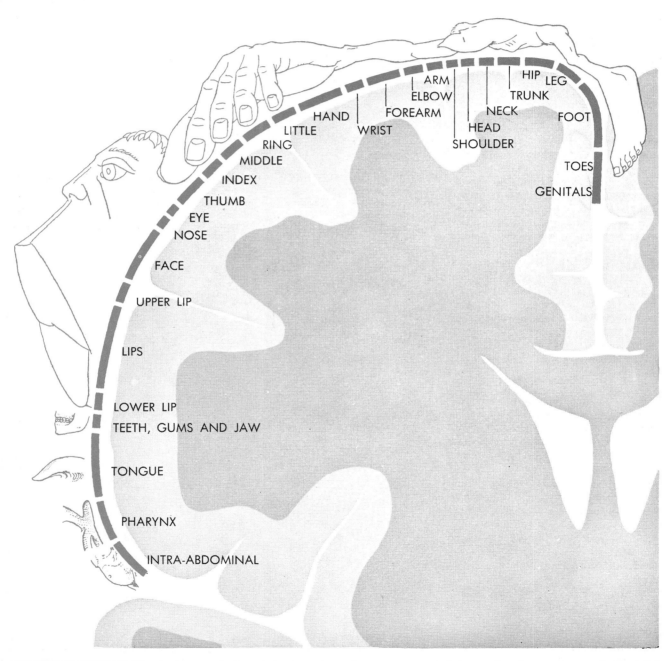

**SENSORY HOMUNCULUS** is a functional map of the sensory cortex of the human brain worked out by Wilder Penfield and his associates at the Montreal Neurological Institute. As in the map of the sensory cortex of the monkey that appears on the preceding page, the distorted anatomical drawing (*color*) indicates the areas of the sensory cortex associated with the various parts of the body.

a family exist that controls sexual activity by custom, that takes care of slow-growing young, and in which—as in the case of primitive human societies—the male and female provide different foods for the family members.

All these family functions are ultimately related to tools, hunting and the enlargement of the brain. Complex and technical society evolved from the sporadic tool-using of an ape, through the simple pebble tools of the man-ape and the complex toolmaking traditions of ancient men to the hugely complicated culture of modern man. Each behavioral stage was both cause and effect of biological change in bones and brain. These concomitant changes can be seen in the scanty fossil record and can be inferred from the study of the living forms.

Surely as more fossils are found these ideas will be tested. New techniques of investigation, from planned experiments in the behavior of lower primates to more refined methods of dating, will extract wholly new information from the past. It is my belief that, as these events come to pass, tool use will be found to have been a major factor, beginning with the initial differentiation of man and ape. In ourselves we see a structure, physiology and behavior that is the result of the fact that some populations of apes started to use tools a million years ago. The pebble tools constituted man's principal technical adaptation for a period at least 50 times as long as recorded history. As we contemplate man's present eminence, it is well to remember that, from the point of view of evolution, the events of the last 50,000 years occupy but a moment in time. Ancient man endured at least 10 times as long and the man-apes for an even longer time.

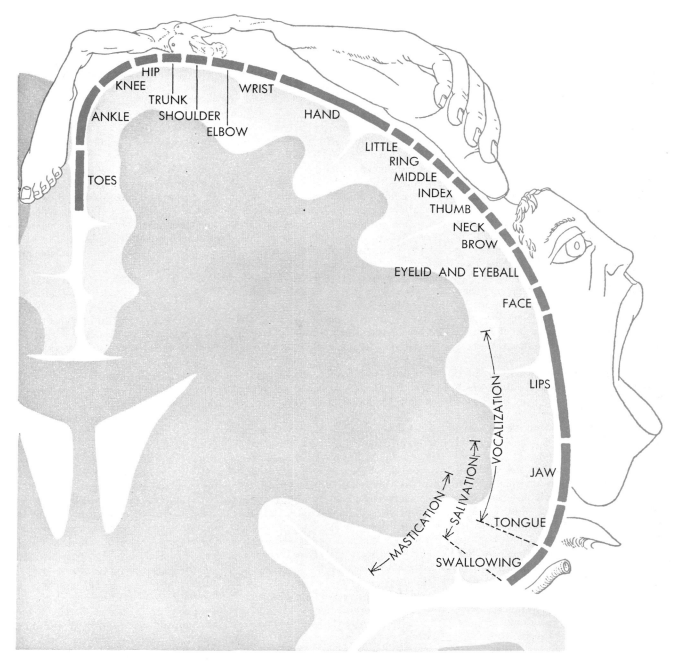

**MOTOR HOMUNCULUS** depicts parts of body and areas of motor cortex that control their functions. Human brain is shown here in coronal (ear-to-ear) cross section. Speech and hand areas of both motor and sensory cortex in man are proportionately much larger than corresponding areas in apes and monkeys, as can be seen by comparing homunculi with diagram of monkey cortex.

# 3

# Homo Erectus

by William W. Howells
*November 1966*

*This species, until recently known by a multiplicity of
other names, was probably the immediate predecessor
of modern man. It now seems possible that the
transition took place some 500,000 years ago*

In 1891 Eugène Dubois, a young
Dutch anatomist bent on discovering early man, was examining a
fossil-rich layer of gravels beside the
Solo River in Java. He found what he
was after: an ancient human skull. The
next year he discovered in the same formation a human thighbone. These two
fossils, now known to be more than
700,000 years old, were the first remains
to be found of the prehistoric human
species known today as *Homo erectus*.
It is appropriate on the 75th anniversary
of Dubois's discovery to review how our
understanding of this early man has
been broadened and clarified by more
recent discoveries of fossil men of similar antiquity and the same general characteristics, so that *Homo erectus* is now
viewed as representing a major stage
in the evolution of man. Also of interest,
although of less consequence, is the way
in which the name *Homo erectus*, now
accepted by many scholars, has been
chosen after a long period during which
"scientific" names for human fossils were
bestowed rather capriciously.

Man first received his formal name
in 1758, when Carolus Linnaeus called
him *Homo sapiens*. Linnaeus was trying
simply to bring order to the world of
living things by distinguishing each
species of plant and animal from every
other and by arranging them all in a
hierarchical system. Considering living
men, he recognized them quite correctly as one species in the system. The two
centuries that followed Linnaeus saw
first the establishment of evolutionary
theory and then the realization of its genetic foundations; as a result ideas on
the relations of species as units of plant
and animal life have become considerably more complex. For example, a species can form two or more new species,
which Linnaeus originally thought was
impossible. By today's definition a spe-

cies typically consists of a series of local
or regional populations that may exhibit minor differences of form or color
but that otherwise share a common
genetic structure and pool of genes and
are thus able to interbreed across population lines. Only when two such populations have gradually undergone so
many different changes in their genetic
makeup that the likelihood of their interbreeding falls below a critical point
are they genetically cut off from each
other and do they become separate species. Alternatively, over a great many
generations an equivalent amount of
change will take place in the same population, so that its later form will be
recognized as a species different from
the earlier. This kind of difference, of
course, cannot be put to the test of interbreeding and can only be judged by
the physical form of the fossils involved.

In the case of living man there is
no reason to revise Linnaeus' assignment: *Homo sapiens* is a good, typical
species. Evolution, however, was not
in Linnaeus' ken. He never saw a human fossil, much less conceived of men
different from living men. Between his
time and ours the use of the Linnaean
system of classification as applied to
man and his relatives past and present
became almost a game. On grasping the
concept of evolution, scholars saw that
modern man must have had ancestors.
They were prepared to anticipate the
actual discovery of these ancestral
forms, and perhaps the greatest anticipator was the German biologist
Ernst Haeckel. Working on the basis of
fragmentary information in 1889, when
the only well-known fossil human remains were the comparatively recent
bones discovered 25 years earlier in the
Neander Valley of Germany, Haeckel
drew up a theoretical ancestral line for
man. The line began among some postu-

lated extinct apes of the Miocene epoch
and reached *Homo sapiens* by way of an
imagined group of "ape-men" (Pithecanthropi) and a group of more advanced but still speechless early men
(Alali) whom he visualized as the
worldwide stock from which modern
men had evolved [*see illustration on
page 30*]. A creature combining these
various presapient attributes took form
in the pooled imagination of Haeckel
and his compatriots August Schleicher
and Gabriel Max. Max produced a family
portrait, and the still-to-be-discovered
ancestor was given the respectable Linnaean name *Pithecanthropus alalus*.

Were he living today Haeckel would
never do such a thing. It is now
requirement of the International Code
of Zoological Nomenclature that the
naming of any new genus or species be
supported by publication of the specimen's particulars together with a description showing it to be recognizably
different from any genus or species previously known. Haeckel was rescued
from retroactive embarrassment, however, by Dubois, who gave Haeckel's
genus name to Java man. The skull was
too large to be an ape's and apparently
too small to be a man's; the name *Pithecanthropus* seemed perfectly appropriate. On the other hand, the thighbone
from the same formation was essentially
modern; its possessor had evidently
walked upright. Dubois therefore gave
his discovery the species name *erectus*.
Since Dubois's time the legitimacy of
his finds has been confirmed by the
discovery in Java (by G. H. R. von
Koenigswald between 1936 and 1939
and by Indonesian workers within the
past three years) of equally old and
older fossils of the same population.

In the 50 years between Dubois's
discovery and the beginning of World

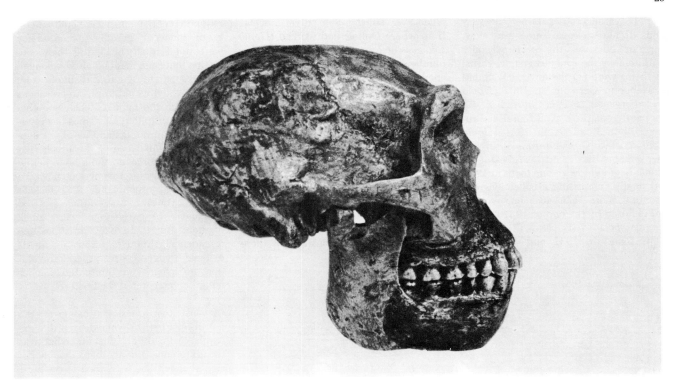

JAVA MAN, whose 700,000-year-old remains were unearthed in 1891 by Eugène Dubois, is representative of the earliest *Homo erectus* population so far discovered. This reconstruction was made recently by G. H. R. von Koenigswald and combines the features of the more primitive members of this species of man that he found in the lowest (Djetis) fossil strata at Sangiran in central Java during the 1930's. The characteristics that are typical of *Homo erectus* include the smallness and flatness of the cranium, the heavy browridge and both the sharp bend and the ridge for muscle attachment at the rear of the skull. The robustness of the jaws adds to the species' primitive appearance. In most respects except size, however, the teeth of *Homo erectus* resemble those of modern man.

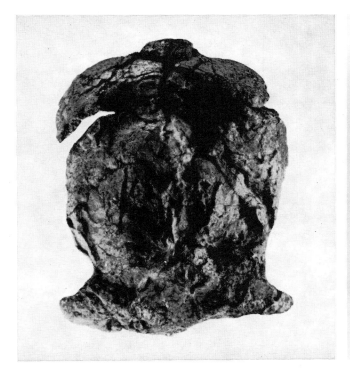

LANTIAN MAN is the most recently found *Homo erectus* fossil. The discovery consists of a jawbone and this skullcap (*top view, browridge at bottom*) from which the occipital bone (*top*) is partially detached. Woo Ju-kang of the Chinese Academy of Sciences in Peking provided the photograph; this fossil man from Shensi may be as old as the earliest specimens of *Homo erectus* from Java.

OCCIPITAL BONE found at Vértesszöllös in Hungary in 1965 is 500,000 or more years old. The only older human fossil in Europe is the Heidelberg jaw. The bone forms the rear of a skull; the ridge for muscle attachment (*horizontal line*) is readily apparent. In spite of this primitive feature and its great age, the skull fragment from Vértesszöllös has been assigned to the species *Homo sapiens*.

War II various other important new kinds of human fossil came into view. For our purposes the principal ones (with some of the Linnaean names thrust on them) were (1) the lower jaw found at Mauer in Germany in 1907 (*Homo heidelbergensis* or *Palaeanthropus*), (2) the nearly complete skull found at Broken Hill in Rhodesia in 1921 (*Homo rhodesiensis* or *Cyphanthropus*), (3) various remains uncovered near Peking in China, beginning with one tooth in 1923 and finally comprising a collection representing more than 40 men, women and children by the end of 1937 (*Sinanthropus pekinensis*), and (4) several skulls found in 1931 and 1932 near

Ngandong on the Solo River not far from where Dubois had worked (*Homo soloensis* or *Javanthropus*). This is a fair number of fossils, but they were threatened with being outnumbered by the names assigned to them. The British student of early man Bernard G. Campbell has recorded the following variants in the case of the Mauer jawbone alone: *Palaeanthropus heidelbergensis*, *Pseudhomo heidelbergensis*, *Protanthropus heidelbergensis*, *Praehomo heidelbergensis*, *Praehomo europaeus*, *Anthropus heidelbergensis*, *Maueranthropus heidelbergensis*, *Europanthropus heidelbergensis* and *Euranthropus*.

Often the men responsible for these

redundant christenings were guilty merely of innocent grandiloquence. They were not formally declaring their conviction that each fossil hominid belonged to a separate genus, distinct from *Homo*, which would imply an enormous diversity in the human stock. Nonetheless, the multiplicity of names has interfered with an understanding of the evolutionary significance of the fossils that bore them. Moreover, the human family trees drawn during this period showed a fundamental resemblance to Haeckel's original venture; the rather isolated specimens of early man were stuck on here and there like Christmas-tree ornaments. Although the arrangements evinced a vague consciousness of evolution, no scheme was presented that intelligibly interpreted the fossil record.

At last two questions came to the fore. First, to what degree did the fossils really differ? Second, what was the difference among them over a period of time? The fossil men of the most recent period—those who had lived between roughly 100,000 and 30,000 years ago—were Neanderthal man, Rhodesian man and Solo man. They have been known traditionally as *Homo neanderthalensis*, *Homo rhodesiensis* and *Homo soloensis*, names that declare each of the three to be a separate species, distinct from one another and from *Homo sapiens*. This in turn suggests that if Neanderthal and Rhodesian populations had come in contact, they would probably not have interbred. Such a conclusion is difficult to establish on the basis of fossils, particularly when they are few and tell very little about the geographical range of the species. Today's general view is a contrary one. These comparatively recent fossil men, it is now believed, did not constitute separate species. They were at most incipient species, that is, subspecies or variant populations that had developed in widely separated parts of the world but were still probably able to breed with one another or with *Homo sapiens*.

It was also soon recognized that the older Java and Peking fossils were not very different from one another. The suggestion followed that both populations be placed in a single genus (*Pithecanthropus*) and that the junior name (*Sinanthropus*) be dropped. Even this, however, was one genus too many for Ernst Mayr of Harvard University. Mayr, whose specialty is the evolutionary basis of biological classification, declared that ordinary zoological standards would not permit Java and Peking man to occupy

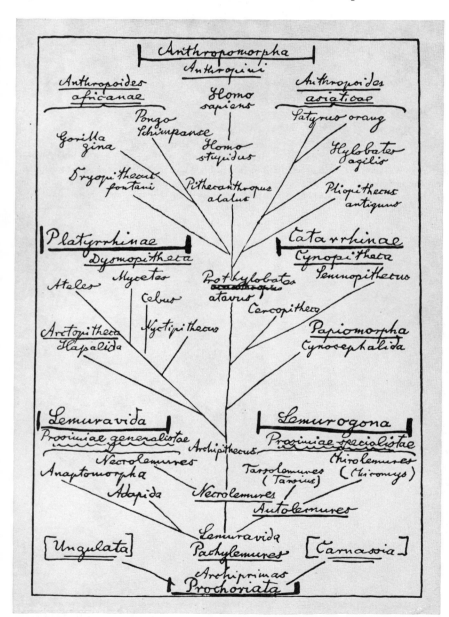

THE NAME "PITHECANTHROPUS," or ape-man, was coined by the German biologist Ernst Haeckel in 1889 for a postulated precursor of *Homo sapiens*. Haeckel placed the apeman genus two steps below modern man on his "tree" of primate evolution, adding the species name *alalus*, or "speechless," because he deemed speech an exclusively human trait.

| GRADE | EUROPE | NORTH AFRICA | EAST AFRICA | SOUTH AFRICA | EAST ASIA | SOUTHEAST ASIA |
|---|---|---|---|---|---|---|
| (5) | *HOMO SAPIENS (VERTESSZÖLLOS)* | | | | | |
| (4) | | | | | | *(HOMO ERECTUS SOLOENSIS)* |
| 3 | *HOMO ERECTUS HEIDELBERGENSIS* | *HOMO ERECTUS MAURITANICUS* | *HOMO ERECTUS LEAKEYI* | | *HOMO ERECTUS PEKINENSIS* | |
| 2 | | | | | | *HOMO ERECTUS ERECTUS* |
| 1 | | | *HOMO ERECTUS HABILIS* | *HOMO ERECTUS CAPENSIS* | *(HOMO ERECTUS LANTIANENSIS)* | *HOMO ERECTUS MODJOKERTENSIS* |

**EIGHT SUBSPECIES** of *Homo erectus* that are generally accepted today have been given appropriate names and ranked in order of evolutionary progress by the British scholar Bernard G. Campbell. The author has added Lantian man to Campbell's lowest *Homo erectus* grade and provided a fourth grade to accommodate Solo man, a late but primitive survival. The author has also added a fifth grade for the *Homo sapiens* fossil from Vértesszöllös (*color*). Colored area suggests that Heidelberg man is its possible forebear.

a genus separate from modern man. In his opinion the amount of evolutionary progress that separates *Pithecanthropus* from ourselves is a step that allows the recognition only of a different species. After all, Java and Peking man apparently had bodies just like our own; that is to say, they were attacking the problem of survival with exactly the same adaptations, although with smaller brains. On this view Java man is placed in the genus *Homo* but according to the rules retains his original species name and so becomes *Homo erectus*. Under the circumstances Peking man can be distinguished from him only as a subspecies: *Homo erectus pekinensis*.

The simplification is something more than sweeping out a clutter of old names to please the International Commission on Zoological Nomenclature. The reduction of fossil hominids to not more than two species and the recognition of *Homo erectus* has become increasingly useful as a way of looking at a stage of human evolution. This has been increasingly evident in recent years, as human fossils have continued to come to light and as new and improved methods of dating them have been developed. It is now possible to place both the old discoveries and the new ones much more precisely in time, and that is basic to establishing the entire pattern of human evolution in the past few million years.

To consider dating first, the period during which *Homo erectus* flourished occupies the early middle part of the Pleistocene epoch. The evidence that now enables us to subdivide the Pleistocene with some degree of confidence is of several kinds. For example, the fossil animals found in association with fossil men often indicate whether the climate of the time was cold or warm. The comparison of animal communities is also helpful in correlating intervals of time on one continent with intervals on another. The ability to determine absolute dates, which makes possible the correlation of the relative dates derived from sequences of strata in widely separated localities, is another significant development. Foremost among the methods of absolute dating at the moment is one based on the rate of decay of radioactive potassium into argon. A second method showing much promise is the analysis of deep-sea sediments; changes in the forms of planktonic life embedded in samples of the bottom reflect worldwide temperature changes. When the absolute ages of key points in sediment sequences are determined by physical or chemical methods, it ought to be possible to assign dates to all the major events of the Pleistocene. Such methods have already suggested that the epoch began more than three million years ago and that its first major cold phase (corresponding to the Günz glaciation of the Alps) may date back to as much as 1.5 million years ago. The period of time occupied by *Homo erectus* now appears to extend from about a million years ago to 500,000 years ago in terms of absolute dates, or from some time during the first interglacial period in the Northern Hemisphere to about the end of the second major cold phase (corresponding to the Mindel glaciation of the Alps).

On the basis of the fossils found before World War II, with the exception of the isolated and somewhat peculiar Heidelberg jaw, *Homo erectus* would have appeared to be a human population of the Far East. The Java skulls, particularly those that come from the lowest fossil strata (known as the Djetis beds), are unsurpassed within the entire group in primitiveness. Even the skulls from the strata above them (the Trinil beds), in which Dubois made his original discovery, have very thick walls and room for only a small brain. Their cranial capacity probably averages less than 900 cubic centimeters, compared with an average of 500 c.c. for gorillas and about 1,400 c.c. for modern man. The later representatives of Java man must be more than 710,000 years old, because potassium-argon analysis has shown that tektites (glassy stones formed by or from meteorites) in higher strata of the same formation are of that age.

The Peking fossils are younger, probably dating to the middle of the second Pleistocene cold phase, and are physically somewhat less crude than the Java ones. The braincase is higher, the face shorter and the cranial capacity approaches 1,100 c.c., but the general construction of skull and jaw is similar. The teeth of both Java man and Peking man are somewhat larger than modern man's and are distinguished by traces of an enamel collar, called a cingulum, around some of the crowns. The latter is an ancient and primitive trait in man and apes.

Discoveries of human fossils after World War II have added significantly to the picture of man's distribution at this period. The pertinent finds are the following:

1949: Swartkrans, South Africa. Jaw and facial fragments, originally given the name *Telanthropus capensis.* These were found among the copious remains at this site of the primitive subhumans known as australopithecines. The fossils were recognized at once by the late Robert Broom and his colleague John T. Robinson as more advanced than the australopithecines both in size and in traits of jaw and teeth. Robinson has now assigned *Telanthropus* to *Homo erectus,* since that is where he evidently belongs.

1955: Ternifine, Algeria. Three jaws and a parietal bone, given the name *Atlanthropus mauritanicus,* were found under a deep covering of sand on the clay floor of an ancient pond by Camille Arambourg. The teeth and jaws show a strong likeness to the Peking remains.

1961: Olduvai Gorge, Tanzania. A skullcap, not formally named but identified as the Bed II Hominid, was discovered by L. S. B. Leakey. Found in a context with a provisional potassium-argon date of 500,000 years ago, the skull's estimated cranial capacity is 1,000 c.c. Although differing somewhat in detail, it has the general characteristics of the two Far Eastern subspecies of *Homo erectus.* At lower levels in this same important site were found the remains of a number of individuals with small skulls, now collectively referred to as "Homo habilis."

1963–1964: Lantian district, Shensi, China. A lower jaw and a skullcap were found by Chinese workers at two separate localities in the district and given the name *Sinanthropus lantianensis.* Animal fossils indicate that the Lantian sites are older than the one that yielded Peking man and roughly as old as the lowest formation in Java. The form of the skull and jaw accords well with this

| GLACIAL STAGES | AFRICA |
| --- | --- |
| PRESENT | |
| WÜRM III | |
| WÜRM II | |
| WÜRM I | |
| RISS-WÜRM INTERGLACIAL | |
| RISS II | |
| RISS I | |
| MINDEL-RISS INTERGLACIAL | |
| MINDEL II | |
| MINDEL I | |
| GÜNZ-MINDEL INTERGLACIAL | |
| GÜNZ | |

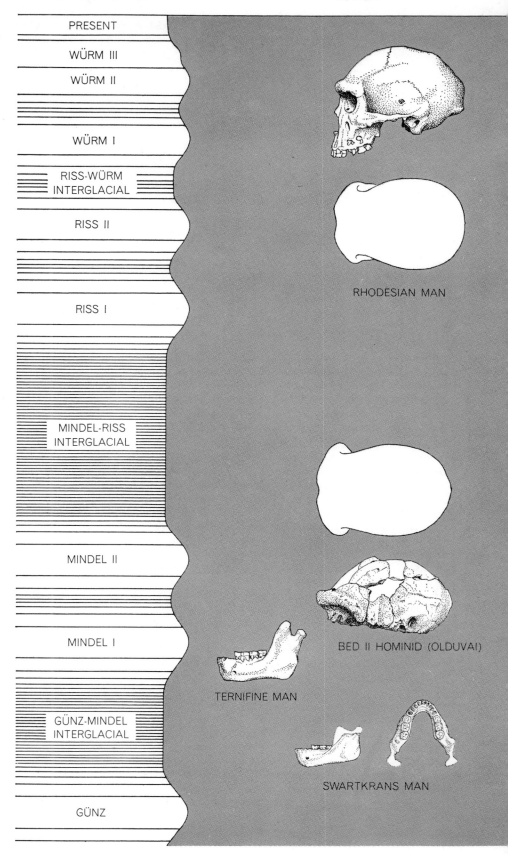

RHODESIAN MAN

BED II HOMINID (OLDUVAI)

TERNIFINE MAN

SWARTKRANS MAN

FOSSIL EVIDENCE for the existence of a single species of early man instead of several species and genera of forerunners of *Homo sapiens* is presented in this array of individual remains whose age places them in the interval of approximately 500,000 years that separates the first Pleistocene interglacial period from the end of the second glacial period (*see scale at left*). The earliest *Homo erectus* fossils known, from Java and China, belong to the first interglacial period; the earliest *Homo erectus* remains from South Africa may be equally

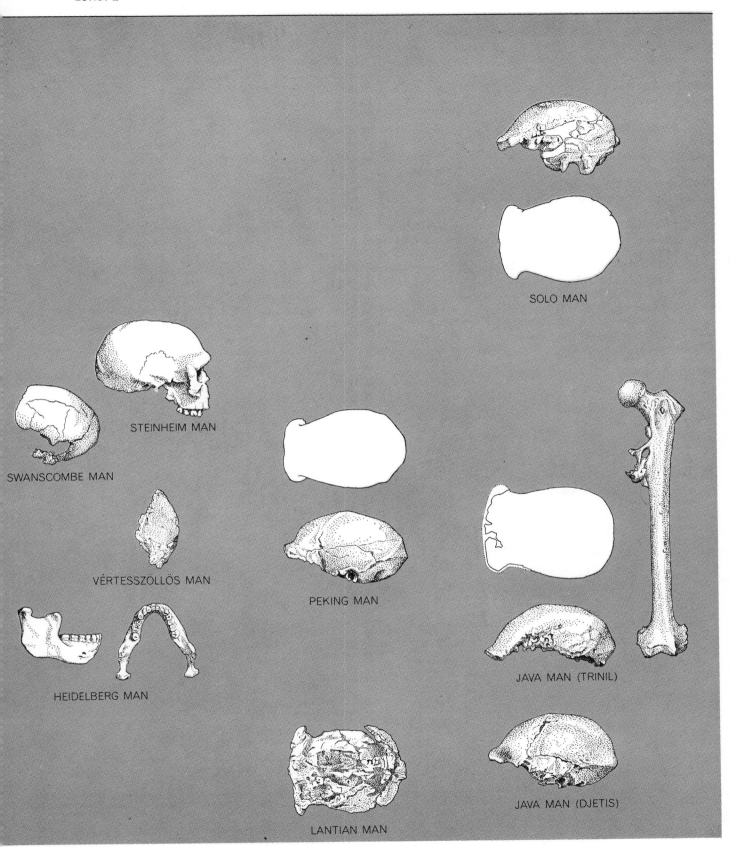

SOLO MAN

STEINHEIM MAN

SWANSCOMBE MAN

VÉRTESSZÖLLÖS MAN

PEKING MAN

JAVA MAN (TRINIL)

HEIDELBERG MAN

LANTIAN MAN

JAVA MAN (DJETIS)

old. Half a million years later *Homo erectus* continued to be represented in China by the remains of Peking man and in Africa by the skull from Olduvai Gorge. In the intervening period this small-brained precursor of modern man was not the only human species inhabiting the earth, nor did *Homo erectus* become extinct when the 500,000-year period ended. One kind of man who had apparent-

ly reached the grade of *Homo sapiens* in Europe by the middle or later part of the second Pleistocene glacial period was unearthed recently at Vértesszöllös in Hungary. In the following interglacial period *Homo sapiens* is represented by the Steinheim and Swanscombe females. Solo man's remains indicate that *Homo erectus* survived for several hundred thousand years after that.

dating; both are distinctly more primitive than the Peking fossils. Both differ somewhat in detail from the Java subspecies of *Homo erectus,* but the estimated capacity of this otherwise large skull (780 c.c.) is small and close to that of the earliest fossil cranium unearthed in Java.

1965: Vértesszöllös, Hungary. An isolated occipital bone (in the back of the skull) was found by L. Vértes. This skull fragment is the first human fossil from the early middle Pleistocene to be unearthed in Europe since the Heidelberg jaw. It evidently dates to the middle or later part of the Mindel glaciation and thus falls clearly within the *Homo erectus* time zone as defined here. The bone is moderately thick and shows a well-defined ridge for the attachment of neck muscles such as is seen in all the *erectus* skulls. It is unlike *erectus* occipital bones, however, in that it is both large and definitely less angled; these features indicate a more advanced skull.

In addition to these five discoveries, something else of considerable importance happened during this period. The Piltdown fraud, perpetrated sometime before 1912, was finally exposed in 1953. The detective work of J. S. Weiner, Sir Wilfrid Le Gros Clark and Kenneth Oakley removed from the fossil record a supposed hominid with a fully apelike jaw and manlike skull that could scarcely be fitted into any sensible evolutionary scheme.

From this accumulation of finds, many of them made so recently, there emerges a picture of men with skeletons like ours but with brains much smaller, skulls much thicker and flatter and furnished with protruding brows in front and a marked angle in the rear, and with teeth somewhat larger and exhibiting a few slightly more primitive traits. This picture suggests an evolutionary level, or grade, occupying half a million years of human history and now seen

to prevail all over the inhabited Old World. This is the meaning of *Homo erectus.* It gives us a new foundation for ideas as to the pace and the pattern of human evolution over a critical span of time.

Quite possibly this summary is too tidy; before the 100th anniversary of the resurrection of *Homo erectus* is celebrated complications may appear that we cannot perceive at present. Even today there are a number of fringe problems we cannot neglect. Here are some of them.

What was the amount of evolution taking place within the *erectus* grade? There is probably a good deal of accident of discovery involved in defining *Homo erectus.* Chance, in other words, may have isolated a segment of a continuum, since finds from the time immediately following this 500,000-year period are almost lacking. It seems likely, in fact practically certain, that real evolutionary progress was taking place,

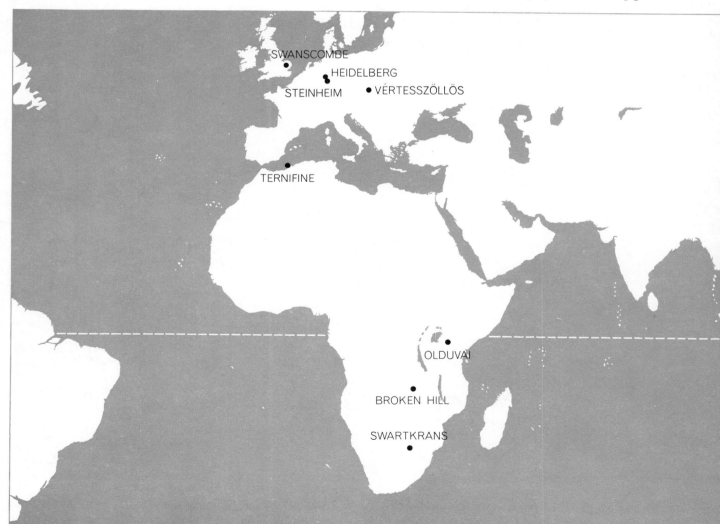

**DISTRIBUTION** of *Homo erectus* seemed to be confined mainly to the Far East and Southeast Asia on the basis of fossils unearthed before World War II; the sole exception was the Heidelberg jaw. Postwar findings in South, East and North Africa, as well as dis-

but the tools made by man during this period reveal little of it. As for the fossils themselves, the oldest skulls—from Java and Lantian—are the crudest and have the smallest brains. In Java, one region with some discernible stratigraphy, the later skulls show signs of evolutionary advance compared with the earlier ones. The Peking skulls, which are almost certainly later still, are even more progressive. Bernard Campbell, who has recently suggested that all the known forms of *Homo erectus* be formally recognized as named subspecies, has arranged the names in the order of their relative progressiveness. I have added some names to Campbell's list; they appear in parentheses in the illustration on page 31. As the illustration indicates, the advances in grade seem indeed to correspond fairly well with the passage of time.

What are the relations of *Homo erectus* to Rhodesian and Solo man? This is a point of particular importance, be-

cause both the African and the Javanese fossils are much younger than the date we have set as the general upward boundary for *Homo erectus*. Rhodesian man may have been alive as recently as 30,000 years ago and may have actually overlapped with modern man. Solo man probably existed during the last Pleistocene cold phase; this is still very recent compared with the time zone of the other *erectus* fossils described here. Carleton S. Coon of the University of Pennsylvania deems both late fossil men to be *Homo erectus* on the basis of tooth size and skull flatness. His placing of Rhodesian man is arguable, but Solo man is so primitive, so like Java man in many aspects of his skull form and so close to Peking man in brain size that his classification as *Homo erectus* seems almost inevitable. The meaning of his survival hundreds of thousands of years after the period I have suggested, and his relation to the modern men who succeeded him in Southeast Asia in recent times, are unanswered questions of considerable importance.

Where did *Homo erectus* come from? The Swartkrans discovery makes it clear that he arose before the last representatives of the australopithecines had died out at that site. The best present evidence of his origin is also from Africa; it consists of the series of fossils unearthed at Olduvai Gorge by Leakey and his wife and called Homo habilis. These remains seem to reflect a transition from an australopithecine level to an *erectus* level about a million years ago. This date seems almost too late, however, when one considers the age of *Homo erectus* finds elsewhere in the world, particularly in Java.

Where did *Homo erectus* go? The paths are simply untraced, both those that presumably lead to the Swanscombe and Steinheim people of Europe during the Pleistocene's second interglacial period and those leading to the much later Rhodesian and Neanderthal men. This is a period lacking useful evidence. Above all, the nature of the line leading to living man—*Homo sapiens* in the Linnaean sense—remains a matter of pure theory.

We may, however, have a clue. Here it is necessary to face a final problem. What was the real variation in physical type during the time period of *Homo erectus*? On the whole, considering the time and space involved, it does not appear to be very large; the similarity of the North African jaws to those of Peking man, for example, is striking in spite of the thousands of

miles that separated the two populations. The Heidelberg jaw, however, has always seemed to be somewhat different from all the others and a little closer to modern man in the nature of its teeth. The only other European fossil approaching the Heidelberg jaw in antiquity is the occipital bone recently found at Vértesszöllös. This piece of skull likewise appears to be progressive in form and may have belonged to the same general kind of man as the Heidelberg jaw, although it is somewhat more recent in date.

Andor Thoma of Hungary's Kossuth University at Debrecen in Hungary, who has kindly given me information concerning the Vértesszöllös fossil, will publish a formal description soon in the French journal *L'Anthropologie*. He estimates that the cranial capacity was about 1,400 c.c., close to the average for modern man and well above that of the known specimens of *Homo erectus*. Although the occipital bone is thick, it is larger and less sharply angled than the matching skull area of Rhodesian man. It is certainly more modern-looking than the Solo skulls. I see no reason at this point to dispute Thoma's estimate of brain volume. He concludes that Vértesszöllös man had in fact reached the *sapiens* grade in skull form and brain size and accordingly has named him a subspecies of *Homo sapiens*.

Thoma's finding therefore places a population of more progressive, *sapiens* humanity contemporary with the populations of *Homo erectus* 500,000 years ago or more. From the succeeding interglacial period in Europe have come the Swanscombe and Steinheim skulls, generally recognized as *sapiens* in grade. They are less heavy than the Hungarian fossil, more curved in occipital profile and smaller in size; they are also apparently both female, which would account for part of these differences.

The trail of evidence is of course faint, but there are no present signs of contradiction; what we may be seeing is a line that follows *Homo sapiens* back from Swanscombe and Steinheim to Vértesszöllös and finally to Heidelberg man at the root. This is something like the Solo case in reverse, a *Homo sapiens* population surprisingly early in time, in contrast to a possible *Homo erectus* population surprisingly late. In fact, we are seeing only the outlines of what we must still discover. It is easy to perceive how badly we need more fossils; for example, we cannot relate Heidelberg man to any later Europeans until we find some skull parts to add to his solitary jaw.

PEKING

LANTIAN

NGANDONG

SANGIRAN

TRINIL

covery of a new *Homo erectus* site in northern China, have extended the species' range.

# 4

# A Paleolithic Camp at Nice

by Henry de Lumley
*May 1969*

*Construction work on the French Riviera has
uncovered the remains of man's earliest-known
construction work: huts put up by hunters who
visited the shore of the Mediterranean some
300,000 years ago*

A Paleolithic site uncovered recently in the south of France contains traces of the earliest-known architecture: huts that were built some 300,000 years ago. The structures were evidently made by nomadic hunters who visited the Mediterranean shore briefly each year. They left behind artifacts and animal bones that, together with the plant pollen found at the site, yield a remarkably detailed picture of the occupants' activities during their annual sojourn by the sea. Because the discovery of the site and its excavation were unusual, I shall give a brief account of both before describing the new evidence the site provides concerning human life during this very early period of prehistory.

The city of Nice, in southeastern France, stands on a basement formation of limestone and marl. The bedrock is covered by layers of sand, clay and soil that mark the glacial oscillations of the ice age. During the construction of a shipyard some years ago certain glacial strata were exposed to view and attracted the attention of several scholars. In one sandy layer in 1959 Georges Iaworsky of the Monaco Museum of Prehistoric Anthropology found a few stone tools of typical Paleolithic workmanship. Two years later in another sandy section he found a tool of the early Paleolithic type known as Acheulean. Acheulean tools take their name from St. Acheul, a site in France where examples were first discovered, but since then Acheulean implements have been found at many other sites in Europe and in Asia and Africa. It had originally seemed that the sands had been deposited in the warm period between the glaciations called the Riss and the Würm, but Iaworsky pointed out that the age of the Acheulean tool indicated that these deposits were much older.

Then, in the course of foundation work during October, 1965, bulldozers cut a series of terraces into the sloping grounds of the Château de Rosemont, on the shoulder of Mont Boron in the eastern part of the city. The area of excavation, near the corner of Boulevard Carnot and an alley romantically named Terra Amata (beloved land), was scarcely 300 yards from Nice's commercial harbor and not far from the shipyard where Iaworsky and others, myself included, had studied the glacial strata. As the excavation proceeded the bulldozers exposed an extensive sandy deposit containing more Paleolithic implements. The significance of the discovery was quickly realized, and the builders agreed to halt operations temporarily. With the help of the French Ministry of Culture, a major archaeological salvage effort was mounted.

Starting on January 28, 1966, and continuing without interruption until July 5 more than 300 workers, including young students of archaeology from the universities and a number of enthusiastic amateurs, devoted a total of nearly 40,000 man-hours to the excavation of the Terra Amata site. The excavated area covered 144 square yards; in the course of investigating the 21 separate living floors found within the area the workers gradually removed a total of 270 cubic yards of fill, using no tools except trowels and brushes. The digging brought to light nearly 35,000 objects, and the location of each object was recorded on one or another of 1,200 charts. In addition, casts were made of 108 square yards of living floor and the progress of the work was documented in some 9,000 photographs.

In stratigraphic terms the deposits at Terra Amata begin at the surface with a layer of reddish clay that is nine feet thick in places and contains potsherds of the Roman period. Below the clay is a series of strata indicative of glacial advances during the Würm, Riss and Mindel periods and the warmer periods that intervened. The site embraces three fossil beaches, all belonging to the latter part of the Mindel glaciation. The youngest beach, marked by a dune and a sandbar, proved to be the site of human habitation.

When the youngest beach was deposited, the level of the Mediterranean was 85 feet higher than it is today. Soon after the beach was formed the sea level dropped somewhat, exposing the sandbar and allowing the wind to build a small dune inland. The hunters must have visited the area during or soon after a major period of erosion that occurred next. The evidence of their presence is found on or in the sands but not in the reddish-brown soil that later covered the eroded sand surface. Numerous shells of land snails, found at the base of the reddish soil, indicate a period of temperate climate.

The landscape of Terra Amata at the time of the hunters' visits differed in a number of respects from today's. The backdrop of the Alps, dominated by Mont Chauve, was much the same, but the sea covered most of the plain of Nice and even penetrated a short distance into what is now the valley of the Paillon River. The climate, though temperate, was somewhat brisker and more humid than the one we know. Pollen studies, undertaken by Jacques-Louis de Beaulieu of the pollen-analysis laboratory at the University of Aix-Marseilles, indicate that fir and Norway pine on the alpine heights grew farther down the slopes than is now the case, and that heather, sea pine, Aleppo pine and holm oak covered Mont Boron and its coastal neighbors.

In the limestone of Mont Boron's western slope the sea had cut a small cove opening to the south. Within the cove a sandy, pebble-strewn beach extended down to the sea, sheltered from the north and east winds. A small spring to one side provided a source of fresh water. A few seashore plants—grasses, horsetails, short-stemmed plantain and various shrubs—grew in the cove. The stream from the spring held water lilies of the genus *Euryale*, which, as De Beaulieu notes, can be found only in Asia today. All things considered, it appears that nothing was lacking even 300 millenniums ago to make Terra Amata a beloved land.

The superimposed living floors at Terra Amata are located in three separate areas. Four are on the section of beach that had formed the sandbar until the sea level dropped; six are on the beach seaward of the bar, and 11 are on the dune inland. The huts that were built on the living floors all had the same shape: an elongated oval. They ranged from 26 to 49 feet in length and from 13

to nearly 20 feet in width. Their outline can be traced with two kinds of evidence. The first is the imprint of a series of stakes, averaging some three inches in diameter, that were driven into the sand to form the walls of the hut. The second is a line of stones, paralleling the stake imprints, that apparently served to brace the walls. One of the earliest of the huts is perfectly outlined by an oval of stones, some as much as a foot in diameter and some even stacked one on the other. The living floor within the oval consisted of a thick bed of organic matter and ash.

The palisade of stakes that formed the walls was not the huts' only structural element. There are also visible the imprints left by a number of stout posts, each about a foot in diameter. These supports were set in place down the long axis of the hut. Evidence of how the palisade and the center posts were integrated to form the roof of the hut has not survived.

A basic feature of each hut is a hearth placed at the center. These fireplaces are either pebble-paved surface areas or shallow pits, a foot or two in diameter, scooped out of the sand. A little wall,

made by piling up cobbles or pebbles, stands at the northwest side of each hearth. These walls were evidently windscreens to protect the fire against drafts, particularly from the northwest wind that is the prevailing one at Nice to this day.

The fact that the hunters built windscreens for their hearths makes it clear that their huts were not draft-free. This suggests that many of the palisade stakes may have been no more than leafy branches. Certainly nothing more permanent was required. As we shall see, the huts were occupied very briefly. As we shall also see, the time of the annual visit can be narrowed down to the end of spring and the beginning of summer, a season when such a building material would have been readily available.

In the huts on the dune the hearths were apparently designed for small fires. If one can judge from the larger amounts of charcoal and ash, the hearths in the huts closer to the sea must have accommodated much bigger fires. It is worth noting that the hearths at Terra Amata, together with those at one other site in Europe, are the oldest yet discovered anywhere in the world. The hearths that

OVAL HUTS, ranging from 26 to 49 feet in length and from 13 to 20 feet in width, were built at Terra Amata by visiting hunters. A reconstruction shows that the hut walls were made of stakes, about three inches in diameter, set as a palisade in the sand and braced on the outside by a ring of stones. Some larger posts were set up along the huts' long axes, but how these and the walls were joined to make roofs is unknown; the form shown is conjectural. The huts' hearths were protected from drafts by a small pebble windscreen.

38

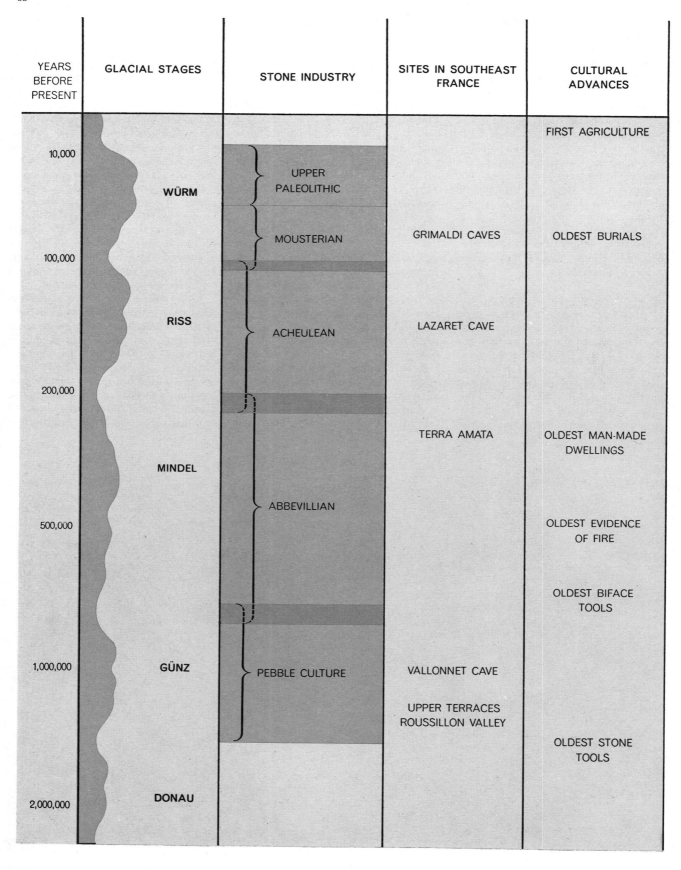

| YEARS BEFORE PRESENT | GLACIAL STAGES | STONE INDUSTRY | SITES IN SOUTHEAST FRANCE | CULTURAL ADVANCES |
|---|---|---|---|---|
| | | | | FIRST AGRICULTURE |
| 10,000 | WÜRM | UPPER PALEOLITHIC | | |
| | | MOUSTERIAN | GRIMALDI CAVES | OLDEST BURIALS |
| 100,000 | RISS | ACHEULEAN | LAZARET CAVE | |
| 200,000 | MINDEL | | TERRA AMATA | OLDEST MAN-MADE DWELLINGS |
| 500,000 | | ABBEVILLIAN | | OLDEST EVIDENCE OF FIRE |
| | | | | OLDEST BIFACE TOOLS |
| 1,000,000 | GÜNZ | PEBBLE CULTURE | VALLONNET CAVE | |
| | | | UPPER TERRACES ROUSSILLON VALLEY | |
| | | | | OLDEST STONE TOOLS |
| 2,000,000 | DONAU | | | |

CHRONOLOGICAL POSITION of Terra Amata in prehistory is indicated on this chart, which shows (*left to right*) the time, given in thousands of years before the present, of the major glacial advances and retreats in Europe, the successive stone industries of the Paleolithic period, sites in southeastern France where the industries have been found and early man's progress in technology.

equal them in age were found by László Vértes in strata of Mindel age at Vértesszölös in Hungary. Like some of the hearths at Terra Amata, those at the Hungarian site are shallow pits a foot or two in diameter.

Also from Vértesszölös comes a significant early human fossil: the occipital bone of a skull that has been assigned to modern man. No such human remains were found in our excavation at Terra Amata, but we came on two indirect sources of information about the site's inhabitants. One is the imprint of a right foot, 9½ inches long, preserved in the sand of the dune. Calculating a human being's height from the length of the foot is an uncertain procedure. If, however, one uses the formula applied to Neanderthal footprints found in the grotto of Toirano in Italy, the individual whose footprint was found at Terra Amata may have been five feet one inch tall.

Our other indirect source of information consists of fossilized human feces found in the vicinity of the huts. De Beaulieu's analysis of their pollen content shows that all of it comes from plants, such as *Genista,* that shed their pollen at the end of spring or the beginning of summer. This is the finding that enables us to state the precise time of year when the hunters came to Terra Amata.

How did the visitors occupy themselves during their stay? The evidence shows that they gathered a little seafood, manufactured stone tools and hunted in the nearby countryside. The animal bones unearthed at Terra Amata include the remains of birds, turtles and at least eight species of mammals. Although the visitors did not ignore small game such as rabbits and rodents, the majority of the bones represent larger animals. They are, in order of their abundance, the stag *Cervus elaphus,* the extinct elephant *Elephas meridionalis,* the wild boar (*Sus scrofa*), the ibex (*Capra ibex*), Merk's rhinoceros (*Dicerothinus merki*) and finally the wild ox *Bos primigenius.* Although the hunters showed a preference for big game, they generally selected as prey not the adults but the young of each species, doubtless because they were easier to bring down.

The visitors did not systematically exploit the food resources available in the Mediterranean. Nevertheless, they were not entirely ignorant of seafood. A few shells of oysters, mussels and limpets at the site show that they gathered shellfish; fishbones and fish vertebrae indi-

cate that on occasion the hunters also fished.

The large majority of all the artifacts found at Terra Amata are stone tools. They represent two different but closely related stone industries. Both appear to be contemporary with the earliest "biface" industries of the Paleolithic period (so named because many of the tools are made out of stone "cores" that are shaped by chipping flakes from both faces rather than from one face only). They bear certain resemblances to the tools of an early Paleolithic biface industry named the Abbevillian (after the site in France where they were first discovered) and to the Acheulean biface indus-

try, which is somewhat more advanced. On balance, both Terra Amata industries should probably be characterized as early Acheulean.

The more primitive of the two Terra Amata industries is represented by the tools found in the huts closest to the sea. Mainly pebble tools, they include many pieces of the type designated choppers, a few of the type called chopping tools and some crude bifaces made by detaching flakes from one end of an oval cobble but leaving a smooth, unflaked "heel" at the other end. Among the other tools found in the seaside huts are cleavers, scrapers, projectile points of a kind known in France as *pointes de Tayac*

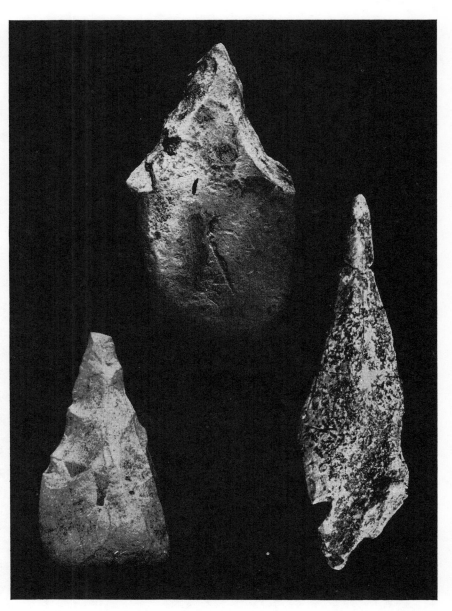

REPRESENTATIVE TOOLS unearthed at Terra Amata include a pebble (*middle*) that has been flaked on one of its faces to form a pick, another stone tool (*left*), flaked on both faces but with one end left smooth, and a bone fragment (*right*) pointed to make an awl.

**FLOOR OF A HUT** at Terra Amata is one of several brought to light by the excavators, revealing the ancient debris left behind by the occupants. The whole pebbles are raw material for tools; the chips and flakes, toolmakers' waste. The antler is from a stag.

and pebble tools flaked on one face only.

The stone industry represented by the tools found in the huts on the dune is more advanced, although it too includes choppers, chopping tools and cobble bifaces with a smooth heel. There are no single-faced pebble tools or cleavers on the dune, however, and tools made from flakes rather than from cores are relatively numerous. The tools made from flakes include those designated scrapers with abrupt retouch, end scrapers with toothed edges and flakes of the kind named Clactonian (after the English site Clacton-on-Sea). Some of the Clactonian flakes have been notched on one edge; others have been made into perforators by chipping out two notches side by side so that a point of stone protrudes. Projectile points from the dunes include, in addition to *pointes de Tayac,* some that are triangular in cross section and others of a kind known in France as *pointes de Quinson.*

Some of the tools found at Terra Amata were probably made on the spot. The hut floors show evidence of tool manufacturing, and the toolmaker needed only to walk along the beach to find workable pebbles and cobbles of flint, quartzite, limestone and other rock. The toolmaker's place inside the huts is easily recognized: a patch of living floor is surrounded by the litter of tool manufacture. The bare patches are where the toolmakers sat, sometimes on animal skins that have left a recognizable impression.

Not all the stone debris represents the waste from finished work. In one instance the excavators found a cobble from which a single chip had been struck. Nearby was a chip that fitted the scar perfectly. In another toolmaker's atelier several flakes had been removed from a cobble by a series of successive blows. Both the core and the flakes were found, and it was possible for us to reassemble the cobble. Scarcely a flake was missing; evidently the toolmaker did not put either the core or the flakes to use.

At least one of the projectile points unearthed at Terra Amata could not have been produced locally. The stone from which it is made is a volcanic rock of a kind found only in the area of Estérel, southwest of Cannes and some 30 miles from Nice. This discovery allows us to conclude that these summer visitors' travels covered at least that much territory in the south of France, although we cannot be sure how much more widely they may have roamed.

A few tools made of bone have been

FIRE PIT (*right*) was protected from drafts and from the prevailing northwest wind in particular by a windscreen built of cobbles and pebbles, seen partially preserved at left.

TOOLMAKER'S ATELIER occupies one section of a hut. It is easily identified by the debris of tool manufacture that surrounds the bare patch of floor where the toolmaker sat.

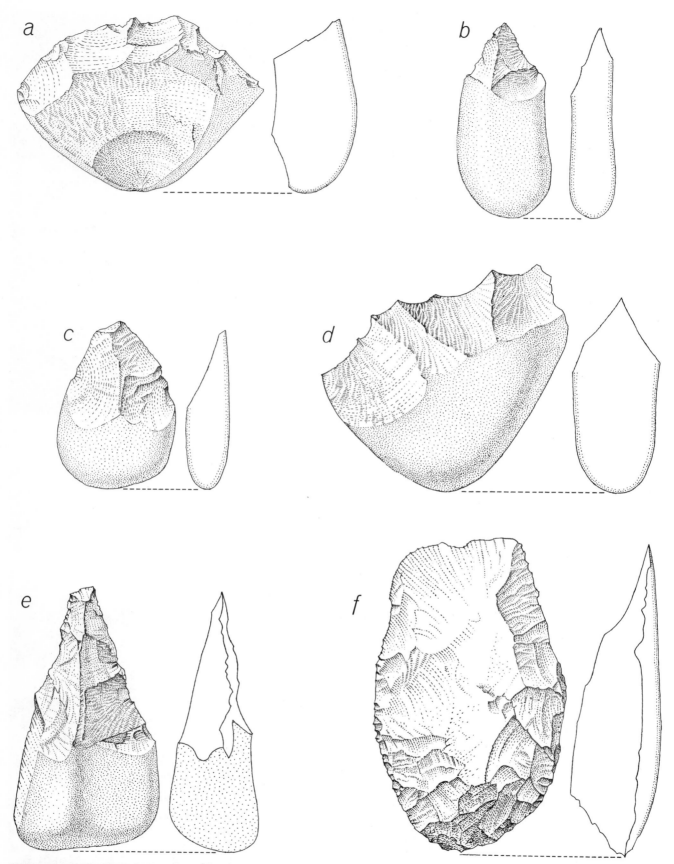

*a*

*b*

*c*

*d*

*e*

*f*

**GROUP OF PRIMITIVE TOOLS** was found in association with the huts closest to the sea at Terra Amata. They include choppers (*a*) and picks (*b,c*), made from pebbles that are flaked on one face only; chopping tools (*d*) that are flaked on both faces; crude bifaces (*e*), made by detaching flakes from one end of a cobble but leaving an unflaked "heel" at the opposite end; cleavers (*f*), and two other kinds of stone artifacts (*illustrated on opposite page*): scrapers and projectile points of a kind known as *pointes de Tayac*.

found at Terra Amata. One leg bone of an elephant has a hammered point at one end. Another bone has a point that was probably hardened in a fire (a technique used today by some primitive peoples to harden the tips of wooden spears). A third bone fragment has one end smoothed by wear; still another may have served as an awl, and some fragments of bone may have been used as scrapers.

As for other kinds of artifacts, there are traces of only two. On the dune a spherical imprint in the sand, filled with a whitish substance, may be the impression left by a wooden bowl. Some pieces of red ocher found at the site obviously belonged to the visitors: the ends are worn smooth by wear. They recall the red ocher found at sites belonging to the much later Mousterian period, which François Bordes of the University of Bordeaux suggests were used for body-painting.

Let us see if the pattern of the hunters' annual visits to Terra Amata can be reconstructed. We know from the pollen evidence that they arrived in the late spring or early summer, and we can assume that they chose the sheltered cove as their camping ground as much because of its supply of fresh water as for any other reason. On arrival they set up their huts, built their hearths and windscreens, hunted for a day or two, gathered some seafood, rested by their fires, made a few tools and then departed. How do we know that their stay was so short? First, the living floors show no sign of the compaction that would characterize a longer occupation. Second, we have independent evidence that the huts collapsed soon after they were built. A freshly chipped stone tool that is left in the sun will quickly become bleached on the exposed side whereas the bottom side retains its original coloring. Many of the tools on the living floors at Terra Amata are bleached in this way. For the implements to be exposed to the full force of the Mediterranean summer sun the huts must have fallen apart soon after they were abandoned.

In the fall the winds covered the living floors, the leveled palisades and the rest of the camp debris with a layer of sand perhaps two inches deep. The rains then spread out the sand and packed it down, so that when the hunters returned to the cove the following year the evidence of their earlier stay had been almost obliterated. Only a few objects, such as the windscreens for the hearths, still protruded from the sand. The visi-

tors then built new huts, often digging the hearth pit exactly where the preceding year's had been and rekindling their fires on the ashes of the previous season. After a day or two of hunting, gathering seafood and making tools the annual visit was ended. The 11 living floors on the dune at Terra Amata are so precisely superimposed that they almost certainly represent 11 consecutive yearly visits, probably involving many of the same individuals.

There is no older evidence of man-made structures than that at Terra Amata. Until this site was excavated the record for antiquity was held by the traces of construction discovered at Latamne, an open-air site in Syria, by J. Desmond Clark of the University of California at Berkeley. An early Acheulean site, Latamne is believed to be as old as the Mindel-Riss interglacial period. Terra Amata, which evidently was inhabited at the end of the Mindel glacial period, is therefore even earlier.

The evidence indicating that the hunt-

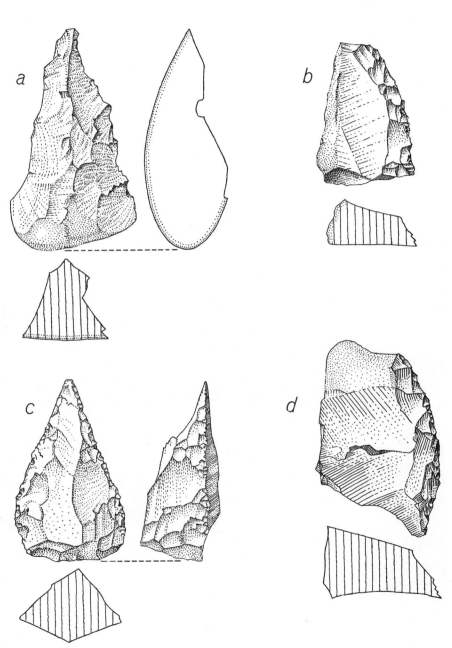

**LESS PRIMITIVE TOOLS** were found in the huts on the dune at Terra Amata. There were no cleavers or single-faced pebble tools and many more of the tools were made from flakes rather than from cores. Tools common to both areas are *pointes de Tayac* (*a*) and flakes made into simple scrapers (*b*), choppers, chopping tools and bifaces like those on the opposite page. Flakes were also made into projectile points (*c*) and more elaborate scrapers (*d*).

ers came to Terra Amata at about the same time year after year, together with the likelihood that the dune huts sheltered some of the same individuals for more than a decade, suggests that the visitors possessed stable and even complex social institutions. It is thus appropriate to conclude with the words of the French historian Camille Jullian, written soon after the Terra Amata living floors had been exposed. "The hearth," Jullian wrote, "is a place for gathering together around a fire that warms, that sheds light and gives comfort. The toolmaker's seat is where one man carefully pursues a work that is useful to many. The men here may well be nomadic hunters, but before the chase begins they need periods of preparation and afterward long moments of repose beside the hearth. The family, the tribe will arise from these customs, and I ask myself if they have not already been born."

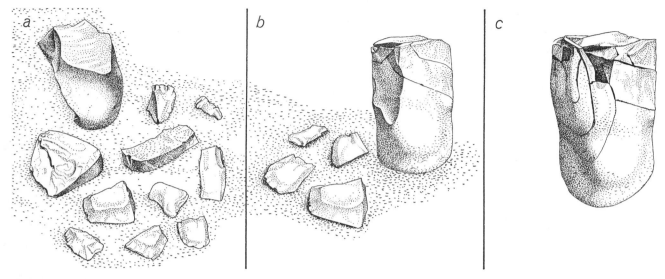

UNUTILIZED RAW MATERIAL was found in one Terra Amata toolmaker's atelier. Near the shattered half of a large cobble lay most of the fragments that had been struck from it (a). They could be reassembled (b) so that the cobble was almost whole again (c).

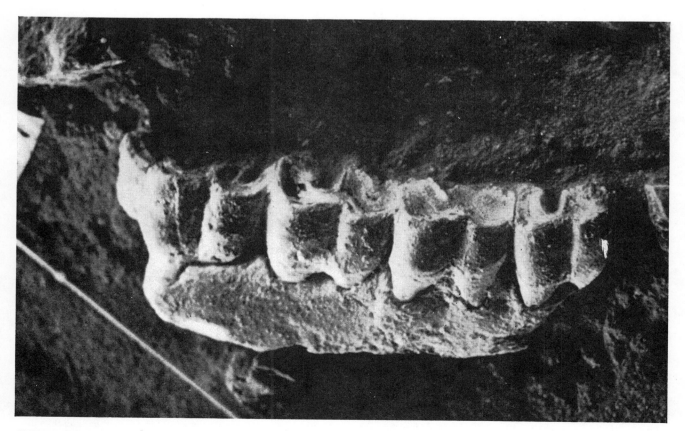

ANIMAL BONE, photographed in situ near one corner of an excavation unit, is a fragment of rhinoceros mandible, complete with teeth. The visitors preferred large mammals to other game. Along with rhinoceros they hunted stag, elephant, boar, ibex and wild ox.

# The Solutrean Culture

5

*August 1964*

*A vigorous hunting culture with a unique tool kit appeared in western Europe 21,000 years ago. Once deemed invaders, the practitioners of Solutrean techniques instead seem to have had their roots in France*

During the last advances and the final retreat of the Pleistocene ice sheets in Europe, between 32,000 and 10,000 years ago, the most vigorous cultures of the Old Stone Age flourished. The hunting peoples of this Upper Paleolithic period enjoyed an abundance of cold-climate game: migrating reindeer by the thousands, herds of horses and wild cattle, and such giants of the subarctic zone as the mammoth and the woolly rhinoceros. The well-fed hunters made these same animals the subjects of sculpture, in the round or in relief, of fine-line engraving on bone, antler and ivory, and of richly colored cave paintings such as those found at Altamira in Spain and Lascaux in France.

Prehistorians generally divide the Upper Paleolithic culture of western Europe into four major components. The two earliest of these, called the Perigordian and the Aurignacian, were roughly contemporary; the distinction between them is based primarily on differences in their assemblages of stone tools and weapons. In western Europe both of these cultural traditions were succeeded some 21,000 years ago by a new array of distinctive stone implements that are assigned to the Solutrean culture. About 17,000 years ago, in turn, the last phase of the Solutrean gave way to the Magdalenian culture, whose members produced many of the most notable examples of Upper Paleolithic art. Finally, as the ice sheets began their last retreat, Magdalenian artifacts disappeared and in southwestern France a comparatively impoverished successor culture, the Azilian, marked the end of an era [*see illustration on page 47*].

These cultural successions have been interpreted in a number of ways.

Thinking in terms of the many waves of migration and conquest that have passed over Europe during historical times, some students argue that each distinctive assemblage of Upper Paleolithic artifacts represents a fresh influx of people from Asia or Africa. Other students point to the enormous time span of the Upper Paleolithic: roughly five times longer than all recorded history. These scholars do not discount the possibility that ideas were imported into western Europe, but they prefer to attribute most of the cultural changes in the region to cultural evolution within a relatively stable population.

It might be less difficult to determine which, if either, of these hypotheses is best supported by the evidence if the history of archaeological research in Europe had been different. For much of its 100-year history the collection of archaeological evidence in some countries has been in the hands not only of scholars but also of amateur antiquarians and professional looters. One result is that few Upper Paleolithic sites have been excavated under controlled conditions. This means that the stratigraphic positions, and thus the age and associations, of many of the period's most significant artifacts have been lost forever.

France is western Europe's greatest Upper Paleolithic treasure-house and the department of Dordogne, in southwestern France, is the country's richest single depository. Thanks to stringent government regulations, looters can no longer mine the limestone caves and shelters in the valleys of the Dordogne and Vézère rivers. During the years since World War II a number of promising sites have been scientifically ex-

cavated. Some are still in the process of long-term excavation; an example is the Pataud rock-shelter near the village of Les Eyzies, where a group from Harvard University has been working for eight years. In the 1950's another rock-shelter at Les Eyzies was reinvestigated by François Bordes of the University of Bordeaux. Known as Laugerie-Haute, it had been shown to be rich in Upper Paleolithic artifacts by the noted French prehistorian Denis Peyrony in the 1920's. More than half of the site was still untouched in the 1950's; the strata containing Upper Paleolithic remains were 10 meters thick in some places, with Solutrean layers occupying more than a meter of this depth.

I worked at Laugerie-Haute with Bordes in 1957. In 1959 he asked me to investigate the site's Solutrean levels to see if some of the problems concerning this comparatively short-lived but remarkable culture could be cleared up by recovering new samples of Solutrean artifacts from a precisely calibrated stratigraphic sequence.

Peyrony's studies of the 1920's were not the first conducted at Laugerie-Haute. A century ago, in 1863, two pioneer prehistorians began a series of now classic investigations at a number of sites in the vicinity of Les Eyzies. One was Édouard Lartet, a French paleontologist whose interests had turned to the new field of archaeology; the other was a British businessman, Henry Christy. Before they were done at such sites as La Madeleine (from which the Magdalenian culture takes its name), the Gorge d'Enfer and Laugerie-Haute the two investigators had discovered the first evidence of prehistoric art—the figure of a mammoth engraved on bone—and had given the name "Reindeer Age" to what we rec-

**PAIR OF WILD CATTLE, attributed to a Solutrean sculptor, was rendered in bas-relief on the surface of a limestone outcropping** on the Dronne River in southwestern France. This Upper Paleolithic work of art was found at a site called Fourneau du Diable.

ognize today as the whole of the Upper Paleolithic. In addition, at Laugerie-Haute they excavated examples of three distinctive Solutrean flint tools: the laurel-leaf blade, the willow-leaf blade and the shouldered point [*see illustration on page 50*].

Lartet and Christy recognized that the exquisite flat flaking of these artifacts was unique, and they christened them the "industry of Laugerie-Haute." This might be the name of the Solutrean culture today except for the fact that other important Upper Paleolithic finds were made at nearby Laugerie-Basse. To avoid confusion prehistorians named the Laugerie-Haute industry after Solutré, a site in eastern France where the same distinctive stone tools were found a few years later.

There were several questions that new excavations at Laugerie-Haute could help to answer. One was that even after 100 years there is little real agreement among prehistorians as to what the Solutrean industry really represents. Some believe, as they do of other Upper Paleolithic cultures, that the Solutrean is merely the grafting of a few foreign ideas onto already existing traditions. Others visualize an invasion of western Europe by groups armed with superior weapons who absorbed or eliminated the earlier inhabitants until they in turn were absorbed or eliminated by the people of the later Magdalenian culture. Finally, still other prehistorians deny both of these hypotheses and assert that the Solutrean culture evolved indigenously in western Europe from one or another of the immediately preceding traditions.

In the past there has been a tendency to overemphasize the exotic and spectacular among Solutrean artifacts, particularly the leaf-shaped blades and the elegantly made projectile points, and to ignore the rest of the Solutrean tool kit: ordinary implements such as burins for engraving and incising, scrapers, perforators and other such tools. Whether special tools were made locally or were introduced from outside is the kind of question that can be answered only by statistical analysis. For this, it is not enough merely to distinguish the major "periods" of a culture. For example, the period named *Solutréen inférieur* in France (and here called early Solutrean) shows five distinct strata at Laugerie-Haute. Careful dissection of these microlayers—each of which may correspond to a separate human occupation of the site—is a prerequisite for sound statistical conclusions.

I began my work in April, 1959, with

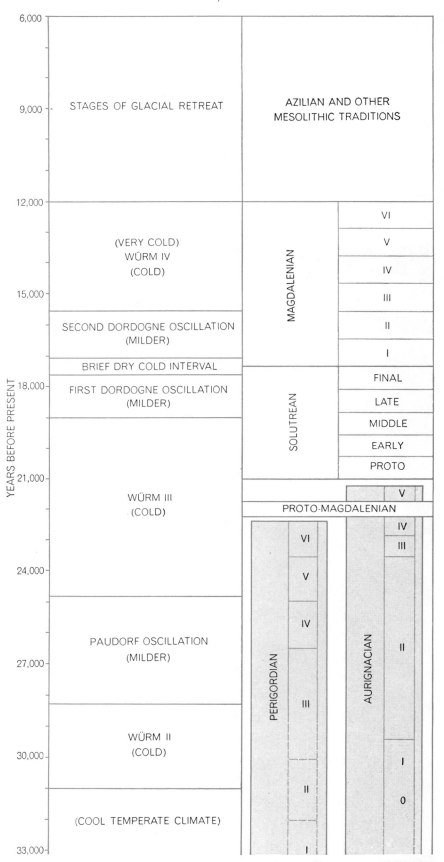

UPPER PALEOLITHIC PERIOD had its inception in western Europe some 32,000 years ago, at a time of retreating ice. The first Solutrean-style tools appeared 11,000 years later, near the end of a cold period. During the next 4,000 years Solutrean culture dominated southwestern France and offshoots appeared in the Iberian Peninsula. It was succeeded some 17,000 years ago by the final Upper Paleolithic culture: the art-rich Magdalenian.

the following questions in mind. Is the Solutrean a continuum with each phase evolving indigenously into the next, or does each phase reflect new stimuli from elsewhere? What clues do the earliest Solutrean levels provide to even earlier ancestral periods? And what was happening at the end of Solutrean times just before the Solutrean culture was replaced by the Magdalenian?

The Laugerie-Haute rock-shelter stretches for about 50 meters under the limestone cliffs bordering the Vézère River. Today the house of the curator of the Museum of Prehistory at Les Eyzies is built directly over the mid-

LAUREL-LEAF BLADE is an example of the remarkable capacity for working in stone that characterizes Solutrean culture.

dle of the site, so that excavating is restricted to the east and west ends. The shelter was inhabited for several thousand years before Solutrean times by people using Perigordian, proto-Magdalenian and Aurignacian tools. After the final Aurignacian occupation there was a short interval during a period of very cold climate when the site and perhaps the whole region was deserted.

This hiatus at Laugerie-Haute is marked by a thick layer of limestone fragments that had fallen from the roof and sides of the shelter. The layer contains no trace of human occupation. Lying directly on this sterile rubble in one small area of the site is a stratum that can be considered proto-Solutrean. The artifacts possess many of the characteristics of later Solutrean assemblages but in a rudimentary form. Very fine, flat flaking is evident on certain flint tools, and a large number of flint blades show the secondary flaking that is called retouching.

Of particular importance are the tools known as unifacial points. These are blades of flint with one surface fully or partially retouched by flat flaking and with the base often chipped to a narrower width as if for mounting on a shaft or handle. The exact use to which these unifacial points were put is unknown. The important thing is that in this proto-Solutrean stratum they are already present but in a form that is heavier and thicker than that in later levels.

There is no doubt that this bottom layer is the earliest evidence of the Solutrean industry in the Les Eyzies region. It probably dates back to somewhere between 21,000 and 22,000 years ago. The proto-Solutrean occupation at Laugerie-Haute seems to have been no more than a brief encampment by a visiting group. The only other site in southwestern France that has yielded a similar assemblage of tools is some 30 kilometers away at Badegoule.

Above this lowest Solutrean stratum there is another short hiatus and then a sequence of five levels, all of which can be classed as early Solutrean. Charcoal from one of these levels gave a radiocarbon date of 18,700 B.C. The discovery of these five strata has allowed a finer subdivision of the early Solutrean than was hitherto possible. The period proves to have evolved by stages from a rather archaic assemblage not much different from proto-Solutrean at the bottom to an uppermost level that is on the point of transforming itself into middle Solutrean. The character-

istic unifacial points become finer and more carefully retouched until, in the final early Solutrean level, the more archaic types disappear and the retouching invades much of the opposite face of the blade. The statistical distribution of other tool types similarly approaches the values typical of the middle Solutrean.

The next strata at Laugerie-Haute belong to the middle Solutrean and consist of at least four layers. In the earliest of these the only real difference from the final early Solutrean lies in the timid appearance of a very few laurel-leaf blades. These elegant implements make up scarcely 3 percent of the total flint inventory, but their appearance may be said to have been heralded by the increasing popularity of bifacial workmanship on the unifacial points in the immediately preceding strata.

In the next three middle-Solutrean levels these laurel leaves increase in numbers and variety and the unifacial points decline proportionately. Flat retouching now becomes an extremely popular flintworking technique. In succeeding strata the Solutrean craftsmen show an amazing flair for experimenting with the forms of the laurel leaves. Some are tiny and delicate; others are long and thick. Many are long and slender, and the retouching consists of fine parallel flaking. Some have such thin cross sections that it is difficult to imagine how they could have served any utilitarian purpose. Indeed, they may have been showpieces and luxury items. This same extravagance is reflected in many bizarre bifacial tools that exhibit notches, stems and asymmetrical shapes [see illustration on page 52]. A count of the laurel-leaf blades found in successive Solutrean levels at Laugerie-Haute shows them to have been scarce at the lowest levels of the middle Solutrean, then increasingly abundant and finally constituting a fourth of all stone tools by the end of that period [see the illustration on page 50]. It has already been noted that a lengthy evolution of bifacial retouching techniques preceded the first appearance of the laurel leaves. Both facts favor the conclusion that these seemingly exotic tools are the result of local evolution rather than an explosive invasion of either new peoples or new ideas.

It is not known exactly how long the middle Solutrean lasted—probably not more than 1,000 years at the most—but

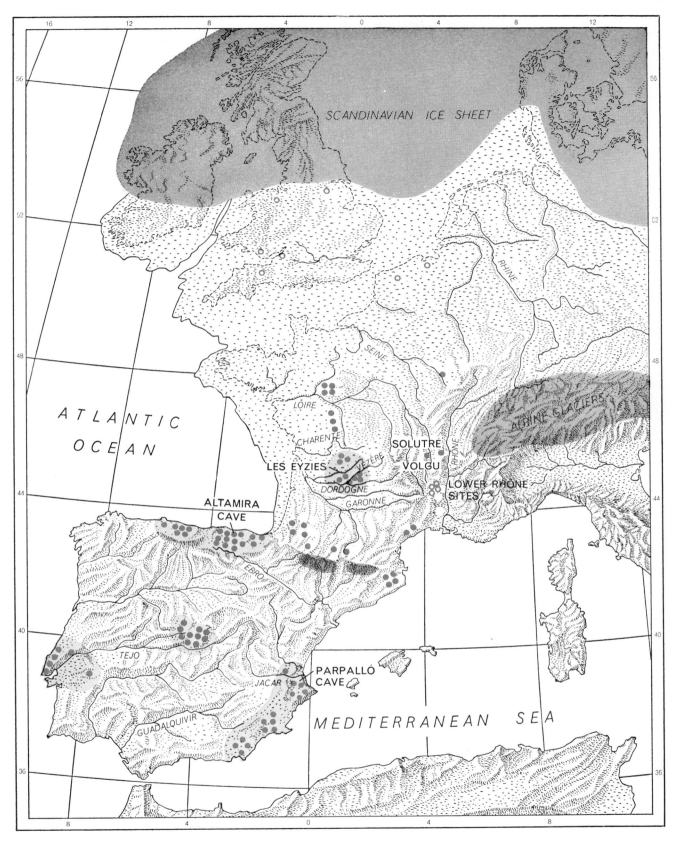

WESTERN EUROPE some 20,000 years ago had approximately today's Mediterranean coastline, but neither the English Channel nor the North Sea existed. Glaciers were extensive in the Alps and the Pyrenees, and the great Scandinavian ice sheet covered most of Ireland and all of Scotland and the Baltic. The third advance of the Würm glaciation was just ending and the weather was cold. Solid dots locate sites where Solutrean materials have been discovered. The five major areas (*light color*) are the classic Solutrean region of the Dordogne in southwestern France and four outlying Iberian regions. The open dots in the lower Rhône valley identify sites from which the earliest Solutrean techniques seem to have dispersed. The other open dots locate sites of less certain affinity.

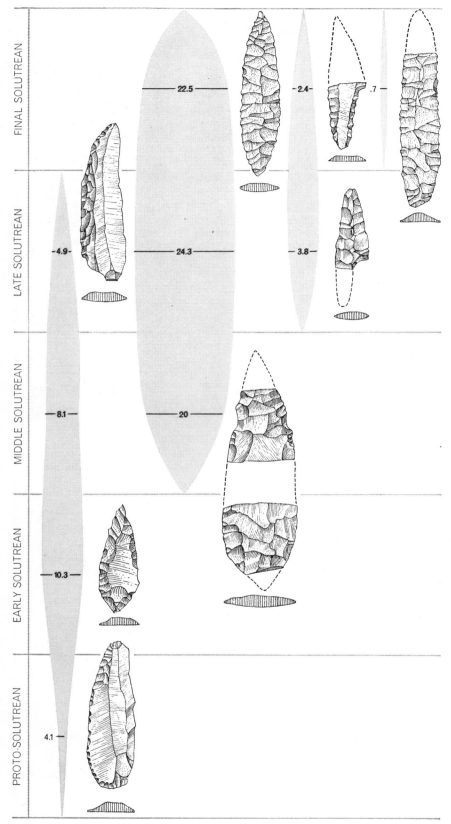

in its uppermost strata there is evidence that new ideas were being introduced or pioneered. Very small flint blades appear, their backs blunted by retouching, perhaps to make them fit into slots in wooden or bone shafts. Equally tiny scrapers are found. Another introduction or invention at the end of this period is the "single-shouldered" point [*see illustration at left*]. Thus, much as in the transition from the early to the middle Solutrean, the top levels of the middle Solutrean grade almost imperceptibly into the next division, the late Solutrean.

At Laugerie-Haute there are four strata that can be assigned to the late Solutrean. One key artifact that marks these layers is an increasingly sophisticated version of the single-shouldered point, which grows longer and shows more elaborate bifacial retouching from layer to layer. In contrast, the unifacial point of the proto-Solutrean and early Solutrean levels has now almost disappeared. The laurel leaves continue, and although they diminish in number and size they exhibit increasingly fine workmanship. Meanwhile a new kind of blade—the willow leaf, with rounded ends and delicate retouching on one face only—is found.

In the middle strata of the late Solutrean at Laugerie-Haute a very practical invention makes its first known appearance: the eyed needle made of bone. This seems to have been a Solutrean innovation; although bone needles are common in the Magdalenian strata that follow, none have been found in earlier Upper Paleolithic levels. The needle eyes are sometimes quite small, and it is a safe supposition that these implements were used for fine stitching or to produce fitted clothing.

Toward the end of the Solutrean period a curious change is evident. In contrast with the thick and rich deposits of earlier age, the sites of human occupation both at Laugerie-Haute and elsewhere in France become thin, restricted in area and impoverished in tools. There seems good reason to suppose that by this time the population of the Dordogne was composed of much smaller or more nomadic bands than before. These bands may even have been single families. Certainly they remained at each site for a shorter time. This phenomenon may be related to the unusually mild climate in the late Solutrean, which may have made the game animals scarcer.

A recent analysis of the strata at Laugerie-Haute has shown that at the

**FOUR KEY STONE TOOLS** appeared during successive Solutrean periods. Unifacial points (flaked on one surface only) are found at Laugerie-Haute from proto-Solutrean through late Solutrean times. They total 10.3 percent of all tools found in the early Solutrean period. Next to appear are laurel-leaf blades, which account for a fourth of all late Solutrean tools found at Laugerie-Haute. The shouldered point is unknown before the late Solutrean. Last of all to appear at Laugerie-Haute are the exquisitely flaked willow-leaf blades. These number less than 1 percent of the tool inventory in the final Solutrean period.

very end of the Solutrean a cold, dry spell struck southern France. This climatic change was brief: it lasted only into the earliest Magdalenian times. It is not yet possible to say whether the preceding mild period, the cold snap or a combination of both was responsible for the disappearance of the Solutrean culture from the Dordogne. In other regions the Solutrean may have lasted longer, but at Laugerie-Haute it was suddenly succeeded by an early Magdalenian industry.

There are as yet no radiocarbon dates for the end of the Solutrean at Laugerie-Haute, but somewhere around 17,000 years ago is probably not far off. Elsewhere, perhaps, there were contacts of some kind between the final Solutrean and the early Magdalenian; the Magdalenian industry not only possesses eyed needles but also shares with the Solutrean the production of carved stone bas-reliefs. There was no such contact at Laugerie-Haute, however. The rock-shelter had already been deserted before the 5,000 years of Magdalenian occupation began.

During the middle and late Solutrean the population of southwestern France was expanding into surrounding areas. A factor in these migrations may have been the mild climate of the period. To judge by widespread finds,

some groups equipped with Solutrean techniques not only occupied sites near the Pyrenees but also spilled over into Spain. The Spanish Solutrean is in some ways distinct from the French, marked by characteristic versions of bifacial blades and stemmed and barbed points.

The expansion was not exclusively to the south; middle Solutrean industries are also found in central France, north of the Loire and almost into Brittany. The Solutrean of this period apparently never reached the Paris basin or the open lands of Belgium and Britain, which was then attached to the Continent. One thriving colony far to the east, however, was the site of Solutré itself in the Rhône valley not far from Lyons. The curious thing about this open-air site, which was discovered in 1866, is that it is the only scene of Solutrean occupation in all that region; if other occupation sites exist, they have yet to be found. In 1873 an isolated cache of 17 very large laurel-leaf blades was found by canal diggers at Volgu, about 50 kilometers west of Solutré, but this hoard was not associated with an occupation site.

After nearly a century of digging at Solutré, there is still no clear knowledge of the length of time the site was occupied or how it ties in chronologically with the Solutrean of other regions. Yet it is clear that Solutré was

by no means the scene of a brief encampment far from some home base. It is a large occupation area that shows two thick and quite separate levels: a middle Solutrean (which corresponds roughly to the middle Solutrean of the Dordogne region) and a later stage. These later strata do not contain the shouldered points, willow-leaf blades or eyed needles typical of the Dordogne; instead they show a local specialization in laurel-leaf blades. Certainly this famous site deserves further investigation.

Combining the specific knowledge gained at Laugerie-Haute with more general information about the Solutrean obtained elsewhere, what can be said in summary about this short-lived Upper Paleolithic culture? First and most important is the fact that the Solutrean does not differ fundamentally from other hunting cultures of western Europe. Almost all Upper Paleolithic peoples were skilled hunters adapted to a rigorous cold environment and living in rock shelters, caves and open-air settlements. They had many kinds of stone implements in common, some of them "secondary" tools intended for fashioning other artifacts in bone, antler, ivory and wood. The ordinary Solutrean tool kit—stone, bone and antler—was not particularly different from that of other hunters. The Solutrean

SITE OF SOLUTRÉ, near Lyons in eastern France, gave the distinctive Upper Paleolithic culture its name. Most Solutrean sites are located in rock-shelters. Solutré, however, was an open-air encampment below a steep precipice. It contains two distinct levels. The earliest one resembles the middle Solutrean of the Dordogne, but the later level shows a local specialization in big blade tools.

subsistence pattern was founded, as was that of the other cultures, on the hunting of large game animals. At Laugerie-Haute more than 90 percent of the animal bones in Solutrean strata belong to reindeer, but horses, wild cattle, ibex and occasionally mammoth and musk-ox were also prey. The bones of salmon and other fishes are sometimes found; at one Solutrean site in Spain hares were the principal game.

Like most other Upper Paleolithic cultures, the Solutrean left an abundance of personal decorations. There are bone and ivory pendants, beads and bracelets: long bone pins with notches may possibly have been used in hair arrangement. Red, yellow and black pigments, found in some sites, could indicate the custom of body or face painting.

For many years it was thought that the Solutrean culture was unlike other Upper Paleolithic cultures of western Europe because it was almost without art. In due course Solutrean decorative work in bone and antler was recognized, but the experts still denied the culture either paintings or sculpture. Then the discovery of Solutrean stone friezes and bas-reliefs added sculpture to the cultural repertoire [*see illustration on page 46*]. Finally, in the 1930's the discovery of paintings on plaques of stone buried in Solutrean strata at the cave of Parpalló in eastern Spain filled the final gap in the artistic inventory. Moreover, associated with early Solutrean remains in the lower valley of the Rhône are paintings and engravings on cave walls that show mammoths, bears and horses in a distinctive style. A case might also be made for viewing the remarkable Solutrean work in flint as a product of some basic Upper Paleolithic artistic drive. In some Solutrean sites, particularly the later ones, the number of such specialized decorative artifacts as laurel leaves and willow leaves reaches amazing proportions—sometimes approaching 50 percent of all stone implements.

How, then, does the Solutrean differ from the other Upper Paleolithic traditions in western Europe? In the first place, its geographical range is surprisingly limited compared with such cultures as the Aurignacian that preceded it or the Magdalenian that followed it. This fact may be related to the culture's relatively short lifetime—a matter of little more than 4,000 years. Negative evidence is perhaps less persuasive, yet the absence of the "Venuses"—female figurines—that are char-

VIRTUOSO FLAKING characterizes four unusual Solutrean tools (*reproduced full-size*). The large bifacial blade (*lower left*) has its base chipped into a neat semicircle. The point (*upper left*) shows two such basal semicircles. At center a small laurel-leaf blade has been given a stemmed base. What use the asymmetrical form (*right*) served is conjectural.

acteristic of other Upper Paleolithic traditions may indicate a distinctive set of Solutrean beliefs or values. The lack of deliberate burials may point in the same direction.

But it is in flintworking techniques that the Solutrean is unique. The passion for fine, flat retouching extended beyond specialized blades and points to many commonplace tools. Moreover, the Solutrean abounds in artifacts not only of flint but also of fine-grained and brightly colored quartzes, jaspers and other fancy stones. Finally, wherever the Solutrean is found there are, in spite of variations due to time or place, quantitative and morphological consistencies in these stone tools. The

proportion of the specialized blades and points is high; the proportion of burins and ordinary blades is low; the proportion of scrapers and perforators is in between. It is this statistical consistency, together with an emphasis on fine retouching and imaginative forms, that gives the Solutrean its distinctive "personality."

Where did the Solutrean culture originate? One school of prehistorians believed it was born in Hungary, where large bifacial flints resembling the laurel-leaf blades have been found, and then expanded across Central Europe to develop into the classic Solutrean of France and Spain. Another school has suggested that its origins lie in a North

African stone-tool industry: the Aterian, which possesses not only bifacial blades but also tanged points that resemble those of the late Solutrean in eastern Spain. The same flaw mars both arguments; each implies that when the Solutrean culture first reached France, it already possessed laurel-leaf blades. The two earliest Solutrean periods in France have no laurel leaves and yet they are fully set in the Solutrean tradition. Therefore few prehistorians any longer believe that there are links between the Solutrean and cultures of eastern Europe or North Africa.

What about the possibility of an indigenous evolution of Solutrean culture from some preceding tradition in western Europe itself? Spain can be ruled out as a birthplace; the earliest levels known there contain an already well-developed middle Solutrean apparently derived from France. As for France itself, some interesting suggestions have come out of the ground in recent years.

The proto-Solutrean at Laugerie-Haute and at two other French sites is the earliest Solutrean identified so far. Any postulated ancestral Solutrean should therefore show certain affinities with proto-Solutrean. In the past decade some curious industries have been found in the lower valley of the Rhône, which is in eastern France. They are earlier in date than the Solutrean of the Dordogne. There are unifacially retouched blades and flakes very reminiscent of the proto-Solutrean; many of the other implements could fit well enough into an early Solutrean tool kit. Ancestral Solutrean may therefore have crystallized in the lower Rhône valley and then branched out, in the form of the proto-Solutrean culture, not only to southwestern France but also to the north. There the site of Le Trilobite in the Yonne valley has yielded suggestions of proto-Solutrean culture. Other possible traces of proto-Solutrean remains are found in northern France, in Belgium and even in Britain.

Why it was that the main Solutrean development took place only in southwestern France remains an unanswered question that only further fieldwork can solve. One fact, however, now seems established: It is no longer necessary to go outside western Europe or indeed outside France itself to locate the birthplace of the Solutrean culture.

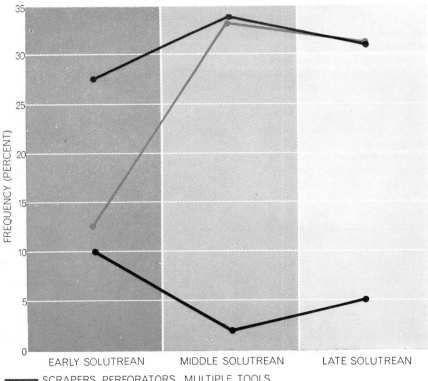

SCRAPERS, PERFORATORS, MULTIPLE TOOLS
BURINS
UNIFACIAL POINTS, LAUREL LEAVES, WILLOW LEAVES, SHOULDERED POINTS

**CONSISTENCY of the Solutrean culture is evident in the quantities of different types of tool. During three successive periods the engraving and chiseling tools called burins never exceeded 10 percent of the stone-tool inventory at Laugerie-Haute. The number of scrapers, perforators and multiple tools at the site, in turn, remained consistently at a higher level. Only the four typically Solutrean blade tools showed a significant quantitative increase.**

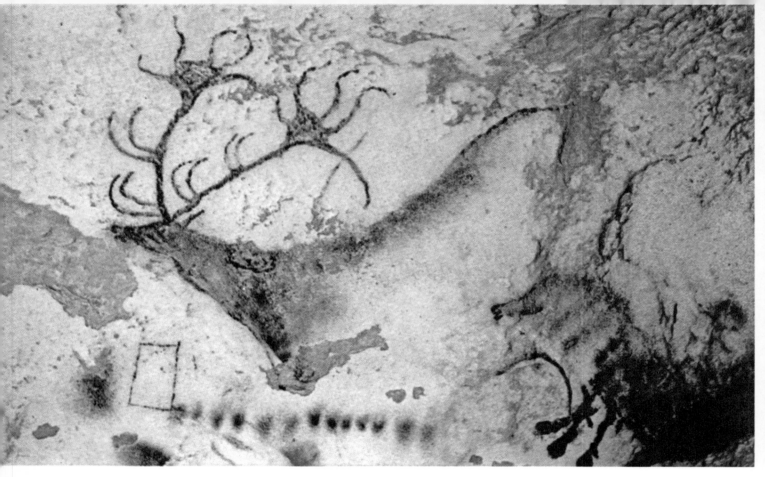

**RED DEER STAG** (*above*) appears on a cave wall at Lascaux, a French Paleolithic site discovered in 1940. Both the stag and the two abstract signs below it, a rectangle and a row of dots, were painted on the rock surface with a manganese pigment; the stag is about five feet high. The painting was made some 15,000 years ago.

**SPOTTED HORSE** (*below*) dominates a cave wall at Pech-Merle, another French Paleolithic site. A hand seen in negative outline indicates the scale of the painting, which, like the stag, belongs to the early Magdalenian period of European prehistory. Abstract signs include many dots and a grill-like red rectangle by the hand.

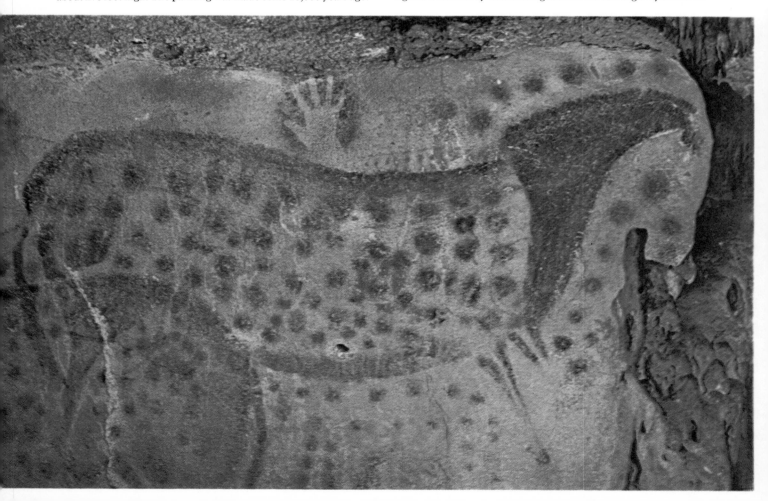

# The Evolution of Paleolithic Art

6

André Leroi-Gourhan
*February 1968*

*The first artistic tradition occupied two-thirds of the period spanned by the entire history of art. How it evolved is studied by the classification of its works in terms of time and space*

The earliest forms of art, at least among those art forms that can be dated with any certainty, were created in Europe between 30,000 and 10,000 B.C. They belong to a time before the oldest civilizations and the earliest agriculture—the Upper Paleolithic period at the end of the last continental glaciation. Paleolithic art has manifested itself in two principal forms: engraved or sculptured objects found by the thousands in excavations from the Urals to the Atlantic, and the awe-inspiring decorations of more than 100 caves in France and Spain. It has now been studied for nearly a century, and such caves as Lascaux and Altamira have become as well known as the most famous art works of historic times.

Until recently studies of Paleolithic art were focused largely on its aesthetic and magico-religious significance. Today attention has turned to the relations among such art forms—to their classification in terms of time and space. As a result we can now begin to perceive how Paleolithic art evolved from its appearance in Aurignacian times to its inexplicable disappearance in Magdalenian times 20,000 years later.

Can an art that embraced all Europe for such a mighty span truly be considered a single art? Should we perhaps speak of prehistoric arts, as we speak of the arts of Africa? The analogy provides the answer to our question: The living arts of Africa south of the Sahara, with all their nuances, are clearly subdivisions of one wholly African art. They cannot be confused with the art of any other region. In the same sense Paleolithic art also constitutes a single episode in art history. Such is the unanimous opinion of its students. This view is based on the continuity that Paleolithic art exhibits in region after region over a span of 20 millenniums. Greek art or Christian art is so identified because its images continuously translate its ideologies. In the same way the term "Paleolithic art" serves to relate various techniques of representation that have undergone changes over a long period of time to a body of figurative themes that has remained remarkably constant. Indeed, consistency is one of the first facts that strikes the student of Paleolithic art. In painting, engraving and sculpture on rock walls or in ivory, reindeer antler, bone and stone, and in the most diverse styles, Paleolithic artists repeatedly depict the same inventory of animals in comparable attitudes. Once this unity is recognized, it only remains for the student to seek ways of arranging the art's temporal and spatial subdivisions in a systematic manner.

## The Problem of Chronology

The task of temporal subdivision is by no means an easy one. To understand its difficulties, let us imagine an art historian who must arrange in their correct chronological order 1,000 statues belonging to every epoch from 500 B.C. to A.D. 1900. Imagine further that his only points of reference are five or six of the statues that are by chance correctly dated. The prehistorian's position is the same—or worse. The large majority of the Paleolithic period's small sculptures (which we classify as "portable art" to distinguish them from "wall art," the paintings, engravings and sculptures of the caves and rock-shelters) were discovered at the beginning of this century, a time when precision in the excavation of stratified sites was far from absolute. As a result there are very few instances in which associations are established between excavated works of art and implements such as scrapers and projectile points that have been firmly dated on the basis of stratigraphy. Even in the few cases where such dating is possible, the style of the object is not always so clear-cut as to allow strong conclusions. Finally, the thousands of wall paintings and engravings created during the period are not stratified at all. If the earth floors of their caves contain the remains of more than one Paleolithic culture, it is difficult to decide to which of these culture periods the art should be assigned. For all these reasons classifying Paleolithic art is a task considerably harder than the classification of prehistoric man's other material remains.

The work of the Abbé Breuil over more than half a century provides the principal source of traditional views concerning the evolution of Paleolithic art. This pioneer prehistorian undertook a prodigious labor of inventory and classification with the limited means available in his day. Except for a few instances in which specific dating was possible, his method of establishing the relative chronology of wall art rested on three assumptions. The first was simply that when two wall paintings are superimposed, the one underneath must be the older. The second, based on the probability that the caves where wall art is found were inhabited continuously for many centuries, was that one should find examples of work from many periods among the decorations. The third assumption was that, since the animal and human forms depicted in the caves were executed individually for magical purposes, there is no order in their arrangement. It follows from this last assumption that such works are not necessarily contemporaneous and that they are not, when taken together, evidence of any organized body of thought.

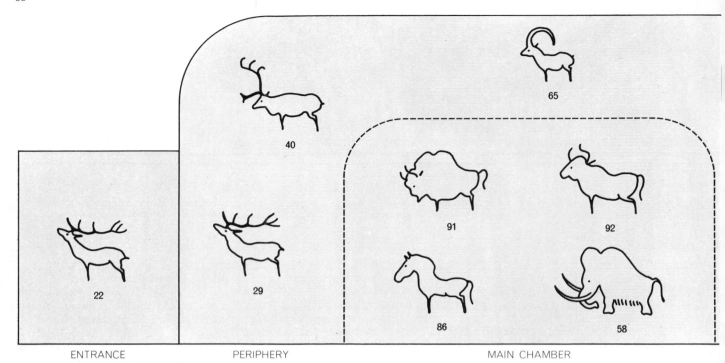

ENTRANCE          PERIPHERY                    MAIN CHAMBER

**METHODICAL ARRANGEMENT** of the animal depictions at various Paleolithic sites was revealed by the author's survey of 62 caves. The diagram shows an idealized cave with an entrance, a main chamber and its periphery and, finally, a back passage to a deep inner area. Numbers below each animal figure show the percent of depictions of that animal present in that part of all the

From this viewpoint (which is still held by some prehistorians) wall art represents the gradual accumulation of isolated pictures, each created by the need of the moment. When one stands before the great wall paintings of Lascaux in France or Altamira in Spain, however, it is hard to imagine how the random accumulation of isolated subjects could possibly have led to an assemblage that impresses the most naïve viewer with its overall balance. Doubts on this score are what inspired Annette Laming-Emperaire to publish her important study of 1962: *The Meaning of Paleolithic Wall Art*. There she vigorously challenges the traditional theories. My own work has been motivated by a similar conviction and is based on the following postulate. If, rather than working haphazardly, the men of the Paleolithic consciously—or

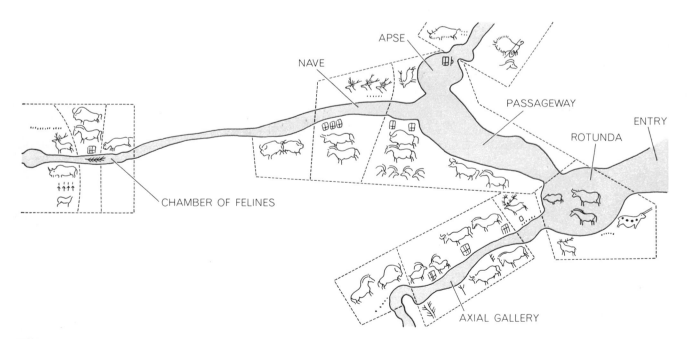

**LASCAUX CAVE**, a famous Paleolithic site in France, is shown in plan view; more than 300 feet separate the cave's deepest recess (*left*) from the entrance (*right*). The broken lines enclosing the groups of depictions suggest how the cave's many decorated areas were originally subdivided. The stag and the two abstract signs just inside the Axial Gallery are reproduced in color on page 54.

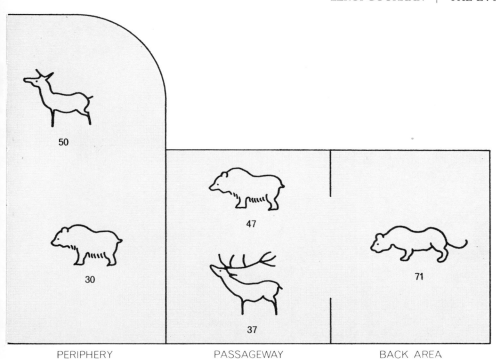

PERIPHERY          PASSAGEWAY          BACK AREA

caves surveyed. More than 90 percent of all bison and wild-ox paintings appear in main chambers, as do most horse paintings. Most stag paintings are located elsewhere: nearly 40 percent are in inner areas, 22 percent are in entrances and 29 percent are in peripheral areas.

even unconsciously—introduced order into the way their pictures are positioned, then an analysis of where various animal paintings are located in a sizable number of caves (say 50 or more out of the 100-odd sites) should reveal what general scheme, if any, the artists had in mind.

To test this postulate I have reviewed the topography of some 60 caves, established the position of more than 2,000 individual animal pictures in them and tabulated the results. The following related facts can be perceived: (1) If one defines "central position" either as the middle of a painted panel or as the most prominent chamber within a cave, it is in this position that more than 85 percent of all pictures of bison, wild oxen and horses are found. (2) The next most prominent animals—deer, ibex and mammoth—appear in positions other than a central one. (3) Three other species—rhinoceros, lion and bear—are found only in the deepest parts of the cave, or far from the central position [see bottom illustration on page 61].

A similar analysis can be made of the subjects other than animals that are depicted in Paleolithic art: representations of humans, male and female, and signs that are more or less abstract. More than 80 percent of all the female figures—and of the symbols that I call "wide" abstract signs, which are evidently related to fe-

male figures—are found in the same central places where bison and wild oxen are depicted. Other symbols designated "narrow" signs are in the same areas where the remaining animal figures are found; that is to say, nearly 70 percent of them are in positions that are peripheral.

This is not the place to consider what such patterns may be able to tell us about the religious beliefs of Paleolithic man. For anyone who is trying to establish a chronology of Paleolithic art, however, the orderliness of these arrays has its own significance. First, one is led to the conclusion that in most of the wall art in most of the caves the separate elements belong to a single period, and that later works were executed in other parts of the cave. Even in those caves where the wall art clearly represents the accumulation of several periods, the later works repeat the elements and order of the earlier ones. Second, in any single assemblage of pictures the wide abstract signs are all much the same, whereas in caves that contain a number of separate picture groups the wide signs differ from group to group. The existence of these differences suggests that the wide signs can serve as chronological guideposts, or at the very least as guides to the relations between the various styles in which the animal figures are executed. Thus, regardless of any hypotheses concerning

prehistoric religion, the fact that there is order in Paleolithic man's art provides a basis for investigating its evolution.

### Discovering Points in Time

All such problems of chronology would have vanished long ago if only one of two things had happened. Each Paleolithic site could have yielded stratified sequences of buried sculptures and the style of the material from each stratum could have shown it to be unmistakably contemporaneous with one after another of the cave's displays of wall art. Alternatively, the examples of the wall art in a number of caves could all have been executed in a single style, and the artifacts excavated from the floors of the same caves could all have been attributed to a single interval of time. In actuality very few examples of wall art can be firmly attributed to a specific period during the many millenniums in which prehistoric art flourished. Still, the few examples that do exist provide us with some degree of chronological framework.

As a starting point, there are no known examples of representational art before the Aurignacian period, beginning about 30,000 B.C. There are, however, firmly dated pieces of Aurignacian sculpture. They are found, for example, in the Aurignacian strata of two sites in the Dordogne valley of France: the Cellier rock-shelter and La Ferassie. They are crudely engraved figures of animals and wide and narrow signs.

Our next bench mark in time is found in strata of Solutrean age (about 15,000 B.C.) at the Roc de Sers site in the Charente valley of France: a low-relief frieze rendered in a vigorous style. It depicts horses, bison, ibexes and men. The date is firmly established because the rock of the frieze had fallen from its original position and was discovered lying face down between two strata containing Solutrean artifacts.

A third bench mark is provided by a number of engraved stone plaques discovered in strata of Upper Magdalenian age (about 10,000 B.C.) in the caves of Teyjat in the Dordogne. The animals depicted on the plaques are the same as those in the Roc de Sers frieze, but they are executed in a more detailed, almost photographic style. The final bench mark, denoting the end of Paleolithic art, is also found in the Dordogne. At Villepin engraved pebbles from strata dating to the very end of the Magdalenian period (about 8000 B.C.) display sketchy, often barely identifiable animal figures.

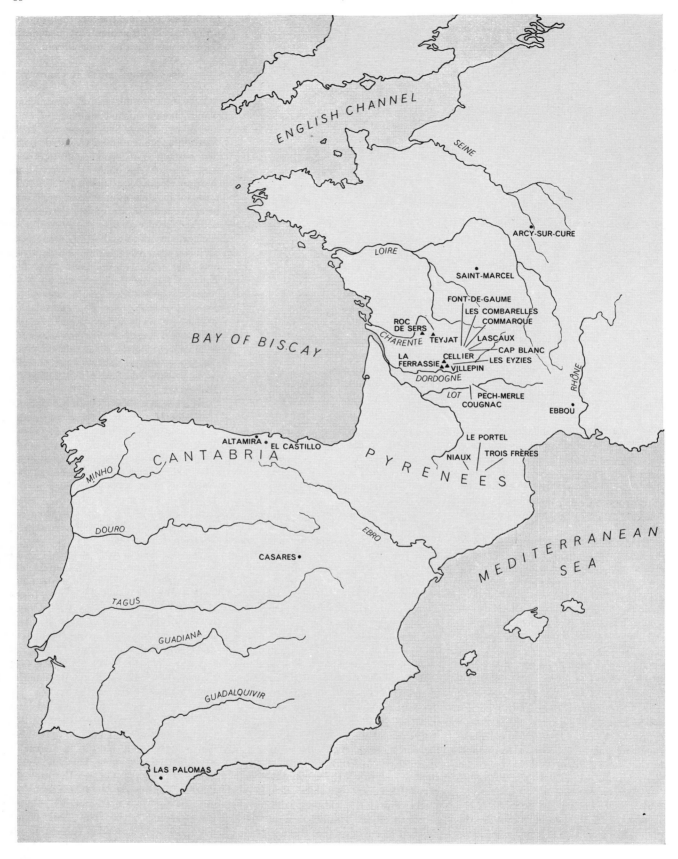

**HEARTLAND** of Paleolithic cave art was western Europe south of the Loire River. Sites mentioned by the author in the valleys of the Charente, the Dordogne and the Lot and in the foothills of the French Pyrenees are shown, as are some with cave art in Canta-brian, central and southern Spain, in France north of the Charente and in the Rhône valley. Cave art has also been found at three sites in Italy and Sicily. Five Charente-Dordogne sites marked with triangles contained sculpture in strata with well-established dates.

Four points in time, all found in the same Dordogne-Charente region, scarcely suffice to establish a chronology for all Europe. Fortunately a number of less exact bench marks are available in France, Spain and Italy. Although these bench marks can be fixed no more exactly than around the start, the middle and the end of the Upper Paleolithic, they are in general accord with the Dordogne-Charente reference points and allow us not only to recognize the entire period's major chronological subdivisions but also to perceive a new and very important fact. Up to now it has been thought that the portable art and the wall art of the Upper Paleolithic evolved in a strictly parallel manner, and that one could find pictures characteristic of each of the period's subdivisions in the caves. It is now apparent that, on the contrary, wall art was extremely rare or even nonexistent early in the Upper Paleolithic, that most of it belongs to a middle phase during which the portable art becomes less abundant, and that portable art catches up with wall art once more in the period's final phase.

## The Evolution of Abstract Signs

Students of Paleolithic art have always been intrigued by certain abstract signs that appear in wall art almost from its beginning to its end, although not so commonly as pictures of animals. In the opinion of some investigators some of the signs represent huts or tents; other signs are interpreted as representing weapons and traps, shields and even primitive heraldic designs. It would seem, however, that only a few signs out of the hundreds known can be explained by their resemblance to actual objects. If instead of selecting a few such examples one makes an inclusive inventory of all the things found in wall art that do not obviously portray animals, a rather different picture emerges. One can even group such representations into general categories.

One category is men and women, sometimes pictured whole and sometimes reduced to a head or torso. To this category can be added numerous realistic representations of the male and female sexual organs, which evidently have the same significance as the fuller figures. The existence of these drawings has suggested to some scholars that a fertility cult existed in Paleolithic times. This is hard to disprove, but given the fact that the male and female representations are as often separate as they are together, they would appear to be at best quite abstract fertility symbols.

| YEARS B.C. | CULTURE | PERIOD | EXAMPLE |
|---|---|---|---|
| 5,000 | | | |
| 10,000 | LATE MAGDALENIAN V–VI | CLASSIC (STYLE IV) | |
| | MIDDLE MAGDALENIAN III–IV | | |
| | EARLY MAGDALENIAN I–II | ARCHAIC (STYLE III) | |
| 15,000 | SOLUTREAN | | |
| | INTER-GRAVETTIAN-SOLUTREAN | PRIMITIVE (STYLE II) | |
| 20,000 | | | |
| | GRAVETTIAN | | |
| 25,000 | | PRIMITIVE (STYLE I) | |
| | AURIGNACIAN | | |
| 30,000 | | | |

**EVOLUTION** of Paleolithic art took place during the era's final 20,000 years, a period known as the Upper Paleolithic. The first examples are dated around 30,000 B.C., when the Aurignacian culture makes its appearance. They were crude outlines cut into rock (*bottom figure is unidentified; the others portray horses*). This Style I work, as it is classified by the author, and later work in Style II comprise the primitive period. The best-known cave art was produced during the archaic (Style III) and the classic (Style IV) periods.

By far the largest number of signs belong to one or the other of the two groups I have mentioned: the wide and narrow signs. The wide signs include rectangles, triangles, ovals and shield shapes. Most of them clearly belong to the category of human representations; they are quite realistic depictions of the female sexual organ. The narrow signs include short strokes, rows of dots and barbed lines. Some of them clearly suggest male sexual organs, although they are extremely stylized. For that matter, the entire inventory of abstract signs could well be nothing but animal and human figures rendered symbolically.

These abstract signs are strikingly diverse in both time and space. One kind of rectangle, for example, accompanies animal figures that themselves have a number of stylistic features in common: the rectangle appears in the Dordogne, in the nearby Lot valley and in Cantabria, beyond the Pyrenees in Spain. This enables us to assign all the cave art in which the rectangle appears to the same time period. At the same time how abstract decoration is used to embellish each rectangle varies sufficiently from cave to cave to establish the fact that the art of Lascaux in the Dordogne, of Pech-Merle in the Lot valley and of Altamira in Spain each belongs to a distinct ancient province. Such a distinction

FOUR QUADRUPEDS, three of them bison, show how styles evolved. Work in Style I (*bottom engraving, cross section at right*) seldom depicted entire animals as here; both line and workmanship are rough. Style II technique (*second from bottom, cross section at left*) remains primitive but forms are more powerful. In Style III (*painting second from top*) line and color have been mastered although anatomical details are unperfected. The work in Style IV (*top painting*) shows both anatomical fidelity and a sense of movement.

cannot be made with equal precision when one must base one's judgment on the style in which the animals are depicted. As a matter of fact, signs remote from realism are a better mirror of local influences than animal portraits are. I have therefore based my use of abstract signs on a twofold principle: first, that as generalized forms they are contemporaneous and, second, that in their details they reveal regional influences.

As in the pictures of animals, the abstract signs do not establish much in the way of precise chronology. Most of the sites where they are found contain nothing that can be rigorously dated. Nonetheless, they make it possible to establish a sequence that is about as reliable as the one based on animal figures. For example, the oldest known abstract signs appear about 30,000 B.C., in Aurignacian times. The wide signs are realistically feminine; the narrow ones are either realistically masculine or are stylized into a series of strokes or dots. In Solutrean times, roughly from 20,000 to 15,000 B.C., full figures of men and women seem to predominate; the style of the latter is familiar to us from the numerous "Venus figurines" that have been found in both western and eastern Europe. The transition between Solutrean and early Magdalenian times (between 15,000 and 13,000 B.C.) is a period of rectangular signs, followed closely by bracket-shaped ones. At this point regional differences in abstract signs make their classification difficult, although a revival in the popularity of small sculptures provides a precise means of determining the chronological position of other animal representations. During the Magdalenian proper, from 13,000 to 9000 B.C., the most important group of abstract signs are "key-shaped" ones, derived from the representation of a woman in profile [*see illustration on page 62*]. In the Dordogne and the Lot Valley it is possible to trace the evolution from early to middle Magdalenian by means of the key-shaped signs. Thereafter these signs become increasingly stylized, both in space (as one moves south) and in time (as the end of the Magdalenian approaches).

Key-shaped signs are by no means the only abstractions of this period. Here a variety of influences appear to have crisscrossed in space and time. At Les Eyzies in the Dordogne, for example, roof-shaped signs (which apparently evolved out of the bracket-shaped ones) seem to take the place of the key shapes. Another trend in symbolism is marked by the appearance of what some scholars have assumed are representations of

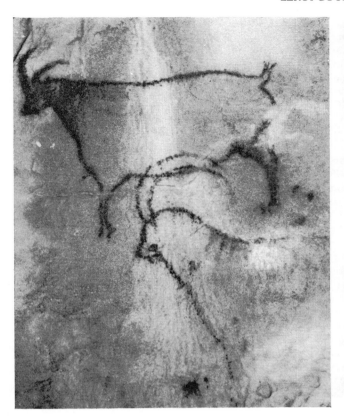

PAINTED IBEXES of the archaic period, a female (*top*) and a male, were done in red ocher at Cougnac, a Lot valley site in France. Painting, engraving and combinations of both are known.

ENGRAVED IBEX, also executed during the archaic period, is one of scores of animal figures cut into the cave walls at Ebbou, a Rhône valley site in France that contains engravings exclusively.

PAINTED RHINOCEROS, one of the animals typically found in the back areas of caves, occupies a niche opening off the main chamber at Lascaux. The work, in manganese, is transitional between Style III and Style IV. Dots by the tail form an abstract sign.

wounds on the bodies of animals. Both symbolic wounds and realistic representations of the female sexual organ are found in a comparable setting in a large number of caves. Since the realistic female representations of the Magdalenian are executed differently from the earliest female representations, it seems likely that the "wounds" are a different kind of female symbol.

### The Time Scale

By putting together all three classes of evidence—from excavations, from the study of reasonably well-dated wall art and from the evolution of human figures and abstract signs—a chronological framework can be erected that begins to approximate reality. The most attractive of all Paleolithic art works, the animal pictures, remain the most difficult to interpret directly. The reason is that any analysis of their evolution is founded on criteria of style, and judgments of style are primarily subjective. When details that allow objective evaluation are scanty, only the most general conclusions are possible. What appears to be an important criterion may reflect nothing more than a regional characteristic or the relative skill of the artist.

In spite of such qualifications, it can be said that the evidence in general allows us to discern the emergence of three great periods of Paleolithic art during the 20,000 years from the Aurignacian to the end of the Magdalenian.

They are, first, a primitive period, then an archaic period (in the same sense that one speaks of archaic Greek art: a well-developed body of art rapidly approaching maturity) and finally a classic period. Where the conditions are most favorable, as in the Dordogne-Charente region, we can point to the succession of four styles in the course of the three major periods. These I have designated Styles I and II (in the primitive period), Style III (in the archaic) and Style IV (in the classic). Even finer subdivisions are possible: the wall art of Lascaux and Pech-Merle, for example, is divisible into early and late Style III, and elsewhere Style IV shows similar early and late stages.

What are the characteristics of each period and style? Style I embraces history's oldest examples of representational art, examples that are precisely dated to the Aurignacian period by virtue of the fact that they are found in association with Aurignacian tools. The Aurignacian sculptures of Cellier and La Ferassie are Style I. As I noted earlier, the representations of animals from this time are very crude; sometimes the whole body is shown but more often the rendering is limited to a head or a forequarter. The inventory of animals includes the horse, the bison, the wild ox, the ibex and the rhinoceros—in other words, the main cast of characters found throughout Paleolithic art. The representations include realistic depictions of the female sexual organ as well as such male symbols as lines and rows of dots.

A long interval, extending from 25,000 to 18,000 B.C. and thus from the late Aurignacian through Gravettian times to early Solutrean ones, is the setting for Style II. In a chronology based on the evolution of techniques this 7,000-year interval is a confused period. One can assume that a number of cultures succeeded one another, but it is hard to equate the changes in one region with those in another. In any case, this was the period in which Paleolithic art attained its greatest geographical range, from the Atlantic coast on the west to the valley of the Don on the east. It is also the period in which the first wall art appears: paintings and engravings executed on the walls of open rock-shelters or on those cave walls that were illuminated by daylight.

The animal forms of Style II are powerful, but the technique of rendering remains quite primitive. The stereotyped curved line representing the neck and back and the line representing the belly are drawn first; the details characteristic of each animal species are then roughly connected to the generalized torsos and are often left unfinished. The abstract signs that are included in the wall art remain close to realism and generally consist of ovals and series of strokes. In the realm of small sculptures the numerous female figurines of this period, usually made of stone or of mammoth ivory, all have much the same shape. The trunk is corpulent and rendered in some detail but the extremities and the

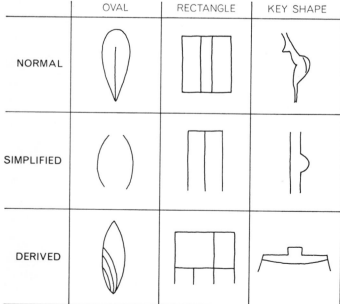

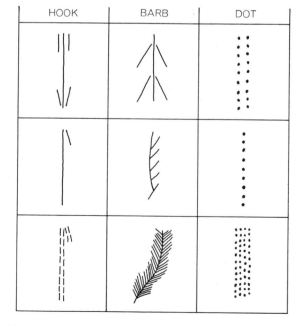

|  | OVAL | RECTANGLE | KEY SHAPE | | HOOK | BARB | DOT |
|---|---|---|---|---|---|---|---|
| NORMAL | | | | | | | |
| SIMPLIFIED | | | | | | | |
| DERIVED | | | | | | | |

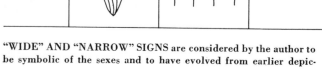

"WIDE" AND "NARROW" SIGNS are considered by the author to be symbolic of the sexes and to have evolved from earlier depictions of female and male figures or sexual organs. Three groups of symbols are shown for each sex, in normal and more abstract forms.

head are stylized and often quite reduced in size.

Style III, which is typical of the entire archaic period, finds its most eloquent expression in the great frieze of the Roc de Sers in Charente, in the equally impressive murals at Lascaux and in some of the Spanish cave paintings. The representations of animals retain a primitive flavor: the bodies are bulky and the small heads and hooves are joined to the bodies without much care for detail or proportion. Line, however, is now handled with great sensitivity, and the control of painting and sculptural technique is complete. The interplay of manganese blacks and ocher reds and yellows in the paintings and the use of color accents on the low reliefs reflect a mastery of both mediums. Representations of humans are scarce and do not compare in quality with the animal pictures. On the other hand, the abstract signs characteristic of Style III, which are rectangular or bracket-shaped, show such a diversity of embellishment that they have been compared to heraldic coats of arms.

Chronologically the style of the archaic period occupies the interval between 18,000 and 13,000 B.C., thus including the late Solutrean and the early Magdalenian. The evolution of animal portrayal can be traced through all five millenniums. At Lascaux and at Pech-Merle, for example, one can differentiate between early Style III animal paintings that are still close to Style II and late Style III paintings that already verge on Style IV.

In western Europe small sculptures are notably rare during the archaic period; of the few works in the category of portable art most are engraved plaques. In eastern Europe, on the other hand, there is no Style III wall art at all but there is a trove of animal and human figurines. Such regional differences probably correspond to ethnic ones. Thus one can readily distinguish between an eastern domain (from what is now Czechoslovakia to the U.S.S.R. west of the Urals) and a western one. Although we are a long way from knowing all the schools of Style III in the western domain, variations in rectangular signs and associated animal figures enable us to detect shades of difference between works from the Dordogne, the Lot valley, the central Pyrenees, Cantabria and the Rhône valley.

The whole of the Magdalenian proper, from 13,000 to 9000 B.C., provides the stage for the classic period of Paleolithic art and Style IV. Outside of western

**THE TWO SEXES** are represented by this array of wide and narrow signs painted on the wall of a cave at El Castillo in Cantabrian Spain during the archaic period. The embellished rectangles belong to one of five groups of female symbols recognized by the author and the rows of dots to one of four male groups (*see illustration on opposite page*).

**"WOUNDED" BISON,** painted during the classic period at Niaux in the French Pyrenees, is interpreted by the author as neither a hunting scene nor a sorcerer's spell but instead as a combination of animal figure and abstract female sign found only in Style IV. Female signs are usually found with bison and wild-ox pictures in the caves' central chambers.

CRUDELY OUTLINED HEAD of an animal from the earliest Aurignacian stratum at the Cellier rock-shelter in the Dordogne valley is typical of the art of the primitive period.

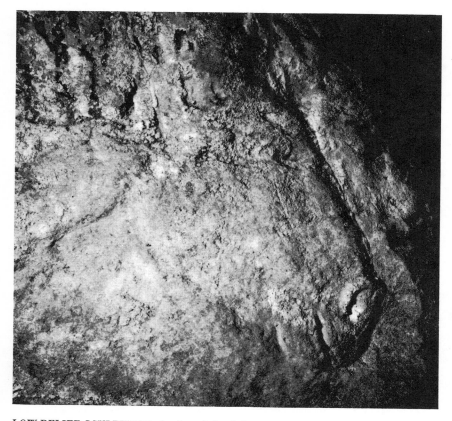

LOW-RELIEF SCULPTURE of a horse's head from Commarque, a Middle Magdalenian cave site in the Dordogne, shows the sophistication of classic period art, 15,000 years later.

Europe, Style IV is not particularly well represented at present, but within that area it is rich in wall art and especially rich in portable art. Small sculptures were widely disseminated in western Europe during the classic period. Toward the end of the period, when an increasingly mild climate allowed occupation of the northern and mountainous areas of Europe, examples of portable art reached the areas of Switzerland, Germany and even Britain. Wall art also extended its boundaries, appearing in Italy for the first time.

The wealth of classic small sculptures makes possible many comparisons between them and Style IV wall paintings that illuminate the main features of the period's art evolution. One result is that a distinction can be made between early and late Style IV animal pictures. In the early period faint traces of the archaic models still remain; regardless of the correctness of their proportions, the animals give the appearance of being suspended in midair. Body contours are filled in with incised lines or splashes of color that convey the texture of the coat. This surface modeling is present in figures found from Spain to the Loire valley in France; each animal species—horse, bison, ibex, reindeer and the like—is rendered by means of the same conventions from one end of this region to the other. In late Style IV representations the rendering of texture is less clear and many animals are presented in simple outline. It is now that anatomical fidelity and a sense of movement reach their peak. If the final art of the Paleolithic lacks the rather solemn grandeur of Lascaux, it nonetheless possesses an extraordinary vitality.

Most of the best-known examples of cave art are either early or late Style IV. These include the wall paintings at Font-de-Gaume, Les Combarelles and Cap Blanc in the Dordogne, the paintings at Le Portel, Trois-Frères and Niaux in the Pyrenees, the great painted ceiling at Altamira and paintings in several other cave sites in Biscay, Cantabria and Asturias. Because Style IV animal pictures are handled in a remarkably uniform manner all the way from Spain to central Europe, regional subdivisions are much harder to establish in the classic period than in the archaic one. Indeed, the uniformity of the classic period suggests not only the existence of contacts between various regional populations but also the existence of a firmly based cosmopolitan artistic tradition. One subdivision that can be detected is a single cohesive Franco-Cantabrian body of early Style IV art; it extends from the Loire valley to the Pyrenees and Asturias and is reflected in the rendering of females in profile and in associated abstract key-shaped signs. The distribution of small Style IV sculptures demonstrates a connection between the Pyrenees-Loire region and areas to the north and east as far as Germany.

What are the main developments during the huge span in which Paleolithic art flourished? At the foot of the evolutionary path a master plan already existed even though techniques were virtually unformed; this was the primitive period. In the extended period of refinement in technique that followed, the key developments involve the delineation of those characteristics that distinguish one species of animal from another; this was the archaic period. Finally both technique and delineation were progressively united in a more and more realistic portrayal of shape and movement; this was the classic period. Then it is all gone, much as the mammoth and the woolly rhinoceros disappeared from the same region. The ideological line uniting an artistic tradition of 20,000 years comes to an end.

Obviously both the long lifetime of Paleolithic art and its disappearance are topics that will occupy generations of investigators. Today, although we know only a fraction of what remains to be learned, we have made some progress. It might be said that historians of Paleolithic art have reached a level of precision comparable to the level achieved by historians of Christian art when they were at last able to fix the date of some object within a century or two. They could be justly criticized for a lack of precision, but they had achieved a clear view of the path along which Christian art had evolved.

**ANATOMICAL FIDELITY is characteristic of Style IV work, produced during the classic period of Paleolithic art. The deftly rendered outline of a wild-ox cow's head is one of the animal engravings in the cave at Teyjat, an Upper Magdalenian site in the Dordogne valley.**

# 7

# Ice-Age Hunters of the Ukraine

by Richard G. Klein
*June 1974*

*In the span between 75,000 and 10,000 years ago men hunted other mammals in the rigorous environment of eastern Europe. At some sites they amassed mammoth bones to build shelters*

Modern man has lived mostly in an ice age. To be specific, the kind of human being we know today arose late in the Pleistocene epoch, or Great Ice Age, that came to a close some 10,000 years ago. The Pleistocene was an epoch of spectacular glacial activity, but it was not one of uniformly cold climates. There were many separate glacial episodes followed by interglacial periods; the total number of these alternations is not known exactly.

During each glacial episode enormous sheets of ice advanced to cover much of North America and Europe. When the ice retreated, the climate during the interglacial interval approximated that of today. The next to last major advance, known to scholars as the Penultimate Glacial (Riss II in the Alpine sequence), marked the end of the Middle Pleistocene some 125,000 years ago. The ensuing 115,000 years are the Upper Pleistocene, a period that includes the Last (Riss-Würm) Interglacial and the Last (Würm) Glacial. At some time during the Last Glacial, perhaps between 45,000 and 35,000 years ago, modern man (*Homo sapiens sapiens*) seems to have made his first appearance.

The systematic study of Pleistocene man began only in the middle of the 19th century. Its first focus was in France. Today, after more than a century of investigation, both the quantity of the discoveries made in France and the high quality of the research undertaken there have placed the French data foremost in most accounts of Pleistocene man. The student learns of the progressively more recent Acheulean, Mousterian, Aurignacian/Perigordian, Solutrean and Magdalenian cultures, whose remains have been found stratigraphically superposed in various French cave sites. He might easily conclude either that the rest of the world was sparsely

populated during the Pleistocene or that few ice-age sites outside France have been investigated.

In both cases the reverse is true. For example, the first occupation sites of Pleistocene man to be discovered in central and eastern Europe, many of them spectacularly rich, were unearthed almost as long ago as the first finds in France. Language barriers have resulted in these sites' being poorly known elsewhere, but the information they contain is vital to an understanding of how early man survived and perhaps even thrived under ice-age climatic conditions in Europe. The point is perhaps best demonstrated by what archaeologists have learned over the past century from a group of nearly 100 Pleistocene sites in and around the Ukraine.

The earliest Pleistocene occupation sites found anywhere in the European U.S.S.R. are roughly between 80,000 and 75,000 years old. They date back to the end of the Last Interglacial [*see illustration on page 70*]. It is possible that older sites will be discovered someday; in Hungary, Poland and Czechoslovakia traces of early man have been

discovered that are hundreds of thousands of years old. Alternatively it is possible that it was only at the end of the Last Interglacial that early man achieved the cultural capacity to survive the harsh climate of the Ukraine. Even today the Ukraine's winters are significantly colder than those of its western neighbors. In any event the vast majority of the Ukrainian ice-age occupation sites belong to the Last Glacial; they are between 75,000 and 10,000 years old. Many of the sites include separate occupation levels, and the intervals between the successive occupations sometimes amount to thousands of years.

Most of the Ukrainian sites lie in the main river valleys of the region [*see illustration on page 68*]. The reason is not only that ice-age men frequented river valleys but also that valleys are places where conditions favor the accumulation of sediments and thus the burial and preservation of ancient occupation sites. Natural erosion or the activities of civilization often expose the buried sites; as is true elsewhere in the world, many of the most important Pleis-

THREE ICE-AGE SHELTERS, built on an ancient terrace of the Dniester River, are shown on opposite page in plan (*far right*) and in hypothetical reconstruction. The first (*top*) was unearthed in the fourth level of the site known as Molodova I; 15 hearth areas (*color*) were surrounded by a rough oval of mammoth bones. Carbon-14 analyses of hearth charcoal show the fourth level is more than 44,000 years old; the associated artifacts are Mousterian. The reconstruction suggests that the shelter consisted of a wood framework covered with skins; mammoth bones evidently helped to hold the skins in place. A second shelter (*middle*) was unearthed in the third level of an adjacent site, Molodova V. A perimeter marked by 64 postholes (*color*) enclosed a single large hearth. Analysis of hearth charcoal shows the third level is about 13,000 years old; the associated artifacts are Upper Paleolithic. The reconstruction suggests a teepeelike wood frame for the shelter; the covering of skins was evidently secured with large wood pegs. The third shelter (*bottom*) is from the next higher level at the same site; the two hearths (*color*) are to one side of the occupational debris. The number of reindeer antlers suggests that these substituted for mammoth bones as a means of securing the skin covering of the teepeelike structure. Carbon-14 dating suggests that it was occupied 1,000 years after the one below it. The grids are one-meter squares.

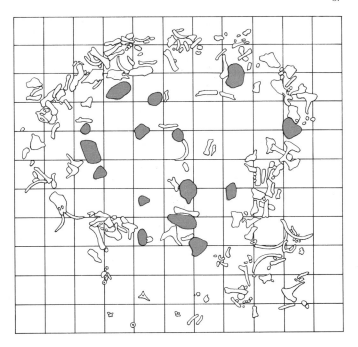

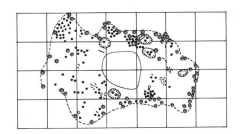

tocene discoveries in the Ukraine were made when road builders or clay diggers happened to uncover strata that contained animal remains and artifacts.

One Ukrainian site that proved to consist of a number of superposed occupation levels is located near the village of Molodova on the Dniester River 150 miles southeast of Lvov. It is one of a cluster of sites in this location and has been designated Molodova V. The most recent of its occupation levels was buried more than 10,000 years ago. The oldest levels, which lie between six and eight meters below the surface, were last inhabited more than 45,000 years ago.

The ages of most Ukrainian sites have been determined primarily by geological analysis. This is partly because of the high cost of carbon-14 dating in the U.S.S.R. and partly because age determinations in excess of 30,000 or 40,000 years are technically difficult to secure by means of carbon-14 assay. At Molodova V, however, a detailed geological analysis by I. K. Ivanova of the Soviet Commission for the Study of the Quaternary period (the period from the present back to the beginning of the Pleistocene) has been supplemented by a large number of carbon-14 determinations.

As at most other Ukrainian sites, the evidence of human occupation is stratified within deposits of sand and silt that were carried to the base of a slope by the combined action of runoff and gravity [see illustration on page 71]. Here the base of the slope is an alluvial deposit laid down at a time when the bed of the Dniester was substantially higher than it is today. This old floodplain can be traced downstream to the point where it grades into marine deposits that were formed when the level of the Black Sea was as high as it is today, or even higher. That, of course, would have been during the Last Interglacial, when just as today the level of the world's seas was not low-

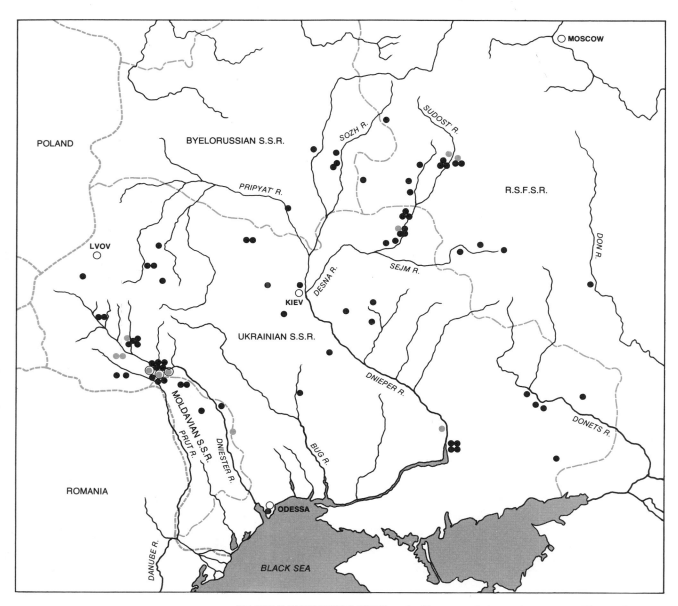

● UPPER PALEOLITHIC

● MOUSTERIAN

◉ BOTH CULTURES

MAJOR PALEOLITHIC SITES in the Ukraine and vicinity lie in river valleys such as that of the Dniester, the Dnieper-Desna region and the Don or near lesser streams and tributaries such as the Prut, the Bug, the Pripyat', the Sejm, the Sozh and the Sudost'. Because many of the sites lie close together their positioning on this map is not exact. Eight of them (*color*) contain Mousterian artifacts only; 72 (*black*) contain only artifacts of the Upper Paleolithic period. At Molodova I and V and at one other site both cultures are found.

ered by the impoundment of vast quantities of water in the ice sheets that covered the northern continents.

As Ivanova's analysis made clear, because the alluvial floodplain had been formed during the Last Interglacial the sands and silts that rest on it are necessarily younger. That the overlying deposits in fact accumulated during the subsequent Last Glacial is suggested by several kinds of evidence. First, some of them appear to have been formed when moisture-laden earth slid downslope over a frozen substratum. The process, known as gelifluction, is commonplace today in subarctic and arctic zones of permafrost, or permanently frozen subsoil. Permafrost could have extended this far south in the Ukraine only during the Last Glacial. Second, the shells of snails that normally inhabit quite cool environments are present in the deposits, and the animal bones unearthed in human occupation levels are those of such subarctic and arctic species as the reindeer and the arctic fox. Moreover, some of the charcoal in the ancient hearths is from the kinds of coniferous trees found today only in much colder environments. Finally, the carbon-14 determinations at Molodova V, although lacking complete internal consistency, indicate that the youngest of the human occupation zones is more than 10,000 years old. Therefore all the occupation levels predate the end of the Last Glacial (conventionally set at some time about 8000 B.C.). The artifacts and other cultural remains sandwiched among the silts at Molodova V are indisputably the work of men who lived during the Last Glacial.

Ivanova's analysis of the Molodova V profile demonstrates a further important point: the Last Glacial was a time not of consistently low temperatures but of fluctuating climate. On several occasions the movement of sand and silt downslope toward the river terrace slowed or stopped altogether. Whenever this happened, the surface layer of sediments was subjected to weathering that led to the development of a soil. The times when deposition slowed or ceased and soils formed evidently represent intervals during the Last Glacial when the climate briefly grew warmer. Substantiation of these episodes is provided by the absence from the soils of Molodova V of the same cold-loving snails that are found in the unaltered sands and silts.

Various kinds of data collected both at Molodova V and at numerous other ice-age sites in the Northern Hemisphere suggest that the Last Glacial was composed of three main parts. The first part

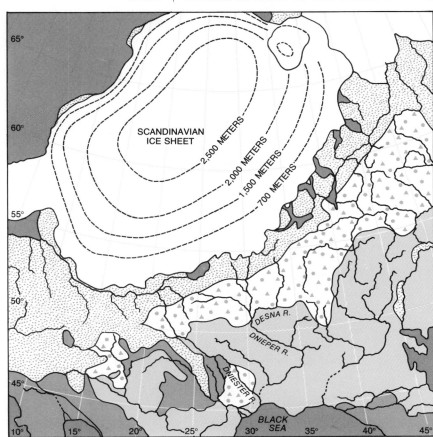

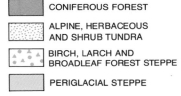

CONIFEROUS FOREST

ALPINE, HERBACEOUS AND SHRUB TUNDRA

BIRCH, LARCH AND BROADLEAF FOREST STEPPE

PERIGLACIAL STEPPE

ICE-AGE LANDSCAPE at the time of maximum cold late in the Würm glacial was made up of a broad belt of tundra along the edge of the ice sheet and an even broader belt of periglacial steppe, separated from the tundra by a zone of forested steppe. In a few areas, including the valleys of the Prut and the Dniester, forests of conifers grew. At that time the Black Sea and Caspian met.

began with the onset of glacial conditions between 75,000 and 70,000 years ago and lasted until about 50,000 years ago. The second part, consisting of a long interval of fluctuating, milder but not really warm climate, lasted from 50,000 to about 30,000 to 25,000 years ago. The third part, which included the cold maximum of the Last Glacial, then began; this episode continued until 10,000 years ago.

Much of the same evidence that indicates the subdivisions of the Last Glacial in and around the Ukraine also makes possible the reconstruction of the landscape. For example, buried pollen grains show that the region was covered by a kind of steppe vegetation characterized by plants reflecting very cold and dry conditions. The plant communities that were present have no exact modern counterparts; they are called periglacial steppe by Russian investigators. Studies of sediments show that the periglacial

steppe was underlain by permafrost that extended almost as far south as the Black Sea. Together with the pollen data, this suggests that the average January temperature, which is below freezing everywhere in the Ukraine today, was then eight or nine degrees Celsius lower.

It may seem surprising that ice-age men could have found a region with such a rigorous climate at all hospitable. The fact is that the periglacial steppe supported a rich and varied fauna. The Ukrainian summers, although short, were warm enough to allow an abundant growth for grazing animals. The winters, although long and cold, were dry; the summer growth was not buried under deep snow and the animals could feed the year round. The bones of no fewer than 13 species of herbivore, large and small, have been found in the Pleistocene sites. Based on the relative abundance of the bones, the primary prey of

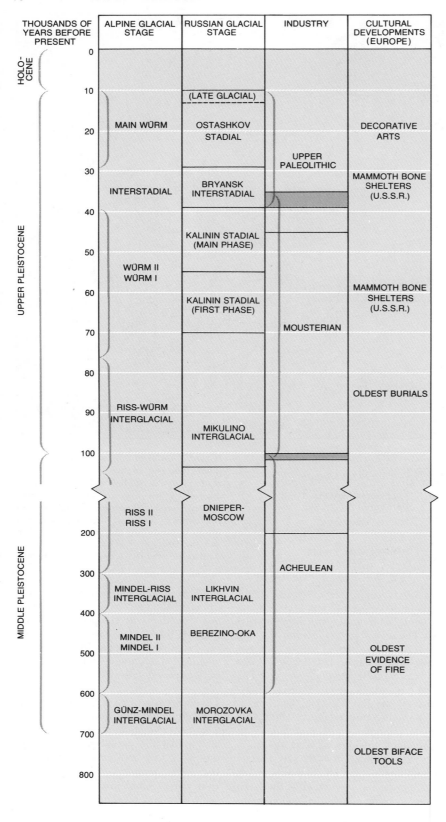

| THOUSANDS OF YEARS BEFORE PRESENT | ALPINE GLACIAL STAGE | RUSSIAN GLACIAL STAGE | INDUSTRY | CULTURAL DEVELOPMENTS (EUROPE) |
|---|---|---|---|---|
| HOLO-CENE | | (LATE GLACIAL) | | |
| MAIN WÜRM | OSTASHKOV STADIAL | | DECORATIVE ARTS |
| | | | UPPER PALEOLITHIC | |
| INTERSTADIAL | BRYANSK INTERSTADIAL | | MAMMOTH BONE SHELTERS (U.S.S.R.) |
| WÜRM II WÜRM I | KALININ STADIAL (MAIN PHASE) | | |
| | KALININ STADIAL (FIRST PHASE) | | MAMMOTH BONE SHELTERS (U.S.S.R.) |
| | | MOUSTERIAN | |
| RISS-WÜRM INTERGLACIAL | MIKULINO INTERGLACIAL | | OLDEST BURIALS |
| RISS II RISS I | DNIEPER-MOSCOW | | |
| | | ACHEULEAN | |
| MINDEL-RISS INTERGLACIAL | LIKHVIN INTERGLACIAL | | |
| MINDEL II MINDEL I | BEREZINO-OKA | | OLDEST EVIDENCE OF FIRE |
| GÜNZ-MINDEL INTERGLACIAL | MOROZOVKA INTERGLACIAL | | OLDEST BIFACE TOOLS |

CHRONOLOGY OF GLACIAL STAGES in the Middle and Upper Pleistocene in the Alps (*left*) and their equivalents in European Russia is shown in thousands of years before the present. Until 100,000 years ago each scale division indicates a 100,000-year interval; thereafter each represents a 10,000-year interval. The earliest Mousterian stone tools known in western Europe are more than 100,000 years old. The Mousterian may not have reached Russia, however, until 75,000 to 80,000 years ago. In Russia tools of the Upper Paleolithic kind probably replaced those of the Mousterian kind between 35,000 and 40,000 years ago.

the Ukrainian hunters were the reindeer and the wild horse in the north and the steppe bison in the south. The distinction between the game taken in the north and that taken in the south probably reflects some unrecognized variation in local vegetation rather than any preference of the hunters.

The other herbivores pursued as game included the woolly rhinoceros, the aurochs, the musk-ox, the saiga antelope, the red deer, the roe deer, the "giant" deer (*Megaloceros*), the moose and either the wild goat or the wild sheep. Rarely, however, are the bones of any of these animals found in large quantities. The bones of carnivores are even rarer. Only the arctic fox and the wolf are represented in significant numbers. The largest and most dangerous of the Pleistocene carnivores, the brown bear and the lion, are virtually unrepresented.

Even less common are the bones of birds and fishes. It is possible that the ice-age occupants of the Ukraine lacked the technology to deal with these animals, but other explanations can be imagined. An intriguing one is that the river valleys, where virtually all the known sites are located, were mainly inhabited only in winter, when frozen rivers prevented fishing and the most desirable birds—migratory waterfowl—had flown south. The fierce winter winds may have made life outside the river valleys all but impossible.

In summer the hunters may have moved away to the uplands between the river valleys. These areas were the grazing lands for the great herds of game on whose meat (possibly dried or smoked for winter use) the occupants of the Ukraine depended. The reason such upland camps have remained undiscovered may be that they were so transitory as to have left little behind to catch the archaeologist's eye or that few of the remains of upland camps have been exposed by road builders or quarriers.

Mammoth bones are virtually the hallmark of ice-age sites in the Ukraine. In more than one instance it was the unearthing of these large and distinctive remains that first made unwitting excavators realize they had discovered an ice-age site. The mammoth bones are present in large numbers. For example, those dug up at eight sites in the Dnieper-Desna basin represent a minimum of 500 individual mammoths. Yet not one Ukrainian site contains clear evidence that a mammoth was actually killed there. Indeed, there is evidence to the contrary: chemical tests of the mammoth bones found at one Dnieper site indicate that the animals probably lived and died in different millenniums. Again, many of these same bones, and the bones from another Dnieper site, had been gnawed by carnivores. The implication is clear. Ice-age men in the Ukraine are at least as likely to have gathered the bare bones of long-dead mammoths as to have hunted and killed the huge beasts. But why would they have wanted the bones?

The answer is clear-cut and surprising. At virtually every Ukrainian site where mammoth bones are common most of them are found in patterned arrangements that look like the ruins of shelters, many of them quite ambitious. The use of mammoth bones as a construction material is further indicated by the presence in disproportionate number of particular bones: skulls, tusks, mandibles, pelvises, scapulas and certain limb bones.

One item of animal-bone evidence indicates the adaptability of the ice-age hunters to winter conditions. It is found among the bones of the wolf, the arctic fox and the hare. Skeletons of these animals are often found intact except that the paws are missing. Groups of paw bones, in turn, are found in other parts of the site. By analogy with modern practices the animals appear to have been skinned for the warmth of their pelts.

In summary, then, the animal remains at the Ukrainian ice-age sites seem to have been accumulated by successful Pleistocene hunters whose diet was rich in protein and fat, who valued furs and who built substantial shelters. The shelters were heated too; there are quantities of charcoal, indicative of hearths, and bits of burned bone as well. All of this should have made the ice-age winters easier to bear.

Who were the hunters? The artifacts that have been found at Ukrainian Last Glacial sites have been assigned to two successive cultural units. The earlier of the two is known as the Mousterian; it is also sometimes called the Middle Paleolithic. (Cultural materials belonging to the preceding Lower Paleolithic have not yet been found in the Ukraine.) The later of the two cultural units is known as the Upper Paleolithic. These successive units characterize the Last Glacial all over Europe; the Upper Paleolithic supplants the Mousterian at some time between 45,000 and 35,000 years ago, the exact time depending on the location of the site.

The commonest Mousterian tool is called a sidescraper. (Its actual function, of course, remains a matter of speculation.) These tools are made from large, irregular flakes of stone that were forcibly detached from a "core," usually of flint, and then "retouched" along one edge or more by removing a series of small flakes. Many different kinds of sidescraper have been recognized on the basis of such factors as the number and shape of the retouched edges and the quality and location of the retouching.

The second most abundant Mousterian implement is a flake with an edge that has been modified so that it has either a single notch or a series of notches on one edge. These are known respectively as notches and denticulates. It has been suggested that they were used as spokeshaves, shredders and saws. Many Mousterian sites also contain roughly leaf-shaped points that are often retouched more or less completely over one face or both [see top illustration on next page].

Inventories of the Mousterian stone tools from various Ukrainian sites reveal that they include certain types, for example special varieties of sidescraper, that are not found elsewhere in Europe. The reverse is also true: artifacts such as the small "hand axes" found in some Mousterian assemblages in France are unknown in the Ukraine. Such differences allow us to infer that the Mousterian was not a single cultural unit but rather a complex of subcultures that varied in time and space.

A Mousterian accomplishment that is more fully evident in the European U.S.S.R. than anywhere else in the world is the one implicit in the collections of mammoth bones: the construction of substantial heated dwellings. A. P. Chernysh has excavated a particularly clear-cut example of one of these Mousterian dwellings at Molodova I, a Dniester River site adjacent to Molodova V [see illustration on page 67]. The remains consist of an oval of mammoth bones surrounding a floor with the considerable area of some 50 square meters. Within the oval Chernysh and his colleagues uncovered 15 separate hearths, hundreds of animal-bone fragments, some 29,000 pieces of flint and one spot of red pigment. As Chernysh recon-

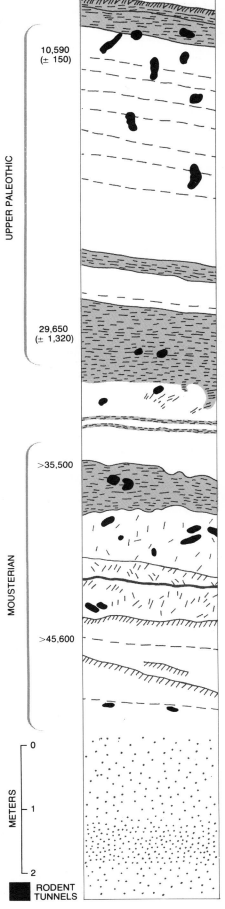

**CROSS SECTION** of strata at Molodova V (*right*) shows 19 cultural horizons within the layers of sand and silt accumulated at the base of a slope. The eight lowest horizons contained Mousterian artifacts; carbon-14 analysis suggests they range from more than 35,000 to more than 45,000 years in age. Upper Paleolithic artifacts from the higher horizons range from 10,500 to more than 30,000 years in age. Areas of color show the soils formed during warmer intervals; the stippling shows alluvium of Last Interglacial.

10,590
(± 150)

UPPER PALEOTHIC

29,650
(± 1,320)

>35,500

MOUSTERIAN

>45,600

0

METERS

1

2

RODENT TUNNELS

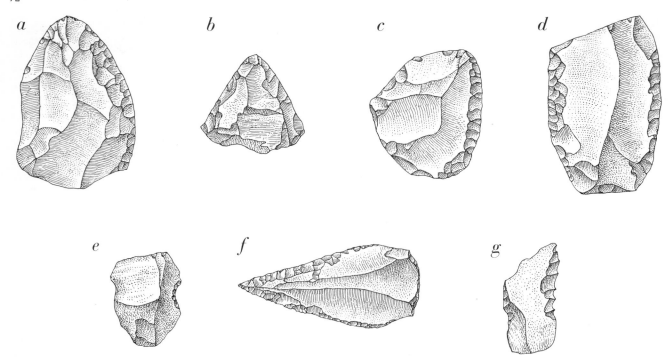

*a*  *b*  *c*  *d*

*e*  *f*  *g*

**TYPICAL MOUSTERIAN TOOL KIT** emphasizes sidescrapers (*a—d*), notches (*e*), points (*f*) and denticulates (*g*). The actual use made of these stone artifacts is not known, but the points may have been hafted to wood shafts and the notches and denticulates could have been used to work wood. The tools illustrated here are from Mousterian sites in western Europe, not from sites in the Ukraine.

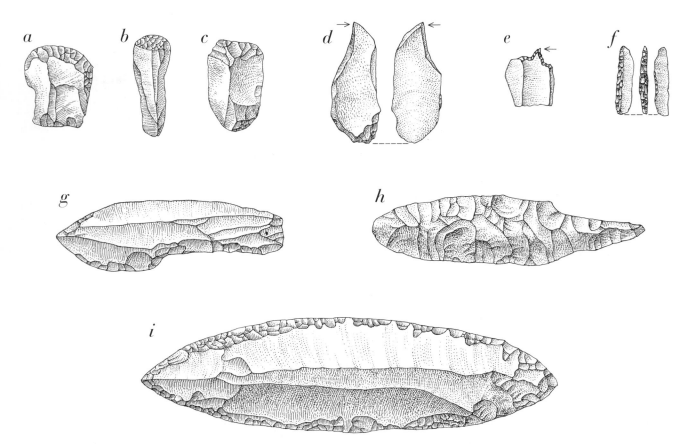

*a*  *b*  *c*  *d*  *e*  *f*

*g*  *h*

*i*

**UPPER PALEOLITHIC TOOLS,** typically made by chipping the desired shape from a narrow flint blade, differ in appearance and in type from Mousterian tools. Shown here are end scrapers (*a—c*), a burin (*d*), a borer (*e*), a backed blade (*f*), a long, leaf-shaped point (*i*) and two shouldered points (*g, h*). All are from Russian sites; *h* and *i* are from the lowermost of the Upper Paleolithic horizons at Molodova V. Like the Mousterian tools illustrated at the top of the page, all artifacts are reproduced at two-thirds actual size.

structs the dwelling, it consisted of animal skins stretched over a wood frame; the mammoth bones served as anchors, securing the edges of the skins at ground level and possibly holding the skins in place elsewhere.

In other parts of Europe and in western Asia the people who made Mousterian tools buried their dead, at least on occasion. No such burials have been found in the Ukraine, although they are known in immediately adjacent areas such as the Crimea. In Europe wherever human remains have been found in association with Mousterian artifacts they invariably belong to the anatomically primitive human subspecies we call Neanderthal man (*Homo sapiens neanderthalensis*). As a result it is now generally accepted that Neanderthals were the makers of Mousterian tools.

Tool assemblages of the Upper Paleolithic kind found at Ukrainian sites, like their counterparts elsewhere, differ sharply from Mousterian assemblages. To make their tools Upper Paleolithic hunters preferred flakes that were at least twice as long as they were wide. Archaeologists call them blades. Instead of consisting primarily of sidescrapers, notches and denticulates, Upper Paleolithic assemblages include end scrapers (blades with one or both narrow ends retouched), burins (blades modified to leave a chisellike corner), backed blades (with one edge deliberately dulled) and borers (blades modified to leave a sharp central protrusion). The assemblages also include different kinds of points, some with one side or both narrowed at one end as if to facilitate hafting, and some retouched over both faces [*see bottom illustration on opposite page*]. Stone tools of the same kind are also found at Mousterian sites, but they are rare or less well formed or both.

Upper Paleolithic assemblages also contain numerous artifacts made from bone and antler; these are virtually unknown at Mousterian sites. The shapes of the objects bring to mind projectile points, hide-burnishers, shaft-straighteners, awls and even needles. The putative needles are particularly interesting. If they were indeed used for sewing, it is highly likely that the Upper Paleolithic hunters of the Ukraine wore fitted skin garments. Outside the Ukraine this conclusion recently became all but inescapable. Three ice-age human skeletons have been excavated at Sungir', northeast of Moscow. The skeletons were girdled with strings of beads that must have been sewn on close-fitting clothing.

One trait that the Upper Paleolithic hunters of the Ukraine shared with their

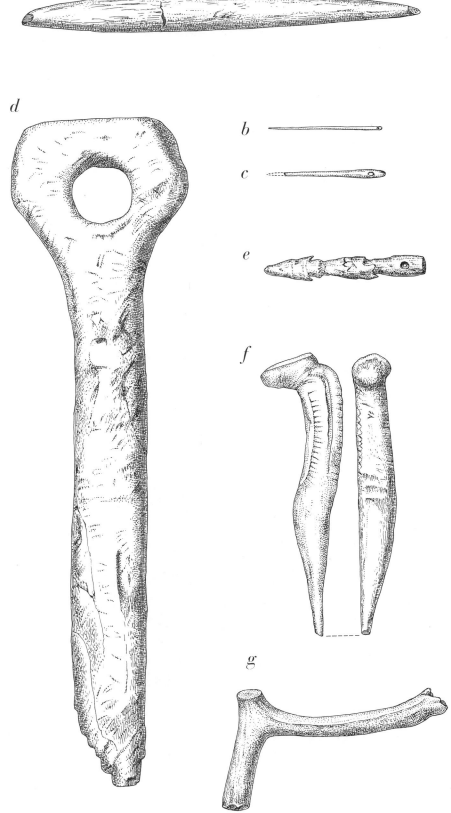

**TOOLS MADE FROM BONE** are found at Upper Paleolithic sites in the Ukraine but rarely at Mousterian sites there or elsewhere in Europe. Illustrated are a projectile point (*a*), two needles (*b, c*), a shaft-straightener (*d*), a harpoon head (*e*), an awl (*f*) and a hammer made from reindeer antler (*g*). The harpoon head is from a horizon near the surface at Molodova V and the shaft-straightener is from an earlier Upper Paleolithic horizon there.

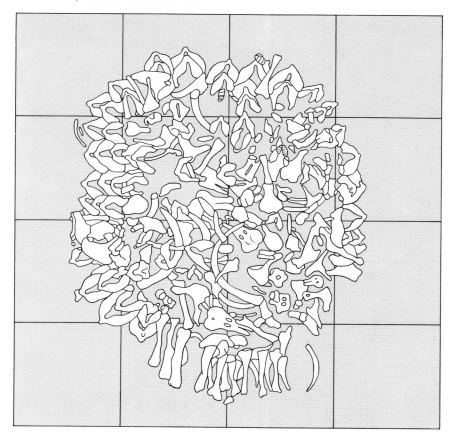

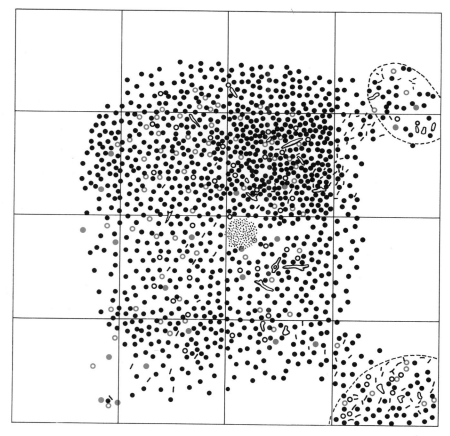

predecessors was the construction of heated dwellings, supported by wood frames and weighted with mammoth bones. In one of the Upper Paleolithic levels at Molodova V even the holes that accommodated the shelter's wood uprights are recognizable. The most spectacular traces of these dwellings are at sites in the Dnieper-Desna basin; there large patterned arrangements of mammoth bones sometimes surround or cover man-made hollows in the ground. In some instances reindeer antlers evidently served in lieu of mammoth bones. The dwelling floors are pockmarked with pits of various shapes and sizes that may have been used for storage or the disposal of refuse.

Evidence from elsewhere in Europe shows that, like the Mousterians, Upper Paleolithic peoples often buried their dead. No such graves, however, have been found in the Ukraine. Where burials have been found in other parts of Europe, including sites in areas adjacent to the Ukraine such as Sungir', the bones are those of the anatomically modern human subspecies *Homo sapiens sapiens*. Evidently at some time during the interval between 45,000 and 35,000 years ago the more primitive human subspecies left the Old World stage, so to speak, and the modern subspecies entered the limelight.

What actually happened to the Neanderthals remains more than a little uncertain. The archaeological record shows that, in terms of material culture as represented by tools and other artifacts, the Mousterian industries were replaced by Upper Paleolithic ones. Does this mean that the Neanderthals were literally shouldered offstage by modern man? Such a conclusion is unacceptable to many authorities, who argue that Neanderthals repeatedly evolved into modern men over a broad front at the same time that Mousterian industries evolved into Upper Paleolithic ones. In the past few years, however, carbon-14 dates

SPECTACULAR RUIN of an Upper Paleolithic shelter, discovered at Mezhirich, a site on the Dnieper south of Kiev, included 385 mammoth bones that covered an oval area some three meters in diameter (*top illustration at left*). When the bones were removed, the excavators uncovered 4,600 flint artifacts, along with nodules of flint, bone artifacts and bits of charred bone, bits of red ocher, pieces of amber and a pit, 20 centimeters deep, filled with ash and charcoal. Two other hearth areas lay beyond the perimeter of the shelter (*bottom illustration*).

● STONE TOOLS AND DEBRIS        ⌇ CHARRED BONE        ● RED OCHER

⌒ BONE ARTIFACTS        ⁙ HEARTH        ○ AMBER

obtained from such sites as Istállóskö Cave in Hungary, taken in conjunction with evidence of where it was that anatomically modern man evolved, have added weight to the hypothesis that modern man and the Upper Paleolithic cultural unit made their first appearance within a geographically narrow region: southwestern Asia and southeastern Europe. On that hypothesis both modern man and Upper Paleolithic material culture, rather than evolving repeatedly in numerous places, radiated outward from this initial heartland.

Regardless of how or where the Upper Paleolithic came into being, the archaeological evidence from the Ukraine and elsewhere in the U.S.S.R. undeniably indicates that it was superior to the Mousterian as an adaptation to Last Glacial climate. This conclusion is supported by the distribution of Mousterian and Upper Paleolithic sites. Systematic reconnaissance in those northern parts of the U.S.S.R. where glaciation has not obliterated all evidence of ice-age man has failed to locate even one Mousterian site north of a latitude of 54 degrees. Upper Paleolithic sites, however, have been found even above the Arctic Circle. The much greater number of Upper Paleolithic sites, particularly ones with "ruins" suggesting a settled or semisettled existence, implies higher overall population numbers and greater population density for Upper Paleolithic peoples.

At this point still another type of evidence needs to be considered. Neither here nor elsewhere in Europe have any Mousterian sites yielded undoubted works of art or decoration. Upper Paleolithic sites in the Ukraine and elsewhere, however, contain numerous figurines of humans and animals made of bone and stone, together with bracelets, beads, pierced shells and teeth and hundreds of bone objects engraved with geometric patterns [*see illustration at right*]. Can the absence of such objects from one material culture and their abundance in a succeeding one be a token of biological change, specifically the evolution of a greater intellectual capacity?

If such a hypothesis is accepted, then the greater adaptive success of the Upper Paleolithic is an example of a feedback interaction between biological change on the one hand and material and sociocultural change on the other. Among other developments, new social structures may now have arisen to allow the integration of larger, denser populations. For example, social innovations may have facilitated intergroup coopera-

tion in the hunting of large mammals. If more meat was available, the hunting economy would support more people. More subtly, new social structures may simply have encouraged greater intergroup food-sharing as a means of mitigating temporary local shortages. If the haves in any one year share with the have-nots, the long-term effect of such an act is a greater total number of both haves and have-nots.

However this may have been, it is reasonable to draw demographic inferences from a numerical comparison of Mousterian and Upper Paleolithic sites. When these inferences are taken together with the differences between the two material cultures, particularly with respect to art objects, one is led to conclude that the Upper Paleolithic represents a quantum advance in human cultural evolution.

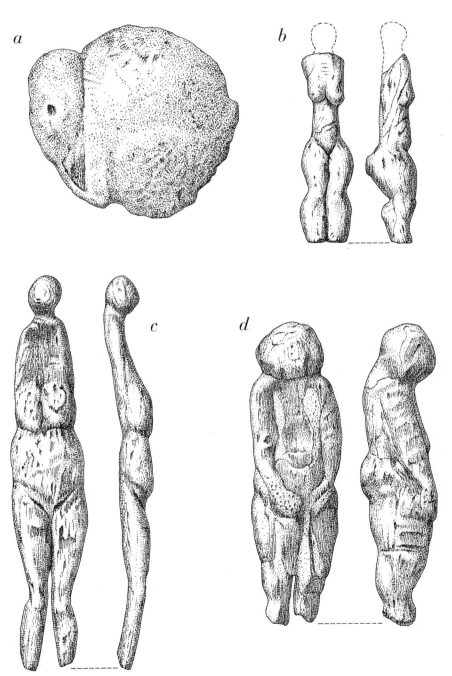

WORKS OF ART from Upper Paleolithic sites in Russia include "Venus" figurines and a representation of a mammoth. The mammoth (*a*) and two of the figurines (*c, d*) are from Avdeevo, on the Sejm 400 kilometers south of Moscow. The headless figurine (*b*) is from Eliseevichi, on the Sudost' some 350 kilometers southwest of Moscow. Whereas objects like these and many geometrically engraved bones are found at Upper Paleolithic sites in Russia, neither there nor elsewhere in Europe have such artifacts been found in Mousterian sites.

# 8

# The Prehistory of the Australian Aborigine

by D. J. Mulvaney
*March 1966*

*The native inhabitants of Australia were long thought to be relatively recent immigrants. In the past decade archaeologists have discovered that man first reached the remote continent at least 16,000 years ago*

The prehistory of Australia ended in 1788, when the British landed at the site of modern Sydney. How many millenniums before that the continent's aboriginal inhabitants arrived has not been precisely established. Only a decade ago their prehistoric period was widely believed to have been no more than a brief prelude to the European colonization. Today it seems certain that the initial migration took place in Pleistocene times—no less than 16,000 years ago and probably much

earlier. Here I shall review the archaeological findings that shed some light on the prehistory of the aborigines and then describe recent field studies that, in my opinion, quite drastically alter earlier views.

Sundered from Asia before *Homo sapiens* evolved, Australia is a land mass almost the size of the U.S. It has 12,000 miles of coastline and extends from 43 degrees South latitude to within 11 degrees of the Equator. A third of its area lies north of the Tropic

of Capricorn. An equally extensive area annually receives less than 10 inches of rainfall. Only 7 percent of the land mass rises above 2,000 feet; indeed, the continent can be traversed from the Gulf of Carpentaria in the northeast to the southern coast without climbing higher than 600 feet. Australia's major mountain and river systems are restricted to its eastern and southeastern parts. These topographic realities must be reckoned with in considering prehistoric patterns of human settlement. Of equal significance are the usually dry watercourses and salt pans of the arid "outback," which testify to a more congenial climate in late Pleistocene or early postglacial times.

In 1788 Australia was inhabited by perhaps 500 aboriginal tribes; they probably mustered a total population of some 300,000. In coastal or river-valley environments, where the population density was comparatively high, there were one or two individuals per square mile. Elsewhere immense tracts supported no more than one person every 30 or 40 square miles. In so large an area one might expect considerable variety in the inhabitants' ecological and technological adaptations, and reports by early European observers and the scantier evidence of archaeology document such differences. For all its variety, however, the prehistoric period had an underlying unity. Over the entire continent the aborigines habitually hunted, fished and gathered wild plants; they had not learned agriculture. The extent of nomadism in each tribal area was largely determined by the local availability of food.

Regional variations in the Australian environment are actually more apparent than real. In other lands differences in topography, rainfall or latitude give

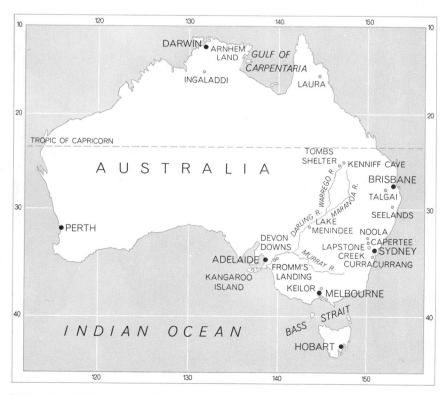

**MAJOR PREHISTORIC SITES** are located on a map of Australia. Devon Downs, in the Murray River valley, was the first stratified site to be found on the continent. Excavated in 1929, its lower levels are 4,500 years old. Kenniff Cave, a site the author found 1,000 miles north of Devon Downs in 1960, contains strata that span some 16,000 years of prehistory.

rise to diversity in plant and animal species; in Australia these factors may result merely in the substitution of one member of the same plant or animal family for another. The eucalyptus and the kangaroo are ubiquitous. Another phenomenon, universal in Australia and unique to it, is the absence in prehistoric times of formidable predatory animals competing with man for the same game. Such factors must have encouraged a degree of human standardization, both in the character of weapons and in the techniques of hunting and foraging. At the same time it can be postulated that these factors discouraged a dynamic experimental attitude within prehistoric Australian societies.

In terms of material culture few Paleolithic peoples were more impoverished than the aboriginal Australians. There were no horned, antlered or tusked species of animals to provide the raw material for the artifacts so valued in hunting societies elsewhere. Flint and similar fine-grained rocks were rare; instead the aborigines made most of their implements out of quartz or quartzite, materials from which even the most skilled knapper has difficulty producing elegant objects. As for the elements of culture beloved of so many writers on archaeology—dwellings, tombs, grave goods, ceramics, metals, precious stones, cultivated crops and domesticated animals (with the exception of the dog)—the aborigines had none.

Accordingly under the best of circumstances the investigator of Australian prehistory is faced with a paucity of archaeological evidence and a limited range of diagnostic cultural traits. To make matters worse, where bone artifacts might have survived, the high acidity of the soil has often eaten them away, and where desert dryness might have preserved wooden artifacts the voracious termite has destroyed them. These disadvantages are partly offset by the rich store of information on living aborigines, beginning with the first European descriptions and extending to the fieldwork of contemporary ethnographers. The prehistorian must guard against an anachronistic fallacy, however; he must not assume that customs and technologies recorded during the past 100 years constitute unambiguous evidence when it comes to interpreting prehistoric remains.

In 1929 a landmark in Pacific archaeology was established. In the valley of the Murray River east of Adelaide, Her-

BASE OF THE CLIFFS bordering the Murray River in South Australia was a popular prehistoric camping ground. Here, at Fromm's Landing rock-shelter No. 2, the excavation of a deep stratified deposit threw new light on earlier discoveries at nearby Devon Downs.

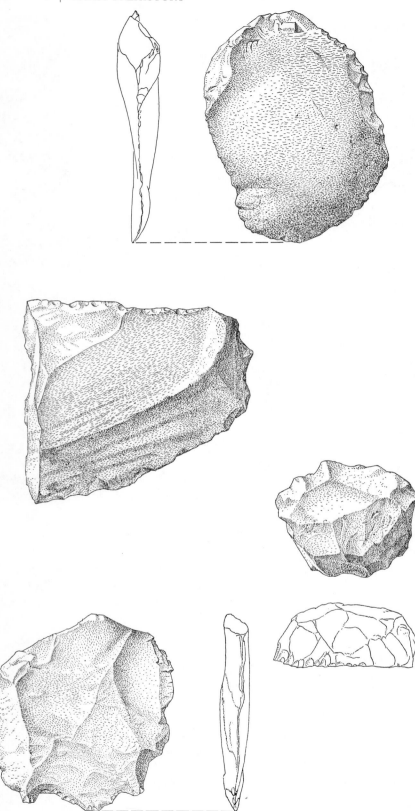

**EARLIEST TOOLS** found at Kenniff Cave were scrapers such as these, shown actual size. Made by trimming the edges of stone flakes, they were hand-held rather than hafted. They are (*top to bottom*) a quartzite side scraper, trimmed along its right edge; a scraper made from a broken quartzite flake, finely trimmed along its top edge; a round scraper, made from chert, that was trimmed very steeply (*see profile*), and a quartzite flake with trimmed projections and concavities on its bottom edge that suggest use in the manner of a spoke-shave to work wood. Eleven thousand years passed before more elaborate tools were made.

bert M. Hale and Norman B. Tindale of the South Australian Museum excavated a rock-shelter site, known as Devon Downs, that contained 20 feet of stratified deposits of human occupation. Hale and Tindale divided the occupation layers into three successive cultural stages on the basis of the presence or absence of stone or bone implements they believed possessed diagnostic significance. They called the earliest culture Pirrian, because the *pirri,* a symmetrical stone projectile point flaked only on one side, was restricted to the lower layers of the site. Pirris are aesthetically perhaps the most pleasing of all the prehistoric aboriginal artifacts [*"c-1" to "c-3" in illustration on opposite page*]. Many of them are found on the surface at sites in the interior of Australia, but it was at Devon Downs that they were first discovered in a stratigraphic context.

The excavators called the second culture Mudukian; *muduk* is the word used by the Murray River aborigines for a short length of bone, pointed at both ends, that resembles the simple kind of fishhook called a gorge [*"f" in illustration on opposite page*]. At Devon Downs muduks were found in the occupation strata above those that contained pirris. Hale and Tindale gave the uppermost occupation layers the label Murundian; this was derived from the subtribal name of the local aborigines. The Murundian layers contain no distinctive objects of either stone or bone; in effect the archaeological definition of the culture is negative. Carbon-14 dating techniques were not available in those days, but charcoal from a sample of earth preserved in the South Australian Museum since 1929 was recently analyzed and yielded a date for one of the Pirrian strata of about the middle of the third millennium B.C.

Within the past decade I have excavated two rock-shelters at Fromm's Landing, a point only 10 miles downstream from Devon Downs. Carbon-14 dating indicates that the lowest levels in these deposits were occupied early in the third millennium B.C. Fromm's Landing and Devon Downs are thus very close, both geographically and temporally. The sequence of three cultures identified by Hale and Tindale at Devon Downs, however, was not evident at Fromm's Landing. This is a matter of more than casual importance because Tindale has asserted—and the assertion has received wide acceptance—that the three cultures are distributed

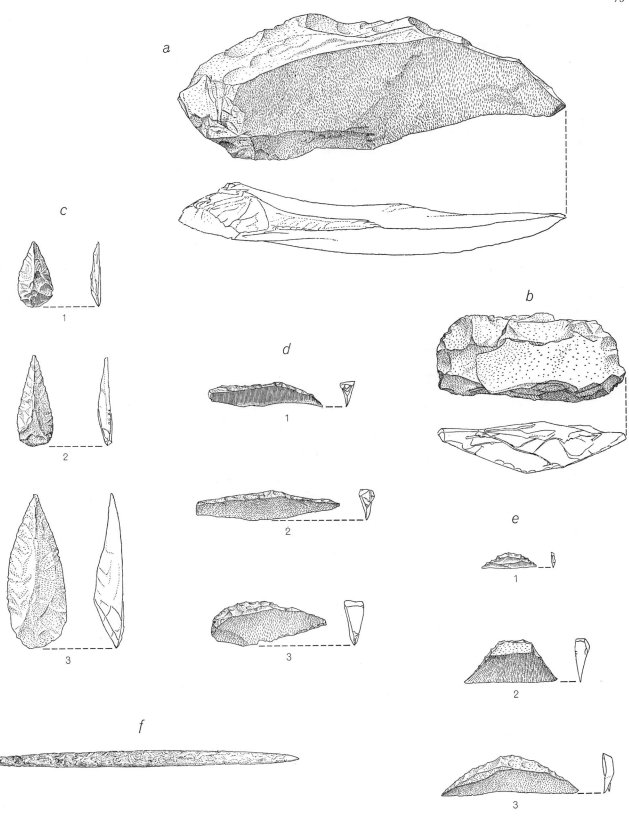

ARTIFACTS FOR HAFTING show a wide variety of forms. All are shown actual size. The knife *a* is from the topmost stratum at Kenniff Cave; stone blades like this, with resin or skin handgrips, were still used by Queensland aborigines early in the 19th century. The step-trimmed adze flake *b* was mounted on the end of a stick and served as a chisel or gouge. The neatly trimmed *pirri* points (*c-1 to c-3*) probably were projectile tips; *c-1* was excavated near Kenniff Cave and is 3,500 years old. The other two are surface finds from South Australia. The three blades (*d-1 to d-3*) are called Bondi points; their backs have been blunted by steep but delicate trimming. The three microliths (*e-1 to e-3*) show similar fine trimming on their backs. All presumably formed the working edges of various composite tools. The pointed bone (*f*) is a 400-year-old *muduk*; it may have served as a fishhook, a spear tip or even a nose ornament.

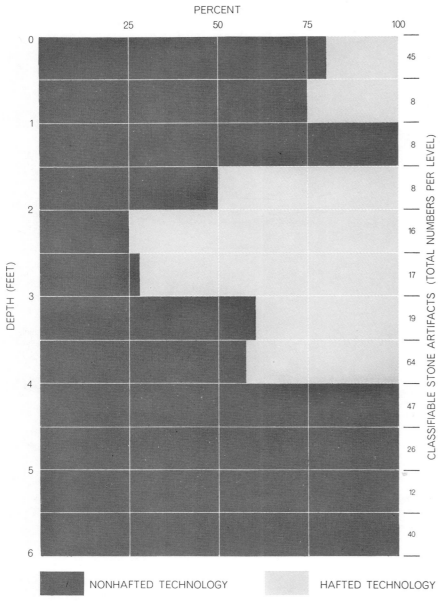

PERCENT

NONHAFTED TECHNOLOGY          HAFTED TECHNOLOGY

**ADVANCE IN TECHNOLOGY** at Kenniff Cave took place about 3000 B.C., when the concept of hafting was introduced. At four feet and deeper only hand-held scrapers (*gray*) were found; above that, entirely new kinds of stone artifact (*color*) appear among the scrapers (*see illustration on preceding page*). These artifacts are evidently parts of composite tools.

across the entire continent. I found the pirris at Fromm's Landing in association with microliths, tiny stone blades of the kind that in Old World cultures are sometimes set in a haft of bone or wood to form a composite tool. The association contradicts Tindale's belief that such microliths are artifacts typical not of the Pirrian but of the later Mudukian culture.

This finding and others at Fromm's Landing led me to question the basis of Tindale's cultural diagnosis at Devon Downs. It seemed more useful to consider the elements the three

Devon Downs assemblages had in common than to isolate discrete traits as Tindale did. Flakes of stone used as adzes, for example, were found in all three Devon Downs culture levels; there was no apparent break in the tradition of stoneworking from the earliest time to the latest. In reporting my findings at Fromm's Landing I suggested that the differences in the inventory of various Devon Downs strata might be attributable to changes in artifact preference on the part of an aboriginal population that was becoming increasingly adapted to life beside a river, with its varied and rich organic re-

sources. Such an interpretation eliminates any need to imagine the successive arrival of separate culture groups, and all the elements of discontinuity that such a succession implies.

By the standards of archaeology in the Old World neither the Devon Downs nor the Fromm's Landing site is particularly ancient. Between 1960 and 1964, however, my associates and I excavated a rock-shelter in southern Queensland that contained 11 feet of stratified deposits; carbon-14 dating showed that the lowest levels at this site—Kenniff Cave on the Mount Moffatt cattle station—are at least 16,000 years old. Troweling and sieving 85 cubic yards of sand and ash, we recovered more than 21,000 stone flakes and waste fragments, most of them quartzite. Among them were some 850 deliberately shaped and retouched artifacts. About 60 percent of the artifacts were either broken or only lightly worked. As a result the total number of artifacts available for rigorous classification and measurement was little more than 350.

The sequence of stone artifacts at Kenniff Cave constitutes the point of departure for any current discussion of Australian prehistory. Two facts give the Kenniff Cave collection its special significance. First, it includes examples of most of the prehistoric implement types known in Australia, arranged in stratigraphic order. Second, the age of the collection ranges from the immediate past back to the late Pleistocene.

For those accustomed to the richness of Old World Paleolithic sites the Kenniff Cave assemblage will seem a small sample, but it is one of the largest Australian collections to be analyzed. Recent work in the vicinity of Sydney and in the Northern Territory (where one excavation has uncovered more than 2,000 worked projectile points) has been more productive, but the results have not yet been published. My experience elsewhere has often been daunting. An excavation in Victoria yielded 2,300 waste pieces and only eight artifacts; the strata of a South Australian site yielded an average of three artifacts per 1,000 years of occupation.

The Kenniff Cave assemblage includes 261 specimens of the generalized tool termed a scraper. Their distribution fluctuated with depth [*see illustration on this page*]. In the uppermost four feet of the deposit scrapers were relatively rare compared with other types of implement. Throughout the lower layers, however, they constituted 100 percent of all classifiable stone artifacts.

An implicit assumption underlies the use of a descriptive label such as "scraper." In this case the assumption is that scrapers were normally held in the user's hand. Scrapers are thus members of the family of nonhafted stone tools. They are technologically distinct from hafted, composite tools of the kind that presumably made use of the microliths unearthed at the Murray River sites in South Australia. Such tools possess handles or other extensions, together with fixatives such as resin or gum or lashings such as hair, vegetable fiber or sinew.

The sandy soil of Kenniff Cave is so acid that, if any such organic constituents of composite tools had once been present, no evidence of them now remains. The distinction between nonhafted and hafted artifacts at Kenniff Cave is therefore a subjective one. Nonetheless, the difference between the percentage of scrapers in the upper strata and in the lower led me to make a basic assumption about the place of nonhafted and hafted tools in Australian prehistory. I postulated that the apparent ignorance of hafting techniques on the part of the early inhabitants of Kenniff Cave was genuine ignorance, and that an extensive phase in the prehistory of the site occupied a period during which this advanced technology was literally unknown. Carbon-14 estimates indicate that this prehafting phase lasted for at least 11,000 years, or from about 14,000 to about 3000 B.C.

When the Kenniff Cave scrapers were set in their stratigraphic sequence and subjected to careful measurement and analysis, the results of the study confirmed that, as postulated, a continuity of tradition had existed during this period of 11 millenniums; the scrapers showed no significant change either in production technique or in size. Such technological stability—or lack of invention—may be relevant when one considers the social dynamics of a prehistoric culture.

In contrast to the long period of stability attested by the lower levels at Kenniff Cave, the upper levels told a sharply different story. Scrapers appear in diminishing percentages, and accompanying them are various types of small, delicately worked stone arti-

fact. Both the size and the shape of these objects—one specimen measuring only 1.7 centimeters by .5 by .1 centimeter is shown at *e-1* on page 5—imply their diverse functions as components of hafted implements. Such is certainly the case with the long stone knives and with the artifacts identifiable as adze flakes [*"a" and "b" in illustration on page 79*]. The latter objects, which have a characteristic stepped appearance, were the stone working edges of gouges or chisels, composite tools that are widely represented in Australian ethnographic collections. It is probably the case with the pirri points (which may have been mounted on projectile shafts) and geometric microliths (a type of artifact whose purpose is debated on other continents but that is everywhere assumed to be part of a hafted tool).

To judge from the level at which these tool types are first found in the stratigraphic sequence at Kenniff Cave, the technology of hafting materialized there about 5,000 years ago. The impact of the new technology was fundamental. During the 2,000 years that followed—until about 1000 B.C.—most of the characteristic types of stone implement that have been unearthed or collected on the surface by prehistorians in southern Australia were deposited in the upper strata of Kenniff Cave. It is of course conjectural that the acquired knowledge of hafting techniques was the factor that enabled the aboriginal populations of this period to develop greater flexibility in the design of tools, but it is unmistakable in the stratigraphic record at Kenniff Cave that the rate of technological advance accelerated during

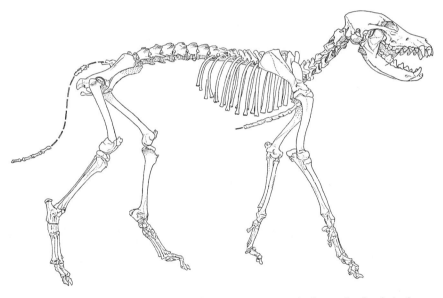

**OLDEST KNOWN DINGO,** the Australian dog, was unearthed at a depth of six feet at Fromm's Landing rock-shelter No. 6. Dating from 1000 B.C., the animal shows no morphological differences from the dingos of today. Man and the dingo were virtually the only predators in prehistoric Australia; they apparently killed off some species of marsupials.

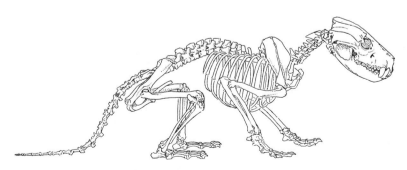

**TASMANIAN DEVIL** is one of two species of marsupials whose bones are found only in the lower strata at Fromm's Landing. Because no major climatic changes occurred during the 5,000 years the site was occupied, the disappearance of this animal and the Tasmanian wolf from the area in the second millennium B.C. may be attributable to man and the dingo.

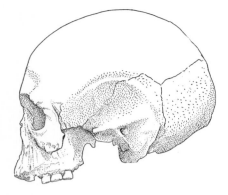
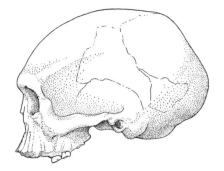
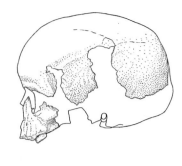

**FOSSIL MAN** in Australia may be most authentically represented by the skull unearthed at Keilor, near Melbourne, in 1940 (*left*); recent additional findings at Keilor suggest that the skull is as much as 18,000 years old. From the time of its discovery the Keilor skull has been considered nearly a twin of a fossil skull from Wad- jak in Java (*center*), discovered in 1890 and of unknown age. The discovery of an adolescent skull, probably 40,000 years old (*right*), in the Niah Caves of Sarawak in 1959 has added another possible precursor to the aboriginal family tree. The scarcity of Australian fossil evidence, however, renders all these conclusions tentative.

the period from 3000 B.C. to 1000 B.C.

Bearing in mind the postulate that a long period of nonhafted-tool technology was followed by a briefer period of the more variable hafted-tool technology, it seems appropriate to review the findings of other archaeologists at a number of sites across the continent. Let us begin with the sites that seem, on the basis of established or assumed chronology, to belong to the nonhafted-tool phase. At the Tombs Shelter in Queensland, near Kenniff Cave, a few artifacts have been found that appear to date back to the eighth millennium B.C. They belong to the nonhafted tradition, and worked stones suitable for hafting are found in the strata above them. At Ingaladdi in the Northern Territory a stone-tool industry that consists of scrapers (and "cores" that were reworked as nonhafted scraping or chopping tools after flakes had been struck from them) yields a date in the fifth millennium B.C. Three sites in New South Wales—Seelands, Curracurrang and Capertee—cover a period from the sixth millennium to early in the second millennium B.C. All three evince non-hafted phases and all are overlain by layers containing artifacts suitable for hafting. These lower-level tool kits contain other nonhafted implements in addition to the ubiquitous scrapers; at least that is how I interpret saw-edged flakes at Capertee and core tools common to all three sites. The cores, flaked on one or both faces, suggest that they were held in the fist for some battering or chopping function. Specimens from Seelands have been measured by the prehistorian J. M. Matthews; he finds them comparable to the Southeast Asian pebble industry named Hoabhinian, after a Vietnamese site.

R. V. S. Wright of the University of Sydney has recently undertaken an important excavation at Laura, on Cape York in northeastern Queensland. The technological sequence he has uncovered may be comparable to that at Kenniff Cave. The same may be true of a ninth-millennium-B.C. occupation site Tindale has found at Noola, near Capertee in New South Wales. The Noola material has not yet been formally described, but Tindale's brief published note allows the relevant finds to be attributed to a nonhafted phase. Some years ago Tindale isolated a stone-tool industry on Kangaroo Island, off the coast of South Australia. No varieties of artifact associated with hafted implements were found there, but flaked pebbles, scrapers and massive core tools were numerous. Tindale postulated a Pleistocene date for the occupation; so far neither excavation nor carbon dating has been attempted. This is an intriguing field for further investigation.

Still another early date is proposed by Tindale and Richard Tedford of the University of California at Riverside for "nondescript" stone flakes found at a surface site at Lake Menindee in New South Wales. Charcoal samples at the site have yielded carbon-14 dates of 17,000 and 22,000 B.C., but detailed evidence for a direct association between the charcoal and the artifacts has not yet been published.

The reconstruction of the most recent 5,000 years of Australian prehistory is further along than the work on the earlier phases, although there is no better agreement on how the evidence from these five millenniums should be interpreted. It is nonetheless possible to relate my hypothesis concerning a significant technological change involv-

ing hafting techniques during this period to the culturally oriented descriptions of findings by other workers. Much of this work is in progress, and since it would be improper to anticipate the results here the survey that follows— like those that have preceded it—draws primarily on published reports and my own experience.

The Kenniff Cave site in Queensland is more than 1,000 miles from the Devon Downs and Fromm's Landing sites in the Murray River valley of South Australia. In comparing the equivalent upper and later levels of the three sites, however, it is worth noting that Kenniff Cave lies in the same system of river valleys as Devon Downs and Fromm's Landing. The upper levels at Kenniff Cave, like those at the South Australian sites, contain pirri points, microliths, adze flakes and other stone artifacts representative of the hafted-tool tradition. There are no bone muduks at Kenniff Cave, but the acid sands of the site would have destroyed any that had been buried. Significantly there is considerable contrast between the size and finish of similar artifacts from the Queensland and the South Australian sites. This tends to confirm my view that artifacts of the same general type were subject to a process of differentiation.

Although many more excavations are needed to bridge existing gaps in knowledge and lay the foundation for valid generalizations, some hint of the rate at which the concept of hafting diffused among the aboriginal populations is provided by the following carbon-14 results. As I have noted, the Fromm's Landing site and the upper strata at Kenniff Cave belong to the early third millennium B.C., and a layer containing pirri points at Devon Downs dates from later in the same millennium. This parallels the age of the oldest hafted types of stone artifact found in New South Wales, those unearthed at Seelands. The Ingaladdi site in the Northern Territory has yielded pirris and other points, some finished on one side and some on both. These points appear with relative suddenness in a layer that has not been dated. A stratum a few inches below the points, however, contains an assemblage of nonhafted artifacts that has been dated to the latter part of the fifth millennium B.C. It begins to look as if the period centered on the fourth millennium B.C. will prove to be a crucial one in the reconstruction of Australian prehistory.

For many years a key figure in the documentation of the prehistory of New South Wales has been Frederick D. McCarthy, principal of the Australian Institute of Aboriginal Studies; his excavations at Lapstone Creek and Capertee have provided a working basis for systematizing evidence from elsewhere in the state. Recent investigations in the Sydney and New England areas of New South Wales have served to test and elaborate McCarthy's pioneering studies. Under the sponsorship of the institute Wright and J. V. S. Megaw of the University of Sydney have carried out important excavations, and Isabel McBryde of the University of New England has undertaken an all-inclusive field survey.

McCarthy believed he had isolated two cultures at Lapstone Creek. The earlier of these he called Bondaian; its characteristic tool is a small, asymmetric, pointed blade reminiscent of a penknife, with a sharp cutting edge and a blunt back edge ["d" in illustration on page 79]. The later culture he named Eloueran; the characteristic tool is a flake shaped like a segment of an orange, with its back heavily blunted and its cutting edge often polished by use. Also found in the Bondaian levels are geometric microliths. This is scarcely surprising when one considers that the skills needed to make microliths and small blades are essentially the same. Both require as their raw material thin blades, one edge of which is then artificially blunted.

Carbon-14 dates from Curracurrang, Capertee and Seelands place the characteristic artifacts of the Bondaian and the Eloueran cultures in the second and first milleniums B.C. Both could be assigned to my hafted phase. This emphasis on technology rather than on any cultural context accords with McCarthy's own observation that, in spite of fluctuations in the fortunes of specific traits, there is an underlying similarity in the stoneworking techniques of the two cultures.

The present rub in classifying Australian artifacts is how to decide where to draw boundaries and what degree of emphasis to give single culture traits. Within each group of artifacts there are variations in size, shape and trimming. What criteria, for example, distinguish a thin Eloueran flake from a large, crescent-shaped microlith? It is unsatisfactory to lump all the pirris together, and there is diversity even among the bone muduks. The truth is that early workers, myself included, selected an ideal type and then blurred the edges of distinction by treating deviations from this ideal as atypical, even though the deviations possessed inherent definable characteristics. Today, in common with the trend in archaeology around the world, the analysis of artifacts in Australia has shifted away from the subjective methods of the past toward laborious quantitative definition. Most assemblages that have been excavated recently are undergoing rigorous statistical investigation. The Bondaian-Eloueran problem should benefit from this objective approach.

I have presented evidence in support of the view that Australian prehistory can be divided into two phases, distinguishable by a change in technology from the exclusive use of nonhafted, hand-held stone artifacts to the employment of many specialized stone artifacts that were hafted to form composite implements. What of the people who used these nonhafted and hafted tools? Some of the most interesting evidence for the antiquity of man in Australia comes from gravel quarries at Keilor on the outskirts of Melbourne, where a creek has cut a series of terraces. A human skull was unearthed there in 1940, but its exact origin became a matter of dispute. In attempting to resolve the controversy, Edmund D. Gill of the National Museum of Victoria has obtained a series of carbon-14 dates for the Keilor quarries; his earliest date, centered around 16,000 B.C., is for charcoal taken from a point some feet below the 1940 level of the quarry floor. The crucial issue is whether this charcoal is from an aboriginal campfire or from some natural conflagration. The fact that a number of stone artifacts have been found in the creek bed and embedded in the banks of the terraces does not automatically mean that the charcoal is also the work of men. These objects lack the authority of artifacts excavated from undisturbed stratified de-

EXCAVATION AT KENNIFF CAVE revealed evidence of human occupation from about the 14th millennium B.C. until the present. The paler strata along the walls of the 11-foot pit represent periods when the shelter was virtually deserted by prehistoric hunters; the darker strata are rich in organic material. The outline paintings of human hands on the overhanging rock were made by aboriginal tribesmen who have used the shelter during recent years.

posits under well-controlled conditions.

In 1965 the evidence favoring the authentic antiquity of the Keilor skull suddenly multiplied. Two miles from the scene of the 1940 discovery earth-moving equipment exposed a human skeleton that was in a fair state of preservation. Preliminary indications are that the skeleton belongs to the same level of terrace as that proposed for the Keilor skull. Charcoal is plentiful at the site, although some of it—tree roots that were burned where they had grown—is clearly the work not of man but of nature. Artifacts are also present. Obviously men lived here during the period of terrace formation, and carbon-14 determinations should establish the age of the site. The National Museum of Victoria is coordinating the investigations now under way at Keilor.

Man may have arrived in Australia at the time of the continent's climatic climax, when inland rivers flowed, lakes brimmed and the giant herbivorous marsupials flourished. In any case he almost certainly played a role in altering the ecological character of the continent (and, less directly, the soil) through selective hunting activities and frequent burning of vegetation. One ecological effect resulted from man's introduction of the dog. Man and the dingo together represented a scourge to the prehistoric fauna; the two were virtually the sole predatory carnivores on the continent. What caused the extermination of numerous marsupial species: man and dog or climatic change? The findings at Fromm's Landing indicate that the two carnivores played their part. There is nothing in the evidence to imply that, during the 5,000 years spanned by the deposits at the site,

there were important fluctuations in climate that might have exerted an ecological influence. Mammal bones identified at Fromm's Landing represent 685 individuals of 31 species. In two cases—*Sarcophilus*, the Tasmanian devil, and *Thylacinus*, the Tasmanian wolf—there are indications that the species became extinct there during the second millennium B.C. It is relevant that a 3,000-year-old stratum at the site has yielded the skeleton of a dingo; this is the earliest authenticated occurrence of the dingo in Australia.

What were the racial origins of the prehistoric Australians? This question has been much debated, but the debate is conducted virtually in a vacuum because of the scarcity of early human fossils in Australia. Until the discovery of the Keilor skeleton there was not one such fossil whose authenticity was unchallengeable. Now the Keilor skull found in 1940—and perhaps a badly crushed skull from Talgai in Queensland—may gain a more respectable status. Still, two or three specimens make a small sample for determining the origin of a race. Two fossil skulls found at Wadjak in Java, to the northwest of Australia, have been proposed as a link in aboriginal evolution; these fossils, however, remain undated. A skull from the Niah Caves in Sarawak, to the north of Java, is possibly 40,000 years old and has also been compared with prehistoric Australian remains. Caution must be the keynote when there are such wide spatial gaps in the fieldwork and so few fossils.

The origin of the prehistoric inhabitants of Tasmania, the large island to the south of Australia, also remains

an open subject. The last Tasmanians (none survived the 19th century) were an ethnographic rarity: a society using stone tools without hafts of any kind. Studies of changes in the sea level during Pleistocene times have made it a tenable theory that the Tasmanians walked to Tasmania from Australia when the intervening strait was dry land; carbon-14 estimates have established their presence in Tasmania 8,000 years ago. During the past two years Rhys Jones of the University of Sydney has achieved striking success in fieldwork in northern Tasmania. When his carbon samples are dated and his human skeletal material is analyzed, Tasmanian archaeology will have entered an objective era.

Now that it seems certain that Australia was colonized in Pleistocene times, the inadequacy of evidence on this period not only in Australia but also in its northern neighbors such as New Guinea is painfully apparent. If we are to retrace the steps of Australia's first colonists, detailed studies of changes in the sea level are required. If we are to seek out their early patterns of settlement, we need far more precise dating of environmental changes in the continent's interior. With much of Australia archaeologically unexplored, with increasing numbers of investigators undertaking fieldwork and with carbon-14 chronologies providing new perspectives, these are exciting times for the study of the continent's prehistory. It is certain that during the next few years the nearly blank outline map of that prehistory will come to be filled with detail.

# EARLY AMERICANS

# II  EARLY AMERICANS

## INTRODUCTION

When the first European explorers landed in the New World, they were amazed at the incredible diversity of human cultures which flourished in the Americas. The aboriginal American became a fashionable topic of inquiry and speculation in European drawing rooms. The concept of the "Noble Savage" came into fashion, depicting the American Indian as enjoying a simple, pastoral life in Eden-like simplicity and comfort. Soon ingenious theories were being invented to explain the flourishing indigenous societies of the New World. All manner of people were alleged to have migrated to North America in remote prehistoric times to become the ancestors of the Indians. Some attributed the Americans to the early migrations of the Ethiopians, others to the Ten Lost Tribes of Israel.

During the nineteenth century more sober judgments began to prevail. Boucher de Perthes' discoveries of stone implements in France provoked such academic excitement that some archaeologists began to look for Stone Age peoples in the Americas. Although no stone handaxes or early Paleolithic tools were found in the New World, Samuel Haven and other sober academics were soon hypothesizing that North America was settled from across the Bering Straits and through Alaska. Most archaeologists now agree with Haven, and considerable research has been directed toward the problem of the date and extent of the first settlement of the Americas.

Little is known of the first Americans, largely because we lack securely dated early archaeological sites. The major research problems revolve around the date of the earliest settlement and the actual problem of peopling the New World once the Bering Straits were crossed. The first necessity was to prove that humans had been living in the Americas at the same time as such large and extinct mammals as the mammoth. It was not until 1926 that the scholarly community accepted the notion that projectile heads and extinct bison bones were truly contemporary, after the discovery of such an association in New Mexico by Dr. Jesse Figgins in 1926. Prior to that, many people believed that the human settlement of the New World began around 3000 B.C. Since 1926 many more discoveries of human artifacts and bones of extinct animals have been made. The development of radiocarbon dating in the late 1940's has enabled the dating of many finds.

In his article, "Early Man in the Andes," Richard MacNeish argues that humankind may have settled in the New World between 40,000 and 100,000 years ago. Securely dated sites are few and far between, especially in Alaska, where research has hardly begun. The basis for MacNeish's bold statement comes from his excavations at Flea Cave in the Andes, where he found stone tools in occupied levels that could be radiocarbon-dated to at least 20,000 years ago. The stone tools found in this level are large and crude choppers and woodworking tools, quite unlike the fine projectile heads so characteristic of later hunting cultures in the Americas. MacNeish has named these occupation levels from the Flea Cave the Paccaicasa Complex, a cultural tradition that lasted in this part of the Andes until about 13,000 years ago. No definite parallels to the Flea Cave tools have been found in North America, although there are some traces of early hunters, in the form of bone tools from a site near Old Crow in the Canadian Yukon, dated to approximately 24,000 years ago, and in a scatter of flakes from Lewisville, Texas, of uncertain age. Some crudely flaked stones and bones of extinct animals have been radiocarbon-dated to around 22,000 years ago at Tlapacaya, near Mexico City.

The logical place to look for the earliest Americans is, of course, Alaska, and it is there that much recent archaeological work has been concentrated. During periods of intense cold, world sea levels fell dramatically below the present coastlines. For example, during the period 50,000 to 40,000 B.C. and 27,000 to 8,000 B.C. the Bering Straits became dry land, so that a land bridge extended between Siberia and the New World. Since no remains of any other humans than *Homo sapiens* have yet been found in the Americas, it seems almost certain that the first Americans crossed the Straits during one of these two periods of colder climate. The earliest known traces of human settlement in Alaska date to around 20,000 B.C., but the artifacts from this "Fisherman's Lake" site are far from sufficient for comparison with Siberian tools. Not much is known of Paleolithic Siberian peoples, either, although the Ushki site on the Kamchatka Peninsula dates to around 14,000 B.C., and contains several layers of human occupation. The difficulties of Alaskan archaeology are well-summarized by Douglas Anderson in his article, "A Stone Age Campsite at the Gateway to America." His Onion Portage site provides one of the few examples of a stratified occupation site in Alaska. Onion Portage was a favorite lookout spot for prehistoric and modern hunters preying on the vast caribou herds that migrate to and from the open tundra immediately to the north of the site. More than seventy levels of human occupation are covered by deposits of silt that could be removed one by one to trace the history of Onion Portage as far back as 8000 B.C., if not earlier. Many of the tools can be compared to Asian artifacts. Onion Portage also provides reliable evidence for the evolution of early Eskimo culture after 500 B.C.

There has been a tendency to think of the first settlement of North America as being achieved by a massive population movement, a migration of many hunting bands at the same time. In fact, however, the process was more gradual, as a well-known Arctic archaeologist, J. L. Giddings, put it: "America was settled by people slowly filtering down from the Arctic population, resorting the genes previously in the New World down through the millennia." The enormously varied environments of the Americas led to a great diversity of adaptations among the hunters and gatherers who were the successors of the first Americans.

Big-game hunting has long been synonymous with Plains Indians in North America. Mass game drives, enormous herds of bison, galloping horsemen thundering across the plains—all these are familiar phenomena on the movie screen. The first widespread big-game hunting dates from the early millennia of American prehistory, and coincides with the appearance of Paleo-Indian hunting bands on the Great Plains and elsewhere before 9500 B.C. Paleo-Indian sites have yielded enormous numbers of carefully flaked projectile heads, a favorite target of artifact collectors. In a few sites, such as the Olsen-Chubbock site described by Joe Ben Wheat in his article, "A Paleo-Indian Bison Kill," these projectile heads have been found in association with the skeletons of bison herds stampeded from narrow arroyos to their death. This wasteful destruction of game herds far in excess of meat requirements was undoubtedly a factor in the extinction of large Pleistocene mammals in the Americas. Joe Ben Wheat's account of the Colorado bison kill gives many details of Paleo-Indian hunting and butchery techniques 8,000 years ago. He describes how they hunted, butchered, cooked, and carried meat in such detail that the atmosphere of the hunt comes to light in vivid detail. He even calculates the direction of the wind on the day of the hunt. American archaeologists are concentrating on studies of this type, reconstructing the diverse ways of life practised by American hunters long before any of the world's population was engaged in agriculture or cattle raising. In the Eskimo and Fuegan Indians of South America, we see a few survivors of a cultural tradition whose roots go back to the first Americans.

# 9

# A Stone Age Campsite
# at the Gateway to America

by Douglas D. Anderson
June 1968

*Onion Portage in Alaska is an unusual Arctic
archaeological site. It provides a record of
human habitation going back at least 8,500 years,
when its occupants were not far removed from their
forebears in Asia*

It seems virtually certain that men first migrated to the New World from Asia by way of the Arctic, yet for some time this fact has presented archaeology with a problem. By 10,000 B.C. Stone Age hunters were killing mammoths on the Great Plains. There is evidence suggesting that man was present in Mexico even earlier, perhaps as early as 20,000 B.C. Until 1961, however, the Arctic gateway region had yielded few traces of man before 3000 B.C. In that year excavations were begun at a site in Alaska where the remains of human occupation are buried in distinct strata, affording the investigators a unique opportunity for reliable dating.

The site is Onion Portage, on the bank of the Kobuk River in northwestern Alaska. It has been intensively excavated from 1964 through 1967. The findings may eventually demonstrate that man was present in Alaska as long ago as 13,000 B.C. Already they show that men with strong Asian affinities were there by 6500 B.C.

Why is the stratified site of Onion Portage so unusual? Archaeological evidence concerning the hunters of sea mammals who lived on the shores of Alaska and northwestern Canada is quite abundant. North of the Aleutian Islands, however, no coastal site has been discovered that is more than 5,000 years old. The reason is that the sea, rising as the last great continental glaciers melted, reached a point close to its present level some 5,000 years ago, thereby drowning the former coastline together with whatever evidence of human habitation it harbored.

The change in sea level would not, of course, have affected early sites in the interior. Such sites are scarce and usually unrewarding for other reasons. One is that the environment of tundra and taiga (treeless barren land and northern forest) could not support as many hunting groups as the game-rich shore. Another reason is that campsites on interior rivers were likely to be washed away or buried as the river shifted its course. In fact, throughout the interior only places where the ground is elevated and dry offer much archaeological promise.

The remains of numerous hunting camps have in fact been found on elevations in the Alaskan interior. These camps were apparently established to enable the hunters to catch sight of caribou on the tundra. As the hunters waited they made or repaired weapons and other implements; the campsites are littered with broken stone projectile points and tools and with the waste chips of their manufacture.

Herein lies another problem. At a rocky site where little or no soil is forming a 6,000-year-old spearpoint may lie beside one discarded only a century ago. It is nearly impossible to prove which is the older or exactly how old either one is. Even where soil has developed and the artifacts have been buried, the Arctic environment plays tricks. The upper layers of soil, soaked with water and lying on top of permanently frozen lower layers, tend to flow and disarrange buried objects. As a result both absolute and relative dating of archaeological material from sites in the Arctic interior was rarely possible before the discovery at Onion Portage.

Some 125 miles upstream from where the Kobuk River enters the Chukchi Sea the course of the river is a lazy meander five miles long. Situated at the upper end of the meander, Onion Portage is bounded by steeply cut banks on the upstream side and by a long natural levee downstream. The terrain has not been radically altered by stream erosion for at least 8,000 years. The name Onion Portage comes from the wild onions that grow profusely along the gravelly shore and from the overland haul across the base of the point, which saves five miles of upstream paddling. Today the boundary between trees and tundra is only a few hundred yards north of Onion Portage. Beyond the trees the open tundra continues all the way to the Arctic Ocean, 270 miles farther north. To the south the terrain is open taiga, dotted with patches of spruce, willow and (in sheltered places) birch.

A sandy knoll dominates the wooded landscape at the site. Hunters both ancient and modern have used this vantage as a lookout for the thousands of caribou that cross the river at Onion Portage, moving north in the spring and south in the fall. From the knoll the approaching animals can be seen soon enough for men to be stationed for the kill at points where the herd is likely to cross the river. The fishing at Onion Portage is also good; several species of salmon migrate upstream during the summer. The prized sheefish, which is scarce in other Alaskan rivers, is also caught by the local Eskimos.

Over thousands of years the lower and flatter parts of Onion Portage have been buried several times under sand eroded from gullies in the knoll. In places the alluvial fans that spread out from the gullies have built up layers of sand as

much as three feet thick. Unusually high spring floods have also engulfed the site from time to time, leaving thin deposits of silt. Windstorms too have spread thin sheets of drifted sand across the site. Each such covering killed the turf buried under it; the new turf that formed on the fresh surface was separated from the dead turf below by a sterile layer of sand or silt. All the deposits combined make up the sequence of strata at Onion Portage. In places the sequence is 20 feet thick. More than 70 of the surfaces show evidence of human occupation. The layers of turf are concentrated in bands, each of which contains from three to 14 occupation levels. The bands have been given consecutive numbers, starting with Band 1 just below the surface and ending with Band 8, the deepest dated series of occupation levels at the site.

The Onion Portage site was discovered in 1941 by the late J. L. Giddings, Jr., of Brown University, who was traveling down the Kobuk on a raft. He stopped and excavated several 500-year-old Eskimo house pits to gather material for an Arctic tree-ring chronology he was then establishing. He returned to the site 20 years later; test digging that year revealed the stratified layers. Giddings began a full-scale excavation in 1964, with the support of Brown University and the National Science Foundation. In the same year he died. Recognizing the uniqueness of the site, both institutions urged that the work be continued the following season. Froelich G. Rainey, director of the University Museum at the University of Pennsylvania, an Arctic specialist and a longtime colleague of Giddings', and I, one of Giddings' former students, were invited to take over the excavation. In the 1966 and 1967 seasons the work at Onion Portage has continued with the same support under my direction.

Our study is by no means complete. Soil samples from various levels at the site, for instance, are still being analyzed at the University of Uppsala, the University of Alaska and the University of Arizona for their chemical constituents, pollen content and even for microscopic diatoms. Samples of charcoal from each of the eight bands have already yielded

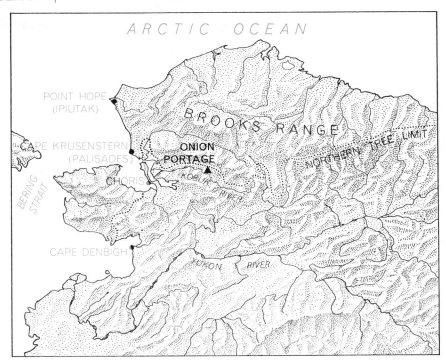

ALASKAN SITES at which artifacts have been found that resemble those unearthed at Onion Portage include the four located on this map. Onion Portage, the first known stratified site in the New World's Arctic interior, was discovered by J. L. Giddings, Jr., in 1941.

carbon-14 dates that will enable us to fit the expected biological and geological information into a sensitive chronology. The chronology now spans a minimum of 8,500 years and may eventually go back another 6,500. Even now a preliminary correlation of the carbon-14 dates with the stone tools, weapons and other remains unearthed at Onion Portage has produced some surprising results. One finding substantially alters assumptions about cultural developments in the New World Arctic.

In presenting our preliminary results I shall start with the earliest of the three main cultural traditions we have found at Onion Portage. American archaeologists use the word "tradition" to describe a continuity of cultural traits that persist over a considerable length of time and often occupy a broad geographical area. A single unifying tradition may be shared by several distinct cultures. The word "complex" is used to describe the distinctive remains of a culture. A tradition usually includes more than one culture complex. It is with the earliest culture complex of the earliest tradition at Onion Portage that I shall begin.

The complex has been named Akmak, after the northern-Alaskan Eskimo word for chert, the flintlike stone that the hunting people of this complex most commonly employed to make tools and

weapons. Most of the Akmak implements have been found on the sandy knoll at the site, between six inches and two feet below the surface. Some have been uncovered along the side of one of the gullies that cuts into the knoll and at the bottom of the gully's ancient channel, which is 10 feet below the bottom of the present channel. Others have been found below Band 8, where, having been carried down the gully, they had lain since before the first levels of Band 8 were formed. The fact that some of the material comes from below Band 8 indicates that the Akmak artifacts are at least 8,500 years old. They may be as much as 15,000 years old. Two fragments of excavated bone are being dated by carbon-14 analysis, but the sample is unfortunately too small to produce a reliable carbon-14 reading. We hope that future work at the site will produce material to settle the matter.

Most Akmak implements are of two classes. Comprising one class are large, wide "blades," the term for parallel-edged flakes of stone that were struck from a prepared "core." The other class consists of "bifaces," so named because the stone from which they were made was shaped by flaking surplus stone from both sides. From the blades the Akmak artisans produced a variety of tools. They include long end scrapers, curved implements with a sharp pro-

DEEP PIT at Onion Portage shows the characteristic layering of soil at the site. Each thin, dark horizontal band was formed when charcoal from hunters' fires or other material was buried under sand or silt. Artifacts found below the lowest band may be as much as 15,000 years old. The measuring stick at right center is three meters long.

ONION PORTAGE SITE is located by the white triangle (*top center*) in this aerial photograph. The site lies on the upstream bank of a point of land enclosed by a wide meander of the Kobuk River, 125 miles from the sea in the interior of northwestern Alaska.

tuberance resembling a bird's beak and knives shaped by flaking one or both faces of a blade. The bifaces, which have the general form of a disk, were usually made by first striking the side of a slab-like core; the detached flakes left scars that end at the center of the disk. Numerous smaller flakes were then removed around the margin of the disk to give it a sharp edge. Nothing like these implements has been found in Alaska before. Indeed, the tools that most resemble Akmak disk bifaces come from the area around Lake Baikal in Siberia, where they are found at sites that are between 12,000 and 15,000 years old.

Using a technique similar to the one for producing large blades, Akmak artisans also made "microblades." Most mi-croblades are about an inch long and quarter of an inch wide. They were struck from a small core prepared in a way that is characteristic of "campus-type microcores," so named because the first to be discovered in America were found at a site on the campus of the University of Alaska. Campus-type microcores have been found in many other parts of Alaska and also in Siberia, Mongolia and Japan. The oldest ones come from the island of Hokkaido in Japan and the Kamchatka Peninsula in the U.S.S.R.

Many Akmak microblades were made into rectangular chips by breaking off both ends of the blade. Prehistoric hunters set such chips in a groove cut in the side of a pointed shaft of wood, bone or antler. The razor-sharp bits of stone gave the pointed weapon a wicked cutting edge. Grooved shafts of antler associated with rectangular microblades have been found both in Siberia and in the Trail Creek caves in western Alaska. Although grooved shafts have not been found at Onion Portage, it is reasonable to assume that the Akmak rectangles were intended for mounting in them.

The Akmak artisans also made burins: specialized stone tools with a sharp corner particularly useful for making grooves in antler and bone. The Akmak technique for producing burins was to strike a blow that left a chisel-like point at the corner of a flake [see illustration on page 95]. Akmak burins show signs of wear both at the tip and along the edge,

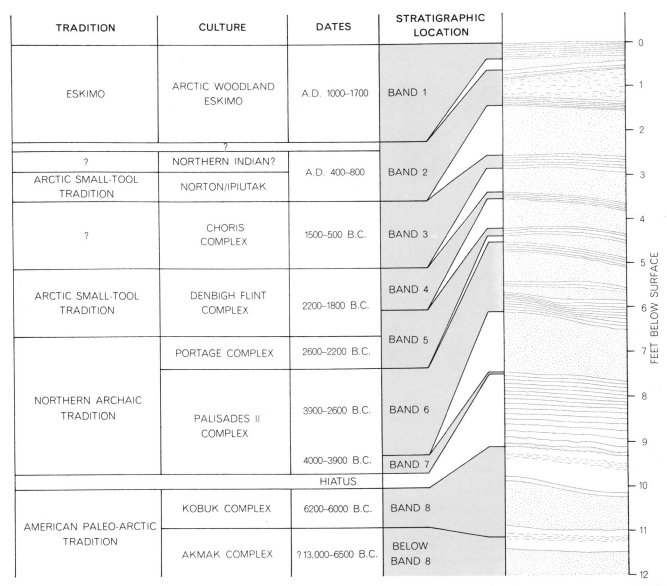

| TRADITION | CULTURE | DATES | STRATIGRAPHIC LOCATION | |
|---|---|---|---|---|
| ESKIMO | ARCTIC WOODLAND ESKIMO | A.D. 1000–1700 | BAND 1 | |
| ? | NORTHERN INDIAN? | A.D. 400–800 | BAND 2 | |
| ARCTIC SMALL-TOOL TRADITION | NORTON/IPIUTAK | | | |
| ? | CHORIS COMPLEX | 1500–500 B.C. | BAND 3 | |
| ARCTIC SMALL-TOOL TRADITION | DENBIGH FLINT COMPLEX | 2200–1800 B.C. | BAND 4 | |
| NORTHERN ARCHAIC TRADITION | PORTAGE COMPLEX | 2600–2200 B.C. | BAND 5 | |
| | PALISADES II COMPLEX | 3900–2600 B.C. | BAND 6 | |
| | | 4000–3900 B.C. | BAND 7 | |
| | HIATUS | | | |
| AMERICAN PALEO-ARCTIC TRADITION | KOBUK COMPLEX | 6200–6000 B.C. | BAND 8 | |
| | AKMAK COMPLEX | ? 13,000–6500 B.C. | BELOW BAND 8 | |

EIGHT MAIN BANDS in the stratigraphic column uncovered at Onion Portage are related in this chart to the evidence of human occupation they contain. Starting before 6500 B.C., and probably much earlier, three major cultural "traditions" succeed one anoth-er. The third tradition, interrupted about 1800 B.C., was initially represented at the site by the culture named the Denbigh Flint complex. It was evidently ancestral to the Eskimo tradition that appeared at Onion Portage about A.D. 1000 and continued thereafter.

III

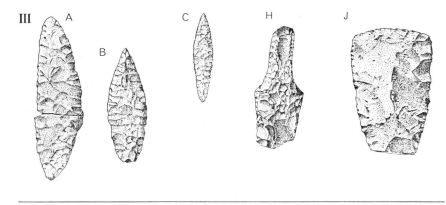

II

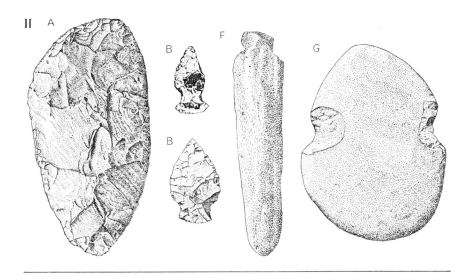

I

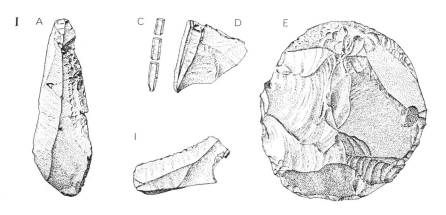

A — KNIFE               D — CAMPUS-TYPE MICROCORE     G — PEBBLE SINKER
B — PROJECTILE POINT    E — DISCOID BIFACE            H — BEAKED TOOL
C — EDGE INSET          F — NEEDLE SHARPENER          I — BURIN
                                                      J — ADZE BLADE

**ARTIFACTS OF THREE PERIODS** at Onion Portage reveal the presence of three separate cultural traditions: the American Paleo-Arctic (I), the Northern Archaic (II) and the Arctic Small-Tool tradition (III). Knives (*A*) are present in all three traditions and stone projectile points (*B*) in the last two. Hunters of all three traditions had projectiles, but the two Arctic traditions favored points made from antler or ivory and inset with tiny stone blades (*C*). Unique to the earliest tradition are "campus-type microcores" (*D*) and disk-shaped bifaces (*E*). Characteristic of the non-Arctic Archaic tradition are stones for sharpening needles (*F*) and sinkers for nets (*G*). Burins appear in both of the Arctic traditions; the one shown (*I*) is Akmak. Unique to the later Arctic tradition are peculiar beaked tools (*H*) and small adze blades (*J*). All the implements are reproduced at one-half natural size.

indicating that they were used not only for grooving but also for cutting.

The Akmak tools suggest relationships between Onion Portage and Asia. Considering the changes in Arctic geography during the past 30,000 years, this is scarcely surprising. At the height of the last continental glaciation Asia and North America were connected across what is now the Bering Strait. The land area that the lowered sea level had exposed was more than a mere isthmus. At its maximum extent between 20,000 and 18,000 years ago it was virtually a subcontinent, a tundra-covered plain 1,300 miles wide that must have been populated by herds of game and hunters pursuing them. The great plain, which has been named Beringia, made Alaska an extension of northern Asia. At the same time two continental glaciers in North America effectively cut ice-free Alaska off from the rest of the New World. The isolation of Alaska did not end until sometime between 14,000 and 10,000 years ago, when the glaciers began to melt rapidly. By then Beringia had already been twice drowned and reexposed by fluctuations in the level of the sea. Then, about 10,000 years ago, Beringia began its final submergence, a process that was not completed until some 5,000 years ago.

To repeat, the Akmak period at Onion Portage ended about 6500 B.C. and may have begun as early as 13,000 B.C. Between these dates dry land connected ice-free Alaska with Siberia while glaciers forbade or at least inhibited contact with the rest of North America. The resemblances between the Akmak culture and Siberian cultures, and the lack of resemblances between the Akmak culture and Paleo-Indian cultures to the south, reflect this geographic history. At the same time there are significant differences between the Akmak culture and the Siberian cultures, suggesting that the Akmak complex resulted from a long period of isolated regional development. Because the tradition of which the Akmak complex is the earliest appears to have been an indigenous development, arising from earlier Arctic-adapted cultures, I have named it the American Paleo-Arctic tradition.

The next evidence of human habitation found at Onion Portage is in two levels of Band 8. Carbon-14 analysis of material from the higher level suggests that the people who camped there did so sometime between 6200 and 6000 B.C. I have termed the remains from Band 8 the Kobuk complex.

The limited variety of Kobuk-complex

artifacts suggests that the material found at Onion Portage represents only a part of a larger assemblage of stone tools. Fewer than 100 worked pieces of stone have been recovered from the two levels. Most of them are rectangles made from microblades. There are also two burins made from flakes, a few remnants of campus-type microcores, a single obsidian scraper and several flakes, some of which have notched edges. All the implements were found adjacent to hearths on deposits of silt. The silt suggests that Onion Portage was a wet and uncomfortable place when the Kobuk hunters camped there. The hearths are probably those of small groups that stayed only briefly.

At a number of surface sites in the Brooks Range I have collected stone implements that are almost identical with those of the Kobuk complex. The only major difference is that the Brooks Range tool assemblage includes biface knives, which are missing from the Kobuk levels at Onion Portage. I suspect that the difference is more apparent than real; if we had unearthed a larger Kobuk inventory at Onion Portage, it probably would have included biface knives. In any case, the presence in both the Akmak and the Kobuk assemblages of microblade rectangles and campus-type microcores suggests that, although the Kobuk complex represents a later period, it is nonetheless a part of the American Paleo-Arctic tradition.

Quite the opposite is true of the ma-terial we have unearthed in Band 7, Band 6 and Band 5. After a hiatus of some 2,000 years an entirely new cultural tradition arrived at Onion Portage. Its lowest levels are dated by carbon-14 analysis at around 4000 B.C. There are no microblades among its tools. Instead of using weapons with microblades inserted in them the newcomers hunted with projectiles tipped with crude stone points that had notched bases and were bifacially flaked. The new assemblage also includes large, irregular knives made from flakes, thin scrapers, notched stone sinkers and large crescent-shaped or oval bifaces. We also unearthed two heavy cobblestone choppers.

The tools from Band 7 and Band 6, which contain the early and middle phases of the new tradition, are nearly identical with a group of tools from a cliff site overlooking Cape Krusenstern on the Alaskan coast 115 miles west of Onion Portage. The cliff site is known as Palisades; the name "Palisades II complex" has been given to these phases of the new tradition at Onion Portage. The tools of the Palisades II complex reflect an uninterrupted continuity, marked only by gradual stylistic changes, for 1,400 years. One such change affected the hunters' projectile points. The notched base characteristic of the early phase gave way in the middle phase to a base with a projecting stem.

The contents of Band 5 indicate that around 2600 B.C. a period of rapid change began at Onion Portage and con-tinued for 300 years. Several new types of tools appear; projectile points, for example, are neither notched nor stemmed but have a straight base. These and other differences in the assemblage indicate that the occupation levels in Band 5 belong to later phases of the new tradition. They warrant a label of their own, and I have named them collectively the Portage complex.

How is the arrival of the new tradition at Onion Portage to be explained? It is noteworthy that the duration of the new tradition coincides almost exactly with a major alteration in the climate of Alaska. About 10,000 years ago, as the region's last glacial period drew to a close, the Alaskan climate entered a warming phase that reached its maximum between 4000 and 2000 B.C. Throughout the period of milder weather the forest margin moved northward, steadily encroaching on the tundra. By the time of the maximum the boundary between tundra and taiga had probably advanced well beyond the position it occupies today. During the 2,000 years of the maximum it seems likely that Onion Portage lay well within the northern forest zone.

Far to the southeast, in the forests of the eastern U.S., an Indian population had pursued a woodland-oriented way of life beginning as early as 6000 B.C. Its weapons and tools reflect a forest adaptation; they belong to what is known as the Archaic tradition, as op-

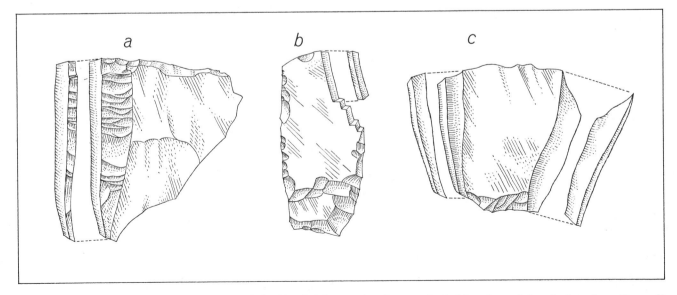

GROOVE-CUTTING TOOLS, or burins, were made by Akmak (*a*) and Denbigh (*b*) knappers at Onion Portage. The Akmak knappers chipped a notch into the edge of a prepared flake before striking a blow (*arrow*) that knocked off a long, narrow spall, giving the flake a sharp, chisel-like corner (*color*). The Denbigh knappers, using the same burin blow (*arrow*), knocked much smaller spalls off flakes carefully prepared in advance. They used the tiny spalls as tools for engraving. Choris knappers (*c*) used the burin blow to strike fine, regular spalls from flakes of irregular shape. This produced no burins; the knappers made tools from the spalls instead.

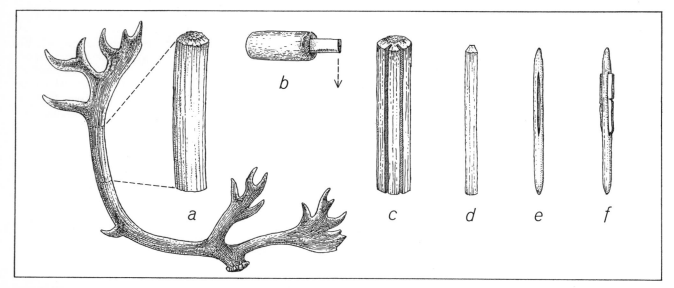

**PROJECTILE POINTS** can be made from antler and microblades as shown here. A length of antler (*a*) is deeply grooved (*c*) with a burin (*b*) mounted in a handle for easy use. The triangular antler segments (*d*) are then rounded and pointed, and grooves are made in one or both sides (*e*). Razor-edged bits of microblade are then set in the grooves (*f*) to form a cutting edge. The Akmak, Kobuk and Denbigh levels at Onion Portage contain edge insets. Akmak and Kobuk insets are rectangles; Denbigh insets are crescents.

posed to the older Paleo-Indian tradition. I find it significant that, during a time when the forest had shifted northward, an assemblage of tools with many resemblances to the Archaic tradition should appear at Onion Portage. Crescent-shaped bifaces, projectile points with notched and stemmed bases, heavy choppers and notched stones that the Indians of the Archaic tradition used as sinkers for nets are among the elements common to the two assemblages.

Up to now evidence for the early diffusion of the Archaic tradition northward and westward from the woodlands of the eastern U.S. does not go much beyond the Great Lakes region. Artifacts that resemble Archaic-tradition tools have been found in central and northwestern Canada and in central Alaska, but their age is undetermined. The fact that the tools are distributed throughout this area nonetheless suggests the possibility that Archaic peoples, or at least the art of making tools in the Archaic tradition, moved northward into the Arctic along with the advancing forest. The findings at Onion Portage seem to support this suggestion. I have therefore named the Palisades II complex and the Portage complex together the Northern Archaic tradition. The differences between the second tradition at Onion Portage and the American Paleo-Arctic tradition that preceded it seem great enough to suggest that they were the products of two different populations. They may have been respectively early Northern Indians and proto-Eskimos.

Almost immediately after 2300 B.C. there was a resurgence of Arctic culture at Onion Portage. The evidence in Band 4 marks the arrival of hunters representing the Arctic Small-Tool tradition. This tradition is well known from other Arctic sites. It is the culture of the earliest people in the New World Arctic who were equally at home on the coast and in the interior. The element of the tradition that is present at Onion Portage is the Denbigh Flint complex, first recognized at an Alaskan coastal site on Cape Denbigh [see "Early Man in the Arctic," by J. L. Giddings, Jr., SCIENTIFIC AMERICAN, June 1954].

The characteristic implements of the Denbigh people are burins and edge insets—the sharp stones shaped for insertion into grooved weapons. Some Denbigh edge insets were made from microblades, but all of them differ from the rectangular Akmak and Kobuk insets in that they are delicately flaked into half-moon shapes. The Denbigh people produced microblades for a variety of other uses. For greater efficiency they devised a new form of microcore. It is wider than the campus-type core, and it allowed them to strike off wider and more easily worked blades.

The people of the Denbigh Flint complex flourished widely in the Arctic between 2500 and 2000 B.C. Many students of Arctic archaeology consider them to be the direct ancestors of today's Eskimos, pointing out that the geographic distribution of Denbigh sites almost exactly coincides with the distribution of Eskimos in historic times. Parallels between the Denbigh Flint complex and the American Paleo-Arctic tradition, including the use of microblades and edge-inset weapons, suggest that the Denbigh culture may well have descended from the Akmak and Kobuk cultures.

After 2000 B.C. the New World Arctic and coastal subarctic area supported a number of Eskimo regional groups, none of which developed along exactly the same lines. Choris is the name given to one regional people that inhabited the Alaskan coast near the mouth of the Kobuk River, hunting caribou and living in large oval houses. The Choris-complex people have an involved history that spans 1,000 years from 1500 to 500 B.C. At Onion Portage, Choris artifacts are found in Band 3.

The earliest known pottery in the New World Arctic comes from Choris sites. The pottery was well made, was decorated by stamping patterns on the surface and was fired at a reasonably high temperature. In the earliest phases of the Choris complex, evidence for which is found at sites on the coast but not at Onion Portage, the pots were decorated by striking the wet clay with a cord-wrapped paddle. The pots are too skillfully made for it to be likely that the Choris people were experimenting with clay for the first time. Instead a fully developed industry must have been introduced from the outside. Exact counterparts have not yet been found abroad, but the basic Choris pottery patterns suggest a source in Asia. This is apparently not the case for Choris-complex tools such as knife blades and skin scrapers. Some of the Choris edge insets for weapons resemble Denbigh types, but the other tools do not. If anything, they resemble Northern Archaic artifacts.

The Choris tool assemblage presents a puzzle in the form of large, regularly flaked projectile points that look very much like the Scottsbluff, Plainview and Angostura points made by the Paleo-Indian hunters of the Great Plains. The nearest Paleo-Indian sites, however, are removed from the Choris complex by some 2,500 miles and 3,000 years. What this likeness means in terms of a possible cultural relation between the Arctic and the Great Plains is a question to which I shall return.

From 500 B.C. to A.D. 500 the hunters who camped at Onion Portage left a record of steady Eskimo cultural evolution that includes evidence of increasing communication between the coast and the interior. Some of the artifacts recovered from the middle levels of Band 2, for example, are typical of those found at the seacoast site of Ipiutak, some 200 miles away on Point Hope. Regional variations nonetheless persist. Tools ground out of slabs of slate are found along with Ipiutak-complex tools at Onion Portage, but ground slate is unknown in the Ipiutak assemblage on Point Hope.

One final break in the continuity of Arctic-oriented cultures is apparent at Onion Portage. It is found in the upper occupation levels of Band 2, which were inhabited around A.D. 500 or 600. The artifacts in these levels are totally unlike those of contemporaneous Eskimo cultures along the coast. It seems logical to assume that forest Indians moving up from the south were responsible for the new cultural inventory. Whatever the identity of the newcomers, they did not stay long. Around A.D. 1000 Onion Portage was again in Eskimo hands.

Measured in terms of the number of artifacts and wealth of information, the modern period recorded in Band 1 is the best-known in the Onion Portage sequence. Our current studies, combined with Giddings' earlier ones, give a remarkably detailed picture of the Kobuk River Eskimos' gradual change from a part-time coastal economy to a full-time way of life adapted to tundra and taiga conditions, in which networks of trade maintained communication with the Eskimos of the coast.

Taken as a whole, the stratigraphic record at Onion Portage has cast much

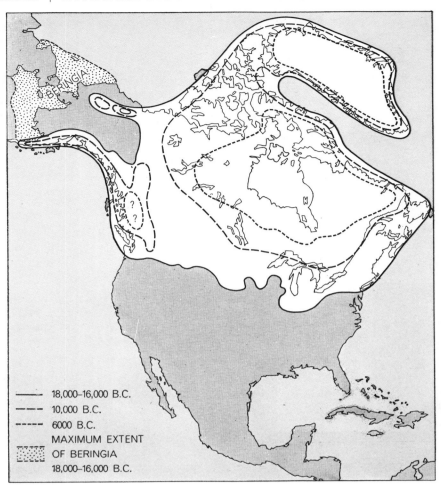

ICE BARRIER, formed by union of two continental glaciers, cut off Alaska from the rest of North America for perhaps 8,000 years. The era's lowered seas exposed Beringia, a vast area that made Alaska into an extension of Siberia. Arctic and Temperate North America were not reunited until the final withdrawal of the two ice sheets had begun (*broken lines*).

Legend:
— 18,000–16,000 B.C.
– – 10,000 B.C.
- - - 6000 B.C.
MAXIMUM EXTENT OF BERINGIA 18,000–16,000 B.C.

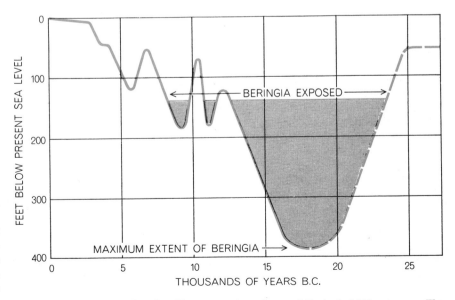

CHANGING SEA LEVEL in late Pleistocene times drowned Beringia 8,000 years ago. The link between Alaska and Siberia had been exposed earlier for two short periods and one long period when it was quite large. The graph is based on one by D. M. Hopkins of the U.S. Geological Survey; dating of sea-level changes before 18,000 B.C. is conjectural.

WORK CREW on the flats below the hill at Onion Portage slowly exposes one of the site's more than 70 levels with traces of human occupation. Silt carried by floodwaters and sand eroded from the hillside had accumulated in the flats to a depth of 20 feet in places.

new light on the relations between various poorly dated or undated Arctic archaeological assemblages. At the start we see Arctic peoples with cultural roots in Siberia adapting themselves to a life of hunting on the treeless tundra of interior Alaska, and later to hunting along the treeless coast. As we can infer from the abundance of microblade edge insets found at Onion Portage, a part of this adaptation involved the efficient use of materials other than wood for weapons, among them antler (and later ivory) spearpoints edged with stone. This indigenous tradition, based on Asian origins, had an uninterrupted development from perhaps as early as 13,000 B.C. until about 6000 B.C.

Sometime before 4000 B.C. we see the arrival at Onion Portage of a forest-adapted tradition that had its origins in the eastern woodlands of the U.S. The advance of the Archaic tradition into Arctic terrain coincided with the postglacial shift in climate that allowed the forests to invade the northern tundra. With the reexpansion of the tundra at the end of the warm period Arctic cultures once again dominated the Kobuk

River region. At the same time they spread rapidly across the entire Arctic area occupied by Eskimos today.

Until Onion Portage was excavated the archaeological record in the Arctic favored the view that early cultural developments there were somehow connected with the Paleo-Indians of the Great Plains. Many scholars suggested that the Arctic and Paleo-Indian cultures shared essentially the same cultural tradition, perhaps originating in the north or perhaps in the Great Plains but in either case occupying northwestern Alaska and Canada sometime between 7000 and 3000 B.C. The suggestion derived its strength primarily from the presence of projectile points almost identical with Paleo-Indian ones at several sites in Alaska and Canada. The projectile points found in the Arctic could not be dated, but it was speculated that they were as much as 7,000 or 8,000 years old. Such antiquity, of course, added strength to the Paleo-Indian hypothesis.

Even before the Onion Portage excavations some contrary evidence had come to light. For example, the Choris complex is rich in projectile points that

are Paleo-Indian in appearance. Yet the Choris complex is firmly dated between 1500 and 1000 B.C.—scarcely half of the minimum age suggested by the Paleo-Indian hypothesis.

The findings at Onion Portage, in my opinion, cast even more doubt on the hypothesis. During the millenniums between 7000 and 3000 B.C.—nearly the entire interval of the postulated contact between (or identity of) the Arctic and the Paleo-Indian cultures—nothing from any occupation level at Onion Portage shows any hint of Paleo-Indian influence. On the contrary, the influence in the earlier part of the interval is Siberian and in the later part Archaic.

We hope that future work at Onion Portage will push the firmly dated record of Arctic prehistory back to even earlier times. We should also like to learn what cultures were developing along the Kobuk River between 6000 and 4000 B.C.— the period for which we have no record at Onion Portage. Meanwhile what we have already learned substantially clarifies the sequence of events at the gateway to the New World.

# Early Man in the Andes

by Richard S. MacNeish
*April 1971*

*Stone tools in highland Peru indicate that men lived
there 22,000 years ago, almost twice the old estimate.
They also imply that the first cultural traditions of the
New World had their roots in Asia*

Recent archaeological discoveries in the highlands of Peru have extended the prehistory of the New World in two significant respects. First, the finds themselves indicate that we must push back the date of man's earliest known appearance in South America from the currently accepted estimate of around 12,000 B.C. to perhaps as much as 20,000 B.C. Second and even more important is the implication, in the nature of the very early Andean hunting cultures now brought to light, that these cultures reflect Old World origins of even greater antiquity. If this is so, man may have first arrived in the Western Hemisphere between 40,000 and 100,000 years ago. The discoveries and the conclusions they suggest seem important enough to warrant this preliminary report in spite of the hazard that it may prove to be premature.

The new findings were made in 1969 and 1970 near Ayacucho, a town in the Peruvian province of the same name. All the sites lie within a mountain-ringed valley, most of it 6,500 feet above sea level, located some 200 miles southeast of Lima [*see top illustration on page 101*]. The valley is rich in prehistoric remains (we noted some 500 sites during our preliminary survey) and archaeological investigations have been conducted there since the 1930's. For me and my associates in the Ayacucho Archaeological-Botanical Project, however, the valley was interesting for other reasons as well.

A number of us had already been involved in a joint archaeological-botanical investigation at Tehuacán in the highlands of Mexico under the sponsorship of the Robert S. Peabody Foundation for Archaeology. Our prime target was early botanical evidence of the origin and development of agriculture in the area. This we sought by archaeological meth-

ods, while simultaneously recording the relation between agricultural advances and the material evidence of developing village life (and ultimately urban life) in Mexico before the Spanish conquest. By the time our fieldwork at Tehuacán had been completed in the mid-1960's we had gained some understanding of the changes that had come about in highland Mesoamerica between its initial occupation by preagricultural hunters and gatherers around 10,000 B.C. and the rise of pre-Columbian civilization [see the article "The Origins of New World Civilization," by Richard S. MacNeish, beginning on page 169].

There was, however, at least one other major New World center that had been the site of a similar development from hunting bands to farmers and city folk. This is western South America. Its inhabitants had cultivated some plants that were unknown to the farmers of Mesoamerica, and they had domesticated animals that were similarly unique to the region. Mesoamerica certainly interacted with South America, but the earliest stages of this second regional development apparently took place in isolation. It seemed logical that the record of these isolated advances might provide the foundation for functional comparisons with the Tehuacán results and perhaps lead us to some generalizations about the rise of civilization in the New World.

This was the objective that brought several veterans of the Tehuacán investigation, myself included, to Peru. The work was again sponsored by the Peabody Foundation, where I now serve as director. Reconnaissance of a number of highland areas led us to select the Ayacucho valley as the scene of our investigations. Our decision was based primarily on ecological grounds: within a radius of 15 miles the varied highland en-

vironment includes areas of subtropical desert, thorn-forest grassland, dry thorn forest, humid scrub forest and subarctic tundra [*see bottom illustration on page 101*]. It is the consensus among botanists who have studied the question that many of the plants first domesticated in western South America were indigenous to the highlands and that their domestication had probably taken place in Peru. The Peruvian ecologist J. A. Tosi had concluded that the most probable locale for the event would be a highland valley that included a wide range of environments. An additional consideration was that the area where we worked should contain caves that could have served as shelters in the past and thus might prove to be the repositories of animal and plant remains. The Ayacucho valley met both requirements.

Two caves in the valley have in fact turned out to be particularly rich repositories. One of them, located about eight miles north of the town of Ayacucho, is known locally as Pikimachay, or Flea Cave. It lies some 9,000 feet above sea level on the eastern slope of a hill composed of volcanic rock; the mouth of the cave is 40 feet high in places and 175 feet wide, and the distance from the front of the cave to the deepest point inside it is 80 feet. Rocks that have fallen from the roof occupy the northern third of the interior of the cave and form a pile that reaches a height of 20 feet. In 1969 Flea Cave yielded the single most dramatic discovery of the season. During our last week of excavation a test trench, dug to a depth of six feet near the south end of the cave, revealed stone tools in association with bones of an extinct ground sloth of the same family as the fossil North American sloth *Megatherium*. One of the bones, a humerus, has

been shown by carbon-14 analysis to be 14,150 (±180) years old.

The other notable cave site, some 11 miles east of the town of Ayacucho, is known locally as Jayamachay, or Pepper Cave. Although Pepper Cave is as high and nearly as wide as Flea Cave, it is only 15 feet deep. Excavations were made at Pepper Cave with rewarding results in both the 1969 and the 1970 seasons. Because the significance of the findings at this site arises largely from a comparison of the material from both caves, I shall first describe the strata at Flea Cave.

What has been revealed in general by our work at all the cave and open-air sites in the Ayacucho valley (a total of 12 excavations) is a series of remains representative of successive cultures in an unbroken sequence that spans the millenniums from 20,000 B.C. to A.D. 1500. The archaeological sequence documents man's progression from an early hunter to an incipient agriculturist to a village farmer and finally to the role of a subject of imperial rule. The material of the most significance to the present discussion, however, is contained in the strata representing the earliest phases of this long prehistoric record. These strata have yielded a succession of stone-tool types that began some 20,000 years ago and continued until about 10,500 years ago. The earliest part of the record is found in the lowest levels at Flea Cave.

The oldest stratified deposit in the cave lies in a basin-like hollow in the lava flow that forms the cave floor. The stratum lies just above the bedrock of the basin. Labeled Zone k, the stratum consists of soils, transported into the cave by natural means, that are mixed with disintegrated volcanic tuffs from the rocks of the cave itself. Zone k is eight inches deep. Just before the deposition of the stratum ended, some animal vertebrae and a rib bone (possibly from an extinct ground sloth) were deposited in it. So were four crude tools fashioned from volcanic tuff and a few flakes that had been struck from tools. One of the flakes is of a green stone that could only have come from outside the cave.

**DEEP CUT** through part of an open-air archaeological site at Puente in highland Peru is seen in the photograph on the opposite page. The record preserved in the successive strata at Puente extends from the first appearance of pottery in the 16th century B.C. to about 7000 B.C., when the Andes were inhabited by hunters specializing in the pursuit of big game.

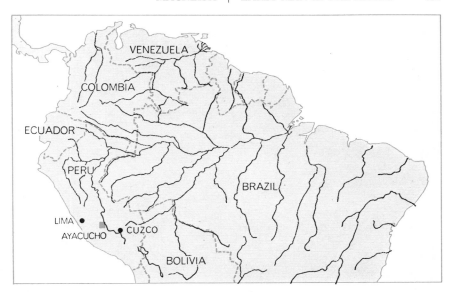

**AYACUCHO VALLEY**, between Lima and Cuzco, is undergoing joint botanical and archaeological investigation that will allow comparisons with a study of Tehuácan, in Mexico. The Robert S. Peabody Foundation for Archaeology is the sponsor of both studies.

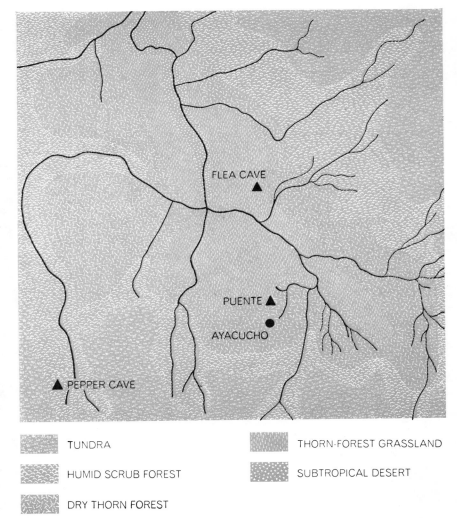

TUNDRA

HUMID SCRUB FOREST

DRY THORN FOREST

THORN-FOREST GRASSLAND

SUBTROPICAL DESERT

**MAJOR SITES** in the Ayacucho valley include Puente, near the town of Ayacucho, Flea Cave, a few miles north of Puente, and Pepper Cave, a few miles southwest. The existence of five distinct zones of vegetation in the valley (*key*) was a factor in its selection for study.

FLEA CAVE, the site that contains the oldest evidence of man's presence thus far unearthed in South America, lies at an altitude of 9,000 feet in an area of intermingled thorn forest and grassland. The mouth of the cave (center) is 175 feet wide and 40 feet high.

PEPPER CAVE, the other major cave site in the Ayacucho area, lies at an altitude of 11,000 feet on a hill where humid scrub forest gives way to upland tundra vegetation. The lowest strata excavated at Pepper Cave are evidently the product of local glacial outwashes.

The soils in Zone k are neutral in terms of acidity, which suggests that the vegetation outside the cave when the soils were formed was of the grassland variety, in contrast to the dry thorn-forest vegetation found today. The period of deposition that formed Zone k may have begun more than 23,000 years ago. It remains to be seen whether the climate at that time, as indicated by the neutral acidity of the soil, can be exactly correlated with any of the several known glacial fluctuations in the neighboring Andes.

Three later strata, all containing the bones of extinct animals and additional stone implements, overlie Zone k. They are labeled, in ascending order, zones j, i1 and i. Zone j is a brown soil deposit 12 inches thick. In various parts of this stratum we unearthed three vertebrae and two rib fragments of an extinct ground sloth and the leg bone of a smaller mammal, perhaps an ancestral species of horse or camel. Zone j yielded 14 stone tools; like those in Zone k, they are crudely made from volcanic tuff. There are in addition some 40 stone flakes, evidently the waste from toolmaking. Carbon-14 analysis of one of the ground-sloth vertebrae shows it to be 19,600 (±3,000) years old.

Zone i1, above Zone j, is a deposit of a more orange-colored soil; it is 15 inches thick, and it contains tools and both fossilized and burned animal bone. Carbon-14 analysis of one of the bones, a fragment of sloth scapula, indicates that it is 16,050 (±1,200) years old. The soils of zones j and i1 are both quite acid, suggesting that they were formed when the climate was less arid and the vegetation outside Flea Cave included forest cover.

The uppermost of the four strata, Zone i, consists of 18 inches of a slightly browner soil. The soil approaches that of Zone k in neutral acidity, suggesting a return to drier climatic conditions. Distributed through the deposit are crude stone artifacts, waste flakes and the bones of sloth and horse. Carbon-14 analysis of one of the bones shows it to be 14,700 (±1,400) years old.

The stone tools from all four of the lowest Flea Cave strata are much alike. There are 50 of them in all, uniformly large and crude in workmanship. The tool types include sidescrapers, choppers, cleavers, "spokeshaves" and denticulate (sawtoothed) forms. Most of them were made from volcanic tuff, which does not flake well, and it takes a skilled eye to distinguish many of them from unworked tuff detached from the

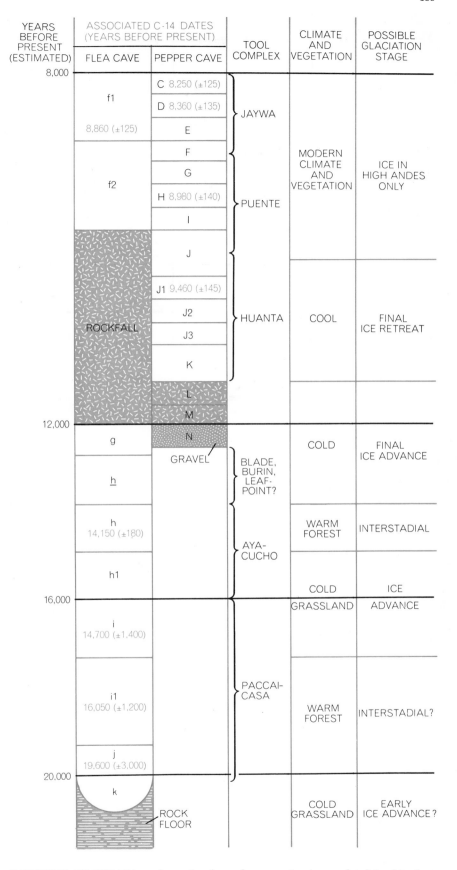

SEQUENCE OF STRATA at the major Ayacucho cave sites is correlated in this chart with the five earliest tool complexes that have been identified thus far. Carbon-14 determinations of the age of certain strata are shown in relation to estimates of the overall temporal sequence. The climate and vegetation are linked to probable stages of glaciation.

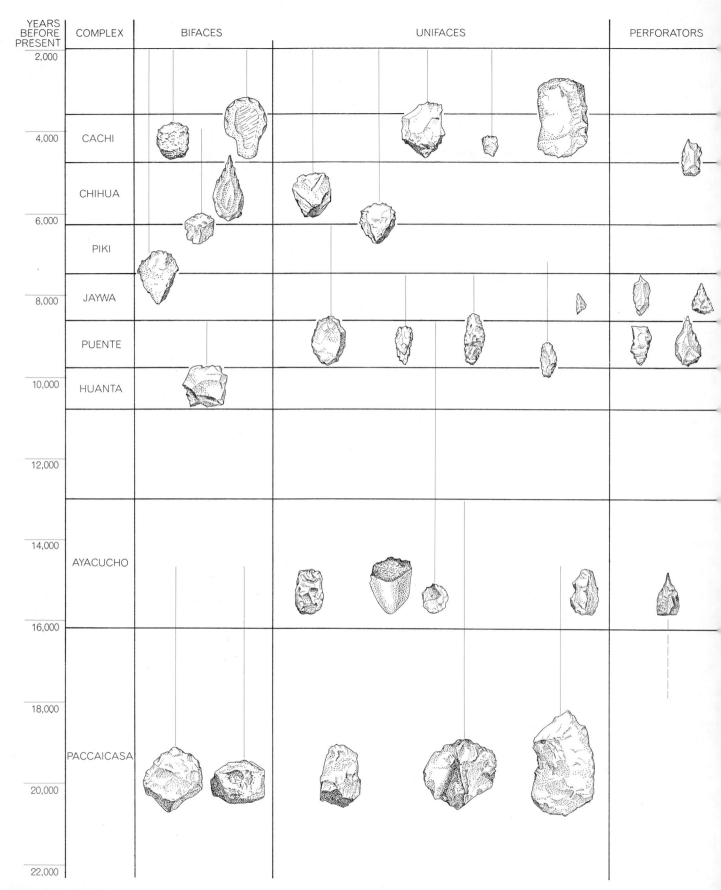

| YEARS BEFORE PRESENT | COMPLEX | BIFACES | UNIFACES | PERFORATORS |
|---|---|---|---|---|
| 2,000 | | | | |
| 4,000 | CACHI | | | |
| | CHIHUA | | | |
| 6,000 | PIKI | | | |
| 8,000 | JAYWA | | | |
| | PUENTE | | | |
| 10,000 | HUANTA | | | |
| 12,000 | | | | |
| 14,000 | AYACUCHO | | | |
| 16,000 | | | | |
| 18,000 | PACCAICASA | | | |
| 20,000 | | | | |
| 22,000 | | | | |

**KINDS OF TOOLS** discovered at 12 excavations in the Ayacucho valley appear in this chart in association with the complex (*names at left*) that first includes them. No complex more recent than the Puente, some 9,000 years old, is relevant to man's earliest arrival

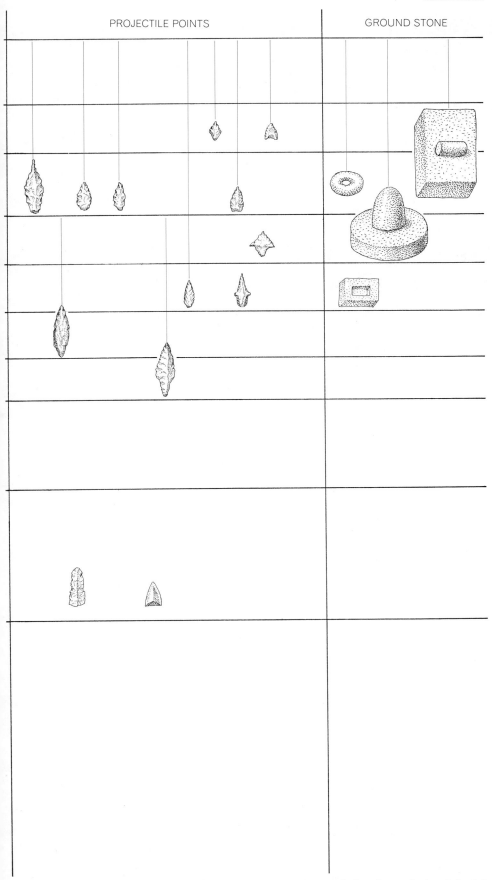

PROJECTILE POINTS

GROUND STONE

**in Peru. The first crude tools (*bottom*) are reminiscent of chopping tools found in Asia. In the next complex projectile points first appear; some were made out of bone (*far right*).**

cave walls by natural processes. A few of the tools, however, were made from other materials, such as rounded pebbles and pieces of basalt, that were collected outside the cave and carried back to be fashioned into implements. The tools in these four levels represent the earliest assemblage of tools, or tool complex, unearthed so far at a stratified site anywhere in South America. We call it the Paccaicasa complex, after a nearby village. The men who fashioned its distinctive tools occupied the Ayacucho valley from as much as 22,000 years ago to about 13,000 years ago.

The strata at Flea Cave that contain the Paccaicasa complex were excavated during the 1970 season. The previous year we thought we had already reached bedrock when we reached the top of the stratum just above Zone i: it was a very hard, yellowish layer of soil that included numerous small flakes of volcanic tuff. With the season nearly at an end we proceeded no farther. The yellow layer, now known as Zone h1, actually turned out to lie just above bedrock over an area of some 150 square yards of cave floor except for the natural basin near the south end of the cave. Digging into this stratum with some difficulty at the start of the 1970 season, we found that its 20-inch depth contained not only the bones of sloth, horse and possibly saber-toothed tiger but also numerous flakes of waste stone and some 70 tools, most of them quite different from the crude tuff artifacts of the strata below. A few tools of the older kind were present in Zone h1, but the majority are made from such materials as basalt, chalcedony, chert and pebbles of quartzite.

The use of new tool materials is also characteristic of Zone h, a 12-inch stratum of softer, light orange soil that overlies Zone h1. Here, however, the animal remains include many not found in the older strata. A kind of ancestral camel appears to be represented in addition to the sloth and the horse. There are also the remains of the puma, the hog-nosed skunk, an extinct species of deer and several unidentified species, possibly including the mastodon. This larger faunal assemblage suggests a return of the countryside around Flea Cave to forest cover. Indeed, the soil of Zone h is strongly acid, unlike the neutral soils of Zone i and Zone h1.

The tools in Zone h are abundant; in addition to more than 1,000 fragments of waste stone there are some 250 finished artifacts. Some of these artifacts are in the "core" tradition of tool manufacture: they were made by removing

LIMB BONE of an extinct ground sloth (*center*) was found at Flea Cave in a stratum that also contained stone and bone tools representative of the Ayacucho complex. Carbon-14 analysis of the bone shows that the stratum was deposited at least 14,000 years ago.

flakes from a stone to produce the desired shape. Among them are both the choppers and spokeshaves typical of the lower strata and new varieties of tool such as split-pebble scrapers and fluted wedges. The core tools are outnumbered, however, by tools consisting of flakes: burins, gravers, sidescrapers, flake spokeshaves, denticulate flakes and unifacial projectile points (points flaked only on one side). The unifacial points are the oldest projectile points found at Ayacucho.

At this stage the inhabitants of Flea Cave were also fashioning tools out of bone: triangular projectile points, polishers, punches made out of antler and "fleshers" formed out of rib bones. There is even one polished animal toe bone that may have been an ornament.

Zone h is the rich stratum that yielded the 14,000-year-old sloth humerus in 1969. The change in tool materials apparent in Zone h1 and the proliferation of new tool types in Zone h suggest that at Flea Cave a second tool complex had taken the place of the earlier Paccaicasa complex. We have named the distinctive assemblage from these two strata the Ayacucho complex.

The stratum immediately overlying Zone h is found in only a few parts of the excavation. It consists of a fine, powdery yellow soil that is neutral in acidity. This sparse formation, labeled Zone h,

has so far yielded only three stone artifacts: a blade, a sidescraper and a large denticulate scraper. The lack of soil acidity suggests that the interval represented by Zone h was characterized by dry grassland vegetation. Further investigation may yield enough artifacts to indicate whether or not the stratum contains a distinctive tool complex suited to the changed environment. For the time being we know too little about Zone h to come to any conclusions.

For the purposes of this discussion the Flea Cave story ends here. Above Zone h at the time our work began was a three-foot layer of fallen rock, including some individual stones that weighed more than three tons. This rock was apparently associated with the much heavier fall in the northern half of the cave. A small stratum above the rock debris, labeled Zone f1, contained charcoal, the bones of modern deer and llamas, and a few well-made bifacial tools (stone tools flaked on both sides). These tools closely resemble tools of known age at Puente, an open-air site near Ayacucho where only the remains of modern animals have been found. On this basis one can conclude that the time of the rockfall at Flea Cave was no later than 10,000 years ago. It is worth mentioning that before any of the strata below the rock layer could be excavated, the rocks had to be

broken up by pickax and carried out of the cave. The three-foot rock stratum was labeled Zone g.

The strata that tell the rest of our story are in a deep deposit in the southeast corner of Pepper Cave. Situated at an altitude of nearly 11,000 feet, this cave is surrounded today by humid scrub forest. It is adjacent to a tributary of the Cachi River, whose bed lies 150 feet below the level of the cave. The bottom stratum of the deep deposit at Pepper Cave consists of stratified sands and gravels close to the top of a high water-built terrace. This fluvial deposit is labeled Zone N. It is overlain by a three-foot layer of rocks that have fallen from the roof of the cave, mixed with stratified sands that indicate a continuation of fluvial terrace building. The mixed stratum comprises zones M and L. Preliminary geological studies suggest that the terrace was formed by outwash from the final advance of the Andean glaciers. There is no evidence of human activity in the three lowest strata at Pepper Cave.

Overlying these sterile layers is a 28-inch stratum of windblown sand and disintegrated volcanic tuff that has been labeled Zone K. Artifacts were found in the upper four inches of the deposit, and a few were also unearthed in one reddish area near the bottom of it. The artifacts represent a new complex of tools that was also found in the next three strata:

floors of human habitation that are labeled in ascending order zones J3, J2 and J1. No animal remains have been recovered from Zone K, but the three J zones contain the bones of horses, of extinct species of deer and possibly of llamas.

The characteristic artifacts of the new tool complex, which we have named Huanta after another town in the valley, include bifacially flaked projectile points with a "fishtail" base, gravers, burins, blades, half-moon-shaped sidescrapers and teardrop-shaped end scrapers. A carbon-14 analysis of one of the animal bones from the uppermost stratum, Zone J1, indicates that the Huanta complex flourished until about 9,500 years ago.

The five strata overlying the Huanta complex at Pepper Cave, like the single layer above the rockfall at Flea Cave, hold remains typical of the Puente complex. These strata have been designated zones J through F. One stratum near the middle, Zone H, is shown by a carbon-14 analysis of charcoal to have been laid down about 9,000 years ago. This date is in good agreement with the known age of material excavated at the Puente site. The contents of the strata above the Puente complex zones at Pepper Cave (zones E through A), like the contents of zones f1 through a at Flea Cave, will not concern us here.

Having reviewed the facts revealed at Ayacucho, let us consider their broader implications. What follows is not only interpretive but also somewhat speculative; it goes well beyond the direct evidence now at our disposal. Stating the implications straightforwardly, however, may serve two useful purposes. First, in doing so we are in effect putting forward hypotheses to be proved or disproved by future findings. Second, in being explicit we help to define the problems that remain to be solved.

Let us first consider the implications of our evidence concerning changes in vegetation and climate. Remains of the Puente complex overlie the sequences of earlier strata at both caves: they are on top of the material of uncertain character at Flea Cave and on top of the Huanta complex at Pepper Cave. To judge from carbon-14 measurements, the earliest appearance of the Puente complex, with its advanced tools and remains of modern animal species, may have been around 9,700 years ago. At about that time, then, the association of early man and extinct animals in this highland area evidently came to an end.

We have not yet completed the soil studies and the analyses of pollens in the soil that will add many details to the record of climate and vegetation. For the time being, however, I tentatively propose that the last of the pre-Puente strata at Flea Cave (Zone *h*) and the sterile zones N through L at Pepper Cave coincide with the last Andean glacial advance. Zone *h* at Flea Cave, with its acid soil and remains of forest animals, appears to represent an earlier "interstadial" period in the glacial record—a breathing spell rather than a full-scale retreat. Zones *h1* and *i*, below Zone *h*, are characterized by the remains of different animals and by soil of neutral acidity, suggesting a colder climate and a glacial advance. Evidence from the still earlier zones *i1* and *j* suggests a second interstadial period of relative warmth. Zone *k*, the lowest in the Flea Cave excavation, apparently represents another period of advancing ice. If the Ayacucho evidence holds true for Andean glacial activity in general, the South American glacial advances and retreats do not coincide with those of the Wisconsin glaciation in North America [*see illustration on this page*]. This apparent lack of correlation presents interesting problems. If glaciation is caused by worldwide climatic change, why are the South American oscillations so unlike the North American ones? If, on the other hand, widespread climatic change is not the cause of glaciation, what is? The precise sequence of Andean glacial advances and retreats obviously calls for further study.

What are the implications of the Aya-cucho findings with respect to early man, not only in South America but also elsewhere in the New World? The results of local studies of the earliest phases of prehistory in South America are all too seldom published, so that the comments that follow are particularly speculative. Having warned the reader, let me suggest that the Paccaicasa complex in the Peruvian central highlands may well represent the earliest stage of man's appearance in South America.

To generalize from Ayacucho material, this earliest stage seems to be characterized by a tool assemblage consisting of large corelike choppers, large sidescrapers and spokeshaves and heavy denticulate implements. This I shall call the Core Tool Tradition; it is certainly represented by the Paccaicasa assemblage in South America and may just possibly be represented in North America by the controversial finds at the Calico site in the Mojave Desert north of Barstow, Calif. In South America the Core Tool Tradition appears to have flourished from about 25,000 years ago to 15,000 years ago.

Man's next stage in South America I call the Flake and Bone Tool Tradition. The only adequate definition of this tradition so far is found in the Ayacucho tool complex. That complex is characterized by a reduction in the proportion of core tools and a sudden abundance of tools made out of flakes: projectile points, knives, sidescrapers, gravers, burins, spokeshaves and denticulate tools.

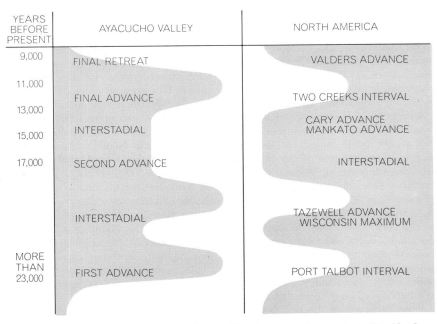

| YEARS BEFORE PRESENT | AYACUCHO VALLEY | NORTH AMERICA |
|---|---|---|
| 9,000 | FINAL RETREAT | VALDERS ADVANCE |
| 11,000 | FINAL ADVANCE | TWO CREEKS INTERVAL |
| 13,000 | | CARY ADVANCE MANKATO ADVANCE |
| 15,000 | INTERSTADIAL | |
| 17,000 | SECOND ADVANCE | INTERSTADIAL |
| | INTERSTADIAL | TAZEWELL ADVANCE WISCONSIN MAXIMUM |
| MORE THAN 23,000 | FIRST ADVANCE | PORT TALBOT INTERVAL |

**PHASE REVERSAL** with respect to the glacial advances and retreats in the Northern Hemisphere during the final period of Pleistocene glaciation appears to characterize the record of fluctuations preserved at Ayacucho. The graph compares estimated Andean advances, retreats and interstadial phases with the phases of the Wisconsin glaciation.

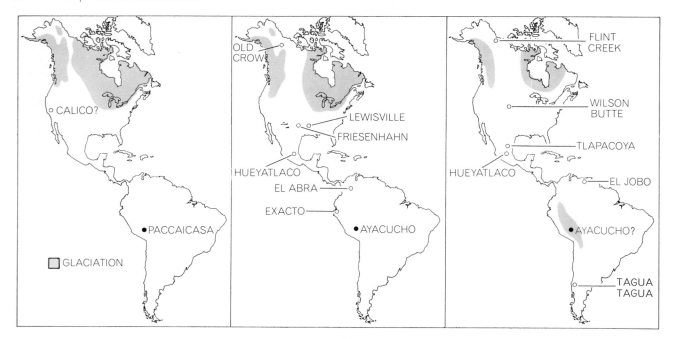

**THREE TRADITIONS** in New World prehistory are the Core Tool Tradition (*left*), the Flake and Bone Tool Tradition (*center*) and the Blade, Burin and Leaf-Point Tradition (*right*). The age of each tradition in North America, in cases where the age of a representative site is known, is substantially greater than it is in South America, suggesting that they stem from earlier Old World roots.

An important element in the tradition is the presence of bone implements, including projectile points, awls and scrapers. The Flake and Bone Tool Tradition apparently flourished from about 15,000 years ago to 13,000 or 12,000 years ago. Elsewhere in South America, although the evidence is scanty, the tradition may be reflected in surface finds attributed to the Exacto complex of coastal Ecuador and in flake tools from the El Abra cave site in highland Colombia; the El Abra material is estimated to be 12,500 years old. Some of the rare worked flakes from the Chivateros "red zone" of coastal central Peru may also represent this tradition [see "Early Man in South America," by Edward P. Lanning and Thomas C. Patterson; SCIENTIFIC AMERICAN, November 1967]. Not all the North American sites that may be representative of the tradition are adequately dated. Where dates are available, however, they are from 10,000 to more than 20,000 years earlier than their South American counterparts.

The third South American stage I call the Blade, Burin and Leaf-Point Tradition. At present it is very poorly represented at our highland sites, consisting only of the three artifacts from Zone *h* at Flea Cave. The tradition is far better defined, however, in the El Jobo phase of Venezuela, where double-ended points, blades, burins and corelike scrapers have been unearthed in association with the bones of extinct animals. The

El Jobo phase is not adequately dated, but estimates suggest that its tool industry flourished roughly between 10,000 and 14,000 years ago. A small amount of material found at Laguna de Tagua Tagua in central Chile may also belong to this third tradition; carbon-14 analysis indicates that the Chilean material is about 11,300 years old. The precise duration of the Blade, Burin and Leaf-Point Tradition is not yet known. My guess is that it flourished from 13,000 or 12,000 years ago until 11,000 or 10,000 years ago. Like the preceding tradition, it is represented at sites in North America that, where age estimates exist, appear to be somewhat older.

Seen from the perspective of the Ayacucho valley, early man's final stage in South America, which I call the Specialized Bifacial Point Tradition, appears to have flourished from 11,000 or 10,000 years ago to 9,000 or 8,000 years ago. At Ayacucho the tradition is defined in the Huanta complex at Pepper Cave and in the later Puente complex there and elsewhere in the valley. It is characterized by bifacially flaked projectile points that evidently represent a specialization for big-game hunting. The tradition's other characteristic implements include specialized end scrapers and knives suited to skinning and butchering. Elsewhere in South America the tradition is represented at Fell's Cave in southern Chile, where a number of carbon-14 determinations suggest ages clustering

around 11,000 years ago. Other artifacts probably in this tradition are those from a stratum overlying the red zone at Chivateros (which are evidently some 10,000 years old), from Toquepala Cave in southernmost Peru (which are about 9,500 years old) and from a number of other South American sites. Sites representative of the Specialized Bifacial Point Tradition in North America are almost too numerous to mention.

What might these four postulated traditions signify concerning man's arrival in the New World from Asia? Considering first the latest tradition—the Specialized Bifacial Point Tradition—we find a bewildering variety of complexes throughout North America at about the time when the late Paleo-Indian stage ends and the Archaic Indian stage begins. Nearly all the complexes have something in common, however: a specialization in bifacially flaked projectile points of extraordinary workmanship. I suggest that these specialized point industries all belong to a single tradition, that for the most part they represent local New World developments and that there is little use in trying to trace them to some ancestral assemblage on the far side of the Bering Strait. Carbon-14 analysis of charcoal from Fort Rock Cave in Oregon indicates that the earliest known specialized projectile points in the New World are some 13,200 years old. On the basis of this finding I propose that the Specialized Bifacial Point Tradition originated in the New World, beginning about 14,000 years ago in North America, and reached South America 3,000 to 4,000 years later.

North American artifacts related to the preceding tradition—the Blade, Burin and Leaf-Point Tradition—in South America include material from Tlapacoya and Hueyatlaco in Mexico, respectively some 23,000 and 22,000 years old, and material at least 15,000 years old from the lower levels of Wilson Butte Cave in Idaho. Some artifacts of the Cordilleran tradition in Canada and Alaska may also be related to the South American tradition. Again there apparently is a lag in cultural transmission from north to south that at its longest approaches 10,000 years. If there was a similar lag in transmission from Asia to North America, it is possible that the Blade, Burin and Leaf-Point Tradition originated with the Malt'a and Buret tool industries of the Lake Baikal region in eastern Siberia, which are between 15,000 and 30,000 years old.

As for the still older Flake and Bone Tool Tradition, adequately dated North American parallels are more difficult to find. Artifacts from Friesenhahn Cave in central Texas and some of the oldest material at Hueyatlaco show similarities to tools in the Ayacucho complex, but in spite of hints that these North American sites are very old the finds cannot be exactly dated. There are bone tools from a site near Old Crow in the Canadian Yukon that carbon-14 analysis shows to be from 23,000 to 28,000 years old. It is my guess that the Yukon artifacts belong to the Flake and Bone Tool Tradition, but many more arctic finds of the same kind are needed to change this guess into a strong presumption. A few flake tools from the site at Lewisville, Tex., may also be representative of the Ayacucho complex. Their estimated age of 38,000 years is appropriate. Figuring backward from the time the tradition appears to have arrived in South America, it would have flourished in North America between 25,000 and 40,000 years ago. Is it not possible that the Flake and Bone Tool Tradition is also an import from Asia? Perhaps it came from some Old World source such as the Shuitungkuo complex of northern China, reportedly between 40,000 and 60,000 years old.

We now come to the most difficult question, which concerns the oldest of the four traditions: the Core Tool Tradition. I wonder if any of my more conservative colleagues would care to venture the flat statement that no Core Tool

Tradition parallel to the one in the Paccaicasa strata at Flea Cave will ever be unearthed in North America? If it is found, is it not likely that it will be from 40,000 to as much as 100,000 years old? To me it seems entirely possible that such a core-tool tradition in the New World, although one can only guess at it today, could be derived from the chopper and chopping-tool tradition of Asia, which is well over 50,000 years old. (An example of such a tradition is the Fenho industry

of China.) I find there is much reason to believe that three of the four oldest cultural traditions in the New World can be derived from specific Old World predecessors. That seems to be the most significant implication of our findings at Ayacucho. However much this conclusion may be modified by future work, one thing is certain: our knowledge of early man in the New World is in its infancy. An almost untouched province of archaeology awaits exploration.

OLD WORLD SOURCES of the three earliest prehistoric traditions in the New World are suggested in this chart. A fourth and more recent tradition, marked by the presence of finely made projectile points for big-game hunting, seems to have been indigenous rather than an Old World import. Although much work will be required to establish the validity of all three proposed relationships, the foremost weakness in the hypothesis at present is a lack in the Northern Hemisphere of well-dated examples of the core-tool tradition.

# 11

# A Paleo-Indian Bison Kill

by Joe Ben Wheat
*January 1967*

*Some 8,500 years ago a group of hunters on the Great Plains stampeded a herd of buffaloes into a gulch and butchered them. The bones of the animals reveal the event in remarkable detail*

When one thinks of American Indians hunting buffaloes, one usually visualizes the hunters pursuing a herd of the animals on horseback and killing them with bow and arrow. Did the Indians hunt buffaloes before the introduction of the horse (by the Spanish conquistadors in the 16th century) and the much earlier introduction of the bow? Indeed they did. As early as 10,000 years ago Paleo-Indians hunted species of bison that are now extinct on foot and with spears. My colleagues and I at the University of Colorado Museum have recently excavated the site of one such Paleo-Indian bison kill dating back to about 6500 B.C. The site so remarkably preserves a moment in time that we know with reasonable certainty not only the month of the year the hunt took place but also such details as the way the wind blew on the day of the kill, the direction of the hunters' drive, the highly organized manner in which they butchered their quarry, their choice of cuts to be eaten on the spot and the probable number of hunters involved.

The bison was the most important game animal in North America for millenniums before its near extermination in the 19th century. When Europeans arrived on the continent, they found herds of bison ranging over vast areas, but the animals were first and foremost inhabitants of the Great Plains, the high, semiarid grassland extending eastward from the foothills of the Rocky Mountains and all the way from Canada to Mexico. Both in historic and in late prehistoric times the bison was the principal economic resource of the Indian tribes that occupied the Great Plains. Its meat, fat and bone marrow provided them with food; its hide furnished them with shelter and clothing;

its brain was used to tan the hide; its horns were fashioned into containers. There was scarcely a part of the animal that was not utilized in some way.

This dependence on big-game hunting probably stretches back to the very beginning of human prehistory in the New World. We do not know when man first arrived in the Americas, nor do we know in detail what cultural baggage he brought with him. The evidence for the presence of man in the New World much before 12,000 years ago is scattered and controversial. It is quite

clear, however, that from then on Paleo-Indian hunting groups, using distinctive kinds of stone projectile point, ranged widely throughout the New World. On the Great Plains the principal game animal of this early period was the Columbian mammoth [see "Elephant-hunting in North America," by C. Vance Haynes, Jr.; SCIENTIFIC AMERICAN, June 1966]. Mammoth remains have been found in association with projectile points that are usually large and leaf-shaped and have short, broad grooves on both sides of the base. These points are typical of the complex

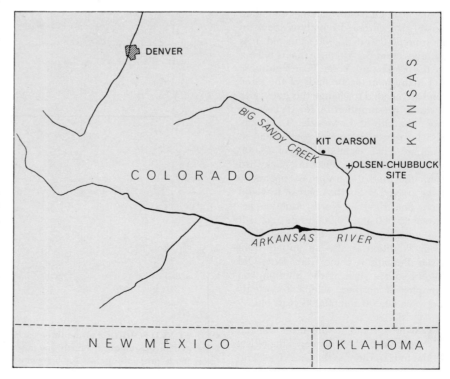

**SITE OF THE KILL** is 140 miles southeast of Denver. It is named the Olsen-Chubbuck site after its discoverers, the amateur archaeologists Sigurd Olsen and Gerald Chubbuck.

of cultural traits named the Clovis complex; the tool kit of this complex also included stone scrapers and knives and some artifacts made of ivory and bone.

The elephant may have been hunted out by 8000 B.C. In any case, its place as a game animal was taken by a large, straight-horned bison known as *Bison antiquus*. The first of the bison-hunters used projectile points of the Folsom culture complex; these are similar to Clovis points but are generally smaller and better made. Various stone scrapers and knives, bone needles and engraved bone ornaments have also been found in Folsom sites.

A millennium later, about 7000 B.C., *Bison antiquus* was supplanted on the Great Plains by the somewhat smaller *Bison occidentalis*. The projectile points found in association with this animal's remains are of several kinds. They differ in shape, size and details of flaking, but they have some characteristics in common. Chief among them is the technical excellence of the flaking. The flake scars meet at the center of the blade to form a ridge; sometimes they give the impression that a single flake has been detached across the entire width of the blade [*see the illustration on page 114*]. Some of the projectile points that belong to this tradition, which take their names from the sites where they were first found, are called Milnesand, Scottsbluff and Eden points. The last two kinds of point form part of what is called the Cody complex, for which there is a fairly reliable carbon-14 date of about 6500 B.C.

Paleo-Indian archaeological sites fall into two categories: habitations and kill sites. Much of our knowledge of the early inhabitants of the Great Plains comes from the kill sites, where are found not only the bones of the animals but also the projectile points used to kill them and the knives, scrapers and other tools used to butcher and otherwise process them. Such sites have yielded much information about the categories of projectile points and how these categories are related in time. Heretofore, however, they have contributed little to our understanding of how the early hunters actually lived. The kill site I shall describe is one of those rare archaeological sites where the evidence is so complete that the people who left it seem almost to come to life.

Sixteen miles southeast of the town of Kit Carson in southeastern Colorado, just below the northern edge of the broad valley of the Arkansas River, lies a small valley near the crest of a low divide. The climate here is semiarid; short bunchgrass is the main vegetation and drought conditions have prevailed since the mid-1950's. In late 1957 wind erosion exposed what appeared to be five separate piles of bones, aligned in an east-west direction. Gerald Chubbuck, a keen amateur archaeologist, came on the bones in December, 1957; among them he found several projectile points of the Scottsbluff type. Chubbuck notified the University of Colorado Museum of his find, and we made plans to visit the site at the first opportunity.

Meanwhile Chubbuck and another amateur archaeologist, Sigurd Olsen, continued to collect at the site and ultimately excavated nearly a third of it. In the late spring of 1958 the museum secured permission from the two discoverers and from Paul Forward, the owner of the land, to complete the excavation. We carried out this work on summer expeditions in 1958 and 1960.

The Olsen-Chubbuck site consists of a continuous bed of bones lying within the confines of a small arroyo, or dry gulch. The arroyo, which had long since been buried, originally rose near the southern end of the valley and followed a gently undulating course eastward through a ridge that forms the valley's eastern edge. The section of the arroyo that we excavated was some 200 feet long. Its narrow western end was only about a foot and a half in depth and the same in width, but it grew progressively deeper and wider to the east. Halfway down the arroyo its width was five feet and its depth six; at the point to the east where our excavation stopped it was some 12 feet wide and seven feet deep. At the bottom of the

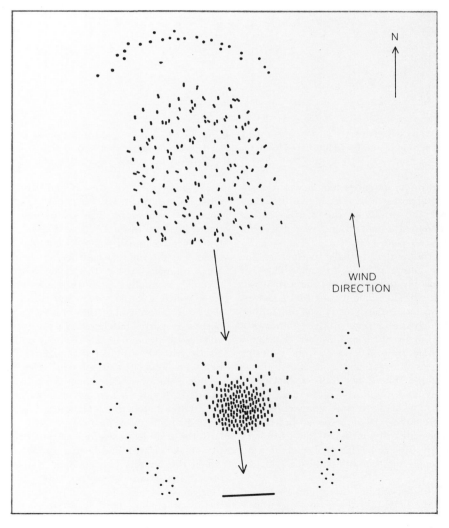

**BISON STAMPEDE** was probably set off by the Paleo-Indian hunters' close approach to the grazing herd from downwind. Projectile points found among the bones of the animals at the eastern end of the arroyo (*bottom*) suggest that some hunters kept the bison from veering eastward to escape. Other hunters probably did the same at the western end of the arroyo.

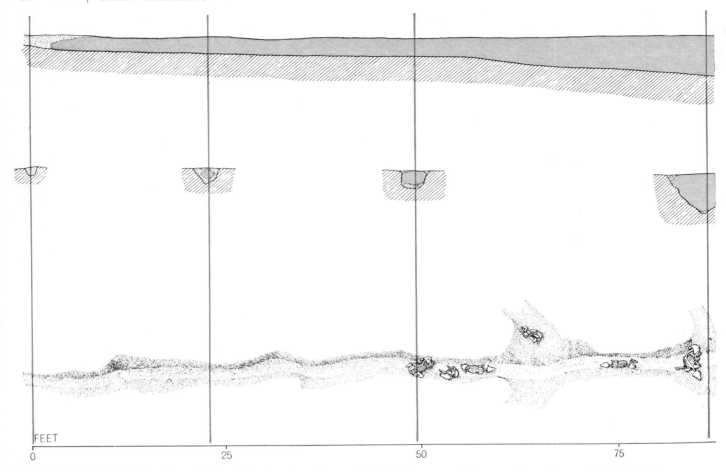

0                          25                          50                          75

**SECTION AND PLAN** of the Olsen-Chubbuck site show how the remains of the dead and butchered bison formed a deposit of bones that lined the center of the arroyo for a distance of 170 feet (*color at top*). One part of the site had been excavated by its discoverers

arroyo for its entire length was a channel about a foot wide; above the channel the walls of the arroyo had a V-shaped cross section [*see top illustration on page 115*].

Today the drainage pattern of the site runs from north to south. This was probably the case when the arroyo was formed, and since it runs east and west it seems certain that it was not formed by stream action. Early frontiersmen on the Great Plains observed that many buffalo trails led away from watering places at right angles to the drainage pattern. Where such trails crossed ridges they were frequently quite deep; moreover, when they were abandoned they were often further deepened by erosion. The similarity of the Olsen-Chubbuck arroyo to such historical buffalo trails strongly suggests an identical origin.

The deposit of bison bones that filled the bottom of the arroyo was a little more than 170 feet long. It consisted of the remains of nearly 200 buffaloes of the species *Bison occidentalis*. Chubbuck and Olsen unearthed the bones of an estimated 50 of the animals; the museum's excavations uncovered the bones of 143 more. The bones were found in three distinct layers. The bottom layer contained some 13 complete skeletons; the hunters had not touched these animals. Above this layer were several essentially complete skeletons from which a leg or two, some ribs or the skull were missing; these bison had been only partly butchered. In the top layer were numerous single bones and also nearly 500 articulated segments of buffalo skeleton. The way in which these segments and the single bones were distributed provides a number of clues to the hunters' butchering techniques.

As the contents of the arroyo—particularly the complete skeletons at the bottom—make clear, it had been a trap into which the hunters had stampeded the bison. Bison are gregarious animals. They move in herds in search of forage; the usual grazing herd is between 50 and 300 animals. Bison have a keen sense of smell but relatively poor vision. Hunters can thus get very close to a herd as long as they stay down-wind and largely out of sight. When the bison are frightened, the herd has a tendency to close ranks and stampede in a single mass. If the herd encounters an abrupt declivity such as the Olsen-Chubbuck arroyo, the animals in front cannot stop because they are pushed by those behind. They can only plunge into the arroyo, where they are immobilized, disabled or killed by the animals that fall on top of them.

The orientation of the skeletons in the middle and lower layers of the Olsen-Chubbuck site is evidence that the Paleo-Indian hunters had initiated such a stampede. Almost without exception the complete or nearly complete skeletons overlie or are overlain by the skeletons of one, two or even three other whole or nearly whole animals; the bones are massed and the skeletons are contorted. The first animals that fell into the arroyo had no chance to escape; those behind them wedged them tighter into the arroyo with their struggles. Many of the skeletons are sharply twisted around the axis of the spinal column. Three spanned the arroyo, deformed into

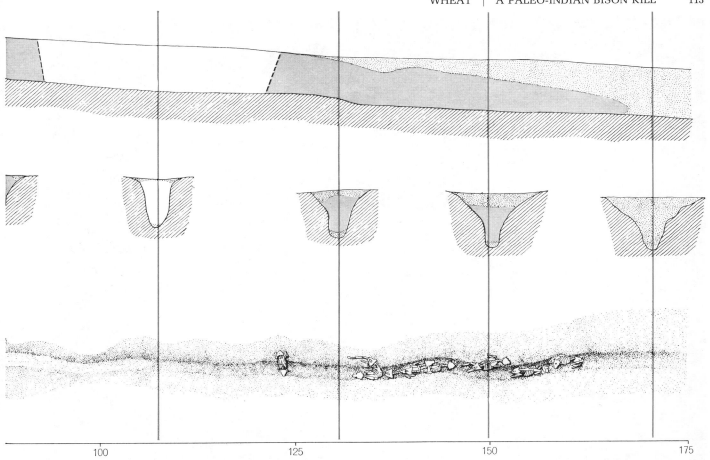

100    125    150    175

before the author and his associates began work in 1958; this area is represented by the 20-foot gap in the deposit. The shallow inner channel at the bottom of the arroyo can be seen in the plan view (*bottom*); outlines show the locations of 13 intact bison skeletons.

an unnatural U shape. Ten bison were pinned in position with their heads down and their hindquarters up; an equal number had landed with hindquarters down and heads up. At the bottom of the arroyo two skeletons lie on their backs.

The stampeding bison were almost certainly running in a north-south direction, at right angles to the arroyo. Of the 39 whole or nearly whole skeletons, which may be assumed to lie in the positions in which the animals died, not one faces north, northeast or northwest. A few skeletons, confined in the arroyo's narrow inner channel, face due east or west, but all 21 animals whose position at the time of death was not affected in this manner faced southeast, south or southwest. The direction in which the bison stampeded provides a strong clue to the way the wind was blowing on the day of the hunt. The hunters would surely have approached their quarry from downwind; thus the wind must have been from the south.

We have only meager evidence of the extent to which the stampede, once started, was directed and controlled by the hunters. The projectile points found with the bison skeletons in the deepest, most easterly part of the arroyo suggest that a flanking party of hunters was stationed there. It also seems a reasonable inference that, if no hunters had covered the stampede's western flank, the herd could have escaped unscathed around the head of the arroyo. If other hunters pursued the herd from the rear, there is no evidence of it.

Even if the hunters merely started the stampede and did not control it thereafter, it sufficed to kill almost 200 animals in a matter of minutes. The total was 46 adult bulls and 27 immature ones, 63 adult and 38 immature cows and 16 calves. From the fact that the bones include those of calves only a few days old, and from what we know about the breeding season of bison, we can confidently place the date of the kill as being late in May or early in June.

As we excavated the bone deposit we first uncovered the upper layer containing the single bones and articulated segments of skeleton. It was soon apparent that these bones were the end result of a standardized Paleo-Indian butchering procedure. We came to recognize certain "butchering units" such as forelegs, pelvic girdles, hind legs, spinal columns and skulls. Units of the same kind were usually found together in groups numbering from two or three to as many as 27. Similar units also formed distinct vertical sequences. As the hunters had removed the meat from the various units they had discarded the bones in separate piles, each of which contained the remains of a number of individual animals. In all we excavated nine such piles.

Where the order of deposition was clear, the bones at the bottom of each pile were foreleg units. Above these bones were those of pelvic-girdle units. Sometimes one or both hind legs were attached to the pelvic girdle, but by and large the hind-leg units lay separately among or above the pelvic units. The next level was usually composed of spinal-column units. The ribs had been removed from many of the chest vertebrae, but ribs were still attached to some of the other vertebrae. At the top

114

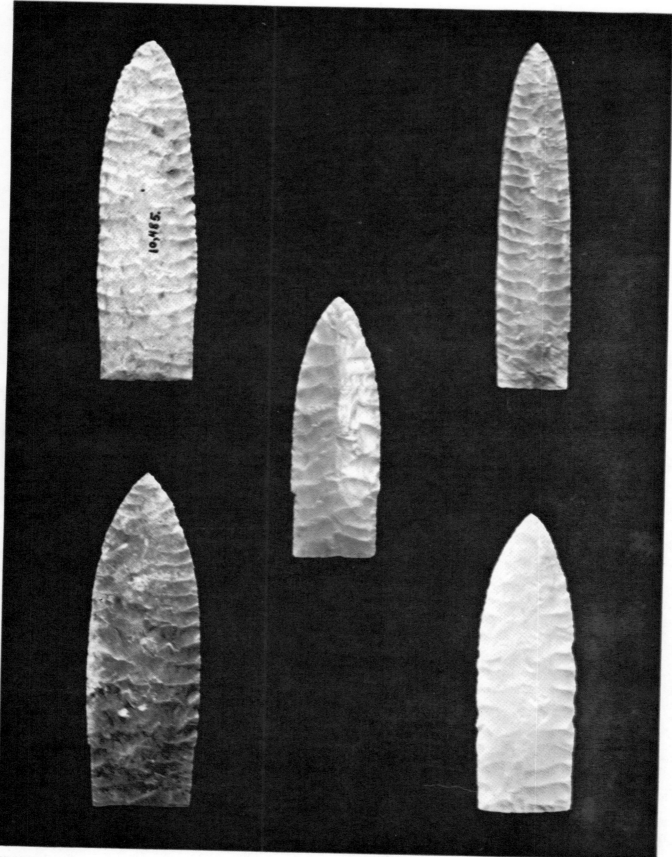

**PROJECTILE POINTS** found at the site show a surprising divergence of form in view of the fact that all of them were used simultaneously by a single group. In the center is a point of the Scottsbluff type. At top left is another Scottsbluff point that shows some of the characteristics of a point of the Eden type at top right. At bottom left is a third Scottsbluff point; it has characteristics in common with a point of the Milnesand type at bottom right. Regardless of form, all the points are equally excellent in flaking.

of nearly every pile were skulls. The jawbones had been removed from most of them, but some still retained a few of the neck vertebrae. In some instances these vertebrae had been pulled forward over the top and down the front of the skull. When the skull still had its jawbone, the hyoid bone of the tongue was missing.

Like the various butchering units, the single bones were found in clusters of the same skeletal part: shoulder blades, upper-foreleg bones, upper-hind-leg bones or jawbones (all broken in two at the front). Nearly all the jawbones were found near the top of the bone deposit. The tongue bones, on the other hand, were distributed throughout the bed. About 75 percent of the single foreleg bones were found in the upper part of the deposit, as were nearly 70 percent of the single vertebrae. Only 60 percent of the shoulder blades and scarcely half of the single ribs were in the upper level.

The hunters' first task had evidently been to get the bison carcasses into a position where they could be cut up. This meant that the animals had to be lifted, pulled, rolled or otherwise moved out of the arroyo to some flat area. It seems to have been impossible to remove the bison that lay at the bottom of the arroyo; perhaps they were too tightly wedged together. Some of them had been left untouched and others had had only a few accessible parts removed. The way in which the butchering units were grouped suggests that several bison were moved into position and cut up simultaneously. Since foreleg units, sometimes in pairs, were found at the bottom of each pile of bones it seems reasonable to assume that the Paleo-Indians followed the same initial steps in butchering that the Plains Indians did in recent times. The first step was to arrange the legs of the animal so that it could be rolled onto its belly. The skin was then cut down the back and pulled down on both sides of the carcass to form a kind of mat on which the meat could be placed. Directly under the skin of the back was a layer of tender meat, the "blanket of flesh"; when this was stripped away, the bison's forelegs and shoulder blades could be cut free, exposing the highly prized "hump" meat, the rib cage and the body cavity.

Having stripped the front legs of meat, the hunters threw the still-articulated bones into the arroyo. If they followed the practice of later Indians, they would next have indulged themselves

EXCAVATION at the eastern end of the arroyo reveals its V-shaped cross section and the layers of sand and silt that later filled it. The bone deposit ended at this point; a single bison shoulder blade remains in place at the level where it was unearthed (*lower center*).

BISON SKULL AND STONE POINT lie in close association at one level in the site. The projectile point (*lower left*) is of the Scottsbluff type. The bison skull, labeled *4-F* to record its position among the other bones, rests upside down where the hunters threw it.

BONES OF BISON unearthed at the Olsen-Chubbuck site lie in a long row down the center of the ancient arroyo the Paleo-Indian hunters utilized as a pitfall for the stampeding herd. The bones proved to be the remains of bulls, cows and calves of the extinct species *Bison occidentalis*. Separate piles made up of the same types of bones (for example sets of limb bones, pelvic girdles or skulls) showed that the hunters had butchered several bison at a time and had systematically dumped the bones into the arroyo in the same order in which they were removed from the carcasses. In the foreground is a pile of skulls that was built up in this way.

by cutting into the body cavity, removing some of the internal organs and eating them raw. This, of course, would have left no evidence among the bones. What is certain is that the hunters did remove and eat the tongues of a few bison at this stage of the butchering, presumably in the same way the Plains Indians did: by slitting the throat, pulling the tongue out through the slit and cutting it off. Our evidence for their having eaten the tongues as they went along is that the tongue bones are found throughout the deposit instead of in one layer or another.

The bison's rib cages were attacked as soon as they were exposed by the removal of the overlying meat. Many of the ribs were broken off near the spine. The Plains Indians used as a hammer for this purpose a bison leg bone with the hoof still attached; perhaps the Paleo-Indians did the same. In any case, the next step was to sever the spine at a point behind the rib cage and remove the hindquarters. The meat was cut away from the pelvis (and in some instances simultaneously from the hind legs) and the pelvic girdle was discarded. If the hind legs had been separated from the pelvis, it was now their turn to be stripped of meat and discarded.

After the bison's hindquarters had been butchered, the neck and skull were cut off as a unit—usually at a point just in front of the rib cage—and set aside. Then the spine was discarded, presumably after it had been completely stripped of meat and sinew. Next the hunters turned to the neck and skull and cut the neck meat away. This is evident from the skulls that had vertebrae draped over the front; this would not have been possible if the neck meat had been in place. The Plains Indians found bison neck meat too tough to eat in its original state. They dried it and made the dried strips into pemmican by pounding them to a powder. The fact that the Paleo-Indians cut off the neck meat strongly suggests that they too preserved some of their kill.

If the tongue had not already been removed, the jawbone was now cut away, broken at the front and the tongue cut out. The horns were broken from a few skulls, but there is little evidence that the Paleo-Indians broke open the skull as the Plains Indians did to take out the brain. Perhaps the most striking difference between the butchering practices of these earlier Indians and those of later ones, however, lies in the high degree of organization displayed by the Paleo-Indians. Historical accounts of butchering by Plains Indians indicate no such efficient system.

In all, 47 artifacts were found in association with the bones at the Olsen-Chubbuck site. Spherical hammerstones and knives give us some idea of what constituted the hunter's tool kit; stone scrapers suggest that the bison's skins were processed at the site. A bone pin and a piece of the brown rock limonite that shows signs of having been rubbed tell something about Paleo-Indian ornamentation.

The bulk of the artifacts at the site are projectile points. There are 27 of them, and they are particularly significant. Most of them are of the Scottsbluff type. When their range of variation is considered, however, they merge gradually at one end of the curve of variation into Eden points and at the other end into Milnesand points. Moreover, among the projectile points found at the site are one Eden point and a number of Milnesand points. The diversity of the points clearly demonstrates the range of variation that was possible among the weapons of a single hunting group. Their occurrence together at the site is conclusive proof that such divergent forms of weapon could exist contemporaneously.

How many Paleo-Indians were pres-

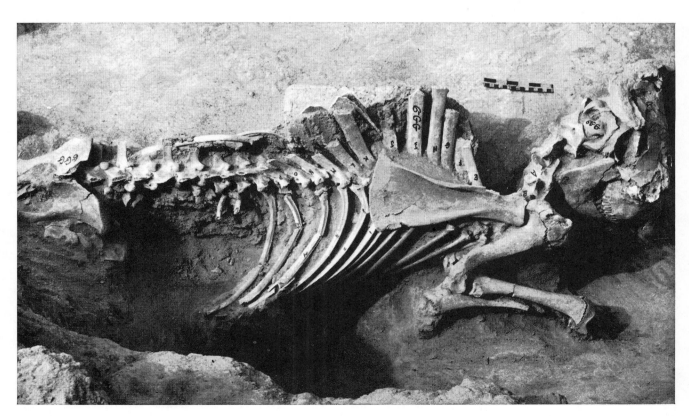

**INTACT SKELETON** of an immature bison cow, uncovered in the lowest level of the arroyo, is one of 13 animals the Paleo-Indian hunters left untouched. The direction in which many bison faced suggests that the stampede traveled from north to south.

ent at the kill? The answer to this question need not be completely conjectural. We can start with what we know about the consumption of bison meat by Plains Indians. During a feast a man could consume from 10 to 20 pounds of fresh meat a day; women and children obviously ate less. The Plains Indians also preserved bison meat by drying it; 100 pounds of fresh meat would provide 20 pounds of dried meat. A bison bull of today yields about 550 pounds of edible meat; cows average 400 pounds. For an immature bull one can allow 165 pounds of edible meat, for an immature cow 110 pounds and for a calf 50 pounds. About 75 percent of the bison killed at the Olsen-Chubbuck site were completely butchered; on this basis the total weight of bison meat would have been 45,300 pounds. The *Bison occidentalis* killed by the Paleo-Indian hunters, however, was considerably larger than the *Bison bison* of modern times. To compensate for the difference it seems reasonable to add 25 percent to the weight estimate, bringing it to a total of 56,640 pounds. To this total should be added some 4,000 pounds of edible internal organs and 5,400 pounds of fat.

A Plains Indian could completely butcher a bison in about an hour. If we allow one and a half hours for the dissection of the larger species, the butchering at the Olsen-Chubbuck site would have occupied about 210 man-hours. In other words, 100 people could easily have done the job in half a day.

To carry the analysis further additional assumptions are needed. How long does fresh buffalo meat last? The experience of the Plains Indians (depending, of course, on weather conditions) was that it could be eaten for about a month. Let us now assume that half of the total weight of the Olsen-Chubbuck kill was eaten fresh at an average rate of 10 pounds per person per day, and that the other half was preserved. Such a division would provide enough fresh meat and fat to feed 150 people for 23 days. It seems reasonable to assume that the Paleo-Indian band was about this size. One way to test this assumption is to calculate the load each person would have to carry when camp was broken.

The preserved meat and fat, together with the hides, would have weighed about 7,350 pounds, which represents a burden of 49 pounds for each man, woman and child in the group (in addition to the weight of whatever other necessities they carried). Plains Indians are known to have borne loads as great as 100 pounds. Taking into account the likeli-

hood that small children and active hunters would have carried smaller loads, a 49-pound average appears to be just within the range of possibility.

A band of 150 people could, however, have eaten two-thirds of the kill fresh and preserved only one-third. In that case the fresh meat would have fed them for somewhat more than a month. At the end the meat would have been rather gamy, but the load of preserved meat per person would have been reduced to the more reasonable average of 31 pounds.

One possibility I have left out is that the Paleo-Indians had dogs. If there were dogs available to eat their share of fresh meat and to carry loads of preserved meat, the number of people in the group may have been somewhat less. In the absence of dogs, however, it seems improbable that any fewer than 150 people could have made use of the bison killed at the Olsen-Chubbuck site to the degree that has been revealed by our excavations. Whether or not the group had dogs, the remains of its stay at the site are unmistakable evidence that hunting bands of considerable size and impressive social organization were supporting themselves on the Great Plains some 8,500 years ago.

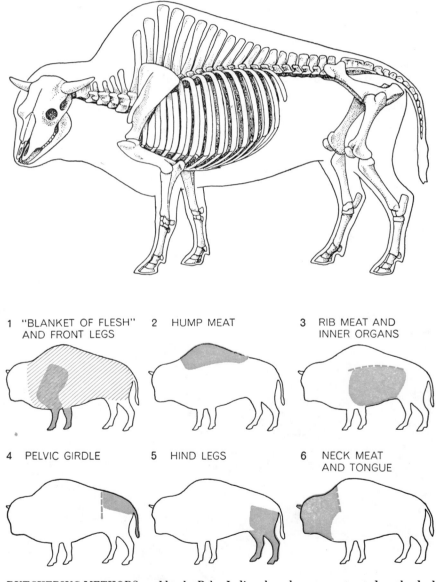

BUTCHERING METHODS used by the Paleo-Indians have been reconstructed on the dual basis of bone stratification at the Olsen-Chubbuck site and the practices of the Plains Indians in recent times. Once the carcass of the bison (*skeleton at top*) had been propped up and skinned down the back, a series of "butchering units" probably were removed in the order shown on the numbered outline figures. The hunters ate as they worked.

# FARMERS AND PEASANTS

# FARMERS AND PEASANTS III

## INTRODUCTION

Agriculture is not to be looked on as a difficult or out-of-the-way invention," wrote the great anthropologist Sir Edward Tylor a century ago. He went on to remark that anyone familiar with food plants knows the secrets of germination. The theory of evolution had a pervasive effect on Victorian thinking, leading people to conceive of human development in terms of universal evolutionary stages. Cultural evolutionary schemes were formulated which envisaged the earliest societies as being based on hunting and gathering. A later stage saw humankind engaged in agriculture or pastoralism. Permanent village settlement, craft specialization, social stratification, and metallurgy were inevitable consequences that led to urban civilization and, ultimately, Western culture and Victorian imperialism. These entirely speculative hypotheses about human development were not tested by much fieldwork until about forty years ago. They owed their most sophisticated and thorough development to V. Gordon Childe, a British archaeologist working in Europe and the Near East.

Childe formulated two great human revolutions, a Neolithic and an Urban Revolution. The Neolithic Revolution took place, so Childe felt, in a period of major climate change at the end of the Pleistocene epoch. With the retreat of the Pleistocene ice sheets, he speculated, the abundant rains that had watered the more temperate Near East shifted northward and widespread desiccation occurred. Both animals and humans moved into basin areas along rivers and new lakes, where the enforced concentrations of animals, plants, and humans in close association ultimately led to the domestication of plants and animals. Childe thought that this Revolution took place about 5000 B.C.

The concept of a Neolithic Revolution has been tested extensively by fieldwork in recent years. Robert J. Braidwood of the University of Chicago excavated at Jarmo and other sites in the Zagros Mountains area of the Near East and found no evidence for catastrophic climatic change. Instead, he saw the economic change as resulting from "ever increasing cultural differentiation and specialization of human communities." In other words, the human capacity for experimentation and receptiveness to change made it possible for domestication to take place. Soon both Braidwood at Jarmo and Kathleen Kenyon at Jericho were finding evidence of early agriculture that in one instance dated back at least 2,500 years before Childe's estimate.

Today, the story of the origins of food production is recognized as being far more complex than either Braidwood or Childe originally suspected: there was not just one locality for the beginnings of agriculture, and early sites such as Jarmo or Jericho are far from unique. The site of Çayönu in Turkey, described by Çambel and Braidwood in their article, "An Early Farming Village in Turkey," is one example. By the time the Çayönu mound was occupied, the inhabitants of the area had domesticated dogs, pigs, sheep, and probably goats, and were cultivating a simple form of wheat, all of this in the eighth millennium B.C. Çayönu is probably typical of many such early farming settlements in the Near East. These small communities were thoroughly familiar with the basic techniques of food production, which had probably evolved during several thousands of years of gradual experimentation with the new techniques, during which time the experimentors still relied heavily on hunting and wild vegetable foods for their diet. The origins of food production do not revolve around the acts of a single genius who had the brilliant idea of planting local grains. Indeed, as American archaeologist Kent Flannery has pointed out, "It is vain to hope for the discovery of the first domestic corn cob, the first pottery vessel, the first hieroglyphic, or the first site where several other major breakthroughs occurred." Flannery urged his colleagues to search for the *causes* of the shift, the numerous and complex interactive factors that caused humankind to make a radical shift in its food-getting strategies. The study of these processes involves large-scale field research, which combines the work of the archaeologist with that of botanists to look at plant remains, zoologists who work on animal bones, and many other specialists studying everything from seashells to metals. Recent investigations have concentrated on three major areas of concern: the nature of the environment where the experimentation that led to agriculture took place; the demographic stresses involved; and the level and type of technology involved in the shift. In other words, people are trying to explain the Neolithic Revolution rather than prove it existed.

The hunters and gatherers of earlier prehistory lived for the most part in small bands, isolated one from another for much of the year, their hunting territory restricted by its carrying capacity and the food resources available within it. Few hunting bands were aware of other peoples living far from their own territory. They were almost entirely self-sufficient in raw materials and foodstuffs, although there are instances, in Australia and elsewhere, of seashells and other ornaments being passed on over long distances. The contacts of early farming villages, however, extended over much wider territory, and in later millennia the first cities developed highly complex trading networks in finished articles, foodstuffs, and raw materials. As is described in the article, "Obsidian and the Origins of Trade," by Dixon, Cann, and Renfrew, one of the most prized materials for early farmers was obsidian, a volcanic glass much valued for its properties in toolmaking and for ornaments. None had suspected how widespread the trade in obsidian had been until a group of archaeologists started examining the trace elements in obsidian from different volcanic deposits. Fortunately, the obsidian from each locality has different trace elements. As many natural sources of the obsidian as possible were identified first, and it was found that no Near Eastern village between northern Iran and Ethiopia was close to an obsidian outcrop. Thus, all obsidian supplied had to be imported. By using spectrographic analysis of the distinctive trace elements in fragments of obsidian found in dozens of sites, the research team was able to show that a widespread obsidian trade had started up around 8,000 B.C. The amount of obsidian traded falls off with geographic distance from the sources, which were located mainly in Anatolia and Armenia. Trade routes connected the villages in a complex network of communications that crossed mountains, deserts, and water. Other commodities than obsidian—salt among them—must have passed between widely scattered village settlements. Without doubt, extensive trading contacts throughout the Near East were a major factor in the development of agricultural economies.

As described in James Mellaart's "A Neolithic City in Turkey," Çatal Hüyük provides an example of the cultural achievement of early farmers. Childe would have been amazed at the cultural diversity of what he called the Neolithic Revolution. The earliest of the great walls of Jericho were built by Stone Age farmers in the seventh millennium B.C. Çatal Hüyük was a sizable town, if not the city that Mellaart would have us call it. It possessed elaborate architecture, a fine religious art, and distinctive fertility-cult shrines. The prosperity of the settlement was based on more efficient agriculture and skillful arts and crafts stimulated by an extensive trade in obsidian, unlimited supplies of which lie within 50 miles of the town. The economy of Çatal Hüyük was based on local agriculture and sheep (and, later, cattle) throughout the town's long prosperity during the seventh millennium B.C. The site gives us a unique insight into the fascinating complexity of early farming life in Turkey only a few millennia after the beginnings of agriculture.

The origins of food production in temperate Europe have been the subject of intensive research for decades. V. Gordon Childe thought that European agriculture originated in the Near East, because the potentially domesticable cultigens of wheat, barley, and other crops were not to be found in their wild state in Europe. No one has yet challenged his basic hypothesis about the origins of agriculture, although the date of early agriculture in Europe is now placed as early as 6000 B.C., a full three millennia earlier than Childe's most optimistic guess.

Nea Nikomedeia in Macedonia is an interesting example of an agricultural village of 8,000 years ago. American archaeologist Robert Rodden, whose article, "An Early Neolithic Village in Greece," appears here, found the low mound in northern Greece in 1960. Unlike Çatal Hüyük, Nea Nikomedeia was a small village of square houses situated five to ten yards apart at the edge of a marshy lake. The village—and there were two phases of occupation—was surrounded by a wall or ditch. The houses were built of timber, with walls of clay and saplings or reeds. Thatched roofs were probably in use. The economy of Nea Nikomedeia rested on wheat and barley, as well as on sheep and goats. Simple bows and arrows, and stone axes and adzes, were in use. Pottery vessels were impressed with fingernail decoration or were painted in red colors. Nea Nikomedeia lies at the gateway of Europe, and its material culture shows signs of cultural contacts with both temperate latitudes and the Near East. The village architecture is no longer of the Near Eastern courtyard type, in which houses were built one against another. It is now adapted to a European climate, where wet and chilly winters are commonplace and timber is more widely used.

For years scientists assumed that the origins of agriculture were to be found in the Near East. So many early farming villages were discovered in that region that it seemed very unlikely that any earlier centers of food production would be found. Agriculture and animal domestication were thought of as having a single origin in the Old World, with the new techniques spreading outward to all parts of Africa, Asia, and Europe. Although a few geographers, like Carl O. Sauer, had long argued that root crops would have been domesticated at an early date in Southeast Asia, there was no archaeological evidence to support this speculation. Chester Gorman of the University of Hawaii has provided the first possible evidence that contradicts the traditional view of Old World agriculture. His excavations at Spirit Cave in the Thai highlands have yielded traces of intensive gathering of wild vegetable foods at least 2,000 years before agriculture began in the Near East. There is but a short step from intensive exploitation of wild foods to incipient agriculture and experimentation with root crops. Wilhelm Solheim, a pioneer in Southeast Asian archaeology, feels that Gorman has found evidence for agriculture, and in his article, "An Earlier Agricultural Revolution," he describes the Spirit Cave finds and evidence for early metallurgy at a lowland site named Non Nok Tha. Both the Near Eastern and the Asian evidence seem to support a multiple origin for agriculture, in various parts of the world where vegetable foods and potential domesticates are abundant. Much of the controversy surrounding early agriculture revolves around various mechanisms that were needed to set early agriculture in motion.

New World agriculture is distinctively American. The domesticated crops grown in the New World were developed from native American cultigens like maize, manioc, sweet and white potatoes, and chili peppers. Tobacco, amaranth, and gourds were in common use. There were few domesticated animals in the Americas except the llama of the Andes, guinea pigs, and dogs. Load-carrying, plowing, and riding animals like the ox or horse were unknown. The gradual transition from hunting and gathering to agriculture is best documented from Robert MacNeish's important excavations in the Tehuacán Valley in the northern highlands of Mexico, as discussed in his article, "The Origins of New World Civilization."

As in the Old World, the major American crops were developed as a result of prolonged experimentation and selective breeding of wild cultigens. Tehuacán is a desert valley, where preservation conditions for seeds and other vegetal materials were exceptionally fine. The rockshelters and open sites of the valley have yielded a cultural sequence extending over 12,000 years of prehistory, beginning in about 10,000 B.C. The small cave of Coxcatlán contained 28 occupation levels, the earliest of which, dating to about 10,000 B.C., contained the seeds of wild vegetable foods and the bones of small animals and birds. These "Ajuerado" people were relying heavily on intensive exploitation of vegetable foods. After 7200 B.C., plant foods were even more important, and the "El Riego" folk, who succeeded their "Ajuerado" predecessors, camped throughout the valley during the dry season, gathering and collecting a whole range of vegetable foods, including squashes, chili peppers, and avocados, some of which may have been cultivated. Between 5200 and 3400 B.C. the people of the succeeding Coxcatlán phase were cultivating a long list of plants, including maize, amaranth, bean, squashes, and chilis. But only about 10 per cent of the diet came from cultivated plants. The rest was derived from intensive collecting. The maize cobs from the Coxcatlán levels are small, and are said to recall the hypothetical wild ancestor of maize, which has never been seen in the wild. Some authorities believe that the wild prototype was a plant named *teosinte*, but the evidence is controversial. After 3000 B.C. agriculture was well-established in the Tehuacán Valley. The history of experimentation and selective breeding of crops in this valley was doubtless repeated at many other localities in Mesoamerica as the new economies were adopted by people accustomed to intensive exploitation of vegetable foods. But, for now, Tehuacán presents us with the most complete history of the development of prehistoric agriculture known anywhere in the world.

# An Early Farming Village in Turkey

by Halet Çambel and Robert J. Braidwood
*March 1970*

*Çayönü Tepesi, a site in a little-studied part of Asia Minor, adds to the growing record of man's agricultural origins. Also revealed there is the earliest evidence of man's use of metal*

When and where did men first turn to farming and animal husbandry as a way of life? This question has increasingly come to occupy the attention of archaeologists in recent years. The first direct attempt to discover just when in human prehistory farming villages appeared was made in the Near East a little more than 20 years ago when a party from the Oriental Institute of the University of Chicago began digging at Jarmo in the foothills of the Zagros Mountains in northeastern Iraq. Today scores of such investigations are in progress in several parts of the Old World and the New World. In the Near East alone the area of interest has grown until it stretches from Turkestan and the Indus valley on the east to the Aegean and the Balkans on the west. This article concerns one Near Eastern investigation that has opened up a new area and has by chance brought to light the earliest evidence of man's use of metal.

Field results in the years since Jarmo allow a few broad generalizations about the dawn of cultivation and animal husbandry. We now know that somewhat earlier than 7500 B.C. people in some parts of the Near East had reached a level of cultural development marked by the production, as opposed to the mere collection, of plant and animal foodstuffs and by a pattern of residence in farming villages. It is not clear, however, when this level of development became characteristic of the region as a whole. Nor do we yet have a good understanding of conditions in the period immediately preceding. The reason is largely that few sites of this earlier period have yet been excavated, and that during the earliest phases of their manipulation the wild plants and animals would not yet possess features indicat-

ing that they were on the way to domestication. Moreover, even the most painstaking excavation may fail to turn up materials that constitute *primary* evidence for domestication, that is, the physical remains of the plants and animals in question. Fragments of plant material and bone—the objects that could tell us exactly which of a number of possible organisms were then in the process of domestication—are often completely missing from village sites.

What should be said of villages that yield plant and animal material that we cannot positively identify as being the remains of domesticated forms? Until recently we tended to believe that if

such sites had every appearance of being permanently settled, and if their inventory of artifacts included flint "sickle" blades, querns (milling stones), storage pits and similar features, then they probably represented the next-earliest level of cultural development; we called it the level of incipient cultivation and animal husbandry. Over the years, however, it has become increasingly probable that early village-like communities of a somewhat different kind may also have existed in the Near East. At these sites the food supply tends at first to include plant and animal forms that were not subsequently domesticated. In other words, even though such items as flint sickles,

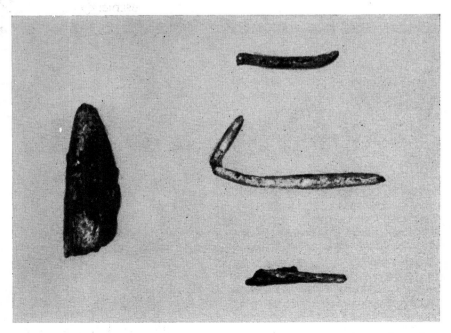

**EVIDENCE OF METALWORKING** at Çayönü Tepesi includes four objects, shown here twice actual size. At left is the point of a reamer, formed from a lump of native copper by hammering. Beside it are two copper pin fragments and a whole pin that has been bent. The pinpoints have been formed by abrasion. A source of native copper lies quite near the site.

querns and the like appear in their inventories, and the architectural traces of their settlement suggest some degree of permanence, it looks as if we are dealing here with villagers living on a level of intensive collection of wild foods alone. Our older notion that villages had to mean farmers has gone by the board.

A prime example of such a non-food-producing community is the village-like site of Mallaha, in northern Israel. The excavator of Mallaha, Jean Perrot of the French Archaeological Mission in Israel, was the first to suggest that when other sites of a similar nature were unearthed, they too might lack any evidence of food production. Mallaha was inhabited about 9000 B.C. The village site of Mureybet, on the middle reaches of the Euphrates in Syria, is somewhat later, say about 8250 B.C. Mureybet, which was excavated by Maurits N. van Loon for the Oriental Institute in 1964 and 1965, also shows no trace of food production. An even later example is the "hunters' village" of Suberde in Turkey, excavated by Jacques Bordaz of the University of Montreal in 1964 and 1965 [see "A Hunters' Village in Neolithic Turkey," by Dexter Perkins, Jr., and Patricia Daly; SCIENTIFIC AMERICAN, November 1968]. As late as 6500 B.C. the people of Suberde fed themselves mainly by killing large numbers of wild sheep and wild cattle.

In very rough outline the available evidence now suggests that both the level of incipient cultivation and animal domestication and the level of intensified food-collecting were reached in the

Near East about 9000 B.C. In contrast to the moderately intensive food-collecting characteristic of the preceding level of development (the level of the late Upper Paleolithic period), what allowed this second kind of community to flourish was collecting of a most intensive kind. We believe such communities can be regarded as being incipiently food-producing, in the sense that their inhabitants were doubtless already manipulating both plants and animals to some extent. It seems to us that in much of the Near East this interval of incipient food production was just before or at the same time as what in Europe is called the Mesolithic period: a phase of cultural readaption, still on a food-collecting level, to the sequence of postglacial forested environments that formed in Europe about 11,000 years ago. (Food production proper did not reach most of Europe until sometime after 5000 B.C.)

The inventory of artifacts known as the Natufian assemblage, after the valley in Palestine where it was first discovered, provides examples, found both in caves and in village-like sites, of communities without food production. The artifacts uncovered at Mallaha, for instance, fit the Natufian classification. A different but contemporary inventory,

found east of the Euphrates and Tigris rivers, is named the Karim Shahirian assemblage, after Karim Shahir, a site on the flanks of the Zagros Mountains. The artifacts from Zawi Chemi, another early site in Iraq, are of this second kind, and Zawi Chemi appears to have the earliest evidence for domesticated sheep (about 9000 B.C.). A somewhat later site in neighboring Iran—Ganj Dareh, near Kermanshah—contains an assemblage that, although it is similar, is somewhat more developed than the basic Karim Shahirian. It is not yet clear, however, either along the Mediterranean littoral or in the regions east of the Euphrates, through how many successive phases the incipient food producer—hunters' village level may have passed before the next developmental step took place.

The early phase of that next step—the level of effective village-farming communities—is now known from sites throughout the Near East. Representative early-phase villages have been unearthed in most of the region's grassy uplands, in some middle reaches of its major river valleys, along the Mediterranean and even beyond the Near East in Cyprus, Crete and Greece. Originally one of us (Braidwood) believed the most ancient evidence of this early phase

● SITES WITH ESTABLISHED
   FOOD PRODUCTION.

○ SITES WITH SEVERAL PERIODS OF
   OCCUPATION, SOME FOOD-PRODUCING.

◆ SITES WITH EVIDENCE OF
   "INCIPIENT" FOOD PRODUCTION.

◇ SITES WITH INSUFFICIENT EVIDENCE
   OR NO EVIDENCE OF FOOD PRODUCTION.

▣ SITES KNOWN FROM BRIEF TESTS OR
   SURFACE COLLECTIONS; NO EVIDENCE
   OF FOOD PRODUCTION.

**SOUTHWESTERN ASIA, from beyond the Caspian (right) to the Mediterranean shore (left), contains many of mankind's earliest farming settlements, most of them in or near the hilly regions flanking the Fertile Crescent of Mesopotamia. The region also contains a number of village-like sites whose inhabitants were only incipient food producers or won a living by means of intensified hunting and gathering (see key above).**

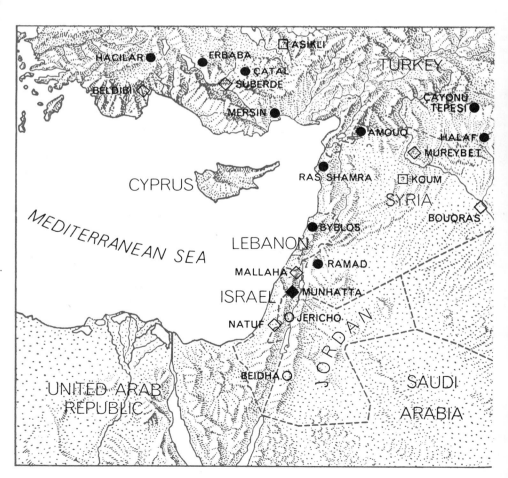

would be found only within a geographically restricted area, which was defined as the hilly flanks of the Fertile Crescent [*see illustration below*]. Moreover, even within this area the expectation was that the evidence would be confined to the zone naturally occupied today by certain wild but potentially domesticable plants and animals. One consequence of this view was that for a time the search for early sites was restricted to the "hilly flank" area, with the result that a large proportion of the early village sites now known are either in that area or immediately adjacent to it.

Recently it has become apparent that in past millenniums the natural range of the potentially domesticable forms of what may be called the "wheat-barley/sheep-goat-cattle-pig complex" extended well beyond the hilly flanks of the Fertile Crescent. For example, while extending earlier investigations by the Oriental Institute in Iran, Herbert E. Wright, Jr., of the University of Minnesota and Willem van Zeist of the University of Groningen have collected samples from the beds of lakes and ponds for analysis of their pollen content. Wright and van Zeist find that since about 17,000 years ago the vegetation and climate along the flanks of the Zagros Mountains have

changed much more than had been supposed. At the same time test excavations by an Oriental Institute group at Koum, in the dry steppe country west of the Euphrates in Syria, have added another site to the growing list of early non-food-producing settlements. Koum, like Mureybet, lies well south of the hilly-flanks zone, just as Suberde in Asia Minor lies well north of it. We have yet to learn precisely how wide the natural range of the domesticable plants and animals constituting this Near Eastern complex was in early times. The question will be answered only with the continued help of our colleagues in the natural sciences.

In the 1950's there was a substantial increase of archaeological activity in the Near East, but not until the 1960's did it become possible to investigate one untouched area that formed a virtual keystone in the arch. This was the southern slopes and the piedmont of the Taurus Mountains in southeastern Turkey, an area that includes the entire northern watershed in the upper reaches of the Tigris and the Euphrates. We reasoned that, however extensive the ancient range of domesticable plants and animals may have been, the upper basin of the Tigris and the Euphrates must have been

somewhere near the center of the zone.

Much of this unexplored territory lay within three Turkish border provinces (Urfa, Diyarbakir and Siirt), which for reasons of national security are normally out-of-bounds to foreign visitors. It seemed to us that if the area was to be reconnoitered, a joint Turkish-American venture was in order. In late 1962 the Oriental Institute joined forces with the department of prehistory of Istanbul University to establish a joint Prehistoric Project, and the authors of this article were made its codirectors. The project received the support of the National Science Foundation and the Wenner-Gren Foundation for Anthropological Research.

We proposed that a surface survey of the three provinces be made in the fall of 1963 and that exploratory digging be undertaken in the spring of 1964. We presently received the necessary approvals, which in this border region meant not only the cooperation of the Directorate of Antiquities of the Turkish Republic but also the active support of the Prime Minister, of many high civil and military authorities and of the governors of the three provinces and their staffs.

Thanks to the interest of all concerned, we were able to begin our sur-

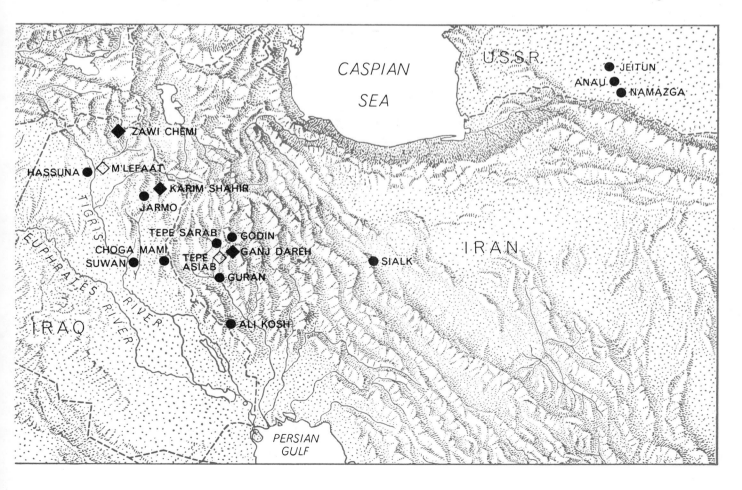

face survey in the province of Siirt early in October of 1963. We moved on to Diyarbakir in mid-November and ended the season with a five-day survey in Urfa in mid-December. Since the three provinces cover a total of more than 46,000 square kilometers, the reconnaissance could scarcely be an intensive one. The most detailed work was done in two valley regions: the plains of Kurtalan in Siirt and the Ergani plain in Diyarbakir. We found a total of 134 archaeological sites, plotted their location and roughly classified the materials we could collect on the surface at the main sites.

Our survey showed that this part of Turkey had been continuously occupied by men at least from the time (between 100,000 and 200,000 years ago) when stone tools of the Acheulean type were commonplace. So far as our particular interests were concerned, sites that looked as though they might be the remains of early farming villages were located in both the Kurtalan and the Ergani valleys. Still other sites in these valleys evidently represented more fully evolved village-farming communities. Some of the sites belonged to the developed village-farming phase termed Halafian (after Tell Halaf in northern Syria).

So far as settlements that might have belonged to the initial level of incipient food production are concerned, the most we can say at the moment is that our survey turned up no artifacts that, even in general terms, could be called representative of either the Natufian or the Karim Shahirian assemblages. Although it is probable that an unrelated third cultural tradition at the general level of incipient food production existed in this part of Turkey, we have yet to identify its traces.

In late April of 1964 we returned to the area of our survey prepared to undertake a number of test excavations. Bruce Howe of Harvard University, who had joined the project with the support of the American Schools of Oriental Research, tackled two small open sites in the area northwest of the provincial capital of Urfa. Named Biris Mezarligi and Söğüt Tarlasi, the sites contained numerous specialized stone tools produced from blades of flint. The inventory seems to represent some end phase of the Paleolithic period in the region. The sites did not yield samples adequate for carbon-14 dating, so that the age of this blade industry is a matter of conjecture; our guess is that the tools were made around 10000 B.C. or perhaps a little later. At Söğüt Tarlasi, but not at Biris Mezarligi, the blade-tool horizon was overlain by material of a time somewhat before 3000 B.C., contemporary with the Uruk phase of Sumerian culture in neighboring Mesopotamia.

While Howe worked in Urfa, the majority of the workers on the project moved on to Diyarbakir in order to investigate a promising mound some five kilometers southwest of the town of Ergani. Known as Çayönü Tepesi, the mound is about 200 meters in diameter;

SUCCESSIVE LEVELS exposed during excavation on the crest of the mound are shown in a drawing based on composite photographs. At the rear of the dig, only a little below the mound surface, are the stone foundations of mud-brick structures that had been built at Level 2. In the middle distance (a, a'), still surrounded by unremoved earth, are the bases of the two stone monoliths found at Level 4. Sections of the cobble pavement found at Level 5 are in the foreground at left. In the foreground at right is the grill-like stone foundation of the elaborate structure exposed at Level 5. The two-by-two-meter pit, foreground, descends beyond Level 6.

it stands on the north bank of a minor tributary of the Tigris. At some time in the past part of the mound's south side was washed away. At the foot of the talus slope on the river side we found fragments of crude and easily crumbled pottery that had been made by hand, rather than with the potter's wheel. Some additional potsherds were present on the northeast slope of the mound and in the top 10 or 15 centimeters of soil in our test excavations (about the depth to which the soil had been disturbed by modern plowing). Below that our 1964 excavations revealed no pottery. The presence in these lower levels of figurines made of clay shows that clay was known and used in the early days of Çayönü Tepesi. Like the people of Jarmo and some other early village-farming communities, however, the inhabitants of Çayönü Tepesi evidently got along without the clay bowls, jars and other containers that are commonplace in the villages of later farmers.

We worked at Çayönü Tepesi for two seasons—in 1964 and again in 1968—and we expect to work there again this year. Our main evidence concerning the early occupation of the site comes from a 10-by-15-meter area we excavated on the crest of the mound and a five-by-eight-meter trench we cut into the mound on the river side; both excavations were undertaken during the 1964 season [see illustrations on page 130]. Those who explore village sites in southwestern Asia come to expect that each new excavation will exhibit an exuberant characteristic that is distinctively its own. Çayönü Tepesi was no exception: its special characteristic is its architecture. Among the buildings we uncovered, several must have been quite imposing. The trench we cut back from the river revealed part of what could have been a building interior or perhaps an open court. The area was floored with a broad pavement of smooth flagstones, around which the stone bases of thick walls rose to a height of a meter or more. Spaced along the main axis of the paved area were the broken bases of a pair of large stone slabs that had once stood upright. From one of the stone walls buttresses projected at the points nearest the broken slabs. Another partly intact slab marked the area's short axis. Unfortunately erosion had eaten away the southern portions of this elaborate structure, so that its full plan is beyond recovery.

At the crest of the mound we dug down to a depth of more than three meters, encountering traces of at least six

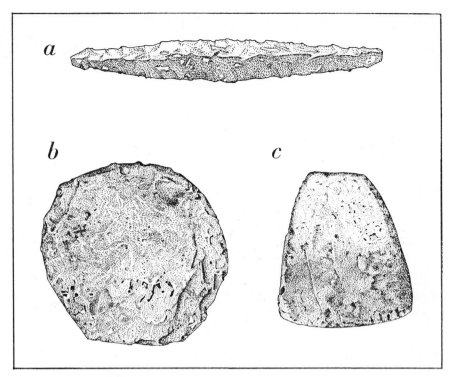

THREE STONE IMPLEMENTS from Çayönü Tepesi are a flint projectile point (a), found during the 1968 season, a scraper of flint (b) and a polished stone celt, the bit of a compound cutting tool (c), unearthed in 1964. The artifacts are shown at their actual size.

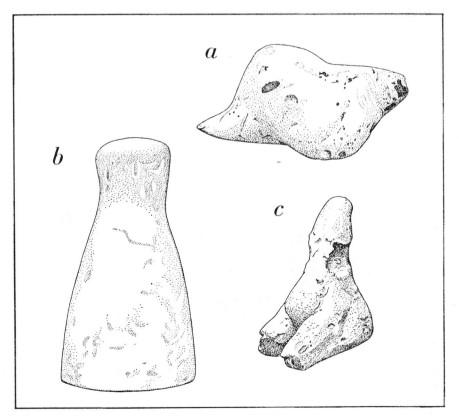

THREE ODDITIES from the site are a snail shell (a), a polished stone object (b) and a crude clay figurine (c). The shell, imported from the Mediterranean, has been smoothed and drilled with holes, presumably for decorative inserts. The stone, about three inches high, is one of 22 found in a cache during the 1968 season; their function is unknown. The figure seems to represent a pregnant woman; it may be a portrayal of the familiar "fertility deity."

AIR VIEW of Çayönü Tepesi, on the bank of a tributary of the Tigris River in southwestern Turkey, shows the work done by the authors in 1964. Near the river (*right*) digging uncovered stone walls and a floor of flagstones. On the crest of the village mound (*left*) six successive levels of occupation have been exposed; the next-to-lowest level contained objects made from copper.

GROUND VIEW of Çayönü Tepesi, from a rise on the south side of the river, shows a stretch of the broad Ergani plain beyond the site. On the northern horizon are the first ranges of the Taurus Mountains, here distinctively marked by light-colored bands of rock.

successive levels of occupation. At the fourth level the bases of two more upright slabs rose from a broad pavement of fist-sized limestone cobbles; the broken upper portion of one slab lay beside its base. The fifth level, also paved with cobbles, contained the stone foundations of still another substantial structure. What we could perceive of the foundation plan showed a curious grill-like pattern [*see illustration on page 128*]. Our work in 1968 exposed another of these grill-like foundations. A similar foundation, although it is smaller and built of sun-dried mud walling rather than stone, was unearthed at Jarmo. We are still puzzled as to the function of such foundations.

The purpose of the upright slabs at Çayönü Tepesi is equally puzzling. We are of two minds about whether they could have been supports for roof beams. Our first notion was that the slabs might have been ceremonial stones set up within unroofed courts, but the actual function of the structures containing them is not yet clear. We are much impressed by the substantial proportions of the buildings and by the relative sophistication of their construction, but we are still loath to press any suggestion that they served a public or a sacred purpose.

In addition to its impressive architecture, Çayönü Tepesi yielded tools chipped from flint and obsidian or fashioned from stone by grinding, ornaments made of polished stone, the clay figurines mentioned above and one shell ornament. The last object indicates contact, direct or indirect, with the Mediterranean coast. If one adds to this inventory evidence what seems to be a primitive form of wheat and the remains of domesticated dogs, pigs, sheep and probably goats, one gains some sense of the quality of life here and in similar communities across southwestern Asia as the arts of farming and animal husbandry became established during the eighth millennium B.C. If that were all Çayönü Tepesi had to tell us, it would be enough. A combination of geological propinquity and archaeological good fortune, however, has made the site even more significant. We have found here what is so far the earliest evidence of man's intentional use of metal.

Turkey is rich in minerals; one of its major mining centers today—a deposit of native copper, copper ores and related minerals such as malachite—is less than 20 kilometers from Çayönü Tepesi. In our excavation at the crest of the mound we noticed, from just below the surface downward, dozens of fragments of a bright green substance that we took to be malachite. Below the fourth occupation level we began to find actual artifacts made of malachite: drilled beads, a carefully smoothed but undrilled ellipsoid and a small tablet. Next we found part of a tool—one end of a reamer with a square cross section—that had been hammered into shape out of a lump of native copper. Finally we uncovered three tiny objects of copper that are perhaps analogous to the ordinary modern straight pin. In two of these pins, which do not appear to be complete, the metal had been abraded to form a point at one end; the third pin was pointed at both ends and was sharply bent [*see illustration on page 125*].

Metallurgy, of course, involves the hot-working of metals, including such arts as smelting, alloying, casting and forging. We are making no assertion that any kind of metallurgy, however primitive, existed at Çayönü Tepesi; there is not even any unanimity of opinion among the experts about whether the reamer, the only article that had certainly been hammered, was worked cold or hot. The fact remains that sometime just before 7000 B.C. the people of Çayönü Tepesi not only were acquainted with metal but also were shaping artifacts out of native copper by abrading and hammering.

What we suggest is that the Çayönü Tepesi copper reveals the moment in man's material progress when he may first have begun to sense the properties of metal as metal, rather than as some peculiar kind of stone. Looking back from the full daylight of our own age of metals, these first faint streaks of dawn are exciting to behold.

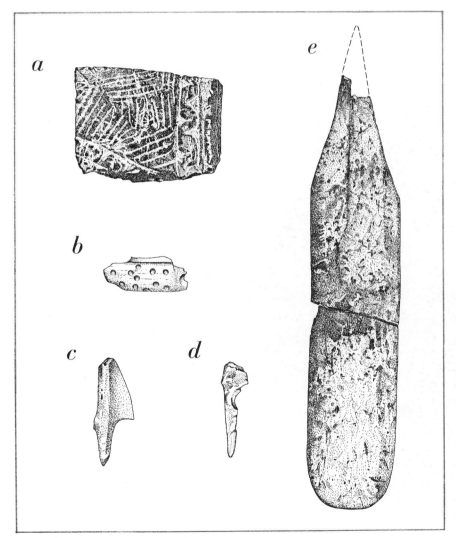

CRAFTSMANSHIP at Çayönü Tepesi included the decoration of stone bowls with incisions (*a*) and bone objects with drilled patterns (*b*). Drills flaked from flint (*c, d*) were used to work the bone. Bone awls (*e*) were probably used to produce wooden and leather items.

# 13 Obsidian and the Origins of Trade

by J. E. Dixon, J. R. Cann, and Colin Renfrew
*March 1968*

*Objects made of this volcanic glass are found at
many Neolithic sites around the Mediterranean.
Spectroscopic analysis indicates that the raw material
often came from hundreds of miles away*

The transition from hunting to farming, which started mankind on the road to civilization, presents a number of interesting questions for investigators, not the least of which is the extent of communication among early human settlements. Archaeological explorations in recent years have unearthed the sites of prehistoric villages that were widely scattered in southwestern Asia and around the Mediterranean. The earliest communities—for example Jarmo in what is now Iraq and Jericho in Jordan—apparently were settled some 10,000 years ago [see "The Agricultural Revolution," by Robert J. Braidwood; SCIENTIFIC AMERICAN, September 1960]. One might suppose the primeval villages, separated by hundreds of miles and often by mountains or water, were isolated developments, not even aware of one another's existence. There have been reasons to suspect, however, that this was not the case, and we have now found definitive evidence that the prehistoric communities throughout the Near East and the Mediterranean region were in active communication.

What kinds of evidence of communication between geographically separated peoples might one look for? Obviously in the case of prehistoric peoples the only materials available for study are the remains of the objects they made or used. In the search for signs of possible contact between two cultures archaeologists have generally depended on a comparative examination of the artifacts. If the two cultures show strong similarities in knowledge or technique—say in the method of working flint or the style of pottery—this is taken to signify mutual contact and perhaps actual trade in objects. At best, however, such evidence is only suggestive and is always subject to doubt; it leaves open the possibility that the similarities, no matter how close they are, may be mere coincidence, the two peoples' having hit independently on a natural and obvious way of doing things.

The raw materials of which the objects were made, on the other hand, may offer an opportunity for a more decisive inquiry. If a material used by a community does not occur locally in the raw state, one must conclude it was imported, and the possibility exists that it was obtained in trade with another population. One can then start on the task

OBSIDIAN BOWL made during the fourth millennium B.C. is seen from above, its spout jutting out at the right. The translucent bowl, which is nearly eight inches in diameter, comes from the Mesopotamian site of Tepe Gawra (*see illustration on page 140*). Trace-element analysis shows that the obsidian comes from Acigöl, 400 miles to the west in Turkey.

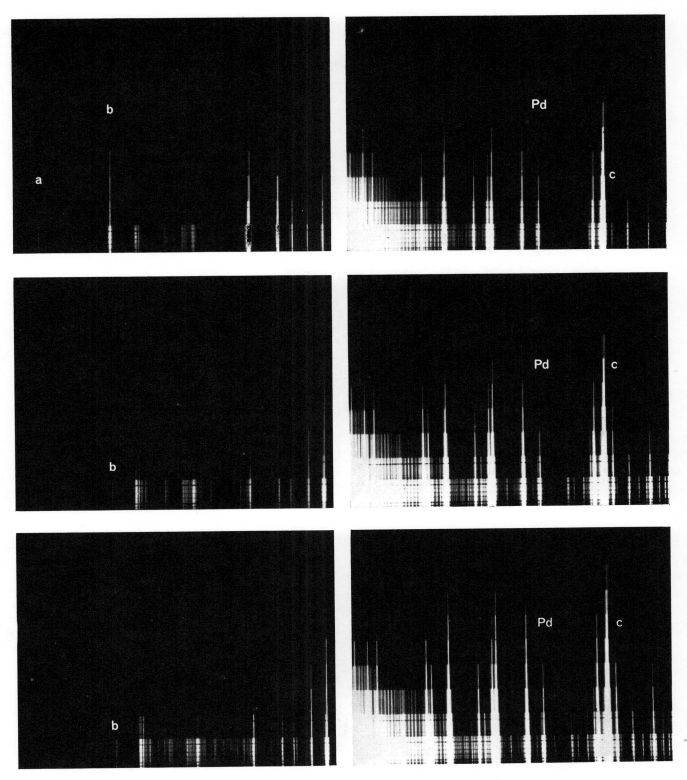

SPECTROGRAMS of three obsidian samples, reproduced here in part, show that differing proportions of trace elements make possible the identification of obsidian from different volcanic deposits. At top are two parts of the spectrogram of raw volcanic glass from Melos in the Aegean Sea. Matching parts of a spectrogram of a piece from an obsidian blade unearthed at Ali Kosh in Iran are at center. Matching parts of a spectrogram of volcanic glass from Nemrut Dağ, near Lake Van in Armenia, are at bottom. In the top specimen the spectral lines of strontium ("a" at left, 4,607.4 angstrom units) and barium ("b" at left, 4,554 angstroms) are relatively long, indicating proportions of some 200 parts per million and 700 parts per million respectively. The same lines are almost invisible in the center and bottom specimens. The spectral line of zirconium ("c" at right, 3,438 angstroms) is relatively short in the top specimen, indicating a concentration of about 50 parts per million. In the other two specimens the long zirconium lines indicate a concentration of about 700 parts per million. Palladium (spectral lines labeled "Pd" to the left of "c") is not a normal trace element in obsidian; the element is added to provide a standard for calibration. The trace-element differences show that the Ali Kosh artifact (center) could not have been made of obsidian from Melos but instead is chemically similar to the obsidian found at Nemrut Dag.

**OBSIDIAN FROM MELOS, in the form of a core from which blades have been flaked, shows the characteristic glistening surface of this volcanic glass. Obsidian was probably traded in the form of glass lumps or cores that the final purchaser turned into tools himself.**

**SCULPTURED SEASHELL, carved from a variety of obsidian with distinctive white spots, was found in a Minoan site on Crete. Sir Arthur Evans, the pioneer student of Cretan prehistory, thought the obsidian had come from Lipari, off Sicily, where similarly spotted volcanic glass is common. Analysis now proves that it came from nearby Giali in the Aegean.**

of tracing the material to its source.

It occurred to us that obsidian might be an ideal material for a tracer investigation of this kind. Obsidian is a hard, brittle volcanic glass that can be chipped like flint and fashioned into a sharp tool. It is known to have been used for knives and scrapers by prehistoric men as early as 30,000 years ago. Obsidian tools have been found in nearly every early village site in the Near East and the Mediterranean region. Yet for most of these sites it was an indubitably foreign material; it can be obtained only in certain areas of recent volcanic activity, which in that part of the world means the region around Italy, some islands in the Aegean Sea and certain areas in modern Turkey and Iran. Some of the ancient villages where obsidian tools were used were many hundreds of miles from the nearest natural source of the material.

How could one identify the particular source from which the obsidian was obtained in each case? Clearly our first task was to determine whether or not obsidian samples showed distinguishable differences that could be connected with their source. We considered several possible criteria. Physical appearance obviously would not be a reliable guide, because obsidian samples from a single volcanic deposit may vary greatly in visible characteristics such as color. Microscopic examination was not helpful: the obsidian tools were generally made of material that is uniform in structure, without crystalline inclusions. Chemical analysis of the main components was also of no avail, because all samples of obsidian are substantially alike from this point of view. We decided finally on a chemical test based on the presence of trace elements. Perhaps the obsidian samples would show distinct differences in their trace-element content that could be identified with the deposits from which they came.

In order to explore this possibility we began by analyzing samples of obsidian collected from various well-known volcanic sources in the Mediterranean area: Lipari, a volcanic island north of Sicily, two areas in Sardinia, the islands of Pantelleria and Palmarola and the island of Melos in the Aegean Sea.

For chemical analysis of the samples we used a convenient spectrographic method that archaeologists have long employed on metal objects. Every element emits characteristic wavelengths of light when it is heated to incandescence; a familiar example is the yellow light of burning sodium. By passing the light

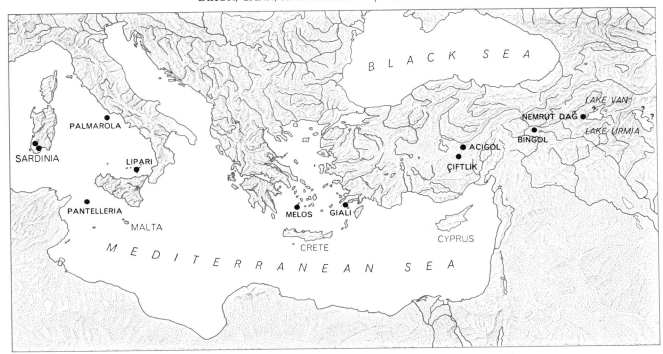

**SOURCES OF OBSIDIAN** in the Mediterranean and the Near East during Neolithic times included volcanic areas in Sardinia and on Palmarola, Lipari and Pantelleria in the central Mediterranean, the islands of Melos and Giali in the Aegean Sea, two central Anatolian sites, Acigöl and Çiftlik, and several places in ancient Armenia, including Bingöl in eastern Turkey and Nemrut Dağ near Lake Van.

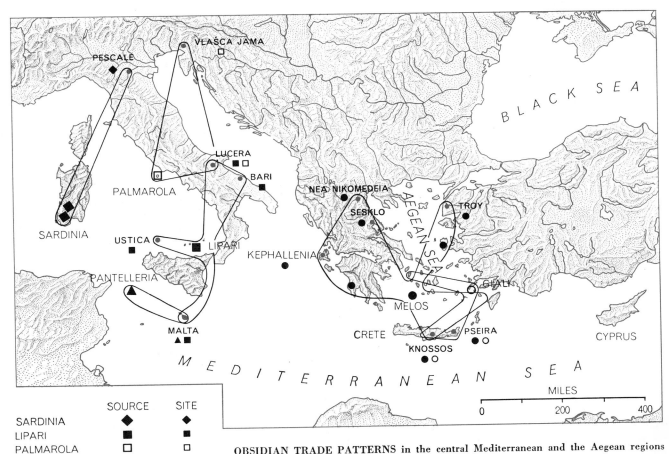

| | SOURCE | SITE |
|---|---|---|
| SARDINIA | ◆ | ◆ |
| LIPARI | ■ | ■ |
| PALMAROLA | □ | □ |
| PANTELLERIA | ▲ | ▲ |
| MELOS | ● | ● |
| GIALI | ○ | ○ |

**OBSIDIAN TRADE PATTERNS** in the central Mediterranean and the Aegean regions show that, although the volcanic glass was often shipped long distances from its sources, trade apparently did not take place between the two regions. Within each region, however, obsidian from two sources is often found at one site. Not all the sites indicated are named.

from a mixture of elements through a prism or diffraction grating that spreads out the wavelengths in a spectrum, one can separate the emissions of the various elements and detect trace elements that are present even in the amount of only a few parts per million. The beauty of the method for studying archaeological specimens is that accurate measurements can be obtained from very small amounts of material. Sixty milligrams taken from a sample is sufficient. Ground to a fine powder, mixed with an equal amount of

carbon and ignited in a carbon arc, this material yields a spectrographic picture that gives a measure of the quantity of each trace element in the sample; the quantity is indicated by the intensity (photographically the height) of the element's spectral lines.

We obtained readings for 16 elements in our samples of obsidian. Among the trace elements found to be present, the two that showed the greatest quantitative variation over the range of samples were barium and zirconium. We there-

fore tried using the relative concentrations of these two elements as a test for identification of the source [*see illustration on this page*]. To our immense satisfaction these quantities were found to indicate the geographical source quite well. Samples from various flows and outcrops at Lipari, for instance, all showed much the same proportion of barium to zirconium; those from Melos had characteristic contents of these elements different from those at Lipari. The Pantelleria and Sardinia samples likewise could be distinguished on the same basis. The Palmarola samples turned out to be similar to the Lipari ones on the barium-zirconium graph, but we found we could distinguish them from the Lipari type by their content of another trace element, cesium.

Having established these markers for identifying the obsidian sources, we were in a position to determine the raw-material origins of obsidian tools found at the sites of ancient settlements. The little island of Malta, south of Sicily, offered objects for a clear-cut test. The remains of a remarkable prehistoric society of 5,000 years ago, marked by colossal stone temples, have been unearthed on this island. The finds include small obsidian tools. There are, however, no natural obsidian deposits on the island. Where, then, did the material come from? Some archaeologists had suggested that it might have been brought there by Minoan traders from the island of Melos, 600 miles to the east. Our trace-element analysis of the Malta tools disclosed that this conjecture was incorrect: the obsidian was of the types found on Lipari and on Pantelleria, a tiny island 150 miles northwest of Malta.

The findings revealed two important facts about the ancient Maltese settlement. They showed that the island people in that early Neolithic period were already accomplished seafarers, traveling frequently to Sicily, Lipari and Pantelleria. On the other hand, the obsidian evidence also indicated that the Maltese people had little or no contact with the contemporary Minoan settlements of the Aegean area. Their stone temples may well have been their own invention.

Our tests resolved another question involving the Minoan culture. Sir Arthur Evans, the illustrious archaeologist who excavated the palace at Knossos on Crete more than half a century ago, found a number of finely carved objects there that were made of a variety of obsidian marked by prominent white spots. He concluded that this material came from

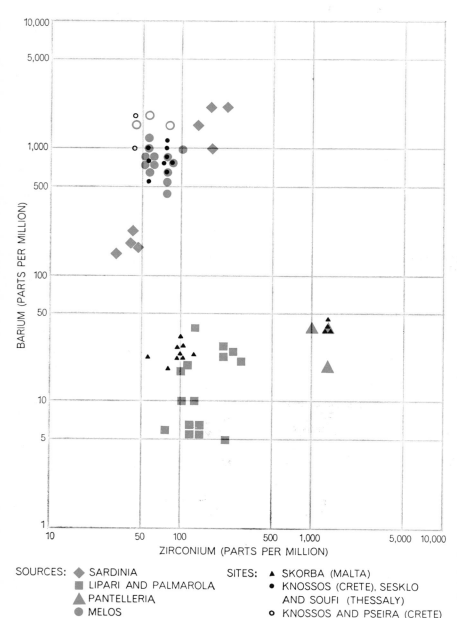

SOURCES: ◆ SARDINIA    SITES: ▲ SKORBA (MALTA)
■ LIPARI AND PALMAROLA    ● KNOSSOS (CRETE), SESKLO
▲ PANTELLERIA    AND SOUFI (THESSALY)
● MELOS    ○ KNOSSOS AND PSEIRA (CRETE)
○ GIALI

**TWO TRACE ELEMENTS,** barium and zirconium, provide the principal means of identifying the sources of obsidian artifacts from central Mediterranean and Aegean sites. Obsidian from both Sardinian sources is richer in barium than obsidian from Pantelleria, Lipari and Palmarola, whereas Pantellerian obsidian is the richest of all in zirconium. Other trace elements, not plotted here, allow additional distinctions to be drawn. Although their barium and zirconium contents are similar, the high calcium content of Gialian obsidian distinguishes it from Melian, whereas Palmarolan obsidian is much richer in cesium than Liparian.

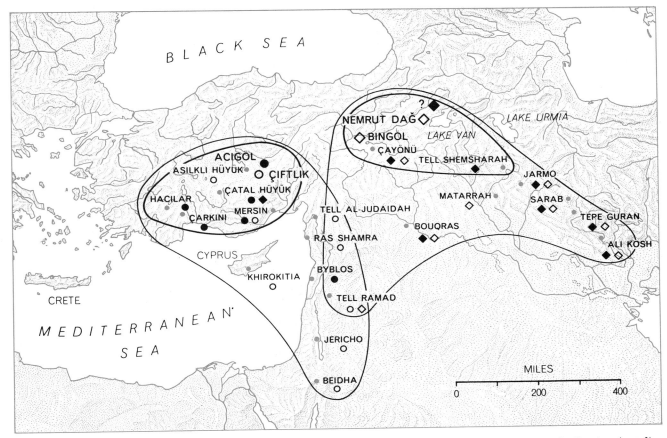

| | | SOURCE | SITE |
|---|---|---|---|
| ARMENIAN OBSIDIAN | 1G | ◆ | ◆ |
| | 4C | ◇ | ◇ |
| ANATOLIAN OBSIDIAN | 1E-F | ● | ● |
| | 2B | ○ | ○ |

NEOLITHIC NEAR EAST was another scene of active obsidian trade. Cypriot, Anatolian and Levant villages obtained obsidian mainly from two sources in Anatolia: Acigöl and Çiftlik. Mesopotamian villages, in turn, depended on sources in Armenia. The locations of two, Nemrut Dağ and Bingöl, are known. A third variety of obsidian, found at many Mesopotamian sites, is also probably Armenian but its source is not yet known. A heavy line surrounds a nuclear zone within each trade area. These are designated "supply zones" by the authors: more than 80 percent of the chipped-stone tools at supply-zone sites are obsidian.

Lipari, some of whose obsidian also has white spots. On trace-element examination, however, it now turns out that the white-spotted obsidian at Knossos came not from Lipari but from the small island of Giali some distance north of Rhodes. The Knossos remains also include tools made of unspotted obsidian. Analysis shows that this material came from Melos, which is to be expected, since Melos is the nearest obsidian source to Crete. In general, the obsidian evidence establishes the early Aegean islanders as skilled sailors and traders, disseminating the material not only among the islands but also to settlements in Greece and Turkey.

The obsidian tracer work, begun only six years ago, has given rise to investigations at various institutions in Britain, the U.S. and elsewhere, and studies are going forward on material from early settlements in Europe, in the Middle East, in Mexico, California and the Great Lakes region of the New World, in New Zealand and in Africa, where early man made hand axes of obsidian as long as 100,000 years ago. Our own group at the University of Cambridge, having verified the validity of the method by the Mediterranean tests, has proceeded to apply it to an investigation of the origins of trade among the earliest settlements of man in the Near East, that is to say, in Mesopotamia and in Turkey, Palestine and Egypt.

The first problem in the study of this region was to locate the natural sources of obsidian. A number of sources (all volcanic, of course) have now been identified in mountainous areas of Turkey and northern Iran [see top illustration on page 135] and in Ethiopia to the south. All the available geological evidence indicates that the entire region between these places, including Egypt, is devoid of natural deposits of obsidian. This means that every prehistoric village in the "fertile crescent," where farming began, had to import its obsidian.

Samples from all the natural deposits and from the obsidian artifacts found in the village sites were analyzed. They were found to be definable in eight different groups, or types, according to their barium-zirconium content, and in some groups the presence of another trace element (like that of cesium in the Palmarola obsidian) served additionally to distinguish the particular source of the material. Some of the obsidian artifacts could not be matched to any known natural source. This necessarily called for searches for the missing sources. The composition of the natural obsidian samples suggested a certain geographical pattern of distribution, and this clue led to the discovery of at least one missing source. A few sources have not yet been located precisely, but the basic pattern of sources and destinations is now clear enough to provide a good picture of the movement and trade routes of obsidian in the period when the first steps toward civilization (variously called the "agricultural revolution" or the "neolithic revolution") were taking place.

By about 9000 B.C. groups of people

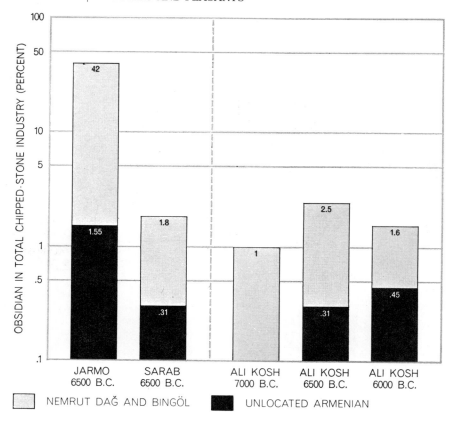

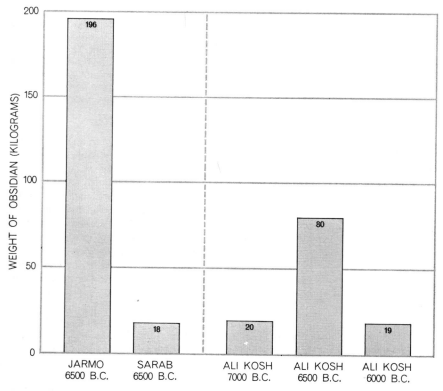

**INFLUENCE OF GEOGRAPHY** on trade in tool materials is apparent from the total obsidian and its proportion to other stone tools at three Zagros villages that imported Armenian obsidian during the seventh to sixth millenniums B.C. Jarmo, although outside the Armenian supply zone (*see illustration on preceding page*), was nonetheless well supplied with obsidian in terms both of percentage (*top graph*) and of estimated total weight of the material (*bottom graph*). The reduction in both percentage and weight at two more distant towns, Sarab and Ali Kosh (*plotted for three periods*), is drastic. Both distance and the difficult terrain apparently contributed to the scantiness of trade in the case of Sarab, a hill town.

in the Near East had begun to practice an incipient agriculture: selectively hunting and perhaps herding sheep and goats and harvesting wild prototypes of wheat and barley. They were not yet using obsidian to any appreciable extent. By the time the first farming villages were founded, probably a little after 8000 B.C., obsidian had come into rather general use. Naturally the extent of adoption of the material varied with distance from the sources of supply, and this is clearly traceable in the obsidian objects found at the sites of the ancient villages.

Within 150 to 200 miles of the obsidian deposits in Turkey and Armenia most of the chipped-stone tools found in the early prehistoric village sites are of obsidian: 80 percent, as against only 20 percent of flint. From that zone the proportion of obsidian falls off nearly exponentially with distance. This is clearly illustrated by the distribution of obsidian from a natural source in the volcanic area around Çiftlik, near the present town of Niğde in Turkey. At Mersin, the site of an early village on the Mediterranean coast not far from Çiftlik, obsidian was the most common chipped-tool material. From there its use diminished rapidly down the Levant coast, until at Jericho, 500 miles from the source, it is found only in very small quantities, most of the chipped tools there being made of flint. A few pieces of Çiftlik obsidian have been found, however, even at a Neolithic settlement on Cyprus, which indicates at least a trading contact across the water. Some of the obsidian from Turkish sources was distributed over distances of more than 600 miles in the early Neolithic period.

The early villages near the sources in Turkey developed a rich art and craftsmanship in obsidian. Particularly impressive are the objects found at Çatal Hüyük, a 6000 B.C. village that was so large it can be called a town. Among its obsidian products were beautifully made daggers and arrowheads and carefully polished mirrors, as sophisticated as any of those made 7,000 years later in Aztec Mexico.

Jarmo, one of the earliest-known villages in the fertile crescent, was favored by proximity to several obsidian sources. At least two of these sources furnished considerable amounts of the material, estimated to total 450 pounds or more, to Jarmo in very early times. From this it appears that well before 6000 B.C. Jarmo must have been conducting a thriving trade across the mountains that brought it into contact with the communities to the north in Armenia. There were then no wheeled vehicles (they were not invented until 3,000 years later) and not even pack animals. Hence all the traded goods, including obsidian, must have been transported on foot, or perhaps part of the way in boats down the Tigris River.

Tracing the varieties of obsidian from their sources to the villages where they turn up in manufactured objects, we can reconstruct the trade routes of that early time in man's economic and social history. The routes, crossing mountains, deserts and water, connect the early settlements with a network of communications that must have influenced their development profoundly. No doubt goods besides obsidian were traded over these routes; indeed, it seems likely that there was a trade in perishable commodities that was much greater in size and economic significance than that in obsidian. Clearly, however, the most impor-

tant traffic must have been in ideas. The network of contacts arising from the trade in goods must have been a major factor in the rapid development of the economic and cultural revolution that within a few thousand years transformed mankind from a hunting animal to a builder of civilization.

Obsidian now furnishes us with a tool for retracing the communications at the beginning of the revolution, more than 3,000 years before the invention of writ-

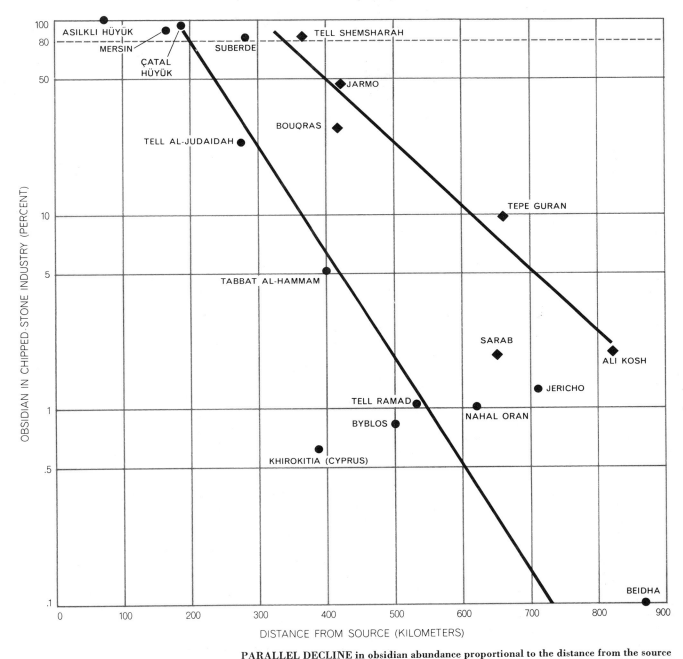

PARALLEL DECLINE in obsidian abundance proportional to the distance from the source is evident in both Near East trade areas during the period from 6500 to 5500 B.C. Not all the sites named here are included in the map on the next page. The boundary between a supply zone and the wider hinterland that the authors call a "contact zone" appears to lie about 300 kilometers from each area's obsidian sources. Poor supply of obsidian at the Cyprus site in spite of its nearness to sources in Turkey is a second example of the influence of geographical factors other than distance. The necessary ocean voyage apparently inhibited trade.

● ANATOLIAN OBSIDIAN

◆ ARMENIAN OBSIDIAN

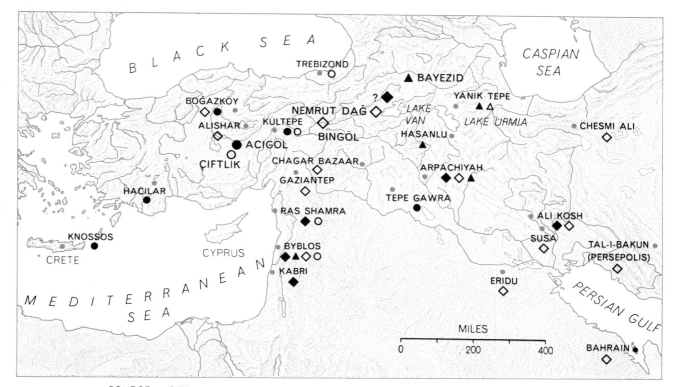

| | | SOURCE | SITE |
|---|---|---|---|
| ARMENIAN OBSIDIAN | 1G | ◆ | ◆ |
| | 3A | ▲ | ▲ |
| | 4C | ◇ | ◇ |
| ANATOLIAN OBSIDIAN | 1E·F | ● | ● |
| | 2B | ○ | ○ |

**POST-NEOLITHIC TRADE**, its directions often traceable by means of luxury items made from obsidian, was cosmopolitan in its extent. Two new sources of supply in the Lake Urmia area of Armenia were developed and Armenian obsidian was traded as far west as the Levant and as far south as Bahrain on the Persian Gulf. Obsidian from Turkey was carried westward to Crete and was transported for the first time across the desert to Mesopotamia. Ethiopian obsidian holds the Near East travel record; a slab of this material, bearing a 16th-century B.C. Egyptian inscription, has been discovered at Boğazköy, a Hittite site in Turkey.

ing. In addition to revealing the pattern and range of contacts among the prehistoric settlements, it gives us a rough picture of trade statistics (through the amounts of material involved) that indicates the strength of the communication links between particular communities. Furthermore, the development of communications over the millenniums after the villages were first established can be traced in the record of the obsidian trade.

As time went on and transportation, aided by the domestication of the ass, improved, the trade in obsidian expanded, both in the number of sources mined and in the distances of distribution. Trade routes developed across the Syrian desert in both directions, and more obsidian began to appear on the Levant coast. Obsidian from Armenia was exported to villages as far distant as Bahrain on the Persian Gulf and the Teheran area near the Caspian Sea. The use of obsidian for tools declined with the coming of the metal ages after 4000 B.C., but it continued to be prized for ornamental objects such as bowls, statuettes and even small articles of household furniture, such as tables. By that time the

Egyptians, apparently obtaining the material from Ethiopia, also had begun to use obsidian for this purpose. A remnant of a little toilette table of obsidian made in Egypt and bearing a hieroglyphic inscription of Pharaoh Chian, of the 16th century B.C., has been found at Bogazköy, the capital of the ancient Hittite kingdom in Turkey. It may have been a gift sent by the Pharaoh to the Hittite king.

By then obsidian itself was no longer an important material of commerce. Nonetheless, the great trade routes that had developed between the cities of the Near East may well have followed the same paths that had first been blazed by the obsidian trade thousands of years earlier.

The analysis of the early obsidian objects now throws new light on the revolution, some 10,000 years ago, that led to man's emergence from the hunter's way of life. There has been a tendency to think of this beginning as an isolated, small-scale phenomenon—of a little tribal group of people settling down somewhere and developing an agricultural system all by itself. In recent years an intensive search has been pursued for

the "birthplace" of this event: Did the first village spring up in the Levant or in the Zagros Mountains on the rim of the fertile crescent or in Turkey? That question now becomes less interesting or significant than it was thought to be. The farming way of life, it appears, originated not at some single location but over whole regions where the peoples of various settlements exchanged ideas and the material means of sustenance.

Throughout the 2,000 years or more during which agriculture was first developing in the Near East the communities dispersed through the region were in more or less continual communication with one another, primarily trading goods but also inevitably sharing their discoveries of agricultural techniques and skills. There is every reason to believe the region functioned essentially as a unit in moving along the road of technological advance. The early villages show considerable diversity in the customs and beliefs that make up what is called a society's "culture," but there can be little doubt that their mutual contact greatly influenced not only their material progress but also their social development and world view.

# A Neolithic City in Turkey

by James Mellaart
*April 1964*

*An ancient mound now known as Çatal Hüyük has
yielded evidence that communities with highly
developed economic structure, religion and art existed
as long ago as 7000 B.C. and perhaps even earlier*

Excavations on the Anatolian plateau of Turkey a few years ago provided an answer to an archaeological question of long standing about Neolithic culture. The Neolithic is the stage of civilization at which men began to cultivate crops and to domesticate animals and as a result of these activities to dwell in permanent settlements; in the Near East this stage occurred roughly between 7000 B.C. and 5000 B.C. The question was how Neolithic culture had moved from the Near East into Europe. The answer was that the movement was overland, by way of the Anatolian plateau. Such a route had long seemed to archaeologists a logical supposition, but until Neolithic communities were excavated on the plateau there had been no direct evidence to support the supposition [see "Hacilar: A Neolithic Village Site," by James Mellaart, SCIENTIFIC AMERICAN, August, 1961].

In answering one question, however, these excavations raised another: What were the origins of the culture of which Hacilar was representative? The Late Neolithic culture found at Hacilar had arrived there fully developed. The long gap between its arrival, probably about 6000 B.C., and the desertion of a prepottery village on the same site some 500 years earlier needed investigation. The gap appeared to correspond to the Early Neolithic period. If an Early Neolithic site could be excavated on the plateau, it might indicate the origin of the Hacilar culture and provide a longer culture sequence.

We had such a site in mind. I had found it about 30 miles southeast of the modern city of Konya in 1958: an ancient mound (*hüyük* in Turkish) bearing the name Çatal. The mound, covered with weeds and thistles, stood in the middle of a great plain. Lying on what

was once the bank of a river (now canalized into other channels to prevent flooding) that flows from the Taurus Mountains onto the plain, it rose gently from the fields to a height of 50 feet.

Çatal Hüyük seemed to be the most promising of some 200 sites we had visited on the Konya plain. A preliminary investigation indicated, to our delight, that the site belonged substantially, if not wholly, to the Early Neolithic period. Small fragments of pottery and broken obsidian arrowheads showed an unmistakable resemblance to those found in the deepest Neolithic levels at Mersin on the southern coast of Turkey, and at Çatal Hüyük they were on top of the mound. Moreover, the pottery looked more primitive than anything we had found at Hacilar.

So it was that Çatal Hüyük's 8,000 years of slumber came to an end on May 17, 1961, when our party began excavations. Ten days later the first Neolithic paintings ever found on man-made walls were exposed, and it was clear that Çatal Hüyük was no ordinary site. Succeeding excavations in 1962 and 1963 have confirmed this impression. With its story only partly revealed by the excavations to date, Çatal Hüyük has already added to the archaeological evidence that the development of towns and cities (as distinct from villages) goes farther back in antiquity than had been thought. Çatal Hüyük deserves the name of city: it was a community with an extensive economic development, specialized crafts, a rich religious life, a surprising attainment in art and an impressive social organization.

For the opportunity to explore this story we are indebted to several organizations. Our excavations have been supported by the Wenner-Gren Foundation for Anthropological Research, the Bol-

lingen Foundation, the British Academy, the University of London, the University of Edinburgh, the Royal Ontario Museum, the Australian Institute of Archaeology, the University of Canterbury in New Zealand and the late Francis Neilson. The Shell Oil Company and British Petroleum Aegean Limited provided technical help. Numerous other institutions have contributed in such ways as sending experts to the site or making analyses of material found at the site.

Çatal Hüyük covers 32 acres and so is easily the largest known Neolithic site, although how much of the site was occupied at any given period cannot be said with certainty. Apparently the settlement grew up from the riverbank, and the substantial part of the mound that spreads back from the river therefore dates from later phases of settlement. Our excavations, covering about one acre, have so far been concentrated on the southwest side of the mound, in a quarter that appears to have been sacred and residential. Because we have found nothing but finished goods in this area, we assume that the bazaar quarter with the workshops lies elsewhere in the mound.

With different quarters for different activities, a clear specialization in crafts and a social stratification that is obvious in both the size of the houses and the quality of burial gifts, this settlement was not a village of farmers, however rich. It was far more than that. In fact, its remains are as urban as those of any site from the succeeding Bronze Age yet excavated in Turkey.

We have found at Çatal Hüyük 12 superimposed building levels, which we have numbered from 0 to VI-A and VI-B to X according to their apparent chronology from latest to earliest [*see illustration on page 147*]. All these levels belong to a single culture that was uninterrupted in development and shows no signs of destruction attributable to outside forces. The entire sequence so far discovered appears to cover the seventh millennium B.C., although radiocarbon dating of Çatal Hüyük materials now in progress at the University of Pennsylvania may provide a more precise time scale. The core of the mound, however, remains to be sounded, and a full 10 meters of deposit there may take the origins of Çatal Hüyük back to the end of the last continental glaciation.

Houses at Çatal Hüyük were built of shaped mud brick of standard sizes. Because the nearest stone was several

miles away and would have been difficult to bring to the site, the foundations of the houses also consist of mud brick, laid in several courses. By these foundations it is possible to recognize buildings even if their floors are gone, as is the case in Level 0. The houses were rectangular, usually with a small storeroom attached [*see the illustration on page 144*]. Apparently these dwellings were one-story structures, perhaps with a wooden veranda.

The houses show a remarkable consistency of plan inside. Along the east wall there were two raised platforms with a higher bench at the southern end. This arrangement constituted a "divan," used for sitting, working and sleeping. The smaller corner platform evidently belonged to the male owner and the

larger central platform to the women and children. This hierarchic convention appears from Level X to Level II and probably existed in Levels I and 0, of which little remains. There are numerous variations on this arrangement of built-in furniture, including situations in which platforms appear along the north or west wall. The hearth was invariably at the south end of the room, sometimes accompanied by an oven and less often by a kiln. There was a reason for this location of the fires: it had to do with the manner in which the houses were entered.

The entrance was, as in some American Indian villages, a hole in the roof, over which there was surely some sort of canopy-like shelter. The roof opening was always on the south side of the

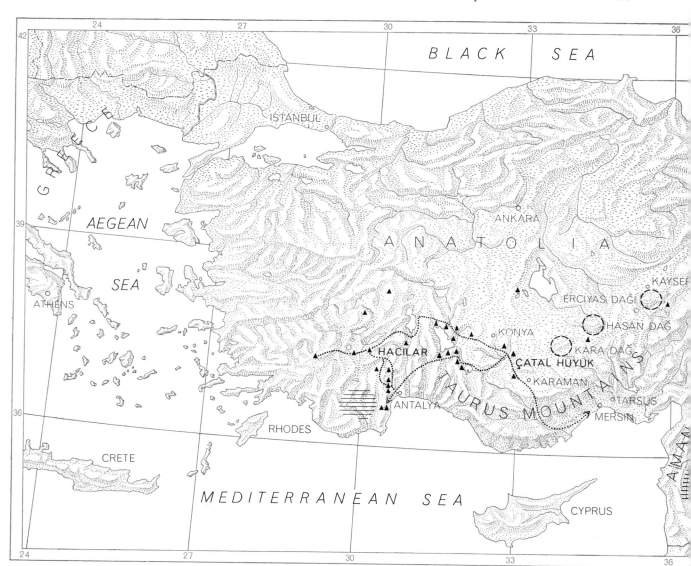

**AREA OF NEAR EAST** in which the culture represented by Çatal Hüyük was located is shown. Triangular symbols show Neolithic sites; circled areas indicate sources of obsidian; hatched areas, sources of flint. Çatal Hüyük was chosen for extensive archaeological work after excavations at Hacilar revealed a Late Neolithic culture that had arrived fully developed from some other place. Çatal

dwelling; thus it served both as a smoke hole and as an entrance. All access from the outside to the roof was by a movable ladder. From the roof into the dwelling the usual access was by a fixed ladder, although some buildings had another entrance through a well-plastered ventilation shaft that apparently had a movable ladder. Communication between dwellings was accomplished over the rooftops. There is little evidence of lanes and passages, and the courtyards that exist (often merely a ruined house) appear to have been used only for rubbish disposal and excreta.

The system of roof entrances meant that the outside of the settlement presented a solid blank wall. This was a check against enemies and also against

Hüyük apparently represents a culture that was a forerunner of Hacilar's and eventually may be traced back farther than 7000 B.C.

floods. It was evidently a successful defense system, as is indicated by the absence of any signs of massacre. About all any attackers could do—armed as they were with nothing more than bow and arrow, slings and stone tools—was to raid the cattle kept in corrals on the edge of the settlement or to set fire to the roofs. The defenders, in contrast, had the advantage of height and probably of superior numbers. In any case, because of the successful defense the only form of destruction suffered by Çatal Hüyük was fire. Most of the buildings in levels from VI to II were destroyed by fire; but with numerous hearths and ovens and the high winds of the region a disastrous fire about once a century is no more than could be expected.

As a result of these fires the carbonized remains of cereal grains and other foods are plentiful at Çatal Hüyük. There are also many animal bones. The food remains and the bones tell a great deal about the domestic economy of the settlement; the studies being made of them by the paleoethnobiologist Hans Helbaek of the National Museum of Denmark and the zoologist Dexter Perkins, Jr., of Harvard University will probably yield important additional information.

On the basis of what is now known Helbaek has described the grain finds as "the largest, richest and best preserved of all early cereal deposits so far recovered," providing "some of the most significant genetical and cultural" data yet obtained about early civilization. The grains, unlike the finds in other early Near Eastern settlements of cultivated plants little removed from their wild ancestors, include such hybrids and mutants as naked six-row barley and hexaploid free-threshing wheat, which were introduced into Europe from Anatolia in the sixth millennium B.C. The use made of the grains is indicated by the grain bins found in every house and the many mortars for dehusking and querns for grinding. In addition to cereals, peas and lentils the community grew bitter vetch and some other crops; the residents also collected nuts, fruits and berries.

The zoological remains are no less interesting: they show the presence of domesticated sheep even below Level X and cows as early as Level VII. Goats and dogs also appear to have been domesticated, but there is no indication that pigs were. Their absence may be due to religious considerations. Although the domesticated animals provided the community with wool, milk, meat and

skins, the people had by no means abandoned hunting. Wild cattle and red deer were extensively hunted, as were wild asses, wild sheep, boars and leopards.

With such an abundant diet it is not surprising to find from the skeletons that the inhabitants were generally healthy. Bone disease was rare, teeth were good and this dolichocephalic (long-headed) people were fairly tall: the males ranged from about five feet six inches to five feet 10 and the females from five feet to five feet eight. Still, as is to be expected of such an ancient era, few individuals reached middle age.

The burials were inside the houses, beneath the platforms. Most of the skeletons we have found are those of women and children; presumably many of the males died away from home on hunting or fighting forays. The dead were buried in a contracted position, usually lying on their left side with feet toward the wall. Isolated burials were rare; some buildings contain several generations of a family, with 30 or more burials. It appears to have been the practice before final burial to strip the bodies of flesh by a preliminary interment, or by exposure to vultures, insects or microorganisms on an outdoor platform, sheltered by gabled structures built of reeds and mats. Thereafter the bones, still more or less held in position by the ligaments, were wrapped in cloth and given final burial, often being laid out on mats of cloth, skin or fur.

The burials provide information about the dress, weapons and jewelry of the Çatal Hüyük people. Male dress consisted of a loincloth or a leopard skin, fastened by a belt with a bone hook and eye; the men appear also to have worn cloaks fastened with antler toggles in the winter. The women wore sleeveless bodices and jerkins of leopard skin, with fringed skirts or string skirts—the ends of the string being encased in copper tubes for weighting. The women used bone pins for fastening garments.

Weapons buried with the men included polished stone maceheads, obsidian arrowheads and javelin heads and sometimes an obsidian spearhead. Frequently there was a fine flint dagger with a chalk or bone handle and a leather sheath.

Jewelry was mainly for the women and children. They wore the necklaces, armlets, bracelets and anklets we found made of beads and pendants in a great variety of stone, shell, chalk, clay, mother-of-pearl and (as early as Level IX) copper and lead. Cosmetics were

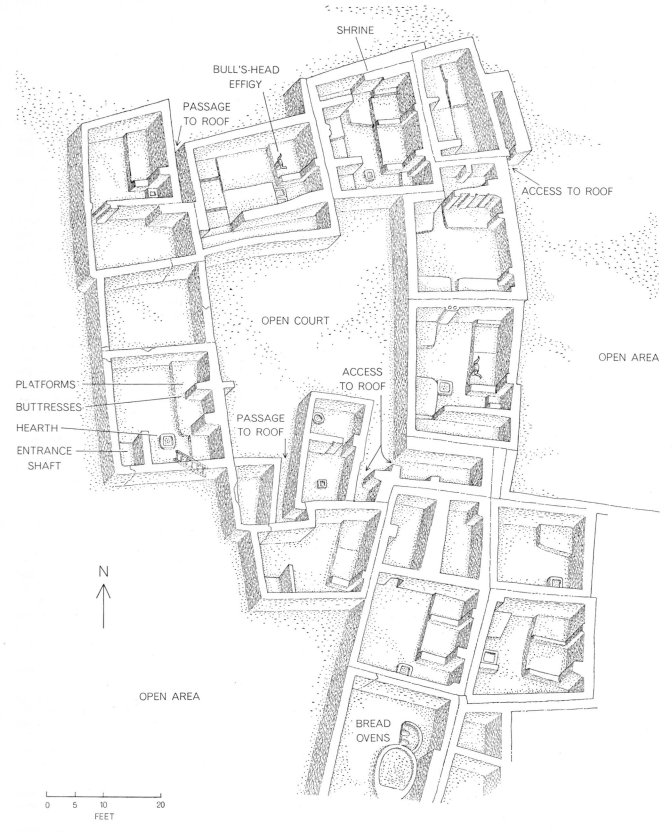

SHRINE

BULL'S-HEAD
EFFIGY

PASSAGE
TO ROOF

ACCESS TO ROOF

OPEN COURT

OPEN AREA

PLATFORMS

BUTTRESSES

HEARTH

ENTRANCE
SHAFT

ACCESS
TO ROOF

PASSAGE
TO ROOF

OPEN AREA

N

BREAD
OVENS

0    5    10         20
FEET

**COMMUNITY ARRANGEMENTS** of 8,000 years ago in a Neolithic city are depicted on the basis of recent excavations. This is a reconstruction of an area in the fifth of 12 building layers so far found at the Çatal Hüyük site on the Anatolian plateau of Turkey. Access to the buildings was solely from the roof, so that the exterior walls presented a solid blank face, which served effectively as a defense against both attackers and floods. Çatal Hüyük showed a surprising evolution of civilization for so early a community.

SITE OF NEOLITHIC CITY is this mound on the Anatolian plateau of Turkey. The Turkish word for mound is *hüyük*, and this one, which rises 50 feet above the plain, has the modern name of Çatal. After the inhabitants left about 6000 B.C. it lay deserted for 8,000 years; when excavations were started in 1961, it was heavily overgrown. In this photograph the view is from west of the site.

GENERAL VIEW OF EXCAVATIONS at Çatal Hüyük shows work in progress in Level VI, which is near the middle of the 12 levels of construction explored to date. The author chose Çatal Hüyük as the most promising of more than 200 sites he visited on the Anatolian plateau in a search for a representative Early Neolithic community. The site proved to have been a major settlement.

EXCAVATED SHRINE is in Level VI. Three plaster heads of bulls appear atop one another on the west wall, with a half-meter scale below them; on the north wall is a ram's head made of plaster. At bottom right is the remaining part of a small pillar.

RECONSTRUCTED SHRINE is the same as that shown above. The drawing represents the author's conception, based on excavations of several shrines at Çatal Hüyük, of how the room might have looked in Neolithic times. The stylized heads of animals and women's breasts probably were fertility symbols. Many of the city's shrines also had wall paintings of remarkable sophistication.

widely used, judging from the number of related articles we found, such as palettes and grinders for their preparation, baskets or the shells of fresh-water mussels for their containers and delicate bone pins for their application. The cosmetics probably consisted of red ocher, blue azurite, green malachite and perhaps galena. The women, once arrayed, used mirrors of highly polished obsidian to see the effect.

Several times we found food remains with the dead: berries, peas, lentils, eggs or a joint of meat put next to the deceased in baskets or in wooden bowls and boxes, which are carved with great delicacy. These wooden vessels are a characteristic of the Çatal Hüyük culture, and even when pottery began to appear in quantity around 6500 B.C., baskets and wooden bowls continued in use and had a strong influence on the pottery. The ovals and boat shapes, the lozenges and rectangles that appear in the pottery, not only from Level VI-A upward at Çatal Hüyük but also in the following Late Neolithic of Hacilar, have their origins in the wood-carving tradition of early Çatal Hüyük. In the same way numerous pottery vessels have features such as handles that derive from the earlier basketry.

The first production of pottery at Çatal Hüyük is found in Levels X and IX, but evidently this soft ware could not compete with traditional wood and woven products. It was not until the end of Level VI-A, when technical improvements had led to the production of an excellent hard baked ware, that pottery came into general use. The pottery was handmade and highly burnished. At first it was all dark brown or black; cooking pots were left that way but other objects were soon turned out in red, buff or mottled tones. In the upper levels of the mound animal heads start to appear on oval cups, and an over-all red slip, or coating, is in use, but painting on pottery was apparently never achieved. This pottery develops without a break into that of Late Neolithic Hacilar.

Another area in which Çatal Hüyük shows a people of remarkable technical competence and sophistication is textiles. We found some carbonized textiles in burials as far down as Level VI. They appear to have been wool, and at least three different types of weaving can be distinguished. These are the earliest textiles yet known; Helbaek has written of them that "we shall be hard put to it to find evidence of more perfect work anywhere within the following thousand years."

It is singular that with all these products of human workmanship we have found so few traces of the workmen. None of the 200 houses and shrines excavated so far has shown any evidence that any art or craft other than food preparation was carried on within. We have much fine woolen cloth but only one or two spindle whorls or loom weights, and these are from fill rather than floor deposits. We have thousands of finely worked obsidian tools but only two small boxes of chips, thousands of bone tools but no piles of waste or splinters. Somewhere in the mound there must be the workshops of the weavers and basketmakers; the matmakers; the carpenters and joiners; the men who made the polished stone tools (axes and adzes, polishers and grinders, chisels, maceheads and palettes); the bead makers who drilled in stone beads holes that no modern steel needle can penetrate and who carved pendants and used stone inlays; the makers of shell beads from dentalium, cowrie and fossil oyster; the flint and obsidian knappers who produced the pressure-flaked daggers, spearheads, lance heads, arrowheads, knives, sickle blades, scrapers and borers; the merchants of skin, leather and fur; the workers in bone who made the awls, punches, knives, scrapers, ladles, spoons, bowls, scoops, spatulas, bodkins, belt hooks, antler toggles, pins and cosmetic sticks; the carvers of wooden bowls and boxes; the mirror makers; the bowmakers; the men who hammered native copper into sheets and worked it into beads, pendants, rings and other trinkets; the builders; the merchants and traders who obtained all the raw material; and finally the artists—the carvers of statuettes, the modelers and the painters.

The unusual wealth of the city of Çatal Hüyük, as manifested by this great variety of sophisticated workmanship, is a phenomenon as yet without parallel in the Neolithic period. At the base of course lay the new efficiency of food production, transplanted from its probable origin in the hills to the fertile alluvial plain. Although that may account for the unprecedented size of the city, something else is needed to explain the community's almost explosive development in arts and crafts.

The key undoubtedly lies in the community's dependence on the import of

CHRONOLOGY OF HABITATION at Çatal Hüyük is indicated in this chart. Each level above VI-B apparently was built because of fire damage to the preceding level; the site appears to have been deserted after a fire in Level 0. Levels may yet be found below X.

**NEOLITHIC ARTIFACTS** found at Level VI of Çatal Hüyük and dating from about 6500 B.C. include bone necklace, bone pin, stone beads, limestone bracelet and obsidian mirror.

**WALL PAINTING** found in Level VI shows children's hands. Çatal Hüyük yielded the earliest known paintings on man-made walls. Most of the painting had a religious purpose.

raw materials (other than clay, timber and food) from near and far. One cannot possibly be wrong in suggesting that it was a well-organized trade that produced the city's wealth. Moreover, it appears likely that the trade in obsidian was at the heart of this extensive commerce. This black volcanic glass, which first appeared in the preceding Mesolithic period, became the most widespread trading commodity during the Neolithic period in the Near East. It has been found in the "proto-Neolithic" and prepottery Neolithic periods at Jericho; it occurs as far south as Beidha near Petra; it reached Cyprus in the sixth millennium. The origin of this obsidian, which was the best material of the time for cutting tools, was almost certainly central Anatolia, and it is extremely likely that the city of Çatal Hüyük controlled this source and organized the trade. The then active volcanoes of Hasan Dağ, Karaca Dağ, Mekke Dağ and others lie on the edge of the Konya plain. The nearest is some 50 miles east of Çatal Hüyük, and all are visible on a clear day. These sources of obsidian were well within the limits of the culture area of which Çatal Hüyük was the undisputed center.

This hegemony was not only economic but also religious and therefore political; in the ancient world no authority could exist without religious sanction. About the political system of Çatal Hüyük one can do little more than guess because there are no writings from the community. It seems likely, however, that at such an early stage of civilization only the priests could have been the bearers of authority.

Of the religious system one can say more because of the shrines and religious art we have found at Çatal Hüyük. In my view they constitute the community's most important archaeological contribution. I would maintain, perhaps wrongly, that the Neolithic religion of Çatal Hüyük (and of Hacilar) was created by women. In contrast to nearly all other earlier and later "fertility cults" of the Near East, it significantly lacks the element of sexual vulgarity and eroticism that is almost automatically associated with fertility and probably is the male's contribution. If the Çatal Hüyük religion is a creation of women, one has the rare opportunity of exploring Neolithic woman's mind by studying the symbolism she used in her effort to comprehend and influence the mysteries of life and death.

Of these symbols there is an abundance. In addition to schematic clay figurines of people and more naturalistic animal figures, there is a unique collection of fine statuettes. Those from the upper layers are modeled in clay; those in the lower layers are carved from stone. Beyond these, which together with burial rites are usually the archaeologist's only sources of information about religion, Çatal Hüyük has produced no fewer than 40 shrines and sanctuaries. They are at every level, but the nine in Level VI-A, the 12 in Level VI-B and the eight in Level VII are particularly rich in information. Wall decorations occur in most: painted scenes with numerous human figures in Levels III and IV; modeled and sometimes painted reliefs in Levels VI-A through X.

The shrines, although frequently large and well appointed, do not differ in plan from the houses, but they are much more lavishly decorated [*see illustration on page 146*]. Even if they were not continuously lived in, they served as burial places, presumably for their priestesses and the priestesses' families. It is only in the shrines that we have found reliefs and symbolism connected with life and death. From these it is possible to reconstruct in some degree the Neolithic pantheon.

The supreme deity was the Great Goddess. Often represented beside her are a daughter and a young son. A bearded god, who is always shown on a bull, was perhaps the Great Goddess' husband. No other deities appear. This group, therefore, probably constitutes the "holy family." Statues and reliefs represent the female deities either as two goddesses or as twins. The idea behind the duplication is evidently that of age and fertility, the whole aim of the religion being to ensure the continuity of life in every aspect: wildlife for the hunter, domesticated life for the civilized communities and finally the life of Neolithic man himself.

It is doubtful that Neolithic thought regarded these as four distinct deities. More likely the representations show aspects of the goddess as mother or as daughter and virgin, with the god as consort or son. The role of the male deity is more pronounced at Çatal Hüyük than it is at Hacilar, perhaps because in Çatal Hüyük hunting and the domestication of wild animals still held major importance, but in general the male plays a subsidiary role.

Scenes dealing with life are generally found on the west wall of the shrines. A typical scene shows the goddess giving birth to a bull or ram. Scenes dealing with death are found on the east

CLAY SEALS, most about the size of a postage stamp, apparently were used for identification. No house had more than one, and all the designs differed. These were in Levels II–IV.

STATUE OF GODDESS, done in clay and about eight inches high, shows her giving birth. Many representations of the goddess were found at Çatal Hüyük; this was in Level II.

wall: in three shrines the east-wall paintings show vultures attacking headless human corpses. Usually, however, the subject of death is expressed in more subtle ways. Representations of women's breasts, for example, which are of course symbolic of life, contained such items as the skulls of vultures, the lower jaws of wild boars and the heads of foxes and weasels—all scavengers and devourers of corpses.

The symbolism of west and east walls, or right and left, is matched by black and red: the red associated with life, the black with death. Panels of red hands are common, and several burial sites show remains of a coating of red ocher, which was evidently intended to be a substitute for blood and so a means of restoring life, at least symbolically. A great black bull covered the vulture paintings; both were symbolic of death. Contrasted with these was another painting of an enormous red bull surrounded by minute jubilant people.

There are some strange figures in the shrines. A stern-looking representation of the goddess was found with a headless bird, probably a vulture. Numerous figures roughly carved out of stalactites suggest a link with the dark world of caves, man's first refuge and sanctuary. An odd painting seems to represent a honeycomb with eggs or chrysalises on boughs and with bees or butterflies, which perhaps symbolize the souls of the dead. It is framed by alternate red and black hands along the top and gray and pink hands along the base. An earlier painting shows alternate red and black lines, resembling a net, similarly framed by hands. Net patterns decorate several other religious scenes, together

with symbols of horns, crosses and hands. Crosses, perhaps a simplified form of a four-petaled flower, were painted on a statuette of the goddess as well as on numerous walls; probably they are to be interpreted as fertility symbols. Rosettes and the double ax (or butterfly) are in the same category.

In several shrines and houses schematized heads of bulls in the form of a pillar serve as a cult symbol for protection. We have found curious benches with one, two, three or seven pairs of the bone cores of horns stuck in the sides. These defy explanation. Perhaps they figured in the burial rites, conceivably serving as a bier while the grave was dug.

Of the rites performed in the shrines little can be said. It is apparent, however, from the absence of blood pits and animal bones that there was no sacrificing of animals in the shrines. There were offerings of other kinds. In a shrine in Level II we found grain that had been burned on the plastered ceremonial altar and then covered by a new coat of plaster; this suggests the first offering after the harvest. In the earlier buildings, particularly in Level VI, there are offerings of all sorts: pots that doubtless contained food and drink; groups of hunting weapons, maces, axes and ceremonial flint daggers; tools; bags of obsidian; beads and many other objects, all unused or in pristine condition.

The wall paintings were mostly created for religious occasions and were covered with white plaster after they had outlived their usefulness. The paint was made of minerals mixed with fat; the painter worked with a brush on a white, cream or pale pink surface. The

range of colors is extensive. Red in all shades, including pink, mauve and orange, is predominant. The other colors are white, lemon yellow, purple, black and (very infrequently) blue. We have yet to find green. In a class apart from the religious paintings are several paintings of textile patterns, which attest the importance attached to weaving. Many of them show kilims, or woven carpets, making carpet weaving an art that can now be traced back to Neolithic times.

Many seasons of work remain at Çatal Hüyük. It is therefore premature to speak definitively about the origins of this remarkable civilization. It can be said, however, that the discovery of the art of Çatal Hüyük has demonstrated that the Upper Paleolithic tradition of naturalistic painting, which died in western Europe with the end of the ice age, not only survived but flourished in Anatolia. The implication is that at least part of the population of Çatal Hüyük was of Upper Paleolithic stock.

These people may not have been the first to learn the arts of cereal cultivation and animal husbandry, but they improved on the techniques to such an extent that they were able to produce the surplus of food that permits the beginning of leisure and specialization. By the seventh millennium they had created the first Mediterranean civilization, of which Çatal Hüyük is such an impressive representative. In time the offshoots of that civilization reached the Aegean shore, and by the sixth millennium Anatolian colonists were laying the foundations for the ultimate development of civilization in Europe.

# An Early Neolithic Village in Greece

by Robert J. Rodden
*April 1965*

*Excavations at Nea Nikomedeia in northern
Greece have uncovered a community of 8,000
years ago. Its remains suggest that agriculture and
animal husbandry came to Europe earlier than
has been supposed*

The Macedonian plain of northern Greece is covered today with orchards and fields of cotton and sugar beets. The aspect of the plain was quite different 8,000 years ago: its central portion was flooded either by an arm of the Aegean Sea or by a shallow lake. Along the shore lived farmer-herdsmen who raised wheat, barley and lentils, tended sheep and goats and may also have herded cattle and pigs. These facts are known because one of the many low-lying mounds on the Macedonian plain has recently been excavated. Called Nea Nikomedeia after a nearby modern village, the mound marks the site of the oldest dated Neolithic community yet found in Europe.

Perhaps even more important than the antiquity of the site is the fact that the patterns of living it reveals, although they are basically similar to the patterns of village life in early Neolithic sites as far east as Iraq and Iran, have their own exclusively European characteristics. The evidence for the existence of a thriving village in northern Greece near the end of the seventh millennium B.C. makes it necessary to reconsider the accepted view that the agricultural revolution of the Neolithic period was relatively late in reaching Europe from its area of origin in the Middle East. In southeastern Europe, at least, the transition from hunting, fishing and food-gathering in scattered bands to farming, herding and permanent village life must have taken place far earlier than has generally been thought.

I first made an archaeological reconnaissance of the Macedonian plain with a fellow graduate student, David Clarke, during the fall of 1960. We were seeking evidence that might clarify the relation between what were then the earliest-known farming communities in Europe—most of which are represented by sites in the Danube valley and in eastern Yugoslavia and central Bulgaria—and those early communities in central Greece whose existence had become known to archaeologists as long ago as the 1900's. Lying between the two regions, the Macedonian plain was an obvious place to look for the remains of communities that might have had connections with the first agriculturists to the north and south.

The Nea Nikomedeia mound had come to the attention of Photios Petsas of the Greek Archaeological Service in 1958, when local road builders bulldozed away three-quarters of an acre of it to use as highway fill. Petsas put a stop to this and, when we consulted him in 1960, directed us to the site. On the bulldozed surface, level with the surrounding plain, we found fragments of pottery and other artifacts that closely resembled the finds from the lowest excavated levels at Neolithic sites in central Greece.

A six-week campaign of exploratory excavation was mounted during the summer of 1961 under the direction of Grahame Clark of the University of Cambridge and myself. The work was done under the auspices of the British School of Archaeology in Athens and in cooperation with the Greek Archaeological Service; the necessary funds were provided by the Crowther-Benyon Fund of the University of Cambridge (which had sponsored my 1960 reconnaissance), the British Academy and the Wenner-Gren Foundation for Anthropological Research. Excavation quickly demonstrated that there was a rich layer of early Neolithic material at Nea Nikomedeia; pottery and other artifacts from this layer showed affinities with material from the earliest pottery-using Neolithic settlements in central Greece and, as we had hoped, with artifacts from the first well-established farming communities to the north.

Impressions of cereal grains, preserved on pottery surfaces, and more than 400 fragments of animal bones demonstrated that the first settlers at Nea Nikomedeia practiced an economy of mixed farming and herding. The 1961 excavations also established the fact that the first houses at the site were rectangular structures with mud walls supported by a framework of wooden poles. Samples of organic material from the site were sent for analysis to the Radiocarbon Dating Laboratory at the University of Cambridge; the analysis yielded a figure of 6220 B.C. ± 150 years. This is the earliest date as yet assigned to Neolithic material from Europe.

It was not until the summer of 1963 that a full-scale excavation could be organized at Nea Nikomedeia. In that year much of the early Neolithic occupation level was uncovered as part of a joint Harvard-Cambridge field project sponsored by the National Science Foundation. As before, the work was done under the auspices of the British School of Archaeology in Athens. It was known from the 1961 excavations that the deposit to be explored was a very shallow one—only a little more than two feet thick at its deepest. This layer was composed partly of accumulated occupation debris but mainly of collapsed and disintegrated mud walls from the site's ancient buildings. Shallow plowing in modern times had disturbed the top four or five inches of the deposit, with the result that only 18 inches or so of undisturbed early Neolithic material remained. The digging began in

CULTURAL SIMILARITIES between Nea Nikomedeia and other early sites in Europe, Asia Minor and the Middle East are indicated by the numbers at each place name. Among the European sites, Karanovo in central Bulgaria is representative of the many Neolithic villages in that northern region; Soufli Magoula and Sesklo in central Greece similarly typify the early sites to the

early June; when it ended in October, this thin layer had been excavated over an area of about half an acre.

Archaeological techniques of the kind normally used in excavating stone or brick buildings could not be applied here. The clay that forms the subsoil at Nea Nikomedeia is the same material the early settlers used to make the walls of their houses; consequently this clay also made up the bulk of the layer being excavated. Any details of ancient structures preserved in the deposit—such as the foundations of walls or the holes that contained timber uprights—would appear only as faint discolorations in the clay. To detect these discolorations and define their outlines clearly it was necessary to apply the painstaking technique of scraping. As the term indicates, scraping involves the removal of wide areas of soil a fraction of an inch at a time. The entire section of the mound to be excavated was laid out in a grid of 12-foot squares; as digging progressed, several adjacent squares would be scraped simultaneously and the pattern of the discolorations noted. All the walls and postholes found at Nea Nikomedeia, as well as the storage and rubbish pits associated with them, were uncovered in this way [see bottom illustration on page 157].

The whole of the mound was not opened during the 1963 season, and some house outlines that continued into the unexcavated portions of the site are not completely revealed. What has been exposed, however, makes it evident that the settlement consisted of individual buildings situated two to five yards apart on a slight knoll at the edge of what was then a marshy lake or inlet. There were two periods of early Neolithic building at Nea Nikomedeia. They are separated in places by a deposit of what appears to be the beginning of a humus soil, so that the second building period evidently represents a reoccupation of the site after a period of abandonment. In any case, the earlier settlement was the smaller of the two, and it was surrounded by a pair of concentric walls on the landward side of the knoll. At the time of the second building period the settlement expanded up to the limit of these walls, which were then replaced by a deep ditch. The ditch shows evidence of having been filled with water; perhaps it served as a moat.

Seven major structures of the earlier building period were uncovered in 1963; six of them are most likely dwellings. Carbonized remains of wood indicate that the frames of the houses were made of oak. The mud walls of the buildings were constructed in the following manner: Sapling uprights were set in place three to four feet apart and the space between them was filled in with bundles of reeds standing on end. The reeds were then plastered on the inside surface with mud mixed with chaff and on the outside with white clay. Many of the footings both for the walls and for the roof supports were

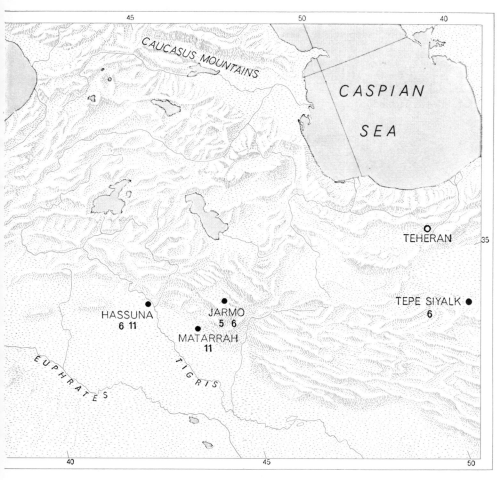

PARALLELS TO NEA NIKOMEDEIA

ARCHITECTURE

1  SQUARE HOUSE PLAN

2  WOOD FRAME AND MUD WALL

3  OPEN SETTLEMENT PLAN

SUBSISTENCE

4  CATTLE?

5  PIGS?

ADORNMENT

6  STUDS AND NAILS

7  CLAY STAMPS

8  BELT-FASTENER

POTTERY DECORATION

9  WHITE-PAINTED AND FINGER-IMPRESSED

10  RED-ON-CREAM PAINTING

11  MODELED FACE

**south. These two areas, the nearest to Nea Nikomedeia, possess the largest number of traits in common with it. Nea Nikomedeia thus exhibits a distinct European character, although it has traits in common with sites as distant as Tepe Siyalk. This suggests that southeastern Europe was not peripheral to the region within which the Neolithic revolution began but was an integral part of it.**

made a yard or so deep, evidently to ensure that the buildings would not be affected by frost heave or by the wetness of the waterfront subsoil. Because the mud-plastered walls would have been subject to damage by rain, it is assumed that the houses of Nea Nikomedeia had peaked and thatched roofs with overhanging eaves that would carry off rainwater [*see illustration on page 155*].

Although the six house plans are different, they have several features in common. The basic unit was evidently a square about 25 feet to a side. Two one-room houses show exactly these dimensions. A third building, consisting of a large main room and a narrow room along one side, was 25 feet wide; its full length could not be determined. The same plan—a large main room with a narrow room attached—is also found in the best-preserved dwelling uncovered at Nea Nikomedeia. At one end of the narrow room in this house stood a raised platform of plaster into which

were sunk a hearth basin and a storage bin; on the opposite side of the house was a fenced-off porch area.

A considerably larger structure, some 40 feet square and divided into three parts by parallel rows of heavy timbers, is also attributable to the first building period at Nea Nikomedeia. It was uncovered in the part of the excavation closest to the center of the mound. Five figurines of women were found within the bounds of its walls. Both its size and its contents suggest that the building served some ritual purpose.

Although much analytical work still remains to be done, preliminary findings by the botanists and zoologists who are working with the expedition provide a good outline of the economy of this early Neolithic community. The fact that the farmers of the first settlement grew wheat, barley and lentils is indicated by carbonized material; the particular varieties of these plants have not yet been identified. A study of the

animal bones recovered in 1961, together with a preliminary analysis of some 25,000 additional specimens recovered in 1963, suggest that sheep and goats played the primary role in animal husbandry. The bones of pigs and cattle were also present, but in far fewer numbers. In addition to tending their flocks the people of Nea Nikomedeia engaged in hunting, fowling and fishing. Deer, hare and wild pig were among the game animals; the presence of fish bones and the shells of both saltwater cockles and freshwater mussels shows that the early settlers also exploited the resources of their coastal environment.

Assuming that the carbon-14 date for Nea Nikomedeia is correct, evidence for the presence of even limited numbers of domesticated cattle and pigs at the site is a matter of considerable importance in the record of animal domestication. For one thing, this would be the earliest dated occurrence of domesticated cattle yet known anywhere in the world. If taken together with the possible evidence of cattle domestication at Fikirtepe in northwestern Turkey and at Çatal Hüyük in southeastern Turkey, this finding would argue for an original center for the domestication of cattle in Asia Minor and southeastern Europe. As for pigs, so early an occurrence of pig bones in Greece suggests that there may have been an independent European center for the domestication of these animals, unconnected with the center implied for the Middle East by the animal-bone findings at such early village sites as Jarmo in Iraq.

It remains possible, although not probable, that the bones of both cattle and pigs found at Nea Nikomedeia represent hunters' prey rather than herdsmen's produce. The remains of both species recovered in 1961 do not all indicate the age of the animal. Of

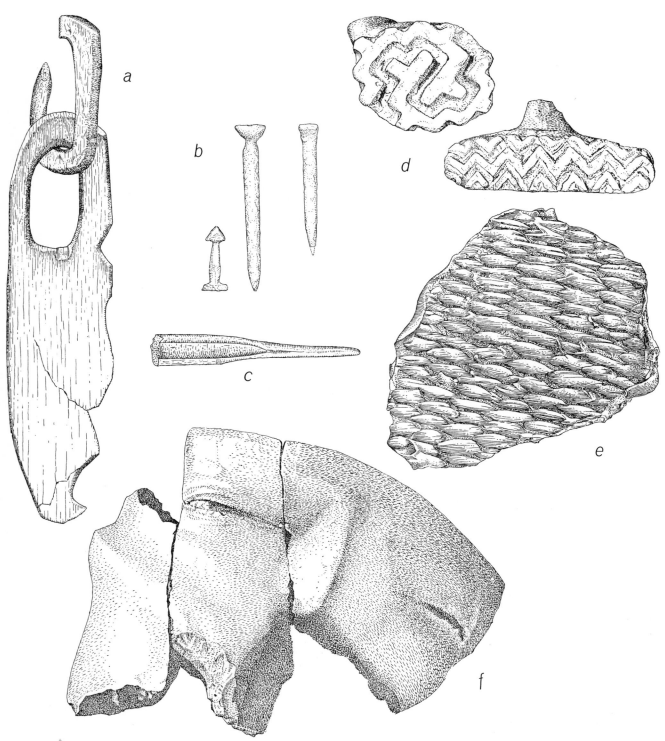

**EARLY NEOLITHIC SKILLS** in working with four varieties of raw material are demonstrated in this illustration. The hook-and-eye belt-fastener (*a*) and the awl (*c*) are made of bone. The two marble nails and the serpentine stud (*b*) show a capacity for fine lapidary work. Examples of the potter's art include geometric stamps (*d*), probably for body-painting, and a human face modeled below the rim of a pot (*f*). The bit of twined matting (*e*) was accidentally preserved in clay. All objects are shown natural size.

the bones that do indicate age, however, more than half belonged to immature animals; only under exceptional circumstances would such a high proportion of young animals be killed as a result of hunting. Nonetheless, the final word on cattle- and pig-domestication at this early Neolithic site must be postponed until the analysis of the vastly larger sample of bones uncovered in 1963 has been completed.

Regardless of the ultimate verdict on this point, it is evident that the economy of Nea Nikomedeia rested on a fourfold base, with wheat and barley as the major cereal crops, and sheep and goats as sources of meat and presumably of hides and milk. There is no reason to doubt that the first inspiration for the cultivation of these cereals and the husbanding of these animals came to Europe from the Middle East, although as yet the earliest links connecting the two regions have not been discovered. The essentials of the economy at Nea Nikomedeia, then, were foreign in origin; what about the other elements of village life? In reflecting on the settlement's tools, pottery, articles of personal adornment and ritual objects, one seeks similarities to material from other sites in Europe and abroad. In this way what was unique at Nea Nikomedeia can be distinguished from what was derived from—or perhaps contributed to—other areas.

The tool kit of the first settlers included both the classic artifacts of polished stone—axes, adzes and chisels—that originally gave the Neolithic, or New Stone, age its name, and a variety of chipped blades of flint and chert from which the farmers made scrapers, arrowheads and the cutting edges of rude sickles. The bow and arrow and the sling were among the hunters' weapons; hundreds of clay slingstones have been unearthed. The settlers also made bone needles (possibly including net-making needles), awls and fishhooks. Such a list, with a few exceptions or additions, would be typical of any other nearly contemporary community in southeastern Europe, Asia Minor or the Middle East. Nonetheless, there are consistent local traditions; as an example, the chipped stone artifacts from Nea Nikomedeia resemble those from sites in central Greece, eastern Yugoslavia and central Bulgaria and differ from those found in southern Greece, Asia Minor and the Middle East.

The earliest pottery at the site shows great technical competence in manufac-

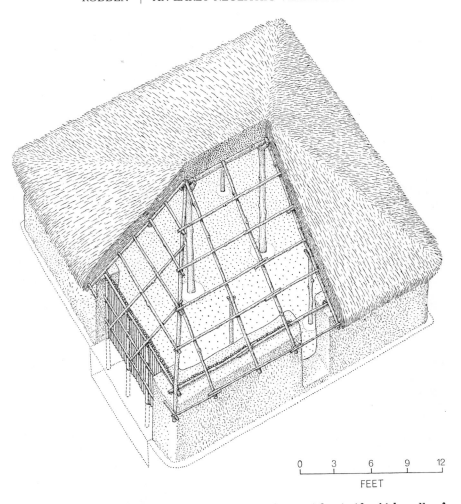

EARLY NEOLITHIC DWELLING consisted of timber uprights inside thick walls of clay plastered onto a frame of saplings and reeds. The foundations for the wall and the footings for the uprights were dug some three feet deep. The peaked pole-and-thatch roof, supported by crotched uprights, is hypothetical, but similar roofs are still built in Greece.

ture, in the range of vessel shapes and in decoration. The settlers made open bowls, large narrow-mouthed storage jars, small ladles, miniature vessels and peculiar shoe-shaped pots that may have been put into a bed of coals to heat their contents. Many of the smaller bowls were provided with lugs, which are perforated vertically or horizontally, so that they could be suspended by cords. Almost all the pots have thin walls and bases that are ring-shaped or disk-shaped. The potters decorated some of their wares by painting and some with finger impressions on the outside surface.

The earliest-known phases of Neolithic settlement in central Bulgaria and eastern Yugoslavia are characterized by pottery that bears finger-impressed decorations or designs in white paint; examples of both can be found at Nea Nikomedeia, but neither is common. That they are found at all, however,

lends weight to the conclusion that connecting links of some kind existed between these early Macedonian farmers and those to the north. The pottery evidence indicates even closer ties between Nea Nikomedeia and the earliest pottery-using settlements in central Greece. Both there and at Nea Nikomedeia wares decorated with block designs, triangles and patterns of wavy lines—all painted in red on a cream-colored background—are commonplace.

These pottery motifs provide an example of the ways in which Nea Nikomedeia may have contributed culturally to areas outside Europe. The tradition of painting pottery with red designs on a cream-colored background appears several hundred years later in southern Asia Minor with the beginnings of the Hacilar culture [see "Hacilar: A Neolithic Village Site," by James Mellaart; SCIENTIFIC AMERICAN, August, 1961]. By the same token, some of the

FIGURINE OF A WOMAN, seven inches high, is one of five similar clay sculptures un-earthed inside the largest early building at Nea Nikomedeia. The presence of so many figurines, which are presumably fertility symbols, suggests that building was used ritually.

pots of Nea Nikomedeia are decorated with human faces made by pinching up a "nose" and adding ovals of clay as "eyes." Similarly decorated pots have been found in post-Neolithic levels at Hacilar and also at the earlier sites of Hassuna and Matarrah in Iraq. In the absence of well-defined intermediate steps, it must remain a matter of conjecture whether or not the presence of pots with human faces at these widely separated sites represents the diffusion of an idea or an independent invention.

Both European and Asiatic characteristics can be found among the articles of personal adornment at Nea Nikomedeia. A bone belt-fastener with a hook-and-eye clasp was uncovered during the 1963 season; a number of such fasteners have been found in the early Neolithic levels at Çatal Hüyük. A bone hook from Soufli Magoula, an early Neolithic site in central Greece, may be another European example of the same kind of object. Clay stamps, each exhibiting a different geometric pattern, are relatively common at Nea Nikomedeia; similar stamps are known from central Greece and elsewhere in southeastern and central Europe. Some of the stamps found at Nea Nikomedeia, however, have designs similar to those on stamps from Çatal Hüyük.

Some Neolithic sites in the Middle East—Tell Judeideh in Syria, Jarmo and Hassuna in Iraq and Tepe Siyalk in Iran—contain curious stone objects that look somewhat like primitive nails. The excavations at Nea Nikomedeia have yielded a great number of these objects, neatly wrought out of white marble, and a lesser number of tiny studs made of green serpentine. It is probable that the nails were headdress decorations and that the studs were earplugs. Such carefully shaped and polished articles of marble and serpentine represent a high level of technical achievement.

Of particular interest is the fact that the settlers made clay figurines of men and women; these stylized sculptures reflect a high level of artistic sensibility. The more sophisticated figurines were made in sections and then pegged together before they hardened; the component parts are the head, the torso (including the arms) and two separate legs. The head usually consists of a slightly flattened cylinder from which a prominent pointed nose is pinched up; as with the faces on the pots, the eyes are often represented by applied lumps of clay. Figurines of women outnumber those of men; in the commonest type of

**MACEDONIAN PLAIN** in northern Greece is level agricultural land today; 8,000 years ago its central portion was underwater and its coastline was marked by farming communities such as the one found at Nea Nikomedeia, the oldest Neolithic site in Europe.

**SCRAPED HALF-ACRE** at the Nea Nikomedeia mound shows the pale discolorations that outline the walls of vanished buildings. Several narrow ridges, composed of unexcavated earth, outline the grid of squares into which the site was divided before digging. Near a zigzag in this grid at the right side of the illustration appears the outline of a square structure that was subdivided into one wide and one narrow room; the disturbed outdoor area opposite the narrow room may have been a porch. Just above this house in the photograph, partly obscured by two grid ridges, is the outline of an undivided house like the one illustrated on page 155.

female figurine the thighs are modeled to an exaggerated roundness. The breasts are mere knobs, supported by the hands [*see illustration on page 156*].

Other clay figurines include rather less elegant models of sheep and goats. It is puzzling that these economically important animals are rendered with such relative crudity whereas three effigies of frogs found at Nea Nikomedeia were beautifully carved in green and blue serpentine and then polished. The site's marshy locale makes it reasonable to suppose that its inhabitants were well acquainted with these amphibians, but what significance the frog may have possessed that inspired the execution of its portrait in stone is unknown.

It is commonly assumed that early societies engaged in the newly discovered art of food production soon developed beliefs about the supernatural in which human, animal and plant fertility were emphasized. The exaggerated forms of the figurines of women uncovered at Nea Nikomedeia, together with the fact that five of them were found together within the confines of the site's largest structure, seem to indicate that fertility beliefs played a part in the life of this particular Neolithic community. The excavations have provided a further insight into the community's spiritual views: There was evidently little or no regard for the dead. Burial pits were located outside the house walls and sometimes in the debris of buildings that had fallen into disuse; the inhabitants appear to have taken little trouble to prepare the graves. In some instances one gains the impression that the dead were crammed into a barely adequate depression. No personal adornment, food offerings or grave goods have been found with the skeletons. In one enigmatic instance, however, a skeleton was found with a large pebble thrust between its jaws.

In summary, the characteristics of early Neolithic village life as it was practiced by the farmers of Nea Nikomedeia show basic parallels with life in similar Neolithic villages in Asia Minor and the Middle East. The most telling of these parallels are the very roots of the Neolithic revolution itself: the cultivation of wheat and barley and the domestication of sheep and goats. This village in the Macedonian marshes, however, was no mere foothold established in Europe by pioneers from the Middle East. Village plans, house plans and building methods comparable to those used at Nea Nikomedeia are known from two nearby regions. The first of these regions includes the early Neolithic sites of Karanovo and Azmak in central Bulgaria; parts of plans of

**SKELETON OF ADULT,** who had been buried in a contracted position, had a large, flat pebble inserted between the jaws for some unknown purpose. The burials at Nea Nikomedeia do not include funeral offerings, and the graves are cramped and shallow.

similar houses have also been exposed at several of the early sites in central Greece. It seems probable, therefore, that a Neolithic pattern of life characterized by a well-established architectural tradition adapted to the European environment and locally available materials stands behind the finds both at Nea Nikomedeia and at the sites of these other early settlements in southeastern Europe.

The precise origins of this architectural tradition remain unknown, but it is one that contrasts strongly with the custom of building houses one against another around the nucleus of a courtyard, which dominates village construction in Asia Minor and the Middle East during the late seventh millennium and early sixth millennium B.C. In the last analysis, such evidence may mean that southeastern Europe will have to be considered a part of that zone—heretofore generally deemed to lie exclusively in Asia Minor and the Middle East—in which were made the primary discoveries that led to the development of Old World civilization.

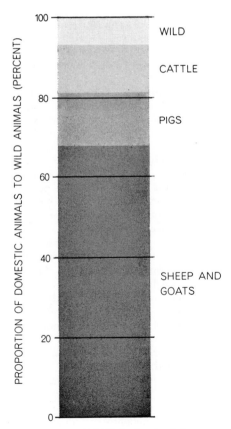

PARTIAL ANALYSIS of animal bones at Nea Nikomedeia shows the preponderance of sheep and goats. If cattle and pigs were domestic rather than wild animals, hunting provided less than 10 percent of the animal produce consumed by the villagers.

# 16

# An Earlier Agricultural Revolution

by Wilhelm G. Solheim II
*April 1972*

*It has generally been assumed that man first domesticated plants and animals in the Middle East. Excavations in Southwest Asia now suggest that there the revolution began some 5,000 years earlier*

Agriculture is known to have been invented at least twice. Plants and animals were domesticated in the Old World and the process was repeated quite independently some millenniums later in the New World. Evidence of a third domestication has now been uncovered. The agricultural revolution, which was thought to have first occurred some 10,000 years ago among the emerging Neolithic societies of the Middle East, seems to have been achieved independently thousands of miles away in Southeast Asia. This separate agricultural revolution involved plants and animals for the most part unknown in the Middle East, and it may have begun as much as 5,000 years earlier.

The fact that some of the most technologically advanced cultures in the world in the period from about 13,000 B.C. to 4000 B.C. flourished not in the Middle East or the adjacent Mediterranean but in the northern reaches of mainland Southeast Asia is not easy to accept. Nonetheless, recent excavations in Thailand have convinced my colleagues and me that somewhere among the forest-clad mountains of the region man's first tentative efforts to exploit wild plants and animals opened the way first to horticulture and then to full-scale agriculture and animal husbandry.

In terms of prehistory mainland and island Southeast Asia are together the largest unknown region in the world. It is only in the past decade that they have been recognized as rewarding areas for archaeological investigation. My own work in the region began in the Philippines in 1949 and has since included investigations both in other island areas and on the mainland. The need for salvage archaeology in advance of construction work in the lower basin of the Mekong River resulted in the excavation of two sites in northern Thailand

by my colleagues and me in 1965–1966. The first of these sites, a prehistoric mound called Non Nok Tha, is close to the area that was flooded by the waters of the Nam Phong Reservoir. Our work there, sponsored jointly by the Thai Government Department of Fine Arts, the University of Otago in New Zealand and my department at the University of Hawaii, began during the 1965–1966 dry season with the support of the National Science Foundation. Simultaneously my department sponsored a second excavation at a promising site in the northwest corner of Thailand. This was Spirit Cave; its discoverer and excavator, Chester F. Gorman, was a student of mine at the University of Hawaii.

The mound called Non Nok Tha was tilled jointly by a few of the farmers of a nearby hamlet. They had almost covered it with plantings of bananas, chili peppers and mulberry bushes, but there were two cleared areas on the mound where the rice from the surrounding paddy fields was threshed at harvesttime. Digging at the edge of a mulberry planting, we found that the uppermost strata of the mound contained a few iron implements and numerous remains of individuals who had been cremated before burial. Below these levels were earlier graves whose occupants had not been cremated; the burials included various grave furnishings. Among them were stone molds for casting bronze axe blades, some of the axes themselves, other bronze objects and a number of polished stone tools. The graves also held pottery that was well made but generally lacked decoration. In the lowest levels of the site we found still more polished stone tools and a few specimens of decorated pottery but no bronze at all.

These were significant discoveries. First, never before had a site been

found in Southeast Asia that contained evidence of a substantial interval when bronze was known but iron was not. Second, the pottery from the lowest strata included two vessels decorated with a pattern that I had first seen in the Philippines and had later observed on pottery from excavations elsewhere in Southeast Asia.

The Non Nok Tha site proved to be so rich in burials that our work went more slowly than we had expected. Eventually we pieced together more than 100 pottery vessels for the Thai National Museum, sent samples off for carbon-14 analysis and packed up a number of other finds for laboratory study back in Hawaii. Several of the site's deepest burials we left untouched but mentally reserved for later excavation. We were convinced that the lowest levels of the mound were quite old, going back perhaps as far as 1000 B.C., but we could not be certain until the carbon-14 results were known.

As we unpacked, cleaned and examined the specimens in Hawaii we continued to find the unexpected. For example, we found among the potsherds from the lowest levels some that bore the imprint of cereal grains and husks. It appeared that the cereal might be rice, and we sent a number of samples to an authority on cereal grains, Hitoshi Kihara of the Kihara Institute for Biological Research in Japan. Kihara concluded that the cereal had been *Oryza sativa*, the common species of rice that is grown throughout Asia today.

We had also found animal bones in many of the burials at Non Nok Tha. They gave the impression that portions had been cut from large animals and placed in the graves. Charles Higham of the University of Otago offered to identify the bones. He found them indistinguishable from the bones of *Bos indicus*, the common species of humped cattle from India.

At last we received the carbon-14 results. They showed that the mound was much older than we had anticipated. The lowest levels we had excavated at the site had been deposited before 3000 B.C., some of them possibly before 4000 B.C. None of the uppermost strata, however, was more than 1,000 years old.

Early in 1968 Donn T. Bayard of the University of Otago was able to excavate in a new area at Non Nok Tha. He opened several deep graves; one contained a remarkably well-preserved human skeleton and, resting on the skeleton's chest, a socketed tool made of copper. This body must have been buried sometime during the fourth millennium B.C., which makes the copper im-

HUMAN BURIAL of the fourth millennium B.C. was unearthed in 1968 at Non Nok Tha, a rich archaeological site in northern Thailand, by Donn T. Bayard of the University of Otago in New Zealand. In addition to a skeleton the burial contained a socketed implement made of copper (*arrow*). The copper contains traces of arsenic and phosphorus, suggesting that, if the tool was not actually a casting, the metal had at least been heat-treated by roasting the ore to prepare it for cold hammering. No older socketed tool is known.

ANIMAL LIMB BONES (*right foreground*) are typical of the many aggregates of animal bone, some of them more than 5,000 years old, found in burials at Non Nok Tha. They are probably the bones of the familiar species of Indian humped cattle, *Bos indicus*.

plement the oldest-known socketed metal tool in the world.

In summary, the findings at Non Nok Tha included several surprises. They showed that rice was an established cereal and that humped cattle were commonplace in mainland Southeast Asia perhaps as early as the fifth millennium B.C. Bronze metallurgy had flourished in the region for a considerable interval before the appearance of iron, and a unique form of copper tool had appeared on the scene even earlier. None of these developments had taken place in a vacuum: some of the earliest pottery in this corner of the mainland bore designs that are found elsewhere in mainland and island Southeast Asia. Even bigger surprises, however, were in store at Spirit Cave.

Gorman's site lies high up on the face of a limestone cliff that overlooks a small stream not far from the border between Thailand and Burma. The cave was last occupied, Gorman found, about 5600 B.C. The levels that underlie the top level span more than 4,000 years, and the earliest strata were formed about 10,000 B.C. The artifacts from all these occupation levels (except for those in the levels of the last 1,200 years or so) proved to be very much the same: simple stone tools representative of a Southeast Asian hunters' and gatherers' culture. The culture is called Hoabinhian because the cave sites where its simple artifacts were first unearthed during the 1920's are in the mountains near the town of Hoa Binh in North Vietnam. Since the initial discovery, many other sites containing Hoabinhian artifacts have been found in the mountainous terrain of northern Southeast Asia, almost always in small caves not far from streams. At first sight Gorman's cave looked like one more Hoabinhian find, remarkable only for being farther west than any previously discovered.

Two findings soon demonstrated the importance of Spirit Cave. The first was the result of Gorman's careful search for plant material. By sifting all the soil as it was removed from his test trench-es, Gorman recovered the fragmentary remains of 10 separate plant genera, among them pepper, butternut, almond, candlenut and betel nut. Of even greater significance was evidence of a species of cucumber, a bottle gourd, the Chinese water chestnut and certain legumes: the pea (*Pisum*), either the bean or the broad bean (*Phaseolus* or *Vicia*) and possibly also the soybean (*Glycine*). Some of these plant remains were present in all levels at the site.

It seems probable that several of the plants were cultivated by the inhabitants of Spirit Cave. The relatively small number of specimens that Gorman recovered in 1966, however, does not make it possible to draw a clear-cut conclusion on this crucial point. Last year Gorman did further work at Spirit Cave and recovered additional specimens. They are now being analyzed by Douglas Yen of the Bernice P. Bishop Museum in Honolulu, so that the question may soon be settled.

Let us assume for the sake of argument that Yen's finding will be negative

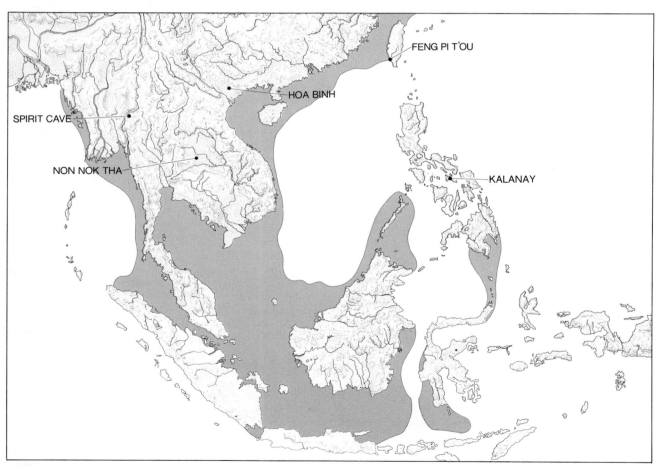

**MAJOR EARLY SITES** in Southeast Asia include Hoa Binh, in North Vietnam, where remains of a hunters' and gatherers' culture were found during the 1930's, and another Hoabinhian site, Spirit Cave in Thailand, where the earliest-known evidence of farming may have been found. Pottery at Spirit Cave, among the oldest in the world, resembles later wares found on Formosa. A second site in Thailand, Non Nok Tha, not only yielded a uniquely early kind of metal tool but also contained pots with designs like those found on Malayan and Philippine pottery. Lower seas in the past greatly enlarged the land area; color shows one estimate of the increase.

and that the plants unearthed at Spirit Cave are merely wild species that had been gathered from the surrounding countryside to supplement the hunters' diet. What should we then conclude? Such a finding would be evidence of an advanced stage in the utilization of wild plants in Southeast Asia, a stage that in my opinion is at least as early as any equivalent stage known in the Middle East. On the other hand, what if Yen's finding is positive? This would be evidence that the inhabitants of Spirit Cave were engaging in horticulture at least 2,000 years before the date that has been suggested for the first domestication of plants in the Middle East.

Gorman's next major finding was evidence that a clearly non-Hoabinhian influence had reached Spirit Cave about 6800 B.C. This was indicated by the presence of new and distinctive artifacts among the simple Hoabinhian tools, including rectangular stone adzes with partially polished surfaces and knives made by grinding both sides of a flat piece of slate to form a wedge-shaped cutting edge. Tools such as these are unknown anywhere else in mainland Southeast Asia at such an early date.

Even more important was the presence in the upper strata of pottery fragments that showed a variety of finishes. Most of the potsherds bore imprints that were probably produced by striking the soft clay with a cord-wrapped paddle before the pot was fired. Other potsherds show evidence of polishing, still others had been incised by cutting into the soft clay with a comblike tool, and a few are coated with what appears to be a resin glaze. Except for certain extremely early examples of pottery that have been unearthed in Japan, these fragments from Spirit Cave are the oldest pottery in the world. Moreover, the variety of decoration and finish they display testifies to the existence of a sophisticated potter's tradition with a considerable past.

In addition to collecting more plant material last year, Gorman found examples of a new class of artifacts to add to the inventory from Spirit Cave. These are small pellets of baked clay. In excavating Non Nok Tha we had found similar pellets that were more recent. Our workmen had suggested that they were projectiles for use with a "pellet bow," a weapon that children in northern Thailand still use to hunt birds. The device is like a conventional bow except that a slingshot-like pouch for the pellet is attached to the bowstring.

It is a peculiarity of Southeast Asian

SPIRIT CAVE, located near the Burma border in northwestern Thailand, is being excavated by Chester F. Gorman of the University of Hawaii. From the start, during 1965–1966, Gorman has found the remains of many kinds of edible plants, including nuts, water chestnuts, a species of cucumber and two or three legumes. Some of the material is 12,000 years old. If cultivated and not picked wild, the plants represent man's earliest farming endeavor.

archaeology that stone projectile points, which are among the most abundant artifacts elsewhere in the world, are rarely found in the region. The reason is presumably that the early hunters in the area made their projectiles of wood, as the Southeast Asians who hunt with the bow and arrow still do; objects made of wood, of course, quickly rot and leave no trace in the archaeological record. If the clay pellets at Spirit Cave were indeed made for pellet bows, then such weapons and possibly conventional bows and arrows could have been in use there 9,000 or more years ago.

Taking into account both the range

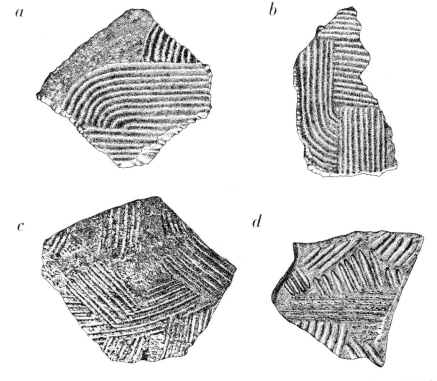

POTTERY FRAGMENTS from Spirit Cave, some nearly 9,000 years old, are decorated with sophisticated incised designs (a, b), suggesting that the potter's art had evolved at a still earlier date elsewhere in Southeast Asia. The designs resemble some on pottery more than 4,000 years old (c, d), found on Formosa in 1964 by Kwang-chih Chang of Yale University.

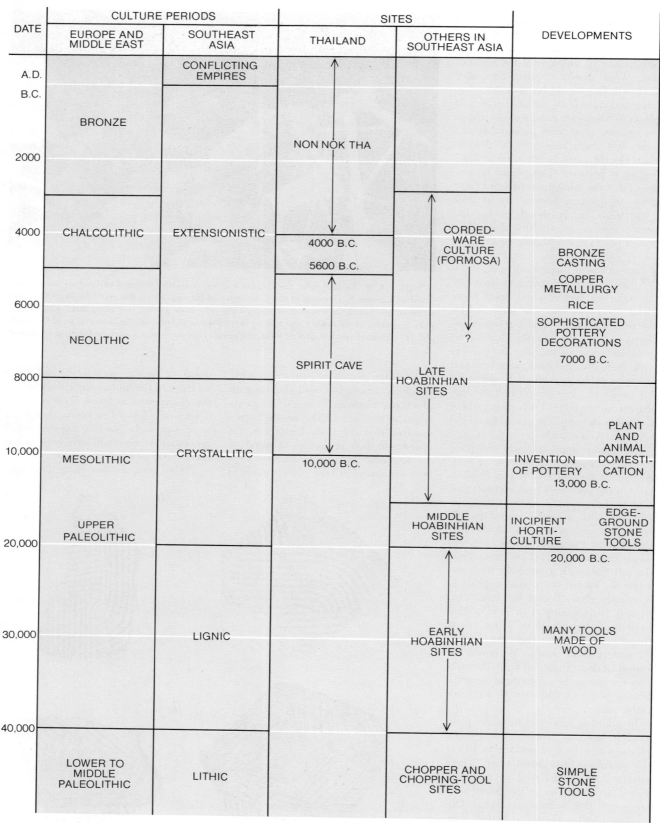

| DATE | CULTURE PERIODS | | SITES | | DEVELOPMENTS |
|---|---|---|---|---|---|
| | EUROPE AND MIDDLE EAST | SOUTHEAST ASIA | THAILAND | OTHERS IN SOUTHEAST ASIA | |
| A.D. | | CONFLICTING EMPIRES | ↕ | | |
| B.C. | BRONZE | | NON NOK THA | | |
| 2000 | | EXTENSIONISTIC | | | |
| 4000 | CHALCOLITHIC | | 4000 B.C. | CORDED-WARE CULTURE (FORMOSA) | BRONZE CASTING |
| | | | 5600 B.C. | | COPPER METALLURGY |
| 6000 | NEOLITHIC | | SPIRIT CAVE | ? | RICE |
| | | | | | SOPHISTICATED POTTERY DECORATIONS |
| 8000 | | | | LATE HOABINHIAN SITES | 7000 B.C. |
| 10,000 | MESOLITHIC | CRYSTALLITIC | 10,000 B.C. | | INVENTION OF POTTERY — PLANT AND ANIMAL DOMESTI-CATION 13,000 B.C. |
| 20,000 | UPPER PALEOLITHIC | | | MIDDLE HOABINHIAN SITES | INCIPIENT HORTI-CULTURE — EDGE-GROUND STONE TOOLS 20,000 B.C. |
| 30,000 | | LIGNIC | | EARLY HOABINHIAN SITES | MANY TOOLS MADE OF WOOD |
| 40,000 | LOWER TO MIDDLE PALEOLITHIC | LITHIC | | CHOPPER AND CHOPPING-TOOL SITES | SIMPLE STONE TOOLS |

**NEW FRAMEWORK** for the prehistory of Southeast Asia has been developed on the basis of recent excavations. The traditional subdivisions of the stone and metal ages of Europe, which cannot be applied in Southeast Asia, are shown at left. Beside them are the five new divisions of the past in Southeast Asia, ranging from prehistoric up to historic times. The names of the earliest periods indicate the kind of material most used for tools: Lithic suggests stone tools; Lignic, wooden ones. The later period names indicate the principal trends during each period. The local cultures of the region took shape during the Crystallitic period. Major population shifts away from mountain habitats occurred in the Extensionistic period. The Period of Conflicting Empires witnessed the rise of states after the start of the Christian Era. Elsewhere the chart shows the relation of five periods to specific sites and basic developments.

of the carbon-14 dates and the rich inventory of remains unearthed at Spirit Cave and Non Nok Tha, it is apparent that a radical revision is needed in our concepts of the prehistory of Southeast Asia. The theoretical outline of a new regional prehistory that follows is based on such a revision. My reconstruction is largely hypothetical; it will need to be tested by further excavation both in mainland and island areas. Much of it is based on the findings at the two Thailand sites, but I have included additional data from my own work and the work of others in the region. Because the outline uses some unfamiliar terms, I shall first briefly review the conventional terminology of prehistory in order to place these new terms in perspective.

For more than a century archaeologists have referred to three stages of the Stone Age: the Paleolithic ("old stone"), the Mesolithic ("middle stone") and the Neolithic ("new stone"). The terms were first defined to fit the prehistory of Europe, but they have since been applied so widely that it is often unthinkingly assumed that cultures all over the world have passed through these three stages. It is quite clear, however, that in many regions the European terms do not correctly describe the sequence of events; this is particularly true of Southeast Asia. The evolution of cultures there has been distinctly different from that in Europe and the Middle East. I am therefore suggesting the substitution of new terms for Southeast Asia.

For the earliest period in Southeast Asia I propose the term Lithic. The term refers to the early human use of chipped and flaked stone for tools. This period, roughly equivalent to the early and middle Paleolithic of Europe, is, I suggest, the only one of the three Stone Age stages that all mankind has shared. In Southeast Asia the technology of chipping and flaking stone developed slowly and never did reach the level of extremely fine workmanship found in many other parts of the world. A possible reason for this seeming backwardness is proposed below. In any event I have arbitrarily set the end of the Lithic period around 40,000 B.C.

For the next period I propose the name Lignic, a term derived from the Latin word for wood. It is part of my hypothesis that during this period tools made of wood—particularly those made of bamboo—became more important to the peoples of Southeast Asia than tools made of stone. Such a change in the preferred material for tools would help to account for the slow progress in stone-working technology during much of the region's prehistory.

Since wood rarely lasts in the ground, we can hardly expect to excavate the ancient wood tools that would prove my hypothesis. It is possible, however, to examine the stone tools for signs of the kind of wear suggestive of woodworking. Gorman has done this with the Hoabinhian tools from Spirit Cave, and he has found several that show edge wear indicating their use to shape both large pieces of wood and wood shafts of small diameter. It may be significant in this connection that a high percentage of the charcoal in the hearths at Spirit Cave consists of charred bamboo.

The period when wood tools proliferated I have arbitrarily defined as beginning about 40,000 B.C. and ending about 20,000 B.C. In terms of the currently known prehistoric cultures of Southeast Asia this dating would equate the Lignic period with early Hoabinhian.

For the third period in the region I propose the name Crystallitic. The term has nothing to do with raw materials but is intended to suggest that during this interval distinct local cultures began to take shape, or crystallize, in Southeast Asia. Before the period ended, sometime around 8000 B.C., I believe there had developed many elements of culture that are still found in the region today. In terms of known prehistoric sites the Crystallitic period equates with middle and late Hoabinhian.

I suggest that it was during Crystallitic times that the technique of shaping stone tools by grinding and polishing was first developed. At the start this method was applied only to a tool's cutting edge; later it was gradually extended over the entire surface. Stone tools that are ground and polished rather than chipped and flaked are typical of the Neolithic stage of the Stone Age in Europe and the Middle East; they make their first appearance about 8000 B.C. in the Middle East. I believe the same technology was being pioneered in Southeast Asia much earlier.

The Crystallitic period is also the interval when plants were domesticated. I suggest that what is called middle Hoabinhian was a culture or cultures whose adherents were experimenting with many different kinds of wild plants for many different reasons. At some point, probably about 13,000 B.C. somewhere in the northern reaches of Southeast Asia, such experiments culminated in the domestication of some of these plants and the consequent appearance of horticulture as a new means of food procurement.

Having advanced this far in the Crystallitic period, we make contact at last with some of our newfound evidence: the contents of the lowest levels at Spirit Cave. I suggest that it was the late Hoabinhian culture, as it is represented in these levels, that achieved the transformation from horticulture to generalized plant and animal domestication and that also achieved the invention of pottery. In different parts of the region different plants would have been selected for cultivation. The same was probably true of the animals involved: the pig, the chicken and possibly even the dog. All these different elements of late Hoabinhian culture spread and accumulated as time passed. When the lowest levels at Spirit Cave were being formed, about 10,000 B.C., the people there appear to have possessed such elements of late Hoabinhian culture as an advanced knowledge of horticulture and perhaps domesticated pigs. They had no pottery, however, nor would they acquire any until an entire spectrum of sophisticated wares arrived at Spirit Cave from elsewhere in Southeast Asia some three millenniums later.

For the fourth period in Southeast Asia I propose the name Extensionistic. The term refers to the major trend during the interval: the movement of peoples out of the mountains where they had previously lived. The Extensionistic trend, which began around 8000 B.C. and ended at about the beginning of the Christian Era, led the mountain peoples not only into the many other hospitable habitats of the mainland but also beyond them; the mountain peoples traveled by overland routes or by water in virtually every direction. I believe future investigation will show that local cultures that were distinctly different from the late Hoabinhian evolved at the start of this period.

At present the only known candidate for one of these newly evolved cultures is the complex of traits that appeared in the upper levels at Spirit Cave, with its rectangular adzes, its slate knives and its sophisticated cord-marked pottery. That complex, however, is not eligible for status as an independent culture; one cannot separate its elements from their late Hoabinhian associations. Is there a similar complex elsewhere, free of a Hoabinhian matrix?

There is on the island of Formosa (Taiwan). Its artifacts include rectangular adzes, polished slate points and cord-marked pottery, some of it decorated with comb incisions like the ware at Spirit Cave. This Formosan complex

**SIMPLE COPPER TOOL,** perhaps used as an adze or an axe, is the one found in 1968 in a deep burial at Non Nok Tha. The socket at one end (*see section*) makes the tool unique.

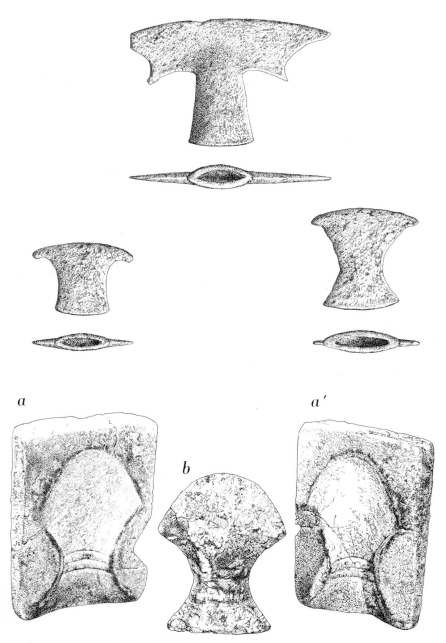

*a*                    *a'*

*b*

**WORK IN BRONZE** at Non Nok Tha included casting axe heads in stone molds. Illustrated are two halves of a mold and a matching axe head (*a, a', b*), and profile and top views of three typical axe heads, showing the sockets for inserting the wooden axe handles.

has been named the Corded-Ware Culture by its discoverer, Kwang-chih Chang of Yale University. Little is known about its age except that, at the two open-air sites where it has been unearthed, the culture ceased to exist sometime before 2500 B.C. Considering the winds of change that marked the Extensionistic period, it is worth emphasizing two points here. First, Formosa is a long way from Spirit Cave. Second, the remains of the Corded-Ware Culture on Formosa are found not in a conventional Hoabinhian cave setting but out in the open.

What were the consequences of the population movements during this period? I suggest that the earliest movements brought the people no farther from the mountains than into the adjacent piedmont. Even this movement led to enough of an environmental change, however, to make the hunting of wild animals and the gathering of wild plants activities of diminishing significance and to make farming much more important. The transition from dependence on wild food resources to dependence on domesticated ones would of course have been gradual. Indeed, the transition is not complete in Southeast Asia even today. People in towns and even in cities still collect wild produce, and many such items are found in the markets. Wild animals are hunted and trapped wherever possible and make an important addition to the limited human intake of protein.

The beginning of the Extensionistic period coincided with the end of the Pleistocene epoch. The lower level of the sea during the Pleistocene ice ages gave Southeast Asia about twice the land area it has today. The seacoast ran along the edge of what is now the Sunda Shelf, and the islands of western Indonesia and the Philippines were connected to the mainland. Few Hoabinhian sites have been found adjacent to the present coastline; it seems logical to expect that many of the Extensionistic settlements were located in river valleys and on shores that are now submerged. The slowly rising sea that accompanied the last retreat of the continental glaciers must have forced some peoples to retreat to the mainland and have left others marooned on the islands. The inhabitants of the Sunda Shelf who retreated to the coast of South China and North Vietnam were probably the ancestors of the people who took readily to the sea starting about 4000 B.C. and ultimately pushed as far as Madagascar off the coast of Africa and Easter Island off the coast of South America.

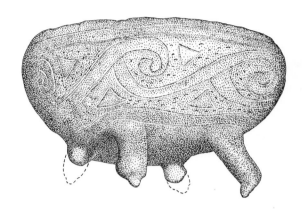

DECORATED POTS, uncommon at Non Nok Tha, were confined to the lower levels of the mound, where the burials are about 5,000 years old. One decorative motif, which combines painted triangles with a curvilinear scroll (*left*), is repeated in the incised decorations on pottery found at offshore sites in the region such as the cave site near Kalanay on the Philippine island of Masbate (*right*).

What material changes would have been evident as various local cultures evolved during this period? Again the material from Spirit Cave and Non Nok Tha is suggestive. The slate knives from the upper levels at Spirit Cave closely resemble the kind used today to harvest rice in parts of Indonesia. Is it possible that rice was one of the plants the final residents of Spirit Cave collected and perhaps cultivated? The cereal was certainly known at Non Nok Tha perhaps no more than 1,500 years later, as the pottery impressions of rice grains and rice husks have demonstrated.

Metallurgical analysis of the copper tool that Bayard unearthed at Non Nok Tha shows that it contains traces of phosphorus and arsenic. This fact suggests that the tool was not merely pounded into shape from a large nugget but that the copper was smelted or otherwise heat-treated, and it implies some degree of metallurgical sophistication among the fourth-millennium inhabitants of the site. Not long afterward the people of Non Nok Tha were casting bronze in the form of socketed tools much like the earlier copper one. No trace of copper, tin or lead ores—the three metals used in this region to make bronze—has been found in association with the bronze-casting equipment at Non Nok Tha. Either the ores were smelted at some other part of the site or the refined metals, or the alloyed bronze itself, reached Non Nok Tha through trade channels.

We are led to the conclusion that the relatively advanced metallurgy practiced at Non Nok Tha during the fourth and third millenniums B.C. had its roots in earlier metallurgical developments elsewhere in the region. If one gives due weight to the evidence that socketed metal tools were unknown outside the region until about 2000 B.C., a further conclusion seems inescapable: The development of metallurgy in Southeast Asia was probably independent of and unrelated to the development of metallurgy in the Middle East.

A major puzzle remains. Given the spread of plant and animal domestication, the advances in metallurgy and the development of trade, it is surprising that the entire Extensionistic period was unmarked by the kind of social evolution that accompanied the same events in the Middle East. We find neither the rise of cities nor the growth of centralized political power. Even as late as the second and first millenniums B.C. fortifications are unknown anywhere in Southeast Asia, which strongly suggests that organized warfare was also unknown. With one possible exception the various cultures of the region seem to have shared much the same kind of economic base and to have enjoyed contact with one another but to have remained politically independent. The exception is the culture of the region of what is now North Vietnam and the adjacent parts of China; during the second millennium B.C. a centralized authority that was quite independent of the imperialistic dynasties in northern China may have arisen in this area. More archaeological investigation is needed, however, before the actual extent of the development can be determined.

The first years of the Christian Era coincided with the start of the most recent period in Southeast Asia, which I call the Period of Conflicting Empires. It was then that, as a result of Indian political and religious influences, the first centralized states finally made their appearance in the region, just as they had in India itself. Once established, a number of petty states flourished in succession for some 1,500 years; they were largely parasitic on the population of the region. Beginning in the 16th century and continuing into the 20th, European imperialism gradually supplanted the native variety; the change in rulers made no appreciable difference to the inhabitants. The occupation of Spirit Cave had of course ended long before the Period of Conflicting Empires began; except for the appearance of iron and the water buffalo the archaeological record at Non Nok Tha was scarcely affected by the events of the period.

Following the withdrawal of the European colonialists after World War II, the Period of Conflicting Empires also came to an end. Southeast Asia today is in an interval of readjustment that has been complicated equally by the collapse of empires and of philosophies. The least one may hope for a region where early man took so many remarkable strides along the road to civilization is a return to the live-and-let-live pattern of cultural independence that characterized much of its prehistory.

# 17

# The Origins of
# New World Civilization

by Richard S. MacNeish
*November 1964*

*In the Mexican valley of Tehuacán bands of hunters
became urban craftsmen in the course of 12,000 years.
Their achievement raises some new questions about the
evolution of high cultures in general*

Perhaps the most significant single occurrence in human history was the development of agriculture and animal husbandry. It has been assumed that this transition from food-gathering to food production took place between 10,000 and 16,000 years ago at a number of places in the highlands of the Middle East. In point of fact the archaeological evidence for the transition, particularly the evidence for domesticated plants, is extremely meager. It is nonetheless widely accepted that the transition represented a "Neolithic Revolution," in which abundant food, a sedentary way of life and an expanding population provided the foundations on which today's high civilizations are built.

The shift from food-gathering to food production did not, however, happen only once. Until comparatively recent times the Old World was for the most part isolated from the New World. Significant contact was confined to a largely one-way migration of culturally primitive Asiatic hunting bands across the Bering Strait. In spite of this almost total absence of traffic between the hemispheres the European adventurers who reached the New World in the 16th century encountered a series of cultures almost as advanced (except in metallurgy and pyrotechnics) and quite as barbarous as their own. Indeed, some of the civilizations from Mexico to Peru possessed a larger variety of domesticated plants than did their European conquerors and had made agricultural advances far beyond those of the Old World.

At some time, then, the transition from food-gathering to food production occurred in the New World as it had in the Old. In recent years one of the major problems for New World prehistorians has been to test the hypothesis of a Neolithic Revolution against native archaeological evidence and at the same time to document the American stage of man's initial domestication of plants (which remains almost unknown in both hemispheres).

The differences between the ways in which Old World and New World men achieved independence from the nomadic life of the hunter and gatherer are more striking than the similarities. The principal difference lies in the fact that the peoples of the Old World domesticated many animals and comparatively few plants, whereas in the New World the opposite was the case. The abundant and various herds that gave the peoples of Europe, Africa and Asia meat, milk, wool and beasts of burden were matched in the pre-Columbian New World only by a half-domesticated group of Andean cameloids: the llama, the alpaca and the vicuña. The Andean guinea pig can be considered an inferior equivalent of the Old World's domesticated rabbits and hares; elsewhere in the Americas the turkey was an equally inferior counterpart of the Eastern Hemisphere's many varieties of barnyard fowl. In both the Old World and the New, dogs presumably predated all other domestic animals; in both beekeepers harvested honey and wax. Beyond this the New World list of domestic animals dwindles to nothing. All the cultures of the Americas, high and low alike, depended on their hunters' skill for most of their animal produce: meat and hides, furs and feathers, teeth and claws.

In contrast, the American Indian domesticated a remarkable number of plants. Except for cotton, the "water bottle" gourd, the yam and possibly the coconut (which may have been domesticated independently in each hemisphere), the kinds of crops grown in the Old World and the New were quite different. Both the white and the sweet potato, cultivated in a number of varieties, were unique to the New World. For seasoning, in place of the pepper and mustard of the Old World, the peoples of the New World raised vanilla and at least two kinds of chili. For edible seeds they grew amaranth, chive, panic grass, sunflower, quinoa, apazote, chocolate, the peanut, the common bean and four other kinds of beans: lima, summer, tepary and jack.

In addition to potatoes the Indians cultivated other root crops, including manioc, oca and more than a dozen other South American plants. In place of the Old World melons, the related plants brought to domestication in the New World were the pumpkin, the

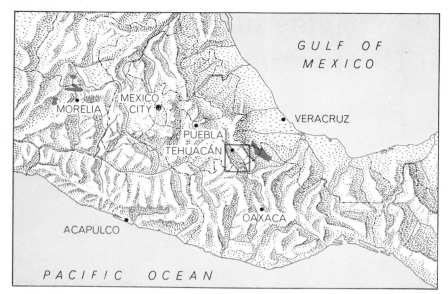

**TEHUACÁN VALLEY** is a narrow desert zone in the mountains on the boundary between the states of Puebla and Oaxaca. It is one of the three areas in southern Mexico selected during the search for early corn on the grounds of dryness (which helps to preserve ancient plant materials) and highland location (corn originally having been a wild highland grass).

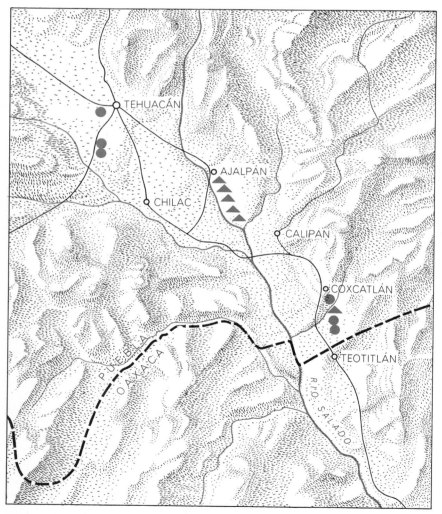

**SIX CAVES** (*dots*) and six open-air sites (*triangles*) have been investigated in detail by the author and his colleagues. Coxcatlán cave (*top dot at right*), where early corn was found in 1960, has the longest habitation record: from well before 7000 B.C. until A.D. 1500.

gourd, the chayote and three or four distinct species of what we call squash. Fruits brought under cultivation in the Americas included the tomato, avocado, pineapple, guava, elderberry and papaya. The pioneering use of tobacco—smoked in pipes, in the form of cigars and even in the form of cane cigarettes, some of which had one end stuffed with fibers to serve as a filter—must also be credited to the Indians.

Above all of these stood Indian corn, *Zea mays,* the only important wild grass in the New World to be transformed into a food grain as the peoples of the Old World had transformed their native grasses into wheat, barley, rye, oats and millet. From Chile to the valley of the St. Lawrence in Canada, one or another of 150 varieties of Indian corn was the staple diet of the pre-Columbian peoples. As a food grain or as fodder, corn remains the most important single crop in the Americas today (and the third largest in the world). Because of its dominant position in New World agriculture, prehistorians have long been confident that if they could find out when and where corn was first domesticated, they might also uncover the origins of New World civilization.

Until little more than a generation ago investigators of this question were beset by twin difficulties. First, research in both Central America and South America had failed to show that any New World high culture significantly predated the Christian era. Second, botanical studies of the varieties of corn and its wild relatives had led more to conflict than to clarity in regard to the domesticated plant's most probable wild predecessor [see "The Mystery of Corn," by Paul C. Mangelsdorf; SCIENTIFIC AMERICAN, July, 1950]. Today, thanks to close cooperation between botanists and archaeologists, both difficulties have almost vanished. At least one starting point for New World agricultural activity has been securely established as being between 5,000 and 9,000 years ago. At the same time botanical analysis of fossil corn ears, grains and pollen, together with plain dirt archaeology, have solved a number of the mysteries concerning the wild origin and domestic evolution of corn. What follows is a review of the recent developments that have done so much to increase our understanding of this key period in New World prehistory.

The interest of botanists in the history of corn is largely practical: they study the genetics of corn in order to produce improved hybrids. After the wild ancestors of corn had been sought for nearly a century the search had narrowed to two tassel-bearing New World grasses—teosinte and *Tripsacum*—that had features resembling the domesticated plant. On the basis of crossbreeding experiments and other genetic studies, however, Paul C. Mangelsdorf of Harvard University and other investigators concluded in the 1940's that neither of these plants could be the original ancestor of corn. Instead teosinte appeared to be the product of the accidental crossbreeding of true corn and *Tripsacum*. Mangelsdorf advanced the hypothesis that the wild progenitor of corn was none other than corn itself—probably a popcorn with its kernels encased in pods.

Between 1948 and 1960 a number of discoveries proved Mangelsdorf's contention to be correct. I shall present these discoveries not in their strict chronological order but rather in their order of importance. First in importance, then, were analyses of pollen found in "cores" obtained in 1953 by drilling into the lake beds on which Mexico City is built. At levels that were estimated to be about 80,000 years old—perhaps 50,000 years older than the earliest known human remains in the New World—were found grains of corn

pollen. There could be no doubt that the pollen was from wild corn, and thus two aspects of the ancestry of corn were clarified. First, a form of wild corn has been in existence for 80,000 years, so that corn can indeed be descended from itself. Second, wild corn had flourished in the highlands of Mexico. As related archaeological discoveries will make plain, this geographical fact helped to narrow the potential range—from the southwestern U.S. to Peru—within which corn was probably first domesticated.

The rest of the key discoveries, involving the close cooperation of archaeologist and botanist, all belong to the realm of paleobotany. In the summer of 1948, for example, Herbert Dick, a graduate student in anthropology who had been working with Mangelsdorf, explored a dry rock-shelter in New Mexico called Bat Cave. Digging down through six feet of accumulated deposits, he and his colleagues found numerous remains of ancient corn, culminating in some tiny corncobs at the lowest level. Carbon-14 dating indicated that these cobs were between 4,000 and 5,000 years old. A few months later, exploring the La Perra cave in the state of Tamaulipas far to the north of Mexico City, I found similar corncobs that proved to be about 4,500 years old. The oldest cobs at both sites came close

to fitting the description Mangelsdorf had given of a hypothetical ancestor of the pod-popcorn type. The cobs, however, were clearly those of domesticated corn.

These two finds provided the basis for intensified archaeological efforts to find sites where the first evidences of corn would be even older. The logic was simple: A site old enough should have a level of wild corn remains older than the most ancient domesticated cobs. I continued my explorations near the La Perra cave and excavated a number of other sites in northeastern Mexico. In them I found more samples of ancient corn, but they were no older than those that had already been discovered. Robert Lister, another of Mangelsdorf's coworkers, also found primitive corn in a cave called Swallow's Nest in the Mexican state of Chihuahua, northwest of where I was working, but his finds were no older than mine.

If nothing older than domesticated corn of about 3000 B.C. could be found to the north of Mexico City, it seemed logical to try to the south. In 1958 I went off to look for dry caves and early corn in Guatemala and Honduras. The 1958 diggings produced nothing useful, so in 1959 I moved northward into Chiapas, Mexico's southernmost state. There were no corncobs to be found,

**EXCAVATION** of Coxcatlán cave required the removal of one-meter squares of cave floor over an area 25 meters long by six meters wide until bedrock was reached at a depth of almost five meters. In this way 28 occupation levels, attributable to seven distinctive culture phases, were discovered. Inhabitants of the three lowest levels lived by hunting and by collecting wild-plant foods.

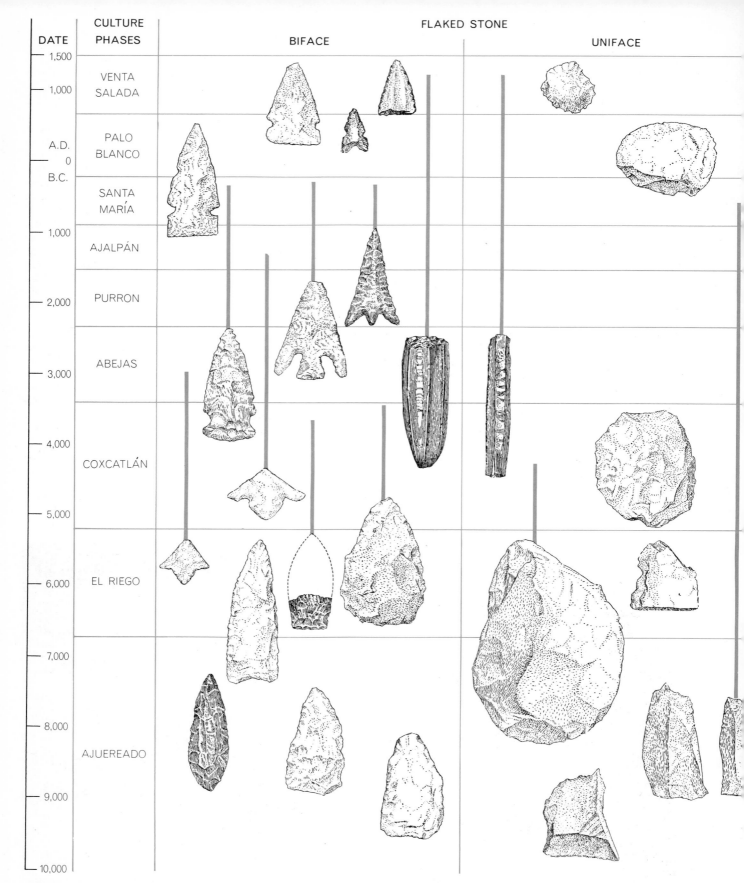

| DATE | CULTURE PHASES | FLAKED STONE BIFACE | UNIFACE |
|---|---|---|---|

DATE

— 1,500
— 1,000

A.D.
0
B.C.

— 1,000

— 2,000

— 3,000

— 4,000

— 5,000

— 6,000

— 7,000

— 8,000

— 9,000

— 10,000

CULTURE PHASES

VENTA SALADA

PALO BLANCO

SANTA MARÍA

AJALPÁN

PURRON

ABEJAS

COXCATLÁN

EL RIEGO

AJUEREADO

**STONE ARTIFACTS** from various Tehuacán sites are arrayed in two major categories: those shaped by chipping and flaking (*left*) and those shaped by grinding and pecking (*right*). Implements that have been chipped on one face only are separated from those that show bifacial workmanship; both groups are reproduced at half their natural size. The ground stone objects are not drawn to a common scale. The horizontal lines define the nine culture phases thus far distinguished in the valley. Vertical lines (*color*) indicate the extent to which the related artifact is known in cultures other than the one in which it is placed. At Tehuacán the evolution of civilization failed to follow the classic pattern established by the Neolithic Revolution in the Old World. For instance, the mortars,

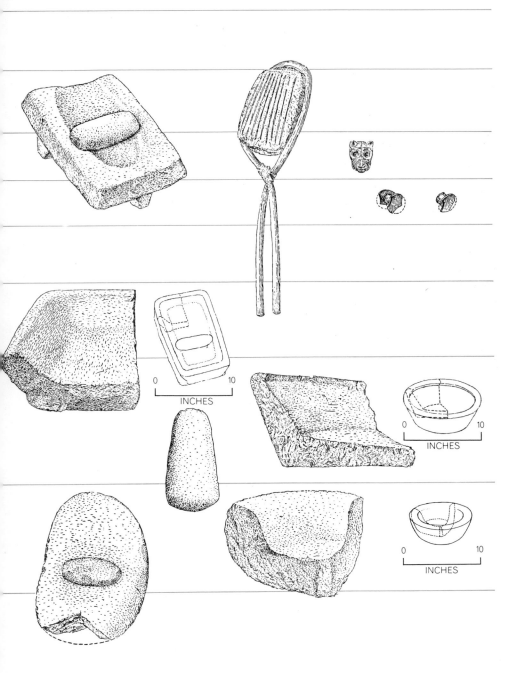

but one cave yielded corn pollen that also dated only to about 3000 B.C. The clues provided by paleobotany now appeared plain. Both to the north of Mexico City and in Mexico City itself (as indicated by the pollen of domesticated corn in the upper levels of the drill cores) the oldest evidence of domesticated corn was no more ancient than about 3000 B.C. Well to the south of Mexico City the oldest date was the same. The area that called for further search should therefore lie south of Mexico City but north of Chiapas.

Two additional considerations enabled me to narrow the area of search even more. First, experience had shown that dry locations offered the best chance of finding preserved specimens of corn. Second, the genetic studies of Mangelsdorf and other investigators indicated that wild corn was originally a highland grass, very possibly able to survive the rigorous climate of highland desert areas. Poring over the map of southern Mexico, I singled out three large highland desert areas: one in the southern part of the state of Oaxaca, one in Guerrero and one in southern Puebla.

Oaxaca yielded nothing of interest, so I moved on to Puebla to explore a dry highland valley known as Tehuacán. My local guides and I scrambled in and out of 38 caves and finally struck pay dirt in the 39th. This was a small rock-shelter near the village of Coxcatlán in the southern part of the valley of Tehuacán. On February 21, 1960, we dug up six corncobs, three of which looked more primitive and older than any I had seen before. Analysis in the carbon-14 laboratory at the University of Michigan confirmed my guess by dating these cobs as 5,600 years old—a good 500 years older than any yet found in the New World.

With this find the time seemed ripe for a large-scale, systematic search. If we had indeed arrived at a place where corn had been domesticated and New World civilization had first stirred, the closing stages of the search would require the special knowledge of many experts. Our primary need was to obtain the sponsorship of an institution interested and experienced in such research, and we were fortunate enough to enlist exactly the right sponsor: the Robert S. Peabody Foundation for Archaeology of Andover, Mass. Funds for the project were supplied by the National Science Foundation and by the agricultural branch of the Rockefeller

pestles and other ground stone implements that first appear in the El Riego culture phase antedate the first domestication of corn by 1,500 years or more. Not until the Abejas phase, nearly 2,000 years later (marked by sizable obsidian cores and blades and by grinding implements that closely resemble the modern mano and metate), do the earliest village sites appear. More than 1,000 years later, in the Ajalpán phase, earplugs for personal adornment occur. The grooved, withe-bound stone near the top is a pounder for making bark cloth.

**EVOLUTION OF CORN** at Tehuacán starts (*far left*) with a fragmentary cob of wild corn of 5000 B.C. date. Next (*left to right*) are an early domesticated cob of 4000 B.C., an early hybrid variety of 3000 B.C. and an early variety of modern corn of 1000 B.C. Last (*far right*) is an entirely modern cob of the time of Christ. All are shown four-fifths of natural size.

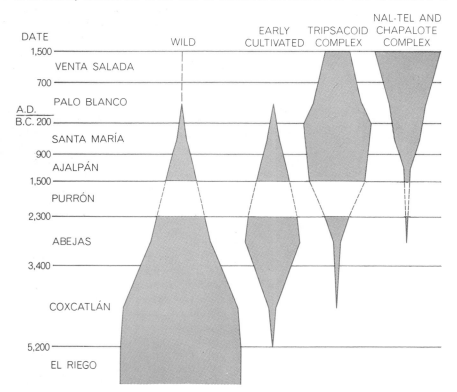

**MAIN VARIETIES OF CORN** changed in their relative abundance at Tehuacán between the time of initial cultivation during the Coxcatlán culture phase and the arrival of the conquistadors. Abundant at first, wild corn had become virtually extinct by the start of the Christian era, as had the early cultivated (but not hybridized) varieties. Thereafter the hybrids of the tripsacoid complex (produced by interbreeding wild corn with introduced varieties of corn-*Tripsacum* or corn-teosinte hybrids) were steadily replaced by two still extant types of corn, Nal-Tel and Chapalote. Minor varieties of late corn are not shown.

Foundation in Mexico, which is particularly interested in the origins of corn. The project eventually engaged nearly 50 experts in many specialties, not only archaeology and botany (including experts on many plants other than corn) but also zoology, geography, geology, ecology, genetics, ethnology and other disciplines.

The Coxcatlán cave, where the intensive new hunt had begun, turned out to be our richest dig. Working downward, we found that the cave had 28 separate occupation levels, the earliest of which may date to about 10,000 B.C. This remarkably long sequence has one major interruption: the period between 2300 B.C. and 900 B.C. The time from 900 B.C. to A.D. 1500, however, is represented by seven occupation levels. In combination with our findings in the Purrón cave, which contains 25 floors that date from about 7000 B.C. to 500 B.C., we have an almost continuous record (the longest interruption is less than 500 years) of nearly 12,000 years of prehistory. This is by far the longest record for any New World area.

All together we undertook major excavations at 12 sites in the valley of Tehuacán [*see bottom illustration on page 170*]. Of these only five caves—Coxcatlán, Purrón, San Marcos, Tecorral and El Riego East—contained remains of ancient corn. But these and the other stratified sites gave us a wealth of additional information about the people who inhabited the valley over a span of 12,000 years. In four seasons of digging, from 1961 through 1964, we reaped a vast archaeological harvest. This includes nearly a million individual remains of human activity, more than 1,000 animal bones (including those of extinct antelopes and horses), 80,000 individual wild-plant remains and some 25,000 specimens of corn. The artifacts arrange themselves into significant sequences of stone tools, textiles and pottery. They provide an almost continuous picture of the rise of civilization in the valley of Tehuacán. From the valley's geology, from the shells of its land snails, from the pollen and other remains of its plants and from a variety of other relics our group of specialists has traced the changes in climate, physical environment and plant and animal life that took place during the 12,000 years. They have even been able to tell (from the kinds of plant remains in various occupation levels) at what seasons of the year many of the floors in the caves were occupied.

Outstanding among our many finds was a collection of minuscule corncobs that we tenderly extracted from the lowest of five occupation levels at the San Marcos cave. They were only about 20 millimeters long, no bigger than the filter tip of a cigarette [*see top illustration on opposite page*], but under a magnifying lens one could see that they were indeed miniature ears of corn, with sockets that had once contained kernels enclosed in pods. These cobs proved to be some 7,000 years old. Mangelsdorf is convinced that this must be wild corn—the original parent from which modern corn is descended.

Cultivated corn, of course, cannot survive without man's intervention; the dozens of seeds on each cob are enveloped by a tough, thick husk that prevents them from scattering. Mangelsdorf has concluded that corn's wild progenitor probably consisted of a single seed spike on the stalk, with a few pod-covered ovules arrayed on the spike and a pollen-bearing tassel attached to the spike's end [*see bottom illustration at right*]. The most primitive cobs we unearthed in the valley of Tehuacán fulfilled these specifications. Each had the stump of a tassel at the end, each had borne kernels of the pod-popcorn type and each had been covered with only a light husk consisting of two leaves. These characteristics would have allowed the plant to disperse its seeds at maturity; the pods would then have protected the seeds until conditions were appropriate for germination.

The people of the valley of Tehuacán lived for thousands of years as collectors of wild vegetable and animal foods before they made their first timid efforts as agriculturists. It would therefore be foolhardy to suggest that the inhabitants of this arid highland pocket of Mexico were the first or the only people in the Western Hemisphere to bring wild corn under cultivation. On the contrary, the New World's invention of agriculture will probably prove to be geographically fragmented. What can be said for the people of Tehuacán is that they are the first whose evolution from primitive food collectors to civilized agriculturists has been traced in detail. As yet we have no such complete story either for the Old World or for other parts of the New World. This story is as follows.

From a hazy beginning some 12,000 years ago until about 7000 B.C. the people of Tehuacán were few in number. They wandered the valley from season to season in search of jackrabbits, rats, birds, turtles and other small animals, as well as such plant foods as be-

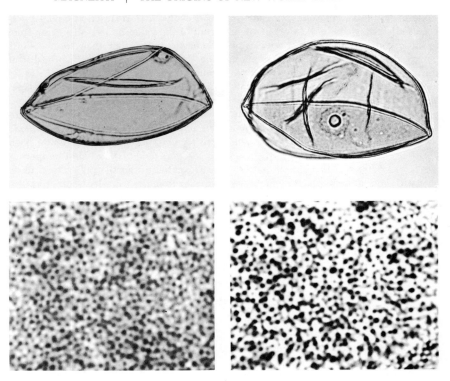

ANTIQUITY OF CORN in the New World was conclusively demonstrated when grains of pollen were found in drilling cores taken from Mexico City lake-bottom strata estimated to be 80,000 years old. Top two photographs (*magnification 435 diameters*) compare the ancient corn pollen (*left*) with modern pollen (*right*). Lower photographs (*magnification 4,500 diameters*) reveal similar ancient (*left*) and modern (*right*) pollen surface markings. The analysis and photographs are the work of Elso S. Barghoorn of Harvard University.

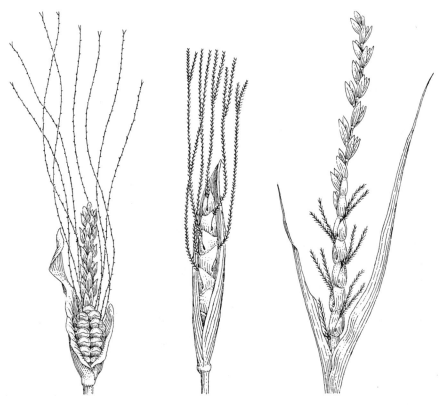

THREE NEW WORLD GRASSES are involved in the history of domesticated corn. Wild corn (*reconstruction at left*) was a pod-pop variety in which the male efflorescence grew from the end of the cob. Teosinte (*center*) and *Tripsacum* (*right*) are corn relatives that readily hybridized with wild and cultivated corn. Modern corn came from such crosses.

came available at different times of the year. Only occasionally did they manage to kill one of the now extinct species of horses and antelopes whose bones mark the lowest cave strata. These people used only a few simple implements of flaked stone: leaf-shaped projectile points, scrapers and engraving tools. We have named this earliest culture period the Ajuereado phase [*see illustration on pages 172 and 173*].

Around 6700 B.C. this simple pattern changed and a new phase—which we have named the El Riego culture from the cave where its first evidences appear—came into being. From then until about 5000 B.C. the people shifted from being predominantly trappers and hunters to being predominantly collectors of plant foods. Most of the plants they collected were wild, but they had domesticated squashes (starting with the species *Cucurbita mixta*) and avocados, and they also ate wild varieties of beans, amaranth and chili peppers. Among the flaked-stone implements, choppers appear. Entirely new kinds of stone tools—grinders, mortars, pestles and pounders of polished stone—are found in large numbers. During the growing season some families evidently gathered in temporary settlements, but these groups broke up into one-family bands during the leaner periods of the year. A number of burials dating from this culture phase hint at the possibility of part-time priests or witch doctors who directed the ceremonies involving the dead. The El Riego culture, however, had no corn.

By about 5000 B.C. a new phase, which we call the Coxcatlán culture,

had evolved. In this period only 10 percent of the valley's foodstuffs came from domestication rather than from collecting, hunting or trapping, but the list of domesticated plants is long. It includes corn, the water-bottle gourd, two species of squash, the amaranth, black and white zapotes, the tepary bean (*Phaseolus acutifolius*), the jack bean (*Canavalia ensiformis*), probably the common bean (*Phaseolus vulgaris*) and chili peppers.

Coxcatlán projectile points tend to be smaller than their predecessors; scrapers and choppers, however, remain much the same. The polished stone implements include forerunners of the classic New World roller-and-stone device for grinding grain: the mano and metate. There was evidently enough surplus energy among the people to allow the laborious hollowing out of stone water jugs and bowls.

It was in the phase following the Coxcatlán that the people of Tehuacán made the fundamental shift. By about 3400 B.C. the food provided by agriculture rose to about 30 percent of the total, domesticated animals (starting with the dog) made their appearance, and the people formed their first fixed settlements—small pit-house villages. By this stage (which we call the Abejas culture) they lived at a subsistence level that can be regarded as a foundation for the beginning of civilization. In about 2300 B.C. this gave way to the Purrón culture, marked by the cultivation of more hybridized types of corn and the manufacture of pottery.

Thereafter the pace of civilization in

the valley speeded up greatly. The descendants of the Purrón people developed a culture (called Ajalpán) that from about 1500 B.C. on involved a more complex village life, refinements of pottery and more elaborate ceremonialism, including the development of a figurine cult, perhaps representing family gods. This culture led in turn to an even more sophisticated one (which we call Santa María) that started about 850 B.C. Taking advantage of the valley's streams, the Santa María peoples of Tehuacán began to grow their hybrid corn in irrigated fields. Our surveys indicate a sharp rise in population. Temple mounds were built, and artifacts show signs of numerous contacts with cultures outside the valley. The Tehuacán culture in this period seems to have been strongly influenced by that of the Olmec people who lived to the southeast along the coast of Veracruz.

By about 200 B.C. the outside influence on Tehuacán affairs shifted from that of the Olmec of the east coast to that of Monte Alban to the south and west. The valley now had large irrigation projects and substantial hilltop ceremonial centers surrounded by villages. In this Palo Blanco phase some of the population proceeded to full-time specialization in various occupations, including the development of a salt industry. New domesticated food products appeared—the turkey, the tomato, the peanut and the guava. In the next period—Venta Salada, starting about A.D. 700—Monte Alban influences gave way to the influence of the Mixtecs. This period saw the rise of true

**COXCATLÁN CAVE BURIAL, dating to about A.D. 100, contained the extended body of an adolescent American Indian, wrapped in** a pair of cotton blankets with brightly colored stripes. This bundle in turn rested on sticks and the whole was wrapped in bark cloth.

cities in the valley, of an agricultural system that provided some 85 percent of the total food supply, of trade and commerce, a standing army, large-scale irrigation projects and a complex religion. Finally, just before the Spanish Conquest, the Aztecs took over from the Mixtecs.

Our archaeological study of the valley of Tehuacán, carried forward in collaboration with workers in so many other disciplines, has been gratifyingly productive. Not only have we documented one example of the origin of domesticated corn but also comparative studies of other domesticated plants have indicated that there were multiple centers of plant domestication in the Americas. At least for the moment we have at Tehuacán not only evidence of the earliest village life in the New World but also the first (and worst) pottery in Mexico and a fairly large sample of skeletons of some of the earliest Indians yet known.

Even more important is the fact that we at last have one New World example of the development of a culture from savagery to civilization. Preliminary analysis of the Tehuacán materials indicate that the traditional hypothesis about the evolution of high cultures may have to be reexamined and modified. In southern Mexico many of the characteristic elements of the Old World's Neolithic Revolution fail to appear suddenly in the form of a new culture complex or a revolutionized way of life. For example, tools of ground (rather than chipped) stone first occur at Tehuacán about 6700 B.C., and plant domestication begins at least by 5000 B.C. The other classic elements of the Old World Neolithic, however, are slow to appear. Villages are not found until around 3000 B.C., nor pottery until around 2300 B.C., and a sudden increase in population is delayed until 500 B.C. Reviewing this record, I think more in terms of Neolithic "evolution" than "revolution."

Our preliminary researches at Tehuacán suggest rich fields for further exploration. There is need not only for detailed investigations of the domestication and development of other New World food plants but also for attempts to obtain similar data for the Old World. Then—perhaps most challenging of all —there is the need for comparative studies of the similarities and differences between evolving cultures in the Old World and the New to determine the hows and whys of the rise of civilization itself.

**SOPHISTICATED FIGURINE** of painted pottery is one example of the artistic capacity of Tehuacán village craftsmen. This specimen, 2,900 years old, shows Olmec influences.

# IV

# CITIES AND CIVILIZATIONS

# CITIES AND CIVILIZATION IV

## INTRODUCTION

The Country Life is to be Preferred," wrote William Penn in the seventeenth century, "for there we see the works of God, but in the cities little else but the works of men." The city is truly a manmade institution, one that has but a 5,000-year history, beginning in Mesopotamia and stretching into modern times. City living is the dominant settlement pattern in the world today, so dominant that the demands of the urban environment have torn apart the millennia-old patterns of social and cultural behavior associated with humankind.

An intense academic curiosity has surrounded the origins of cities and urban civilization for centuries. Notions of human progress, from savagery to the pinnacle of achievement represented by literate civilization, haunt many theories about the beginnings of urban life. Modern research into the origins of civilization began with V. Gordon Childe, who thought that the Urban Revolution in the Near East followed closely on the Neolithic Revolution. Childe centered his definition of the Urban Revolution on the development of a city, a densely populated settlement whose farmers supported a small army of craftsmen, priests, and traders with massive surpluses. Metallurgical industries were developed, which provided superior weapons and led to the emergence of a class society, including both an elite and fulltime specialists. Writing was essential for recordkeeping and development of exact sciences and astronomy. "A unifying religious force" dominated urban life, as priest-kings and despots rose to power over huge populations of peasants and craftsmen.

Childe thought that the Urban Revolution was a critical turning point in human cultural, economic, and social change. This bold concept dominated archaeological thinking for years, but was eventually shown to have serious flaws. Some of Childe's criteria for cities and civilization are far from universal, for some civilizations, among them the Maya and the Mycenaean, did not have cities. Others, like the Inca of Peru, never developed writing. The only things common to all civilization seem to be a degree of craft specialization and a well-formulated religious structure.

The debate about the origin of cities and civilization has been concerned both with critiques of Childe's Urban Revolution hypothesis and with attempts to understand the actual processes which led to the emergence of the city. Robert Adams, whose article, "The Origin of Cities," leads off this section, has emphasized the importance of the development of social organization and craft specialization during the Urban Revolution. Adams has oriented his research toward the changes in social organization in Mesopotamia and in central Mexico that he described as following "a fundamental course of development in which corporate kin groups, originally predominating in the control of land, were gradually supplanted by the growth of private estates in the hands of urban elites." A class society, political and religious hierarchies to administer the state, and a very complex division of labor, including military units, craftsmen, slaves, and bureaucrats, are all essential ingredients of Adams' definition of the processes that led to urban civilization.

But so far no one has succeeded in defining civilization itself. Archaeologists and historians have developed many different working definitions, of which one of the most widely accepted is that of the anthropologist Clyde Kluck-hohn, who defined three essential criteria for civilization: towns with a population of more than 5,000 persons; writing; and monumental ceremonial architecture, including ceremonial centers.

Gideon Sjoberg's article, "The Origin and Evolution of Cities," discusses the origin and evolution of cities on rather a wide canvas. He defines three levels of human organization, each characterized by its own technological, economic, social, and political patterns. The pre-urban folk society is one that generates few food surpluses, certainly none capable of supporting a class of fulltime specialists. The world's first cities developed in the context of what Sjoberg calls the "civilized preindustrial stage of organization." Writing was a key to the keeping of simple accounts and records, and preindustrial societies did have writing. But they had few energy sources, even though an abundant food surplus provided both labor specialization and the development of a class structure capable of organizing irrigation schemes and other major public works. Sjoberg's third level is the fully literate industrial civilization, with a fluid class system and access to "new sources of inanimate energy that produced and still sustains the industrial revolution."

The development of cities as envisaged by Sjoberg is probably a simplistic account of a highly complex system of interacting processes and factors. More recently archaeologists have been looking at systems models, regarding human society as one class of living system. Under this notion, the state appears as a very complex system, with many different subsystems, such as technology and social organization, interacting one with another. Complex mechanisms involving both decision-making and societal policy keep the system as a whole in equilibrium. Those who favor the systems approach have to be able to isolate a series of rules by which the origins of a state system might be simulated; investigating the mechanisms of decision making lies at the center of these efforts. Systems research in archaeology is still in its infancy, but some idea of the greater complexity explanations for the origins of civilization can be obtained from the Lamberg-Karlovskys' article, "An Early City in Iran." They describe their excavations at Tepe Yahya, a large occupation mound in southeastern Iran, where they found evidence of widespread trading connections between several centers of early civilization. The Lamberg-Karlovskys feel that the Sumerians, Proto-Elamites, Egyptians, and Harappans of the Indus Valley were already maintaining a pattern of cultural and economic exchange among themselves by 3500 B.C. All these societies showed "distinctive sets of the interrelated phenomena that Adams used to define civilization." It is the economic dialog between these various societies that stimulated intense political and social development in each region.

Economic development in later prehistory depended heavily on some startling technological innovations. Surprisingly little attention has been paid to many of the great inventions of prehistory—fire is one example; the bow and arrow is another; and the early history of the wheel and wheeled transport is a third—partly because the remains of such inventions are often among the first to perish when preservation conditions are anything but perfect. For wheeled transport, little survives for the archaeologist to work with in his excavations. Professor Stuart Piggott, an English archaeologist of long experience, has spent his career studying the early history of farming and metallurgy in the temperate zones of Europe. He turned his attention to the history of the wheel when he realized the critical importance of the cart and the wagon for trade and transport. Wheels mean a much greater capacity for load-carrying. Prerequisites for the development of wheeled transport include both domesticated cattle to pull the wagon and abundant timber for the carts. In his article, "The Beginning of Wheeled Transport," Piggott describes new discoveries in the U.S.S.R. which extend the history of the wheel back to at least 5,000 years ago. He feels the wheel was invented and developed throughout a wide area of eastern Europe, wherever the necessary tools and materials were available. The article is an admirable example of the use of many different and scattered finds to hypothesize about a major issue in prehistory.

Much of the debate surrounding the origins of cities and civilizations in the Old World has been echoed for the Americas. Although equivalents to the great literate civilizations of the Near East never evolved in the New World, a remarkable series of indigenous and distinctively American polities developed in Mesoamerica and Peru. The great empires of the Aztec and Inca were destroyed by the Spanish *conquistadores* in the sixteenth century and vanished into oblivion within a few generations. Only a few sketchy eyewitness accounts of the Aztecs and Incas have survived, together with some ethnographic notes by early Spanish chroniclers. We have to rely on archaeology for primary information on New World civilization.

The institutions of the American states were centered around vast ceremonial complexes and were based on subsistence agriculture and a strongly unifying religious force that dominated all strata of society. Great empires like that of the Maya or the Moche rose to power and then collapsed with bewildering rapidity. The processes of rise and decline are still imperfectly understood, largely because archaeologists have been preoccupied with chronologies and artifact patterning until recent years, by which time a broad outline of Mesoamerican and Peruvian chronology had been agreed upon. Some of the best studies in Mesoamerican civilization are concerned with the reconstruction of minor details of ceremonial centers of vast urban complexes.

One of the most thoroughly investigated cities of the New World is the largest city of pre-Colombian America, Teotihuacán. Professor René Millon is in the final stages of a huge research project which has involved the compilation of a complete city plan, plotting the structures within the city limits. Teotihuacán covered an area of eight square miles, and probably supported a population of between 50,000 and 100,000 at the height of its prosperity. The top strata of society were religious leaders, bureaucrats, and soldiers. A closely integrated society of craftsmen, peasants, and other workers manned Teotihuacán's enormous markets, and pottery and obsidian tool manufacture were important activities. Millon's article, describing the many facets of Teotihuacán and the extraordinary political and religious niche it occupied in classic Mesoamerica, enables us to glimpse the mechanisms which led to the rise, prosperity, and fall of the greatest of Mesoamerica's early cities. Millon concludes by remarking that "Teotihuacán was as influential in its collapse as in its long and brilliant flowering." This comprehensive long-term research project is typical of the detailed field studies essential to the understanding of New World civilization.

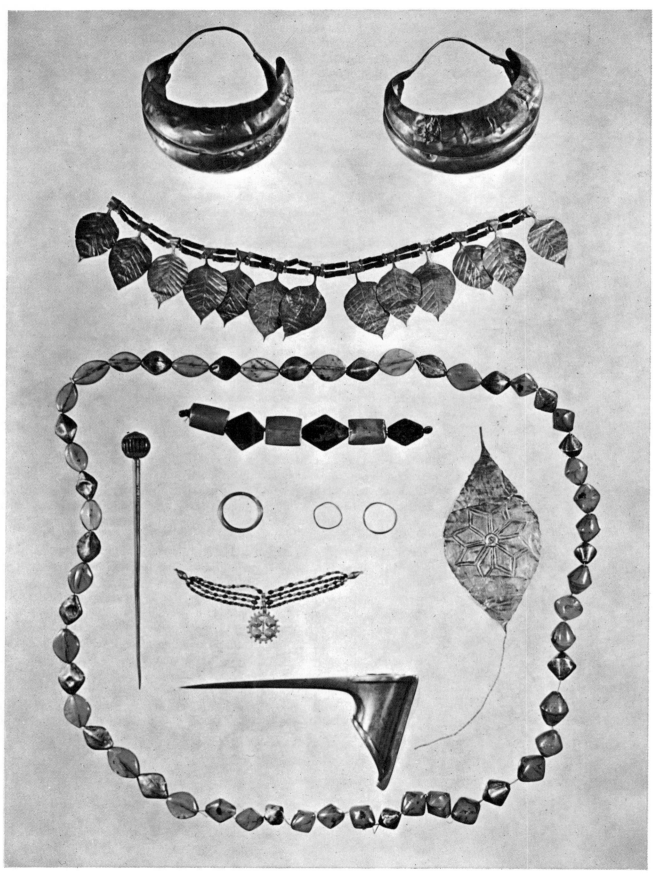

**ROYAL GRAVE OFFERINGS** from later tombs at Ur indicate the concentration of wealth that accompanied the emergence of a kingly class. Dated at about 2500 B.C., the objects include large gold earrings (*top*); a headdress with gold leaves; beads of gold, lapis and carnelian; gold rings; a gold leaf; a hairpin of gold and lapis; an ornament with a gold pendant; an adz head of electrum.

# The Origin of Cities

by Robert M. Adams
*September 1960*

*The agricultural revolution ultimately made it possible for men to congregate in large communities, and to take up specialized tasks. The first cities almost certainly arose in Mesopotamia*

The rise of cities, the second great "revolution" in human culture, was pre-eminently a social process, an expression more of changes in man's interaction with his fellows than in his interaction with his environment. For this reason it marks not only a turning but also a branching point in the history of the human species.

Earlier steps are closely identified with an increasing breadth or intensity in the exploitation of the environment. Their distinguishing features are new tools and techniques and the discovery of new and more dependable resources for subsistence. Even in so advanced an achievement as the invention of agriculture, much of the variation from region to region was simply a reflection of local differences in subsistence potential.

In contrast the urban revolution was

MAP OF NIPPUR on a clay tablet dates from about 1500 B.C. Two lines at far left trace the course of Euphrates River; adjacent lines show one wall of the city. Square structures at far right are temples; the two vertical lines at right center represent a canal.

EARLY GRAVE OFFERINGS from Mesopotamian tombs of about 3900 B.C. consist mainly of painted pottery such as two vessels at left. Vessels of diorite (*center and right center*) and alabaster (*far right*), found in tombs of about 3500 B.C. and later, reflect growth of trade with other regions and increasing specialization of crafts. These vessels and objects on opposite page are in the University Museum of the University of Pennsylvania.

a decisive cultural and social change that was less directly linked to changes in the exploitation of the environment. To be sure, it rested ultimately on food surpluses obtained by agricultural producers above their own requirements and somehow made available to city dwellers engaged in other activities. But its essential element was a whole series of new institutions and the vastly greater size and complexity of the social unit, rather than basic innovations in subsistence. In short, the different forms that early urban societies assumed are essentially the products of differently interacting political and economic—human—forces. And the interpretive skills required to understand them are correspondingly rooted more in the social sciences and humanities than in the natural sciences.

Even the term urban needs qualification. Many of the qualities we think of as civilized have been attained by societies that failed to organize cities. At least some Egyptologists believe that civilization advanced for almost 2,000 years under the Pharaohs before true cities appeared in Egypt. The period was marked by the development of monumental public works, a formal state superstructure, written records and the beginnings of exact science. In the New World, too, scholars are still searching the jungles around Maya temple centers in Guatemala and Yucatán for recognizably urban agglomerations of dwellings. For all its temple architecture and high art, and the intellectual achievement represented by its hieroglyphic writing and accurate long-count calendar, classic Maya civilization apparently was not based on the city.

These facts do not detract from the fundamental importance of the urban revolution, but underline its complex character. Every high civilization other than possibly the Mayan did ultimately produce cities. And in most civilizations urbanization began early.

There is little doubt that this was the case for the oldest civilization and the earliest cities: those of ancient Mesopotamia. The story of their development, which we will sketch here, is still a very tentative one. In large part the uncertainties are due to the state of the archeological record, which is as yet both scanty and unrepresentative. The archeologist's preoccupation with early temple-furnishings and architecture, for example, has probably exaggerated their importance, and has certainly given us little information about contemporary secular life in neighboring precincts of the same towns.

Eventually written records help overcome these deficiencies. However, 500 or more years elapsed between the onset of the first trends toward urbanism and the earliest known examples of cuneiform script. And then for the succeeding 700 or 800 years the available texts are laconic, few in number and poorly understood. To a degree, they can be supplemented by cautious inferences drawn from later documents. But the earliest chapters rest primarily on archeological data.

Let us pick up the narrative where Robert J. Braidwood left it in the article on page 71, with the emergence of a fully agricultural people, many of them grouped together in villages of perhaps 200 to 500 individuals. Until almost the end of our own story, dating finds little corroboration in written records. Moreover, few dates based on the decay of radioactive carbon are yet available in Mesopotamia for this crucial period. But by 5500 B.C., or even earlier, it appears that the village-farming community had fully matured in southwestern Asia. As a way of life it then stabilized internally for 1,500 years or more, although it continued to spread downward from the hills and piedmont where it had first crystallized in the great river valleys.

Then came a sharp increase in tempo. In the next 1,000 years some of the small agricultural communities on the alluvial plain between the Tigris and Euphrates rivers not only increased greatly in size, but changed decisively in structure. They culminated in the Sumerian city-state with tens of thousands of inhabitants, elaborate religious, political and military establishments, stratified social classes, advanced technology and widely extended trading contacts [see "The Sumerians," by Samuel Noah Kramer; SCIENTIFIC AMERICAN, October, 1957]. The river-valley agriculture on which the early Mesopotamian cities were established differed considerably from that of the uplands where domestication had begun. Wheat and barley remained the staple crops, but they were supplemented by dates. The date palm yielded not only prodigious and dependable supplies of fruit but also wood. Marshes and estuaries teemed with fish, and their reeds provided another building material. There was almost no stone, however; before the establishment of trade with surrounding areas, hard-fired clay served for such necessary agricultural tools as sickles.

The domestic animals—sheep, goats, donkeys, cattle and pigs by the time of the first textual evidence—may have differed little from those known earlier in the foothills and northern plains. But they were harder to keep, particularly the cattle and the donkeys which were needed as draft animals for plowing. During the hot summers all vegetation withered except for narrow strips along the watercourses. Fodder had to be cultivated and distributed, and pastureland was at a premium. These problems of management may help explain why the herds rapidly became a responsibility of people associated with the temples. And control of the herds in turn may have provided the stimulus that led temple officials frequently to assume broader control over the economy and agriculture.

Most important, agriculture in the alluvium depended on irrigation, which had not been necessary in the uplands. For a long time the farmers made do with small-scale systems, involving breaches in the natural embankments of the streams and uncontrolled local flooding. The beginnings of large-scale canal networks seem clearly later than the advent of fully established cities.

In short, the immediately pre-urban society of southern Mesopotamia consisted of small communities scattered along natural watercourses. Flocks had to forage widely, but cultivation was confined to narrow enclaves of irrigated plots along swamp margins and stream banks. In general the swamps and rivers provided an important part of the raw materials and diet.

Where in this pattern were the inducements, perhaps even preconditions, for urbanization that explain the precocity of the Mesopotamian achievement? First, there was the productivity of irrigation agriculture. In spite of chronic water-shortage during the earlier part of the growing season and periodic floods around the time of the harvest, in spite of a debilitating summer climate and the ever present danger of salinity in flooded or over-irrigated fields, farming yielded a clear and dependable surplus of food.

Second, the very practice of irrigation must have helped induce the growth of cities. It is sometimes maintained that the inducement lay in a need for centralized control over the building and maintaining of elaborate irrigation systems, but this does not seem to have been the case. As we have seen, such systems came after the cities themselves. However, by engendering inequalities in access to productive land, irrigation contributed to the formation of a stratified society. And by furnishing a reason for border disputes between neighboring communities, it surely promoted a warlike atmosphere that drew people together in offensive and defensive concentrations.

Finally, the complexity of subsistence pursuits on the flood plains may have indirectly aided the movement toward cities. Institutions were needed to medi-

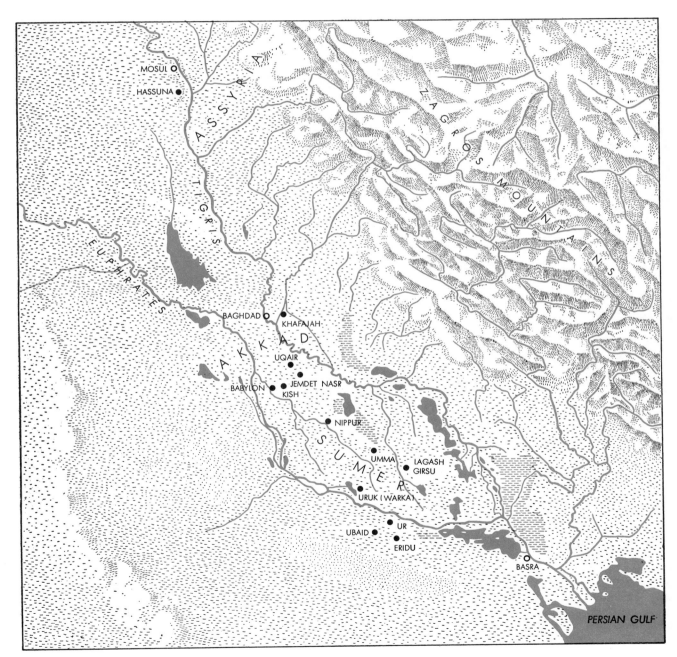

**ANCIENT CITIES** of Mesopotamia (*black dots*) were located mainly along Tigris and Euphrates rivers and their tributaries. In ancient times these rivers followed different courses from those shown on this modern map. Modern cities are shown as open dots.

CITY OF ERBIL in northern Iraq is built on the site of ancient city of Arbela. This aerial view suggests the character and ap- pearance of Mesopotamian cities of thousands of years ago, with streets and houses closely packed around central public buildings.

ate between herdsman and cultivator; between fisherman and sailor; between plowmaker and plowman. Whether through a system of rationing, palace largesse or a market that would be recognizable to us, the city provided a logical and necessary setting for storage, exchange and redistribution. Not surprisingly, one of the recurrent themes in early myths is a rather didactic demonstration that the welfare of the city goddess is founded upon the harmonious interdependence of the shepherd and the farmer.

In any case the gathering forces for urbanization first become evident around 4000 B.C. Which of them furnished the initial impetus is impossible to say, if indeed any single factor was responsible. We do not even know as yet whether the onset of the process was signaled by a growth in the size of settlements. And of course mere increase in size would not necessarily imply technological or economic advance beyond the level of the village-farming community. In our own time we have seen primitive agricultural peoples, such as the Yoruba of western Nigeria, who maintained sizable cities that were in fact little more than overgrown village-farming settlements. They were largely self-sustaining because most of the productive inhabitants were full-time farmers.

The evidence suggests that at the beginning the same was true of Mesopotamian urbanization: immediate economic change was not its central characteristic. As we shall see shortly, the first clear-cut trend to appear in the archeological record is the rise of temples. Conceivably new patterns of thought and social organization crystallizing within the temples served as the primary force in bringing people together and setting the process in motion.

Whatever the initial stimulus to growth and reorganization, the process itself clearly involved the interaction of many different factors. Certainly the institutions of the city evolved in different directions and at different rates, rather than as a smoothly emerging totality. Considering the present fragmentary state of knowledge, it is more reasonable here to follow some of these trends individually rather than to speculate from the shreds (or, rather, sherds!) and patches of data about how the complete organizational pattern developed.

Four archeological periods can be distinguished in the tentative chronology of the rise of the Mesopotamian city-state. The earliest is the Ubaid, named for the first site where remains of this period were uncovered [*see map on page 187*]. At little more than a guess, it may have lasted for a century or two past 4000 B.C., giving way to the relatively brief Warka period. Following this the first written records appeared during the Protoliterate period, which spanned the remainder of the fourth millennium. The final part of our story is the Early Dynastic period, which saw the full flowering of independent city-states between about 3000 and 2500 B.C.

Of all the currents that run through the whole interval, we know most about religious institutions. Small shrines existed in the early villages of the northern plains and were included in the cultural inventory of the earliest known agriculturalists in the alluvium. Before the end of the Ubaid period the free-standing shrine had lost its original fluidity of plan and adopted architectural features that afterward permanently characterized Mesopotamian temples. The development continued into the Early Dynastic period, when we see a complex of workshops and storehouses surrounding a greatly enlarged but rigidly traditional arrangement of cult chambers. No known contemporary structures were remotely comparable in size or complexity to these establishments until almost the end of the Protoliterate period.

At some point specialized priests appeared, probably the first persons released from direct subsistence labor. Their ritual activities are depicted in Protoliterate seals and stone carvings. If not immediately, then quite early, the priests also assumed the role of economic administrators, as attested by ration or wage lists found in temple premises among the earliest known examples of writing. The priestly hierarchies continued to supervise a multitude of economic as well as ritual activities into (and beyond) the Early Dynastic period, although by then more explicitly political forms of organization had perhaps become dominant. For a long time, however, temples seem to have been the

SPEARHEADS of copper and bronze from the royal cemetery at Ur date back to the third millennium B.C. The workmanship of these weapons matches that of the jewelry shown on page 184.

largest and most complex institutions that existed in the communities growing up around them.

The beginnings of dynastic political regimes are much harder to trace. Monumental palaces, rivaling the temples in size, appear in the Early Dynastic period, but not earlier. The term for "king" has not yet been found in Protoliterate texts. Even so-called royal tombs apparently began only in the Early Dynastic period.

Lacking contemporary historical or archeological evidence, we must seek the origins of dynastic institutions primarily in later written versions of traditional myths. Thorkild Jacobsen of the University of Chicago has argued persuasively that Sumerian myths describing the world of the gods reflect political institutions as they existed in human society just prior to the rise of dynastic authority. If so, they show that political authority in the Protoliterate period rested in an assembly of the adult male members of the community. Convoked only to meet sporadic external threat, the assembly's task was merely to select a short-term war leader.

Eventually, as the myths themselves suggest, successful war leaders were retained even in times of peace. Herein lies the apparent origin of kingship. At times springing up outside the priestly corporations, at times coming from them,

ROYAL WAR-CHARIOT carved on limestone plaque from city of Ur reflects increasing concern of Mesopotamian cities about methods of warfare in middle of third millennium B.C.

RELIGIONS of ancient Mesopotamia were dominated by the idea that man was fashioned to serve the gods. Here a worshipper followed by figure with pail brings a goat as an offering to goddess seated at right. A divine attendant kneels before her. This impression and the one below were made from stone cylinder-seals of Akkadian period (about 2400 B.C.).

new leaders emerged who were preoccupied with, and committed to, both defensive and offensive warfare against neighboring city-states.

The traditional concerns of the temples were not immediately affected by the new political leadership. Palace officials acquired great landed estates of their own, but the palace itself was occupied chiefly with such novel activities as raising and supplying its army, maintaining a large retinue of servants and entertainers and constructing a defensive wall around the city.

These undertakings took a heavy toll of the resources of the young city-states, perhaps too heavy to exact by the old "democratic" processes. Hence it is not surprising that as permanent, hereditary royal authority became established, the position of the assembly declined. In the famous epic of Gilgamesh, an Early Dynastic king of Uruk, the story opens with the protests of the citizenry over their forced labor on the city walls. Another episode shows Gilgamesh manipulating the assembly, obviously no longer

depending on its approval for his power. Rooted in war, the institution of kingship intensified a pattern of predatory expansionism and shifting military rivalries. The early Mesopotamian king could trace his origin to the need for military leadership. But the increasingly militaristic flavor of the Early Dynastic period also can be traced at least in part to the interests and activities of kings and their retinues as they proceeded to consolidate their power.

As society shifted its central focus from temple to palace it also separated into classes. Archeologically, the process can best be followed through the increasing differentiation in grave offerings in successively later cemeteries. Graves of the Ubaid period, at the time when monumental temples were first appearing, hold little more than a variable number of pottery vessels. Those in the cemetery at Ur, dating from the latter part of the Early Dynastic period, show a great disparity in the wealth they contain. A small proportion, the royal tombs

(not all of whose principal occupants may have belonged to royal families), are richly furnished with beautifully wrought weapons, ornaments and utensils of gold and lapis lazuli. A larger number contain a few copper vessels or an occasional bead of precious metal, but the majority have only pottery vessels or even nothing at all. Both texts and archeological evidence indicate that copper and bronze agricultural tools were beyond the reach of the ordinary peasant until after the Early Dynastic period, while graves of the well-to-do show "conspicuous consumption" of copper in the form of superfluous stands for pottery vessels even from the beginning of the period.

Early Dynastic texts likewise record social and economic stratification. Records from the main archive of the Baba Temple in Girsu, for example, show substantial differences in the allotments from that temple's lands to its parishioners. Other texts describe the sale of houseplots or fields, often to form great estates held by palace officials and worked by communities of dependent clients who may originally have owned the land. Still others record the sale of slaves, and the rations allotted to slaves producing textiles under the supervision of temple officials. As a group, however, slaves constituted only a small minority of the population until long after the Early Dynastic period.

Turning to the development of technology, we find a major creative burst in early Protoliterate times, involving very rapid stylistic and technical advance in the manufacture of seals, statuary and ornate vessels of carved stone, cast copper or precious metals. But the number of craft specialists apparently was very small, and the bulk of their products seems to have been intended only for cult purposes. In contrast the Early Dynastic period saw a great increase in production of nonagricultural commodities, and almost certainly a corresponding increase in the proportion of the population that was freed from the tasks of primary subsistence to pursue their craft on a full-time basis. Both stylistically and technologically, however, this expansion was rooted in the accomplishments of the previous period and produced few innovations of its own.

Production was largely stimulated by three new classes of demand. First, the burgeoning military establishment of the palace required armaments, including not only metal weapons and armor but also more elaborate equipment such as chariots. Second, a considerable vol-

GILGAMESH, early Mesopotamian king and hero of legend, may be figure attacking water buffalo (right center). Figure stabbing lion may be his companion, the bull-man Enkidu.

ume of luxury goods was commissioned for the palace retinue. And third, a moderate private demand for these goods seems to have developed also. The mass production of pottery, the prevalence of such articles as cylinder seals and metal utensils, the existence of a few vendors' stalls and the hoards of objects in some of the more substantial houses all imply at least a small middle class. Most of these commodities, it is clear, were fabricated in the major Mesopotamian towns from raw materials brought from considerable distance. Copper, for example, came from Oman and the Anatolian plateau, more than 1,000 miles from the Sumerian cities. The need for imports stimulated the manufacture of such articles as textiles, which could be offered in exchange, and also motivated the expansion of territorial control by conquest.

Some authorities have considered that technological advance, which they usually equate with the development of metallurgy, was a major stimulant or even a precondition of urban growth. Yet, in southern Mesopotamia at least, the major quantitative expansion of metallurgy, and of specialized crafts in general, came only after dynastic city-states were well advanced. While the spread of technology probably contributed further to the development of militarism and social stratification, it was less a cause than a consequence of city growth. The same situation is found in New World civilizations. Particularly in aboriginal Middle America the technological level remained very nearly static before and after the urban period.

Finally we come to the general forms of the developing cities, perhaps the most obscure aspect of the whole process of urbanization. Unhappily even Early Dynastic accounts do not oblige us with extensive descriptions of the towns where they were written, nor even with useful estimates of population. Contemporary maps also are unknown; if they were made, they still elude us. References to towns in the myths and epics are at best vague and allegorical. Ultimately archeological studies can supply most of these deficiencies, but at present we have little to go on.

The farming villages of the pre-urban era covered at most a few acres. Whether the villages scattered over the alluvial plain in Ubaid times were much different from the earlier ones in the north is unclear; certainly most were no larger, but the superficial appearance of one largely unexcavated site indicates that they may have been more densely built up and more formally laid out along a regular grid of streets or lanes. By the end of the Ubaid period the temples had begun to expand; a continuation of this trend is about all that the remains of Warka and early Protoliterate periods can tell us thus far. Substantial growth seems to have begun toward the end of the Protoliterate period and to have continued through several centuries of the Early Dynastic. During this time the first battlemented ring-walls were built around at least the larger towns.

A few Early Dynastic sites have been excavated sufficiently to give a fairly full picture of their general layout. Radiating out from the massive public buildings of these cities, toward the outer gates, were streets, unpaved and dusty, but straight and wide enough for the passage of solid-wheeled carts or chariots. Along the streets lay the residences of the well-to-do citizenry, usually arranged around spacious courts and sometimes provided with latrines draining into sewage conduits below the streets. The houses of the city's poorer inhabitants were located behind or between the large multiroomed dwellings. They were approached by tortuous, narrow alleys, were more haphazard in plan, were less well built and very much smaller. Mercantile activities were probably concentrated along the quays of the adjoining river or at the city gates. The marketplace or bazaar devoted to private commerce had not yet appeared.

Around every important urban center rose the massive fortifications that guarded the city against nomadic raids and the usually more formidable campaigns of neighboring rulers. Outside the walls clustered sheepfolds and irrigated tracts, interspersed with subsidiary villages and ultimately disappearing into the desert. And in the desert dwelt only the nomad, an object of mixed fear and scorn to the sophisticated court poet. By the latter part of the Early Dynastic period several of the important capitals of lower Mesopotamia included more than 250 acres within their fortifications. The city of Uruk extended over 1,100 acres and contained possibly 50,000 people.

For these later cities there are written records from which the make-up of the population can be estimated. The overwhelming majority of the able-bodied adults still were engaged in primary agricultural production on their own holdings, on allotments of land received from the temples or as dependent retainers on large estates. But many who were engaged in subsistence agriculture also had other roles. One temple archive, for example, records that 90 herdsmen, 80 soldier-laborers, 100 fishermen, 125 sailors, pilots and oarsmen, 25 scribes, 20 or 25 craftsmen (carpenters, smiths, potters, leather-workers, stonecutters, and mat- or basket-weavers) and probably 250 to 300 slaves were numbered among its parish of around 1,200 persons. In addition to providing for its own subsistence and engaging in a variety of specialized pursuits, most of this group was expected to serve in the army in time of crisis.

Earlier figures can only be guessed at from such data as the size of temple establishments and the quantity of craft-produced articles. Toward the end of the Protoliterate period probably less than a fifth of the labor force was substantially occupied with economic activities outside of subsistence pursuits; in Ubaid times a likely figure is 5 per cent.

It is not easy to say at what stage in the whole progression the word "city" becomes applicable. By any standard Uruk and its contemporaries were cities. Yet they still lacked some of the urban characteristics of later eras. In particular, the development of municipal politics, of a self-conscious corporate body with at least partially autonomous, secular institutions for its own administration, was not consummated until classical times.

Many of the currents we have traced must have flowed repeatedly in urban civilizations. But not necessarily all of them. The growth of the Mesopotamian city was closely related to the rising tempo of warfare. For their own protection people must have tended to congregate under powerful rulers and behind strong fortifications; moreover, they may have been consciously and forcibly drawn together by the elite in the towns in order to centralize political and economic controls. On the other hand, both in aboriginal Central America and in the Indus Valley (in what is now Pakistan) great population centers grew up without comprehensive systems of fortification, and with relatively little emphasis on weapons or on warlike motifs in art.

There is not one origin of cities, but as many as there are independent cultural traditions with an urban way of life. Southern Mesopotamia merely provides the earliest example of a process that, with refinements introduced by the industrial revolution and the rise of national states, is still going on today.

# 19

# The Origin and Evolution of Cities

by Gideon Sjoberg
*September 1965*

*The first cities arose some 5,500 years ago; large-scale urbanization began only about 100 years ago. The intervening steps in the evolution of cities were nonetheless a prerequisite for modern urban societies*

Men began to live in cities some 5,500 years ago. As the preceding article relates, however, the proportion of the human population concentrated in cities did not begin to increase significantly until about 100 years ago. These facts raise two questions that this article proposes to answer. First, what factors brought about the origin of cities? Second, through what evolutionary stages did cities pass before the modern epoch of urbanization? The answers to these questions are intimately related to three major levels of human organization, each of which is characterized by its own technological, economic, social and political patterns. The least complex of the three—the "folk society"—is preurban and even preliterate; it consists typically of small numbers of people, gathered in self-sufficient homogeneous groups, with their energies wholly (or almost wholly) absorbed by the quest for food. Under such conditions there is little or no surplus of food; consequently the folk society permits little or no specialization of labor or distinction of class.

Although some folk societies still exist today, similar human groups began the slow process of evolving into more complex societies millenniums ago, through settlement in villages and through advances in technology and organizational structure. This gave rise to the second level of organization: civilized preindustrial, or "feudal," society. Here there is a surplus of food because of the selective cultivation of grains—high in yield, rich in biological energy and suited to long-term storage—and often also because of the practice of animal husbandry. The food surplus permits both the specialization of labor and the kind of class structure that can, for instance, provide the leadership and command the manpower to develop and maintain extensive irrigation systems (which in turn make possible further increases in the food supply). Most preindustrial societies possess metallurgy, the plow and the wheel—devices, or the means of creating devices, that multiply both the production and the distribution of agricultural surpluses.

Two other elements of prime importance characterize the civilized preindustrial stage of organization. One is writing: not only the simple keeping of accounts but also the recording of historical events, law, literature and religious beliefs. Literacy, however, is usually confined to a leisured elite. The other element is that this stage of organization has only a few sources of energy other than the muscles of men and livestock; the later preindustrial societies harnessed the force of the wind to sail the seas and grind grain and also made use of water power.

It was in the context of this second type of society that the world's first cities developed. Although preindustrial cities still survive, the modern industrial city is associated with a third level of complexity in human organization, a level characterized by mass literacy, a fluid class system and, most important, the tremendous technological breakthrough to new sources of inanimate energy that produced and still sustains the industrial revolution. Viewed against the background of this three-tiered structure, the first emergence of cities at the level of civilized preindustrial society can be more easily understood.

Two factors in addition to technological advance beyond the folk-society level were needed for cities to emerge. One was a special type of social organization by means of which the agricultural surplus produced by technological advance could be collected, stored and distributed. The same apparatus could also organize the labor force needed for large-scale construction, such as public buildings, city walls and irrigation systems. A social organization of this kind requires a variety of full-time specialists directed by a ruling elite. The latter, although few in number, must command sufficient political power—reinforced by an ideology, usually religious in character—to ensure that the peasantry periodically relinquishes a substantial part of the agricultural yield in order to support the city dwellers. The second factor required was a favorable environment, providing not only fertile soil for the peasants but also a water supply adequate for both agriculture and urban consumption. Such conditions exist in geologically mature mid-latitude river valleys, and it was in such broad alluvial regions that the world's earliest cities arose.

What is a city? It is a community of substantial size and population den-

FAINT OUTLINES of a forgotten Persian city appear in the aerial photograph on the opposite page. The site is on the south bank of the Gurgan River, east of the Caspian Sea near the present border between Iran and the U.S.S.R. A natural frontier between Persia and the steppe country to the north, the Gurgan region served as a barrier to penetration by nomads at least since the Iron Age. The citadel on the opposite bank of the river (*top right*) defended the city from steppe raiders. The photograph is one of many made in Iran by Erich F. Schmidt for the Oriental Institute of the University of Chicago.

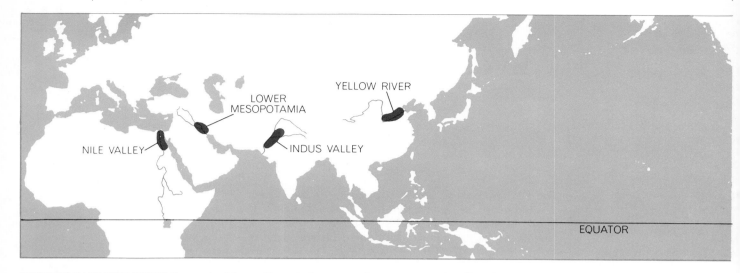

**WORLD'S EARLIEST CITIES** first evolved from villages in lower Mesopotamia and in the Nile valley (*left*). Soon thereafter cities also arose in similar alluvial regions to the east, first in the Indus valley and then along the Yellow River; Mesopotamian influences

sity that shelters a variety of nonagricultural specialists, including a literate elite. I emphasize the role of literacy as an ingredient of urban life for good reasons. Even though writing systems took centuries to evolve, their presence or absence serves as a convenient means for distinguishing between genuinely urban communities and others that in spite of their large size and dense population must be considered quasi-urban or nonurban. This is because once a community achieves or otherwise acquires the technological advance we call writing, a major transformation in the social order occurs; with a written tradition rather than an oral one it is possible to create more complex administrative and legal systems and more rigorous systems of thought. Writing is indispensable to the development of mathematics, astronomy and the other sciences; its existence thus implies the emergence of a number of significant specializations within the social order.

As far as is known, the world's first cities took shape around 3500 B.C. in the Fertile Crescent, the eastern segment of which includes Mesopotamia: the valleys of the Tigris and the Euphrates. Not only were the soil and water supply there suitable; the region was a crossroads that facilitated repeated contacts among peoples of divergent cultures for thousands of years. The resulting mixture of alien and indigenous crafts and skills must have made its own contribution to the evolution of the first true cities out of the village settlements in lower Mesopotamia. These were primarily in Sumer but also to some extent in Akkad, a little to the

north. Some—such as Eridu, Erech, Lagash and Kish—are more familiar to archaeologists than to others; Ur, a later city, is more widely known.

These early cities were much alike; for one thing, they had a similar technological base. Wheat and barley were the cereal crops, bronze was the metal, oxen pulled plows and there were wheeled vehicles. Moreover, the city's leader was both king and high priest; the peasants' tribute to the city god was stored in the temple granaries. Luxury goods recovered from royal tombs and temples attest the existence of skilled artisans, and the importation of precious metals and gems from well beyond the borders of Mesopotamia bespeaks a class of merchant-traders. Population sizes can only be guessed in the face of such unknowns as the average number of residents per household and the extent of each city's zone of influence. The excavator of Ur, Sir Leonard Woolley, estimates that soon after 2000 B.C. the city proper housed 34,000 people; in my opinion, however, it seems unlikely that, at least in the earlier periods, even the larger of these cities contained more than 5,000 to 10,000 people, including part-time farmers on the cities' outskirts.

The valley of the Nile, not too far from Mesopotamia, was also a region of early urbanization. To judge from Egyptian writings of a later time, there may have been urban communities in the Nile delta by 3100 B.C. Whether the Egyptian concept of city living had "diffused" from Mesopotamia or was independently invented (and perhaps even earlier than in Mesopotamia) is a matter of scholarly debate; in any case

the initial stages of Egyptian urban life may yet be discovered deep in the silt of the delta, where scientific excavation is only now being undertaken.

Urban communities—diffused or independently invented—spread widely during the third and second millenniums B.C. By about 2500 B.C. the cities of Mohenjo-Daro and Harappa were flourishing in the valley of the Indus River in what is now Pakistan. Within another 1,000 years at the most the mid-

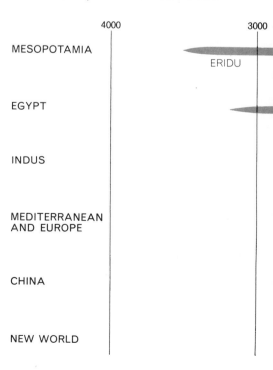

|  | 4000 | 3000 |
|---|---|---|
| MESOPOTAMIA | | ERIDU |
| EGYPT | | |
| INDUS | | |
| MEDITERRANEAN AND EUROPE | | |
| CHINA | | |
| NEW WORLD | | |

**SEQUENCE** of urban evolution begins with the first cities of Mesopotamia, makes its

may have reached both areas. The cities of Mesoamerica (*right*) evolved independently.

dle reaches of the Yellow River in China supported urban settlements. A capital city of the Shang Dynasty (about 1500 B.C.) was uncovered near Anyang before World War II; current archaeological investigations by the Chinese may well prove that city life was actually established in ancient China several centuries earlier.

The probability that the first cities of Egypt were later than those of Sumer and the certainty that those of the Indus and Yellow rivers are later lends weight

to the argument that the concept of urban living diffused to these areas from Mesopotamia. Be this as it may, none will deny that in each case the indigenous population contributed uniquely to the development of the cities in its own area.

In contrast to the situation in the Old World, it appears certain that diffusion played an insignificant role or none at all in the creation of the pre-Columbian cities of the New World. The peoples of Mesoamerica—notably the Maya, the Zapotecs, the Mixtecs and the Aztecs—evidently developed urban communities on a major scale, the exact extent of which is only now being revealed by current investigations. Until quite recently, for example, many New World archaeologists doubted that the Maya had ever possessed cities; it was the fashion to characterize their impressive ruins as ceremonial centers visited periodically by the members of a scattered rural population. It is now clear, however, that many such centers were genuine cities. At the Maya site of Tikal in Guatemala some 3,000 structures have been located in an area of 6.2 square miles; only 10 percent of them are major ceremonial buildings. Extrapolating on the basis of test excavations of more than 100 of these lesser structures, about two-thirds of them appear to have been dwellings. If only half the present-day average household figure

for the region (5.6 members) is applied to Tikal, its population would have been more than 5,000. At another major Maya site—Dzibilchaltun in Yucatán—a survey of less than half of the total area has revealed more than 8,500 structures. Teotihuacán, the largest urban site in the region of modern Mexico City, may have had a population of 100,000 during the first millennium A.D. [*see illustration on next two pages*].

Although only a few examples of writing have been identified at Teotihuacán, it is reasonable to assume that writing was known; there were literate peoples elsewhere in Mesoamerica at the time. By the same token, the achievements of the Maya in such realms as mathematics and astronomy would have forced the conclusion that they were an urban people even in the absence of supporting archaeological evidence. Their invention of the concept of zero (evidently earlier than the Hindus' parallel feat) and their remarkably precise calculation of the length of the solar year would surely have been impossible if their literate elite had been scattered about the countryside in villages rather than concentrated in urban centers where a cross-fertilization of ideas could take place.

Mesoamerica was by no means the only area of large, dense communities in the New World; they also existed in the Andean region. A culture such as

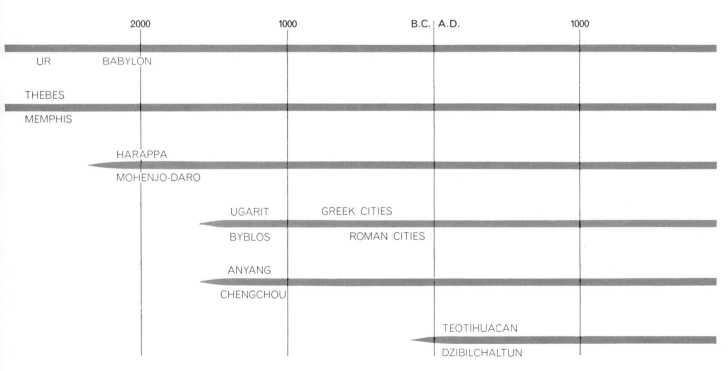

next appearance in the Nile valley, then extends to the Indus, to the eastern Mediterranean region and at last to China. In each    area, the independently urbanized New World included, cities rose and fell but urban life, once established, never wholly disappeared.

**TEOTIHUACAN is an extensive urban site near modern Mexico City that flourished during the first millennium A.D. Only the center of the city is seen in the photograph, but the precise grid layout of the city is partly revealed. The full extent of the grid, based on** 60-meter-square city blocks, is not yet known, but it continues for miles beyond the city center. Aerial and ground surveys of the region by René Millon of the University of Rochester show that the north-south axis of the city was formed by a broad avenue (the

the Inca, however, cannot be classified as truly urban. In spite of—perhaps because of—their possession of a mnemonic means of keeping inventories (an assemblage of knotted cords called a quipu) the Incas lacked any conventionalized set of graphic symbols for representing speech or any concepts other than numbers and certain broad classes of items. As a result they were denied such key structural elements of an urban community as a literate elite and a written heritage of law, religion and history. Although the Incas could claim major military, architectural and engineering triumphs and apparently were on the verge of achieving a civilized order, they were still quasi-urban at the time of the European conquest, much like the Dahomey, Ashanti and Yoruba peoples of Africa.

The New World teaches us two lessons. In Mesoamerica cities were created without animal husbandry, the wheel and an extensive alluvial setting. One reason for this is maize, a superior grain crop that produced a substantial

food surplus with relatively little effort and thus compensated for the limited tools and nonriverine environment. In the Andean region imposing feats of engineering and an extensive division of labor were not enough, in the absence of writing, to give rise to a truly urban society.

In spite of considerable cultural diversity among the inhabitants of the Near East, the Orient and the New World, the early cities in all these regions had a number of organizational forms in common. The dominant pattern was theocracy—the king and the high priest were one. The elite had their chief residences in the city; moreover, they and their retainers and servants congregated mainly in the city's center. This center was the prestige area, where the most imposing religious and government buildings were located. Such a concentration had dual value: in an era when communications and transport were rudimentary, propinquity enhanced interaction among the

elite; at the same time it gave the ruling class maximum protection from external attack.

At a greater distance from this urban nucleus were the shops and dwellings of artisans—masons, carpenters, smiths, jewelers, potters—many of whom served the elite. The division of labor into crafts, apparent in the earliest cities, became more complex with the passage of time. Artisan groups, some of which even in early times may have belonged to specific ethnic minorities, tended to establish themselves in special quarters or streets. Such has been characteristic of preindustrial cities in all cultural settings, from the earliest times to the present day. The poorest urbanites lived on the outskirts of the city, as did part-time or full-time farmers; their scattered dwellings finally blended into open countryside.

From its inception the city, as a residence of specialists, has been a continuing source of innovation. Indeed, the very emergence of cities greatly accelerated social and cultural change; to

Street of the Dead) that starts at the Pyramid of the Moon (*far left*), runs past the larger Pyramid of the Sun (*left of center*) and continues more than three miles beyond the Ciudadela (*far right*). The east-west axis of Teotihuacán was formed by similar avenues that can be traced outward for two miles on either side of the central Ciudadela area. Although primarily a market and religious center for the surrounding countryside, Teotihuacán probably contained a resident population of 100,000 or more within its 16 square miles.

borrow a term from the late British archaeologist V. Gordon Childe, we can properly regard the "urban revolution" as being equal in significance to the agricultural revolution that preceded it and the industrial revolution that followed it. The city acted as a promoter of change in several ways. Many of the early cities arose on major transportation routes; new ideas and inventions flowed into them quite naturally. The mere fact that a large number of specialists were concentrated in a small area encouraged innovation, not only in technology but also in religious, philosophical and scientific thought. At the same time cities could be strong bulwarks of tradition. Some—for example Jerusalem and Benares—have become sacred in the eyes of the populace; in spite of repeated destruction Jerusalem has retained this status for more than two millenniums [see "Ancient Jerusalem," by Kathleen M. Kenyon; SCIENTIFIC AMERICAN, July 1965].

The course of urban evolution can be correctly interpreted only in relation to the parallel evolution of technology and social organization (especially political organization); these are not just prerequisites to urban life but the basis for its development. As centers of innovation cities provided a fertile setting for continued technological advances; these gains made possible the further expansion of cities. Advanced technology in turn depended on the increasingly complex division of labor, particularly in the political sphere. As an example, the early urban communities of Sumer were mere city-states with restricted hinterlands, but eventually trade and commerce extended over a much broader area, enabling these cities to draw on the human and material resources of a far wider and more diverse region and even bringing about the birth of new cities. The early empires of the Iron Age—for instance the Achaemenid Empire of Persia, established early in the sixth century B.C., and the Han Empire of China, established in the third century B.C.—far surpassed in scope any of the Bronze Age. And as empires became larger the size and grandeur of their cities increased. In fact, as Childe has observed, urbanization spread more rapidly during the first five centuries of the Iron Age than it had in all 15 centuries of the Bronze Age.

In the sixth and fifth centuries B.C. the Persians expanded their empire into western Turkestan and created a number of cities, often by building on existing villages. In this expansion Toprak-kala, Merv and Marakanda (part of which was later the site of Samarkand) moved toward urban status. So too in India, at the close of the fourth century B.C., the Mauryas in the north spread their empire to the previously nonurban south and into Ceylon, giving impetus to the birth of cities such as Ajanta and Kanchi. Under the Ch'in and Han dynasties, between the third century B.C. and the third century A.D., city life took hold in most of what was then China and beyond, particularly to the south and west. The "Great Silk Road" extending from China to Turkestan became studded with such oasis cities as Suchow, Khotan and Kashgar; Nanking and Canton seem to have attained urban status at this time, as did the settlement that was eventually to become Peking.

At the other end of the Eurasian land mass the Phoenicians began toward the end of the second millennium B.C. to spread westward and to revive or establish urban life along the northern coast of Africa and in Spain. These coastal traders had by then developed a considerable knowledge of shipbuilding; this, combined with their far-reaching commercial ties and power of arms, made the Phoenicians lords of the Mediterranean for a time. Some centuries later the Greeks followed a rather similar course. Their city-states—actually in a sense small empires—created or rebuilt numerous urban outposts along the Mediterranean shore from Asia Minor to Spain and France, and eastward to the most distant coast of the Black Sea. The empire that did the most to diffuse city life into the previously nonurban regions of the West—France, Britain, the Low Countries, Germany west of the Rhine, central and even eastern Europe—was of course Rome.

Empires are effective disseminators of urban forms because they have to build cities with which to maintain military supremacy in conquered regions. The city strongholds, in turn, require an administrative apparatus in order to tap the resources of the conquered area and encourage the commerce needed both to support the military garrison and to enhance the wealth of the homeland. Even when a new city began as a purely commercial outpost, as was the case under the Phoenicians, some military and administrative support was necessary if it was to survive and function effectively in alien territory.

There is a significant relation between the rise and fall of empires and the rise and fall of cities; in a real sense history is the study of urban graveyards. The capitals of many former empires are today little more than ghostly outlines that only hint at a glorious past. Such was the fate of Babylon and Nine-veh, Susa in Persia, Seleucia in Mesopotamia and Vijayanagar in India. Yet there are exceptions. Some cities have managed to survive over long periods of time by attaching themselves first to one empire and then to another. Athens, for example, did not decline after the collapse of Greek power; it was able to attach itself to the Roman Empire, which subsidized Athens as a center of learning. Once Rome fell, however, both the population and the prestige of Athens dwindled steadily; it was little more than a town until the rise of modern Greece in the 19th century. On the other hand, nearby Byzantium, a city-state of minor importance under Roman rule, not only became the capital of the Eastern Roman Empire and its successor, the Ottoman Empire, but as Istanbul remains a major city to this day.

In the light of the recurrent rise and decline of cities in so many areas of the world, one may ask just how urban life has been able to persist and why the skills of technology and social organization required for city-building were not

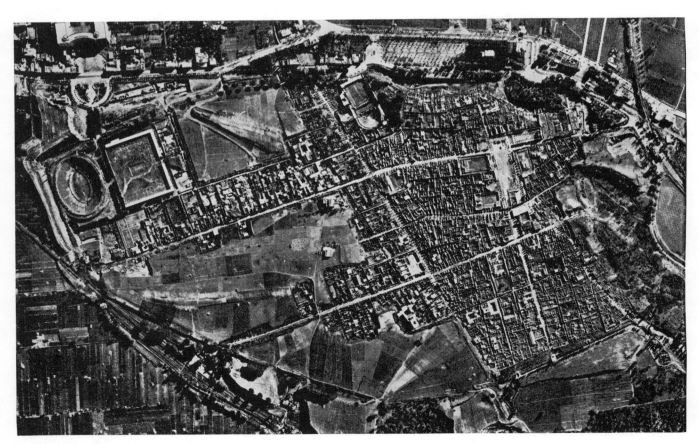

**A ROMAN RESORT** in Italy, Pompeii was buried by 18 feet of ash from Vesuvius in A.D. 79 after a lifetime of at least 400 years. Its rectangular ground plan was presumably designed by the Etruscans, who were among the city's first residents in pre-Roman days. Population estimates for the resort city are uncertain; its amphitheater (*far left*), however, could seat 20,000 people. Forgotten soon after its burial, Pompeii was rediscovered in 1748; systematic excavation of the site began in the middle of the 19th century.

lost. The answer is that the knowledge was maintained within the framework of empires—by means of written records and oral transmission by various specialists. Moreover, all empires have added to their store of skills relating to urban development as a result of diffusion—including the migration of specialists—from other civilized areas. At the same time various civilized or uncivilized subjects within empires have either been purposely educated by their conquerors or have otherwise gained access to the body of urban lore. The result on occasion is that the subjects challenge the power of the dominant ruling group.

The rise and fall of the Roman Empire provides a highly instructive case study that illuminates several relations between the life-span of cities and the formation and decline of empires. The Romans themselves took many elements of their civilization from the Etruscans, the Greeks and other civilized peoples who came under their sway. After Rome's northward expansion in western Europe and the proliferation of Roman cities in regions inhabited by so-called "barbarians"—in this instance preliterate, or "noncivilized," peoples—the Roman leaders were simply unable to staff all the bureaucratic posts with their own citizens. Some of the preliterates had to be trained to occupy such posts both in their own homelands and in the cities on the frontier. This process made it possible for the Romans to exploit the wealth of conquered regions and may have pacified the subjugated groups for a time, but in the long run it engendered serious conflicts. Eventually the Ostrogoths, Vandals, Burgundians and others—having been partially urbanized, having developed a literate elite of their own and having acquired many Roman technological and administrative skills—turned against the imperial power structure and engineered the collapse of Rome and its empire. Nor is this a unique case in history; analogies can be perceived in the modern independence movements of such European colonies as those in Africa.

With the breakup of the Roman Empire, not only did the city of Rome (which at its largest may have had more than 300,000 inhabitants) decline markedly but many borderland cities disappeared or shrank to small towns or villages. The decline was dramatic, but it is too often assumed that after the fall of Rome cities totally disappeared from western Europe. The historian E. Ewig has recently shown that many cities continued to function, particularly in Italy and southern France. Here, as in all civilized societies, the surviving cities were the chief residences and centers of activity for the political and religious elite who commanded the positions of power and privilege that persisted during the so-called Dark Ages.

In spite of Rome's decline many of the techniques and concepts associated with literate traditions in such fields as medicine and astronomy were kept alive; this was done both in the smaller surviving urban communities of Europe and in the eastern regions that had been ruled by the Romans—notably in the cities of the succeeding Eastern Roman Empire. Some of the technology and learning associated with Rome also became the basis for city life in the Arab empires that arose later in the Near East, North Africa, Spain and even central Asia. Indeed, the Byzantine and Arab empires—which had such major intellectual centers as Constantinople, Antioch, Damascus, Cairo and Baghdad—advanced beyond the knowledge inherited from antiquity. The Arabs, for example, took from the Hindus the concept of zero and the decimal system of numerals; by utilizing these concepts in both theory and practice they achieved significant advances over the knowledge that had evolved in the West. Eventually much of the new learning was passed on to Europe, where it helped to build the foundations for the industrial revolution.

In time Europe reestablished extensive commercial contact with the Byzantine and Arab empires; the interchange that followed played a significant role in the resurgence of urban life in southern Europe. The revitalization of trade was closely associated with the formation of several prosperous Italian city-states in the 10th and 11th centuries A.D. Venice and other cities eventually were transformed into small-scale empires whose colonies were scattered over the Mediterranean region—a hinterland from which the home cities were able to extract not only many of their necessities but also luxury items. By A.D. 1000 Venice had forged com-

A ROMAN OUTPOST in Syria, Dura Europos was founded on the Euphrates about 300 B.C. by the Seleucid successor to Alexander the Great. At first a center of Hellenism in the East, it was later a Roman stronghold until Valerian lost it in A.D. 257. Yale University archaeologists have studied the site since 1922; finger-like ramps are their excavation dumps.

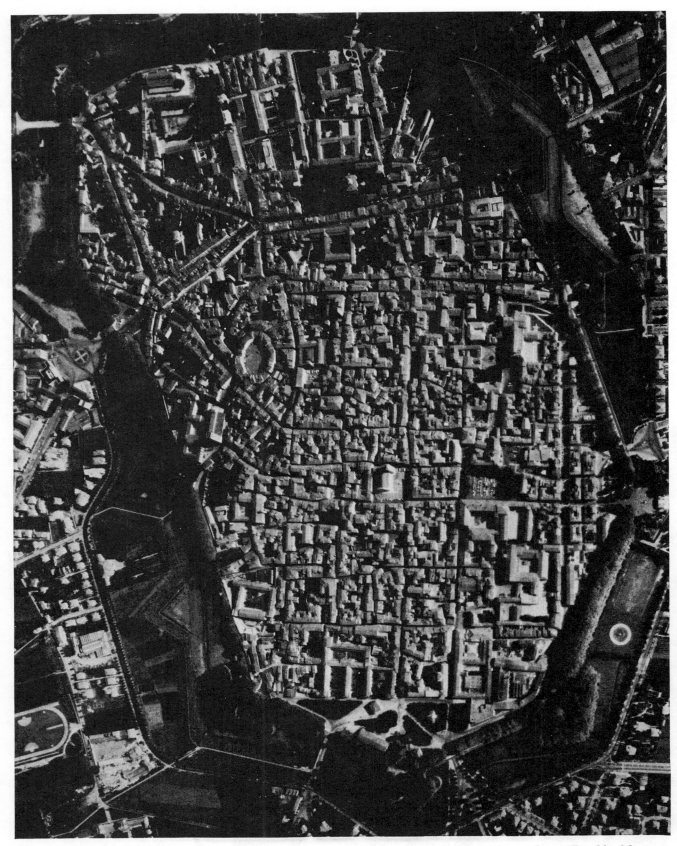

A RENAISSANCE CITY, Lucca in northern Italy is no longer contained within the bastioned circuit of its walls, which were begun in 1504 and completed in 1645. Lucca's seesaw history is like that of many other southern European cities. A Roman town during the Punic wars, it was the site of Caesar's triumvirate meeting with Pompey and Crassus in 60 B.C. and was pillaged by Odoacer at the fall of the Roman Empire in A.D. 476. A fortress city once again by the seventh century A.D., Lucca had become a prosperous manufacturing center, specializing in the weaving of silk textiles, by the 12th century. It continues to produce silk and other textiles today.

mercial links with Constantinople and other cities of the Eastern Roman Empire, partly as a result of the activities of the Greek colony in Venice. The Venetians were able to draw both on the knowledge of these resident Greeks and on the practical experience of sea captains and other specialists among them. Such examples make it clear that the Italian city-states were not merely local creations but rather products of a multiplicity of cultural forces.

Beginning at the turn of the 11th century A.D. many European cities managed to win a kind of independence from the rulers of the various principalities and petty kingdoms that surrounded them. Particularly in northern Italy urban communities came to enjoy considerable political autonomy. This provided an even more favorable atmosphere for commerce and encouraged the growth of such urban institutions as craft guilds. The European pattern is quite different from that in most of Asia (for instance in India and China), where the city was never able to attain a measure of autonomy within the broader political structure. At the same time the extent of self-rule enjoyed by the medieval European cities can be exaggerated and often is; by the close of the Middle Ages urban self-rule was already beginning to be lost. It is therefore evident that the political autonomy of medieval cities was only indirectly related to the eventual evolution of the industrial city.

It was the industrial revolution that brought about truly far-reaching changes in city life. In some nations today, as Kingsley Davis notes in his first introduction, the vast majority of the inhabitants are city dwellers. Nearly 80 percent of the people in the United Kingdom live in cities, as do nearly 70 percent of the people of the U.S. Contrast this with the preindustrial civilized world, in which only a small, socially dominant minority lived in cities. The industrial revolution has also led to fundamental changes in the city's social geography and social organization; the industrial city is marked by a greater fluidity in the class system, the appearance of mass education and mass communications and the shift of some of the elite from the center of the city to its suburban outskirts.

Although there are still insufficient data on the rise of the industrial city—an event that took place sometime between 1750 and 1850—and although scholars disagree over certain steps in the process, the major forces at work in the two or three centuries before the industrial city emerged can be perceived clearly enough. Viewed in the light of Europe's preindustrial urban era, two factors are evident: the expansion of European power into other continents and the development of a technology based on inanimate rather than animate sources of energy. The extension of European trade and exploration (which was to culminate in European colonialism) not only induced the growth of cities in Asia, in parts of nonurban Africa and in the Americas but also helped to raise the standard of living of Europeans themselves and made possible the support of more specialists. Notable among the last was a new occupational group—the scientists. The expansion abroad had helped to shatter the former world view of European scholars; they were now forced to cope with divergent ideas and customs. The discoveries reported by the far-ranging European explorers thus gave added impetus to the advance of science.

The knowledge gained through the application of the scientific method is the one factor above all others that made the modern city possible. This active experimental approach has enabled man to control the forces of nature to an extent undreamed of in the preindustrial era. It is true that in the course of several millenniums the literate elite of the preindustrial cities added significantly to man's store of knowledge in such fields as medicine, astronomy and mathematics, but these scholars generally scorned mundane activities and avoided contact with those whose work was on the practical level. This meant that the scholars' theories were rarely tested and applied in the everyday realm. Moreover, in accordance with prevailing religious thought, man was not to tamper with the natural order or to seek to control it, in either its physical or its social aspect. For example, medical scholars in Greek and Roman cities did not dissect human cadavers; not until the 16th century in Europe did a physician—Andreas Vesalius of Brussels—actually use findings obtained from dissection to revise ancient medical theories.

In the field of engineering, as late as the 17th century most advances were made by artisans who worked more or less on a trial-and-error basis. With the development of the experimental method, however, the learning of the elite became linked with the practical knowledge of the artisan, the barber-surgeon and the like; the result was a dramatic upsurge of knowledge and a fundamental revision of method that has been termed the scientific revolution. Such was the basis of the industrial revolution and the industrial city.

That the first industrial cities appeared in England is hardly fortuitous; England's social structure lacked the rigidity that characterized most of Europe and the rest of the civilized world. The Puritan tradition in England —an ethical system that supports utilitarianism and empiricism—did much to alter earlier views concerning man's place in nature. In England scholars could communicate with artisans more readily than elsewhere in Europe.

The advent of industrialism brought vast improvements in agricultural implements, farming techniques and food preservation, as well as in transportation and communication. Improved water supplies and more effective methods of sewage disposal allowed more people to congregate in cities. Perhaps the key invention was the steam engine, which provided a new and much more bountiful source of energy. Before that time, except for power from wind and water, man had no energy resources other than human and animal muscle. Now the factory system, with its mass production of goods and mechanization of activity, began to take hold. With it emerged a new kind of occupational structure: a structure that depends on highly specialized knowledge and that functions effectively only when the activities of the component occupations are synchronized. This process of industrialization has not only continued unabated to the present day but has actually accelerated with the rise of self-controlling machines.

The evolution of the industrial city was not an unmixed blessing. Historians have argued through many volumes the question of whether the new working class, including many migrants from the countryside, lost or gained economically and socially as the factory system destroyed older social patterns. Today, as industrialization moves inexorably across the globe, it continues to create social problems. Many surviving traditional cities evince in various ways the conflict between their preindustrial past and their industrial future. Nonetheless, the trend is clear: barring nuclear war, the industrial city will become the dominant urban form throughout the world, replacing forever the preindustrial city that was man's first urban creation.

# 20

# An Early City in Iran

by C. C. and Martha Lamberg-Karlovsky
June 1971

*Tepe Yahyā, midway between Mesopotamia and India, was a busy center of trade 5,500 years ago. An outpost of Mesopotamian urban culture, it played a key role in the spread of civilization from west to east*

The kingdom of Elam and its somewhat better-known neighbor, Sumer, were the two earliest urban states to arise in the Mesopotamian area during the fourth millennium B.C. Archaeological findings now show that the Elamite realm also included territory at least 500 miles to the east. For more than 10 centuries, starting about 3400 B.C., the hill country of southeastern Iran some 60 miles from the Arabian Sea was the site of a second center of Elamite urban culture.

Today all that is left of the city that stood halfway between the Euphrates and the Indus is a great mound of earth located some 4,500 feet above sea level in the Soghun Valley, 150 miles south of the city of Kerman in the province of the same name. Known locally as Tepe Yahyā, the mound is 60 feet high and 600 feet in diameter. Its record of occupation begins with a 6,500-year-old Neolithic village and ends with a citadel of the Sassanian dynasty that ruled Persia early in the Christian Era. Intermediate levels in the mound testify to the connections between this eastern Elamite city and the traditional centers of the kingdom in the west.

Such a long archaeological sequence has much value for the study of man's cultural development from farmer to city dweller, but three unexpected elements make Tepe Yahyā a site of even greater significance. First, writing tablets made of clay, recovered from one of the lower levels in the mound, have been shown by carbon-14 analysis of associated organic material to date back to 3560 B.C. (±110 years). The tablets are inscribed with writing of the kind known as proto-Elamite. Proto-Elamite inscriptions and early Sumerian ones are the earliest known Mesopotamian writings, which are the oldest known anywhere. The Tepe Yahyā tablets are unique in

that they are the first of their kind that can be assigned an absolute date. It comes as a surprise to find these examples of writing—as early as the earliest known—in a place that is so far away from Mesopotamia.

The second surprise is evidence that Elamite trade with neighboring Sumer in an unusual commodity—steatite, the easily worked rock also known as soapstone—formed a major part of the commerce at Tepe Yahyā. Unlike Sumer, which was surrounded by the featureless floodplains of lower Mesopotamia, Elam was a hill kingdom rich in natural resources. Elamite trade supplied the Sumerians with silver, copper, tin and lead, with precious gems and horses, and with commoner materials such as timber, obsidian, alabaster, diorite and soapstone. To find that the soapstone trade reached as far east as Tepe Yahyā adds a new dimension to our knowledge of fourth-millennium commerce.

Third, the discovery of Tepe Yahyā has greatly enlarged the known extent of ancient Elam, which was hazily perceived at best. Susa, the most famous Elamite city, lies not far from such famous Sumerian centers as Ur and Eridu. As for other Elamite cities named in inscriptions (Awan, for example, or Madaktu), their location remains a mystery. To discover a prosperous Elamite city as far east of Mesopotamia as Tepe Yahyā is both a surprise and something of a revelation. It suggests how urban civilization, which arose in lower Mesopotamia, made its way east to the valley of the Indus (in what is now West Pakistan).

The British explorer-archaeologist Sir Aurel Stein was the first to recognize that southeastern Iran is a region with important prehistoric remains. Two sites that Stein probed briefly in the 1930's—Tal-i-Iblis near Kerman and Bampur in Per-

sian Baluchistan—have recently been excavated, the first by Joseph R. Caldwell of the University of Georgia and the second by Beatrice de Cardi of the Council for British Archaeology. Although it is the largest mound in southeastern Iran, Tepe Yahyā remained unknown until the summer of 1967, when our reconnaissance group from the Peabody Museum at Harvard University discovered it during an archaeological survey of the region.

We have now completed three seasons of excavation at Tepe Yahyā in coopera-

LARGE EARTH MOUND, over a third of a mile in circumference, was raised to a

tion with the Iran Archaeological Service and have established a sequence of six principal occupation periods. The site was inhabited almost continuously from the middle of the fifth millennium B.C. until about A.D. 400. Following the end of the Elamite period at Tepe Yahyā, about 2200 B.C., there is a 1,000-year gap in the record that is still unexplained but finds parallels at major sites elsewhere in Iran. Tepe Yahyā remained uninhabited until 1000 B.C., when the site was resettled by people of an Iron Age culture.

Our main work at Tepe Yahyā began in the summer of 1968 with the digging of a series of excavations, each 30 feet square, from the top of the mound to the bottom [see illustration below]. Small test trenches were then made within the series of level squares. During our second and third season the excavations were extended by means of further horizontal exposures on the top of the mound and to the west of the main explorations. In addition we opened a stepped trench 12 feet wide on the opposite face of the mound as a check on the sequences we had already exposed.

The earliest remains of human occupation at Tepe Yahyā, which rest on virgin soil in a number of places, consist of five

superimposed levels of mud-brick construction. We have assigned them to a single cultural interval—Period VI—that is shown by carbon-14 analysis to lie in the middle of the fifth millennium B.C. The structures of Period VI seem to be a series of square storage areas that measure about five feet on a side. Most of them have no doorways; they were probably entered through a hole in the roof. The walls are built either of sun-dried mud bricks that were formed by hand or of hand-daubed mud [see top illustration on page 207]. Fragments of reed matting and timber found on the floors of the rooms are traces of fallen roofs.

The tools of Period VI include implements made of bone and flint. Many of the flints are very small; they include little blades that were set in a bone handle to make a sickle. The most common kind of pottery is a coarse, hand-shaped ware; the clay was "tempered" by the addition of chaff. The pots are made in the form of bowls and large storage jars and are decorated with a red wash or painted with red meanders. Toward the end of Period VI a few pieces of finer pottery appear: a buff ware with a smooth, slip-finished surface and a red ware with decorations painted in black.

Human burials, all of infants, were found under the floor in a few of the

structures. The limbs of the bodies had been tightly gathered to the trunk before burial, and accompanying the bodies are unbroken coarse-ware bowls. In one room a small human figurine was found face down on the floor, resting on a collection of flint and bone tools. The sculpture is 11 inches long and was carved out of dark green soapstone [see illustration on next page]. The carving clearly delineates a female figure. Its elongated form and the presence of a hole at the top of the head, however, suggest a dual symbol that combines male and female characteristics.

The Neolithic culture of Period VI evidently included the practice of agriculture and animal husbandry. Identifiable animal bones include those of wild gazelles and of cattle, sheep and goats. Camel bones are also present, but it is not clear whether or not they indicate that the animal had been domesticated at this early date. The domesticated plants include a variety of cereal grains. In the Tepe Yahyā area today raising crops involves irrigation; whether or not this was the case in Neolithic times is also unclear. At any rate the Neolithic occupation of the mound continued until about 3800 B.C.

The transition from Period VI to the Early Bronze Age culture that followed

height of 60 feet over a 5,000-year period as new settlements were built on the rubble of earlier ones. Located in southeastern Iran and known locally as Tepe Yahyā, the site was first occupied by a Neolithic community in the middle of the fifth millennium B.C.

**NEOLITHIC FIGURINE** was found in one of the storerooms in the earliest structure at Tepe Yahyā, associated with tools made of flint and bone. The sculpture was apparently intended to be a dual representation: a female figure imposed on a stylized phallic shape.

occurred without any break in continuity. The structures of Period V contain coarse-ware pottery of the earlier type. The finer, painted pottery becomes commoner and includes some new varieties. One of these, with a surface finish of red slip, has a decorative geometric pattern of repeated chevrons painted in black. We have named this distinctive black-on-red pottery Yahyā ware, and we call the material culture of Period V the Yahyā culture.

The commonest examples of Yahyā ware are beakers. These frequently have a potter's mark on the base, and we have so far identified nine individual marks. Evidence that outside contact and trade formed part of the fabric of Early Bronze Age life at Tepe Yahyā comes from the discovery at Tal-i-Iblis, a site nearly 100 miles closer to Kerman, of almost identical painted pottery bearing similar potter's marks. There is other evidence of regional contacts. Yahyā ware shows a general similarity to the painted pottery at sites elsewhere in southeastern Iran, and a black-on-buff ware at Tepe Yahyā closely resembles pottery from sites well to the west, such as Bakun. Moreover, the Period V levels at Tepe Yahyā abound in imported materials. There are tools made of obsidian, beads made of ivory, carnelian and turquoise, and various objects made of alabaster, marble and mother-of-pearl. One particularly handsome figure is a stylized representation of a ram, seven inches long, carved out of alabaster [see top illustration on page 210]. No local sources are known for any of these materials.

Although the architecture of Period V demonstrates a continuity with the preceding Neolithic period, the individual structures are larger than before. Several of them measure eight by 11½ feet in area and are clearly residential in character. Some rooms include a hearth and chimney. In the early levels the walls are still built of hand-formed mud bricks. Bricks formed in molds appear in the middle of Period V, which carbon-14 analyses show to have been around 3660 B.C. (±140 years).

The bronze implements of Period V, like much of the earliest bronze in the world, were produced not by alloying but by utilizing copper ores that contained "impurities." This was the case in early Sumer, where the ore, imported from Oman on the Arabian peninsula, contained a high natural percentage of nickel. Early bronzesmiths elsewhere smelted copper ores that were naturally rich in arsenic. Chisels, awls, pins and spatulas at Tepe Yahyā are made of such an arsenical bronze.

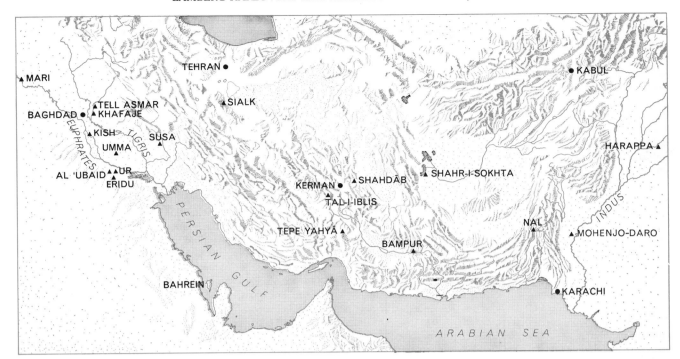

FIRST CITIES arose in the kingdom of Sumer in lower Mesopotamia (*left*). The earliest known forms of writing appeared in Sumer and in nearby Elam at cities such as Susa and Sialk. The discovery of proto-Elamite writing at Tepe Yahyā (*center*), which is 500 miles to the east, suggests that trade between the region and the early cities of Mesopotamia led to the rise of cities in this part of ancient Persia in the fourth millennium B.C. and to the later development of the urban Harappan civilization in the Indus region.

Six artifacts from the site have been analyzed by R. F. Tylecote and H. McKerrell of the University of Newcastle upon Tyne. They found that the bronze had been produced by smelting, which shows that the metalworkers of Period V were able to obtain the high temperatures needed to smelt copper ores into molten metal. The final shapes were not made by casting, however, but by hot and cold forging, a more primitive technique. One of the articles, a chisel, proved to contain 3.7 percent arsenic, which leads us to believe that the metalworkers consciously selected for smelting ores with a high arsenic content. This finding is further testimony in support of trade at Tepe Yahyā; none of the copper deposits native to the region could have been used to make arsenical bronze.

With the beginning of Period IV, around 3500 B.C., the appearance of writing at Tepe Yahyā allows the city to be identified as a proto-Elamite settlement. Much of the pottery representative of the first two phases of this period, IV-C and IV-B, is typical of the preceding Yahyā culture in both shape and decoration. Although there is plentiful evidence of external contact, the transition to Period IV at Tepe Yahyā, like the one that preceded it, occurred without any break in continuity. There is no need at Tepe Yahyā to conjure up that hackneyed instrument of cultural change: a new people arriving with luggage labeled "Proto-Elamite."

Architecture, however, was considerably transformed. The site ceased to be a residential area and became an administrative one. A large structure we have unearthed at the IV-C level of the mound is carefully oriented so that its walls run north-south and east-west. The walls consist of three courses of mold-formed brick in a new size. The earlier mold-formed bricks had been six by six by 12 inches; the new ones were 9½ by 9½ by 4¾ inches—a third wider and less than half as thick. So far we have identified five of an undetermined number of rooms within the large structure, although we have fully cleared only part of one room. Both the structure and the partially excavated room continue toward the center of the mound; the size of each remains to be determined.

The part of the room that has been cleared measures about 10 by 20 feet. Its contents strongly suggest a commercial function. Among the objects in the room are bowls with beveled rims made of a coarse ware. The vessels have counterparts at numerous sites in Mesopotamia. They are believed to have served as standard measures. Three large storage jars, which proved to be empty, were also found in the room; near them were some 24 "sealings": jar stoppers made of clay and marked with a seal impression. The seals used to mark the sealings were cylindrical; the designs resemble those on cylinder seals found at Susa, the Elamite capital in the Mesopotamian area. The finding creates the possibility that goods from Susa were reaching Tepe Yahyā early in Period IV.

Lying on the floor of the room were 84 blank clay tablets and six others that bore inscriptions. The tablets are all the same shape; they are made of unbaked dark brown clay, are convex in profile and measure 1⅛ by two inches. The six inscribed tablets bear a total of 17 lines of proto-Elamite writing. The inscriptions were impressed in the soft clay with a stylus; they read from right to left along the main axis of the tablet and from top to bottom. When an inscription continues from one side of a tablet to the other, the writer rotated the tablet on its main axis so that the bottom line of the obverse inscription and the top line of the reverse inscription lie opposite each other.

The Tepe Yahyā inscriptions are being deciphered now. Preliminary examination indicates that they are records or receipts dealing with goods. The fact that inscribed and otherwise identical blank tablets were found in the same room is strong evidence that the writing was done on the spot. Therefore the goods they describe must have been either entering or leaving the administrative area.

Until the discovery at Tepe Yahyā the only other proto-Elamite tablets known were from Susa or from Sialk in northwestern Iran. Susa yielded nearly 1,500 such tablets, Sialk only 19. Proto-Elamite writing has been found recently at Shahdāb, a site north of Kerman that is being excavated by the Iran Archaeological Service. The writing there is not on tablets but consists of brief inscriptions, with a maximum of seven signs, incised on pottery.

A second change in architectural style is evident in the single IV-B structure examined so far. It is a building, nine by 24 feet in area, that is oriented without reference to north-south and east-west. It is built of bricks of a still newer size and shape. They are oblong rather than square, and are either 14 or 17 inches long; the other two dimensions remained the same. The structure is subdivided into two main rooms and a few smaller rooms that contain large storage bins built of unbaked clay. Its walls are only one brick thick, and their inside surfaces are covered with plaster.

Storage vessels in one of the main rooms still held several pounds of grain. The grain was charred, which together with the fact that the matting on the floor and the bricks in the wall were burned indicates that the building was destroyed by fire. Amid the debris on the floors were cylinder seals and, for the first time at Tepe Yahyā, stamp seals as well.

Some bronze tools of the IV-B period have also been discovered. Needles and chisels, unearthed in association with soapstone artifacts, were probably used to work the soapstone. A bronze dagger some seven inches long was found by Tylecote and McKerrell to have been made by forging smelted metal, as were the bronze tools of Period V. Analysis showed that the dagger, unlike the earlier artifacts of arsenical bronze, was an alloy comprising 3 percent tin. Tin is not found in this part of Iran, which means that either the dagger itself, the tin contained in it or an ingot of tin-alloyed bronze must have been imported to Tepe Yahyā.

The proof that writing was known at Tepe Yahyā as early as it was known anywhere is a discovery of major importance to prehistory. Perhaps next in importance, however, is the abundant evidence suggesting a unique economic role for the city beginning late in the fourth millennium B.C. The IV-B phase at Tepe Yahyā is known from carbon-14 analyses to have extended from near the end of the fourth millennium through the first two centuries of the third millennium. During that time the city was a major supplier of soapstone artifacts.

Objects made of soapstone, ranging from simple beads to ornate bowls and all very much alike in appearance, are found in Bronze Age sites as far apart as Mohenjo-Daro, the famous center of Harappan culture on the Indus, and Mari on the upper Euphrates 1,500 miles away. Mesopotamia, however, was a region poor in natural resources, soapstone included. The Harappans of the Indus also seem to have lacked local supplies of several desired materials. How were the exotic substances to be obtained? Sumerian and Akkadian texts locate the sources of certain luxury imports in terms of place-names that are without meaning today: Dilmun, Maluhha and Magan.

Investigations by Danish workers on the island of Bahrein in the Persian Gulf have essentially confirmed the belief that the island is ancient Dilmun. There is also a degree of agreement that the area or place known as Maluhha lay somewhere in the valley of the Indus. Even before we began our work at Tepe Yahyā it had been suggested that the area known as Magan was somewhere in southeastern Iran. Our excavations have considerably strengthened this hypothesis. A fragmentary Sumerian text reads: "May the land Magan [bring] you mighty copper, the strength of . . . diorite, 'u-' stone, 'shumash' stone." Could either of the untranslated names of stones stand for soapstone? Were Tepe Yahyā and its hinterland a center of the trade? Let us examine the evidence from the site.

**TWO CYLINDER SEALS from the level at Tepe Yahyā overlying the first proto-Elamite settlement appear at left in these photographs next to the impressions they produce. The seal designs, which show pairs of human figures with supernatural attributes, are generally similar to the designs on seals of Mesopotamian origin but appear to be of local workmanship.**

More soapstone has been found at Tepe Yahyā than at any other single site in the Middle East. The total is more than 1,000 fragments, unfinished pieces and intact objects; the majority of them belong to Period IV-B. Among the intact pieces are beads, buttons, cylinder seals, figurines and bowls. Unworked blocks of soapstone, vessels that are partially hollowed out and unfinished seals and beads are proof that Tepe Yahyā was a manufacturing site and not merely a transshipment point.

Some of the soapstone bowls are plain, but others are elaborately decorated with carvings. The decorations include geometric and curvilinear designs, animals and human figures. Among the decora-

**EARLIEST STRUCTURE** at Tepe Yahyā is a storage area consisting of small units measuring five feet on a side. Few of the units have doorways; apparently they were entered through a hole in the roof. The walls were built either of sun-dried mud bricks, formed by hand rather than in molds, or simply of hand-daubed mud. White circle (*left*) shows where female figurine was found.

**TWO ELAMITE BUILDINGS** at Tepe Yahyā left the traces seen in this photograph. The walls of the earlier building (*left*) were built sometime around 3500 B.C. of mold-formed mud bricks 9½ inches on a side. The walls run from north to south and from east to west. The walls of the later structure (*right*) are not oriented in these directions. It was built sometime after 3000 B.C. of oblong mold-formed mud bricks of two lengths. Both structures seem to have been administrative rather than residential. The earlier one contained storage pots and measuring bowls. Near one angle of its walls a pile of 84 unused writing tablets is visible.

tions are examples of every major motif represented on the numerous soapstone bowls unearthed at Bronze Age sites in Mesopotamia and the Indus valley. Moreover, motifs found on pottery unearthed at sites such as Bampur, to the east of Tepe Yahyā, and Umm-an-Nai on the Persian Gulf are repeated on soapstone bowls from IV-B levels.

During our 1970 season we located what was probably one of the sources of Tepe Yahyā soapstone. An outcrop of the rock in the Ashin Mountains some 20 miles from the mound shows evidence of strip-mining in the past. This is unlikely to have been the only source. Soapstone deposits are often associated with deposits of asbestos and chromite. There is a chromite mine only 10 miles from Tepe Yahyā, and we have noted veins of asbestos in stones unearthed during our excavation of the mound. Reconnaissance in the mountains to the north might locate additional soapstone exposures.

Taking into consideration the large quantities of soapstone found at the site, the evidence that many of the soapstone articles were manufactured locally, the availability of raw material nearby and the presence in both Mesopotamia and Harappan territory of soapstone bowls that repeat motifs found at Tepe Yahyā, it is hard to avoid the conclusion that the city was a major producer of soapstone and a center of trade in the material. Before turning to the broader significance of such commercial activity in this geographically remote area, we shall briefly describe the remaining occupation periods at Tepe Yahyā.

At present there is little to report concerning the final phase of Period IV, which drew to a close about 2200 B.C. It is then that the break occurs in the continuity at Tepe Yahyā. The Iron Age reoccupation of the site, which lasted roughly from 1000 to 500 B.C., comprises Period III. It is evidenced by a series of living floors and by pottery that shows strong parallels to wares and shapes produced during the same period in northwestern Iran. We have not yet uncovered a major structure belonging to Period III; both the nature of the culture and Tepe Yahyā's relations with its Iron Age neighbors remain unclarified.

Period II at Tepe Yahyā, which consists of more than 200 years of Achaemenian occupation, was a time of large-scale construction. The building material remained mud brick, but we have yet to uncover a complete structure. The appearance of the two large rooms excavated thus far suggests, however, that the site had once more become at least partly residential.

A subsequent 600 years or so of Parthian and Sassanian occupation, representing Period I, is the final period of urban civilization at Tepe Yahyā. We have uncovered suggestions of large-scale architecture, including courtyards and part of a massive mud-brick platform made by laying four courses of brick one on the other. By Sassanian times (early in the third century) the accumulated debris of thousands of years had raised the mound to an imposing height; the structure that has been partly exposed probably was a citadel standing on the summit.

Most of the Sassanian pottery consists

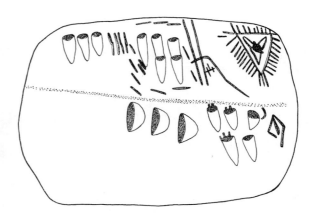

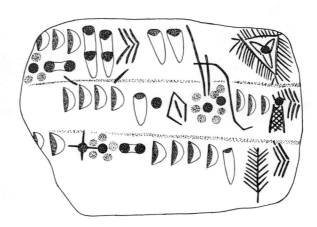

**INSCRIBED TABLETS** from Tepe Yahyā (*photographs*) are shown next to drawings that reproduce the written symbols. Only six inscribed tablets have been found so far. The inscriptions are in proto-Elamite, written from right to left across the length of the tablet by pressing the blunt or sharp end of a stylus into the soft clay. Similar written tablets have been unearthed at Susa and Sialk.

of coarse, thick-walled storage jars. An abundance of beads and several small glass and pottery bottles, perhaps containers for perfume, suggest a degree of prosperity during Period I. The presence of iron and bronze swords, axes and arrowheads adds a military flavor. A single work of art, a small clay figurine, represents a warrior with a distinctive headdress [*see bottom illustration on next page*]. Thereafter, from sometime in the fifth century on, Tepe Yahyā was occupied only by occasional squatters or transient nomads. The few scattered surface finds are of early Islamic age; none of the visitors lingered or built anything of substance.

What role did Elamite Tepe Yahyā play in the transmission of the urban tradition from west to east? The city's position suggests that Elamite culture, which is now revealed as being far more widespread than was realized previously, was instrumental in the contact between the first urban civilization in Mesopotamia and the civilization that subsequently arose in the Indus valley. It appears that the Elamites of eastern Persia may have accomplished much more than that. To assess this possibility it is necessary to examine the evidence for direct contact, as distinct from trade through middlemen, between Mesopotamia and the Indus valley.

A small number of artifacts that are possibly or certainly of Harappan origin have been found at sites in Mesopotamia. Because much of the archaeological work there was done as long as a century ago, it is not surprising that both the age and the original location of many of these artifacts can only be roughly estimated. Nonetheless, Mesopotamia has yielded six stamp seals, one cylinder seal and a single clay sealing, all of the Harappan type, that are evidence of some kind of contact between the two civilizations. Certain seals are engraved with Harappan writing. On others the writing is combined with animal figures that are indisputably Harappan in style: a "unicorn," an elephant, a rhinoceros. Evidence of contact, yes. But was the contact direct or indirect?

The single Indus sealing found in Mesopotamia was discovered by the French archaeologist G. Contenau at Umma in southern Iraq during the 1920's. It suggests the arrival there of freight from Harappan territory that had been identified with the sender's personal mark before shipment. The seven seals, however, are evidence of a more equivocal kind. Mesopotamian contact with the Indus evidently did not resemble the later trade

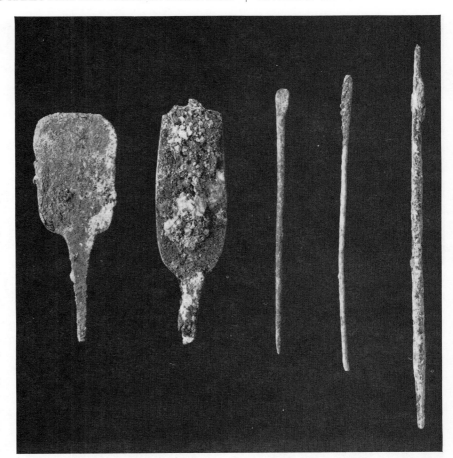

BRONZE OBJECTS contemporaneous with peak of work and trade in soapstone at Tepe Yahyā include two chisels (*left*) and three needle-like forms; the longest object measures 6½ inches. The bronze was not produced by alloying but by utilizing copper that naturally included significant amounts of arsenic. The enriched ores were obtained through trade.

SOAPSTONE BOWLS, many of them elaborately decorated, were among the numerous objects made at Tepe Yahyā and traded eastward and westward during the first half of the third millennium B.C. Fragments of bowls with decorations like the ones on these bowl fragments from Tepe Yahyā have been found from Mesopotamia to the Indus valley.

FIGURINE OF A RAM carved out of alabaster is one of the numerous articles made from imported materials that are found at Tepe Yahyā at the time of its first urban settlement about 3800 B.C. Evidences of trade between the city and outlying areas include, in addition to alabaster, mother-of-pearl from the Persian Gulf, marble, turquoise and carnelian.

FIGURINE OF A WARRIOR modeled in clay is from the final period of occupation at Tepe Yahyā, when a Sassanian military outpost stood on the top of the mound from sometime in the third century B.C. to about A.D. 400. Thereafter only nomads visited the dead city.

between Mesopotamia and, say, the Hittite realm to the west. In that instance Assyrian trading colonies were housed within special quarters of such Hittite strongholds as Kültepe and Hattusha [see the article "An Assyrian Trading Outpost," by Tahsin Özgüç, beginning on page 243]. There is simply no good evidence that Mesopotamians ever visited the Indus to set up residence and trade or that Harappans did the reverse.

What, then, were the seals of Harappan traders doing in Mesopotamia? What was the function of the three unearthed at Ur, the two at Kish and the two at Tell Asmar? So far there is no persuasive answer to these questions. It is tempting to look on these seals not as credentials but as souvenirs of indirect trade contact; all of them are handsome objects. At the same time another equally puzzling question presents itself. Some objects of Indus origin have been found in Mesopotamia. Why has nothing of any kind from Mesopotamia been found at any Indus site?

Evidence of direct trade contact between the two civilizations thus remains almost entirely absent. Other kinds of trade, however, are equally well known. One of the oldest and most widespread is simple exchange, which can interpose any number of witting or unwitting intermediaries between two principals. Exchange is notable for presenting the archaeologist with difficulties of interpretation; intangibles such as style and function are likely to travel along with the goods.

A system of exchange that involves a single intermediary seems to provide the theoretical model that best approximates the situation at Tepe Yahyā. Such a system is known as "central place" trade; we suggest that Tepe Yahyā was just such a central place in southeastern Persia during Elamite times.

A central place can lie outside the sphere of influence of either principal and at the same time produce goods or control natural resources desired by both. In addition to (or even instead of) exporting its own products, a central place can transship goods produced by either principal. Bahrein—ancient Dilmun—provides a good example of a central place whose prosperity was based on the transshipment of goods bound for Mesopotamia. Whether or not transshipment was important at Tepe Yahyā, the city's basic central-place role in Elamite times was clearly that of a producer manufacturing and exporting articles made of soapstone.

The names of the Mesopotamian sites that contain soapstone bowls identical in shape and decorative motif with those we unearthed at Tepe Yahyā read like an archaeologist's checklist: Adab, Mari, Tell Asmar, Tell Aqrab, Khafaje, Nippur, Telloh, Kish, Al 'Ubaid and Ur. Bowls of Tepe Yahyā style have also been found at Mohenjo-Daro on the Indus and at Kulli-Damb in Pakistani Baluchistan. In addition to bevel-rim bowls of the Uruk type at Tepe Yahyā as evidence of contact with the west, the mound has yielded Nal ware, a kind of Indus painted pottery that predates the rise of Harappan civilization, as evidence of contact with the east.

Tepe Yahyā was not, however, the only central place in eastern Persia. It seems rather to have been one of several that comprised a local loose Elamite federation astride the middle ground between the two civilizations. Shahr-i-Sokhta, a site 250 miles northeast of Tepe Yahyā, appears to have been another central place, exporting local alabaster and transshipping lapis lazuli from Afghanistan. The links between Tepe Yahyā and other possible central places in the region such as Tal-i-Iblis, Shahdāb and Bampur—mainly demonstrated by similarities in pottery—have already been mentioned.

How did this remote Elamite domain, which in the case of Tepe Yahyā predates the appearance of Harappan civilization by at least three centuries, influence developments in the Indus valley? In spite of exciting new evidence that trade networks existed as long ago as the early Neolithic, a strong tendency exists to view trade exclusively as an ex post facto by-product of urbanism. Trade, however, has certainly also been one of the major stimuli leading to urban civilization. This, it seems to us, was exactly the situation in ancient Kerman and Persian Baluchistan.

We suggest that trade between resource-poor Mesopotamia and the population of this distant part of Persia provided the economic base necessary for the urban development of centers such as Tepe Yahyā during the fourth millennium B.C. It can further be suggested that, once an urban Elamite domain was established there, its trade with the region farther to the east provided much of the stimulus that culminated during the third millennium B.C. with the rise of Harappan civilization. Sir Mortimer Wheeler has declared that "the idea of civilization" crossed from Mesopotamia to the Indus. It seems to us that the Elamite central places midway between the two river basins deserve the credit for the crossing.

# 21

# The Beginnings of Wheeled Transport

by Stuart Piggott
*July 1968*

*Mankind has traveled on wheels for at least 5,000 years. The recent discovery of ancient wagons at sites in the U.S.S.R. casts doubt on the accepted hypothesis that vehicles were invented in Mesopotamia*

Professor Marshall McLuhan, in one of his oracular pronouncements, defined the relationship of the automobile to modern man as that of the mechanical bride. Recent archaeological studies help to trace the earliest stages in man's romance with the wheel that ultimately led to this strange, if not unholy, consummation. Like all first courtships, it was inexpert and tentative in its beginnings, but more than 5,000 years ago the bride of wheeled transport had been won in Eurasia. For whatever reason, the early Americans failed to duplicate this invention.

It is not excessively determinist to suggest that certain prerequisites are needed for the development of wheeled vehicles. The vehicles will be invented only in societies that have a need to move heavy or bulky loads considerable distances over land that is fairly flat and fairly firm. A suitable raw material, such as timber, must be on hand for building the vehicle. And a prime mover stronger than a man must be available to make the wheels turn. In the Old World the power problem had been solved at least 7,000 or 8,000 years ago by the domestication of cattle. Once it was realized that castration produced a docile, heavy draft animal, oxen were available for traction; their strength and patience more than compensated for their slowness. Timber was available in quantity in the parts of the Near East that were neither desert nor steppe. These are the regions that saw the emergence of the earliest agricultural communities, beginning about 9000 B.C. The same communities were among the first to possess polished stone axes and adzes and, soon thereafter, copper and bronze tools suitable for elaborate carpentry.

The archaeological evidence shows that the first stages of wheeled transport depended on heavy vehicles with disk (as opposed to spoked) wheels. The wheels were either cut from a single massive plank or were made from three (and occasionally more) planks doweled and mortised together. Light vehicles with spoked wheels, harnessed to swift draft animals, were a later development that combined an advanced technology in bronze tools—and thus in the wheelwright's craft—with the domestication of the small wild horse of the steppe. Such vehicles first appear in the Near East in response to military needs during the first half of the second millennium B.C. Here, however, we are concerned mainly with developments earlier than the second millennium, when vehicles were usually drawn by oxen.

From the standpoint of the archaeologist wood is a miserable material; it is resistant to decay only in exceptional conditions of waterlogging or desiccation. Under normal circumstances to detect and recover traces of wood encountered in an excavation calls for a high degree of technical skill. It may therefore surprise the reader to learn that in Europe and Asia nearly 50 wheeled vehicles—or their wheels—have been recovered from sites that predate the second millennium B.C. This type of direct evidence concerning early vehicles is supported by discoveries of other kinds, such as models of vehicles or their wheels made from pottery, which of course is much less susceptible to disintegration than wood.

The earliest examples of wheeled vehicles have all been found within a region no more than 1,200 miles across centered between Lake Van in eastern Asia Minor and Lake Urmia in northern Iran. Presumably the first wheeled vehicle originated somewhere within this region. The oldest evidence dates back to the final centuries of the fourth millennium B.C., indicating that wheeled transport came into existence somewhat more than 5,000 years ago.

The region within which wheeled vehicles made their first appearance embraces desert and open steppe as well as forested slopes along the mountain belt that includes the ranges of the Taurus, the Caucasus and the Zagros. Deciduous timber does not grow below the 1,000-foot contour of these mountains and often not below 3,000 feet. A mosaic of communities, with economies based on mixed agriculture and copper or bronze metallurgy, flourished in the region from about 3000 B.C. onward. In Mesopotamia to the south the population was already literate and urban societies were beginning to form. To the north the zone of farming communities probably merged gradually into the area occupied by the pastoralists of the steppe beyond the Caucasus. All three societies were ones in which wheeled transport would constitute a valuable technological addition to the existing economy.

Our earliest evidence for vehicles with wheels, as opposed to simple sledges that could be dragged overland, is provided by symbols in the pictographic script of Uruk, a Sumerian city in southern Mesopotamia. The Uruk pictographs represent man's earliest known writing; they are believed to date from somewhat before 3000 B.C. Some Uruk signs depict a schematized profile view of a sledge; others show the sledge pictograph with two little disks added below it—an abbreviated symbol for a four-wheeled vehicle. Beginning about 2700 B.C. in Mesopotamia the evidence is no longer symbolic but concrete. By that time the Sumerians and their neighbors buried vehicles along with their dead; sometimes the vehicles even contained the dead. The vehicle remains often survive as nothing more than stains in the soil such as have been de-

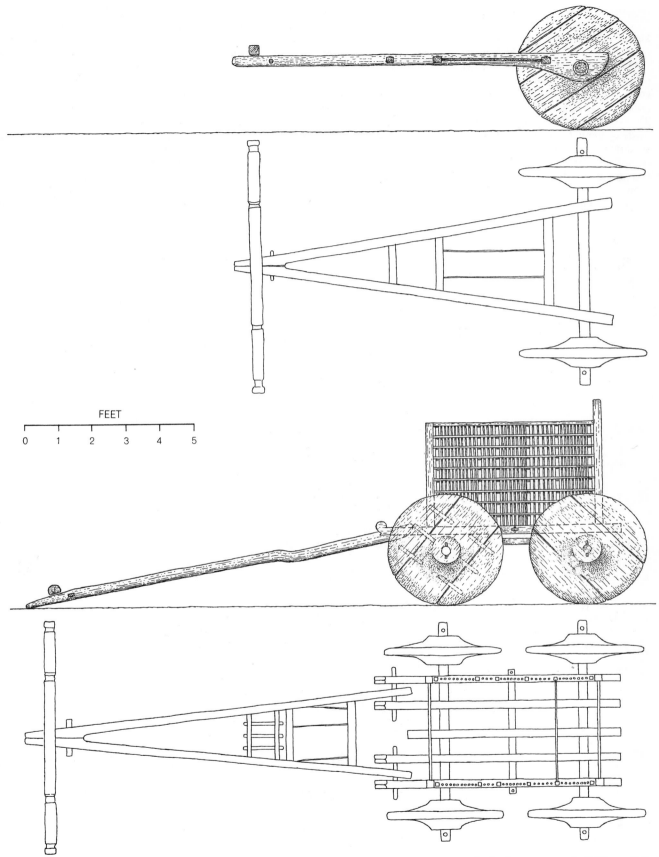

FEET

| 0 | 1 | 2 | 3 | 4 | 5 |

CART AND WAGON from the latter half of the second millennium B.C. were found by Soviet archaeologists in tombs at Lake Sevan in the Armenian S.S.R. They closely resemble the wheeled vehicles of much earlier times. The simple design of the A-frame cart (*top*) suggests that these vehicles came into being through the addition of an axle and wheels to a two-pole "slide car" that was formerly dragged along the ground by draft animals. The wagons at Lake Sevan (*bottom*) were complex and utilized mortise-and-tenon joining. Their draft poles, however, were apparently nothing more than cart A-frames, pegged to the wagon's chassis.

tected in the Royal Tombs at Kish and Ur and at Susa in Elam. They are of two kinds: vehicles with two wheels (carts) and vehicles with four wheels (wagons).

Carts and wagons alike were drawn by oxen or by Asiatic asses (*Equus onager*), cousins of the horse that the early Mesopotamians had managed to domesticate. The vehicles' wheels were light disks made by joining three planks. The representations in Mesopotamian art and the model vehicles that have survived from this period and the periods that follow it show that disk-wheeled vehicles were known both in Mesopotamia and among

the nonliterate peoples along the Mesopotamian frontier, from Asia Minor on the west to Turkmenia on the east. The vehicles were present along most of the periphery before 2000 B.C.; soon thereafter they were common throughout it.

It had been assumed until recently that the adoption of wheeled transport among peoples to the north and west of the central zone outlined above, as well as the eventual adoption of vehicles by the peoples who inhabited Europe, were events that took place measurably later than adoption of vehicles within the

central zone. Indeed, the spread of wheeled transport is often cited as a classic example of diffusion from a primary center. Since World War II, however, the picture has changed as archaeologists in southern Russia and in the Soviet republics of Georgia and Armenia have unearthed large quantities of new prehistoric material.

Among the discoveries are more than 25 burials in which vehicles were included; these apparently date from at least 2500 B.C. up to about 1200 B.C. Indirect evidence from several Soviet sites for even earlier knowledge of wheeled

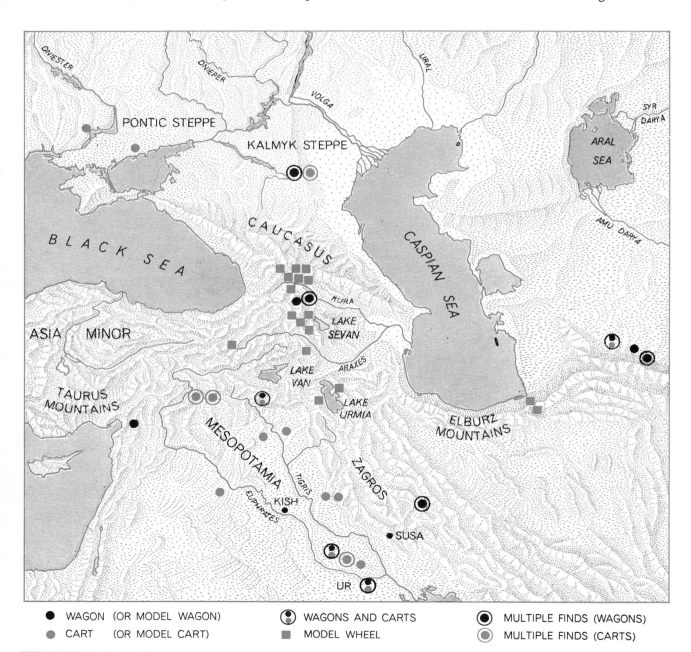

WAGON (OR MODEL WAGON)    ● WAGONS AND CARTS    ◉ MULTIPLE FINDS (WAGONS)
CART (OR MODEL CART)    ■ MODEL WHEEL    ◉ MULTIPLE FINDS (CARTS)

**VEHICLES** built before 2000 B.C. in a zone between the Black Sea and central Asia are found in two main concentrations. One is Transcaucasia and the open steppe to the north. The other is Mesopotamia, including the headwaters of the Tigris and Euphrates. It was formerly believed that the first wheeled vehicles were made in Mesopotamia. The discovery that such vehicles were made in Soviet Georgia and Armenia before the second millennium B.C. diminishes the probability of a Mesopotamian origin of wheeled transport.

vehicles—in the form of model wheels made from pottery—pushes the starting date back perhaps as far as 3000 B.C. Nothing has been found at the new Soviet sites that is demonstrably as old as the pictographs from Uruk. Nonetheless, the Soviet evidence considerably weakens the case for absolute priority in the invention of wheeled transport previously conceded to Mesopotamia. The challenge is a serious one because the Mesopotamian claim rests on the pictograph of a modified sledge and on nothing else.

Because the recent evidence from the U.S.S.R. is little known outside that country it is worth describing in some detail. By way of preface I should explain that a number of excavations in Transcaucasia—the region between the Black Sea and the Caspian Sea lying south of the greater Caucasus—have made it evident that this region was once occupied by a single homogeneous culture. Marked by a complex of sedentary mixed farming, village settlements and some copper-working, the culture extended from the river valleys of the Kura and the Araxes in Georgia and Armenia, southward to Lake Urmia and westward well beyond Lake Van [see illustration on opposite page]. The period during which the Kura-Araxes culture flourished is known on the basis of carbon-14 determinations. It began about 3000 B.C., continued until sometime after 2500 B.C. and may even have lasted down to the end of the third millennium B.C. Pottery models of disk wheels with well-marked hubs are found at a number of Kura-Araxes sites. They are identical with the wheels of model vehicles unearthed in the Near East; evidently the existence of wheeled transport was at least known in Transcaucasia at the same time that actual vehicles were being entombed at Kish and Ur.

As a matter of fact the Kura-Araxes culture possesses vehicle burials of its own. One tomb at Zelenyy, in the Tsalka region of the Georgian S.S.R., was found to have contained a wagon. It had evidently been interred in working order, since the floor of the tomb bore long grooves made by the vehicle's wheels. The burial at Zelenyy, a pit grave covered by a round kurgan, or barrow mound, belongs to a style of burial that moved into the Caucasus from the southern Russian steppe. On the steppe the burials have given their name to the Pit Grave culture, which flourished during much of the third millennium B.C. Similar burials—including in two instances the remains of wagons—have been unearthed at Trialeti, another site in the Tsalka district.

The waterlogged soil of one of these tombs, excavated in 1958, contained a wagon with massive three-piece wheels. The wagon had an A-shaped draft pole, of which the stumps were preserved. It had apparently been equipped with an arched canopy to shelter its occupants. As we shall see, several more or less complete examples of similar "covered wagons" have been found elsewhere. The Trialeti burial probably took place sometime before 2000 B.C., although the date is not known precisely.

Some 350 miles north of the Tsalka district, beyond the passes of the greater Caucasus range and well into the southern Russian steppe, Soviet archaeologists have unearthed several other buried carts and wagons. The sites are located in the Elista region of the Kalmyk Steppe, no more than a month's ox-trek distant from Transcaucasia. The first Elista burials were found in 1947; others were located in 1962 and 1963. They belong to the final phase of the Pit Grave culture or to a culture that overlapped and succeeded it, and appear to be dated between 2400 and 2300 B.C.

The carts buried in the Elista graves are represented by pairs of wheels and by one pottery model of a cart with an arched canopy. The most interesting of the Elista burials, however, are those containing four-wheeled wagons. Like the model cart, the Elista wagons had arched canopies; in some cases remains of the wickerwork of which the canopies were made have survived. The Soviet excavators maintain that one of the Elista wagons had a pivoted front axle, a device that would have permitted steering the wagon. This is remarkable. If accepted, the Elista innovation antedates by many centuries the first previously known appearance of a most important advance in vehicle design. Heretofore no ancient vehicle was known to have a pivoted front axle until the time of the Celtic ritual wagons at Djebjerg in Denmark, in the first century B.C. Indeed, the very existence of the feature before medieval times has sometimes been called into question, and we are certain of pivoted axles only from the Middle Ages onward.

The resemblance between the Elista vehicle burials and vehicle burials in the Georgian S.S.R. is not the only evidence that implies contact between the steppe and Transcaucasia. Near the Black Sea and the Dnieper River in southern Russia, an area that also lies within the ancient boundaries of the Pit Grave culture, two more vehicle burials

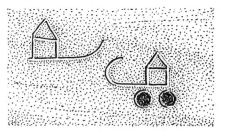

OLDEST PORTRAYAL of a vehicle with wheels is a Sumerian pictograph used shortly before 3000 B.C. It is derived from the sign for a sledge (left). The addition of two circles (right) turns it into the sign for a wagon.

CHINESE PICTOGRAPHS for a chariot or cart, apparently with spoked wheels, are first seen in inscriptions of the Shang dynasty, somewhat later than 1500 B.C. Two inverted "y" strokes (top right) represent the horses.

have been found. The graves were dug late in the third millennium B.C.; in both instances the vehicles are carts with one-piece disk wheels.

In 1956 the initiation of a hydroelectric project at Lake Sevan in the Armenian S.S.R. lowered the lake's level by many feet. Near Lchashen, as the level fell, a number of formerly submerged tombs were revealed; in them were found nearly a dozen carts and wagons. The vehicles are comparatively recent, having been buried over a period of some centuries, beginning about 1400 B.C. They are so well preserved, however, and have so many features in common with carts and wagons of much greater age that they merit special attention. Each burial was made in a huge boulder-lined pit, originally with a sloping ramp at one end. The vehicles were apparently maneuvered down the ramps and the pits were then covered with stone cairns. Soon afterward the level of Lake Sevan rose and immersion preserved the wood of the vehicles. In addition to vehicles with three-part disk wheels some of the tombs contained light carts—virtually chariots—that had spoked wheels.

From the viewpoint of technological development two-wheeled vehicles are more primitive than four-wheeled ones. In spite of their relatively late date the

**MESOPOTAMIAN CHARIOT, pulled by Asiatic asses, was modeled in copper by an artisan at Tell Agrab around 2800 B.C. Although such vehicles were used for sport and war rather than for cartage, their three-piece disk wheels are identical with earlier cart wheels.**

Lchashen carts reflect this. They are of the simplest kind and embody a design that is still found today among nonindustrialized peoples in parts of Europe and Asia from the Iberian peninsula and the Mediterranean coast to Asia Minor, the Crimea, the Kalmyk Steppe and the Caucasus. (The same simple carts are found even farther east, of course, but their distribution in the Orient need not concern us here.) The basic design is an A-frame. The design presumably evolved from a simple travois, or slide car, made by lashing the butts of two poles together and letting the tips of the poles trail along the ground behind the draft animals. The addition of an axle and a pair of wheels near the wide end of the A-frame turns such a travois into a cart.

Wagons, on the other hand, are comparatively complex structures. With their intricate frames and often elaborate ornamentation, the Lchashen wagons were plainly vehicles of prestige just as much as today's Cadillac. The tombs at Lchashen contained six wagons in all. Four of them had arched canopies and one had upright wickerwork sides and a decorated panel at the back. Their complicated carpentry testifies to the need for adequate coachbuilders' tools. One covered wagon was an assembly of 70 component parts; the parts were either pegged together or joined by a mortise-and-tenon system that required cutting no fewer than 12,000 mortises. (The frame

of the canopy alone required 600.) In spite of the excellence of their workmanship, the Lchashen wagons must have been slow and clumsy: the estimated unloaded weight of the wagon with the wickerwork sides is two-thirds of a ton.

Although the covered wagons of Lchashen are nearly 1,000 years younger than the steppe vehicles of the Elista region, they have counterparts among them. Moreover, the same form of wagon was common in the Near East during the third millennium B.C., as is indicated by pottery models unearthed in northern Iraq and Syria. The draft poles of the Lchasen wagons provide a lesson in vehicle evolution. They are plainly derived from cart A-frames; each wagon looks as if a cart A-frame had been pegged to the front of its chassis [see illustration on page 213]. This suggests continued use the familiar A-frame cart was the earliest form of vehicle known and that, when four-wheeled wagons came to be built, the designers continued to use the familiar A-frame shape instead of devising a single central pole for the draft animals.

What do the various Soviet discoveries signify as far as the beginning of wheeled transport is concerned? One way of interpreting this evidence is to suggest that during the third millennium B.C. the wagon found its way to Transcaucasia from the Russian steppe to the north, along with a funeral rite that re-

quired the burial of the vehicles in pit graves. At the time of the wagons' emergence, however, wheeled transport must already have existed in Transcaucasia, perhaps in the form of A-frame carts (the evidence for this being the pottery models of wheels found in Kura-Araxes sites of earlier date). Another interpretation might suggest instead that the covered wagons came to Transcaucasia from the south and that their presence in the Pit Grave sites represents an exotic intrusion into the steppe that has its ultimate origins in the early civilizations of the Near East.

The problems presented by such alternative explanations will be discussed later. Meanwhile one should remember that the Caucasus do not in fact form an insuperable barrier to movement across them in either direction. There are good passes through the greater Caucasus, particularly the one through which the Georgian Military Highway runs from Tiflis to Ordzhonikidze. Whichever way the current of diffusion may have run between urban and barbarian zones during the third millennium B.C., carts and wagons with one-piece and three-piece wheels certainly were in use throughout the region well before 2000 B.C.

Let us now turn to the spread of wheeled transport into prehistoric Europe and see how, if you will, the West was won by the covered wagons of antiquity. Recently a number of large one-piece disk wheels have been discovered in the Netherlands. Carbon-14 determinations indicate that they were made a century or so before 2000 B.C. Two similar disk wheels, slightly earlier in date, have been found in Denmark. The wheels that most closely resemble the Dutch and Danish discoveries are ones found in the cart burials of the Pontic Steppe in southern Russia. This area is some 2,500 miles removed from the North Sea, even as the crow flies, and is considerably farther in terms of feasible overland routes of travel. What connections can be found between two such widely separated areas?

In all the land between the steppe and the North Sea the only direct evidence of the ancient use of wheeled vehicles consists of model wheels made of pottery and of a single model wagon. The pottery objects all appear to have been made before the end of the third millennium B.C., although precise dating is difficult. The model wagon, equipped with disk wheels, was found in a cemetery of the copper-using Baden culture, located at Budakalasz, on the outskirts of Budapest. It has a stunted one-piece draft pole. Above the chassis the wagon's sides rake outward; their concave upper edges suggest a body made of matting, supported by four corner poles [*see lower illustration on page 219*].

The Baden culture appears to have flourished in the period between 2700 and 2300 B.C. Chronologically this is not far removed from the era that saw wagons being buried at Ur, and it is contemporary with the vehicles found to the north and south of the Caucasus. The pottery models of single wheels are distributed at random. The one found deepest in central Europe was unearthed near Brno in Czechoslovakia; in general they are all contemporary with the later centuries of the Baden culture.

These few bits of clay constitute our only direct evidence of linkages between Europe and the steppe, but they are not the only evidence. In the Baden culture and in other roughly contemporaneous societies that flourished in what are now

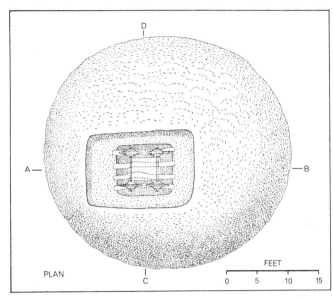
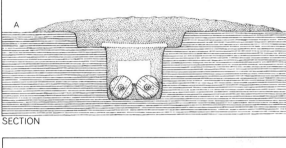
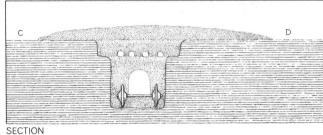

WAGON IN A TOMB was unearthed by Soviet archaeologists at Trialeti, in the Tsalka district of the Georgian S.S.R., in 1958. The wagon's wooden wheels and parts of its draft pole and chassis were preserved in the burial pit's waterlogged soil (*see illustration below*). Traces were found of an arched canopy that sheltered the occupants. The wagon probably was buried before 2000 B.C.

TRIALETI BURIAL PIT resembles a bog as the diggers probe for remnants of an entombed wagon. The vehicle's distinctive three-piece wheels have been almost wholly exposed. Trialeti is one of two Caucasus sites containing vehicles that predate 2000 B.C.

Poland and East Germany it was not uncommon to give ceremonial burial to animals as well as to men and women. Frequently the buried animals were pairs of cattle; more than 15 such burials belonging to the third millennium B.C. have been unearthed. One of them was found in the same Hungarian cemetery that yielded the model wagon. There a pair of oxen occupied one end of a long grave and human remains occupied the other end. In other cases paired oxen have been found lying at one end of a grave that was dug longer than necessary to accommodate the animals alone.

One inference to be drawn from the burials is that we are seeing pairs of draft animals; the discovery in Poland of two models of yoked pairs of oxen, of about the same age as the animal burials, lends weight to the inference. It is uncertain, however, whether we are seeing burials that originally included wheeled vehicles. The vehicles might have decayed without leaving a trace, or the traces could have gone unrecognized by the excavators. There also could have been no buried vehicles at all; the oxen may have been plow teams or animals that pulled a sledge. Nonetheless, if we take into account the burials of vehicles that have survived elsewhere, it seems most probable that burial of pairs of oxen is

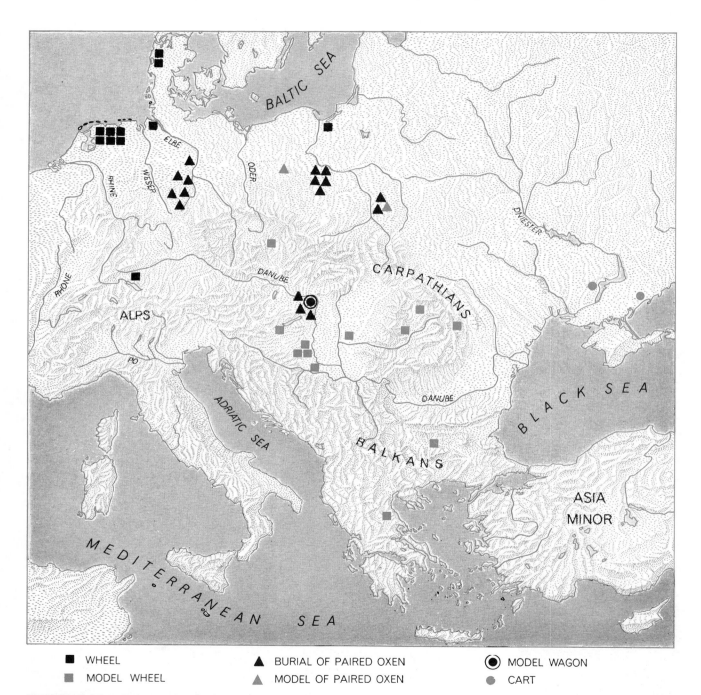

| ■ | WHEEL | ▲ | BURIAL OF PAIRED OXEN | ◉ | MODEL WAGON |
| ■ | MODEL WHEEL | ▲ | MODEL OF PAIRED OXEN | ● | CART |

**PRESENCE OF WAGONS** in Europe before 2000 B.C. is shown by the discovery of one-piece disk wheels in the Netherlands and in Denmark that yield carbon-14 dates earlier than the second millennium B.C. Direct evidence, in the form of pottery models of wheels and a single pottery model of a wagon, suggests that some vehicles entered central Europe via the Ukraine, the Romanian plain and Hungary. Indirect evidence, in the form of buried pairs of oxen and models of yoked oxen, suggests that another influx of wagons moved northwest from the Ukraine, skirting the Carpathian Mountains and arriving in the forested plain of northern Europe.

another variant of a general funeral rite in which at times a vehicle and its animals were buried together (as at Uruk), and at other times the animals were buried alone as a token representation. Accepting such an interpretation tentatively, we find that the indirect evidence of the animal burials fits in well with the direct evidence provided by the model wagon and model wheels. Both lines of evidence give added substance to a picture of Europe in which wheeled transport was used from the middle Danube to the Low Countries and Jutland at least by 2500 B.C. and probably earlier.

Thus, as in the Soviet excavations, we see that new or reassessed archaeological evidence, given the secure dating provided by carbon-14 analysis, is serving to narrow the ancient Near East's supposed margin of priority in the innovation of wheeled transport. What remains to be seen is whether valid inferences can be drawn with respect to two interlinked questions. The first question is whether or not the available evidence is sufficient to test the traditional diffusionist hypothesis about wheeled vehicles. This is the contention that the first such transport originated in a restricted region of western Asia where other technological innovations were under way among the precociously developing societies that immediately preceded the literate civilization of Sumer and Elam. The other question is more restricted in scope but is nevertheless important: Assuming that the area can be found in which wheeled vehicles were first used, by what routes and in what context of prehistory was the technology transferred from the point of innovation to Europe?

The answers to both questions depend heavily on the acceptability of the estimated ages of many archaeological finds and even of the actual dates of past events. In the context where the evidence is most needed, alas, it is not precise. For example, the date assigned to the earliest Uruk pictographs is derived from reasoned guesses and historical computation backward from the 24th century B.C., the point at which history of a sort begins in Mesopotamia, along with a glance at one or two relevant carbon-14 dates. Yet physicists have recently questioned whether "carbon-14 years" are exactly equivalent to calendar years during the period in question. The carbon-14 readings apparently give "true" dates that are several centuries earlier than the ones now in use, and correlation of the historical time scale with the carbon-14 time scale is fraught with difficulties. Even if carbon-14 dates themselves are no more than expressions

of statistical probabilities, comparison of one with another should still provide a good relative scale. In this way, for example, one could validly equate part of the Kura-Araxes culture with part of the Baden culture. The scarcity of carbon-14 determinations for the Soviet vehicles is particularly regrettable when one considers the wealth of wood available for analysis. In spite of these handicaps, however, it is hard to escape the conclu-

sion that the closely spaced dates of early wheeled vehicles unearthed from the Caucasus to the Netherlands must reflect a basic reality that indicates a rapid transmission of ideas over great distances.

Where was the first wheeled vehicle made? Let us return briefly to some of the factors considered at the outset. Timber would be needed both for the

HEAVY WHEEL, fashioned from a single massive plank of wood, was found by Dutch archaeologists in Overijssel in 1960. Carbon-14 analysis dates it earlier than 2000 B.C.

MODEL OF A WAGON was found in a Hungarian cemetery that contains remains of the Baden culture. The Baden culture flourished in the middle of the third millennium B.C.

wheels and for the chassis; thus one is inclined to look toward regions adjacent to natural woodlands. In the case of Mesopotamia, timber would have had to come from the Zagros Mountains or from the Kurdish highlands. In support of Mesopotamia as the scene of the invention we should bear in mind that the Sumerians themselves seem to have come down from hill country, perhaps as early as the sixth millennium B.C.

Alternatively, the first wheeled vehicles could have been made within easy reach of the timber of the Caucasus. From there the invention could have been transmitted on the one hand to Mesopotamia (in the context of long-standing Sumerian ancestral relationships with the mountain peoples) and on the other into the treeless steppe to the north. Without drawing on resources beyond its bounds, however, the steppe itself certainly could not have been the birthplace.

In the light of our limited present knowledge it seems prudent to assume that the invention of wheeled vehicles took place in a wide area rather than a narrow one. The area should include Transcaucasia. Furthermore, the inventors should have not only access to raw materials but also suitable draft animals and adequate metal tools. Finally, the possibility of multiple invention is not beyond imagining. A vehicle of Sumerian design, with small one-piece wheels, could have provided a starting point. Later such developments as the covered wagon, with its heavy three-piece wheels, may well have taken place elsewhere and then been introduced into Mesopotamia. Mesopotamian wagon wheels are of noticeably lighter construction than those of the steppe; they

can hardly have been the prototypes of the massive, doweled and mortised wheels of Transcaucasia. They could, however, represent a timber-saving version of a Transcaucasian original.

As for tracing the routes by which a knowledge of vehicles, or for that matter the vehicles themselves, moved westward into Europe, we must depend largely on inference. The evidence for cultural connections between the southern Russian steppe and the areas to the north and west is general rather than specific. Moreover, a new technological addition to a culture, such as the use of wheeled transport, does not necessarily carry any other traits of the parent culture with it. In spite of these caveats it has long been recognized that the cultures of the Hungarian plain in the late third millennium B.C. possess features that are difficult to explain on a basis of evolution from indigenous antecedents alone. A likely source for at least some of the obviously intrusive elements, such as new types of copper implements that resemble Caucasus copperwork, is southern Russia. The route of the intrusion could have been by way of the Ukraine and the plains of Romania, and thence into Hungary either over the mountains or by way of the Danube's Iron Gate. Along this route too could have come knowledge of the first wheeled vehicles.

The evidence of buried oxen in Poland and buried wheels in the Netherlands and Denmark may be related to an entirely separate intrusion. The pattern of cultures in the northern European plain around the middle of the third millennium B.C. includes a culture complex characterized by cord-ornamented pottery, stone battle axes and the custom of burying the dead in single graves cov-

ered by earth barrows. It has long been held that the complex is an intrusive one and is ultimately to be derived from sources in southern Russia related to the Pit Grave culture, although this interpretation has recently been disputed, and a case has been made instead for indigenous evolution.

The championing of local origins arises perhaps in part as a healthy reaction to earlier, overworked models of European prehistory that too strongly emphasized "invasions" and "folk movements." Nevertheless, even if some features of early northern European cultures can better be explained in terms of local growth, there still remains ample evidence of contact between southern Russia and northern Europe during the period. Dutch archaeologists have sought the origin of their disk-wheeled vehicles in Russia with good reason. A practicable route for the contact would also involve the Ukraine steppe, but from there it would cross the forest steppe and run beside the Dniester River, skirting the northern slopes of the Carpathian Mountains until it reached northern Europe's forested plain.

As in all questions of prehistory, we can at most advance working hypotheses that seem, in accordance with Occam's law, to account most economically for the archaeological facts. Indeed, what we call the facts are themselves only inferences derived from the surviving material culture of extinct communities. The investigation is nonetheless worthwhile, since it was during prehistoric times that the foundations of all our technology were laid down. No innovation was more fraught with ambiguous consequences than the invention and development of wheeled transport.

# Teotihuacán

by René Millon
June 1967

*The first and largest city of the pre-Columbian New World arose in the Valley of Mexico during the first millenium A.D. At its height the metropolis covered a larger area than imperial Rome*

When the Spaniards conquered Mexico, they described Montezuma's capital Tenochtitlán in such vivid terms that for centuries it seemed that the Aztec stronghold must have been the greatest city of pre-Columbian America. Yet only 25 miles to the north of Tenochtitlán was the site of a city that had once been even more impressive. Known as Teotihuacán, it had risen, flourished and fallen hundreds of years before the conquistadors entered Mexico. At the height of its power, around A.D. 500, Teotihuacán was larger than imperial Rome. For more than half a millennium it was to Middle America what Rome, Benares or Mecca have been to the Old World: at once a religious and cultural capital and a major economic and political center.

Unlike many of the Maya settlements to the south, in both Mexico and Guatemala, Teotihuacán was never a "lost" city. The Aztecs were still worshiping at its sacred monuments at the time of the Spanish Conquest, and scholarly studies of its ruins have been made since the middle of the 19th century. Over the past five years, however, a concerted program of investigation has yielded much new information about this early American urban center.

In the Old World the first civilizations were associated with the first cities, but both in Middle America and in Peru the rise of civilization does not seem to have occurred in an urban setting. As far as we can tell today, the foundation for the earliest civilization in Middle America was laid in the first millennium B.C. by a people we know as the Olmecs. None of the major Olmec centers discovered so far is a city. Instead these centers—the most important of which are located in the forested lowlands along the Gulf of Mexico on the narrow Isthmus of Tehuantepec—were of a ceremonial character, with small permanent populations probably consisting of priests and their attendants.

The Olmecs and those who followed them left to many other peoples of Middle America, among them the builders of Teotihuacán, a heritage of religious beliefs, artistic symbolism and other cultural traditions. Only the Teotihuacanos, however, created an urban civilization of such vigor that it significantly influenced the subsequent development of most other Middle American civilizations—urban and nonurban—down to the time of the Aztecs. It is hard to say exactly why this happened, but at least some of the contributing factors are evident. The archaeological record suggests the following sequence of events.

A settlement of moderate size existed at Teotihuacán fairly early in the first century B.C. At about the same time a number of neighboring religious centers were flourishing. One was Cuicuilco, to the southwest of Teotihuacán in the Valley of Mexico; another was Cholula, to the east in the Valley of Puebla. The most important influences shaping the "Teotihuacán way" probably stemmed from centers such as these. Around the time of Christ, Teotihuacán began to grow rapidly, and between A.D. 100 and 200 its largest religious monument was raised on the site of an earlier shrine. Known today as the Pyramid of the Sun, it was as large at the base as the great pyramid of Cheops in Egypt [*see bottom illustration on page 228*].

The powerful attraction of a famous holy place is not enough, of course, to explain Teotihuacán's early growth or later importance. The city's strategic location was one of a number of material factors that contributed to its rise. Teotihuacán lies astride the narrow waist of a valley that is the best route between the Valley of Mexico and the Valley of Puebla. The Valley of Puebla, in turn, is the gateway to the lowlands along the Gulf of Mexico.

The lower part of Teotihuacán's valley is a rich alluvial plain, watered by permanent springs and thus independent of the uncertainties of highland rainfall. The inhabitants of the valley seem early to have dug channels to create an irrigation system and to provide their growing city with water. Even today a formerly swampy section at the edge of the ancient city is carved by channels into "chinampas": small artificial islands that are intensively farmed. Indeed, it is possible that this form of agriculture, which is much better known as it was practiced in Aztec times near Tenochtitlán, was invented centuries earlier by the people of Teotihuacán.

The valley had major deposits of obsidian, the volcanic glass used all over ancient Middle America to make cutting and scraping tools and projectile points. Obsidian mining in the valley was apparently most intensive during the city's early years. Later the Teotihuacanos appear to have gained control of deposits of obsidian north of the Valley of Mexico that were better suited than the local material to the mass production of blade implements. Trade in raw obsidian and obsidian implements became increasingly important to the economy of Teotihuacán, reaching a peak toward the middle of the first millennium A.D.

The recent investigation of Teotihuacán has been carried forward by specialists working on three independent but related projects. One project was a monumental program of excavation and reconstruction undertaken by Mexico's National Institute of Anthropology, headed by Eusebio Dávalos. From 1962 to 1964 archaeologists under the direction of Ignacio Bernal, director of the

National Museum of Anthropology, unearthed and rebuilt a number of the structures that lie along the city's principal avenue ("the Street of the Dead"); they have also restored Teotihuacán's second main pyramid ("the Pyramid of the Moon"), which lies at the avenue's northern end. Two of the city's four largest structures, the Pyramid of the Sun and the Citadel, within which stands the Temple of Quetzalcoatl, had been cleared and restored in the 1900's and the 1920's respectively. Among other notable achievements, the National Institute's work brought to light some of the city's finest mural paintings.

As the Mexican archaeologists were at work a group under the direction of William T. Sanders of Pennsylvania State University conducted an intensive study of the ecology and the rural-settlement patterns of the valley. Another group, from the University of Rochester, initiated a mapping project under my direction. This last effort, which is still under way, involves preparing a detailed topographic map on which all the city's several thousand structures will be located. The necessary information is being secured by the examination of surface remains, supplemented by small-scale excavations. One result of our work has been to demonstrate how radically different Teotihuacán was from all other settlements of its time in Middle America. It was here that the New World's urban revolution exploded into being.

It had long been clear that the center of Teotihuacán was planned, but it soon became apparent to us that the extent and magnitude of the planning went far beyond the center. Our mapping revealed that the city's streets and the large majority of its buildings had been laid out along the lines of a precise grid aligned with the city center. The grid was established in Teotihuacán's formative days, but it may have been more intensively exploited later, perhaps in relation to "urban renewal" projects undertaken when the city had become rich and powerful.

The prime direction of the grid is slightly east of north (15.5 degrees). The basic modular unit of the plan is close to 57 meters. A number of residential structures are squares of this size. The plan of many of the streets seems to repeat various multiples of the 57-meter unit. The city's major avenues, which run parallel to the north-south axis, are spaced at regular intervals. Even the river running through the center of the city was canalized to conform to the grid. Miles from the city center the remains of buildings are oriented to the grid, even when they were built on slopes that ran counter to it. A small design composed of concentric circles divided into quadrants may have served as a standard surveyor's mark; it is sometimes pecked into the floors of buildings and sometimes into bare bedrock. One such pair of marks two miles apart forms a line

exactly perpendicular to the city's north-south axis. The achievement of this kind of order obviously calls for an initial vision that is both audacious and self-confident.

A city planner's description of Teotihuacán would begin not with the monumental Pyramid of the Sun but with the two complexes of structures that form the city center. These are the Citadel and the Great Compound, lying respectively to the east and west of the city's main north-south avenue, the Street of the Dead. The names given the various structures and features of Teotihuacán are not, incidentally, the names by which the Teotihuacanos knew them. Some come from Spanish translations of Aztec names; others were bestowed by earlier archaeologists or by our mappers and are often the place names used by the local people.

The Street of the Dead forms the main axis of the city. At its northern end it stops at the Pyramid of the Moon, and

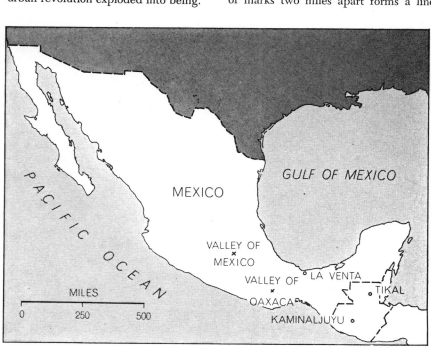

EARLY CIVILIZATION in Middle America appeared first in the lowlands along the Gulf of Mexico at such major centers of Olmec culture as La Venta. Soon thereafter a number of ceremonial centers appeared in the highlands, particularly in the valleys of Oaxaca, Puebla and Mexico. Kaminaljuyu and Tikal, Maya centers respectively in highlands and lowlands of what is now Guatemala, came under Teotihuacán's influence at the height of its power.

CEREMONIAL HEART of Teotihuacán is seen in an aerial photograph looking southeast toward Cerro Patlachique, one of a pair of mountains that flank the narrow valley dominated by the city. The large pyramid in

we have found that to the south it extends for two miles beyond the Citadel-Compound complex. The existence of a subordinate axis running east and west had not been suspected until our mappers discovered one broad avenue running more than two miles to the east of the Citadel and a matching avenue extending the same distance westward from the Compound.

To make it easier to locate buildings over so large an area we imposed our own 500-meter grid on the city, orienting it to the Street of the Dead and using the center of the city as the zero point of the system [see bottom illustration, p. 227]. The heavy line defining the limits of the city was determined by walking around the perimeter of the city and examining evidence on the surface to establish where its outermost remains end. The line traces a zone free of such remains that is at least 300 meters wide and that sharply separates the city from the countryside. The Street of the Dead,

East Avenue and West Avenue divide Teotihuacán into quadrants centered on the Citadel-Compound complex. We do not know if these were formally recognized as administrative quarters of the city, as they were in Tenochtitlán. It is nonetheless possible that they may have been, since there are a number of other similarities between the two cities.

Indeed, during the past 25 years Mexican scholars have argued for a high degree of continuity in customs and beliefs from the Aztecs back to the Teotihuacanos, based partly on an assumed continuity in language. This hypothetical continuity, which extends through the intervening Toltec times, provides valuable clues in interpreting archaeological evidence. For example, the unity of religion and politics that archaeologists postulate at Teotihuacán is reinforced by what is known of Aztec society.

The public entrance of the Citadel is a monumental staircase on the Street of the Dead. Inside the Citadel a plaza

opens onto the Temple of Quetzalcoatl, the principal sacred building in this area. The temple's façade represents the most successful integration of architecture and sculpture so far discovered at Teotihuacán [see bottom illustration on page 124].

The Great Compound, across the street from the Citadel, had gone unrecognized as a major structure until our survey. We found that it differs from all other known structures at Teotihuacán and that in area it is the city's largest. Its main components are two great raised platforms. These form a north and a south wing and are separated by broad entrances at the level of the street on the east and west. The two wings thus flank a plaza somewhat larger than the one within the Citadel. Few of the structures on the platforms seem to have been temples or other religious buildings. Most of them face away from the Street of the Dead, whereas almost all the other known structures along the avenue face toward it.

the foreground is the Pyramid of the Moon. The larger one beyond it is the Pyramid of the Sun. Many of the more than 100 smaller religious structures that line the city's central avenue, the Street of the Dead, are visible in the photograph. South of the Pyramid of the Sun and east of the central avenue is the large enclosure known as the Citadel. It and the Great Compound, a matching structure not visible in the photograph, formed the city's center. More than 4,000 additional buildings, most no longer visible, spread for miles beyond the center. At the peak of Teotihuacán's power, around A.D. 500, the population of the city was more than 50,000.

One therefore has the impression that the Compound was not devoted to religious affairs. In the Citadel there are clusters of rooms to the north and south of the Temple of Quetzalcoatl, but the overall effect conveyed by the temples and the other buildings that surround the Citadel's plaza is one of a political center in a sacred setting. Perhaps some of its rooms housed the high priests of Teotihuacán.

The plaza of the Compound is a strategically located open space that could have been the city's largest marketplace.

The buildings that overlook this plaza could have been at least partly devoted to the administration of the economic affairs of the city. Whatever their functions were, the Citadel and the Compound are the heart of the city. Together they form a majestic spatial unit,

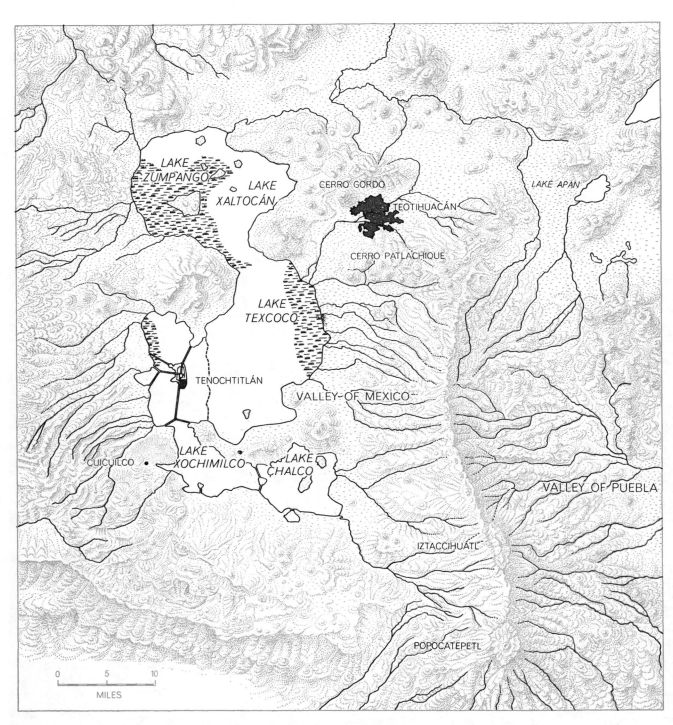

VALLEY OF MEXICO was dominated by shallow lakes in late pre-Hispanic times; in the rainy season they coalesced into a single body of water. Teotihuacán was strategically located; it commanded a narrow valley a few miles northeast of the lakes that provided the best route between the Valley of Mexico and the Valley of Puebla, which leads to the lowlands along the Gulf of Mexico (*see map at bottom of page 222*]. It was an important center of trade and worship from 100 B.C. until about A.D. 750. Centuries after its fall the Aztec capital of Tenochtitlán grew up in the western shallows of Lake Texcoco, 25 miles from the earlier metropolis.

a central island surrounded by more open ground than is found in any other part of Teotihuacán.

The total area of the city was eight square miles. Not counting ritual structures, more than 4,000 buildings, most of them apartment houses, were built to shelter the population. At the height of Teotihuacán's power, in the middle of the first millennium A.D., the population certainly exceeded 50,000 and was probably closer to 100,000. This is not a particularly high figure compared with Old World religious-political centers; today the population of Mecca is some 130,000 and that of Benares more than 250,000 (to which is added an annual influx of a million pilgrims). One reason Teotihuacán did not have a larger population was that its gleaming lime-plastered residential structures were only

SOUTH ELEVATION

**APARTMENT HOUSE** typical of the city's many multiroomed dwellings was excavated in 1961 by Laurette Séjourné. The outer walls of the compound conform with the 57-meter module favored by the city's planners. Within its forbidding exterior (*see south façade at bottom of illustration*) individual apartments comprised several rooms grouped around unroofed patios (*smaller white areas*).

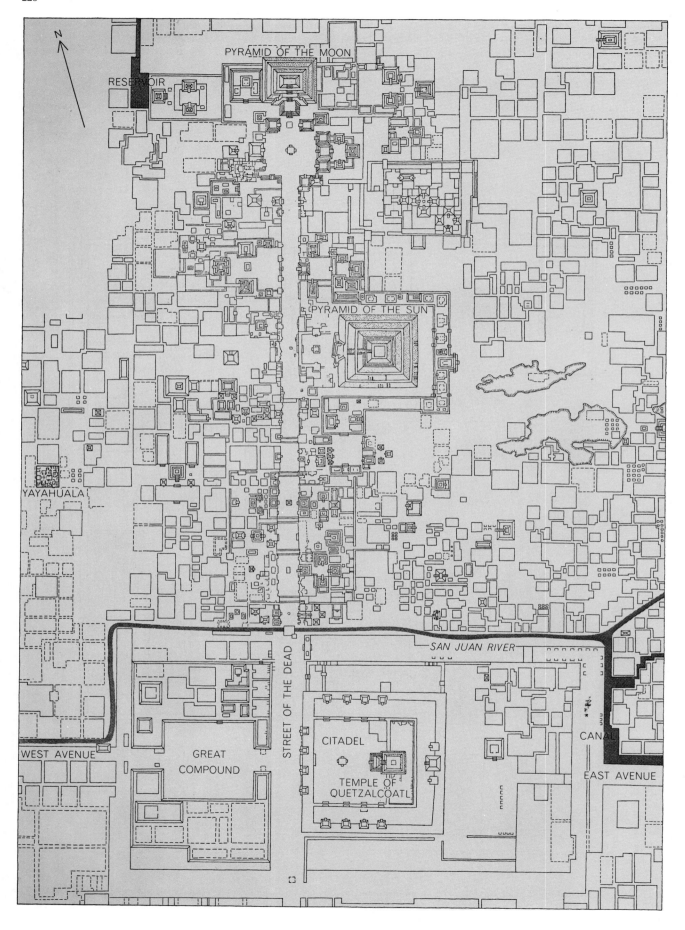

N

RESERVOIR

PYRAMID OF THE MOON

PYRAMID OF THE SUN

YAYAHUALA

STREET OF THE DEAD

SAN JUAN RIVER

WEST AVENUE

GREAT COMPOUND

CITADEL

TEMPLE OF QUETZALCOATL

CANAL

EAST AVENUE

one story high. Although most of the inhabitants lived in apartments, the buildings were "ranch-style" rather than "high-rise."

The architects of Teotihuacán designed apartments to offer a maximum of privacy within the crowded city, using a concept similar to the Old World's classical atrium house [*see illustration on page 225*]. The rooms of each apartment surrounded a central patio; each building consisted of a series of rooms, patios, porticoes and passageways, all secluded from the street. This pattern was also characteristic of the city's palaces. The residential areas of Teotihuacán must have presented a somewhat forbidding aspect from the outside: high windowless walls facing on narrow streets. Within the buildings, however, the occupants were assured of privacy. Each patio had its own drainage system; each admitted light and air to the surrounding apartments; each made it possible for the inhabitants to be out of doors yet alone. It may be that this architectural style contributed to Teotihuacán's permanence as a focus of urban life for more than 500 years.

The basic building materials of Teotihuacán were of local origin. Outcrops of porous volcanic rock in the valley were quarried and the stone was crushed and mixed with lime and earth to provide a kind of moisture-resistant concrete that was used as the foundation for floors and walls. The same material was used for roofing; wooden posts spaced at intervals bore much of the weight of the roof. Walls were made of stone and mortar or of sunbaked adobe brick. Floors and wall surfaces were then usually finished with highly polished plaster.

What kinds of people lived in Teotihuacán? Religious potentates, priestly bureaucrats and military leaders presumably occupied the top strata of the city's society, but their number could not have been large. Many of the inhabitants tilled lands outside the city

and many others must have been artisans: potters, workers in obsidian and stone and craftsmen dealing with more perishable materials such as cloth, leather, feathers and wood (traces of which are occasionally preserved). Well-defined concentrations of surface remains suggest that craft groups such as potters and workers in stone and obsidian tended to live together in their own neighborhoods. This lends weight to the hypothesis that each apartment building was solely occupied by a "corporate" group, its families related on the basis of occupation, kinship or both. An arrangement of this kind, linking the apartment dwellers to one another by webs of joint interest and activity, would have promoted social stability.

If groups with joint interests lived not only in the same apartment building but also in the same general neighborhood, the problem of governing the city would have been substantially simplified. Such organization of neighborhood groups could have provided an intermediate level between the individual and the state. Ties of cooperation, competition or even conflict between people in different neighborhoods could have

created the kind of social network that is favorable to cohesion.

The marketplace would similarly have made an important contribution to the integration of Teotihuacán society. If the greater part of the exchange of goods and services in the city took place in one or more major markets (such as the one that may have occupied the plaza of the Great Compound), then not only the Teotihuacanos but also the outsiders who used the markets would have felt a vested interest in maintaining "the peace of the market." Moreover, the religion of Teotihuacán would have imbued the city's economic institutions with a sacred quality.

The various social groups in the city left some evidence of their identity. For example, we located a walled area, associated with the west side of the Pyramid of the Moon, where large quantities of waste obsidian suggest that obsidian workers may have formed part of a larger temple community. We also found what looks like a foreign neighborhood. Occupied by people who apparently came to Teotihuacán from the Valley of Oaxaca, the area lies in the western part of the city. It is currently under study by

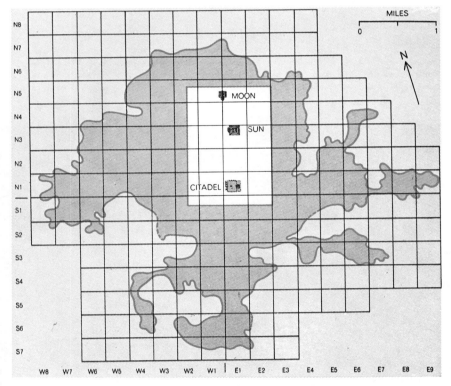

IRREGULAR BOUNDARY of Teotihuacán is shown as a solid line that approaches the edges of a grid, composed of 500-meter squares, surveyed by the author's team. The grid parallels the north-south direction of the Street of the Dead, the city's main avenue. One extension of the city in its early period, which is only partly known, has been omitted. A map of Teotihuacán's north-central zone (*light color*) is reproduced on page 226.

CITY CENTER is composed of two sets of structures, the Great Compound and the Citadel (*bottom of illustration on opposite page*). They stand on either side of the Street of the Dead, the main north-south axis of the city. A pair of avenues approaching the center of the city from east and west form the secondary axis. The city's largest religious monuments were the Pyramid of the Sun, the Pyramid of the Moon and the Temple of Quetzalcoatl, which lies inside the Citadel. Yayahuala (*left of center*) was one of many residential compounds. Its architecture is shown in detail on page 225.

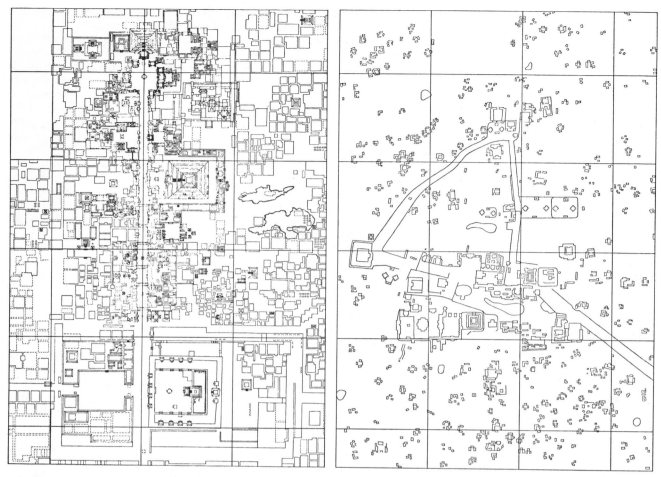

**DENSITY OF SETTLEMENT** at Teotihuacán is compared with that at Tikal, largest of the lowland Maya ceremonial centers in Middle America. The maps show the central area of each settlement at the same scale. The data for Teotihuacán (*left*) are from surveys by the author and the Mexican government. Those for Tikal (*right*) are from a survey by the University of Pennsylvania. Even though its center included many public structures, Teotihuacán's concentrated residential pattern shows its urban character.

**PYRAMID OF THE SUN** is as broad at the base as the great pyramid of Cheops in Egypt, although it is only half as high. It was built over the site of an earlier shrine during Teotihuacán's first major period of growth, in the early centuries of the Christian era.

John Paddock of the University of the Americas, a specialist in the prehistory of Oaxaca. Near the eastern edge of the city quantities of potsherds have been found that are characteristic of Maya areas and the Veracruz region along the Gulf of Mexico. These fragments suggest that the neighborhood was inhabited either by people from those areas or by local merchants who specialized in such wares.

We have found evidence that as the centuries passed two of the city's important crafts—the making of pottery and obsidian tools—became increasingly specialized. From the third century A.D. on some obsidian workshops contain a high proportion of tools made by striking blades from a "core" of obsidian; others have a high proportion of tools made by chipping a piece of obsidian until the desired shape was obtained. Similar evidence of specialization among potters is found in the southwestern part of the city. There during Teotihuacán's period of greatest expansion one group of potters concentrated on the mass production of the most common type of cooking ware.

The crafts of Teotihuacán must have helped to enrich the city. So also, no doubt, did the pilgrim traffic. In addition to the three major religious structures more than 100 other temples and shrines line the Street of the Dead. Those who visited the city's sacred buildings must have included not only peasants and townspeople from the entire Valley of Mexico but also pilgrims from as far away as Guatemala. When one adds to these worshipers the visiting merchants, traders and peddlers attracted by the markets of Teotihuacán, it seems likely that many people would have been occupied catering to the needs of those who were merely visiting the city.

Radical social transformations took place during the growth of the city. As Teotihuacán increased in size there was first a relative and then an absolute decline in the surrounding rural population. This is indicated by both our data from the city and Sanders' from the countryside. Apparently many rural populations left their villages and were concentrated in the city. The process seems to have accelerated around A.D. 500, when the population of the city approached its peak. Yet the marked increase in density within the city was accompanied by a reduction in the city's size. It was at this time, during the sixth century, that urban renewal programs may have been undertaken in areas

HUMAN FIGURE, wearing a feather headdress, face paint and sandals, decorates the side of a vase dating from the sixth century A.D. Similar figures often appear in the city's murals.

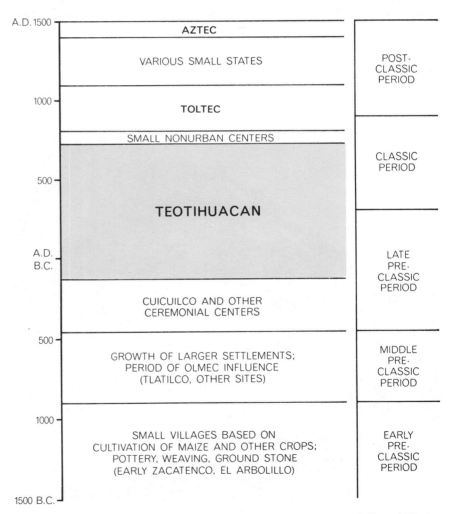

CITY'S BIRTH took place during the late pre-Classic Period in the Valley of Mexico, about a century before the beginning of the Christian era. Other highland ceremonial centers such as Cuicuilco in the Valley of Mexico and Cholula in the Valley of Puebla were influential at that time. Although Teotihuacán fell in about A.D. 750, near the end of the Classic Period, its religious monuments were deemed sacred by the Aztecs until Hispanic times.

**PYRAMID OF THE MOON, excavated in the early 1960's by a Mexican government group under the direction of Ignacio Bernal, stands at the northern end of the Street of the Dead. The façade presented to the avenue (above) consists of several interlocking, truncated pyramids thrusting toward the sky. The structure, 150 feet high and 490 feet wide at the base, is smaller than the Pyramid of the Sun but is architecturally more sophisticated.**

**TEMPLE OF QUETZALCOATL is the major religious structure within the Citadel, the eastern half of Teotihuacán's city center. The building is believed to represent the most successful integration of sculpture and architecture to be achieved throughout the city's long history. A covering layer of later construction protected the ornate facade from damage.**

where density was on the rise.

Such movements of rural and urban populations must have conflicted with local interests. That they were carried out successfully demonstrates the prestige and power of the hierarchy in Teotihuacán. Traditional loyalties to the religion of Teotihuacán were doubtless invoked. Nevertheless, one wonders if the power of the military would not have been increasingly involved. There is evidence both in Teotihuacán and beyond its borders that its soldiers became more and more important from the fifth century on. It may well be that at the peak of its power and influence Teotihuacán itself was becoming an increasingly oppressive place in which to live.

The best evidence of the power and influence that the leaders of Teotihuacán exercised elsewhere in Middle America comes from Maya areas. One ancient religious center in the Maya highlands—Kaminaljuyu, the site of modern Guatemala City—appears to have been occupied at one time by priests and soldiers from Teotihuacán. Highland Guatemala received a massive infusion of Teotihuacán cultural influences, with Teotihuacán temple architecture replacing older styles. This has been recognized for some time, but only recently has it become clear that Teotihuacán also influenced the Maya lowlands. The people of Tikal in Guatemala, largest of the lowland Maya centers, are now known to have been under strong influence from Teotihuacán. The people of Tikal adopted some of Teotihuacán's artistic traditions and erected a massive stone monument to Teotihuacán's rain god. William R. Coe of the University of Pennsylvania and his colleagues, who are working at Tikal, are in the midst of evaluating the nature and significance of this influence.

Tikal provides an instructive measure of the difference in the density of construction in Maya population centers and those in central Mexico. It was estimated recently that Tikal supported a population of about 10,000. As the illustration at the top of page 228 shows, the density of Teotihuacán's central area is strikingly different from that of Tikal's. Not only was Teotihuacán's population at least five times larger than Tikal's but also it was far less dispersed. In such a crowded urban center problems of integration, cohesion and social control must have been of a totally different order of magnitude than those of a less populous and less compact ceremonial center such as Tikal.

What were the circumstances of Teotihuacán's decline and fall? Almost certainly both environmental and social factors were involved. The climate of the region is semiarid today, and there is evidence that a long-term decline in annual rainfall brought the city to a similar condition in the latter half of the first millennium A.D. Even before then deforestation of the surrounding hills may have begun a process of erosion that caused a decrease in the soil moisture available for crops. Although persistent drought would have presented increasingly serious problems for those who fed the city, this might have been the lesser of its consequences. More ominous would have been the effect of increasing aridity on the cultivators of marginal lands and the semisedentary tribesmen in the highlands north of the Valley of Mexico. As worsening conditions forced these peoples to move, the Teotihuacanos might have found themselves not only short of food but also under military pressure along their northern frontier.

Whether or not climatic change was a factor, some signs of decline—such as the lowering of standards of construction and pottery-making—are evident during the last century of Teotihuacán's existence. Both a reduction in population and a tendency toward dispersion suggest that the fabric of society was suffering from strains and weaknesses. Once such a process of deterioration passed a critical point the city would have become vulnerable to attack.

No evidence has been found that Teotihuacán as a whole had formal defenses. Nonetheless, the valley's drainage pattern provides some natural barriers, large parts of the city were surrounded by walls or massive platforms and its buildings were formidable ready-made fortresses. Perhaps the metropolis was comparatively unprotected because it had for so long had an unchallenged supremacy.

In any case, archaeological evidence indicates that around A.D. 750 much of central Teotihuacán was looted and burned, possibly with the help of the city's own people. The repercussions of Teotihuacán's fall seem to have been felt throughout civilized Middle America. The subsequent fall of Monte Alban, the capital of the Oaxaca region, and of many Maya ceremonial centers in Guatemala and the surrounding area may reasonably be associated with dislocations set in motion by the fall of Teotihuacán. Indeed, the appropriate epitaph for the New World's first major metropolis may be that it was as influential in its collapse as in its long and brilliant flowering.

**FEATHERED SERPENT,** from one of the earlier murals found at Teotihuacán, has a free, flowing appearance. The animal below the serpent is a jaguar; the entire mural, which is not shown, was probably painted around A.D. 400. It may portray a cyclical myth of creation and destruction. The city's principal gods were often represented in the form of animals.

**LATER SERPENT GOD,** with a rattlesnake tail, is from a mural probably painted less than a century before the fall of Teotihuacán. The figure is rendered in a highly formal manner. A trend toward formalism is apparent in the paintings produced during the city's final years.

# V

# ARCHAEOLOGY AND ARCHAEOLOGICAL ISSUES

# ARCHAEOLOGY AND ARCHAEOLOGICAL ISSUES

V

## INTRODUCTION

Modern archaeology encompasses a multitude of different activities: investigations into the campsites of the earliest humans, excavations in Paleolithic caves, studies of Mediterranean shipwrecks, ancient Mesoamerican temples, and Classical cities. Archaeologists work on Medieval cities, Viking coinage, even buildings of the Industrial Revolution. The articles reprinted in this section cover both some of the major archaeological problems of international interest and some of the diverse issues of preservation and chronology that confront any archaeologist, whatever time period he studies. It is impossible to link all the articles in this section into a coherent survey narrative; so we will look briefly at the significance of each contribution in the order in which they appear.

An overriding concern of any archaeologist is that of accurate chronologies. "How old is it?" is a fundamental question asked by anyone looking at a prehistoric site or a long-buried artifact for the first time. The measurement of accurate chronologies for the multitude of prehistoric sites and cultures of the past 50,000 years has come a long way since the 1950's, when Willard Libby's radiocarbon dating technique first came into widespread use. Radiocarbon dating took prehistoric chronologies, for both the Americas and the Old World, from the realm of informed guesswork into a new era in which archaeologists could begin to construct reliable chronologies for the rapidly accelerating tempo of human cultural evolution at the end of the Pleistocene epoch. For the first time, people hoped, they would be able to study culture change in prehistory with an accurate chronological dimension. Colin Renfrew, an English archaeologist who has worked in the Aegean and Greece, has long been concerned with the accuracy of radiocarbon dates. In his article, "Carbon-14 and the Prehistory of Europe," he describes the $C^{14}$ method itself and shows how radiocarbon laboratories have been trying to improve on the accuracy of radiocarbon samples by calibrating dates obtained from such samples with readings from tree-ring chronologies whose accuracy is known. He describes some rather startling discrepancies between the long-established chronology for the later prehistory of Europe and that obtained from calibrated dates. His new readings reverse many long-held notions about the influence of the Near East and eastern Mediterranean on central and western European prehistory which considered the Europeans to be the recipients of new technological and religious innovations rather than innovators of major cultural change in their own right. Renfrew's article is of interest, not only on account of the academic controversies that it raises, but also because of the close relationships it draws between the study of chronology and cultural process in archaeology, a fundamental concern of all archaeologists today.

The Scythians were one of the scourges of the ancient world, referred to with dread by Greek writers (Herodotus, for example) as cannibals and fierce warriors. Their constant forays into settled farming land on the northern shores of the Black Sea led them into contact with the Classical world. But their homeland extended far northward into the great steppes of Central Asia.

Scythian culture was based on the horse, and a highly specialized knowledge of animal husbandry. The Scyths were predominantly nomads, constantly on the move, for their existence depended on the pastures of the steppe, where enormous tracts of land were needed to support their herds. They lived on mare's milk and cheese, as well as game and fish. Scythian horsemen rode on fine horses, upon whose harnesses they lavished skilled workmanship and a vigorous art tradition. Their felt tents were richly decorated with fine rugs and lavish wall hangings. Jewelry and bronze mirrors were both imported from the Mediterranean and copied by Scythian craftsmen.

Nomadic peoples traditionally leave little for the archaeologist to find. Their material possessions tend to be highly portable, and mainly of such light materials as wood and leather. But the Scythians have come down to us in vivid detail, thanks to their elaborate burial mounds, permanently refrigerated by the arctic climate of the steppe. In "Frozen Tombs of the Scythians," M. I. Artamonov describes some of the most important of these tombs, found by Soviet archaeologists at Pazyryk and elsewhere, where all the elaborate panoply of Scythian horsemen has survived the ravages of time. The findings of Sergei Rudenko and other archaeologists confirm the observations of Herodotus, who described the great burial rites of the Scythian chiefs in a remote corner of their vast and savage territory, where each ruler vied with the others in erecting larger and larger burial mounds.

The vagaries of archaeological preservation, especially in drier parts of the world, have led to the survival of astonishingly complete evidence for the diet of early humans. One rich source of information on early diet is the human coprolite, which, when analysed microscopically, can yield a wealth of startling information about the hunting, gathering, and agricultural practices of prehistoric peoples. In "The Coprolites of Man," Bryant and Williams-Dean describe some of the basic techniques used to obtain dietary information from human coprolites. For example, pollen analysis recovered both insect-borne and wind-borne pollens, and showed that the Indians of one southwestern Texas rockshelter were ingesting several kinds of flowers as an essential part of their diet. Coprolites from settlements dating to as early as the Middle Pleistocene (about 300,000 years ago) have been analysed, and more recent specimens have produced traces of parasites and bugs as well as evidence for seasonal occupation of prehistoric settlements. The study of human feces is now a routine part of archaeology, a specialized archaeological technique that is widely applied, especially in the New World.

Norman Hammond's study, "The Planning of a Maya Ceremonial Center," is not only a useful sequel to René Millon's Teotihuacán study in Part IV, but also an excellent example of modern settlement archaeology. Lubaantún in British Honduras is a huge Maya ceremonial center consisting of eleven major structures and at least twenty plazas. The investigation of the site was a long-term research project, using a systems approach both to the research and to the cultural elements and mechanisms involved in planning and implementing such a vast communal effort. Lubaantún was built with an enormous investment of labor over a 150-year period on a pattern of plazas and stone structures common to all Maya ceremonial centers. Those responsible for the construction used the labor of a scattered rural population supported by subsistence agriculture to erect Lubaantún's vast structures. Hammond made accurate plans of the site and measured the heights and other dimensions of the major structures. At least five stages of growth were identified, throughout which the builders adhered, regardless of expense, to a fixed plan laid down by the original planners. In answering some of the basic questions about Lubaantán, Hammond looked closely at the site in relation to its environment, potential trade routes, and sources of raw materials. This type of "settlement pattern" archaeology is very prevalent in New World prehistory, and demonstrates the importance of using not only archaeological data but also that from geology, pedology, and cultural anthropology (to mention only a few relevant disciplines) to look at the motives and social and cultural mechanisms behind the construction of prehistoric cities and ceremonial centers.

Underwater archaeology has become a familiar part of the academic scene since the development of the aqualung, which made it possible for archaeologists to search for shipwrecks and burial sites in quite substantial depths of water. Regrettably, much underwater archaeology has become little more than a treasure hunt for artifacts and valuable coins to be sold as treasure trove or as collectors' loot. But much valuable research has been carried out as well by highly qualified underwater archaeologists, resulting in the development of new recovery and recording techniques, many of which have become familiar to readers of the *National Geographic* and other popular periodicals.

The objectives of underwater archaeology can ultimately be defined as a search for a history of seafaring, of ship design from the earliest times. Indeed, a magnificent volume of essays on this very subject has recently been published by George F. Bass, one of the most skilled and celebrated underwater archaeologists in the United States. As editor of *A History of Seafaring*, Bass has commented on the dangers facing underwater archaeology, especially the damage perpetrated by unscrupulous divers and the casual amateur. Recently he has been concerned with "A Byzantine Trading Venture," described in his article here. The venture ended in tragedy, for the 40-ton ship struck a reef near Halicarnassus in A.D. 625. Fortunately for science, the shipwreck was discovered intact in 120 feet of water, in conditions where an excavation was possible. The dig involved, among other things, plotting the position of every nail hole and scored mark on the ship's hull fragments that could be recovered. The divers recovered more than 900 amphorae, many of them without stoppers. Perhaps the ship was carrying its cargo of fine jars to wine-producing islands, such as Kos and Rhodes, where they would be filled. No less than eleven anchors were lying in the wreck, and Bass gives possible explanations for their presence. By judicious use of literary sources and analogies from other shipwrecks, in this detailed study of a single ship he has painted a remarkably complete picture of early Mediterranean trade. It is an admirable example of a vignette of history recorded by archaeological techniques unknown a quarter of a century ago.

Underwater archaeology has much wider applications than merely to shipwrecks. The coastal shelves of many of the world's oceans have been submerged since late prehistoric and Classical times, as the oceans continue their adjustments to the end of the last (Weichsel) glaciation. Numerous archaeological sites have been found beneath the coastal waters of the Mediterranean and Western Europe, and many prehistoric shell middens are known to occur in shallow water near the Southern California coast. As described in "The Excavation of a Drowned Greek Temple," Michael Jameson recovered an entire Greek temple complex from shallow water, part of the city of Halieis in southern Greece. Halieis was abandoned about 323 B.C., and much of the ruins of the settlement are still to be found on land. But a sizeable sector of the town lay in the shallow water offshore. Its stone foundations were still largely intact, for stone robbers were unable to reach the boulders below water. A plan of the streets and houses was recovered by aerial photography and high-pressure water jet, and a complete temple complex dedicated to Apollo was found outside the town walls. The Halieis project is an example of an intelligent use of underwater archaeology to recover the plan and general layout of a settlement. Dating evidence was obtained from objects found in the temple, and careful dredging assisted in the excavations. This was systematic archaeological investigation of a high standard, in which the basic techniques of a landborne science were adapted to an underwater environment.

No characters on the stage of world history have excited more popular interest than the Vikings. Their prowess as seafarers, their magnificent ships, warlike personalities, and long recognition as the first European visitors to North America, centuries before Columbus, have made them naturals for movie epics and popular novels. But the Viking sagas are but a small part of Scandinavia's rich history, and archaeology has done much to correct the myths that have surrounded the Vikings in the past century. The Vikings emerged as a recognizable group at the end of a period of constant political upheaval around A.D. 750. Their first recorded raid was on June 8, 793, on the monastery of Lindisfarne in the North Sea, the first of many such forays that gained the Vikings their reputation as bloodthirsty pirates.

Eric Oxenstierna, in his article "The Vikings," concentrates on the activities of the Vikings in the Baltic area. He looks at the trade in glassware, coins, slaves, and other materials, at their incredibly farflung contacts, as far south as Byzantium, where only small parties of unarmed Vikings were permitted to visit the city. Much of his research is concerned with coins, which are an important facet of archaeological research, for they often provide valuable evidence for dating buildings, fortifications, or caches of buried treasure (particularly in large cities like Winchester, where the strata are highly disturbed, and it is difficult to tell different phases of occupation from one another). Oxenstierna uses coins as a means of looking at Viking trading groups and their various spheres of influence. The scholars involved in the research are fortunate to have about 57,000 Arab silver coins (found in Scandinavia alone) to work with. Underwater archaeology has been used to look at the anatomy of Viking ships, not only their famous long ships, but also the humble merchant vessels used to voyage from fjord to fjord. Well-designed ships were one of the mainstays of Viking trade and power, for their voyages reached not only to North America but also to as far afield as Morocco. Oxenstierna's article gives a useful summary of the uses and limitations of archaeology in a late historical period, for he relies heavily on historical records. It should be noted that the Vinland map is now known to be a forgery.

Martin Biddle's long-term research project at Winchester, England, as described in "The Archaeology of Winchester," is an attempt to examine the reason why a city is born and why it dies. The Winchester Project is remarkable in that it is a major research effort supported not only by the city authorities but also by many universities and individuals. The objective is to write the history of Winchester from its Roman beginnings up to modern times. Historians and archaeologists have collaborated not only on rescue efforts to save archaeological remains from massive development, but also in carrying out work on unthreatened sites. The first thousand years of Winchester's history are barely touched by written records. After A.D. 1200, the records are often very complete, to the extent that the ownership of individual houses found in the excavations can be linked to title deeds.

Urban archaeology of this type is increasingly commonplace in Europe, where the age-old centers of major cities and even small towns are being ripped apart by massive redevelopment schemes. Biddle's article gives one an impression not only of the long and ever-changing face of an early English town, but also a notion of the tremendous intellectual challenges facing scholars in Medieval archaeology, where complex rebuilding efforts, disturbances, and modern development disturb archaeological stratigraphy and render interpretation especially difficult. Such research is urgent, before an entire, little known phase of European history is destroyed forever by the developers' bulldozers. The Winchester Project shows what can be done with dedicated scholarship, a sympathetic public, and a supportive City Council. Let us hope it is the blueprint for many more such ventures.

# 23

# Carbon 14 and the Prehistory of Europe

by Colin Renfrew
*October 1971*

*Tree-ring measurements have shown that early carbon-14 dates are off by as much as 700 years. As a result the view that cultural advances diffused into Europe from the east is no longer tenable*

Our knowledge of European prehistory is currently being revolutionized. The immediate cause of the revolution is a recently discovered discrepancy between the actual ages of many archaeological sites and the ages that have been attributed to them on the basis of carbon-14 analysis. Some sites are as much as seven centuries older than they had been thought to be. This revelation has destroyed the intricate system of interlocking chronologies that provided the foundation for a major edifice of archaeological scholarship: the theory of cultural diffusion.

For more than a century a basic assumption of prehistorians has been that most of the major cultural advances in ancient Europe came about as the result of influences from the great early civilizations of Egypt and Mesopotamia. For example, megalithic tombs in western Europe feature single slabs that weigh several tons. The prevailing view of their origin was that the technical skills and religious motivation needed for their construction had come from the eastern Mediterranean, first reaching Spain and Portugal and then France, Britain and Scandinavia. To take another example, it was generally supposed that the knowledge of copper metallurgy had been transmitted by Mediterranean intermediaries to the Iberian peninsula and to the Balkans from its place of origin in the Near East. The revolution in chronology shows, however, that the megalithic tombs of western Europe and the copper metallurgy of the Balkans are actually older than their supposed Mediterranean prototypes.

When the scholars of a century ago wanted to date the monuments and objects of prehistoric Europe, they had

little to help them. C. J. Thomsen, a Danish student of antiquities, had established a "three ages" frame of reference in 1836; structures and objects were roughly classified as Stone Age (at first there was no distinction between Paleolithic and Neolithic), Bronze Age or Iron Age. To assign such things an age in years was a matter of little more than guesswork.

Prehistoric finds are of course by their nature unaccompanied by written records. The only possible recourse was to work from the known to the unknown: to try to move outward toward the unlettered periphery from the historical civilizations of Egypt and Mesopotamia, where written records were available. For example, the historical chronology of Egypt, based on ancient written records, can be extended with considerable confidence back to 1900 B.C. because

**MEGALITHIC MONUMENT** near Essé in Brittany is typical of the massive stone structures that were raised in France as long ago as the fifth millennium B.C. Called "Fairies' Rock," it is made of 42 large slabs of schist, some weighing more than 40 tons. Because of the great effort that must have been required to raise such monuments, scholars traditionally refused to credit the barbarian cultures of prehistoric Europe with their construction and instead attributed them to influences from civilized eastern Mediterranean.

the records noted astronomical events. The Egyptian "king lists" can then be used, although with far less confidence, to build up a chronology that goes back another 11 centuries to 3000 B.C.

The need to establish a link with Egypt in order to date the prehistoric cultures of Europe went naturally with the widespread assumption that, among prehistoric sites in general, the more sophisticated ones were of Near Eastern origin anyway. In 1887, when the brothers Henri and Louis Siret published the results of their excavations in the cemeteries and settlements of "Copper Age" (late Neolithic) Spain, they reported finding stone tombs, some roofed with handsome corbeled stonework and others of massive megalithic construction. In the tombs there were sometimes human figurines carved in stone, and daggers and simple tools made of copper. That these structures and objects had evolved locally did not seem likely; an origin in the eastern Mediterranean—in Egypt or the Aegean—was claimed for all their more exotic features.

In the first years of this century this method of building up relationships and using contacts with the early civilized world to establish a relative chronology was put on a systematic basis by the Swedish archaeologist Oskar Montelius. In 1903 Montelius published an account of his "typological method," where the development of particular types of tools or weapons within a given area was reconstructed and the sequence was then compared with those of neighboring areas. Adjacent regions could thus be linked in a systematic manner, until a chain of links was built up stretching from the Atlantic across Europe to Egypt and Mesopotamia. It was still assumed that most of the innovations had come from the Near East, and that the farther from the "hearthlands" of civilization they were found, the longer it would have taken them to diffuse there.

Some diffusionist scholars went to extremes. In the 1920's Sir Grafton Smith argued the view that nearly all the innovations in the civilizations around the world could be traced back to Egypt. In this hyperdiffusionist theory the high cultures of the Far East and even the early civilizations of Central America and South America had supposedly stemmed from Egypt. Today very few continue to suppose that the essential ingredients of civilization were disseminated from Egypt to the rest of the world, perhaps in papyrus boats. There were, of course, scholars whose views lay at the other extreme, such as the German ultranationalist Gustaf Kossinna, whose chauvinist writings fell into a predictable pattern. For these men the truly great advances and fundamental discoveries always seem to have been made in the land of their birth. The *Herrenvolk* fantasies of Aryan supremacy in the Nazi era were rooted in Kossinna's theory of Nordic primacy.

Appalled by both of these extremes, the British prehistorian V. Gordon Childe tried to steer a middle course. In *The Dawn of European Civilisation,* published in 1925, Childe rejected Smith's fantasy that the ancient Egyptians were responsible for all the significant advances in prehistoric Europe. Working in the same framework as Montelius but with a detailed and sympathetic consideration of the prehistoric cultures of each region, he built up a picture in terms of what one colleague, Glyn E. Daniel, has termed "modified diffusionism."

Childe saw two main paths whereby a chronological link could be established between Europe and the Near East. First there were the Spanish "Copper Age" finds. Earlier writers had likened the megalithic tombs of Spain, particularly those with corbeled vaults, to the great tholos tombs of Mycenae, which were built around 1500 B.C. Childe saw that the Mycenaean tombs were too recent to have served as a model, and he suggested instead a link between the Spanish tombs and the round tombs of Bronze Age Crete, which had been built

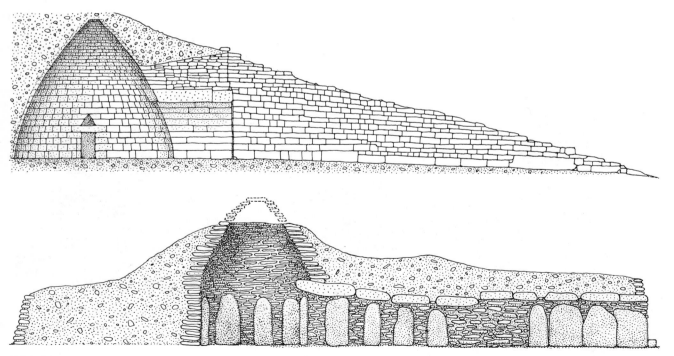

TWO SIMILAR STRUCTURES with corbeled domes are the famous "Treasury of Atreus," a Mycenaean tomb built around 1500 B.C. (*top*), and a megalithic passage grave, Île Longue in Brittany, which is probably some 6,000 years old (*bottom*). Unaware of the true age of the French passage graves, the prehistorian V. Gordon Childe nonetheless dismissed the notion that they were inspired by a civilization as recent as Mycenae. He suggested that they were probably modeled on earlier Minoan tombs built around 2500 B.C.

about 2500 B.C. As subsequent work provided more detail, it was even suggested that colonists from the Aegean had set up settlements in Spain and Portugal. With them they would have brought their knowledge of architecture, their custom of collective burial, their belief in a "mother goddess" and their skill in metallurgy. The fortifications at one or two of these early Iberian sites resemble those at the settlement of Chalandriani on the Aegean island of Syros [*see bottom illustration at right*].

It was on this basis that the earliest megalithic tombs of the Iberian peninsula were assigned an age of around 2500 B.C. The similar French and British tombs, some of which also have stone vaults, were assigned to times a little later in the third millennium.

Similar logic was used in assigning dates to the striking stone temples of Malta. Sculptured slabs in some of the island's temples are handsomely decorated with spirals. These spirals resemble decorations from Crete and Greece of the period from 1800 to 1600 B.C. The Maltese temples were therefore assumed to date from that time or a little later.

Childe's second path for chronological links between western Europe and the Near East was the Danube. Artifacts of the late Neolithic period found at Vinča in Yugoslavia were compared by him to material from the early Bronze Age "cities" at Troy. The Trojan finds can be dated to within a few centuries of 2700 B.C. It was concluded that metallurgy had arisen in the Balkans as a result of contacts with Troy. This view was strengthened by certain similarities between the clay sculptures found at Vinča and various artistic products of the early Bronze Age Aegean.

These twin foundations for the prehistoric chronology of Europe have been accepted by most archaeologists since Childe's day. The appearance of metallurgy and of other striking cultural and artistic abilities in the Balkans, and of monumental architecture on the Iberian peninsula, were explained as the result of contacts with the Aegean. Such skills make their appearance in the Aegean around 2500 B.C., a point in time that is established by finds of datable Egyptian imports in Crete and of somewhat later Cretan exports in datable contexts in Egypt. The chronology of Crete and the southern Aegean is soundly based on the chronology of Egypt and has not been affected by the current revolution.

It should be noted that, as Childe himself pointed out, these conclusions rested on two basic assumptions. First, it

TWO SIMILAR SPIRALS are the decorations on a stele from a Mycenaean shaft grave (*top*) and decorations at temple of Tarxien in Malta (*bottom*). Mycenaean spirals were carved about 1650 B.C. Maltese ones were held on grounds of resemblance to be same age.

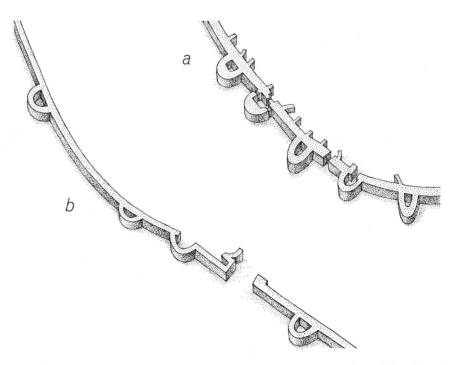

TWO SIMILAR FORTIFICATIONS are the bastioned walls at Chalandriani (*a*), a site on the Aegean island of Syros, and the walls of Los Millares (*b*), a "Copper Age" site near Málaga in Spain. The likeness was once attributed to the work of Aegean colonists in Spain.

was assumed that "parallel" developments in different regions—the appearance of metallurgy or the beginning of monumental tomb architecture—were not entirely independent innovations. Second, it was assumed that if the developments had indeed diffused from one region to another, the ancient civilizations of the Near East were the innovators and the barbarians of Europe were the beneficiaries. Childe realized that these assumptions could be questioned, but in the absence of any independent dating method the only way prehistoric Europe could be dated at all was to relate it to the dated civilizations of the Near East. In practice this meant full acceptance of the assumptions. As Childe remarked of his work, "the sole unifying theme was the irradiation of European barbarism by Oriental civilization."

The discovery of carbon-14 dating in 1949 offered, in principle at least, the possibility of establishing a sound absolute chronology without the need for the assumptions that Childe had had to make. Even without carbon-14 dating, however, some of the arguments of the modified diffusionist school were susceptible to criticism. For example, there are no megalithic tombs in the Aegean, so that some special pleading is needed to argue a Near Eastern origin for those of western Europe. Again, detailed studies in the Aegean area show that the resemblances between the pottery and fig-

urines of the Iberian peninsula and those of Greece, the supposed homeland of the "colonists," are not as close as had been supposed. Nor are the Balkan Neolithic finds really very closely related to the Aegean ones from which they were supposedly derived. There was certainly room for doubt about some of the details in the attractive and coherent picture that diffusionist theory had built up.

Although the introduction of carbon-14 dating did not disrupt the diffusionist picture or the chronology based on it, the dates did produce a few anomalies. A decade ago there were already hints that something was wrong. The carbon-14 method, originated by Willard F. Libby, ingeniously exploits the production of atoms of this heavy isotope of carbon in the upper atmosphere. The carbon-14 atoms are produced by the absorption of neutrons by atoms of nitrogen 14. The neutrons in turn are produced by the impact of cosmic ray particles on various atoms in the atmosphere. Carbon 14 is radioactive, and like all radioactive elements it decays in a regular way. Its half-life was originally estimated by Libby to be some 5,568 years.

The manufacture of the radioactive isotope by cosmic radiation and its diminution through decay sets up a balance so that the proportion of carbon 14 to carbon 12, the much more abundant nonradioactive isotope, is approximately constant. The atoms of the radioactive isotope in the atmosphere, like the atoms

of normal carbon, combine with oxygen to form carbon dioxide. This substance is taken up by plants through photosynthesis and by animals feeding on the plants, and in that way all living things come to have the two kinds of carbon in the same proportion in their tissues while they are alive. At death, however, the cycle is broken: the organisms no longer take up any fresh carbon and the proportion of the two isotopes steadily changes as the radioactive isotope decays. Assuming that the proportion of the two isotopes in the atmosphere has always been constant, one can measure how much carbon 14 is left in plant or animal remains (in charcoal, say, or bone) and, knowing the half-life of the radioactive isotope, can calculate how long the decay process has been going on and therefore how old the sample is.

This, put rather simply, is the principle of the dating method. In practice it is complicated by the very small number of carbon-14 atoms in the atmosphere and in living things compared with the number of carbon-12 atoms: approximately one per million million. The proportion is of course further reduced in dead organic material as the rare isotope decays, making accurate measurement a delicate task. Nonetheless, samples from archaeological sites began to yield coherent and consistent dates soon after 1949. In general the carbon-14 dates in Europe tallied fairly well with those built up by the "typological method"

CONVENTIONAL CARBON-14 DATES IN CARBON-14 YEARS

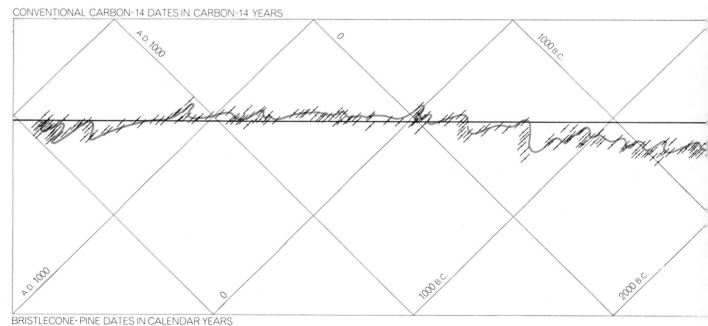

BRISTLECONE-PINE DATES IN CALENDAR YEARS

**BRISTLECONE-PINE CALIBRATION** worked out by Hans E. Suess of the University of California at San Diego makes it possible to correct carbon-14 dates. The dates running across the top and the lines on which they rest refer to carbon-14 dates in carbon-14 years; the dates running across the bottom and the lines on which they rest refer to bristlecone-pine dates in calendar years. The col-

back to about 2500 B.C. The great surprise was how early the Neolithic period, defined by the appearance of farming villages, began everywhere. Instead of yielding the expected dates of around 4000 or 4500 B.C., the earliest villages in the Near East proved to date back to as early as 8000 B.C.

These dates for the early Neolithic period were most important. Indeed, their impact on prehistoric archaeology can be regarded as the first carbon-14 revolution. The sharp increases in age did not, however, actually disrupt the diffusionist picture. Farming developments in the Near East remained in general earlier than those in Europe. The pattern did not change nor did the Near East lose its primacy; it was just that all the dates were earlier than had been expected. Everyone had always been aware that, for the period before 3000 B.C., which is when the Egyptian chronology begins, all dates were guesswork. What the first carbon-14 dates demonstrated was that the guesses had not been bold enough.

Thus the first carbon-14 revolution did not seriously challenge the relationships that had previously been established in terms of relative chronology between the different areas of Europe and the Near East. Even with respect to the crucial period after 3000 B.C., for which the Egyptian historical chronology provided a framework of absolute rather than relative dating, the new dates seemed to harmonize fairly well with the traditional ones. Just three troublesome problems hinted that all was not yet well. First, whereas many of the early carbon-14 dates for the megalithic tombs in western Europe fell around 2500 B.C., which fitted in with Childe's traditional chronology, the dates in France were somewhat earlier. In Brittany, for example, the dates of several corbeled tombs were earlier than 3000 B.C. This did not agree with the established picture of megalithic tombs diffusing from Spain to France sometime after 2500 B.C. Most scholars simply assumed that the French laboratories producing these dates were no better than they ought to be, and that the anomaly would probably disappear when more dates were available.

Second, the dates for the Balkan Neolithic were far too early. Sites related to the Vinča culture gave carbon-14 readings as early as 4000 B.C. This implied that not only copper metallurgy but also the attractive little sculptures of the Balkans were more than a millennium older than their supposed Aegean prototypes. Clearly something was wrong. Some archaeologists, led by Vladimir Milojčić, argued that the entire carbon-14 method was in error. Others felt that some special factor was making the Balkan dates too early, since the dates in other regions, with the exception of Brittany, seemed to be in harmony with the historical dates for the third millennium B.C.

Third, the dates for Egypt were too late. In retrospect this now seems highly significant. Egyptian objects historically dated to the period between 3000 and 2000 B.C. consistently yielded carbon-14 dates that placed them several centuries later. With the early inaccuracies and uncertainties of the carbon-14 method these divergences could at first be dismissed as random errors, but as more dates accumulated such an excuse was no longer possible. The archaeologists kept on using their historical dates and did not bother too much about the problems raised by the new method.

The physicists were more concerned, but they supposed, to use Libby's words, "that the Egyptian historical dates beyond 4000 years ago may be somewhat too old, perhaps five centuries too old at 5000 years ago, with decrease in error to [zero] at 4000 years ago.... It is noteworthy that the earliest astronomical fix is at 4000 years ago, that all older dates have errors and that these errors are more or less cumulative with time before 4000 years ago." For once, however, the archaeologists were right. The discrepancy was to be set at the door of the physicist rather than the Egyptologist. The consequences were dramatic.

Remote as it may seem from European archaeology, it was the venerable pine trees in the White Mountains of

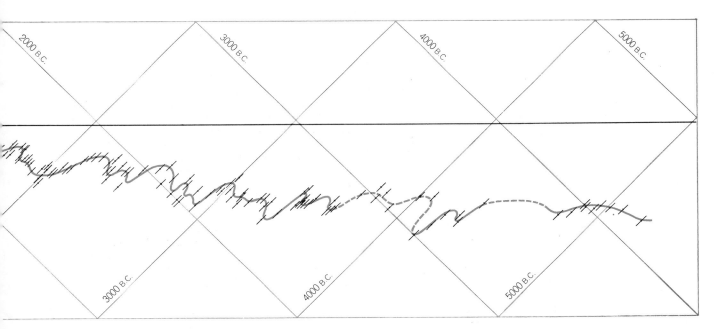

ored curve, which follows many individual measurements, shows how the carbon-14 dates go off with time. To calibrate a carbon-14 date, say 2000 B.C., one follows the line for that date until it meets the colored curve. At that point a diagonal is drawn parallel to the bristlecone-pine lines and the date is read off on the bristlecone-pine scale. The corrected date would be about 2500 B.C.

| YEARS B.C. | EGYPT | AEGEAN | BALKANS | ITALY | MALTA |
|---|---|---|---|---|---|
| 1500 | DYNASTY XVIII | MYCENAE | | | TARXIEN CEMETERY |
| | | MIDDLE BRONZE AGE | FÜZESABONY | POLADA | |
| 2000 | | EARLY BRONZE AGE | NAGYREV | | |
| 2500 | PYRAMIDS | LERNA III | | | TARXIEN |
| 3000 | DYNASTY I | TROY I | | REMEDELLO | |
| | | EARLY HELLADIC I | | | GGANTIJA |
| 3500 | GERZEAN | FINAL NEOLITHIC | LATE GUMELNITSA | LAGOZZA | ZEBBUG |
| 4000 | | LATE NEOLITHIC | | CHIOZZA | |
| 4500 | AMRATIAN | | LATE VINČA | | RED SKORBA |
| | | EARLY VINČA | | | |

**REVISED CHRONOLOGY, taking the Suess calibration into account, destroys the basis for the diffusionist theory of European** prehistory. Colored area at left marks the portion of Egyptian and Aegean chronology that is related to historical records. Colored

California that brought about the revolution in Old World prehistory. These trees have provided a reliable check of the carbon-14 method and have produced significant modifications. By 1960 one major assumption of the method was already coming into question. This was that the rate of production of carbon 14 in the atmosphere, and hence its proportion in all living things, had been constant over the past 40,000 years. The assumption was first really checked when Eric H. Willis, Henrik Tauber and Karl Otto Münnich analyzed samples of wood from the stump of a giant sequoia that could be dated exactly by counting its annual growth rings. Although the carbon-14 dates and the tree-ring dates agreed to within 100 years all the way back to A.D. 650, some minor but real fluctuations were observed. This suggested that there had been definite small changes in the rate of carbon-14 production in the past.

It was obviously desirable to check back to even earlier periods. Fortunately the fantastically long life of the California bristlecone pine (*Pinus aristata*) was known to the late Edmund Schulman of the Laboratory of Tree-Ring Research at the University of Arizona. Bristlecone pines as old as 4,600 years had been authenticated. Since Schulman's death the study of the trees has been energetically pursued by Charles Wesley Ferguson of the same laboratory. With ring sequences from many bristlecones, Ferguson has succeeded in building up a continuous absolute chronology reaching back nearly 8,200 years. The compilation of such a chronology, with due provision for multiple growth rings and missing rings, is a formidable task. Ferguson and his colleagues have developed computer programs for the comparison and matching of the ring sequence of different trees. This admirably systematic work has been the indispensable foundation of the second carbon-14 revolution.

Ferguson supplied wood samples whose absolute age had been determined by ring-counting to three independent carbon-14 laboratories: one at the University of Arizona, one at the University of Pennsylvania and one at the University of California at San Diego. The carbon-14 determinations, which in general agree fairly well with one another, reveal major discrepancies between previously accepted carbon-14 dates and actual dates. At San Diego, Hans E. Suess has analyzed more than 300 such samples and has built up an impressively clear and coherent picture of these discrepancies.

The divergence between the carbon-14 and tree-ring dates is not serious after 1500 B.C. Before that time the difference becomes progressively larger and amounts to as much as 700 years by 2500 B.C. The carbon-14 dates are all too young, but Suess's analysis can be used to correct them [see illustration on preceding two pages].

One problem that has emerged is that, in addition to a large first-order divergence, Suess's calibration curve shows smaller second-order fluctuations or "kinks." Sometimes the rate of carbon-14 production has fluctuated so rapidly that samples of different ages show an identical concentration of carbon 14 in spite of the fact that the older sample allowed more time for radioactive decay. This means that a given carbon-14 date can very well correspond to several different calendar dates.

The reasons for the fluctuations are not yet known with certainty, but the Czechoslovakian geophysicist V. Bucha has shown that there is a striking correlation between the divergence in dates and past changes in the strength of the earth's magnetic field. The first-order variation is probably due to the fact that as the strength of the earth's field changed it deflected more or fewer cosmic rays before they could enter the atmosphere. There are strong indications that the second-order fluctuations are correlated with the level of solar activity. Both the low-energy particles of the "solar wind" and the high-energy particles that are the solar component of the cosmic radiation may affect the cosmic ray flux in the vicinity of the earth. Climatic changes may also have influenced the concentration of carbon 14 in the atmosphere.

To the archaeologist, however, the reliability of the tree-ring calibration is more important than its physical basis. Libby's principle of simultaneity, which states that the atmospheric level of carbon 14 at a given time is uniform all

| IBERIA | FRANCE | BRITISH ISLES | NORTH EUROPE |
|--------|--------|---------------|--------------|
| EL ARGAR | | MIDDLE BRONZE AGE | BRONZE HORIZON III |
| | EARLY BRONZE AGE | STONEHENGE III | HORIZON II |
| | | | HORIZON I |
| BEAKER | | | |
| | BEAKER | STONEHENGE I | |
| | SEINE-OISE-MARNE CULTURE | | MIDDLE NEOLITHIC (PASSAGE GRAVES) |
| LOS MILLARES | | NEW GRANGE | |
| ALMERIAN | LATE PASSAGE GRAVE | NEOLITHIC | TRICHTERBECKER "A" |
| EARLY ALMERIAN | | | ERTEBØLLE |
| | EARLY CHASSEY | EARLY NEOLITHIC | |

area at right indicates periods when megalithic monuments were built in the European areas named. Lines and names in color show "connections" now proved to be impossible.

over the world, has been in large measure substantiated. Tests of nuclear weapons have shown that atmospheric mixing is rapid and that irregularities in composition are smoothed out after a few years. The California calibration should therefore hold for Europe. There is no need to assume that tree growth or tree rings are similar on the two continents, only that the atmospheric level of carbon 14 is the same at a given time.

There remains the question of whether some special factor in the bristlecone pine itself might be causing the discrepancies. For example, the diffusion of recent sap across the old tree rings and its retention in them might affect the reading if the sap were not removed by laboratory cleaning procedures. Studies are now in progress to determine if this is a significant factor; present indications are that it is not. Even if it is, it would be difficult to see why the discrepancy between carbon-14 dates and calendar dates should be large only before 1500 B.C.

The general opinion, as reflected in the discussions at the Twelfth Nobel Symposium at Uppsala in 1969, is that the discrepancy is real. Suess's calibration curve is the best now available, although corrections and modifications can be expected. It is particularly satisfying that when the carbon-14 dates for Egypt are calibrated, they agree far better with the Egyptian historical calendar. Further work is now in progress at the University of California at Los Angeles and at the British Museum on

Egyptian samples specially collected for the project, so that a further check of the extent to which the calibrated carbon-14 dates and the historical chronology are in harmony will soon be available.

The revision of carbon-14 dates for prehistoric Europe has a disastrous effect on the traditional diffusionist chronology. The significant point is not so much that the European dates in the third millennium are all several centuries earlier than was supposed but that the dates for Egypt do not change. Prehistorians have always used the historical dates for Egypt because they seemed more accurate than the carbon-14 dates. They have been proved correct; the calibrated carbon-14 dates for Egypt agree far better with the historical chronology than the uncalibrated ones did. Hence the Egyptian historical calendar, and with it the conventional Egyptian chronology, remains unchanged. The same is true for the Near East in general and for Crete and the southern Aegean. The carbon-14 dates for the Aegean formerly seemed too young; they too agree better after calibration.

For the rest of Europe this is not true. Over the past decade prehistorians in Europe have increasingly been using carbon-14 dates to build up a chronology of the third millennium B.C. Except in Brittany and the Balkans, this chronology had seemed to work fairly well. The dates had still allowed the megalithic tombs of Spain to have been built around 2500 B.C. There was no direct contradiction between the diffusionist

picture and the uncalibrated carbon-14 chronology.

All that is now changed. A carbon-14 date of about 2350 B.C. for the walls and tombs at Los Millares in Spain must now be set around 2900 B.C. This makes the structures older than their supposed prototypes in the Aegean. Whereas the carbon-14 inconsistency in western Europe was formerly limited to Brittany, it now applies to the entire area. In almost every region where megalithic tombs are found the calibrated carbon-14 dates substantially predate 2500 B.C. The view of megalithic culture as an import from the Near East no longer works.

The same thing seems to be happening in Malta, although there are still too few carbon-14 dates to be certain. A date of 1930 B.C. for the period *after* the temples now becomes about 2200 B.C. Clearly the spirals in the temples cannot be the result of Aegean influence around 1800 B.C.

The Balkans are affected too. The figurines of the Vinča culture now have dates earlier than 4500 B.C.; to associate them with the Aegean of the third millennium becomes ludicrous. The revision of dates also shows that in the Balkans there was a flourishing tradition of copper metallurgy, including such useful artifacts as tools with shaft holes, before metal production was well under way in the Aegean.

Similar changes are seen all over Europe. Stonehenge was until recently considered by many to be the work of skilled craftsmen or architects who had come to Britain from Mycenaean Greece around 1500 B.C. The monument is now seen to be several centuries older, and Mycenaean influence is clearly out of the question.

All is not confusion, however. As we have seen, the chronology of Egypt, the Near East, Crete and the Aegean is not materially changed in the third millennium B.C. Although the actual dates are altered in the rest of Europe, when we compare areas dated solely by carbon 14 the relationships between them are not changed. The great hiatus comes when we compare areas that have calibrated carbon-14 dates with areas that are dated by historical means. The hiatus may be likened to a geological fault; the chronological "fault line" extends across the Mediterranean and southern Europe.

On each side of the fault line the relationships and the successions of cultures remain unaltered. The two sides have shifted, however, *en bloc* in relation to each other, as the geological stra-

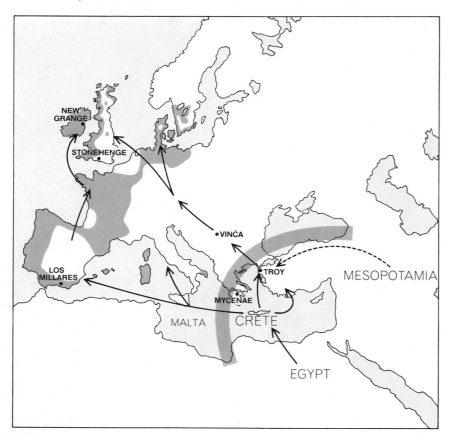

CHRONOLOGICAL "FAULT LINE" (*curved bar*) divides all Europe except the Aegean from the Near East. Arrows above the fault line are supposed chronological links now discredited. Areas of Europe that contain megalithic chamber tombs are in color at left.

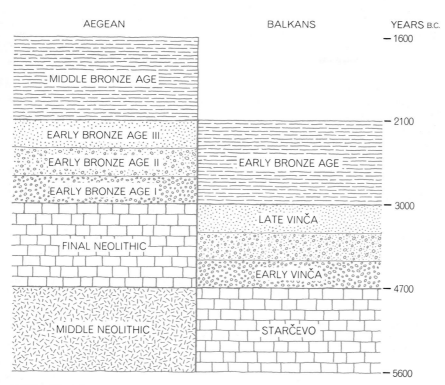

FAULT-LINE SLIPPAGE is shown schematically as it affects the chronological connection between the barbarian Balkans and the civilized Aegean. Strata with the same markings were once thought to be contemporary. Estimated Balkan dates, however, were too recent.

ta on two sides of a fault might. As a result much of what Montelius and Childe wrote about relationships and relative chronologies within continental Europe still stands. It is only the absolute chronology in calendar years and certain key links—between Spain and the Aegean and between the Balkans and the Aegean—that are ruptured. The dates for Europe as a whole have moved back in time, and the old diffusionist view of links connecting Europe and the Near East is no longer tenable.

The really important effect of tree-ring calibration is not that it changes the dates for prehistoric Europe by a few centuries. What matters is that it transforms our picture of what happened in prehistoric Europe and of how Europe developed. No longer can the essential theme of European prehistory be Childe's "irradiation of European barbarism by Oriental civilization." Indeed, the very early dates for some of the achievements of the prehistoric inhabitants of Europe make the term barbarism quite inappropriate.

Now it is clear that megalithic chamber tombs were being built in Brittany earlier than 4000 B.C., a millennium before monumental funerary architecture first appears in the eastern Mediterranean and 1,500 years before the raising of the pyramids. The origins of these European burial customs and monuments have to be sought not in the Near East but in Europe itself. The temples of Malta must likewise be viewed as remarkable, indeed unique, local creations: the oldest freestanding stone monuments in the world.

Even metallurgy may have been independently invented in the Balkans, and possibly in Spain as well. Certainly it was flourishing in the Balkans earlier than it was in Greece. The possibility remains, however, that the art of metalworking was learned from the Near East, where it was known even earlier than in the Balkans.

The central moral is inescapable. In the past we have completely undervalued the originality and the creativity of the inhabitants of prehistoric Europe. It was a mistake, as we now can see, always to seek in the Near East an explanation for the changes taking place in Europe. Diffusion has been overplayed. Of course, contact between prehistoric cultures often allowed ideas and innovations to pass between them. Furthermore, evidence might easily emerge for occasional contacts between western or southern Europe and the Near East in very early times. This, however, is not an adequate model for the explanation of culture change. Nor is there any case for turning the tables on the old diffusionists by suggesting that the early monuments and innovations in Europe inspired the pyramids of Egypt or other achievements in the Near East. That would merely be to reverse the arrows on the diffusionist map, and to miss the real lesson of the new dating.

The initial impact of the carbon-14 revolution will be to lead archaeologists to revise their dates for prehistoric Europe. This is the basic factual contribution that the tree-ring calibration has to make, although inevitably it will be some years before we can develop a definitive and reliable calibrated chronology for the entire area. The more profound impact, however, will be on the kind of explanation that prehistorians will accept in elucidating cultural change. A greater reluctance to swallow "influences" or "contacts" as sufficient explanations in themselves, without a much more detailed analysis of the actual mechanisms involved, is to be expected. This is in keeping with much current archaeological thinking. Today social and economic processes are increasingly seen as more important subjects for study than the similarities among artifacts.

When the textbooks are rewritten, as they will have to be, it is not only the European dates that will be altered. A shift in the basic nature of archaeological reasoning is necessary. Indeed, it is already taking place in Europe and in other parts of the world. This is the key change that tree-ring calibration, however uncertain some of its details remain, has helped to bring about.

ANCIENT PINE, its trunk scarred and its branches twisted, is one of the many trees of the bristlecone species (*Pinus aristata*) that grow in the White Mountains of California. An analysis of this tree's growth rings proves it to be more than 4,500 years old. Using this and other specimens, Charles Wesley Ferguson and his co-workers at the University of Arizona have built up a continuous tree-ring chronology with a span of more than 8,000 years.

SCYTHIAN HORSEMAN, with flying cloak and bold moustache, is one of two figures used repeatedly to decorate the largest piece of cloth found in the frozen burial chambers in the Pazyryk valley of the Altai Mountains. Made of felt, the cloth was probably used as a rug. The preserved portion measures 15 by 21 feet; horse and rider occupy 16 square feet. The tombs were built about 300 B.C.

# Frozen Tombs of the Scythians

by M. I. Artamonov
*May 1965*

*Soviet archaeologists, examining several 2,000-year-old
graves in Siberia, have found rich stores of normally
perishable cloth, leather and wood artifacts almost
perfectly preserved by cold*

Judging by the remains of ancient cultures, one might suppose that the material creations of prehistoric men were limited to objects made of stone, clay, bone and a few metals such as copper, gold and iron. Archaeologists are of course aware that this is a false impression, attributable to the fact that nature is hostile to the preservation of organic materials. Normally anything made of wood, leather, cloth or the like cannot long survive exposure to the disintegrating effects of weather or burial. This circumstance has caused a certain distortion of our view of the everyday life and activities of peoples of the distant past.

Occasionally archaeologists have been fortunate enough to discover ancient settlements at sites where their contents have been preserved by conditions of permanent wetness or permanent dryness—for example in the lake bottoms and peat bogs of Switzerland, in the marshes of the northwestern U.S.S.R. and in the deserts of Egypt. These rare finds give us quite a different picture of ancient life. As if a black-and-white photograph were suddenly rendered in color to reveal a richness of detail not previously visible, they bring to light an astonishing profusion of garments, furnishings and other creations in wood, fur, leather and fiber. In short, they show that the trappings of life in prehistoric civilizations included many of the materials we consider modern.

In central Siberia, a land whose prehistory has been almost completely unknown, Soviet archaeologists have in recent years uncovered the remains of an ancient people kept remarkably intact by still another means of preservation: refrigeration. The find consists of a number of burial mounds high in the Altai Mountains on the border between Siberia and Outer Mongolia. Through an accident of their construction these graves have been frozen virtually since they were made more than 2,000 years ago. In each of the mounds the burial chambers were covered with a layer of massive boulders. This layer was not airtight, and the burial chambers were soon filled with freezing air during the cold Altai winter. Because cold air is heavier than warm, the frigid air below the boulders was not penetrated by warm air during the short Altai summers; only still colder, denser air could settle into the chambers. Thus the graves became natural refrigerators. Here, in these chambers of eternal frost, the bodies of ancient chieftains, with their horses, clothing and varied possessions, have been preserved from decay.

The Altai finds have opened up a significant ancient culture. These buried horsemen belonged to one of the great tribes of "barbarians"—nomads who roamed the steppes of Eurasia in the time of ancient Greece and Persia and were called by ancient writers the Scythians. Little has been known about the Scythians—if we may call them that —of central Asia. Now the graves in the Altai Mountains show that these remote and nearly forgotten people were in surprisingly close contact with the cultures of Greece, Iran and China. What is more, the artifacts from these graves reveal that the people who made them had an unexpected sophistication and creativeness in art.

Let us note first that there has been much speculation about the origins and migrations of the Eurasian tribes. Whatever their origin, throughout the first millennium B.C. these peoples hovered at the entire northern frontier of the established civilizations of Greece and western Asia, ranging the steppes from the Black Sea all the way to China. They traded with the Greeks and Iranians when they had to and raided their cities when they could. But the wandering tribes of the steppes also developed a common way of life of their own, with the same kind of economy (mainly pastoral) and common cultural characteristics. This was the culture described by ancient writers as "Scythian."

Herodotus and other Greek writers give something of a picture of the life of the Scythians, based mainly on the tribes living in contact with Greek colonists on the northern shore of the Black Sea. The Greek accounts, however, are inconsistent and become vaguer as they reach further into the continent of Asia beyond the northern shore of the Black Sea, until finally they fade off into pure legend. They picture central Asia as inhabited by a series of fabulous baldheaded creatures: the Argippaei, the one-eyed Arimaspi and the gold-guarding griffins (beings with the head of an eagle and the body of a lion).

It remained for modern archaeologists to reconstruct a clearer and more accurate account of the Scythians. Excavations of ancient Scythian burial mounds near the Black Sea, beginning in the 19th century, have turned up an extraordinary collection of objects that are considered to be among the greatest treasures of the State Hermitage Museum in Leningrad. Unfortunately most of these graves, like burials elsewhere, had been plundered by treasure hunters before archaeological workers found them. Nevertheless, the archaeologists recovered many remarkable pieces, fashioned in gold, silver, bronze and ceramic materials. Some of these objects had been produced by craftsmen of Greece and Asia Minor, but most were the work of Scythian artists. They were distinguished by their depiction of animal forms—the so-called "animal style" now

**ALTAI MOUNTAIN REGION** of Siberia (*color*) lies near the boundary between Mongolia and Chinese Turkestan. The Scythian treasures in Siberia first came to light in the 18th century, when some 200 pieces of gold sculpture were sent to Peter the Great.

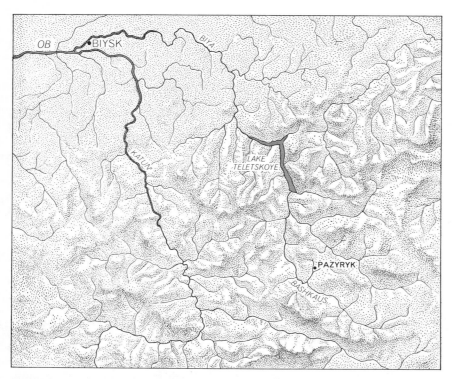

**RICHEST ALTAI SITE** is the highland valley of Pazyryk, south of Lake Teletskoye. Six Scythian tombs in the area were excavated by Soviet archaeologists between 1947 and 1949.

famous as a trademark of Scythian art.

The study of these treasures by scholars at the Hermitage has steadily added to our knowledge of the Scythians and their easterly cousins. For example, for a long time the collection has included a most unusual group of finds from Scythian graves in western Siberia. These objects were extracted from burial mounds by gold hunters around the end of the 17th century and found their way into the possession of Peter I ("Peter the Great"). The more than 200 assorted gold items include plates with extraordinary pictures of fighting beasts and other animals in the distinctive Scythian animal style; they differ from the objects found near the Black Sea only in that they show Iranian rather than Greek influence and picture local animal life of the Siberian region.

It is against this background that we can now place the discoveries in the Altai Mountains, part of the region that the Greek historians supposed to be populated by one-eyed men and griffins. Strangely enough, objects of the Altai type have been known for more than a century and a half, but their significance was not realized until fairly recently. Around the beginning of the 19th century an engineer in the Altai area named P. K. Frolov collected from various sources a number of local art objects of bronze, bone and wood. Some of them were particularly notable wood carvings; all were executed in the typically Scythian animal style. No doubt Frolov realized that the objects were old, but there is no indication that he connected them with the distant past. Then in the 1860's an archaeologist, V. V. Radlov, excavated two big burial mounds in the same region. Among his finds in these mounds were some fur garments in excellent condition and some carved wood like the items in Frolov's collection. Apparently it did not occur to Radlov or anyone else to wonder how it was that these things were so well preserved; at any rate, no effort was made to follow up the discoveries by searching for other graves.

The present scientific interest in digging up the past of the Altai area began in 1927. In that year a Soviet archaeologist, M. P. Gryaznov, went to work on a stone mound in the vicinity of Shiba in the Altai Mountains. In it he found objects of metal, wood and bone like those in the Frolov and Radlov collections. This time the discoveries inspired a systematic and carefully scientific investigation of similar mounds in the region. In 1929 S. I. Rudenko opened a large boulder-roofed mound in the Pazyryk valley, which was to become celebrated for the richness of archaeological finds in it. World War II interrupted Rudenko's work, but he returned to the Pazyryk valley in 1947 and soon excavated six more mounds there. He went on to uncover two others at Bash Adar and two at Tuekte. All these graves were protected by the perpetual frost and their contents were remarkably well preserved. Several other mounds with shallower layers of boulders have also been excavated in the same region; in these the burials had suffered further decay.

The archaeologists found the big, stone-roofed graves partly filled with layers of ice. In the process of excavating them the ice had to be melted bit by

bit with boiling water and bailed out. When the diggers finally cleared and examined the burial chambers, they found that every one had been thoroughly looted by plunderers many centuries before. There was clear evidence of the manner and extent of the lootings, and certain clues allow us to guess even the approximate time they took place.

As an example of the construction of the burial mounds, let us take those of the Pazyryk type [see illustrations below]. The builders first dug a rectangular pit approximately 15 feet deep and some 25 feet on a side. In this excavation they erected a wood framework, leaving a space between the frame and the earth wall on the north side large enough to receive the dead chieftain's horses, which were slaughtered in the

funeral rites; from five to 22 horses were found in this space in the Pazyryk graves. Inside the first framework the grave builders usually constructed a second, filling the space between the two with earth or stone. The inner structure enclosed the burial chamber itself, which was a shallow room no more than five feet high with a board floor and walls and ceiling, all covered with a thick layer of felt. The body of the dead man, sometimes with that of his wife or concubine, was placed in a single large coffin made of the hollow trunk of a larch tree. (Occasionally two smaller coffins were found in a grave.) The coffin was covered with carved figures of animals or with designs cut out of leather or birch bark [see bottom illustration on next page]. In the cham-

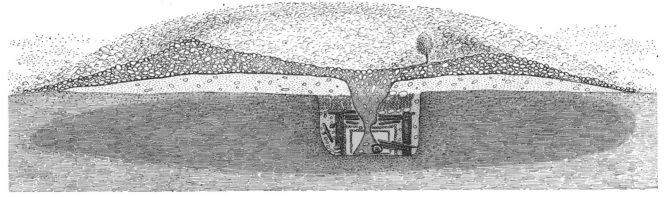

**PAZYRYK TOMB**, shown in cross section, was built of wood at the bottom of a pit 15 feet deep. A thick layer of logs over the roof of the chamber served to fill the pit up to the original level of the ground, after which the earth from the excavation was used to make a low, wide mound. The Scythians then carted large numbers

of boulders to the site and piled them high on the earth mound. The empty spaces between the boulders collected chill winter air that did not reheat during the brief summer. Eventually the earth below the mound became frozen (color) and the contents of the tomb were thus preserved. This is mound No. 5 at Pazyryk.

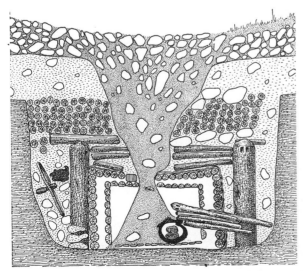

**UNDERGROUND STRUCTURE** consists of a heavy wood frame within which was built a double-walled burial chamber where the coffin and household goods were placed. Horses were sacrificed and piled along the north side of the pit. Every burial chamber at Pazyryk was looted by robbers, who dug down to the layer of logs and then chopped their way inside (note the disturbed area).

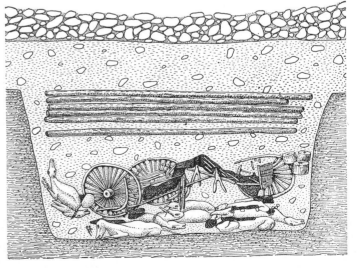

**HORSE SACRIFICE** at mound No. 5 included the wheels and the frame of a four-horse carriage, as well as saddles, harness and other trappings. Mares evidently were seldom ridden or driven; all the slain horses were geldings. Because the ancient looters did not usually dig up the horse sacrifices modern archaeologists have found many of the finest Scythian artifacts among these burials.

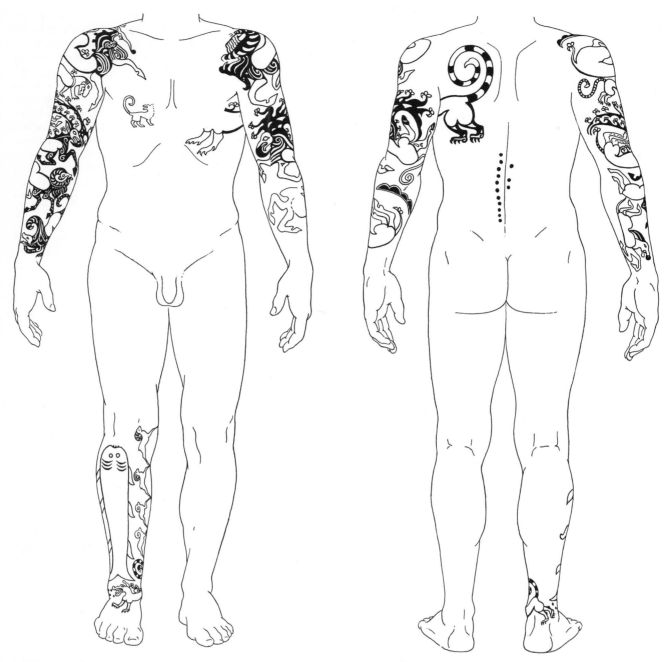

**TATTOOED CHIEF,** most of his skin preserved by the freezing temperature of mound No. 2 at Pazyryk, had both arms and one leg decorated with designs in the celebrated "animal style" of the Scythians. The figures were formed by first pricking the skin and then rubbing in soot. The various carnivores portrayed seem to be mythical felines; the herbivores (*for example the row of mountain sheep on the leg*) are more realistically rendered. The chief's head was scalped and crushed, suggesting death in battle.

**ANIMAL STYLE** in Scythian art is further exemplified by this quartet of wildcats incised on a coffin made from the trunk of a larch tree. Other tree-trunk coffins in Altai tombs display carvings of deer, mountain sheep, moose, and even roosters arrayed in rows.

ber with the dead were placed various funeral goods—low tables with carved legs, wooden stools, dishes containing food and so on. The chamber was then roofed with several layers of bark and logs. On this was heaped the soil from the excavation, topped by a stone platform some 120 to 150 feet in diameter. The entire mound sometimes rose as high as 13 or 14 feet above ground level.

All the burial mounds discovered in the Altai region had been broken into by plunderers in exactly the same way, evidently by men who knew their construction quite well. The looters first dug a shaft into the mound to the timbered ceiling of the burial chamber, then cut a hole in the ceiling large enough for a man to lower himself through it into the room. They generally took everything of value that was not too heavy to move. They seldom bothered, however, to dig into the space where the horses were buried, because it was too difficult to search through the stones and earth heaped on them and nothing very valuable was interred with them.

It appears that the robbers must have looted these graves some considerable time after they were built—a time probably measured in generations. In the first place, their digging operations were done quite openly, which indicates that there were no living relatives of the dead on hand to stop them. A second clue is presented by the peculiar stratification of the ice in several of the burial chambers. In each case the bottom layer was made up of clean ice in which the archaeologists found funeral objects still embedded. This ice must have formed from moisture wrung by the cold from the thin, dry mountain air. That it took some time for the ice to form can be deduced from the fact that sacrificial meats left at the time of burial had rotted away, leaving only bones, before the burial chamber chilled and the ice accumulated. Above this layer of clean ice the archaeologists found a mass of ice containing dirt and rubbish, which was washed into the chamber by ground water leaking through the hole in the ceiling by which the looters made their entry.

All of this indicates a substantial lapse of time between the burials and the plundering of the graves. On the other hand, the timbers through which the robbers hacked their way into the graves give evidence that they had been cut by primitive metal axes, which means that the robberies must have

occurred long ago. In all probability the looters were Turks who invaded the Altai Mountains sometime after the third century B.C.

The ransacked burial chambers were in great disorder, with the bodies of the dead scattered about, their clothing stripped off and their extremities sometimes amputated, evidently so that the thieves could remove necklaces and other ornaments. In one grave, for example, both the man and the woman were beheaded by the looters, and from the woman's body both feet, one leg and the right hand were cut off. The felt coverings were torn from the walls of the chamber, apparently in order to remove the copper nails that had suspended them.

No doubt what the archaeologists

have found in the Altai graves is only a small part of their original contents. Nevertheless, even the plundered remains make up a picture incomparably more detailed and more revealing than other graves have yielded, thanks to the permanent frost that preserved these remains.

The bodies of the dead, in the first place, were in remarkable condition, with even the hair and skin still in a good state of preservation. They had been carefully embalmed. The brains, internal organs and sections of muscle had been removed, and to maintain the shape of the body the corpses had been stuffed with grass or hair and the skin was then sewed up with threads made of hair or tendons. One man's skin was covered with tattoos of animals in the

PREDATORS IN ACTION are typical subjects of Scythian art. Both figures are cut from leather; the griffin seizing a moose (*top*) is repeated 20 times along the border of a hide rug from mound No. 2 at Pazyryk. The tiger or leopard striking down a mountain sheep (*bottom*) decorates a saddle; it is also from mound No. 2. The most common predators are felines; the figures are distinctively Scythian but the theme was derived from Persia.

PHEASANTS were embroidered in silk on a saddlecloth found at Pazyryk mound No. 5. Both the use of silk and the style of the figures strongly suggest a Chinese origin.

HEADDRESS for a horse, from mound No. 2, combines a mountain sheep's head and a bird. Such objects were not special funeral wares; they show clear signs of daily use.

typical style of Scythian decoration [see top illustration on page 252]. All the corpses had had their heads either partly or entirely shaved, but before their burial hair had been attached artificially to the heads of the women and beards to the faces of the men.

Enough scraps and remnants of clothing were found in the graves to give a fairly good idea of the people's wearing apparel. All the clothing was made of leather, fur or felt, except for some shirts that were woven of hemp or a hemplike fiber. Apparently wool was not used for clothing (although, as we shall see, a woolen rug was one of the items found in the Altai remains). The men wore narrow trousers made of many pieces of chamois-like leather, felt stockings, high boots with soft soles, and a spacious, capelike tunic with long, decorated sleeves. Their headgear was a felt hat with leather-covered earflaps or a peaked felt cap. The women's garments included a similar tunic, with a bib worn over the chest, and felt stockings. They wore dress boots made of leopard fur and elaborately embroidered with beads even on the soles—obviously not practical for walking but clearly suggesting that the women must have been in the habit of sitting cross-legged so that the soles of their boots showed. Their headwear, then as now, was more varied than the men's. One woman had a kind of cap topped with a crown of jagged teeth; another wore a little cap of carved wood attached to a complicated coiffure. Several belts were found, one of them decorated with silver plaques.

Although the looters had stripped practically every piece of jewelry from the graves, a few small items that escaped their notice remain as samples of the rich adornment that must have been buried with the bodies. The Altai Mountains have always been famous as a gold-mining area. In the pillaged remains of the graves the archaeologists recovered only one example of solid gold jewelry—a pair of finely wrought earrings. They also found some gold-covered fragments of a necklace (with representations of griffins!), a few gilded bronze plaques bearing animal figures, which were sewed on clothing, and a small quantity of beads, some of them made of turquoise. There were a few toilet articles, including a comb of horn and three mirrors—one made of bronze, one of silver with a long horn handle and one of a white metal, a kind of Chinese zinc.

Very few weapons were found in the graves. There were fragments, however, which showed that weapons were deposited originally in the burials—pieces of pikestaffs from which the looters had removed the bronze heads, remains of shields made of wooden frames covered with leather (and one made of wood carved to look like leather) and fragments of a short iron sword and a dagger.

Among the more or less intact items of domestic goods were wooden tables, wooden serving dishes with little feet, wooden headboards for beds, wooden and pottery plates, felt mats and a stone lamp. There were bags, flasks, purses and cases made of leather, sacks made of fur and rugs and shawls made of felt and leather. There were also some musical instruments—drums made of horn and an instrument like a harp. One particularly interesting apparatus was a kind of cone-shaped miniature tent, covered with a felt or leather rug, standing over a copper censer. Hemp seeds found on the spot suggest that this contrivance was a special enclosure that could be filled with narcotic smoke from the burning seeds. The use of other drugs was also indicated by the presence of horn containers, in one of which was a small wooden spoon such as is still commonly used with snuffboxes in central Asia.

It is in the horse burials that the archaeologists have unearthed the most complete and best-preserved picture of the materials and art of the people who built these mounds. As already noted, the plunderers scarcely touched the part of the mound where the horses were buried. Furthermore, this section too was protected by the frost. The horses were found in excellent condition, and so were the accouterments interred with them.

The animals were a mixed collection —some large and of high breeding, others just run-of-the-herd. Almost all were riding horses, and they were all geldings between two and 20 years old. All had their manes clipped and their tails bobbed; some of the tails were plaited and smartly tied in a knot. Before burial with their master each had been killed by an ax blow on the head.

Some of the horses still wore blankets of felt and had leather covers over their tails, but most of the trappings had been removed and merely piled in the grave with the animals. These trappings are in every way remarkable. Each saddle consists of two pillows, stuffed with deer hair or grass and sewed together, combined with a saddlecloth, a girth and a strap passing under the horse's tail. The saddle and saddlecloth are decorated in almost unbelievably elaborate fashion: they are covered with cutouts of colored felt or leather depicting fights between wild animals, with details in colored thread and insets of beaten gold or tin. The saddle and bridle are also festooned with pendants carved out of leather or wood in a great variety of designs. Many of these beautiful and intricate carvings were covered with thin sheets of gold or tin and were found intact. Signs of wear and of repairs show that the gilded equipage was not mere funeral decoration but the regular gear that riders used on their mounts.

This was not all: the horses also wore, even on ordinary occasions, a still more spectacular item of dress in the form of a decorated slipcover, or mask, over the head. One of those found on a horse's head in the Altai graves had two large antlers attached to the top and a picture of a tiger outlined in fur along the muzzle. Another mask depicted a tiger attacking a winged griffin with tooth and claw. A third had a sculptured mountain sheep's head, and on the sheep's neck stood a big bird stretching its wings [*see bottom illustration on opposite page*].

In one of the burial mounds at Pazyryk (the fifth one excavated) two most unusual rugs were found buried with the horses. One is of woven wool, and it has the distinction of being the oldest known article in the world made of wool fiber. Measuring six by six and a half feet, it is woven in many colors and in an incredibly complicated fashion: in an area of 100 square centimeters (about 15½ square inches) 3,600 knots can be counted. The central panel of the rug contains a pattern consisting of four-pointed stars, and its wide border has figures of griffins, spotted deer and horsemen. The other rug is made of felt, with designs applied in color. The main feature is a frieze with a repeated composition representing a horseman with a flying cloak [*see the illustration on page 248*] before a goddess who sits on a throne and holds a plant in her hand. In its theme and its technique this rug is strongly reminiscent of the Greco-Scythian art in the Black Sea region.

The materials found with the horses tell us something about the technology, as well as the art, of the ancient Altai horsemen. Along with the horses were found parts of primitive wagons. The wheels were of solid wood, cut from the trunks of larch trees. Judging by

**USE OF NARCOTICS** by the Scythians is evidenced by these objects from mound No. 2. The stoollike device is a censer for burning hemp; the pot contained hemp seeds. The six sticks formed the frame of an 18-inch-high tent in which the hemp smoke was collected.

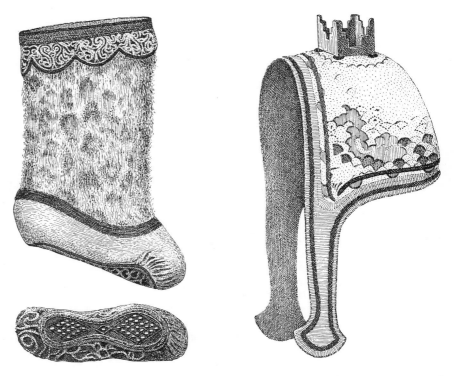

**HAT AND BOOTS** found at Pazyryk demonstrate a high level of craftsmanship in furs and skins. The crested hat is a man's, the fur boot a woman's. The sole of a second boot (*bottom left*) is embroidered with glass beads and pyrite crystals; it was obviously not for walking.

the signs of heavy wear in the axle holes, it appears that these wagons were used to drag up the boulders for the barrows and were then thrown into the pit when it was filled in. The fifth Pazyryk mound yielded up pieces of a much more complex wagon—evidently a kind of coach with four large, spoked wheels and a body consisting of latticed sides and a flat roof [see illustration at bottom right on page 251]. The shaft's yoke and traces show that the coach was pulled by four horses.

I have given only a quick survey of the finds in the Altai burial mounds; they make up a large collection that has been described in full detail in archaeological journals. We now ask: Who were these people—these artistic "barbarians" who lived in the Altai Mountains well over 2,000 years ago?

It can be said at once that they were clearly of Iranian origin. The woolen rug found in the fifth Pazyryk mound and many of the other objects can definitely be identified as Iranian in style. Beyond this, the obvious Black Sea influence and the general features that run through all the artifacts, particularly the familiar animal style, place the group within the overall Scythian culture that prevailed among the tribes of Eurasia.

At the same time the Altai remains also show a close contact with China. Although most of the individuals buried in the graves are of European stock, some are plainly Mongoloid. Moreover, some of the objects—such as a mirror and a saddlecloth with fine silk embroidery—are Chinese in origin [see top illustration on page 254]. There is every indication, indeed, that the Altai area was a meeting place between the Scythian nomads and ancient China. Here, it seems, was one of the ultimate extensions of the great Indo-European migration that stopped at China's doorstep.

Chinese documents of the third and second centuries B.C. tell of an Indo-European people in this region whom they call the Yueh-chih. In all probability these were the same people who built at least some of the Altai burial mounds. The Yueh-chih transmitted the Scythian art style to the Huns of Mongolia and northern China. Eventually they were dislodged from the region and driven westward by the Huns or the Turks.

Estimates of the dates of the Altai graves differ rather widely. From comparisons of the tree-growth rings in the excellently preserved timbers of the burial mounds it has been possible to judge the relative ages of the mounds pretty well. Apparently the difference between the oldest (the first mound at Tuekte) and the most recent (the fifth mound at Pazyryk) is about 200 years. We can be fairly confident about the accuracy of this relative chronology, because the tree-ring results agree with carbon-14 analyses of the wood, but the absolute dates are much more uncertain. The margin of error in the carbon-14 absolute dating is plus or minus 130 years, and the estimates of various authorities on the dates of the individual mounds range all the way from the seventh century B.C. to the first century of our era. The seventh-century date seems to me unlikely. The oldest examples of the Scythian animal style found in Iran and in the Black Sea area go back no further than the end of the seventh century B.C., and it is not to be expected that the style would have appeared earlier in a region near the extreme limit of the nomadic migrations; there is no basis whatever for supposing that the style originated in Siberia rather than at the fountainheads of Scythian culture near ancient Greece and Iran. The most probable dates for the burial mounds in the Altai Mountains are between the fifth (or at the earliest the sixth) and the third centuries B.C. The artistic styles in the Pazyryk mounds, for example, seem closely similar to those found in Iranian burials near the Black Sea (at Semibratny), which date from the fifth and fourth centuries B.C. Like the Semibratny burials, the successive Pazyryk graves show a gradual evolution of the animal style from realistic, three-dimensional forms to stylized, ornamental designs. This no doubt was a delayed but parallel reflection of the Black Sea development.

In any case, we are deeply indebted to the intervention of nature that preserved for us, in the frozen graves of the Altai Mountains, examples of ancient Scythian art in a great variety of materials that elsewhere have been effaced by the destructive processes of time. The Altai remains demonstrate clearly that art has been important to man in all times and among all peoples. Even in the so-called barbaric state man has enriched his life, from the cradle to the grave, with artistic creations. In every culture and age art has served not only to fulfill his aesthetic needs but also to shape his ideological concepts within the framework of his environment, his economy and his social relations.

# 25

# The Coprolites of Man

by Vaughn M. Bryant, Jr., and Glenna Williams-Dean
*January 1975*

*Archaeologists have unearthed fossil human feces
that range in age from a few hundred to 300,000 years.
Analysis of their contents is yielding information on
prehistoric diet, environment and behavior*

The human fossil record is short and scant, but it does offer a source of information about behavior that is not available to those who study the fossils of, say, dinosaurs. Where conditions favor the preservation of organic matter archaeologists frequently uncover desiccated human feces in or near prehistoric camps and dwellings. Objects of this kind, known to paleontologists as coprolites, are not uncommon among the remains of animals older than man; in fact, some sedimentary rocks consist largely of the fecal pellets of certain marine animals. These ancient coprolites, however, have become petrified, which makes it virtually impossible to analyze their original organic contents. Such analysis can now be routinely undertaken with human coprolites, thanks to laboratory techniques developed in the past decade. Analysis of coprolites ranging in age from the middle Paleolithic period to late prehistoric times is providing scholars with remarkably specific evidence on the diets and seasonal activities of early hunters and farmers in both the Old World and the New.

The excavator in the field may be unable to distinguish between the coprolites of man and those of other animals, but laboratory analysis as it is practiced today almost always yields a correct identification. The key step in the procedure, pioneered in the 1960's by the late Eric O. Callen of Macdonald College in Canada, is the immersion of the specimen in a dilute solution of trisodium phosphate. In the Anthropological Research Laboratories of Texas A&M University, where we have done most of our own work, we immerse the specimen for a minimum of 72 hours. If the specimen originated with an omnivorous or carnivorous mammal, the fluid usually remains translucent; if it is colored at all, the color is a pale brown. If the specimen originated with a herbivorous mammal, the fluid is translucent and sometimes yellowish. If the specimen is of human origin, the fluid is opaque and dark brown or black. Only one mammal other than man, the raccoonlike coatimundi, is known to leave feces that give rise to a similar chemical reaction.

If the results of the reaction are not conclusive, further steps are almost certain to dispel doubt. The sample is passed through a 20-mesh brass screen, which passes particles smaller than 850 microns, and then through a 100-mesh screen, which passes particles smaller than 150 microns. At both stages the retained material is gently washed with distilled water so that any fine particles, such as plant pollen, that still adhere to the larger debris can also pass through the mesh. The solid residues trapped on both screens are dried and prepared for examination under the microscope. The liquid fraction is centrifuged to collect pollen grains, plant crystals and any other small objects it contains.

Since the human diet characteristically consists of both plant and animal material, and since human beings have for at least half a million years processed their food by fire, the solid residues retrieved by screening include materials from a wide variety of sources. Along with bits of charcoal picked up in the course of cooking there may be plant fibers, cracked or milled seeds, hairs and fragments of bone, nutshell, eggshell, mollusk shell, feathers and the hard parts of insects. A few of these materials may be present in nonhuman coprolites, but when they are found in great variety, the specimen is almost certainly human. Moreover, if the specimen's pollen content is taken into account, the possibility of confusion between a human source and a nonhuman one can be still further reduced.

In principle it is possible to glean from such material information not only about the dietary preferences of groups and individuals but also about an individual's state of health (as indicated by the presence or absence of parasites), about techniques of food preparation, about the seasons of the year when a site was inhabited and about contemporary environmental conditions. In practice most of the information concerns dietary preferences and seasonal activities. For example, pollen analysis reveals that some 2,800 years ago the Archaic Indians of southwestern Texas collected and consumed the flowers of a number of desert and semidesert plants. Whether the flowers were sucked or chewed for the nectar they contained, were brewed into tea or were put into salads is more difficult to determine; perhaps they were consumed in all three ways.

Seeds have a hard test, or outer coat, that resists digestion. A test or even a fragment of one usually has a characteristic shape or surface pattern that makes it possible to identify the plant family, and perhaps the genus and species. An example of seed-fragment analysis that illuminated ancient food-preparation techniques is Callen's study of coprolites from Tehuacán, a site in Mexico that embraces some 12,000 years of New World prehistory. Some of the fragments of millet tests Callen recovered showed evidence of crushing, indicating that the grain had been prepared by pounding. Other fragments showed evidence of splitting, indicating that the grain had been prepared not by pounding but by being rolled back and forth on a stone *metate*.

We ourselves gathered interesting information on techniques of food preparation in a study of coprolites from a rock-shelter in southwestern Texas. Fragments of cactus-seed tests in speci-

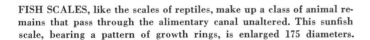

FISH SCALES, like the scales of reptiles, make up a class of animal remains that pass through the alimentary canal unaltered. This sunfish scale, bearing a pattern of growth rings, is enlarged 175 diameters.

FEATHERS are also little changed by the digestive process; the pattern of their barbules often identifies the species of bird. This specimen is a chicken feather, enlarged 550 diameters.

mens from five of the eight strata at the site showed that the cactus seeds had been prepared for eating by either pounding or grinding. The seed tests of other plants, particularly millet and goosefoot, were charred, indicating that the seeds had not been milled but roasted. Many coprolite seed tests are unbroken; when a seed is not itself valued as a food, it may still be ingested whole when the fruit of a plant is eaten. As a result it has been possible to demonstrate that the diet of prehistoric hunters and farmers at a number of sites in the New World included such food items as chili peppers, grapes, tomatoes, guavas, blackberries and squashes.

A subtler form of dietary evidence, usually confined to regions where the ground water is rich in dissolved minerals, is the phytolith, or plant crystal. Unlike animals, plants cannot excrete the inorganic substances in their water supply. The calcium and silicon that are taken up along with ground water are deposited in the plant tissue in crystalline form, most often as salts of calcium and anhydrides of silica. The form of a particular crystal is not usually associated with any one plant species. Nonetheless, we have found, in the

course of examining the phytoliths in plants of the same family or genus that grow in southwestern Texas, certain crystals that have similar forms. For example, the crystals of calcium oxalate that appear in four species of the prickly-pear cactus (*Opuntia*) are quite similar in appearance. Furthermore, one phytolith is species-specific. It is a rhomboidal crystal that is found only in the tissue of one species of agave, *Agave lecheguilla* [*see illustration on page 265*]. Identification of these crystals has enabled us to demonstrate that several individuals among the succession of Archaic Indians who visited the rock-shelter in southwestern Texas had eaten prickly-pear cactus and agave, even though the coprolites in which the crystals were found did not contain identifiable fibers, seeds or pollen from the plants.

Information is of course provided by animal material as well as plant material. For example, at one site in Nevada, Lovelock Cave, Lewis K. Napton and O. A. Brunetti of the University of California at Berkeley were able to identify the various species of waterfowl that the occupants had eaten from an investigation of the fragments of feathers they found in coprolites. The local diet had included the heron, the grebe, the mud

hen and the goose. In our own analysis of materials from the Texas rock-shelter we have recognized various animal remains, including fragments of grasshoppers and other insects, and the bones of small mammals, reptiles and fishes [*see illustration on page 263*].

When the prey is large, for example deer or bison, butchering and cooking practices are likely to minimize the chance that bones or bone fragments will be ingested. Almost inevitably, however, a few hairs will adhere to the meat and will be swallowed. We have recognized hair from one small mammal, the field mouse, in some rock-shelter coprolites, and we have even recovered such seemingly perishable items of animal material as insect larvae.

Still another kind of animal material makes its way through the alimentary tract largely unaltered: the scales of fishes and reptiles. The two kinds of scale can be told apart without great difficulty. Fish scales show a pattern of concentric growth rings and are generally rounded. Reptile scales have no growth rings and are often pointed at one end. Under ideal circumstances, and with an adequate reference collection for purposes of comparison, more can be learned than simply whether a

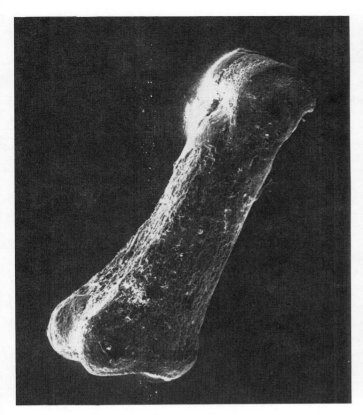

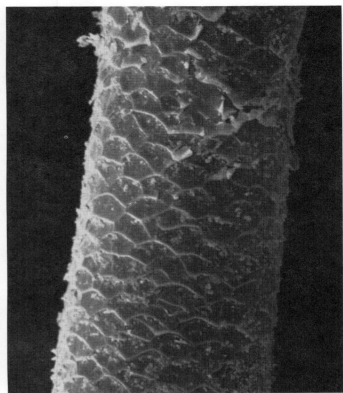

SMALL BONES, if not too fragmented by chewing, are often identifiable. This limb bone of a small rodent, enlarged 45 diameters, is from a coprolite found at a rock-shelter in Texas.

ANIMAL HAIR, like scales and feathers, resists digestion. This hair, from the coat of a white-tailed deer, shows a scale pattern that is characteristic of ruminants. The specimen is seen enlarged 1,100 diameters.

scale represents a fish or a reptile. Napton and another Berkeley colleague, Robert F. Heizer, were able to identify three different species of fish eaten by the occupants of Lovelock Cave.

Evidence of parasitic infestation appears occasionally in the course of coprolite analysis. Specimens between 3,000 and 5,000 years old from a Peruvian cave site, Huaca Prieta, were shown by Callen and T. W. M. Cameron to contain tapeworm eggs. Specimens from a 10,000-year-old stratum at Danger Cave in Utah were found by Gary F. Fry of Youngstown State University and Edwin Englert, Jr., of the University of Utah to contain the eggs of another intestinal parasite, the thorny-headed worm. Coprolites from Mesa Verde in Colorado contained pinworm eggs. As for the ticks, mites, lice and fleas that infest human body hair, ethnographic evidence regarding human grooming behavior is enough to dispel any surprise that their remains are also found in coprolites. Callen has identified ticks in specimens from one Tehuacán stratum that dates back some 6,000 years. Specimens from Mesa Verde and from Salts Cave in Kentucky contain mites, and those from the Utah cave site contain lice and louse eggs.

It is only in recent decades that archaeologists have come to appreciate how much information can be provided by pollen analysis. As botanists are well aware, the exine, or outer wall, of the pollen grain has a remarkable chemical stability, and so buried pollen grains are virtually indestructible. Moreover, the morphology of the exine is genetically determined, so that the form of a pollen grain will often indicate the plant species that gave rise to it, or at the least the genus or family. Putting aside the information that conventional pollen analysis can give the archaeologist, pollen grains that have been accidentally or purposely ingested are still another class of objects that pass through the alimentary tract virtually unaltered. Under the microscope pollen can be as informative about prehistoric diet as any other kind of plant material. The species the pollen represents can indicate the season of the year when a site was occupied and even give a general picture of the environment at the time.

Let us describe what the identification of pollens and other plant materials has revealed about the activities of the people who lived in the Texas rock-shelter we have mentioned. The coprolites found at the site are the result of inter-

mittent human occupation over a period of some 1,300 years, from 500 B.C. to A.D. 800. A total of 43 specimens were recovered from the various occupation levels; all but nine contained pollen. One of the pollen analyst's first tasks is to separate the grains into three classes: those grains that the wind carries from flower to flower, those that are transported by animals (most of them insects) and those that come from plants that are self-pollinating. (Certain aquatic plants release their pollen under water, but these grains generally lack an exine and are rarely preserved; they do not play a role here.)

Windborne pollens are released in vast quantities. As an example, the spruce forests of central and southern Sweden are estimated to release 75,000 tons of pollen per year. One anther of a wind-pollinated plant can produce as many as 70,000 grains of pollen and rarely produces fewer than 10,000. In insect-pollinated plants the production is smaller, about 1,000 grains per anther; in self-pollinating plants it can be fewer than 100 grains per anther.

The six principal windborne pollens found in the specimens from the Texas rock-shelter belonged to three plant genera and to three broader groups of plants; the morphology of the latter three kinds of pollen did not allow identification of the species or genus that produced them. Depending on the season, a more or less steady "rain" of all six pollens fell on the site. Some grains were probably ingested because they had fallen on articles of food; others may have accumulated in the drinking water or may even have been inhaled and then swallowed.

The three plant genera that contributed to the pollen were hackberry (*Celtis*), oak (*Quercus*) and pine (*Pinus*). Both hackberry (the species *C. laevigata* and *C. reticulata*) and oak (the shin oak, *Q. pungens*) still grow in the comparatively well-watered bottomland near the site. The nearest pines known, however, are isolated stands of pinyon (*P. cem-*

**PRINCIPAL POLLENS** found in 34 of the coprolites unearthed at a rock-shelter in southwestern Texas came from plants belonging to six groups that broadcast windborne pollens (*left*) and to eight groups with insect-transported pollens (*right*). In many specimens no pollen grains or only trace amounts were present. The presence of large amounts of pollen in other specimens, however, indicates

*broides*) found some 80 miles to the east.

The plants from two of the three less well-defined groups that contributed to the rain of pollen included members of the large family of composite-flowered plants (the Compositae) and members of the equally large family of seed-bearing grasses (the Gramineae). The third group consists of a constellation of plants well known to botanists in the southwestern U.S. It is called the Cheno-Am group because the formal names of its two principal constituents are the Chenopodiaceae (the goosefoot family) and the genus *Amaranthus* (pigweed). The pollens produced by the many species in the two groups of plants are almost impossible to tell apart. Much the same is true of the many species of Compositae, except that the exines of the windborne composite pollens have short spines

that the Archaic Indians who periodically visited the site ingested several kinds of flowers, either sucking or chewing them for their nectar, brewing them into tea or eating them in salads. In only one instance was a windborne pollen present in a specimen in association with evidence that the plant yielding the pollen was used as food; the ingestion of these pollens was largely accidental.

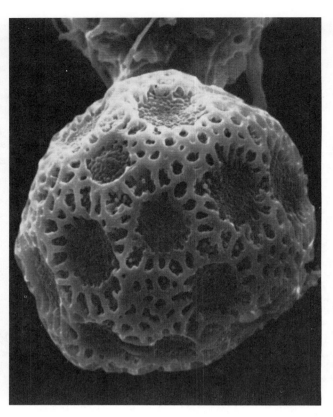

GRAINS OF POLLEN from mesquite (*left*) and prickly-pear cactus (*right*) are representative of insect-borne pollens found in ancient coprolites. These scanning electron micrographs, made in the electron-microscope center at Texas A&M University, are respectively enlarged 3,100 and 1,350 diameters. Both grains are modern; they are from the authors' collection of specimens for comparison.

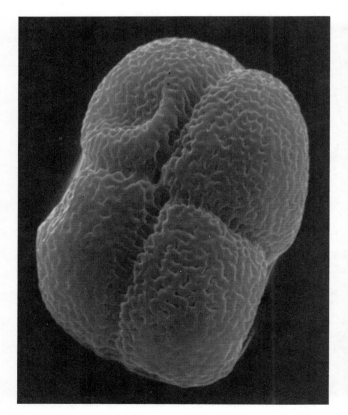

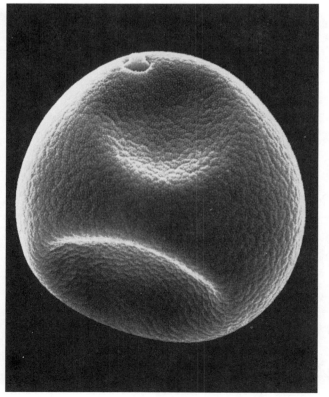

WINDBORNE POLLENS are represented here by a four-grained cluster of cattail pollen (*left*) and one grain of a wild sorghum, Johnson grass (*right*). They are respectively enlarged 4,500 and 2,250 diameters in these scanning electron micrographs. Windborne pollens are broadcast seasonally, and anyone who prepares food or drinks water during that season is likely to swallow a few grains.

whereas the exines of the animal-transported pollens have long ones.

The amount of windborne pollen in the rock-shelter coprolites ranged from none or mere trace amounts to as much as 48 percent of the pollen present. With one exception there is no evidence that the ingestion of any of the windborne pollen was related to diet. The exception is represented by the specimen that contained 48 percent windborne pollen. The pollen was of Cheno-Am origin, and many goosefoot seeds were also present in the specimen. The goosefoot has a long flowering season, so that pollen from late blossoms might easily have mixed with early-maturing seeds when the seeds were being collected for food.

Analysis of the windborne pollens at the rock-shelter provides the basis for one generalization about the local environment during the period from about 500 B.C. to A.D. 800. At least trace amounts of all six windborne pollens were present in one specimen or more from each of the eight strata at the site. Although pine is missing from the vicinity of the site today, with that one exception it appears that the plants of the present were also the plants of the past. The windborne pollen data do not, however, tell us anything about the relative numbers of plants of each kind during the 1,300-year interval. It is even possible that pines did not grow near the rock-shelter and that the pine pollen found there was wafted in from distant stands of pinyon.

Eight genera or larger groups of plants that bear insect-transported pollen also contributed plant materials to the contents of the rock-shelter coprolites. Among them were representatives of the Compositae that are characterized by long-spined pollen grains, but the balance of the flora was typical of arid and semiarid environments. One recognizable species was the desert agave *A. lecheguilla*. The other six pollens define genera only: the lead tree (*Leucaena*), the mesquite (*Prosopis*), the prickly-pear cactus (*Opuntia*), the pincushion cactus (*Mammillaria*), the yucca-like sotol (*Dasylirion*) and a showy genus of the lily family, the yucca itself (*Yucca*).

Evidence that the blossoms of the agave, the sotol and the yucca were sucked or chewed for their nectar, brewed into tea or eaten in salads is overwhelming. One specimen or more from the seven lens-shaped upper strata in the rock-shelter contained at least trace amounts of agave pollen; in Lens 1 the proportion of agave pollen in one speci-

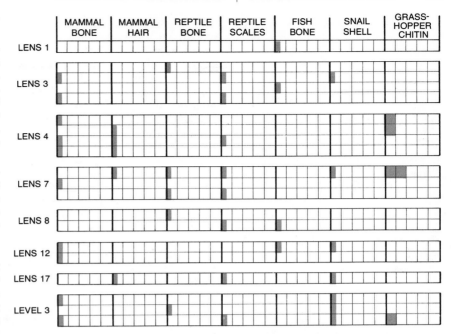

ANIMAL REMAINS in the coprolites from the Texas rock-shelter are not abundant. Rather than reflecting any shortage of animal protein in the Archaic Indians' diet, however, this is probably attributable to the more efficient digestion of meat. Quantitatively the item most in evidence is the grasshopper; rodents, lizards and fishes were also eaten.

men reached 81 percent [*see illustration on pages 260 and 261*]. Sotol pollen was found in at least one specimen from all but two strata. In the earliest deposit at the site the proportion of sotol pollen in two specimens exceeded 90 percent. Five of the eight strata yielded specimens that contained yucca pollen; in Lens 3 and Lens 8 the proportion was greater than 80 percent, and in Lens 4 the proportion in four of the six specimens exceeded 90 percent.

Cactus flowers appear to have been less popular. Pollen from pincushion-cactus blooms was found only in specimens from three strata. Lens 3 contained the maximum concentration: 57 percent. Prickly-pear flowers were somewhat more highly valued; only Lens 1 lacked any trace of their pollen. Nevertheless, only Lens 4 (with a specimen content of 71 percent) and the earliest deposit (with a content of 20 percent) show evidence of significant consumption of this cactus flower. When one considers that the two cacti grow in similar habitats and bloom in the same season, it is puzzling to find that only four specimens contained both pollens in trace amounts or more. The scanty evidence for the simultaneous consumption of the two flowers may reflect some unknown dietary preference or may simply be due

to the limited size of the coprolite collection.

In addition to the goosefoot seeds associated with the Cheno-Am pollen the collection contained many other macroscopic plant materials. The inhabitants of the rock-shelter ate not only the flowers but also the leaves of several monocotyledonous plants such as yucca, sotol and agave. They also ingested flowers from the lead tree and the mesquite. As one of us (Bryant) knows from personal experience, mesquite flowers are quite bitter when they are eaten raw. Perhaps the blossoms were boiled to make tea or were allowed to ferment to render them more palatable. Some specimens were found to contain tree bark in considerable quantities; what treatment, if any, made bark an acceptable item of diet is not known. Perhaps its use was medicinal.

The amount of animal protein eaten by the inhabitants of the shelter, except for that in grasshoppers, may have been quite limited [*see illustration above*]. Among the fragments of animal material identified in our analysis are the bones of fishes the size of minnows, the scales of small reptiles (probably lizards) and the shells of land snails.

The evidence of the plant materials bearing on the seasons when the rock-shelter was occupied included some variables. In Lens 1, near the surface, the limited number of coprolite specimens at first raised doubts about the adequacy of the sample. Nonetheless, the 81 percent proportion of agave pollen in one of the two specimens and the 66 percent proportion of lead-tree pollen in the other suggest that the shelter was tenanted in late spring and early summer. The flowers of those plants bloom at that time of the year. Occupation in late spring and early summer is also suggested by the quantities of cactus and yucca pollen and of wild-onion bulbs in the two specimens. The content of windborne pollen similarly supports this conclusion; hackberry and pine are both spring-pollinating plants.

With two exceptions much the same kind of late-spring and early-summer residence seems to hold true for the other strata at the site. Lens 8 contained only two specimens; the lack of plant material in one of the two makes any judgment about the season of occupation impossible. In Lens 12, although the data for pollen other than the windborne varieties are skimpy, many of the other plant materials in the specimens, such as cactus fiber and yucca fiber, could have been collected and ingested at any time of the year. Because cactus fruits ripen late in summer and because prickly-pear seeds are present in several specimens from Lens 12, it seems reasonable to assume that at the time this deposit was formed the site was occu-

pied in middle and late summer. All in all the coprolite evidence indicates that the Texas rock-shelter was visited annually during the warmer months by a nomadic population of primitive hunters and gatherers.

The most ancient coprolites recovered at the shelter were less than 3,000 years old. What might one learn from specimens of much greater antiquity? Before Callen's untimely death he examined four supposedly human specimens from the Neanderthal site of Lazaret in France. The context of the discovery of the Lazaret specimens suggests that they were between 50,000 and 70,000 years old. Callen found on immersing the specimens that all four of them failed to

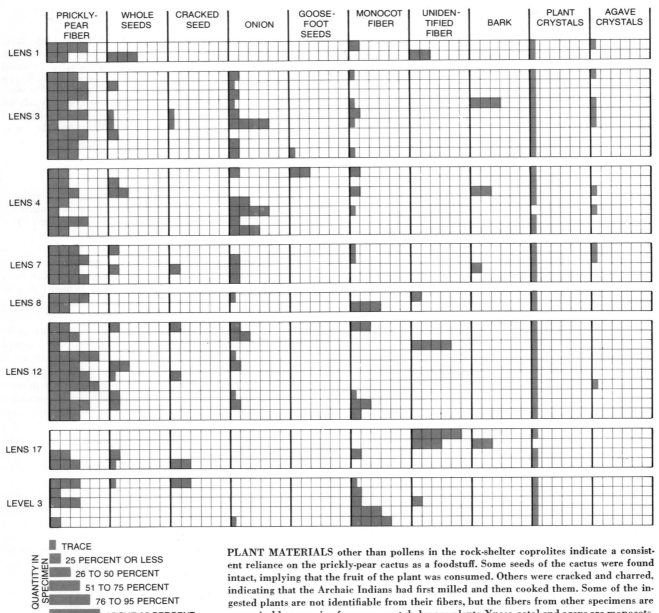

PLANT MATERIALS other than pollens in the rock-shelter coprolites indicate a consistent reliance on the prickly-pear cactus as a foodstuff. Some seeds of the cactus were found intact, implying that the fruit of the plant was consumed. Others were cracked and charred, indicating that the Archaic Indians had first milled and then cooked them. Some of the ingested plants are not identifiable from their fibers, but the fibers from other specimens are recognizable as coming from monocotyledonous plants. Yucca, sotol and agave are monocots.

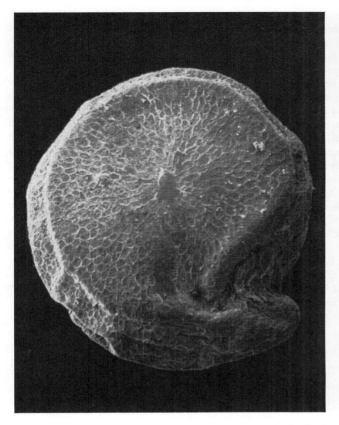

SEEDS, frequently found in coprolites, may identify the kind of plant that bore them. This quinoa seed is enlarged 70 diameters.

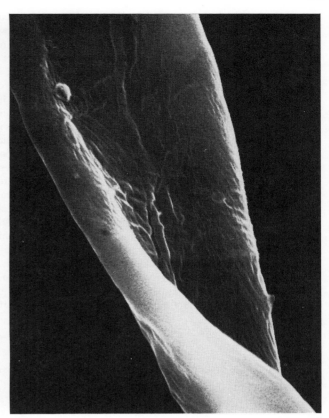

FIBERS make up another class of plant materials with forms indicative of origins. This is a cotton fiber, enlarged 6,000 diameters.

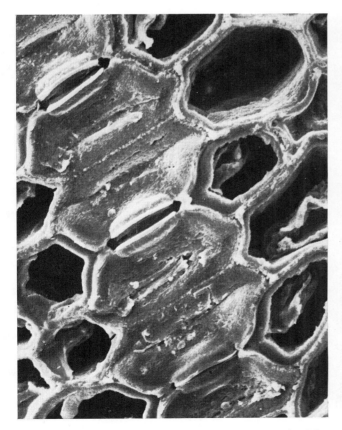

STOMATES on leaf surfaces also make identification possible. This agave leaf fragment, from a coprolite, is enlarged 800 diameters.

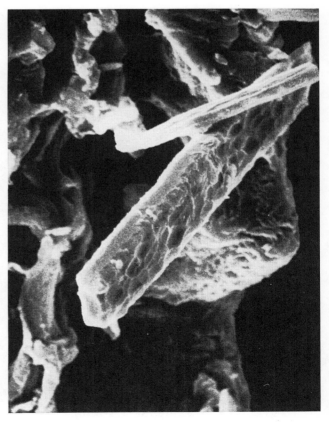

PLANT CRYSTALS can reveal details of diet. Enlarged 3,000 diameters is a crystal (*long rod*) present only in *Agave lecheguilla*.

color the solution. In two of them he could identify fragments of bone, hairs and bits of charcoal. This evidence for the use of fire in the preparation of meat convinced him that at least these two specimens were probably of human origin. He did not find plant materials in any of the specimens.

Recently in our laboratory we began work on a large sample of much older material: some 500 supposedly human coprolites from a French Mediterranean site, Terra Amata. The specimens were made available to us by the excavator, Henry de Lumley [see the article "A Paleolithic Camp at Nice," by Henry de Lumley, beginning on page 36]. Apart from coprolites no human remains were found at the site, but the kinds of stone tools that were uncovered imply that the residents of this seaside camp probably represented the species *Homo erectus*, the precursor of modern man. De Lumley believes that the strata unearthed at Terra Amata may be as much as 300,000 years old. Whereas Callen found his much younger Neanderthal specimens were chemically unreactive when they were immersed, some of the Terra Amata specimens have faintly colored the solutions in our laboratory.

Much work remains to be done with de Lumley's specimens. Nonetheless, preliminary analysis has identified grains of sand, which are almost inevitably ingested at the seashore, flecks of charcoal, which indicate the use of fire in the preparation of food, and fragments of mollusk shell, which point to one food resource that may have been exploited by the inhabitants. So far we have found no bone and no plant remains, even though analyses of other Terra Amata specimens, undertaken some years ago in the laboratory at the University of Aix-Marseilles, showed the presence of several windborne pollens and the insect-transported pollen of the broom plant (*Genista*).

The potential of analyses such as these for giving the archaeologist both a detailed inventory of preferred foodstuffs in a variety of prehistoric contexts and a relatively precise indication of the time of the year when transient sites were occupied has gained increasing recognition. Today our laboratory regularly receives for analysis specimens that have been unearthed by investigators in all parts of the world. As the work continues perhaps we can provide other glimpses of prehistoric human behavior as unexpected as our discovery that the Archaic Indians of southwestern Texas were, at least in a dietary sense, "flower people."

# 26

# The Planning of a Maya Ceremonial Center

by Norman Hammond
*May 1972*

*The center at Lubaantún in British Honduras called
for a huge investment in labor and materials. When
a choice had to be made between cutting costs and
adhering to the plan, the plan won out*

Among the pre-Columbian civilizations of the New World the Aztec and Inca empires that the conquistadors overthrew are commonly believed to have been the most advanced, but this distinction may well belong to the Maya, whose culture reached its apogee in the first millennium of the Christian Era during what is known as the Classic period. The brilliance of Maya aesthetics is apparent in Classic stucco work, vase-painting and fresco; the intellectual achievements of the Classic period include not only a written language but also calendric and astronomical studies of a high order. Classic Maya civilization was centered in the lowland jungle province of Petén in Guatemala and in adjacent Belize (British Honduras), extending northward and westward into Mexico and southward and eastward into Honduras and El Salvador.

The civilization of the Classic period flourished within a surprisingly loose framework compared, for example, with the partly contemporaneous pre-Columbian culture centered on Teotihuacán a few hundred miles away in the Valley of Mexico. In the first half of the first millennium the rulers of Teotihuacán built one of the largest and most precisely planned urban complexes known in ancient times [see the article "Teotihuacán," by René Millon, beginning on page 221]. Where the Maya held sway in the tropical lowlands, however, there were no such cities. The numerous population was scattered among widely dispersed farmers' hamlets. Living in relative isolation and sheltered in dwellings built of perishable materials, the great majority of the Maya supported themselves by raising crops (principally maize and beans) in forest clearings they prepared for planting by the slash-and-burn method. At intervals were a few clusters of more permanent structures built of stone, but these were not cities in any conventional sense; the most spectacular of their masonry edifices are lofty pyramids like those the first Spaniards saw used as temples in Aztec Mexico. As a result it has become customary to call these clusters of stone buildings "ceremonial centers."

From an economic viewpoint the construction of a Maya ceremonial center constituted an enormous investment in energy and materials. More than a century of archaeological investigation has shown that within a range of regional variation the centers are all much alike architecturally. Where uneven terrain had to be leveled, this was achieved by building foundation platforms of rough stone rubble retained by masonry walls. Rising from these foundations are stone structures arrayed around a number of open plazas.

Each structure consists of a freestanding masonry wall that encloses a more or less rectangular area, filled with rubble up to the height of the retaining wall; in general the greater the area enclosed, the higher the wall. On top of these structures stood superstructures of various kinds. It is customary to call the superstructures on high pyramidal substructures "temples" and those on lower and more extensive substructures "palaces." Most of the superstructures on lower and smaller substructures, having been made of perishable materials, have entirely disappeared; many are known to have been residences, whereas others are buildings of unknown purpose.

Amid the cluster of interconnected plazas with structures grouped around them, each Maya center is likely to have one or more "ball courts." Unlike the term palace, the term ball court is not guesswork. It is known from sculptured monuments that these distinctive structures were used for playing a game that might be described as a cross between volleyball and soccer. Each ball court consists of a pair of steep rubble mounds faced with masonry; these mounds form the sides of a long, narrow field of play where the Maya engaged in the ritual contest they called *pok-ta-pok*.

In most Maya centers built during the Classic period the plaza in front of the major temple pyramid contained sculptured stone monuments that archaeologists call by the Greek name "stelae." These bear the images of rulers, some of them shown with their captives, and long hieroglyphic inscriptions that seem to contain historical information. The portions of the inscriptions that record dates in Maya calendric notation can be read. The dates inscribed on stelae and on sculptured altars at the Classic sites of Piedras Negras and Yaxchilán, two ceremonial centers on the Usumacinta River in the Petén region, and Quiriguá, a third center to the southeast, seem to record events in the lives of several rulers. The first of these dated monuments was erected during the third century of the Christian Era and the last at the end of the ninth century.

The emphasis in recent years on settlement-pattern research in the Maya area has resulted in the common presumption that the location and layout of ceremonial centers and the distribution of settlements around them are due solely to environmental dictates, without the deliberate planning apparent in such places as Teotihuacán. On the other hand, the social investment in labor and materials required for the construction of such a center suggests that a certain amount of consideration must have gone into the work: the marshaling of labor, the specification of dimensions, the collecting of vast amounts of rubble fill and masonry facing blocks, and the feeding of all these things into the construction program. The successful integration of such elements and the abilities of a range of specialized artisans argues strongly in favor of a preordained plan, and one that specified the layout and subsequent function of the site.

My opportunity to seek evidence for Maya planning came recently. The occasion was the surveying and excavation of Lubaantún, a small Maya ceremonial center in the Rio Grande basin of southern Belize. Field studies were pursued there, primarily under the sponsorship of the University of Cambridge and the Peabody Museum of Archaeology and Ethnology of Harvard University, in 1970. Three main programs were undertaken. The first was the detailed mapping of the center and of a sample of the surrounding settlement area; this work was done by Michael Walton, a professional architect, and Basilio Ah, a local Mopan Maya Indian with previous mapping experience. The second program called for excavation at the center to determine both the sequence of construction and the dates of occupation.

The third was an ecological survey of the Rio Grande region, including a study of the local geology by John Hazelden of the University of Cambridge, to determine what kinds of natural resources—building stone, materials for tools, forest products for construction, plants for medicine and ritual, wild game and other foodstuffs—were or had once been locally available.

Lubaantún lies in the foothill zone of the Maya Mountains [see illustration on opposite page]; it occupies a long sloping ridge that runs from north to south. To the east and west the ridge falls away steeply and is bounded by creeks. The slope of the ridge is gradual, eventually descending sharply to the level of the Rio Columbia, a branch of the Rio Grande that passes a few hundred meters south of the site. Stream erosion has carved the surrounding land into a maze of low, round-topped hillocks; as a result the ridge is the only fairly level tract of any size in the area.

The region around Lubaantún is well endowed with natural resources. The Rio Columbia contains an abundance of freshwater mollusks. It also provides a waterway, navigable by canoe, that runs

via the Rio Grande all the way to the Caribbean; the seacoast is some 25 kilometers east of Lubaantún as the crow flies. Hazelden's survey showed that thinly bedded sandstone, limestone and siltstone are available along the riverbanks and in the nearby foothills, and that all the stone needed for the center could have been quarried within a radius of three kilometers. Potter's clay is also found along the river, and such forest products as copal gum, valued by the Maya as incense, can be gathered on the wooded coastal plain. Moreover, the foothill zone where Lubaantún is situated has some of the most fertile soil in all southern Belize. There is game in the hills and on the coastal plain, waterfowl in swampy areas, and mollusks, crustaceans and fish along the coast. The canoe route to the coast covers 90 kilometers, or almost four times the straight-line distance, and might be thought to have been traveled infrequently by the people of Lubaantún. When Elizabeth S. Wing of the Florida State Museum analyzed the animal remains we recovered at the ceremonial center, however, she found that nearly 40 percent of them were of marine origin.

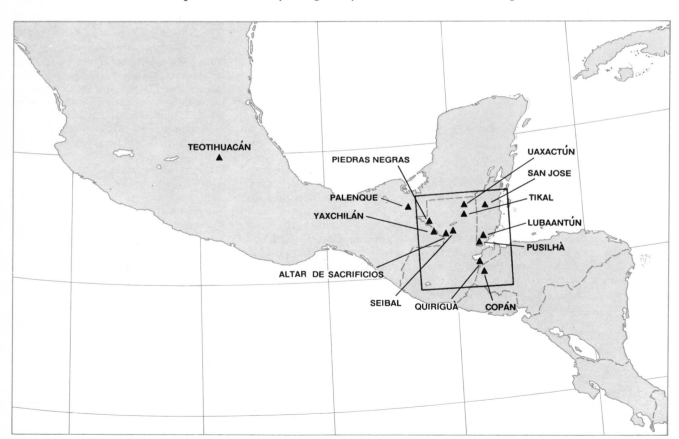

**PETÉN LOWLANDS** of northern Guatemala border on Mexico to the north and west and on Honduras and British Honduras to the south and east. Twelve lowland Maya centers of the Classic period are shown; the region is shown in more detail on the opposite page.

Our excavations showed that when the Lubaantún center was founded early in the eighth century, it consisted of a single large platform covering an area of some 2,500 square meters on the part of the ridge that was later occupied by an open plaza we have designated Plaza IV [see "b" in illustration on pages 272 and 273]. On the north side of this first platform stood a series of narrow rubble-filled substructures faced with stone. We were surprised to find that the original construction had begun so late; by early in the eighth century the Late Classic florescence of Maya civilization was already at its height. As will be seen, the lateness of the date has important historical implications.

In any event the first platform at the center was almost completely buried under later construction. In the second phase of the work two more large platforms were built north and south of the first, and large plaza areas were laid out beyond the north platform [see "c" in illustration on pages 272 and 273], quadrupling the area of Lubaantún. At one side of the north platform, facing what was later to be Plaza IV, the builders raised their first temple pyramid. We have designated it Structure 12. Its present size is the result of later construction that has entirely engulfed the original pyramid. Construction of a ball court on the southern extension completed the second-phase work at Lubaantún.

The first undeniable evidence that planning outweighed expediency in the building of the center appeared during the third phase of construction. Early work during the third phase had extended the north platform southward until it covered most of the 2,500-square-meter platform built in the first phase. It was then decided to enlarge the first pyramid and add two new ones. The size of these, as planned, meant that space in the center of the site was going to be very short indeed; for the first time a crucial decision was forced on the rulers of Lubaantún. Was the site to be extended still farther north and south along the ridge, where the shallow curve of the crest meant that a large surface area could be gained with the construction of a relatively shallow platform? Or was centralization more important than economy and should the center be expanded laterally even though the acquisition of a small area meant the construction of high platforms and the investment of a prodigious amount of labor and material resources? The latter decision was taken, and the growth of Lubaantún changed

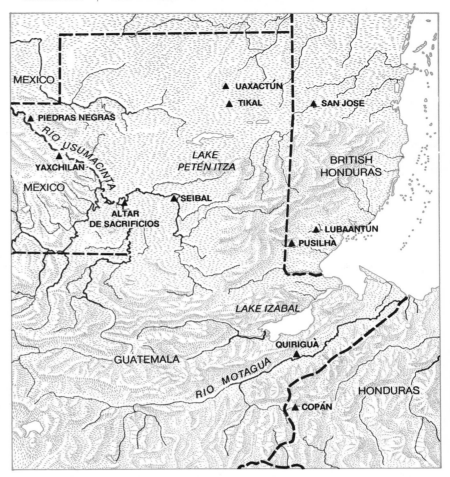

LUBAANTÚN IS SITUATED in the foothills of the Maya Mountains, an isolated highland area in southern British Honduras. It is among the last of the centers built by the Maya.

from modification of the local topography to the creation of an artificial topography [see "d" in illustration on pages 272 and 273]. The retaining walls that gained the builders six meters' horizontal space to the east and west are multiterraced and more than 11 meters high. The amount of rubble that fills the space between ridge slope and wall must exceed 3,000 cubic meters. It is hard to imagine clearer proof that the planned layout of Lubaantún was sufficiently important to force the builders to overcome the limitations of local topography.

In the fourth phase of construction at the center still more artificial topography was created. Just beyond the newly extended main platform was a gully cut by a small stream on the west side of the ridge. This watercourse was now covered by rubble-filled platforms, forming a series of broad plazas that led down the steep slope almost to the bank of the creek at the bottom [see "e" in illustration on pages 272 and 273]. Whether the most southerly part of this extension was built during the fourth phase or the fifth

remains uncertain. In any event the major enterprise during the fifth and final phase of construction at Lubaantún was the refurbishing of the central part of the site. Broad staircases were built at the north and south ends of Plaza V, and a second ball court was constructed on a new platform east of the plaza. At the same time a new staircase was added to Structure 12, the largest of the temple pyramids at the site.

The building of Lubaantún, which had been in progress for between 100 and 150 years, was now essentially complete. Begun early in the eighth century, the work ended not long before the ceremonial center was abandoned sometime between A.D. 850 and 900. The plan of Lubaantún that we have now is a palimpsest, so to speak, of all five periods, but it is essentially the plan of the site as it was functioning at the time of its abandonment. It is only at this period that we can fully comprehend the zonal structure and traffic pattern within the ceremonial center.

As a result of the mapping project we

know not only the total number of edifices that were built at Lubaantún but also exactly where they stood in relation to one another and the exact dimensions of each. The structures range in height from as little as 20 centimeters to more than 12 meters and in basal area from 40 square meters to more than 500 square meters. As at other Maya ceremonial centers, each structure served as a foundation for some kind of superstructure. Elsewhere a number of these superstructures, in particular the temples and palaces, were built of stone and still survive. At Lubaantún, however, all the superstructures apparently were built of wood and no longer exist. They presumably had walls of poles and roofs of palm thatch, like the Maya houses in the vicinity today. Fragments of the clay that was daubed on the pole walls of one temple have been preserved by fire; the impressions show that the poles were a little over three inches in diameter.

When we compared the dimensions of the various foundation structures, we found that they fell into four distinct clusters. The pyramids are at the top of the scale; the smallest of the three has a basal area of more than 500 square meters and is more than five meters high. Our system of classification placed structures this large or larger in the "religious" category. At the bottom of the scale are numerous small, low structures, all less than 1.2 meters high and 100 square me-

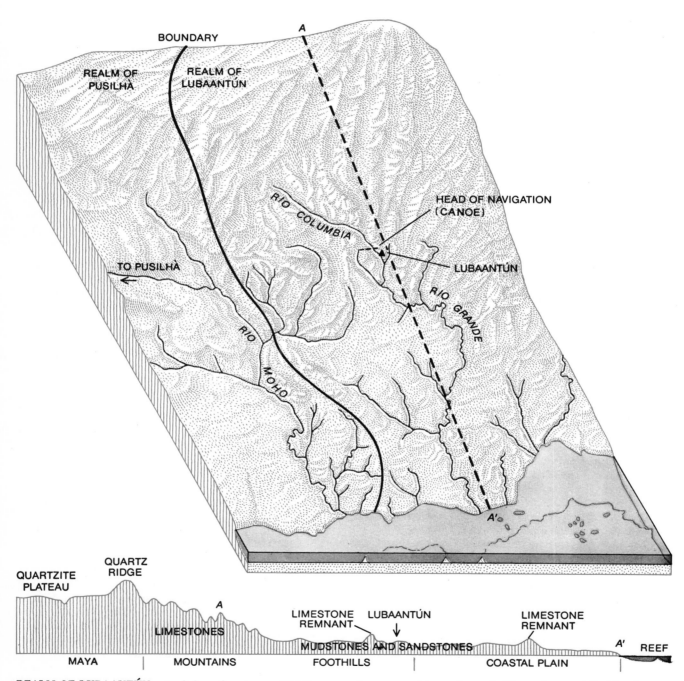

REALM OF LUBAANTÚN extended northwest some 25 kilometers from the foothills of the Maya Mountains to the highland plateau and southeast another 25 kilometers to the low-lying Caribbean coast and the sheltered waters of the barrier reef offshore (*see cross section at bottom*). The region controlled by the ceremonial center consisted of some 1,600 square kilometers, and the population may have numbered 50,000. The soil in the foothills was fertile, and the realm was rich in raw materials and wild foods.

ters in area. We assume that they were house foundations and have classified them as "residences." Between these extremes are two groups of structures with dimensions that overlap with respect to area but not with respect to height. The structures of the smaller group range from more than 1.2 meters in height to less than two meters; none is less than 150 or more than 280 square meters in basal area. On the basis of size and location we have dubbed this group of structures "elite residences." The structures of the larger group, ranging in height from two to 3.6 meters with a basal area as large as 330 square meters, include the two Lubaantún ball courts and a number of other structures that are neither obviously residential nor obviously ritual. We have placed all of them in a nonspecific category: "ceremonial structures."

When we marked the structures on the site map according to this four-category classification, an interesting correlation emerged. The structures surrounding any particular plaza usually belonged in the same category. Plaza IV, with its three pyramids, is a prime example; it is the only one of the 20 plazas at Lubaantún that belongs in the "religious" category. Furthermore, the five plazas immediately contiguous to Plaza IV all belong to the "ceremonial" category, and six of the seven most remote plazas at the site fall in the "residential" category. The master plan for Lubaantún seems to have called for a religious core surrounded by an inner zone of ceremonial plazas and an outer zone of residences. Such a layout follows a simple concentric-zone model, modified at Lubaantún only by the requirements of topography.

Common sense suggests that the traffic plan for such a concentric-zone model would call for residential areas with low accessibility and public areas with high accessibility. Religious areas would be either accessible or secluded depending on the nature of the cult. For example, if access to a central religious area was restricted, this fact would suggest worship of an exclusive and elitist nature.

In order to test this hypothesis we conducted a topological analysis of the potential traffic flow at Lubaantún without regard for the presumed functions of the plazas as deduced from the categories of structures surrounding them. Our first step was to reduce the pattern of the major plazas and their interconnections to a planar graph [see graph in bottom illustration at right]. The graph en-

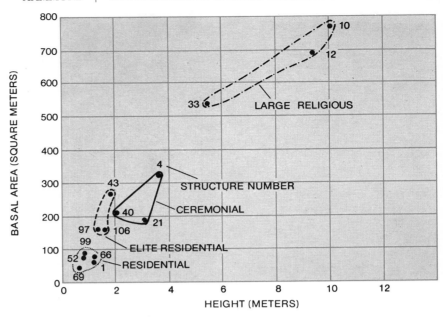

MEASUREMENT OF THE STRUCTURES at Lubaantún showed a proportional relation between height and basal area. When both measurements are plotted on a graph, the structures typically fall within one of four clusters. The pyramids of Plaza IV cover the most area and are the highest of all the structures at the site. Adjacent to the more remote plazas were the lowest and smallest structures; these had presumably been house foundations. Of the structures in two intermediate clusters, the higher were probably foundations for buildings that served "ceremonial" purposes; the lower may have been occupied by the elite.

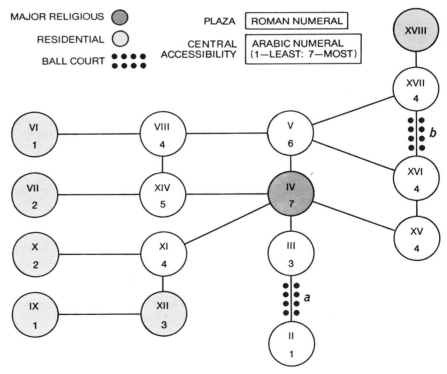

PLANAR GRAPH OF THE PRINCIPAL PLAZAS at Lubaantún and their interconnections allowed a topological analysis of the accessibility and centrality of each. An index of central accessibility showed that Plaza IV, the religious center of the site, was the most centrally accessible, with a maximum index value of 7. Of the eight least accessible plazas, all with an index value no greater than 3, six were bordered by small, low structures that were probably occupied by houses. A major difference is evident between the first ball court at the site, which was quite private (a), and the second, which was more public (b).

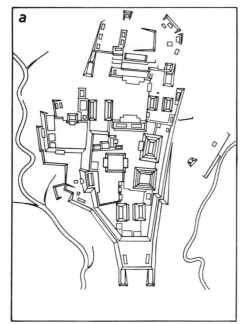

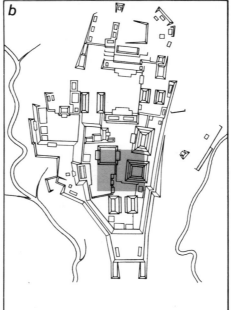

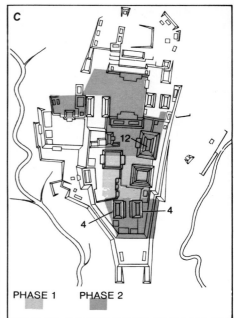

LUBAANTÚN GREW in the five phases outlined in this sequence of illustrations. The center after its completion is shown schematically at far left (*a*). In the first construction phase (*b*) a rectangular platform covering 2,500 square meters was built astride the north-south ridge that forms the long axis of the site. During the second phase (*c*) another platform was added to the south of the first, and plaza areas and a third platform were added to the north. The first pyramid at the site was built on one side of the north platform and the first ball court was built on the south platform. During the third phase (*d*) a southerly addition to the north plat-

abled us to calculate for each plaza an index of centrality and an index of accessibility. Combined, these indexes provided a rating of central-accessibility that ranged from a minimum value of 1 to a maximum value of 7.

We then compared the topological analysis with our estimates of the functions served by the various plazas. Our hypothesis of low accessibility in residential areas was confirmed. The most secluded of all the plazas, with the minimum rating of 1, were the plazas numbered VI, IX and XVIII, which we had classified as residential, and Plaza II, which we had classified as ceremonial. The next most secluded, with ratings of 2 or 3, were the residential plazas numbered VII, X and XII and a second ceremonial plaza, Plaza III. The most centrally accessible plaza at the site, with the maximum rating of 7, proved to be Plaza IV, the religious center of the site.

The fact that two ceremonial plazas, Plaza III and Plaza II, were among those with minimal accessibility ratings meant that the site layout called for a striking decline in accessibility southward along the central axis of Lubaantún. The accessibility rating of Plaza III is four points lower than the rating of its neighboring plaza to the north, and the rating of Plaza II is the minimum possible. Since these two plazas form the end zones of

the first ball court built at Lubaantún and because the ball court can only be reached by way of Plaza IV, the site's religious center, the question arises: Were playing and watching the ball game restricted activities?

It is known from early Spanish accounts that the Maya ball game had ritual overtones; sculptures at Chichén Itzá indicate that some matches even ended with the sacrifice of the losing players. Taking this evidence and the restricted access at Lubaantún into consideration, it seems probable that if any part of the religious practice during the early days at the ceremonial center was confined to the elite, that part was the ball game.

The Spanish accounts, however, indicate that for all its ritual overtones the ball game was open to public view. This suggests that the fact the second ball court at Lubaantún, the one constructed late in the history of the center, is located in a much more public part of the center is significant. The second court lies just off Plaza V, a highly accessible area: plazas XVII and XVIII, which are its end zones, also rate high in accessibility. Perhaps a change in Maya attitudes regarding the esoteric nature of the game occurred in the interval between the building of the first court and the building of the second. If that is what hap-

pened, the trend toward a more public ritual that seems evident in the middle of the ninth century at Lubaantún persisted throughout the post-Classic period and on down to the time of the Conquest.

In summary, the traffic-flow analysis confirmed our commonsense hypothesis that the center's residential areas were secluded and its public areas more accessible. Concerning the question of whether the religious observances were public or restricted, common sense had identified Plaza IV, with its three pyramids, as the religious center of Lubaantún. By showing that Plaza IV was also the most accessible plaza at the site, traffic analysis suggests unrestricted public access to religious activities.

Plaza V, just to the north, ranks next in accessibility. This open area, with its broad stairways, is perhaps the most spacious of all the plazas at Lubaantún, and its high accessibility strengthens our suspicion that, with or without the contiguous Plaza VIII, this was the marketplace for the center. Finally, the fact that for a century or more the only ball court at Lubaantún was an area with sharply restricted access suggests that, at least until very late in Classic times, the ball game was confined to an elite group within a well-stratified society.

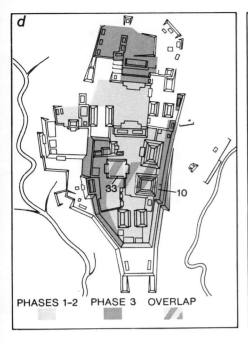

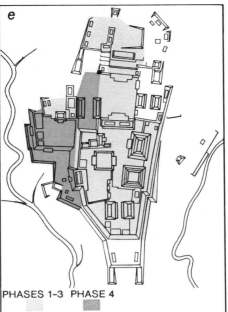

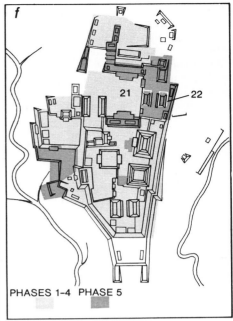

form covered up most of the first-phase platform at the site, and adequate foundations for two more pyramids were provided by new platforms built over the steep east and west slopes of the ridge. Construction in the fourth phase (e) included a series of platforms on the west slope that descended almost to the creek at the bottom of the ridge. In the final phase the main construction (f) consisted of a second ball court east of Plaza V and new staircases for Plaza V and for Structure 12, the first of the pyramids at the center. Growth of the center to the east and west regardless of the immense cost indicates the builders' adherence to a fixed plan.

Perhaps it is not too much to propose here a wider archaeological application of assessments of this kind. Analysis of the centrality and accessibility of the different areas that make up "palace" complexes in, for example, Mesopotamia or Crete or Mycenaean Greece might suggest functions quite different from those enshrined in long accepted but essentially poetic phrases such as "the queen's antechamber" or "lustral area."

Why was Lubaantún built where it was? The answer to the question is suggested by the results both of our mapping and ecological surveys and of our excavations. These show that the influence of the ceremonial center was felt not only adjacent to but well away from the site itself. Most of the low, round-topped hills on all sides of Lubaantún are surmounted by small masonry and rubble platforms; the dressed-stone retaining walls are one or two meters high and the rubble serves to level off the summit. These structures, on a smaller scale, are exactly like the great platforms at Lubaantún. Furthermore, they support house foundations in numbers sufficient to indicate that 1,200 to 1,300 people resided within a one-kilometer radius of the ceremonial center. This is scarcely a large population, but it is as densely concentrated as the local topography permits.

These hill platforms and house foundations represent a social investment in labor and materials that, although it is dispersed, is comparable to the more concentrated investment that produced the complex structures of the ceremonial center. The scale of the work also implies an adequate supply of food for the inhabitants of the district, which suggests in turn that location of the center in the belt of fertile soil along the foothills of the Maya Mountains was scarcely accidental.

Why was the center built, however, at precisely this place? The soil zone extends a considerable distance to both the northeast and the southwest, which suggests that factors in addition to the prospect of good crops must have entered into the decision to build the center here. One of the factors must have been the propinquity of the site to the Rio Columbia. Not only was the stream a source of water and the mollusks from it a reliable source of protein (their shells appeared by the thousands in our excavations) but also the head of navigation by canoe lies near Lubaantún. Goods coming upstream from the Caribbean would have been transferred from canoe to porter in this area. Moreover, this spot is also where the main overland trail along the base of the foothills crosses the river. Lubaantún was thus in a position to

control canoe traffic to and from the coast and overland traffic along the foothills. In effect, the center dominated the entire Rio Grande basin, a "realm" extending for some 50 kilometers from the high plateau of the Maya Mountains southeastward to the Caribbean shore. The entire realm is some 1,600 square kilometers in extent; its population may have numbered as many as 50,000.

Our excavations made it clear that Lubaantún was the center of a flourishing regional marketing system. From the Maya Mountains came the metamorphic rock used to make not only axe heads of stone but also the *manos,* or stone rollers, and *metates,* or shallow stone troughs, that are used together to grind maize. From the Caribbean coast, which was as far away in the opposite direction, came marine shells used for ornaments and the seafood that forms such a high percentage of the animal remains at the site. In addition, trade extended far beyond the frontiers of the realm. Two sources in the highlands of Guatemala, identified by Fred H. Stross of the University of California at Berkeley, provided obsidian, which can be flaked into fine blades with a razor-sharp edge. Also from the highlands came tripod *metates* made of lava. From the south came plumes from the cock quet-

**CEREMONIAL CENTER at Lubaantún consisted of 11 major structures and many minor ones grouped around 20 plazas. A number of these are identified in the map on the opposite page by Arabic and Roman numerals respectively. Construction of the center began in the eighth century after Christ, late in the Classic Maya period, and continued for 150 years.**

zal to adorn the rulers of Lubaantún and from an unidentified highland source came jade for their jewels.

In exchange for these imports the inhabitants of Lubaantún evidently traded the beans of the cacao tree, which are used to make chocolate and were the universal currency of Middle America in pre-Columbian times. As I have noted, the soil around Lubaantún is fertile. A study of all the soils in the region in terms of their utility to the Maya of the Classic period was conducted recently by Charles Wright of the United Nations Food and Agriculture Organization. He found that Lubaantún stands in the center of the largest zone of top-quality soil for cacao-tree culture in all of southern Belize. As Spanish records attest, cacao beans were traded between this lowland area and the highlands of Guatemala in post-Conquest times. That the tree and its fruit were known in Lubaantún is apparent from a figurine of the Classic period excavated there; it depicts a musician wearing a cacao-pod pendant [*see illustration at left*]. It seems clear that the prosperity of the realm was in large measure due to its possession of one of the sources of this scarce product, which was in constant demand. The trade with the Guatemalan highlands, where a completely different range of resources was available, was in many ways a form of economic symbiosis, existing for the mutual benefit of both partners and fostering diplomatic as well as commercial contacts that it was mutually useful to maintain.

The question of why Lubaantún was built when it was remains unanswered. The entire Rio Grande basin appears to have been unoccupied territory until the eighth century, when the center was founded. So far not a single object made before Late Classic times, not even a potsherd, has been discovered at any site in the region. To the southwest of the Rio Grande basin another Maya site, a ceremonial center named Pusilhà, has been discovered in the basin of the Moho River. Some 20 stelae have been found there; the dates they bear range from A.D. 573 to 731. Pusilhà was therefore functioning as a ceremonial center during all of the seventh century. Moreover, the most recent of the Pusilhà stelae dates and the presence there of Lubaantún-style figurines show that the center was still occupied well after the foundation of Lubaantún.

Pusilhà was flourishing before Lubaantún was even built. This fact has given rise to a number of cause-and-effect hypotheses. According to one of them, the Maya who built Lubaantún were former residents of the Pusilhà realm who migrated northward as a re-

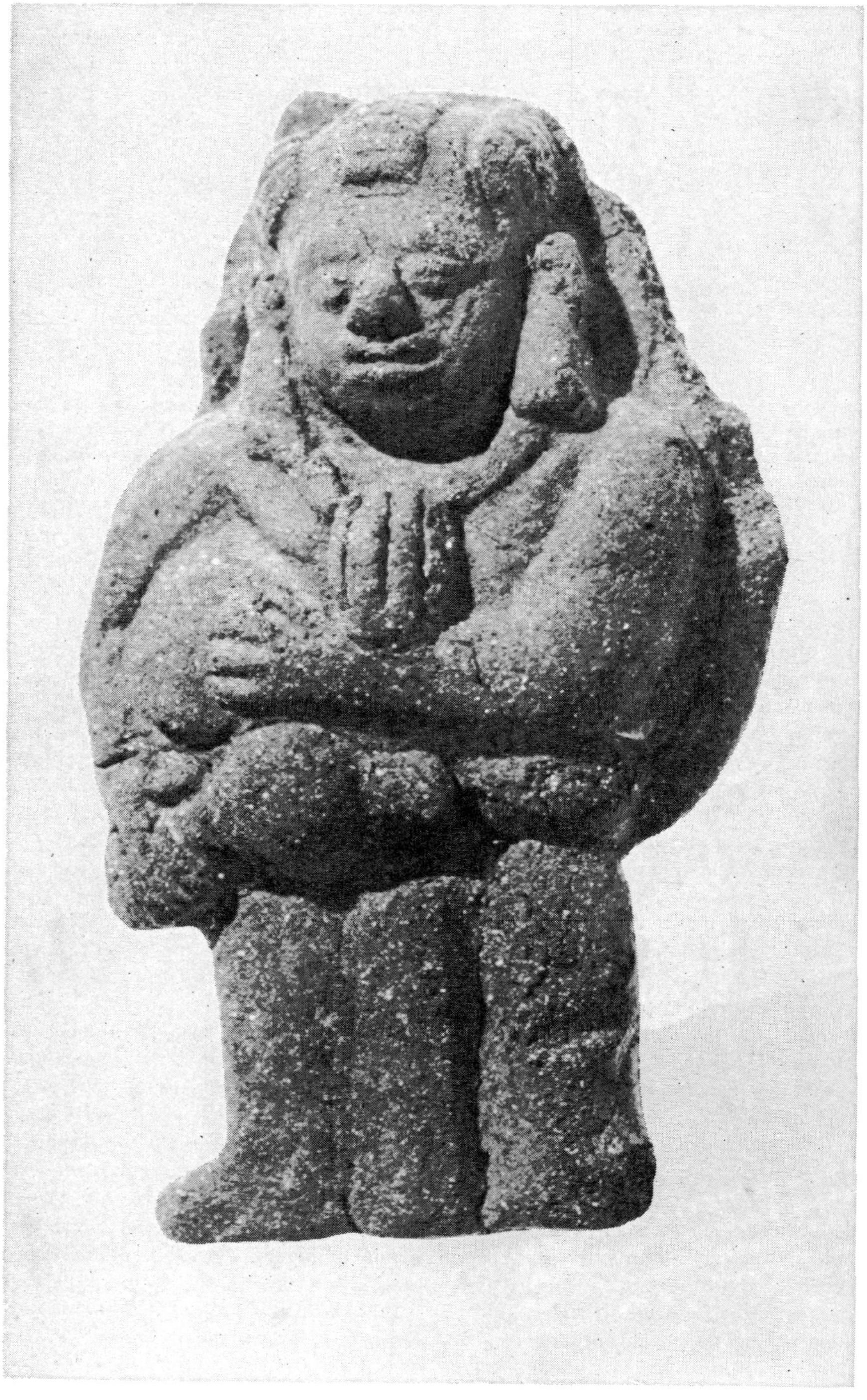

**MUSICIAN WEARING A PENDANT in the form of a pod from the cacao tree is the subject of a figurine of the Classic period found at Lubaantún. Evidence that cacao was known to the people of Lubaantún, taken together with evidence that local soils are particularly suited to raising cacao trees, suggests that cacao beans were exchanged for foreign imports.**

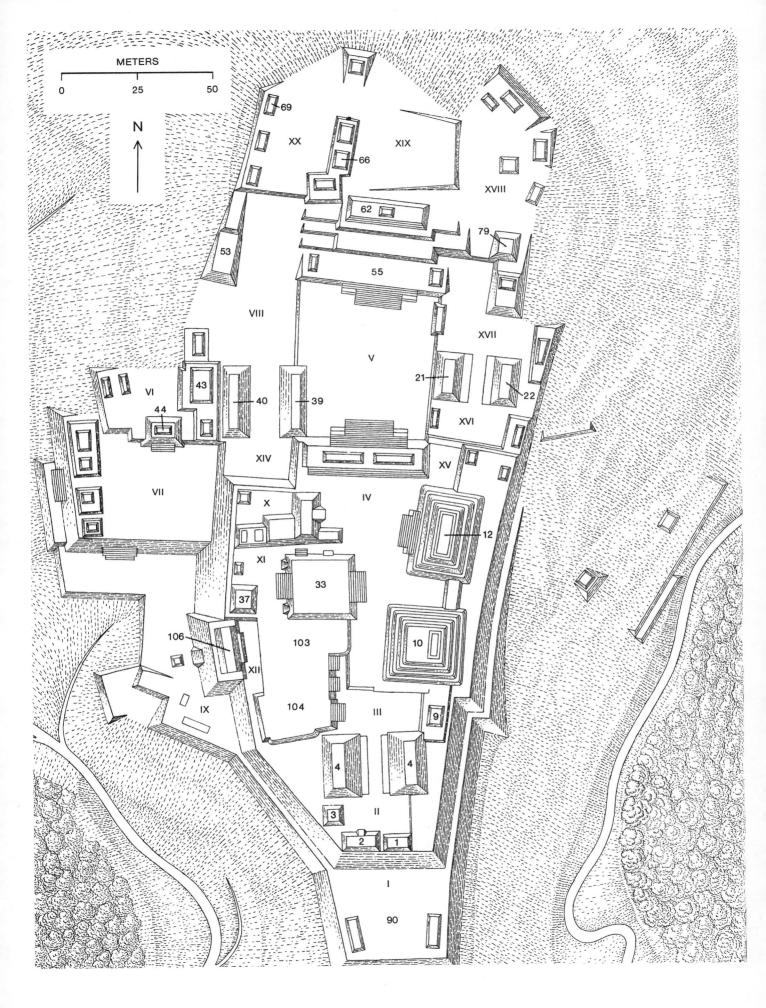

METERS

0   25   50

N

sult of population pressure or political expansion within or beyond that realm. Another hypothesis, first advanced in 1938 by Sylvanus Griswold Morley, suggested that political control had been transferred from Pusilhà to Lubaantún in the eighth century, the time when the Maya at Pusilhà ceased to raise stelae. According to the Morley hypothesis, the halt in stela-raising was evidence that the use of Pusilhà as a ceremonial center had also ceased.

The Morley hypothesis, applied more generally, has been the controlling model for much of the speculation about the collapse of Classic Maya civilization. In this view the end of the "stela cult" at each ceremonial center marked the end of the religious, political, administrative and commercial control exerted by the realm's rulers. Our studies at Lubaantún cast doubt on that line of specula-

tion. Although this Late Classic ceremonial center exerted control over a wide realm for some 150 years, not one stela, sculptured or plain, appears to have been raised there. It thus seems clear that the presence of the stela cult was not crucial to the exercise of effective religious, political and commercial control. If a center such as Lubaantún could flourish without instituting such a cult, then other ceremonial centers could have continued to exercise authority after stelae were no longer raised. Excavation at Maya sites of the Classic period to obtain articles for carbon-14 or thermoluminescence analysis might well shed more light on the decline of Maya civilization than do hypotheses that depend on the terminal dates preserved on stelae.

The stelae cult might better be viewed as a product of ideological fashion than

as an integral part of the social and economic infrastructure that supported the culture of the Maya for more than 2,000 years. Maya ceremonial centers, if Lubaantún is a fair example, drew their power not so much from the gods as from the integration of a broad range of economic resources. The economic effort may often have included, as it did at Lubaantún, the exploitation of a commodity in great demand. Seen in this light the Maya ceremonial center seems to have been more the focus of a regional marketing system and, as a result, a seat of administrative and political power than the headquarters of a primarily religious institution. In almost every aspect except population density the Maya centers equate in form and function with the preindustrial cities of the Old World.

# A Byzantine Trading Venture

by George F. Bass
*August 1971*

*Early in the seventh century a small cargo ship went
down in the eastern Mediterranean. Four seasons of
underwater investigation have reconstructed the
vessel's last voyage*

In A.D. 625 or 626 a Greek merchant vessel of 40 tons' burden was sailing south along the coast of what is now Turkey when it struck a reef some 20 miles from Halicarnassus and sank in 120 feet of water. In 1958 the wreck was discovered during a diving reconnaissance by Peter Throckmorton, and from 1961 to 1964 the underwater site was excavated by my group from the University Museum of the University of Pennsylvania. Analysis of our findings, which is now reaching completion, provides a vivid picture of a trading venture in the eastern Mediterranean during the days of the Byzantine Empire. This is the story of the ship and its last voyage.

Ten years or so before the ship went down a cypress keel had been laid in a shipyard probably located in the Aegean, in the Black Sea or in the waters between. On the keel, which was about 40 feet long, was mounted a high, curved sternpost of the same wood. (The ship's stem was probably also made of cypress, but that part of the vessel was not preserved.) Once the spine of the hull had been completed the shipwrights went on to construct the sides.

They did not, as we would today, first build a complete skeleton by adding ribs to the spine and then cover the frame with planking. Neither did they follow the practice, customary in earlier centuries, of stiffening the hull by fastening

DIVING ARCHAEOLOGISTS from the University Museum of the University of Pennsylvania, working at a depth of 120 feet off the small Turkish coastal island of Yassi Ada, guide a wire basket to the surface from the site of the seventh-century Byzantine shipwreck (*see page 284*). The basket contains timbers from the hull of the vessel.

its planks edge to edge with a series of mortise-and-tenon joints no more than four inches apart along the full length of each strake, or strip of planking. Seventh-century construction fell somewhere between these two methods; it represents the continuation of a trend, starting two or three centuries earlier, that cut down the investment in labor required to build hulls in the earlier Greco-Roman style.

Selecting pine planks, the shipwrights cut mortises in them every three feet or so and fastened the planks together edge to edge by inserting loosely fitted tenons made of oak. The hull was built up from the keel in this fashion, one strake at a time, until the waterline was reached. The builders then scored the inside of the planks to mark where ribs, made of elm, should be placed. The ribs, which rose from the keel to well above the waterline, were secured in place with iron nails driven through the pine strakes from the outside. Four pairs of heavier strakes were then run along each side of the ship; three pairs were nailed in place and the fourth pair was bolted. The uppermost pair ran along the top of the ribs. The spaces between the heavier strakes were filled by nailing additional planks to the ribs without mortise-and-tenon joining.

We know that this kind of compromise with earlier Greco-Roman practice was on the rise because we have also studied a sunken vessel that is some 250 years older than the seventh-century wreck. The hull of the older ship was made with carefully mortised planking; the mortising continued at least up to deck level and possibly all the way to the gunwale. The planks were fixed to the ribs with treenails—long wooden dowels—rather than with iron nails, and

smaller dowels held each tenon securely in place. Even by this time, however, the mortise-and-tenon joints were spaced about seven inches apart, or considerably farther apart than before. The trend was destined to continue. The practice of fastening the planks to the ribs with iron nails and omitting mortise-and-tenon joints, found only above the waterline in the seventh-century ship, advanced until the strength of a hull came to depend exclusively on the bonds between the ribs and the planking, as is true today, and mortise-and-tenon hull-stiffening disappeared.

Once the hull was entirely planked, deck beams were inserted across the width of the ship. They were supported at the ends by short L-shaped timbers and elsewhere probably by posts [*see top illustration on page 280*]. The ship was now completely decked except for the galley area at the stern and a hatch aft of the single, centrally located mast. There may also have been a smaller hatch forward, but like the stem timber this part of the vessel was not preserved. Deck beams near the stern projected beyond the hull on each side to form a pair of rectangular structures where the steering oars were mounted.

Frederick van Doorninck, Jr., of the University of California at Davis has plotted the position and angle of every nail hole and scored mark visible on the fragments of ship's hull that were salvaged. Largely on the basis of this evidence he has produced a restoration of the ship [*see illustration on next two pages*]. He was helped to visualize some of the ship's less certain features by the work of a gifted amateur marine architect, J. Richard Steffy, who has constructed a series of scale models on van Doorninck's data.

Van Doorninck calculates that the

ship was some 63 feet long, with a streamlined hull and a beam of only 17 feet. This is a length-to-width ratio of 3.6 to one, which is quite slender for a cargo vessel. The fourth-century vessel mentioned above had been beamier; its ratio was three to one. It is interesting to note in this connection that several years before either wreck was known a historian, Robert S. Lopez of Yale University, suggested the development of slimmer and swifter merchant vessels in the seventh century because of the need at that time "to dodge or outrun the hostile ships that lurked along every route." Lopez also believes the rise of the independent shipowner in the seventh century must have led to the building of small, single-deck vessels in place of the great cargo ships characteristic of the imperial Roman merchant fleet. Our seventh-century vessel seems to bear out Lopez' contentions. A ship of twice its burden was considered small in Greco-Roman times; many of the vessels plying between Alexandria and Rome carried more than 1,200 tons.

When the slim merchantman was ready for launching, its owner must have visited a ship chandler to buy the gear needed to outfit the vessel. A site recently excavated at the ancient Black Sea port of Tomis—Constanza in modern Romania—has shown us what such a shop must have been like early in the Christian Era. Stacked against a wall in a large vaulted chamber at Tomis were iron anchors with removable anchor stocks, almost identical with the ones found in the wreckage of our seventh-century ship. The owner must have obtained at least 11 such anchors from the chandler, since this is the number we recovered. He also bought a grapnel, probably for use with the ship's boat.

Why were there so many anchors? There are at least two possible explanations. First, the theory and practice of anchoring with the help of heavy anchor chain was unknown to Byzantine seamen, who did not realize that an anchor alone, without the added weight represented by a length of stout chain, is not an efficient bottom-holding device. With only rope for their anchors the mariners probably lost anchors frequently, and they may have been accustomed to carrying spares. The second possible explanation is that the ship was required by statute to carry a specified number of anchors. Such statutes are known to have been in force a few centuries later.

I mentioned that we recovered 11 an-chors. What we actually brought to the surface were 11 featureless concretions; the iron that had been at the core of each concretion had corroded away hundreds of years before. We found it possible, however, to cut into the hollow concretions with a jeweler's saw and were thus able to make exact casts of nine of the 11 anchors. Working with the anchor casts, van Doorninck was able to calculate the weight of the originals. Six of the anchors were small, each weighing about 250 Roman pounds (327.45 grams per pound); each of the three larger ones weighed about 450 pounds. The uniformity among the two

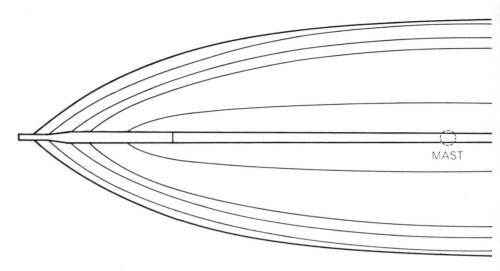

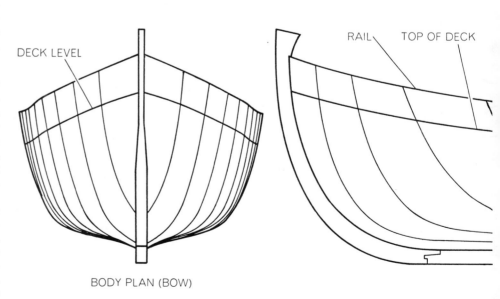

APPEARANCE OF SHIP wrecked at Yassi Ada was reconstructed after detailed study of the wood fragments (*color*) that still remained after more than 1,300 years of submersion. The study was conducted by Frederick van Doorninck, Jr., of the University of California

kinds suggests that in the seventh century, as in later times, there were regulations requiring vessels of various classes to carry a minimum number of anchors of specified sizes.

The chandlery at Tomis offered a variety of resins for sale. So, evidently, did the one patronized by our owner. His ship had already been coated with resin below the waterline, inside and out. Now he obtained a smaller amount to be melted on board in a cheap cooking pot and applied as needed to seal the pores of clay pitchers and other containers for liquids. The chandlery at Tomis also offered pigments for paint and jars full of iron nails. We do not know whether or not the owner painted his ship, although literary accounts of earlier and later times speak of many ships as being brightly colored. He did buy several bags of nails, probably with shipboard repairs in mind.

Literary accounts of the period men-

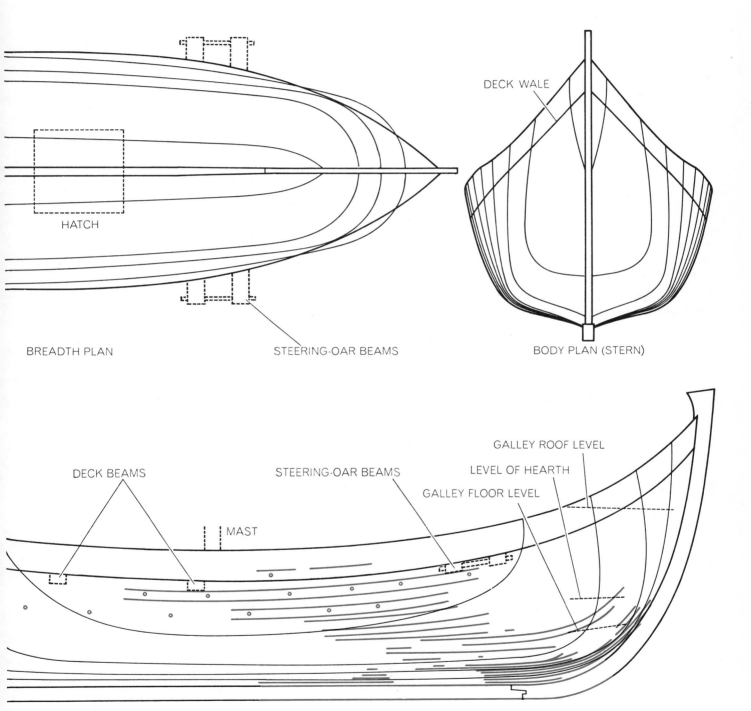

HATCH

BREADTH PLAN

STEERING-OAR BEAMS

DECK WALE

BODY PLAN (STERN)

DECK BEAMS

MAST

STEERING-OAR BEAMS

GALLEY ROOF LEVEL

LEVEL OF HEARTH

GALLEY FLOOR LEVEL

SHEER PLAN

at Davis. The pair of beams projecting outboard just forward of the galley area (*broken lines*) supported the ship's two steering oars. Between the oar beams and the vessel's single mast a deck hatch gave access to the cargo hold; there may have been another hatch forward, but no wood from this part of the ship has survived. The length of the ship at the waterline was some 55 feet.

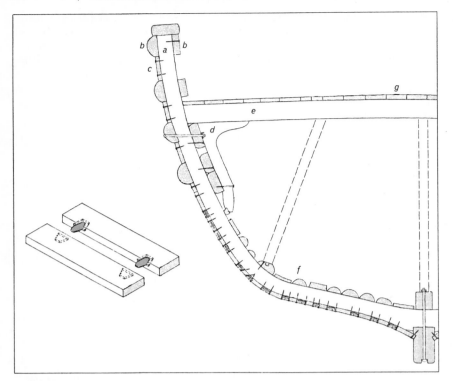

**HULL WAS BUILT** by laying planks upward from the keel. The planks were fastened edge to edge with mortise-and-tenon joints (*color*) spaced as far apart as three feet (*detail at left*). When the planking reached waterline height, the ship's ribs (*a*) were inserted and fixed to the hull planking with nails. Four pairs of heavier timbers (*b and b'*) were then laid along each side of the ship, and the exterior was completed with more planking (*c*). *L*-shaped timbers (*d*) were set inside to support deck beams (*e*), which may have needed added bracing (*broken lines*). Hold stringers (*f*) and deck planks (*g*) finished the job.

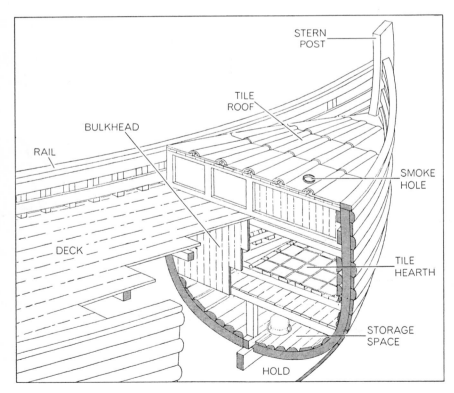

**GALLEY AREA** occupied the extreme stern of the vessel and was roofed with flat and curved tiles. The tile hearth was located to port. Its form remains conjectural. One of several arrangements (*not shown*) may have used an iron grid to brace pots against ship's motion.

tion skins for covering deck cargo in foul weather, as well as sails and cordage, and all of these the owner may have got at the chandlery. We are certain that he bought 24 oil lamps, because we found them in the wreck. It seems probable that this was another chandlery purchase; in the shop at Tomis were found not only lamps but also the molds for producing them.

With the new ship almost ready for sea it would have been time to assemble a crew. We need not depend entirely on our imagination in reconstructing the roster; a document of the seventh century or slightly later, known as the Rhodian sea law, lists a regular ship's company of the day and assigns to each member his proper share in the profits of a successful venture. First is the *naukleros,* the shipowner or the captain or both, who receives two shares. Next are the *kybernetes,* the helmsman; the *proreus,* the "prow officer"; the *naupegos,* the ship's carpenter, and the *karabites,* the boatswain. Each receives a share and a half. This completes the list of officers; the *nautai,* or seamen, who follow on the roster receive a single share each. Last is the lowliest member of the crew, the *parascharites.* The approximate meaning of the word is "gut-slitter," and in this context it may mean cook. At any rate, his stake in the voyage is only half a share.

We know that the captain of the vessel was named Georgios. He was probably also the shipowner, or perhaps a part owner. The finest scale on the ship, a bronze balance of the kind called a steelyard beam, has his name punched in it in Greek letters to read *Georgiou Presbyterou Nauklerou.* That is to say "Georgios Elder (or Senior), Owner/Sea Captain." The inscription presents problems in spite of its simplicity. Christianity was a strong element in every aspect of Byzantine life; was Captain Georgios a *presbyteros,* an elder of the church? Or does the word have some other meaning here?

Several passages in the Rhodian sea law indicate that sometimes there was more than one captain aboard a vessel. How would one have distinguished between two captains? Should Georgios' title perhaps be read as "Georgios, Senior Sea Captain"? At the same time that we were excavating the wreck, Martin Harrison of the University of Newcastle discovered an inscribed baptismal basin in Turkey (in a sixth-century church in Lycia). The inscription reads: *Nicholas Naukleros Mesatos. Mesatos* is derived from *mesos,* meaning middle. and Harrison has tentatively suggested that the term might mean something such as "middling sea captain," that is, an officer junior to a senior sea captain. No one, Harrison included, accepts this suggestion completely. In its support, however, it should be noted that *mesonautai* are mentioned in the literature of the sixth century and it has been suggested that the term applied to a junior grade of *nautai* or regular seamen.

Our ship had steering oars and therefore surely carried a helmsman, but no evidence of his presence survived in the wreck. The same is true of the post of prow officer, unless he was in charge of the anchors (and a conical sounding lead, with a hollow for the tallow or wax that picked up samples of the bottom). The presence of the ship's carpenter is more easily demonstrated. This officer evidently stored his tool chest on deck. A little forward of the galley area at the ship's stern we found a number of shapeless concretions. Here again careful cutting enabled us to cast what proved to be perfect replicas of the tools in a Byzantine tool chest. Michael L. Katzev, who made casts of the hollow cores and analyzed the collection, found that it included an axe, adzes, a hammer-adze, a claw hammer, hammers for metalworking, chisels, gouges, punches, files, drill bits, dividers, an awl, assorted knives and numerous nails and tacks [*see bottom illustration on next two pages*]. A folded sheet of lead and some waste from lead casting that we also recovered from the wreck suggest that various lead fittings could be made on board ship; this may have been part of the carpenter's duties.

If Byzantine boatswains were responsible for the ship's boat, then the grapnel we found is evidence of a kind that Georgios' crew included a boatswain. As for any ordinary seamen who may have served aboard, no evidence of them has survived. In American days of sail, however, square-rigged ships only slightly smaller than Georgios' merchantman often had a crew of no more than three men and a boy. There need not have been many ordinary seamen in the crew to eat further into the profits from the venture. Indeed, there may have been none.

Whether or not *parascharites* stands for cook, there was certainly a cook aboard the ship, and the galley where he worked contained some of our richest finds. Located at the extreme stern of the ship, it was set as low as possible

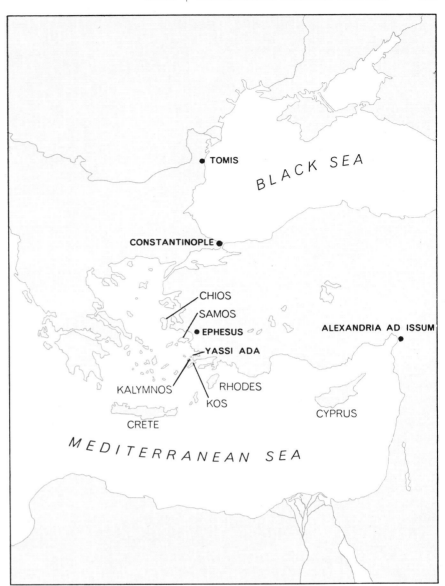

ISLAND OF YASSI ADA, where the ship went down, lies off the southwestern coast of Turkey. It is between the mainland and the larger island of Kalymnos, which is some 20 miles to the west of the ancient city of Halicarnassus. The vessel was evidently sailing from north to south, perhaps bound for one of the celebrated wine-producing centers in the area.

within the hull and was separated from the cargo hold by a bulkhead scarcely eight feet forward of the sternpost. The galley roof stood two and a half feet above the level of the deck and was made of tiles, including one tile with a circular hole that was probably to let the smoke from the galley fire escape. The precise arrangement of the hearth where the fire burned has not yet been reconstructed to everyone's satisfaction. It was built of tiles and iron bars, and it stood in the port half of the galley. Perhaps the tiles formed a low firebox, open at the top and covered by a grill of iron rods that supported the round-bottomed pots used for cooking.

The cook had at his disposal 22 such pots, two copper cauldrons and a large water jar that was stowed at the extreme rear of the galley. A further array of 17 storage jars of various shapes and sizes, doubtless including one or two filled with lamp oil, was kept in a kind of pantry to starboard and forward of the hearth. Elsewhere in the galley, perhaps on shelves and perhaps also in a cupboard of which only a bronze handle has survived, were eight large red plates, two cups, three jars with spouts (two with lids) and 18 pitchers. Most of the pitchers were coated inside with resin, which indicates that they were used to hold wine. Georgios was evident-

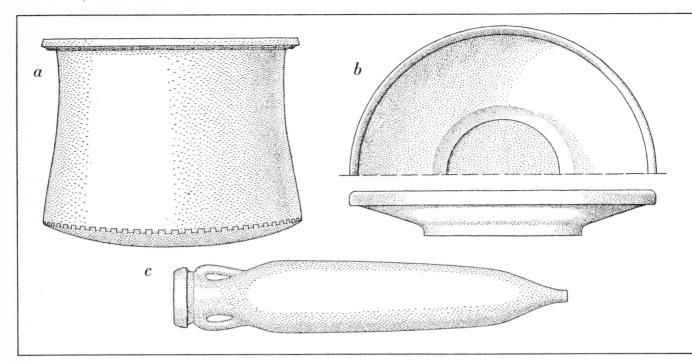

**GALLEY EQUIPMENT** included several copper cooking utensils. One, a cauldron (*a*), had a bottom ingeniously dovetailed to the body. Eight of the large red-ware dinner plates (*b*) were found in the wreck, as were three of the slender amphoras (*c*), possibly containers for cooking oil. A jug (*d*) that was coated with resin to seal the porous clay was probably used to hold wine. An oil lamp typical

ly not laggard in the fashions of the day: the oldest precisely dated Byzantine lead-glazed pottery consists of four small bowls that we found in the galley area.

The galley may have doubled as a storage area for the officers' gear or indeed as a kind of wardroom. It was in this part of the wreck, clearly separated from the carpenter's kit, that we found the grapnel and a group of iron tools: axes, a pickaxe, pruning hooks and a shovel. These look like boatswain's stores that would have been needed by a landing party to collect firewood for the cook and to enlarge springs to obtain fresh water. The galley area also contained, probably originally stored in the cupboard, a supply of money, a set of balance-pan weights, a bronze censer with wick pin, three bronze belt buckles and a metal belt-tip sheath, the bowl of

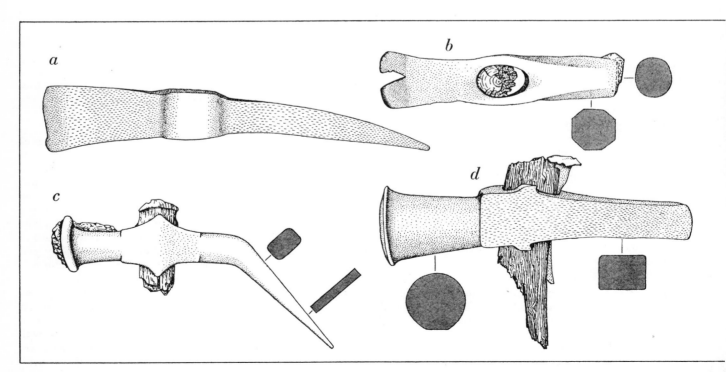

**CARPENTER'S TOOLS**, destroyed by corrosion, were replicated by making rubber casts of the cavities within the concretions that had formed around them. Among other tools, the ship's carpenter had brought with him a mattock (*a*), a claw hammer (*b*), a ham-

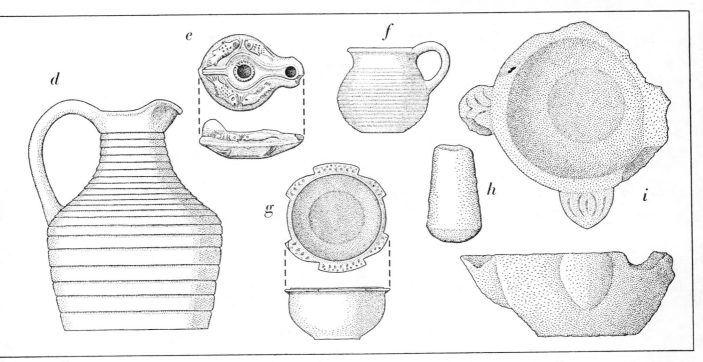

of the 24 found in the wreck (*e*) had been decorated with fish. The single-handled drinking cup (*f*) is one of two such cups that were recovered. The bowl (*g*) is one of four made of glazed ware found aboard the ship and is the earliest precisely dated example of lead-glaze ware from Byzantine times. A stone pestle (*h*) and a matching stone mortar (*i*) were also among the furnishings of the galley.

a lead spoon, a copper tray and several copper vessels. Other cook's gear included a whetstone, a milling stone and a stone mortar and pestle.

What can be said about the ship's last voyage? We have noted that Georgios, in addition to being the captain, may have been the owner and a merchant-venturer as well. The basis for this conjecture is the fact that the scale bearing his name is an item of merchant's equipment. It should be mentioned that later Venetian statutes required that ship-owners supply every vessel with a weighing device; perhaps even during Byzantine times a captain may have needed to carry his own balance to show that his freight charges were correct. If we may assume, however, that Georgios was owner as well as master, we can calculate with some confidence his total in-

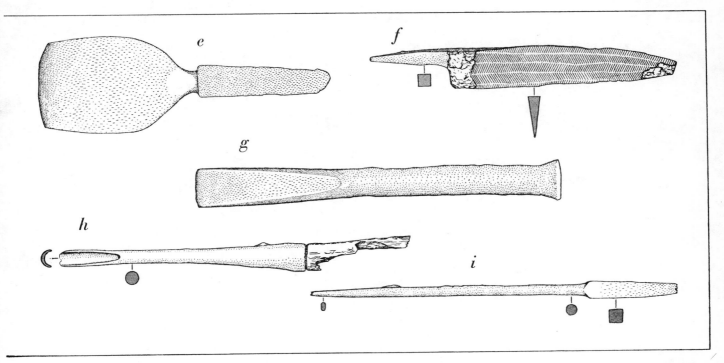

mer-adze (*c*) and a metalworking hammer that fitted its handle loosely and had been fixed in place with a nail (*d*). Other tools included a hand adze (*e*), a file (*f*), a chisel (*g*), a gouge (*h*) and, to judge by its haft, a wood-boring bit for a brace (*i*). All are half-size.

vestment in the ship and all its stores.

The Rhodian sea law indicates that the seventh-century cost of fully outfitted shipping ran about 50 *solidi* (gold coins) per six and a half tons' capacity. On this basis Georgios' investment would have been some 300 *solidi*, a substantial sum in times when a shipyard caulker might earn 18 *solidi* for a year's work and less skilled laborers might receive only seven or eight. Might this investment have been all Georgios could afford, leaving him with no capital to invest in a cargo? A shipload of wine, for example, would have cost 200 or 300 *solidi* more. One piece of evidence suggests that such was the case.

We found a single lead seal in the wreck; it bears a cross-shaped monogram that we read as the name Ioannes, or John. Such a seal could of course have belonged to a passenger or crew member, but the fact that it was the only seal we found suggests at least the possibility of more official use. Perhaps Ioannes was the *emporos*, or merchant, aboard Georgios' ship, traveling with him to pay the freight charge and handle the sale of goods at the vessel's destination.

If Ioannes was indeed a merchant or merchant's agent, he would have asked other merchants who had sailed previously with Georgios whether or not, as specified by law, the ship was in good condition. When he had heard that it was, he and Georgios would have entered into a contract. Just where Ioannes or his employer had raised the money to buy a cargo was no one else's affair as long as he could pay Georgios the required freight charge.

We know exactly what external shape the cargo took. Loaded aboard the ship were 900-odd amphoras, or storage jars, most of them large and globular but some smaller and more elongated. The large jars could hold as much as 40 liters of liquid, the small ones around nine liters. We cannot be sure what, if anything, the jars contained. Not all of them were lined with resin, the customary method of waterproofing the porous clay. However, if all the jars had been filled with liquid, say wine, the cargo would have weighed some 37 tons. In any event, we can visualize a procession of porters carrying aboard the amphoras, full or empty, and passing them down through the hatch into the hold.

The cook's stores would have been loaded at the same time. Presumably he saw to it that his large jar had been filled with fresh water and checked his supply of lamp oil. We know that his fresh rations included a basketful of

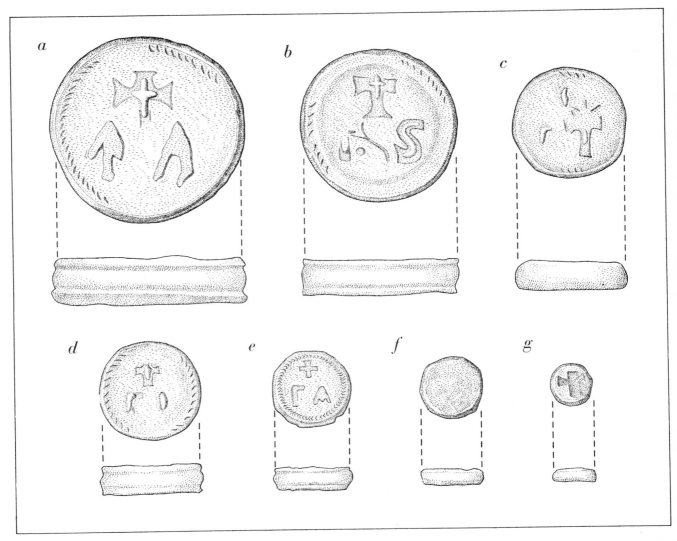

**WEIGHTS** for a balance scale are made of bronze inlaid with silver. They range from one pound (*a*) to a seventh of an ounce (*g*). The ounce was 20.45 grams; a pound consisted of 14 ounces. They were not standard weights, and their purpose is not known.

**CAPTAIN'S SCALE** made of bronze was of the fulcrum-and-counterpoise type later called a steelyard beam. The object to be weighed was suspended from the short end of the beam, and the counterpoise was moved outward until the scale balanced. The weight was then read from calibrations along the beam. Scale was calibrated for both heavy and light loads.

**COUNTERPOISE** for the steelyard beam was a hollow bronze bust of the goddess Athena weighted with lead. The Gorgon's head on the breastplate identifies the goddess. Athena's image was often used in this way even though the Byzantine Empire was officially Christian.

dark, gleaming Bosphorus mussels: we found piles of their shells in the wreck and they are not native to these waters. We know too that the bow officer—if such was his responsibility—had lashed a pair of anchors to the port gunwale and another to the starboard gunwale near the bow and had stowed the remaining seven just forward of the mast.

Meanwhile the captain placed in the galley certain valuables, including a money purse or two. We found 54 copper *folles* (coins worth a small fraction of a *solidus*) and 16 small gold pieces; the total value of the coins was just a little more than seven *solidi*. Was this a ship's fund or money deposited by a passenger? The Rhodian sea law declares: "If a passenger comes on board and has gold, let him deposit it with the captain. If he does not deposit it and says 'I have lost gold or silver,' no effect is to be given to what he says, since he did not deposit it with the captain." If one is to try to answer the question, one needs to know something about the purchasing power of the *solidus*.

As we have noted, seven *solidi* represented a year's wage for some kinds of labor; early in the eighth century, for example, a blacksmith earned three-quarters of a *solidus* per month. Early in the seventh century a cloak might cost from one to three *solidi*, and later in the century one *solidus* would buy four cheap blankets. Food was much less dear. One sixth-century figure gives five *solidi* as the cost of a year's rations for one man; in the years when our ship made its final voyage a loaf of bread cost three *folles*. The money found in the wreck would have fed a crew of 15 for a month with something left over, not even taking into consideration the evidence (lead weights for fishing lines and nets) that the ship's company supplemented its provisions en route. It therefore seems likely that the contents of the purse or purses were the ship's victualing money.

The 70 coins, by the way, are what enable us to pinpoint the date of the voyage at A.D. 625 or 626. Six of the coins were too badly preserved to allow identification. Of the remainder Joan Fagerlie of the American Numismatic Society finds that only two were minted earlier than the reign of the Emperor Heraclius (A.D. 610–641). The latest coin in the group was minted in the 16th year of the emperor's reign, that is, in A.D. 625. We may safely assume that the ship sank in the same year or quite soon thereafter.

The weighing equipment for the voy-

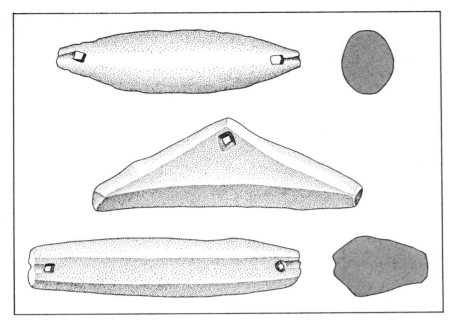

**FISHING WEIGHTS** found in the wreck were used with both lines and nets. Their presence implies that the crew members fished during the voyage to supplement their rations.

age was also stowed in the galley cupboard or close to it. The balance-pan weights, made of bronze inlaid with silver, came in a wooden tray that held them in a graduated series in cylindrical pockets. Seven of the original nine weights were recovered. In addition we found what may be a fragment of the balance itself. The bronze steelyard beam that bears Georgios' name was one of three scales of this kind in the wreck; one of the other two was made of iron and was therefore poorly preserved. All this equipment has been studied in detail by G. Kenneth Sams of the University of North Carolina.

Georgios' steelyard beam is decorated with a boar's head at one end and the head of another animal, possibly a dog or a lion, at the other [*see top illustration on opposite page*]. It has two fulcrum points and two calibrated scales, for heavy or light loads; the counterweight is a lead-filled bronze bust of the goddess Athena. (Two similar counterweights in Athena's image have been discovered in wrecks, one off Sicily and the other in the Bosphorus.)

Both bronze steelyard beams are calibrated in terms of a pound that was equal to 315 grams. (Our pound troy, which is 373 grams, is the closest modern equivalent; our pound avoirdupois is 453 grams.) Van Doorninck has found that the same lightweight pound was the unit of measurement for the ship's anchors. The same unit is very close to one determined earlier from weights of fifth-century and sixth-century Byzantine times.

Curiously the balance-pan weights represent an entirely different system. Most are clearly marked; they include a one-*litra*, or one-pound, weight; a six-*unciae*, or six-ounce, weight, and three-ounce, two-ounce and one-ounce weights. Two smaller weights are unmarked: one of three *nomismata* (six *nomismata* normally equaled one *uncia*) and the other of one *nomisma*. This is possibly the most complete set of Byzantine weights in existence, and their pound is not the standard "light" 315-gram one. It is superlight: 287 grams. Furthermore, it is a pound divided into 14 ounces rather than the customary 12, and its ounce is divided into seven *nomismata* rather than six.

These unusual values are not the result of any alteration in the original weights as a consequence of their long submersion. Each of the weights in the set, give or take a fraction of a gram, is consistent with all the others; in every case the ounce is 20.45 grams. It happens that an ounce of this weight was the Byzantine standard for gold coinage; the standard was established in the time of Constantine the Great (A.D. 272–337) on the basis of the old Roman pound (327.45 grams). In this coinage-weight system, however, there were 16 ounces to the pound rather than 12 or 14. Only one other 14-ounce pound is known: during the fourth century a "heavy" pound divided into 14 ounces rather

than 12 was used in the mining of gold in order to increase state revenue from mine leases. All of this, however, can have nothing to do with the standard of the balance-pan weights from the wreck. At present it remains unexplained.

The wreck contained one more balance weight. It is a small pendant of yellow glass that is pierced for stringing. It is so similar in appearance to other Byzantine glass weights that it must have been one. The pendant is shaped like a coin, and pressed into the glass is another cruciform monogram; this one gives the name Theodoros. Such weights are thought to have been used to check gold coins, although the weights of the glass pieces seldom correspond to the weights of any coins then in circulation. The discrepancy is explained on the grounds that the glass pieces have lost weight as a result of corrosion.

So far we have seen Georgios' ship built, supplied, loaded and under way. What was its home port, its course and its intended destination? It seems safe to state, on the basis of the coins alone, that the voyage was from north to south. With a single exception every one of the identifiable copper coins had been struck at mints in the northern part of the Byzantine Empire: Constantinople, Thessalonika, Nikomedia, Cyzicus. Only one copper coin, and it is one of the oldest, is from a mint in another part of the empire; it was struck at Alexandria ad Issum on what is now the Levantine coast of Turkey. Since the copper coins are overwhelmingly northern, the home port of the ship should probably be sought in the same direction.

The pottery from the galley strengthens this assumption. Karen D. Vitelli of the University of Maryland at Baltimore has found that fully half of the oil lamps we recovered are "Asia Minor" types. Seven are of a kind common in Bulgaria, Romania, Thrace and the Hellespont; others find their closest counterparts at Samos, Ephesus, Smyrna, Troy, Miletos, Delos and Chios. A probable origin cannot yet be assigned to the rest of the lamps, but as with the coins few if any appear to have come from the parts of the empire west, south or east of the shipwreck. Other wares from the galley also find their best parallels to the north. The lead-glazed bowls speak of Constantinople, and other pottery is similar to the ware of Chios and of two Black Sea ports: Histria and Tomis.

The presence of Bosphorus mussels among the ship's victuals provides still another piece of evidence suggesting a

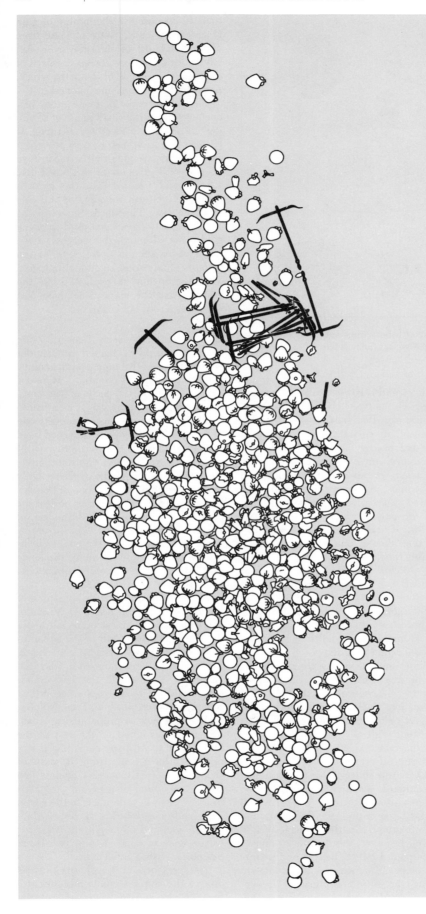

northern home port for the ship, perhaps in the Hellespont itself. Finally, the place where the ship went down is compatible with a course running from north to south. The wreck lay on the southeast side of a treacherous reef off a small coastal island named Yassi Ada. Throckmorton, who found the ship, is of the opinion that it was running southward before a wind from the north when the reef tore a hole in its bottom; evidently it sank so fast that there was no time to salvage valuables from the galley or to drop even a single anchor.

In the light of all this evidence it seems reasonable to assign the ship a home port not too far from Constantinople. It is virtually certain that the vessel was on a southward course when it sank. There remains the question of its destination. Today one sees vessels plying the Aegean whose hold and deck are crowded with pottery containers. The pots are empty; they are the cargo.

We have seen that many but not all of the amphoras aboard Georgios' ship were lined with resin. A potful of congealed resin was also found in the galley. This suggests that resin was being melted during the voyage; perhaps the purpose was to coat the unlined amphoras. Moreover, although the ship carried some 900 amphoras, we found in the wreck only 100 amphora stoppers. (It is of course possible that the missing stoppers were made of some perishable material.) The ship's course was carrying it toward Kos, Knidos and Rhodes, all of them celebrated wine-producing centers. It is not illogical to suggest that Georgios was carrying a load of the best wine jars available on the Constantinople (or Black Sea) pottery market for the use of vintners in the south, and that the merchant Ioannes had decided to cut costs a little by having some of the unlined pots coated with resin on the voyage.

There are of course other questions, some of which may be answered and some not. The main thing we have learned is how much a single shipwreck—and not a particularly well-preserved one—can tell us.

CARGO OF AMPHORAS littered the sea floor off Yassi Ada as they spilled from the decaying shipwreck. More than 900 were recovered by the excavators. The majority were globular, with a maximum diameter of about 18 inches. A few, more elongated in shape, were only 10 inches in diameter. If all had been filled with liquid, the weight of the cargo would have been some 37 tons.

# 28

# The Excavation of
# a Drowned Greek Temple

by Michael H. Jameson
*October 1974*

*Geological changes in the level of the Mediterranean
shoreline have submerged a number of classical sites.
The investigation of one of these shallow-water
ruins suggests that they would all reward study*

The introduction of self-contained underwater breathing apparatus some 20 years ago opened up the new domain of underwater archaeology. Now it seems that certain geological events of the past open up an extension of that domain into what can be called shallow-water archaeology. So far the principal beneficiaries of this kind of archaeology have been students of classical Greek and Roman times. The reason is that the sites that have been investigated are all in the Mediterranean area.

The shoreline of the Mediterranean has had its geological ups and downs over the past few thousand years. For example, the ruins of the port of Ephesus in Turkey today lie some miles inland from the coast. An even more dramatic example is the Temple of Serapis at ancient Puteoli, near Naples. The temple now stands, as it did when it was built, on dry land. High up on its stone columns, however, are numerous holes that were cut into the stone by burrowing marine animals; evidently the temple was once submerged for a considerable length of time.

My own acquaintance with shallow-water archaeology began at a site in Greece. At the beginning of the classical Greek period a small city-state arose near the tip of the Argolid peninsula in the Peloponnesus. The town grew up along the shoreline of a sheltered circular harbor that was smaller then than it is today. The settlement was called Halieis, or "the salty places," probably because nearby sea-level flats were used as salt pans. The population of Halieis probably never exceeded 4,000; the inhabitants presumably supplemented their agricultural resources, meager in this arid peninsula, by fishing, exporting salt and dealing in the valuable purple dye of antiquity that came from the marine snail *Murex*, which was plentiful in their waters.

About 470 B.C. the town opened its gates to a company of refugees from Tiryns, a neighboring principality that had been overrun by forces from the larger city-state of Argos. The newcomers seem to have invigorated Halieis. For most of the next two centuries the port, protected by a system of walls and a hilltop citadel, served as a valuable naval base during a period that witnessed continual struggles among larger Greek powers. Then, sometime after the death of Alexander the Great in 323 B.C., Halieis was mysteriously abandoned.

Beginning in 1962 my department at the University of Pennsylvania, the Department of Classical Studies, undertook with the support of the University Museum a conventional dry-land excavation of the ruins of Halieis, which lie in and around the modern town of Porto Cheli [*see bottom illustration on page 291*]. Tracing the line of the ancient city walls down to the water's edge, we soon found that a considerable part of Halieis, some four and a half acres in extent, was now submerged in the harbor. The depth of water over the ruins ranged from a few inches to more than 10 feet. As we were to learn later, another 40-acre area outside the city walls was similarly covered by the harbor shallows.

To a dry-land archaeologist a drowned site seems at first a total loss. Actually it has certain compensating advantages. For one thing, wood and other organic materials are better preserved under water than on land. Furthermore, Halieis, like most such cities, was built mostly of sun-dried mud bricks that were set on stone foundations. On land when such buildings fall into ruins, the mud brick eventually melts away, and as often as not the foundation stones themselves are later stolen to be used in other construction. At Halieis submersion had protected many of the foundation stones from thieves, and at the same time wave action had swept away such remnants of the mud-brick superstructures as had not already been broken down by rain. To clear the debris from a comparable area on land, using normal archaeological methods, would take years of work, whereas in the harbor, under the right conditions, entire sections of the city lay waiting to be revealed.

The question was how. The octopus fisherman who slowly sculls across the harbor at dawn knows how to find the large blocks of stone in whose crevices his quarry hides. The shallow harbor waters, however, are made murky by rich

**SANCTUARY OF APOLLO**, built outside the walls of ancient Halieis, is seen in the aerial photograph on page 295. Constructed on what was at the time a harborside site, the sanctuary was later drowned by subsidence. Many of the foundation stones of sanctuary structures escaped later reuse because of their inaccessibility under water, making the original ground plan relatively easy to reconstruct. Out-of-focus object leading to the small boat is the tether for the balloon that suspended the remotely controlled camera above the site.

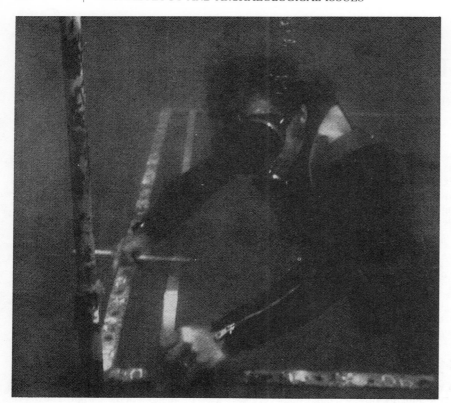

**CONTROLLED EXCAVATION** under water was achieved by placing a square frame, mounted on adjustable legs, over each intended trench. Here a diver is seen adjusting the horizontal orientation of a frame with a carpenter's level. The position of each two-meter-square frame was noted with respect to the overall site grid, and its depth below sea level was determined. As the excavation under each frame progressed the location of uncovered artifacts was recorded with respect to both horizontal coordinates and vertical position.

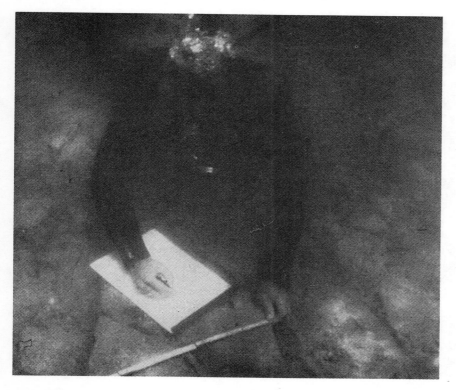

**FOUNDATION PLANS** were prepared by noting the size, shape and position of each of the foundation stones on waterproof paper. Here a diver, having measured a stone, sketches its position on a sheet that already shows the location of foundation stones surveyed earlier.

organic growth and are easily rendered altogether opaque by wave action. Only occasionally does the combination of a flat calm and sunlight at the right angle provide a glimpse of the drowned streets and houses. Indeed, most of Porto Cheli's inhabitants had no suspicion of what lay just below the harbor surface.

In 1967, following an earlier season of snorkel surveying, our group at Porto Cheli was joined by a team from Indiana University. The work load was divided; we would be responsible for the shallow-water research and the Indiana team for the work ashore. Julian and Eunice Whittlesey provided the perspective we needed for our endeavors by suspending a camera from a tethered hydrogen balloon, which a swimmer would guide into position in the early-morning hours when the harbor was at its calmest. The very first roll of film showed us a detail of the drowned city wall, the outline of one of a pair of towers, that we had not been able to make out because we had been too close to it in the shallow water. The Whittleseys' balloon-supported camera has provided similar insights for five seasons now.

Our shallow-water work in both 1967 and 1968 was concentrated on recovering the plan of the drowned part of Halieis by a combination of surveying and utilizing a high-pressure water jet to clear away the silt and sand that obscured many of the foundation stones. The motor, pump and hose for the water jet we kept aboard a chartered local fishing boat. The boat's owner, an octopus fisherman, took us across the harbor one day and showed us a large complex of drowned buildings that he had located in his fishing. The complex lay about half a mile from the main gate in the city wall, and its presence had not been suspected up to that time. The Whittleseys promptly made balloon photographs that gave us some notion of the extent of the new find: We left Porto Cheli determined to survey the complex in the near future and if possible to excavate it.

When we returned in 1970, we carried with us new means of clearing away bottom debris: light, portable dredges that had originally been developed for gold miners and that had already proved to be particularly useful in shallow-water work undertaken by archaeologists from the University of Chicago and Indiana University at Kenchreai on the Isthmus of Corinth. The pump for each dredge, which we mounted on a scaffold near the shore, sent a stream of seawater through a hose to the working head of the dredge. The head was a galvanized iron pipe; the pumped water entered the pipe at a 45-degree angle, producing a powerful suction at the rear of the working head. This part of the apparatus was kept 100 feet or so away from the area under excavation in order to avoid having the discharge wash back and obscure the excavator's vision. Lengths of quick-clamping irrigation pipe led from the dredge head to the work area; the last length of the suction apparatus was made of corrugated rubber, thus allowing the excavator flexibility of movement. The diver could feed mud, small stones and any plant debris that he freed from the bottom into the rubber tube; the suction promptly deposited the waste materials a good distance away. As an added benefit the suction also continuously drew off the obscuring silt that clouded the water as a result of a diver's least motion, so that the area being excavated remained relatively clear.

We began work at the complex by establishing over the target area a submerged grid of 10-meter squares that was tied into the Greek ordnance survey grid ashore. The intersections of the grid lines were marked by nails, each identified by colored flagging, driven into the harbor bottom. The grid provided a framework for the stone-by-stone plan of all the foundations in the complex and also fixed the location of the various trenches we intended to excavate in order to sample the stratigraphy of the site.

Stratigraphic excavation is, of course, the *sine qua non* of all archaeology. It requires the removal of successively deeper layers of earth and the assignment of the artifacts discovered in each layer to a general time interval. Often the excavator's downward progress is dictated by minor variations in soil texture and color that, for example, make possible the detection of intrusions from above, such as storage pits or the foundation trenches for later walls, which may cut into older strata. In shallow-water excavation all these considerations can be taken into account, although detection of soil differences is more difficult and allowance must be made for disturbances in levels caused by the incoming water. The uppermost level of mud and sand under water corresponds to the disturbed plow soil of a cultivated field on land and needs to be cleared before the significant levels in a trench are reached.

Over each proposed trench we fitted an iron frame two meters square, secured in position by a two-meter leg at each corner. The frame was free to ride up or down on the legs. The legs in turn had

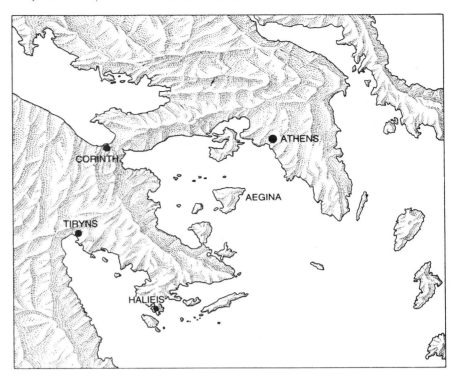

ANCIENT HALIEIS stood near the southern tip of the Argolid peninsula, a region of the Peloponnesus roughly equidistant between Athens and Corinth. Today its sheltered harbor is the site of the modern town of Porto Cheli, where few knew of the drowned ruins.

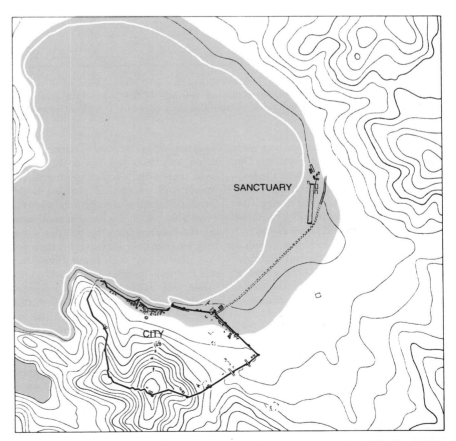

SUBMERGED PART of the harbor at Porto Cheli today that was dry land during the first millennium B.C. is the area between the innermost contour line (*white*) and the present shoreline (*color*). A considerable part of the city wall and the settlement within it (*bottom*) was thus preserved, as were traces of the road from city to sanctuary and much of the sanctuary complex (*right of center*). A plan of the sanctuary appears on the next two pages.

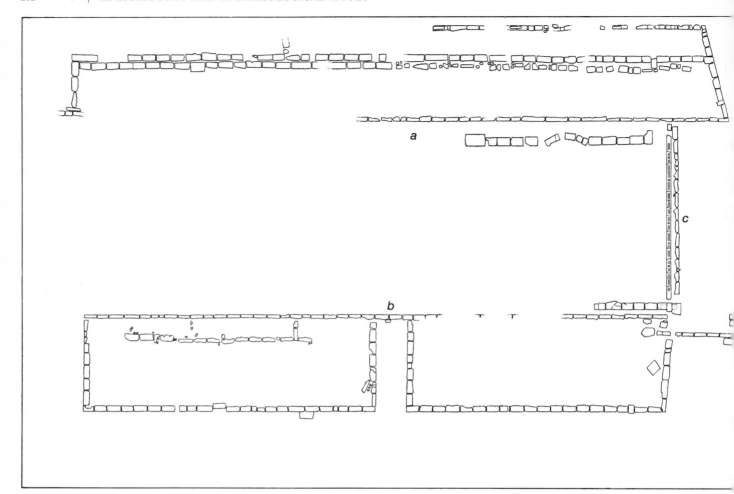

**PRINCIPAL COMPONENTS** of the sanctuary of Apollo are (*from left*) "grandstand" foundations (*a, b*) to the east and west of the near end of a footrace track; one track starting line (*c*); foundations of an open-air altar (*d*) that stood between the starting line and the front of an early three-chambered temple of Apollo (*e*), with an entrance porch (*f*); massive foundations of a later, more

been set up in a known position with respect to the overall grid system. The frame was made horizontal with the help of a carpenter's level, and its depth below the surface, which we called its negative elevation, was determined. This required placing the bottom end of a stadium rod on the leveled frame and then taking a reading on the part of the rod that projected above the water, using a transit set up at a known elevation on the shore.

The frame method and the excavation procedures associated with it, mainly devised by James A. Dengate, were ingenious adaptations of techniques that had been developed under other circumstances. Each diver worked from one to two hours at a time, no more than twice a day. Floating at neutral buoyancy under the frame, he would dig up the bottom with a small hand pick, a knife or his bare hands. For the most delicate work, where the excavator ashore might use a small trowel or a brush, the underwater excavator moves his hand back and forth to establish a light current. When an object is located, its position

with respect to the frame's edges is measured and recorded (on a waterproof form that bears a scale drawing of the frame) and its vertical position is determined by dangling a plumb bob from a movable bar on the frame and measuring the distance from the bob to the bar with a meterstick. The object is then put in a plastic bag with a numbered tag, and the same number is recorded on the waterproof paper next to its indicated position. Large objects such as roofing tiles and rubble are not bagged but are put in tagged baskets for later examination ashore. Potentially perishable objects such as those made of wood or metal are freed of most of their salt content by immersion in a tank of fresh water ashore and then are subjected to various techniques of preservation. The diver types up his notes immediately on returning to shore, so that each three-diver team's series of notes provides a consecutive record of the excavation of the trench. One man from each team is responsible for writing a final report on each trench, for drawing sections of the

four vertical trench faces and for analyzing the finds.

As we surveyed the site, sluicing away mud and sand from the foundation stones and digging test trenches here and there, the character of the structures that had once stood between the edge of the harbor and the ancient coast road leading to the main gate of Halieis gradually became clear. They had formed a sanctuary outside the city: a large open-air altar for animal sacrifices, a temple to shelter the deity in whose honor the sacrifices were made, various auxiliary buildings and, quite unexpectedly, a runners' racecourse that must have been built for the quasi-religious athletic games so beloved of the classical Greeks.

Indirect evidence suggested that the sanctuary's deity was Apollo, the prophet-musician son of Zeus who was widely worshiped throughout Greece. He is known to have been the chief god of Halieis, and his image often appeared on the city's coins. Furthermore, in a treaty between Halieis and Athens, in-

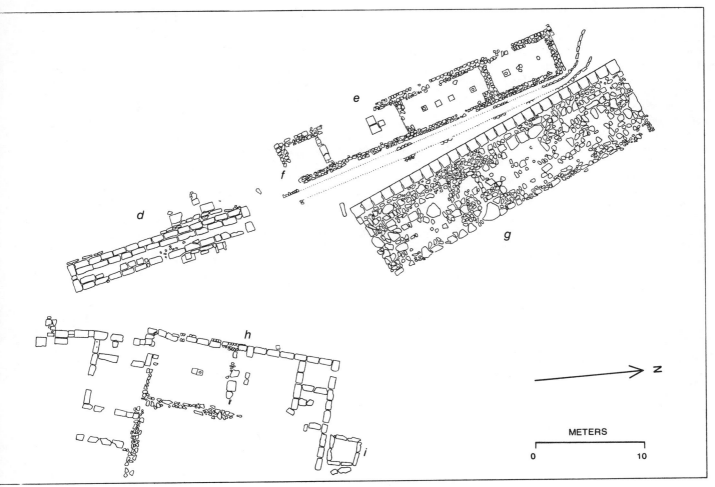

ambitious building (*g*) that probably replaced the early temple; foundations of a third building (*h*) that may have housed competitors in the games at the racecourse or served as dining quarters for those attending religious festivals, and a well (*i*) that held many drinking cups. The southern starting line of the racecourse was only 167 meters away, making it one of the shortest in Greece.

scribed on stone in 423 B.C., the text provides that another copy of the treaty be erected in the sanctuary of Apollo at Halieis, so that we know he had a temple there. A marble statue found in fragments among the temple ruins points to the same conclusion. A discovery made during our second season resolved the question beyond further doubt. The divers recovered the remains of three long pieces of angled iron, welded together by corrosion [*see top illustration on page 297*]. We identified them as a set of three temple keys; in Greek art such keys are often shown in the hands or on the shoulder of priests. In spite of the corrosion it was just possible to make out, inscribed at the top of one key, the name Apollo.

Today, after our third season of excavation, the history of the Halieis sanctuary can be reconstructed in considerable detail. The harborside settlement that was to become a city-state started to expand during the eighth century B.C., just as Greece in general was reawakening after its dark ages. It was at this time

that the first two elements in the future complex were built. A narrow, south-facing temple that measured 27 meters from end to end but only 4.46 meters from side to side was raised adjacent to a flat stretch of shore suitable for footraces and other sports. The outdoor altar was placed between the front of the temple and the racecourse. No doubt some primitive wood statue of Apollo looked out through the entrance of the temple, overseeing both the altar and the racecourse beyond it.

At later times other buildings were added to the sanctuary, farther to the east and facing the altar. A formal entranceway was also built, leading from the coast road to the open space between the altar and the racecourse. Although added buildings are regularly encountered at most Greek sanctuaries, their architecture is rarely specialized enough to provide a clue to their function. Here the additional buildings near Apollo's temple contained a series of small rooms. This suggests that the buildings provided facilities for dining in connection with

religious festivals or were used to house competitors in the games. The remains of many drinking cups, found in a nearby well, would support either interpretation.

All the later structures to the east of the temple testify to the disadvantage of a site's not being sufficiently drowned. They were built on higher ground and were therefore more exposed than the other buildings as the shoreline sank. It must have been all too easy to bring in a boat and load it with the largest and best blocks of stone. In any event we can speak only tentatively about what once stood in that part of the complex. In this connection the original temple, which was the earliest structure at the site and was built of the simplest materials, is also the best preserved; because it was sunk the deepest it was the least pillaged. Certainly a part of the original temple survived into the fourth century B.C., when the city met its end.

We found it possible to re-create many details of the temple's original appearance by studying the debris of the collapsed walls and roof. From the base upward the temple walls were built of two rows of limestone slabs; as many as four courses of the slabs are still standing in some places. The slabs were roughly finished on their outer face only. Judging by the heavy fall of masonry along the outer face of the walls their upper courses may also have been stacked stone slabs rather than the more usual mud brick. In any event solid single blocks of stone ran through the width of the walls at the four corners. The lowest course included a narrow projecting ledge, and on the inside of the building semicircular pieces of limestone were set at 1.5-meter intervals. These bases were evidently the supports for wood columns; the upper part of the columns must have lent additional strength to the upper part of the walls.

The temple floor was paved in places with irregularly shaped slabs of sandstone, but in the main it was composed of chunks of soft, clayey limestone that formed a hard-packed layer. Round slabs of stone stood along the main axis of the temple; these were evidently the bases for a central row of wood columns that helped to support the roof. Considerable support must have been required: the

roof was made of heavy tiles. Many of these were found where they had fallen when the roof collapsed. Flat rectangular "pan tiles," 30 inches long, 20 inches wide and two inches thick, were arranged side by side; the joints between adjacent rows were concealed under narrow, angular "cover tiles" some six inches wide. Not all pan tiles and cover tiles are of the same size, shape and fabric, a fact that suggests roof repairs at intervals of many years. As a finishing touch the temple walls were plastered on the inside and perhaps on the outside too. On the inside, at least, the plaster bore painted designs; the remains of the designs, however, are too fragmentary to allow reconstruction.

The narrow temple building had a porch at the south end, facing the altar, and was divided into three chambers. The front chamber would have held a now vanished image of Apollo. The broken marble statue we found there evidently represents a much later replacement. Between the stone base for the statue and the rear wall of the first chamber is a space that seems to have served as a temple treasury. There we found quantities of iron spits, which

would have been indispensable for roasting the meat of sacrificed animals. Spits also served as a primitive form of money that continued in circulation in nearby Sparta long after conventional coinage had been introduced elsewhere in Greece. In addition to the spits we found 18 silver coins of various denominations that had been minted between 550 and 525 B.C. on the island of Aegina (modern Aiyina), which lies between Halieis and Athens. The coinage of Aegina was widely circulated throughout Greece up to the time of the island's subjugation by Athens in the middle of the fifth century B.C.

Sunk into the floor of the temple treasury were two large masses of heavily corroded iron. An X-ray plate of one of the masses shows the outline of two axe-adze heads and one double-axe head. Like the iron spits, these tools would have had some monetary value, but another interpretation of their presence in the treasury is possible. One of my colleagues, an Orientalist, tells me that in the ancient Near East the tools that were used in the building of a temple were often thereafter dedicated to the resident deity; such may have been the case here.

Among other finds in the treasury area

**ALTAR AND TEMPLE** are shown in this reconstruction as they may have appeared in the fifth century B.C. The temple porch has been omitted. The temple walls were built of roughly dressed stone and were smoothly plastered on the inside. The roof, covered with heavy terra-cotta tiles, was supported by the walls and by pillars along the walls and along the central axis of the building. Animals were sacrificed to Apollo both on the plastered top of the outdoor altar and within the second of the three temple chambers.

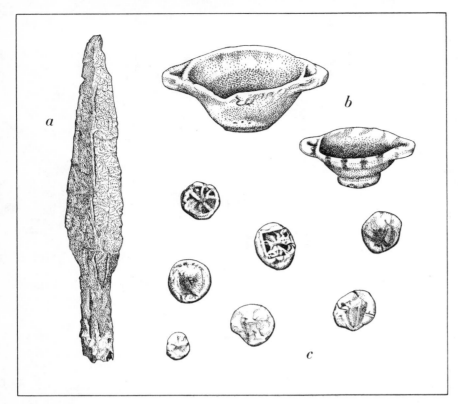

**ARTIFACTS** recovered from the early temple include weapons made of iron (*a*), probably the offerings of well-to-do worshipers, and miniature wine cups (*b*), a common temple offering of the poor. Silver coins (*c*) were found in the part of the first chamber that appears to have been a repository for temple treasure; they had been minted on the island of Aegina.

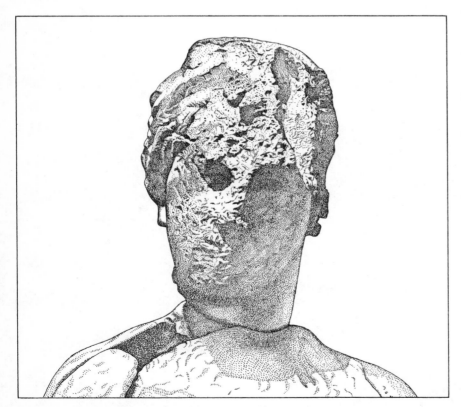

**STATUE OF APOLLO**, found in fragments in the first chamber of the temple, imitates the sculptural style of the early fifth century B.C. but was actually made at some later date. It may have replaced an earlier statue, possibly destroyed in an Athenian attack in 460 B.C.

were some pieces of amber, evidently imported from the Baltic, bits of ostrich eggshell imported from Africa and an inscribed bronze plaque made early in the fifth century B.C. Most of the inscription is illegible, but the parts of the text that can be clearly read refer to the imposition of fines. Presumably the plaque contained a warning not to misuse the temple treasures.

The middle chamber of the temple may have served as an inner sanctum where oracular and purification rites were performed. The presence there of numerous horn cores from sheep or goats and the bones of young pigs is suggestive of such a ritual function. A shrine of Apollo on Crete and also one of Hermes there had altars made of piled-up horns; Apollo's altar of horns on Delos was known throughout classical Greece. Similarly, the sacrifice of piglets was a common practice, particularly in a purification context; that was how Orestes was purged of guilt in Apollo's celebrated shrine at Delphi after slaying his mother, Clytemnestra. Also found in the middle chamber were the heads and torsos of three bronze animal figurines: a goat, a ram and a bull. The bronzes were designed to fit as finials on the tips of wood shafts, but their function is open to speculation.

The temple's third and last room was evidently a storage area. There we found the remnants of at least 5,000 miniature pottery wine cups, a common offering of the poor. Throughout the temple we also found knives, swords and spearheads of iron. These evidently represented the offerings of people of greater means.

The arrival of the refugees from Tiryns early in the fifth century B.C. may have prompted certain temple renovations. At about this time the old circular bases for the temple's axial row of pillars were for the most part replaced with rectangular blocks of a finer stone and some of the new bases were topped with circular plinths. The columns they supported, however, continued to be made of wood; no stone column drums have been found in the ruins. The positions of the new pillar bases make it plain that not all was well with the temple roof. They are located irregularly, probably wherever the sagging roof most needed support.

Other changes perhaps inspired by the refugees from Tiryns include a new temple entrance, built from the porch into the forechamber and distinguished by a handsome stone threshold. It is tempting to see in a rectangular loop of iron found nearby the keyhole of a vanished wood entrance door into which the

**CORRODED IRON BARS,** curiously bent, are the remains of three temple keys. It proved possible in spite of the corrosion to read the name Apollo inscribed on one of the keys.

great iron temple keys fitted and to identify a second iron object as a door pull. That the people from Tiryns were involved in these various innovations is suggested by the fact that the letters on both the temple key and the bronze treasury plaque are written in the alphabet of the Argive plain, the Tirynthians' former home, and not in the alphabet in common use at this end of the Argolid peninsula.

When was the temple of Apollo built and how long did it stand? We were able to salvage some of the pine timbers used in the construction of the temple. After treatment for the effects of long immersion a sample of the wood provided a carbon-14 date (adjusted for correlation with tree-ring dates) of $780 \pm 59$ B.C. The date is indicative of the time the pine was felled. If we assume that the construction utilized newly cut timbers rather than reused ones, this range of dates suggests that the temple was built in the period from the latter part of the ninth century B.C. to the latter part of the eighth century. The more recent date seems the most plausible: the oldest pottery recovered from the ruins dates back

to the late eighth century and early seventh. In the more advanced parts of Greece at that time cult buildings as primitive as the Halieis temple were being replaced by the first of the Doric temples, built of well-cut masonry and surrounded by a colonnade of pillars. In the quiet backwater of Halieis, Apollo's old shrine was to be preserved for centuries longer. Few objects found in the ruins, however, can be dated later than the middle of the fifth century B.C.

We know from recorded history that Athens made an unsuccessful assault on Halieis in 460 B.C., and it may be that the unprotected sanctuary by the shore was damaged at that time. Whether or not the Athenians desecrated Apollo's temple, it appears to have received little attention thereafter. At some later time a small building was constructed in what had been the temple entrance. Either before or after that (the chronology is still not clear) the marble statue we found was placed on a foundation of reused blocks in the outermost chamber and marble lustral basins were set on each side of it. The statue imitates early fifth-century sculpture in its style but it was clearly made at a later time. The impression one has is that the old temple was now a kind of antique, damaged but not destroyed, that was being preserved more as a sacred relic than as a functioning religious building. Eventually, as we know from the condition of the timbers we recovered, the temple was destroyed by fire.

Meanwhile the town of Halieis flourished, and considerable money and energy were invested elsewhere in the sanctuary. The outdoor altar in front of the old temple was rebuilt on a grander scale, and four pillars were erected there, probably to support a canopy near one end. The blocks of fine, hard limestone that composed the upper part of the rebuilt altar were almost all pillaged in later years for use elsewhere.

Immediately to the east of the old temple a larger and more ambitious building was constructed. Like the rebuilt altar, this modern structure was later robbed of much of its stone; today even its orientation is in doubt. I would guess that it was a new temple that faced the rebuilt altar in much the same way the old temple did, and that it was intended to fill the same function. Its foundation was massive: some of the stone blocks are three meters long. We assume that the building walls were made of mud brick because in the vicinity we recovered heavy baked bricks: 30 inches long, 20 inches wide and nearly four inches thick. These bricks were probably

**X-RAY PLATE** of one large mass of corroded iron found with the temple treasure reveals two axe-adzes and one double axe. The tools may have been used in constructing the temple.

used to make the top course of the wall on which the roof beams rested. The roof itself was tiled, but the tiles differ in design from those used in the old temple. Wide and curved, they are of the type known as Lakonian. The few artifacts we recovered from the ruins—wine cups and iron weapons—are some support for the interpretation that the structure was a temple.

The racecourse was also improved by the construction of a starting line at each end. The starting lines consisted of fitted stone blocks, one for each of the track's six lanes; parallel grooves indicated where the runners should place their feet and sockets allowed the mounting in each lane of a wood *hysplex,* or starting gate. The starting lines are 167 meters apart, which makes the Halieis stadium one of the smallest in classical Greece; a one-lap race would have covered little

more than 180 yards, whereas the Olympic *stade* was more than 200 yards. The existence of two starting lines allowed a one-lap race to begin at the city end and finish near the sanctuary altar and a two-lap race to begin and end near the altar. Foundations were built for some kind of spectator accommodation on each side of the starting line at the altar end. We found the starting line at the city end of the stadium by probing along the east wall of the sanctuary until the wall ended; the line at the altar end was discovered by accident when the discharge from one of our dredges exposed one of the starting-line blocks.

The fate that befell Apollo's sanctuary remains as unexplained as the fate of Halieis itself. As far as we know the sea did not encroach on the sanctuary and the city until well after the beginning of the Christian era. Before then, of course,

minor changes in the height of the land could have contaminated the local wells with salt water and forced abandonment of the area. It is perhaps more likely that some powerful warlord, perhaps Demetrius Poliorcetes, the "Besieger of Cities," deciding about 300 B.C. to eliminate a naval base that might be used against him, destroyed the fortifications and drove out the inhabitants.

Halieis was a modest town with a modest sanctuary. By an accident of geological change it has been possible to study there aspects of a classical Greek city-state that are seldom accessible at dry-land sites. In the course of the work, methods of reconnaissance and of excavation in shallow water have been advanced. Our experience suggests that many more rich opportunities for archaeology exist in the precarious zone between the sea and the land.

# The Vikings

by Eric Oxenstierna
*May 1967*

*For 400 years beginning in the ninth century A.D.
these seafaring nomads shaped history from the
Middle East to North America. Such finds as coin
hoards and buried ships trace their rise and decline*

To most Americans, I would venture to say, the Vikings are known as redoubtable seafarers who raided England and France, colonized Iceland and Greenland and even landed in North America centuries before Columbus. Much less known are the Scandinavian traders and settlers who colonized parts of England and France and the whole of Sicily, established the first Russian state, traveled by inland waterways to the Black Sea and the Caspian, manned the Byzantine fleet and traded slaves and furs in the bazaars of Bagdad for Arab silver and Chinese silks.

In this article I shall emphasize these less familiar aspects of Viking history. A review of the subject is timely because much new archaeological evidence concerning these Scandinavian peoples has

| | NUMBER OF COINS | |
|---|---|---|
| YEAR | ARABIC | GERMAN |
| 950–980 | 2,336 | 22 |
| 980–1000 | 738 | 457 |
| 1000–1020 | 129 | 1,184 |
| 1020–1050 | 20 | 2,994 |
| 1050–1070 | 4 | 3,030 |

**ARAB AND GERMAN COINS** found in Danish hoards show that Viking trade with the East via Russian waterways collapsed between A.D. 970 and 1070 (*see illustration, p. 300–301*). During this interval the proportion of Arab coins to German coins fell from more than 99 percent to less than 1 percent.

recently been uncovered, illuminating a period of history that is poorly represented in written records.

The Vikings emerged as a recognizable group at the end of a restless period, lasting almost 1,000 years, during which many peoples of northern Europe had migrated to almost every corner of the continent. For example, the Burgundians had moved to France from the island of Burgundarholm (now Bornholm) in the Baltic Sea. The Vandals had gone from Vandilsyssel in what is now Denmark all the way to Andalusia in southern Spain; the Lombards from the mouth of the Elbe on the Baltic to Lombardy in Italy, and the Angles and the Saxons from what is now northern Germany to England.

Not all these movements were to the south. A number of grave sites recently excavated on the Scandinavian peninsula indicate that early in the seventh century A.D. a farming population moved into mountain valleys and deep forests where no one had ever lived before. Even the poorest of these immigrant farmers had enough iron at his disposal—in terms of hoes, spades, plows, axes, knives and, not least, a good sword—to enable him to clear the forest and cultivate his fields. Within a few generations, however, the newly cleared forest soil was exhausted, and there was hunger all over Scandinavia.

During this same period a significant technological change took place: the oared galleys that had provided water transportation in Scandinavia were replaced by ships with sails. An excavation at Kvalsund in Norway shows that by about A.D. 600 sizable sailing vessels were being built. They were shallow-draft vessels with a planked deck but no keel.

It is no accident that, at a time when a new mobility at sea coincided with hunger at home, history should record

the first Viking raid. It occurred on June 8, 793. The action took place on the island of Lindisfarne, in the North Sea near the border of Scotland and England. The number of ships that came up over the horizon that day is not recorded, but the actions of their crews were noted in detail by the English monks who were their victims. The Vikings slaughtered the monastery's herd of cattle and loaded the carcasses into their ships. They killed anyone who resisted. After removing everything in the monastery that was made of silver and gold they set fire to all the buildings. From the Christian viewpoint the episode was an atrocity. For the pagan Vikings it had been a routine *strandhugg* (victualing raid) in which the unexpected haul of precious metal and the absence of armed resistance must have been agreeable surprises.

The word of the raiders' easy success evidently spread through Scandinavia like wildfire. The next summer "dragon ships" (named for their dragon-shaped figurehead) attacked two monasteries along the same North Sea coast of Britain. The summer after that monasteries on three islands off the western coast of Scotland—Rechru, Iona and Skye—were plundered. By A.D. 799 raids on the British Isles were common, and similar attacks on the Continent compelled the Emperor Charlemagne to organize a coast-watching force.

Thus began the activities that gained the Vikings a reputation as pirates. As I have indicated, however, these peoples had other interests. Let us turn from the North Sea to the Baltic, particularly to the Svea people of the area around the modern Swedish city of Uppsala, to the inhabitants of the island of Gotland and to the petty kings who controlled the base of the peninsula of Jutland. Both the Svea and the Gotlanders had established coastal settlements in Latvia and elsewhere across the Baltic before the middle of the seventh century. Indeed, the excavation of a large seventh-century cemetery at Grobin in Latvia has uncovered ornaments typical of both Gotlander men and women—proof that their trans-Baltic enclave was a genuine colony inhabited by married couples and not a mere outpost.

From the trans-Baltic settlements trade goods (the most important were furs) flowed back to Gotland and the main Svea centers of commerce: the island towns of Helgö and Birka in Lake Mälar, near modern Stockholm. Excavations at Helgö have revealed trade goods manufactured far to the south (for example glassware made in Cologne on the Rhine) that had no doubt been received

in exchange for pelts or for the iron that also was an export of the Svea.

Items of even more distant origin have been uncovered by the digging at Helgö, which began in 1953. The bronze head of a crosier—the ornate shepherd's crook carried by abbots, bishops and other church officials as a symbol of their pastoral duties—is among the finds. It is of Irish manufacture; we can assume that it

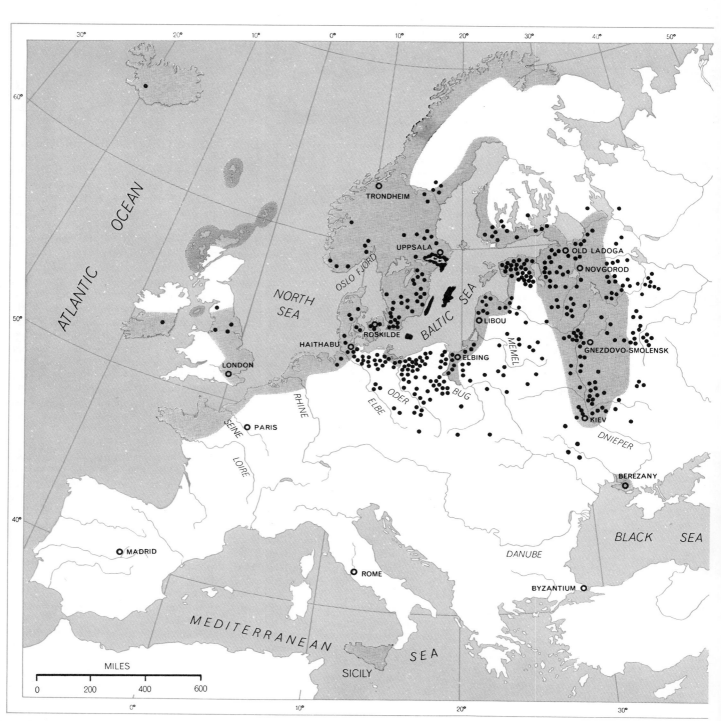

**VIKING SPHERE** during four centuries of trade, settlement and piracy extended from the Volga River and the Caspian Sea in Asia, through the Mediterranean and western Europe to the British Isles, Iceland and beyond (*see illustrations on page 309*). The areas where the Vikings established permanent colonies are indicated in gray; areas of passing conquest or other brief residence have been omit-

reached the Norwegian coast as part of some raider's loot and was then traded eastward to Helgö. A greater surprise was the discovery in 1955 of a small bronze figure of Buddha, complete with a golden caste mark on the forehead.

One of the way stations along this trade route between the north and Charlemagne's Europe was a Danish town at the base of the Jutland penin-

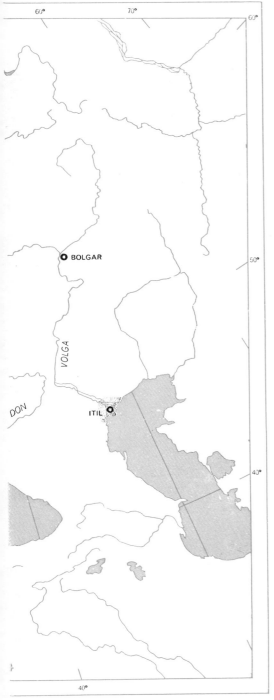

ted. The pervasive effect of Viking trade with the East is shown by the wide distribution of Arab coins (dots mark coin finds).

sula. Founded by King Godfred in A.D. 808, it stood near the present Kiel Canal at a point where only eight miles of land separate the Treene River and the North Sea from the Schlei River and the Baltic. Not only could goods moving north and south be easily transshipped here; the light dragon ships could themselves be hauled from one sea to the other on log rollers or mattresses of brushwood.

On all this traffic the Danes levied a profitable tariff. The town was Haithabu (modern Hedeby) and by A.D. 1000 it had grown as large as Cologne. Some of this area, which today lies in West Germany, was excavated before World War II; the work was resumed in 1960. Haithabu's cosmopolitan character during the last centuries of the first millennium can be judged by the kinds of objects that have been uncovered there. The excavators found, for example, a gold coin from Byzantium minted during the rule of the joint emperors Theophilus and Constantine (A.D. 829 to 842) in association with a gold-plated bronze buckle acquired in a raid on Ireland.

In 829 Charlemagne's son Louis the Pious received an embassy from the king of the Svea at a conclave that assembled at Worms on the Rhine. A regularization of trade was probably in the minds of both parties. In any case, Louis took advantage of the Svea delegation's return to Uppsala to send with them a missionary, a Benedictine monk. Accounts of the monk's mission indicate that he built a church but was not very successful in winning converts among the Vikings.

## Overland to Byzantium

Meanwhile in their colonies across the Baltic the Svea were doing more than farming and trading. They advanced in their light ships across eastern Europe as if its meadows and forests were the open sea. Sailing up the Düna and Memel rivers, they beached their shallow-draft vessels and carried them overland to launch them again in rivers flowing south—the Dnieper and the Volga. Scarcely 10 years after the Svea embassy had visited the Emperor of the West at Worms, Vikings who had sailed the inland waterways to the Black Sea paid their respects to the Emperor of the East at Byzantium. Indeed, one such Svea group traveled back to its own land not the way it had come but by way of the Mediterranean and Italy, traveling with the Eastern emperor's embassy to the new ruler of the West (Lothar, who succeeded Louis the Pious in 840). A contemporary chronicle introduces us to a new word: the returning Svea are re-

ferred to as "some men calling themselves and their people Rus."

It is worth a digression to consider this word. The coastal district east of Uppsala in Sweden is Roslagen, and to this day its inhabitants are called Rospiggar. (The word rus itself means "oarsman.") The Svea kings certainly raised levies in this district, each locality traditionally furnishing a ship and crew. It is at least plausible to suggest that the trans-Baltic Viking settlements included many such complements of rus from Roslagen. Further weight is lent to this suggestion by the fact that the Finnish name for Sweden is Ruotsi. It is not surprising, therefore, that the oldest political entity in eastern Europe, the city of Kiev and its surrounding lands on the Dnieper, should have come to be known as Rusland and eventually as Russia.

In czarist times, and even today, some Russian scholars have challenged this derivation of "Russia." In my view the archaeological record strongly supports the Viking origin of "Rusland." As in the Gotland graves in Latvia, graves in Russia have yielded a large number of women's ornaments that show typical Svea workmanship. Nearly 100 oval Svea clasps have been unearthed, for example. I take this to be clear proof that the same Viking warrior-merchants who traveled the inland waterways also settled, with their wives, the fertile Russian countryside. Moreover, an excavation in Kiev has uncovered a chamber tomb of typical Svea design, and on the chest of the entombed man was found a Svea "Thor's hammer." It takes little imagination to reach the conclusion that the man was a worshiper of the Norse gods and in all probability a Viking colonist.

At least at first, however, the inland voyagers must have considered trade more important than colonization. Soon many of the Svea knew all the details of the journey southward from Kiev. They knew the names of the seven rapids of the Dnieper where travelers had to portage, and had chosen an island (Berezany) in the Dnieper delta as a place to stop before sailing on across the Black Sea. Soon treaties were written between the Byzantine authorities and the Svea, mainly to restrict the voyagers' freedom of action. The Vikings were not allowed to spend the winter in Byzantium. No more than 50 Vikings at a time could enter the city, and then only unarmed. Purchases of silk, a highly prized commodity, were not to exceed 50 aurei in value. The traders may not have spent long periods at the island of Berezany, but one of them found time to leave a

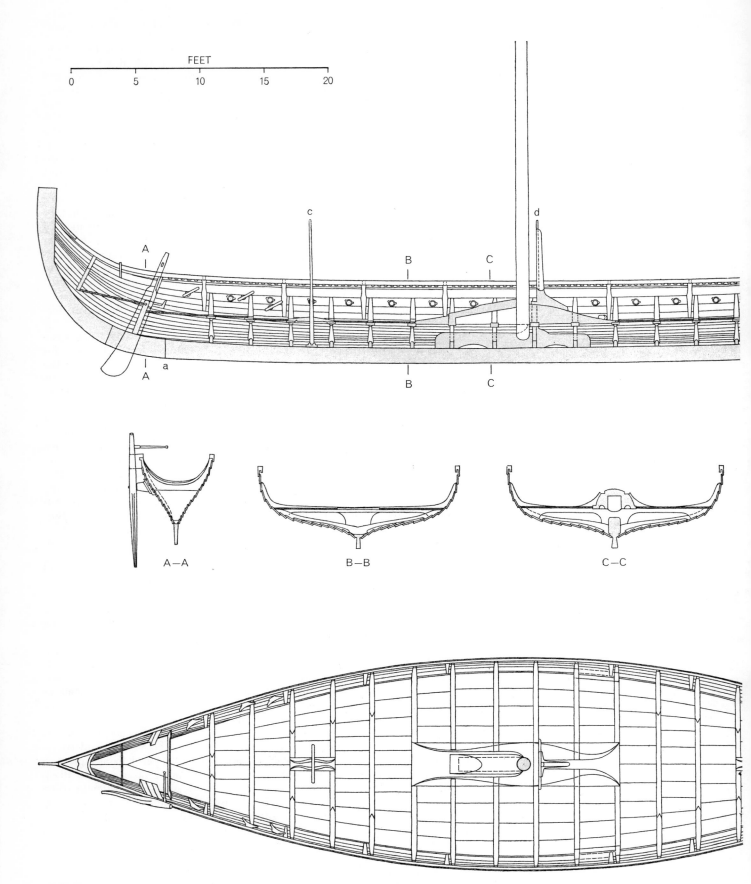

**GOKSTAD SHIP,** smaller than most of the dragon ships with which the Vikings harried the British Isles and western Europe, preserves their main features. For the better part of its 78-foot length (*from "a" to "b"*) the keel is one piece of oak, hewn from a tree that must have stood more than 75 feet high. The ship had 16 pairs of oars, and 32 overlapping shields filled the spaces between the oar holes on each side when the ship was in port. The three uprights ("*c*," *"d" and "e"*) may have supported tentlike shelters in

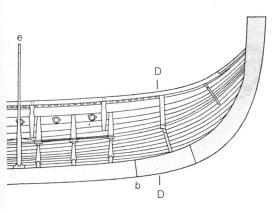

D—D

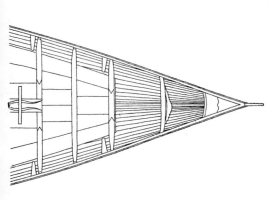

**foul weather. Little is known, however, about the accommodations the Vikings enjoyed while at sea, how the ships' sails were rigged or what rigging braced their masts.**

memorial stone there. Its runic inscription reads: "Grane raised this arch for his comrade Karl."

## Contact with Islam

The route to Byzantium down the Dnieper was only one of the inland waterways used by the Viking traders. They also reached the Volga by way of the Gulf of Finland and Lake Ladoga, and descended to the Caspian Sea, a gateway to the world of the Turks and the Arabs. It was not even necessary to go all the way to the Caspian; at a halfway point on the Volga stood the rich trading city of Bolgar. The 10th-century Arab geographer Muqqadasi names some of the goods sold in the market there: "Sable, squirrel, ermine, corsac, martin, foxes, beaver pelts, colorful hare, goatskin, wax, arrows, birchbark, caps, fish-lime, fish teeth, beaver-gall, amber, horny leather, honey, hazel nuts, hawks, swords, armor, acorns, Slavonic slaves, small cattle and oxen—all this from Bolgar."

Another market town, at the mouth of the Volga, was equally colorful. There, near present-day Astrakhan, a 10th-century representative of the Bagdad caliphate named ibn Fadlan met a Viking trading party. "I have never seen humans more nobly built," he wrote. "They are tall as palm trees, red blond, with light skins. The man wears a cape slung over one shoulder, so that one hand is free. Every man carries an axe, a dirk and a sword. Each one has a bench on which he sits with his beautiful slaves who are for sale. [To worship] a man goes up to [a wooden] pillar and throws himself down on the ground and says, 'O my god, I come from far off and bring with me so and so many women and so and so many skins of martin.... Grant me a purchaser who has many gold and silver coins and buys everything from me.... When a man possesses 10,000 silver coins he has a [necklace] made for his wife. If he has 20,000 she gets a second necklace.... Many chains therefore hang around the neck of a Rus woman."

There is no reason to doubt the importance of slaves as articles of trade. Who the slaves were is suggested by the fact that the Svea word for such human chattels, *trälar,* was soon abandoned in favor of the word *slavar.* Evidently most of the slaves were Slavs. Yet the Vikings' slaves would not have been exclusively Slavs; one wonders how many Franks, Irish and Anglo-Saxons served as involuntary oarsmen on the dragon ships' homeward voyages and then moved on

to the slave markets of the Scandinavian peninsula. Not all the slave markets were strictly in Viking country. Recent studies have shown that three of them were on the European mainland: Haithabu on the Baltic, Magdeburg on the Elbe and Regensburg on the Danube. One Viking merchant, called "Gille the Russian" because he always wore a Russian cap, was a common sight in the slave market of Göteborg, in what is now Sweden. His specialty was Irish girls; it is recorded that he sold one of them for three times the usual price, in spite of the fact that the girl was deaf. She must have been very beautiful.

The total number of Arab silver coins so far discovered in Scandinavia is about 57,000. The way in which these coins are distributed brings out an important fact about the various Viking groups and their separate areas of operations. It is apparent that the hoards were not a normal place of storage but a temporary refuge for treasure. Probably only when the possessors of precious metal believed they were about to be raided would they hastily dig a hole and hide their treasure, always in the expectation of reclaiming it when the trouble was past. This helps to explain why Gotland, which was a favorite target of raiders, has yielded not only the two largest hoards in Scandinavia but also the largest number of Arab coins—some 40,000 in all. Doubtless the hoards remained buried when their owners were victims of the very raids that caused them to hide their wealth.

In any case, only 17,000 additional Arab coins have been recovered from the Swedish mainland and modern Denmark, and Norway has yielded a mere 400. The geography of Scandinavia explains why this is so. For the Gotlanders and the peoples of the Swedish mainland the Baltic was virtually a private lake. They usually left it only to take to the inland waterways of Russia. The Danish peoples, on the other hand, faced both the North Sea and the Baltic. When they raided, England and the coast of Germany and France were their primary targets. When they traded, it was into the Baltic. It is not surprising that much Arab coinage should have come into Danish hands. As for the peoples of what is now Norway, their harbors on the North Sea were best suited to island-hopping operations that led them by way of the Shetland and the Orkney islands to the Irish Sea and the rich prizes along both its eastern and its western shore. It is therefore not surprising that they possessed very little Arab silver.

that had divided Europe into three quarrelsome kingdoms after the death of Charlemagne, he gave the king of France, Charles the Bald, a bad scare in 845 by sailing a 120-ship force up the Seine and capturing Paris. Charles's army was divided by the river. Ragnar routed the French troops on one bank while their comrades-in-arms on the other bank did nothing. Whatever aggressiveness may have remained in the French ebbed away when Ragnar hanged more than 100 of his prisoners as a sacrifice to Odin. Shortly thereafter Charles the Bald sent Ragnar a gift of 7,000 pounds of silver and asked him to desist.

Yet Ragnar's three sons, with a minimum of bloodshed in 876, successfully seized and colonized the eastern part of England—a region called the Five Boroughs after the five strongholds (Lincoln, Stamford, Leicester, Derby and Nottingham) from which the Danes administered it. The district remained populous and prosperous until William the Conqueror—himself of Viking descent—found that a "harrying of the north" was necessary if his new kingdom was to

**DRAGON HEAD** carved out of wood provides an example of more intricate Viking workmanship than the stone carving shown on page 308. This is one of several dragon heads found aboard the ship in which a Norwegian Viking queen was buried near Oslo in A.D. 850.

No one of these three main Viking spheres of influence was held exclusively. Consider the example of Harald Haadraade (Hard-Ruler), who commanded the Byzantine fleet under the Empress Zoë and even fought a naval engagement (off Monopoli, near Naples, in 1042) against fellow Vikings who had entered the Mediterranean from the west. Although a dominant figure among the eastern Vikings, Harald himself was a Norwegian who had spent his boyhood in Russia and had thus gravitated toward Byzantium. When he eventually returned home to occupy the Norwegian throne, he was no less active in western affairs. It was fighting off his raid on England in 1066 that wore out the English king Harold's troops and assured the Norman Conquest. Another example is provided by the Danish Vikings who moved into the normally Norwegian preserve of Ireland in the middle of the ninth century. The Danes fought beside the Irish to repulse the next Norwegian raiders to appear. On the whole, however, the Swedish Vikings stayed in the Baltic and the East, leaving the North Sea, the Atlantic and the parts of the Mediterranean that were unclaimed by

Byzantium to the Norwegians and the Danes.

## The Norwegian and Danish Vikings

In describing the activities of the Norwegians and the Danes during the ninth century one can draw a legitimate distinction between the occasions when they were raiding and those in which they were colonizing. The Norwegians certainly settled the northern islands they used as stepping-stones to the Irish Sea. Once established in western waters, they founded settlements in the Hebrides and on the islands nearer the western coast of Scotland and also made the Isle of Man a base of operations. Although the Norwegians began raiding Ireland as early as 820, their intentions were more ambitious than mere piracy. By the middle of the century they had established a royal line in Dublin and held extensive Irish lands.

Nor were the Danes—who, as we shall see, were second to none as raiders—exclusively piratical. Ragnar Lodbrok (Hairy-Breeches) was clearly a man of large plans. One of the first Danish Vikings to take advantage of the civil strife

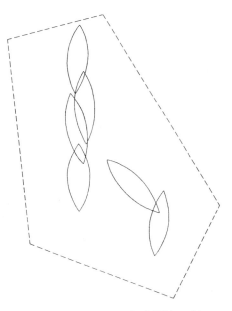

**WATERLOGGED HULLS** of Viking ships, sunk 1,000 years ago to block the mouth of Roskilde Fjord in Denmark, appear in the aerial photograph on the opposite page. In 1962 a cofferdam was built around the stone-laden hulks, the seawater was pumped out and the timbers were salvaged from the muddy bottom. Positions of the six ships partly visible in the photograph are shown in the illustration above. Most of the Roskilde ships were freighters; the success of the Vikings in trade and war, however, depended more on their swift "dragon ships" (*see illustrations, pages 302, 303, and 307*).

SILVER PENDANTS are examples of simple and elaborate Viking work in metal. Both objects are so-called Thor hammers. The simple one recognizably mimics a socketed hammerhead mounted on a short shaft, but the maker of the ornate one did not attempt realism.

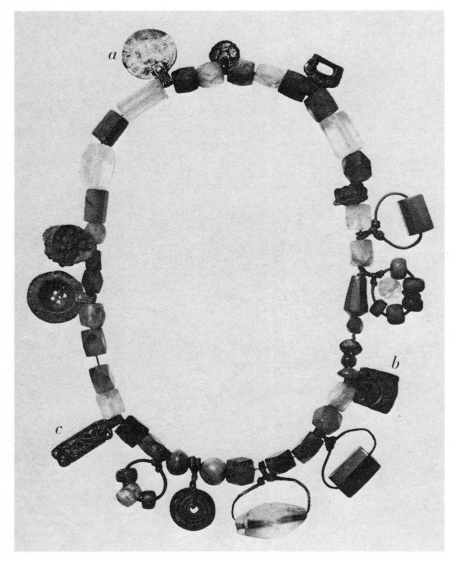

VIKING NECKLACE, found near Stockholm, shows the wide geographical range of Viking trade. Clockwise, the coin ("a," at top) is Byzantine, the silver fragment (b) is from an Arab bowl and the bronze flange (c) is a portion of a book mounting made in Great Britain.

be free from Scandinavian interference.

Ragnar was not the first Viking to raid mainland Europe. Four years earlier, in May of 841, a Danish force under one Asgeir sailed up the Seine toward Paris. It sacked Rouen and advanced as far as St. Denis before turning back. Two years later another Viking force with 67 ships sailed up the Loire, ravaged Nantes and sailed downstream again to pass the winter in Noirmontier at the river's mouth.

The Vikings remained active on the North Sea coast. The Frisian city of Dorestad was looted almost yearly. In 845, the same year in which Ragnar attacked Paris, another Viking force burned Hamburg. The chronicles of the unsuccessful defense of Hamburg state that the assault was mounted by 600 dragon ships. If we give each vessel a complement of 40 men, we must assume a Viking force of 24,000! It seems more likely that the Viking fleet numbered perhaps 60, rather than 600, vessels.

The year 845 also saw the customary Viking raids on Ireland and, far more significant, the dispatch of a fleet (said to number 100 ships) that sailed south past France and Spain into the Mediterranean to trade or raid along the coast of Arab North Africa. The record of this first entry into the Mediterranean by the western Vikings is obscure. More information is available on these activities four years later, in 859. In that year Ragnar's son Björn Ironsides, together with a Viking named Hastings, sailed 62 dragon ships into the Mediterranean for a raid that lasted 36 months. Using an island at the mouth of the Rhone as their base, they plundered Nimes, Arles and Valence. Then, pushing eastward into Italy, they sacked Pisa, Fiesole and Luna (a harbor town that no longer exists). On the way home Björn's Vikings stopped at Pamplona in Spain. There they happened to find the Prince of Navarre, for whom they were given a large ransom. The Vikings counted it a successful voyage, even though they lost 40 of their ships in a storm off Gibraltar. Among other things, their peaceable visit to Morocco during the voyage resulted in the Maghreb caliphate's dispatching an ambassador to Denmark. It is reported that he did not enjoy his visit.

In the winter of 878, two years after Ragnar's three sons had established the Five Boroughs in England, other Viking raiders gathered to see what could be accomplished elsewhere in the British Isles. Fortunately for England, but unfortunately for the continent of Europe, Alfred, a young English ruler in Wessex,

**VIKING SHIP BURIAL,** unearthed in 1880 at Gokstad in Norway, served as the grave of King Olaf, who died in 880. Although its royal treasure had been looted centuries earlier, the Gokstad ship's timbers were so well preserved that it could be reconstructed in full detail (*see illustration on pages 302 and 303*). The ship's single mast was secured to the hull by means of a set of interlocking braces that are visible amidships in the photograph. The twin sets of upright planks that form inverted V's to the rear of the mast bracing were parts of the framework of the burial chamber rather than components of a deckhouse. The ship could carry a load of 20 tons.

defeated the invading force at Ethandun. The following spring the defeated Vikings landed en masse at the mouth of the Schelde River, gradually assembled a "Great Army" that finally numbered 700 ships and 40,000 men, and proceeded to ravage the Continent for the next 13 years.

At last, having gathered all the loot it could and finding little prospect for more in a famine year, the Great Army withdrew. The Viking force then sailed for England once again, but Alfred (now known as "the Great") was more than ready for them, this time with his own fleet. By 896, in the final years of Alfred's reign, the remnants of the Great Army sailed back to the Continent, reduced to little more than a band of mercenaries.

In the opening years of the 10th century European towns were no longer regularly sacked by major Viking forces, but the Viking influence on the Continent remained considerable. Fresh Viking forces continued to leave Denmark and Norway, seeking lands to occupy. One such emigré—Rollo—eventually became leader of all western Europe's Vikings.

The king of France, Charles the Simple, saw a solution to the Viking problem. In exchange for Rollo's baptism and an oath of fealty in 911, Charles granted the Viking leader all Normandy. It was from this Viking enclave that a

century and a half later emerged both the leader and the troops who conquered England and reshaped its history.

## The Dragon Ships

What single element in Viking history can be deemed most responsible for these northerners' success in battle, trade and emigration? It must surely be the dragon ship. The tallies of the Viking fleets of the ninth and 10th centuries make it clear that these ships were built in large numbers, but the fact remains that only a few of the vessels uncovered by the archaeologist's spade are typical dragon ships. From the remains we have and from literary descriptions, however, it is possible to reconstruct the Vikings' seafaring warships with reasonable accuracy.

The earliest-known Scandinavian ship, uncovered on a moor near Nydam in Denmark, dates back to about A.D. 300. Built of oak planks, it had a rounded bottom and a comparatively deep draft; it had no keel or mast. There were positions for 30 oars—15 on each side—and therefore 15 oarsmen's benches. The second-known Scandinavian ship, built some 300 years later and unearthed at Kvalsund, I have already mentioned. It shows considerable evolution, being wider in beam and shallower in draft than the Nydam ship. Although it lacks

a true keel, it has a deck and provision for a mast.

The finest Viking ships discovered so far are all from sites near Oslo in Norway: Gokstad and Oseberg on the western shore of Oslofjord and Tune on the eastern shore. The Gokstad ship, uncovered in 1880, is 78 feet long, has a mast and also a keel consisting of a single oak timber. Its carrying capacity is estimated at 20 tons. It has 16 rowing benches, 32 oars in all. The Norwegian notable whose grave it marks appears to be one Olaf, a king who lived from about 810 to 880.

The Oseberg ship, which was discovered in 1904, is shorter by some six feet, has one less rowing bench and a mast that gives the impression of being small and weak. This ship is the burial place of Olaf's stepmother, Queen Asa, whose husband ruled from about 780 to 820. Both the ship and its contents are decorated with carvings of remarkable beauty and intricacy. Nonetheless, the Oseberg ship appears not to have been an oceangoing craft but a coastwise one. The third vessel, found near Tune in 1867, is the least well preserved of the three. It is estimated to have been some 66 feet long and to have had 11 or 12 rowing benches. All three vessels are preserved today in a special museum at Bygdöy, outside Oslo.

How closely do these Norwegian ves-

**LEGEND OF SIEGFRIED,** popular among the Vikings, is the subject of this Viking memorial inscription. The body of the huge dragon, Fafner, forms the lower margin of the rock carving; within its outline is a runic inscription honoring one Holmger. The legend starts (*lower right*) with Siegfried driving his sword into Fafner's body. Next (*left of center*) Siegfried sits cooking the dragon's heart on a spit. Burning his thumb with the hot fat, he puts the thumb in his mouth. The taste of dragon fat works wonders; he now understands animal languages and overhears the birds in the tree beside his horse (*right*). The birds are discussing the treacherous plans of the smith Regin. Siegfried at once slays Regin; the headless corpse (*far left*) is identified as the smith's by the hammer, tongs, anvil and bellows that lie nearby. The doglike animal above the smith's hammer is Rodmar's son, the otter; in its mouth is Nibelung's ring.

sels resemble the Viking dragon ships? The Gokstad ship has passed an impressive empirical test: a faithful replica of it was sailed across the Atlantic in 1893 to be exhibited at the Chicago World's Fair. Not only was the voyage successful but also the crew found they could make a speed of as much as 10 to 11 knots in a brisk wind. It is therefore possible that some dragon ships were as small as the Gokstad ship. On the basis of literary descriptions, however, it appears that most dragon ships were larger.

The ships built for royalty at the turn of the millennium, although known only through oral tradition, were apparently larger still. At the Battle of Svolder in A.D. 1000 King Olaf of Norway appeared aboard the *Ormen Lange* (*Long Snake*), which was some 164 feet long and had 34 rowing benches. The last of the royal Norwegian ships, built by the shipwrights of Trondheim in 1263, had three more rowing benches than the *Ormen Lange*. Sang a skald: "[It] shall carry thee, majestic friend, like a keen hawk on the quarterdeck. Never did more beautiful ship sail with more magnificent king."

Not all Viking vessels were dragon ships. Viking freighters, called *knarr*, were known only from literary references, however, until 1962. In that year Danish archaeologists recovered several incomplete Viking ships from Roskilde Fjord on the Danish island of Seeland. For reasons at which we can only guess, the people of Roskilde had blocked their harbor by filling several ships with stones and sinking them in the mouth of the fjord. One of them, 53 feet long, was apparently a fast cargo vessel. Another vessel is almost 65 feet long and is notable for its breadth of beam and the stoutness of its timbers. It was evidently a carrier of heavy freight. To judge by the low railing and the number of oar holes of the third ship, it may have been a fast passenger vessel. A fourth appears to be a onetime dragon ship that was converted into a freighter late in its career. The remains of the other Roskilde ships are too fragmentary to tell us much about them.

Meanwhile other ships that may belong to the Viking period have been found in northern Germany. In 1953 a volunteer diver working with the director of the Schleswig Museum located one large vessel and parts of a smaller one in the harbor of Haithabu. All of us who are particularly interested in such matters look forward to what will be learned from these remains when the funds necessary for their recovery become available.

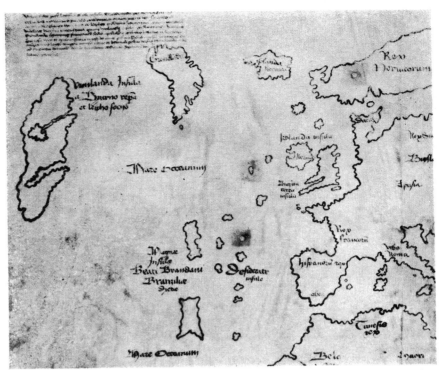

VINLAND MAP, drawn 52 years before Columbus discovered America, shows a surprisingly accurate outline of Greenland to the west of Iceland and a larger island, labeled Vinland, to the west of Greenland. A notation on the map, prepared for an ecclesiastical council at Basel in 1440, declares that Eric Gnuppson, a bishop of Greenland, visited "this very rich land" (Vinland) in 1118. The map maker dotted the Atlantic with fictitious islands.

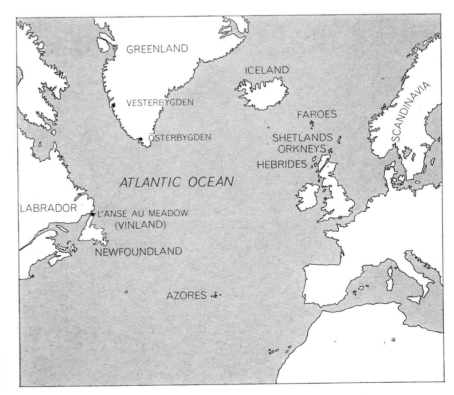

MODERN MAP of the same regions shown in the Vinland map shows the remarkable correctness of the earlier document's outline of Greenland. Although the shape given to Vinland bears no obvious relation to the shape of northeastern North America, its two bays (*see top illustration*) may indicate a knowledge of Hudson Bay and the Gulf of St. Lawrence.

When and why did Viking fortunes—in trade if not in war—decline? To the first of these questions Scandinavian archaeology provides a remarkably detailed answer. The silver hoards recovered in Denmark, for example, contained no coins but Arab ones until 950. The hoards of the next 30 years contain both Arab coins and a few German ones. A century later exactly the opposite is true: of some 3,000 silver coins found in hoards that were buried between 1050 and 1070 only four are Arab. Evidently Viking contacts with the Moslem world dwindled to nothing within the span of a century.

As to the question of why, it is probably pertinent to note three historical developments that fall within the same period. First, the silver mines of central Asia (on which the Moslem rulers of the East depended for their metal) seem to have become exhausted at about this time. Second, a general advance of Turkish tribes in the Middle East and Near East denied the Russian waterways to the Swedish Vikings and severed their connections with Byzantium. Finally, the European powers on the Mediterranean halted the advance of Islam during this period and soon no longer needed the hardy Viking merchant-warriors to act as middlemen.

## The Vikings in North America

Our knowledge of one other important series of events in Viking history—the voyages west from Iceland—has also been increased as a result of recent archaeological research. The story of Eric the Red and his son Leif is too well known to need retelling here. Less well known, perhaps, is the tradition that another Greenlander, Thorfinn Karlsefni, took three ships and 160 men and in 1020 established a colony in what they called Vinland on the coast of North America. When Thorfinn's house in Greenland was excavated in 1930, the diggers came on a lump of anthracite coal that has been identified as having originated in the vicinity of Rhode Island.

At Brattalid, in Greenland's "eastern settlement," archaeologists have uncovered Leif Ericson's homestead. In 1965 these workers came on the remains of Leif's mother's chapel, a few hundred yards from the foundation of his house. Beside the chapel are 150 graves, from which 96 skeletons have been disinterred. It seems more than likely that one of them is Leif's.

For some centuries the New World settlement established by Leif—called Leifsbodarna in the Viking sagas—had been sought, without success. During the 1950's, however, a Norwegian investigator, Helge Ingstad, began to reconnoiter the coasts of Labrador and Newfoundland with a fresh idea in mind. Could the "vin" in Vinland mean something other than "wine," as had been generally supposed? Ingstad preferred to think that it meant "grass" or "pasturage." In 1961, near the isolated fishing village of L'Anse au Meadow in northern Newfoundland, an expedition under Ingstad uncovered traces of several buildings, including the foundation of a "great hall" identical with the one Leif had built for himself in Greenland. Charcoal associated with iron and slag at the site—evidently the remains of a smithy—has yielded a carbon-14 date of A.D. 1060 ± 70, which agrees reasonably well with the dates that are given in the sagas.

Three years' work at the Newfoundland site has yielded Ingstad a number of architectural details but very few artifacts. Perhaps the most significant one is a spindle whorl—the weight that acts as a flywheel when a spindle is used to twist yarn from raw wool—made of soapstone. Soapstone spindle whorls are common at Norse sites in Greenland and Iceland, as well as in Scandinavia.

## Greenland's Decline

The Greenland colonies from which the Viking visitors to North America came numbered some 300 homesteads at their height. They were cut off from contact with Iceland and Europe sometime during the 15th century, but before that they had had a bishop, two cloisters and 16 churches. They had even sent a tithe of walrus tusks to the Vatican (the record shows that 250 tusks were received in 1327). The only vessel regularly in the Greenland trade was wrecked in 1367 and not replaced, but archaeological evidence shows that contacts continued after that date. In Greenland graves are found woolen caps, peaked in a manner that became fashionable in Burgundy during the latter half of the 15th century.

Less than a century later, in 1540, a voyaging Icelander happened to sail past one of Greenland's settled fjords. He saw people, including a man lying dead on the ground, and decided not to land. A few years later a ship out of Hamburg called at Greenland but its captain was unable to find any signs of life.

# The Archaeology of Winchester

by Martin Biddle
*May 1974*

*This English cathedral city was faced with the loss of
its past as a result of urban redevelopment.
Excavation has now revealed the pattern of its
growth since its birth some 2,000 years ago*

How is a city born and how does it grow? If it is long dead, like Troy or royal Ur, archaeology can readily provide some of the answers. If the city is still very much alive, like Rome or London, the evidence is harder to obtain. Nonetheless, over the past 12 years an intensive archaeological campaign has uncovered the early periods and amplified the recorded history of one such city. The site was a major defended settlement during the latter part of the British Iron Age, was the island's fifth-largest town in Roman times, was a prosperous bishopric from the seventh century, was a royal seat until well after the Norman Conquest and is today one of England's leading cathedral cities, with a population of 33,000. The city is Winchester, and what more than a decade of urban archaeology has revealed about it is a fair indication of how much can be achieved elsewhere in the world when the work is begun before the past is irretrievably destroyed.

The River Itchen, the trout stream made famous by Izaak Walton in *The Compleat Angler,* rises in central Hampshire and flows south through a range of chalk downs on its way to Southampton Water, behind the Isle of Wight. Since remote antiquity the river valley and the grassy downs have provided natural lines of communication, the one north-south and the other east-west. At the point where the two routes cross and the alluvial valley floor is narrowest a spur of the chalk downs slopes more gently than elsewhere toward the riverbank.

A mile or so southeast of this spur the valley of the Itchen is commanded on its opposite eastern side by an Iron Age hill fort: St. Catharine's Hill [*see illustration on page 313*]. Built during the third or second century B.C. and enclosing an area of more than 20 acres, the defenses give evidence of having been reconstructed several times before being burned in the first century B.C. By then a settlement had appeared on the western side of the valley, on the same chalk spur where Winchester would later lie. In about the middle of the first century B.C. the new settlement was formally defined by the construction of a rampart and ditch that enclosed an area of just over 40 acres, or nearly twice the area of the eastern hill fort. This enclosure was the dominant feature of the valley in the later Iron Age. It lay astride the east-west route and commanded the river crossing.

Although little is known of the interior of the western settlement, its central area seems to have been densely occupied. The economy of the inhabitants was based on agriculture, but there is also evidence for long-distance trade connections. Fragments of southern Italian wine amphoras of the first century B.C. have been found, and the enclosure and its immediate vicinity have produced nine large bronze Ptolemaic coins of the third century B.C. from Egypt. These, of course, may have been imported for the value of their metal long after the time when they were first minted.

The size of the western enclosure is impressive, but there is not yet enough evidence to suggest that it contained an urban or even a proto-urban community. Moreover, the settlement appears to have been a false start; there is a break of as much as 100 years in its habitation. When the area was reoccupied soon after the Roman conquest of Britain in A.D. 43, the settlement was on the valley floor near the river, outside and downhill from the Iron Age enclosure.

Much of what we know about the growth of the settlement in Roman times is the result of emergency excavations first undertaken in 1961, when preparations were being made for the building of a new hotel in the center of the city. The rescue excavation soon revealed two facts. The first was the immense and virtually untapped wealth of Winchester's archaeological record. The second was the rate at which that record would be destroyed by the modern developments then planned for the decade ahead.

The city today is an important administrative, judicial, military, ecclesiastical and business center. The pressures generated by these urban functions find expression in plans for new roads and buildings, all potentially destructive of the buried remains of the city's past. A special body, the Winchester Excavations Committee, was set up in 1962 to deal with the problem of investigating and recording the archaeological evidence before its destruction. During the next 10 years the committee administered the largest program of urban excavation yet undertaken in Britain (or elsewhere in Europe for that matter). For seven years the work has been a joint Anglo-American venture, done in collaboration with the University of North Carolina and Duke University and supported by government and foundation funds from both sides of the Atlantic.

The project had from the start the principal objective of studying the origin and changing character of the urban community throughout its entire existence, from the first permanent settlement down to the emergence of the modern city in the reign of Victoria. The city itself was to be the subject, rather than any one period or aspect of its past. We hoped to try to grasp the totality of the urban phenomenon and the interaction of the city and its setting, both at distinct moments in time and between one period of its development and another.

The project involved not only rescue

excavations on threatened sites but also excavations on unthreatened ones, some of them large enterprises that yielded information essential to any balanced concept of the city's evolution. The project also required the integrated utilization of all the available evidence, whether it was from archaeology, from the natural sciences or from written records (in which the city is immensely rich from the 12th century on).

In 1968 the Winchester Research Unit was set up to prepare this large body of-material for publication. A series of perhaps 12 volumes of *Winchester Studies* is planned. They will come from the Clarendon Press at Oxford and the University of North Carolina Press. The first volume will appear late this year or early in 1975.

The new Romano-British settlement on the Itchen was peopled not by Romans from Italy but by Romanized Celts. Their settlement may have grown up in a rather formless way at the junction of the new Roman roads that met close to the old river crossing. These roads, built shortly after the Roman conquest, were perhaps protected by a detachment of troops housed in a fort at or near their junction. If the fort ever existed, and the evidence is still unclear, its life was no more than 20 years. The development of the civil settlement was in contrast rapid: by the end of the first century it had become a walled city with a chessboard street plan and public buildings. The earth-and-timber ramparts of the city defenses enclosed an area of more than 143 acres. Their line was followed by all subsequent walls of the city down to the end of the Middle Ages.

The size of the enclosed area made Winchester the fifth-largest city in Roman Britain. Two long-distance Roman roads formed the axes of the rectilinear street system that divided the city into *insulae,* or blocks. A central block was occupied by the forum and basilica, constructed by about A.D. 100 to house the judicial, administrative and principal commercial functions of the city. The city was now known as Venta Belgarum. As "Venta" may imply, it was the market center of its region, and as "Belgarum" indicates, that region was populated by the Celtic tribesmen known as the Belgae, from among whose principal landowners the city's chief citizens were drawn.

Little is known of the detailed development of Roman Winchester. At first its houses, even if they were provided with such amenities as glazed windows, painted walls, tiled roofs and mosaic floors, were built of timber. Increasing prosperity in the later second century led to their being rebuilt in stone. About A.D. 200 the defenses, which must long have been out of repair, were totally remodeled. Within a generation the earth-and-timber perimeter was strengthened by the addition of a stone wall that was to stand for 1,500 years. The influence of the stone ramparts is still reflected in the traffic problems of the modern city.

The Romano-Britons left behind one common kind of archaeological evidence: the remains of their dead. In the Roman fashion the cemeteries lay along the roads outside the city gates. Here in the mid-fourth century, among the burials of the native population, is found the first clear evidence of the arrival of aliens at Winchester. Some graves, distinguished by the leather belts with bronze fittings they contained, are apparently those of soldiers. Their equipment is of a kind well known along Rome's frontiers on the Rhine and the Danube.

During the second half of the fourth century, following the barbarian ravaging of Britain in A.D. 367, the defenses of the island provinces were reorganized. An important element in the revised strategy was a system of "defense in depth," which was to be provided by walled towns. The towns' fortifications were strengthened by the addition of projecting towers, evidently to mount catapults that could rake attackers with arcs of intersecting fire. Winchester was included in the defense system. The maintenance and use of such artillery probably required the services of specialized troops; the alien element now recognized in burials of this period at Winchester and at other towns may well indicate the presence of such specialists. They were foreigners (perhaps Germans), either regular soldiers or mercenaries.

The movement of troops and even of entire peoples in the interests of frontier defense was a normal part of Roman policy. That policy was evidently continued even after the departure of the Roman administration of Britain at the beginning of the fifth century. In A.D. 410 the Emperor Honorius told the cities of Roman Britain to look after their own defense; this they did by continuing to hire mercenaries. The foreign levies now came not from the distant frontiers of the empire but from the barbarian shores around the North Sea, the traditional homeland of the Anglo-Saxon peoples.

The presence of Anglo-Saxons among the Romanized Celts of Winchester shortly after A.D. 400 is indicated by the

**WINCHESTER LIES** beside the River Itchen near the center of Hampshire, some 12 miles to the north of Southampton and 60 miles southwest of London, the city that eclipsed it.

presence of pottery identical with the pottery used in their home settlements along the lower reaches of the German rivers Weser and Elbe. Together with the evidence from the cemeteries, the pottery shows that the population of late Roman Winchester was already mixed and that before the end of Roman Britain the first forerunners of the English were already established in and around the city that was eventually to emerge as the capital of an English kingdom: Wessex.

It appears that urban life in Roman Winchester came slowly to an end during the fifth century. At every site of excavation the evidence of decay, the abandonment of buildings and the loss of streets is the same. No objects and only a little pottery of the period from A.D. 450 to 650 have been found. The ruined Roman city nonetheless remained an important focal point as Anglo-Saxon settlement of the region progressed, and this is indicated by two lines of evidence.

First, comparatively few Anglo-Saxon cemeteries of the pagan period from the fifth to the seventh century have been found in the county of Hampshire. The most striking cluster of these cemeteries lies in the immediate area of Winchester, outside the city walls to the east and west. Moreover, an early cemetery that was in use by A.D. 500 lies two miles upstream from the city. Unless the former Roman center was still a focus of some kind, why should these cemeteries, each of which presumably holds the burials of a farm or a small village, be concentrated in its vicinity?

Second, in about A.D. 648 Cenwalh, king of Wessex, founded a church dedicated to St. Peter and St. Paul inside the still standing Roman walls of Winchester. About a decade later this church became the see of the bishop of Wessex. Cenwalh had built the Winchester church not as a bishop's see but simply as a minster, that is, a church served by a group of priests and clerks not necessarily living under monastic rule. One may ask what function and what community this church in the center of a ruined city was intended to serve.

The Anglo-Saxon cemeteries suggest that from the late fifth century into the seventh Winchester was still an important place. (The Saxons transformed the name Venta into Wintancæster.) King Cenwalh's church may indicate the nature of that focus. Excavation of the seventh-century church has shown that it lies adjacent to the Roman forum. In the late Saxon period the Anglo-Saxon royal palace was immediately west of the church and was intimately associated

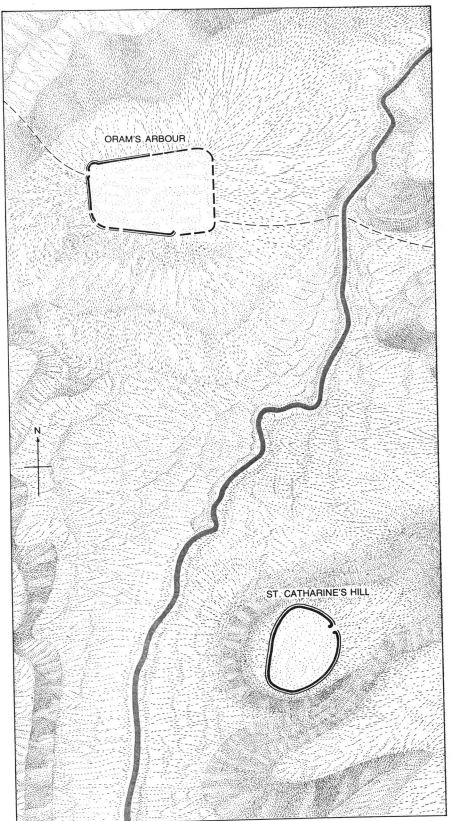

EARLIEST SETTLEMENTS in the Winchester area were two Iron Age defended enclosures. The earlier of the two (*bottom*), the hill fort now known as St. Catharine's Hill, was built in the third or second century B.C. By the time it was abandoned a second defense, twice the size of the first, had been constructed to the north on the opposite side of the river. Commanding the east-west route across the chalk downs, the new enclosure, now known as Oram's Arbour, has yielded pottery made in Italy and large bronze coins minted in Egypt. Both the route location and parts of earthworks shown at Oram's Arbour are hypothetical.

with it. The royal palace also lay close to the forum, in particular to the south end of the basilica, the principal public building of Roman Venta. The origins of the royal palace are unknown, and the site has not been excavated. The relationship of these structures may nonethe-

less support the following interpretation.

We know that the Germanic mercenaries serving in post-Roman Britain revolted against their native masters, thereby destroying the fabric of the life they had been engaged to protect. Power passed to the victorious rebels, who did

not entirely forget, even when they were augmented by successive waves of settlers from barbarian Europe, that they were in some sense heirs of Rome. Continental analogies, for example the towns of Trier and Cologne, show that the buildings that had been the seat of Ro-

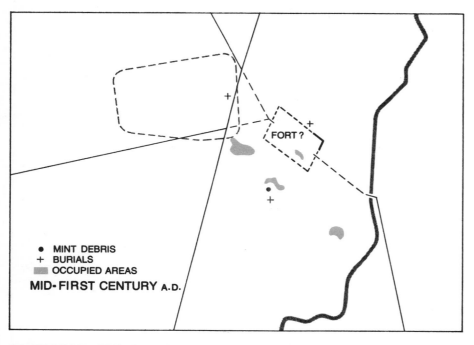

- • MINT DEBRIS
- + BURIALS
- ▨ OCCUPIED AREAS

**MID-FIRST CENTURY** A.D.

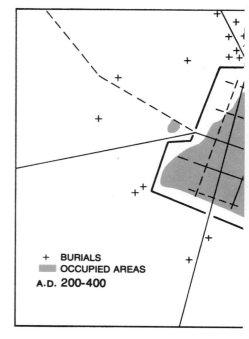

- + BURIALS
- ▨ OCCUPIED AREAS

**A.D. 200-400**

**THREE MAJOR CYCLES** of urban efflorescence at Winchester are illustrated on these two pages. The city's first roots were planted (*above*), perhaps in the form of a military post, to the east of the abandoned Iron Age enclosure (*light gray*) at the juncture of five Roman roads; this took place in the middle of the first century B.C. Broken lines indicate conjectural restoration.

**VENTA BELGARUM**, as the growing settlement was known in Roman times, was a fortified town with its streets comprising a rectangular

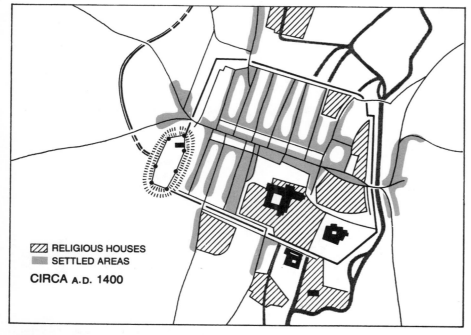

- ▨ RELIGIOUS HOUSES
- ▨ SETTLED AREAS

**CIRCA** A.D. **1400**

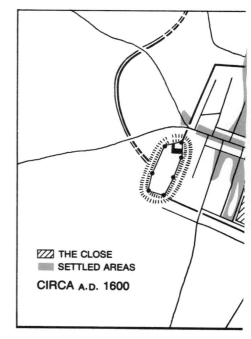

- ▨ THE CLOSE
- ▨ SETTLED AREAS

**CIRCA** A.D. **1600**

**MEDIEVAL REVIVAL**, first under English and then under Norman rule, raised Winchester above its former eminence as a Roman town. As seen here, some two centuries after the Conquest it had already begun to diminish in importance in spite of the great new Norman cathedral that had obliterated Old Minster. Growth of city in this period is illustrated on next two pages.

**SECOND SLUMP** saw the city drop to 37th place among English towns by the 1520's. Winchester fell even lower after England's monasteries

man authority sometimes survived as the residences of the new rulers. The same may have happened at Winchester. Germanic peoples of Saxon origin were established in the Roman city before its collapse. To them authority over the city and its lands may have passed by conquest or by survival, and their leaders, later to be kings, may have taken up residence in or next to the basilica that was the symbol of that authority.

On that hypothesis the Anglo-Saxon cemeteries outside the walls would reflect the presence of this ruling element within the old walled city, and the founding of the church by a king of Wessex in the middle of the seventh century would represent the establishment of a chapel to serve the royal household. The lack of archaeological material from this period is negative evidence of a certain

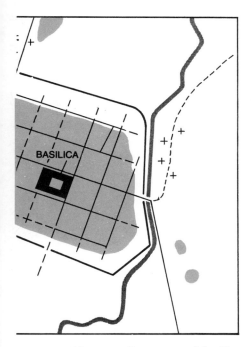

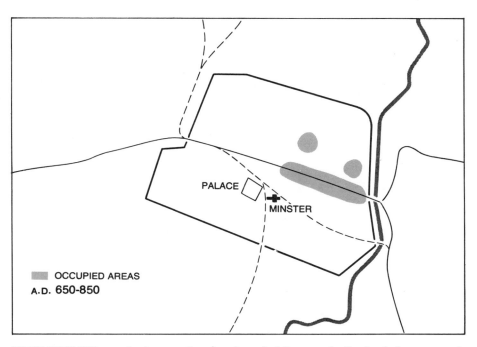

grid surrounding a central basilica and forum. In the third and fourth centuries A.D. it was the fifth-largest of the settlements in Roman Britain.

FIRST DECLINE came in the centuries after the end of Roman rule. By the sixth century only the wall and a single road bisecting the enclosed area remained of Venta Belgarum. For the next three centuries the town, called Wintancæster by the Saxons, may have sheltered a "king's hall" near the ruined basilica; the bishop's minster nearby could also have served as a royal chapel.

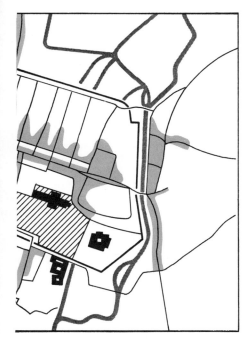

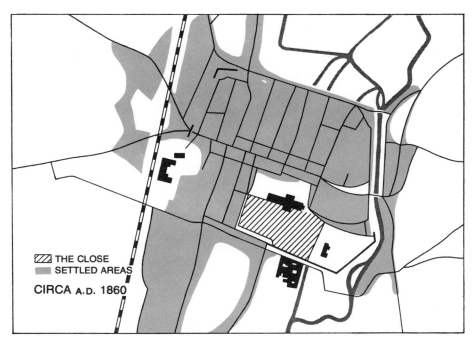

were dissolved during the 1530's. Depressed for 300 years thereafter, the cathedral city largely marked time until early in the 19th century.

VICTORIAN REVIVAL of Winchester included construction of a railway just west of the city, which now stretched beyond the bounds of its Roman walls although only slightly exceeding its maximum extent in medieval times. The southeast quadrant of the old walled area remained dominated by the cathedral and its "close." Just south stands Winchester College, a public school.

value: it shows that the greater part of the walled area was uninhabited. On the other hand, it has nothing to say about the Anglo-Saxon royal palace that has been buried under the cathedral graveyard for eight centuries and remains unexcavated.

With the founding of the church, which later became known as Old Minster, the city of Winchester entered a new phase. A few contemporary written records, an increasing amount of archaeological evidence and comparisons with other English and continental centers make it possible to present a less hypothetical picture of the character of the city in the two centuries following A.D. 648.

Within the walled area of Winchester four components become evident. One is the bishop's church and its community.

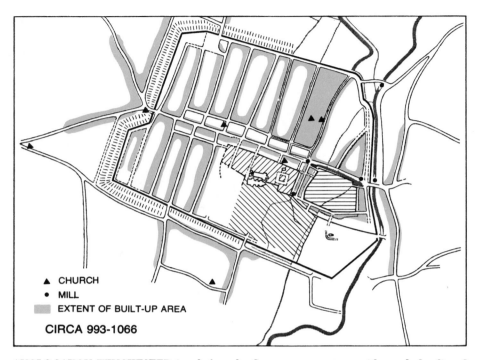

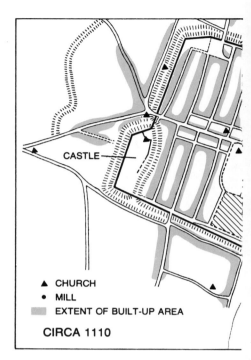

ANGLO-SAXON WINCHESTER just before the Conquest was a town with regularly aligned streets, elaborate defenses and many churches in addition to the Old and New Minsters and Nunnaminster. The illustration directly below shows the city's southeast quadrant in detail.

POST-CONQUEST DECADES were notable for Norman expansion. A new castle (lower left) enhanced the

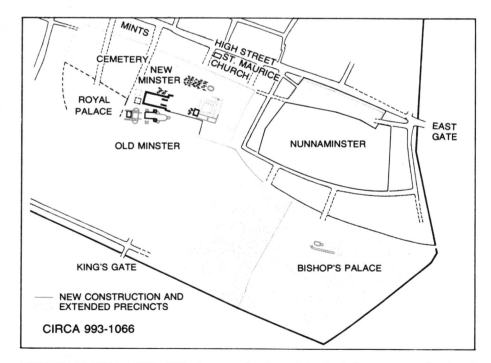

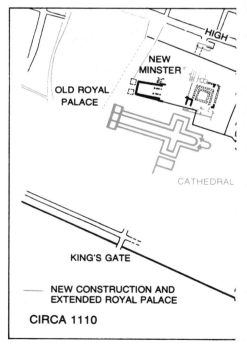

SOUTHEAST QUADRANT of Winchester at the close of the Anglo-Saxon era was the site of the royal palace, the bishop's palace and, in addition to lesser churches, the cathedral church or Old Minster, New Minster and Nunnaminster (nuns' church). Mints may have been located here.

NORMAN CHANGES doubled the size of the royal palace, rebuilt and extended the bishop's palace and also

Another is the royal residence; there is more circumstantial evidence for its existence during this period, when the church was the burial place of the Wessex kings. A third component is the presence of an unknown number of private residences; there is evidence of two such residential complexes. Of one, only the name survives as a description of an area within the city's East Gate: Coitburi. Names of this type, the second element signifying a defensible enclosure, are known from early London. The other private residence has actually been excavated in part; its earliest feature is a small private cemetery of the seventh century, probably adjacent to the earliest buildings, which remain unexcavated. The area of the cemetery was eventually built up; the first structures here were of timber, and in about A.D. 800 a stone

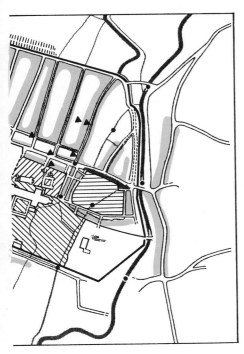

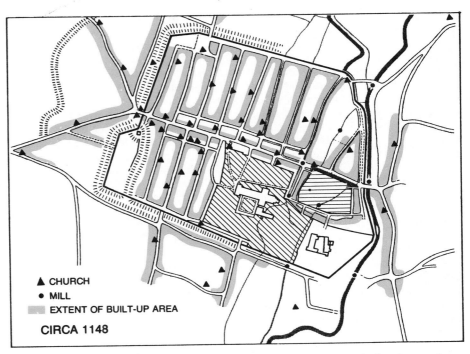

defenses and a great new cathedral rose. As a Norman seat the city stood second among English towns.

NORMAN APOGEE at Winchester came in the 12th century, when the city's churches numbered more than 50. Winchester's decline began that same century with a loss of close contact with the court. The trend was accelerated by removal of the royal treasury to London during the 1180's.

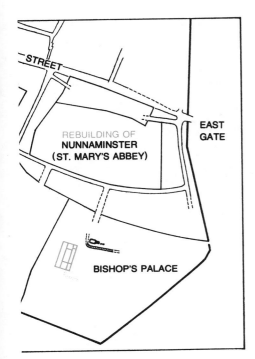

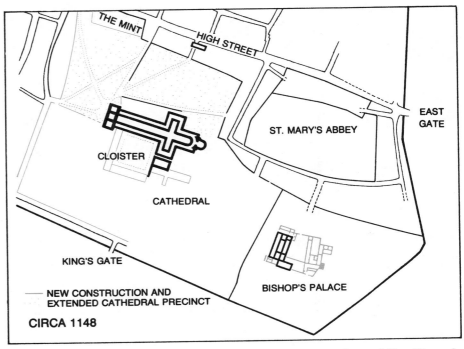

raised a great new cathedral. At the time of completion the cathedral was the longest church in all England.

CATHEDRAL PRECINCT had extended over the sites of the royal palace and New Minster by 1148. Nunnaminster, now called St. Mary's Abbey, was rebuilt once again. The bishop's palace, one of the greatest houses of its age, had by now almost reached its ultimate dimensions.

house was built [*see illustration on opposite page*]. Its remains contain evidence for the working and assaying of gold. The wealth of the burials in the private cemetery (one contained a necklace with gold and garnet pendants and 27 silver rings), the construction of a stone building and the working of precious metal all suggest occupants of high social status.

The fourth component is more problematical. It seems likely that the royal, ecclesiastical and private residences must have been supported by some service population, perhaps in the form of a developing street market along the eastern part of High Street, in the area known by about A.D. 900 as *ceapstræt,* or market street. As extensive excavations have shown, much of the walled area of the city was certainly uninhabited at this time, but contemporary records and the archaeological evidence both indicate that some of the walled acres were used for the grazing of livestock and the raising of crops.

The existence of these four components does not make Winchester an urban community at this time; there is no evidence of industry, of a dense population, of trade or of a full social hierarchy. Indeed, only the higher levels of society

seem to be present. Comparisons with Anglo-Saxon Hamwih (modern Southampton), some 12 miles downstream, are instructive. At Winchester we have a royal residence and royal burials, a bishop and his church, the homes (two at least) of subjects of substance and just possibly a mint. Southampton had a mint but no other obvious marks of social greatness. At this time, however, Southampton had a substantial population, much industrial activity and the elements of a regular street plan. Moreover, there is evidence of long-range trade. In contrast, none of these is found in Winchester.

Here are two different kinds of settlement: the old royal and ceremonial center, limited in its extent and functions, and the complementary port and industrial settlement emerging as a true town at the head of a superb natural harbor. Now, Anglo-Saxon kings had many residences, and the primitive apparatus of government moved with the king as he journeyed among his estates. Winchester therefore was not at this time a capital any more than it was an urban community. It was, however, one of the more important royal residences, perhaps because of its church and the city's close association with the royal house.

Beginning toward the close of the

eighth century England was subjected to a series of Viking attacks that steadily increased in severity. By the middle of the ninth century these had evolved into a phase of extensive Scandinavian settlement. Alone among the English kingdoms Wessex survived. After the Battle of Edington in 878 and the Treaty of Wedmore in the same year King Alfred, who ruled Wessex from 871 to 899, set about bolstering the defenses of his kingdom. Alfred's strategy was based on a series of "burhs," or fortified places, so located that no part of Wessex was more than 20 miles from one of them. The burhs were of several kinds: simple forts, refurbished Roman fortresses, newly created towns and former Roman towns that had been refortified and replanned. Winchester was in the last category.

The Roman defenses of the city were brought back into commission and the city gates repaired or rebuilt. Within the walls a new street system was laid out along the axis of the main east-west street; this street had survived in modified form from the Roman period. The other new streets, however, had no connection with the Roman pattern, which had long since vanished. The elements of the new pattern—the east-west High Street, the back streets parallel to it and the intersecting north-south streets—

ROW OF SMALL DWELLINGS, built in the 13th century, lies exposed by excavation. Only the earth floors and the clay sills of walls have survived. Medieval records place cloth-finishing works in this area; the cottages may have housed workers in the industry.

have remained in use with minor changes down to the present. A fourth element, a street running around the entire city inside the wall and providing direct access to the city's perimeter defenses in time of war, is partly lost today. As its original function became unnecessary it was built on in many places.

The ninth-century street plan shows that the entire walled area of the Roman city—143 acres—was brought back into use by the end of the century. Similar street systems can be seen in many of the other burhs set up by Alfred, and there can be no doubt that they represent a deliberate intent to establish urban communities; this English episode of organized town foundation is without parallel in early medieval Europe. The blocks formed by the new streets seem to have represented land apportioned for permanent settlement. In such places military effectiveness was to be secured by economic success.

Not all Alfred's burhs were successful, but Winchester never looked back. By the 960's the privacy of its monasteries had to be protected against a rising tide of urban life. Before the end of the century several city streets were named after the trades practiced in them. There was a Tanner Street, a Fleshmonger Street, a Shieldmaker Street and later a Shoemaker Street (to give their names in modern English), and suburbs were growing outside each of the city's five gates.

The southeastern quarter of Winchester gave the city its unique character. Here, 100 years before the Norman Conquest, was the most remarkable group of royal and ecclesiastical buildings in Anglo-Saxon England. Edward the Elder (899–924) founded New Minster and Nunnaminster, that is, a "nuns' minster." In the reign of King Edgar (959–975), Old Minster, New Minster and Nunnaminster were reformed and reconstructed. The bishop's palace was established in the same quarter of the city at about the same time, and between 971 and 994 Old Minster was entirely rebuilt. By this time written evidence at last confirms the existence of the royal palace immediately east of the cathedral.

It was in these buildings toward the end of the Anglo-Saxon period that the apparatus of a centralized English state began to emerge. By the reign of Cnut, or Canute (king of both England and Denmark from 1016 to 1035), Winchester had become the permanent repository of the king's treasure. The time of Edward the Confessor (1042–1066) may have seen the emergence of an embryo

ANGLO-SAXON HOUSE, some 23 feet square, may have been built around A.D. 800. The four corners and the doorway incorporate masonry, much of it taken from Roman buildings, but the walls are mainly courses of flint rubble. The two graves (*right*) continue under wall; antedating the house construction, they form part of a cemetery of seventh century.

financial and secretarial administration. The cathedral continued its ancient association with the ruling house: Cnut was buried in it in 1035 and Edward was crowned there at Easter, 1043, thus formalizing his accession the preceding year. Even before the Norman Conquest the custom seems to have been established of the king of England's wearing his crown in Winchester Cathedral at Easter, the most important feast of the Christian year.

No other place in England and few places in all Europe played such a central role in the life of a state during the 11th century. Yet Winchester was not the largest city in the realm. It was perhaps fourth in size and economic power, being surpassed by London, York and Lincoln in that order. Yet it was emerging as a kind of national capital, a distinction that was destined to pass to Westminster and London in the century that followed.

Victorious at Hastings on October 14, 1066, William the Conqueror seized Winchester without opposition in November, opening the way for the surrender of London and his coronation in Westminster Abbey on Christmas Day. The effects of the Conquest on Winchester were as complex as they were considerable. In the larger buildings, in the composition of the upper levels of urban society and in social fashion there were profound changes. In administration, in

the bulk of the population and in the basic fabric of the houses and the streetscape there was essential continuity. If for many in Winchester the immediate dislocation caused by the Conquest and the appropriation of land for new buildings was serious, the massive Norman financial investment in major public works during the remainder of the century and the presence of royal officials, barons and magnates of the newly rich Anglo-Norman aristocracy ensured for the city a rapid recovery and a clear improvement in its wealth and status.

By about 1100 the ancient role of Winchester as a royal center had been given new emphasis. In February, 1067, a Norman castle had been begun at the point where the Roman defenses at the southwest corner of the city formed a salient. In about 1070 the Anglo-Saxon royal palace was extended northward to High Street and doubled in area, the additional space being required for the construction of the Conqueror's hall and palace. East of the palace the total rebuilding of Old Minster was begun in 1079. The eastern part of the new cathedral was dedicated 14 years later, in 1093, and the entire project was completed in 30 or 40 years.

The Norman cathedral demonstrated most clearly, as perhaps its builders had intended, not only the eminent role of the city but also the finality of the Norman acquisition of the Anglo-Saxon

**SITE OF OLD MINSTER,** the principal cathedral church of the Anglo-Saxon kingdom of Wessex, is seen under excavation (*left*) in this aerial photograph. The excavation lies to the north of the cathedral built by the Normans following their conquest of England.

MORE THAN 1,100 REINTERRED SKELETONS were found near the west end of the cathedral. In digging foundations for the Norman cathedral the builders disturbed many burials. In filling the trench dug to gather stone from Old Minster for use in the new building they disposed of the disturbed remains. Skulls were placed toward west according to tradition, but other bones were jumbled.

state. The new cathedral was more than 500 feet long, making it larger than any other church in England or Normandy, longer than old St. Peter's or any of the churches on the pilgrims' route to Santiago de Compostela in Spain. Only the contemporary abbey church built by St. Hugh at Cluny in Burgundy was longer.

With the building of the castle, the rebuilding of the palace and the cathedral, the repair and reconstruction of New Minster and Nunnaminster (renamed St. Mary's Abbey), Winchester in about 1100 was a principal residence of the Norman kings, the seat of the royal administration and a center of great ecclesiastical importance. Englishmen had yielded place to Normans in the houses along the most important streets of the city. The English had also adopted Norman fashions to such an extent that 70 percent of the citizens' names recorded in about 1110 were foreign, whereas only 15 percent had been before the Conquest. The English were nonetheless still prominent in affairs. Winchester's

mint was now second in importance only to London's, and the moneyers, whose ranks included the leading burgesses and property owners in the city, were almost all English.

Winchester probably reached its zenith in the early years of the 12th century. After 1104 Henry I abandoned the custom of the annual Easter crown-wearing at the cathedral, a practice that had been regularly observed by his predecessors. Royal interest shifted from the palace in the center of the city, in intimate contact with the cathedral, to the new castle on the hill beside the wall. By the 1130's the palace was no longer a royal residence; it may by then have passed to the bishop, whose role in city affairs was now increasing. At that time the rebuilding of the episcopal palace at Wolvesey in the southeastern corner of the city was undertaken. Successive kings also extended the period over which the bishops of Winchester might enjoy the profits of St. Giles Fair, held on

the hill east of the city. The three days originally granted by William Rufus in 1098 were increased to 16 days under Henry II. Although the fair was probably of pre-Conquest origin, its heyday came in the 13th century, when it was one of the most important fairs in England and was attended by traders from many parts of Europe.

In the civil war of 1141 Winchester was seriously damaged. The old royal palace was burned down, and St. Mary's and Hyde Abbey and many parish churches and private houses suffered severely when the city was sacked by the London contingent supporting the king. By that time London had been the largest and wealthiest city in England for some 200 years. Westminster had emerged as a royal residence in the 11th century and increased greatly in importance with the rebuilding of the Abbey by Edward the Confessor and his burial there in 1066. By the middle of the 12th century an increasing number of administrative functions were located at Westminster. Finally in the 1180's even the tradition of Winchester as the site of the royal treasury gave way, and the king's treasure was transferred to London.

The close link between Winchester and the crown was now severed. The castle remained an important royal residence, often embellished and often visited, but it was of no more importance than many another great house. The economy of the city held up during the rest of the 12th century, but there are signs of trouble in the 13th century, as first the western suburb and then the western neighborhood within the walls began to decline. Large areas of the city passed into religious hands. By the 14th century considerable tracts within the walls were no longer built up. A petition of 1440 cited the destruction of 11 streets, 17 parish churches and 987 houses as a result of pestilence and the withdrawal of trade. Where Winchester had occupied second place among English cities at the end of the 11th century, by 1200 it was sixth or lower. By 1334 it was 14th, by 1377 it was 29th and by 1527 it was 37th. Many of the city parishes were amalgamated in the early 16th century, but it was the suppression of the monasteries in 1536–1539 that wrought the greatest changes, removing three monastic communities, four friaries and several lesser institutions.

The built-up area of the city was by now confined to the central and eastern parts of High Street, to the adjacent areas of the side streets, to the main north-south street and to the eastern and southern suburbs. So it was to remain for three centuries. By the early 19th century a revival had begun, encouraged by the growing role of Winchester as a garrison town and by the advent of the railway in 1839.

Ancient Winchester now lies under the streets and buildings of an active and dynamic modern urban center. Reconstruction, redevelopment and the redesign of approach roads and internal streets are destroying the evidence of the city's past at a quantifiable rate. The pattern of the city's Roman-built defenses was effectively breached for the first time only in 1939. By 1950, 2 percent of the defenses had been destroyed and by 1965, 8 percent. By 1980 completion of the city's traffic plan will have raised this figure to 35 percent. A third of the 2,000-year-old defensive system will have been removed in 40 years. There are many similar examples.

In such a situation the raw material for the study of urban evolution has to be rescued now or not at all. Winchester is exceptionally rich in written records, but they barely touch the first 1,000 years of the community's existence, its Iron Age and Roman cycles and its Anglo-Saxon rebirth. Historical data only become full during the time of Winchester's long medieval decline. This is a pattern that is repeated all over Europe. The basic evidence for the study of urban origins and growth, for the waxing and waning of our towns and cities, has not been recognized until the last moment before its destruction. In London not more than 15 years remain in which to undertake an inquiry that will never again be possible. The example of Winchester may show what can be won. It also shows how much may be lost.

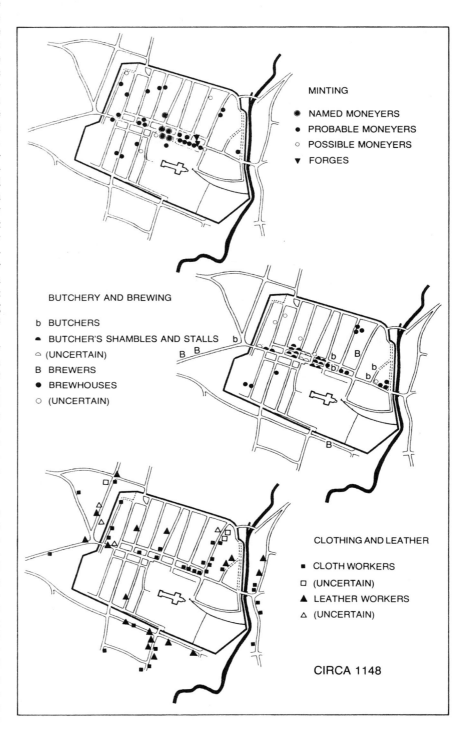

URBAN TRADES AND INDUSTRIES in mid-12th-century Winchester included victualing and manufacture in addition to the minting of coins. Five properties, four of them on High Street, were occupied by moneyers whose names appear in an 1148 survey. Another 27 properties are identifiable as probably or possibly moneyers', and two moneyers' forges are known.

# BIBLIOGRAPHIES

I give here some key references which can lead you further into the complex literature of archaeology, listing first some general works, then some relevant to each article here.

## Surveys of World Prehistory

MAN IN PREHISTORY, 2nd Ed. Chester S. Chard. McGraw-Hill Book Company, 1975. (A succinct account of the major events in world prehistory. Useful tables and maps.)

WORLD PREHISTORY: A NEW OUTLINE. Grahame Clark. Cambridge University Press, 1969. (Inexpensive paperback, with relatively few illustrations, strong on Near East and Europe.)

MEN OF THE EARTH. Brian M. Fagan. Little, Brown and Company, 1974. (Wide geographic coverage and comprehensive bibliographies. Many illustrations.)

## Method and Theory in Archaeology

INVITATION TO ARCHAEOLOGY. James Deetz. Natural History Press, 1967. (Short, paperback summary of the basic principles of archaeology. Lucid and sometimes controversial.)

IN THE BEGINNING, 2nd Ed. Brian M. Fagan. Little, Brown and Company, 1975. (Covers New and Old World archaeology. Major emphasis on methods. Numerous illustrations and references.)

AN INTRODUCTION TO PREHISTORIC ARCHAEOLOGY, 2nd Ed. Robert F. Heizer. Holt, Rinehart, & Winston, 1973. (For the more advanced student. Major emphasis on systems. Lengthy bibliography.)

# I  EARLY PREHISTORY

## 1. The Idea of Man's Antiquity

ONE HUNDRED YEARS OF ARCHAEOLOGY. Glyn Daniel. Duckworth and Company, Ltd., 1950. (A useful general account of the history of archaeology and of the controversies surrounding the antiquity of man.)

A HISTORY OF AMERICAN ARCHAEOLOGY. Gordon R. Willey and Jeremy A. Sabloff. W. H. Freeman and Company, 1974. (Covers the story of New World prehistory in some detail.)

## 2. Tools and Human Evolution

THE EVOLUTION OF PRIMATE BEHAVIOR. Alison Jolly. Macmillan Publishing Company, 1972. (This and the following three publications cover the basic ground most admirably. The Washburn and Moore volume is a good basic introduction.)

THE ASCENT OF MAN. David Pilbeam. Macmillan Publishing Company, 1972.

PRIMATE EVOLUTION. Elwyn L. Simons. Macmillan Publishing Company, 1972.

APE INTO MAN. S. L. Washburn and Ruth Moore. Little, Brown and Company, 1973.

## 3. Homo Erectus

THE ASCENT OF MAN. David Pilbeam. Macmillan Publishing Company, 1972.

MANKIND IN THE MAKING. W. W. Howells. Doubleday and Company, Inc., 1967.

## 4. A Paleolithic Camp at Nice

DECOUVERTE D'HABITATS DE L'ACHEULEEN ANCIEN, DANS LES DEPOTS MINDELIENS, SUR LE SITE DE TERRA AMATA (NICE). Henry De Lumley in *Comptes Rendus de l'Academie des Sciences*, No. 264, pages 801–804; 1967.

LES NIVEAUX QUATERNAIRES MARINS DES ALPES MARITIMIES: CORRELATIONS AVEC LES INDUSTRIES PREHISTORIQUES. Henry De Lumley in *Comptes Rendus Sommaires des Seances de la Société Geologique de France*, Vol. 5, Series 7, pages 163–164; 1963.

## 5. The Solutrean Culture

LAUGERIE-HAUTE PRÈS DES EYZIES (DORDOGNE). Denis and Elie Peynony in *Archives de L'Institut de Paleontologie Humaine*, Memoire 19; 1938.

LE SOLUTREEN EN FRANCE. Philip E. L. Smith in *Institute de Prehistoire, Bordeaux;* 1966. (The monograph on Smith's research.)

## 6. The Evolution of Paleolithic Art

400 CENTURIES OF CAVE ART. Henri Breuil. Centre d'Etudes et de Documentation Préhistoriques, 1952. (A classic summary of Breuil's work.)

PALEOLITHIC ART. Paulo Graziosi. Faber and Faber, Ltd., 1956. (A compendium of Paleolithic art.)

TREASURES OF PREHISTORIC ART. André Leroi-Gourhan. Harry N. Abrams, Inc., 1967. (The author's detailed account of his work.)

## 7. Ice-Age Hunters of the Ukraine

MAN AND CULTURE IN THE LATE PLEISTOCENE. Richard Klein. Chandler Publications, 1969. (An account of the hunters described in this article for the advanced student.)

ICE-AGE HUNTERS OF THE UKRAINE. Richard Klein. University of Chicago Press, 1973. (Detailed and specific account of Ukrainian hunters.)

## 8. The Prehistory of the Australian Aborigine

THE PREHISTORY OF AUSTRALIA. Derek Mulvaney. Praeger Publications, 1969. (The most comprehensive synthesis of Australian prehistory yet available.)

ABORIGINAL MAN IN AUSTRALIA. Edited by Ronald M. and Catherine H. Berndt. Angus and Robertson, 1965.

# II  EARLY AMERICANS

## 9. A Stone Age Campsite at the Gateway to America

THE ARCHAEOLOGY OF CAPE DENBIGH. J. L. Giddings. Brown University Press, 1964.

THE BERING LAND BRIDGE. David Moody Hopkins. Stanford University Press, 1967.

AN INTRODUCTION TO AMERICAN ARCHAEOLOGY, VOL. I: NORTH AND MIDDLE AMERICA. Gordon R. Willey. Prentice-Hall, Inc., 1966. (The best synthesis of North American culture history yet available.)

## 10. Early Man in the Andes

AMERICAN PAST: A NEW WORLD ARCHAEOLOGY. Thomas C. Patterson. Scott, Foresman and Company, 1973. (A basic text on New World prehistory, informative for the beginner.)

AN INTRODUCTION TO AMERICAN ARCHAEOLOGY, VOL. II: SOUTH AMERICA. Gordon R. Willey. Prentice-Hall, Inc., 1966. (The latest continent-wide synthesis of early prehistory south of Mexico.)

## 11. A Paleo-Indian Bison Kill

THE HIGH PLAINS AND THEIR UTILIZATION BY THE INDIAN. Waldo R. Wedel in *American Antiquity*, Vol. 1, No. 1, pages 1–16; 1963.

THE OLSEN-CHUBBOCK SITE: A PALEO-INDIAN KILL. Joe Ben Wheat in *Memoirs of the Society for American Archaeology*, Vol. 26; 1972. (This is the site report.)

# III FARMERS AND PEASANTS

## 12. An Early Farming Village in Turkey

PREHISTORIC INVESTIGATIONS IN IRAQI KURDESTAN. Robert J. Braidwood and Bruce Howe. University of Chicago Press, 1950. (Summarizes Braidwood's early work.)

THE ORIGINS OF AGRICULTURE. Kent V. Flannery. *Biannual Review of Anthropology*, pages 271–310; 1973. (An up-to-date summary of the evidence for early food production world wide.)

ORIGINS OF FOOD PRODUCTION IN SOUTHWESTERN ASIA. Gary A. Wright in *Current Anthropology*, Vol. 12, No. 45, pages 447–478; 1971. (A survey of the literature and major theories.)

## 13. Obsidian and the Origins of Trade

OBSIDIAN AND EARLY CULTURE CONTACT IN THE NEAR EAST. Colin Renfrew and J. E. Dixon in *Proceedings of the Prehistoric Society*, Vol. 32, No. 2, pages 30–72; 1966.

OBSIDIAN IN THE AEGEAN. Colin Renfrew and J. R. Carr in *The Annual of the British School at Athens*, No. 60, pages 225–242; 1965.

## 14. A Neolithic City in Turkey

THE EARLIEST CIVILIZATIONS OF THE NEAR EAST. James Mellaart. McGraw-Hill Book Company, 1965.

CATAL HÜYÜK. James Mellaart. McGraw-Hill Book Company, 1967. (The most complete account available.)

## 15. An Early Neolithic Village in Greece

ANCIENT EUROPE. Stuart Piggott. Aldine Publishing Company, 1967. (The definitive summary of later European prehistory.)

EXCAVATIONS AT THE EARLY NEOLITHIC SITE AT NEA NIKOMEDEIA, GREEK MACEDONIA (1961 SEASON). Robert J. Rodden in *Proceedings of the Prehistoric Society*, Vol. 28, pages 267–288; 1961.

## 16. An Earlier Agricultural Revolution

EXCAVATIONS AT NON NOK THA, THAILAND. Donn T. Baynard in *Asian Perspectives*, Vol. 13; 1973.

THE HOABHINIAN AND AFTER: SUBSISTENCE PATTERNS IN SOUTHEAST ASIA DURING THE LATE PLEISTOCENE AND EARLY RECENT PERIODS. Chester Gorman in *World Archaeology*, Vol. 2, No. 3, pages 300–320; 1971.

## 17. The Origins of New World Civilization

THE ORIGINS OF AGRICULTURE. Kent V. Flannery in *Biannual Review of Anthropology*, pages 271–310; 1973. (Updates the Tehuacán monograph.)

# IV CITIES AND CIVILIZATION

## 18. The Origins of Cities

THE EVOLUTION OF URBAN SOCIETY. Robert M. Adams. Aldine Publishing Company, 1966. (Reviews Adams's hypothesis.)

WHAT HAPPENED IN HISTORY. V. Gordon Childe. Penguin Books, 1946. (Summarizes Childe's basic hypotheses.)

## 19. The Origin and Evolution of Cities

THE CULTURAL EVOLUTION OF CIVILIZATIONS. Kent V. Flannery in *Annual Review of Ecology and Systematics*, Vol. 3, pages 399–426; 1972. (A fascinating essay on the mechanics of urban life.)

THE EMERGENCE OF CIVILIZATION. Colin Renfrew. Methuen & Company, Ltd., 1972. (Another study of mechanisms, this time in an Aegean context.)

THE PREINDUSTRIAL CITY: PAST AND PRESENT. Gideon Sjoberg. The Free Press, 1960.

## 20. An Early City in Iran

THE SUMERIANS: THEIR HISTORY, CULTURE, AND CHARACTER. Samuel Noah Kramer. The University of Chicago Press, 1963. (The classic work.)

Excavations at Tepe Yahya, Southeastern Iran, 1967–1969. C. C. Lamberg-Karlovsky in *Bulletin of the American Journal of Prehistoric Research,* No. 27; 1970. (Describes the excavations mentioned here.)

The Indus Civilization. Sir Mortimer Wheeler. Cambridge University Press, 1968. (Another classic.)

## 21. The Beginnings of Wheeled Transport

The First Wagons and Carts: From the Tigris to the Severn. V. Gordon Childe in *Proceedings of the Prehistoric Society,* Vol. 17, Part 2, pages 177–194. (A useful, if a little outdated, survey article.)

Ancient Europe. Stuart Piggott. Edinburgh University Press, 1965. (Rapidly becoming a classic source on European prehistory. A thoroughly literate and well-researched study.)

Before Civilization. Colin Renfrew. Alfred A. Knopf, 1973. (Assesses the impact of new radiocarbon dates on the prehistory of Europe. Complements Piggott.)

## 22. Teotihuacán

Mexico. Michael Coe. Praeger Publications, 1962. (A succinct summary of Mexican prehistory including Teotihuacán.)

Urbanization at Teotihuacán, Mexico. Edited by René Millon. University of Texas Press, 1974. (The multivolume report on Millon's project, which will appear over a number of years.)

# V ARCHAEOLOGY AND ARCHAEOLOGICAL ISSUES

## 23. Carbon-14 and the Prehistory of Europe

Before Civilization. Colin Renfrew. Alfred A. Knofp, 1971. (A popular account of the controversies described in this article for the general reader. Contains full information on the technical literature of $C^{14}$ and European prehistory.)

## 24. Frozen Tombs of the Scythians

Frozen Tombs of Siberia: the Pazyryk Burials of Iron Age Horsemen. Sergei Rudenko. Translated by M. W. Thompson. University of California Press, 1970. (The best and most comprehensive description, and about the only one in English.)

## 25. The Coprolites of Man

Prehistoric Diet in Southwest Texas: the Coprolite Evidence. Vaughn M. Bryant, Jr. in *American Antiquity,* Vol. 38, No. 3; pages 407–420.

Analysis of the Tehuacán Coprolites. Eric O. Callen in *The Prehistory of the Tehuacán Valley, Vol. I: Environment and Substance.* Douglas O. Byers. University of Texas Press, 1967. (One of the best coprolite reports yet available.)

Biological and Cultural Evidence from Prehistoric Human Coprolites. Robert F. Heizer and Lewis K. Napton in *Science,* Vol. 165, No. 3893, pages 563–568; 1969.

Pollen Analysis of Prehistoric Human Feces. Paul S. Martin and Floyd W. Shanock in *American Antiquity,* Vol. 30, No. 2, pages 168–180. (Basic description of pollen analysis techniques.)

## 26. The Planning of a Maya Ceremonial Center

Excavations at Lubaatun, 1970. Norman Hammond in *Antiquity,* Vol. 44, pages 216–223; 1970.

The Aztecs, the Maya, and their Predecessors. Muriel Porter Weaver. Seminar Press, 1972. (A useful summary of the field.)

## 27. A Byzantine Trading Venture

Archaeology Under Water. George F. Bass. Penguin Books, 1972. (The best summary of the subject.)

A History of Seafaring. Edited by George F. Bass. Thames & Hudson, Ltd., 1972. (A series of essays on all aspects of underwater archaeology, designed to be a first attempt at tracing the hitherto little-known history of early seafaring. Destined to become a classic.)

A Fourth Century Shipwreck at Yassi Ade. George F. Bass and Frederick H. van Doorminck, Jr. in *American Journal of Archaeology,* Vol. 75, No. 1, pages 27–37; 1971.

## 28. The Excavation of a Drowned Greek Temple

Archaeology Under Water. George F. Bass. Penguin Books, 1972.

Excavations at Porto Cheli and Vicinity, Preliminary Report, I: Halieis, 1962–1968. Michael H. Jameson in *Hesperia,* Vol. 38, No. 2, pages 311–342; 1969. (A report on the findings at Halieis over a six-year period.)

Balloon over Halieis. Julian Whittlesey in *Archaeology*, Vol. 21, No. 1, pages 66–67; January, 1968. (Describes a survey technique used at the site.)

## 29. The Vikings

The Norsemen. Eric Oxenstierna. New York Graphic Society, 1965. (A widely read popular account.)

The Age of the Vikings. P. H. Sawyer. Edward Arnold, Publishers, 1962. (A useful summary with excellent bibliographies.)

## 30. The Archaeology of Winchester

The Winchester excavations have been summarized in a series of preliminary reports written by Martin Biddle in *The Antiquarian Journal*, Vol. 44–54; 1964–1974. The articles appear annually except for 1971, 1972, and 1973.

Winchester: The Brooks. Andrew and Wendy Selkirk in *Current Archaeology*, No. 20, pages 250–255. (A brief account of one part of the excavations. Reprinted in *Corriders in Time*. Edited by Brian M. Fagan. Little, Brown and Company, 1974.)

# INDEX